TEACHING WITH THE NORTON ANTHOLOGY OF

WESTERN

LITERATURE

NINTH EDITION

A GUIDE FOR INSTRUCTORS

The Editors

Martin Puchner, General Editor
HARVARD UNIVERSITY

Suzanne Akbari
UNIVERSITY OF TORONTO

Wiebke Denecke
BOSTON UNIVERSITY

Barbara Fuchs
UNIVERSITY OF CALIFORNIA, LOS ANGELES

Caroline Levine
UNIVERSITY OF WISCONSIN, MADISON

Pericles Lewis
YALE UNIVERSITY

Emily Wilson
UNIVERSITY OF PENNSYLVANIA

TEACHING WITH THE NORTON ANTHOLOGY OF

WESTERN LITERATURE

NINTH EDITION

David Boyles
UNIVERSITY OF NEVADA, LAS VEGAS

Zander Brietzke
COLUMBIA UNIVERSITY

Rachel Disney
UNIVERSITY OF NEVADA, LAS VEGAS

Scott Hollifield
UNIVERSITY OF NEVADA, LAS VEGAS

Dana Milstein
BARUCH COLLEGE, CITY UNIVERSITY OF NEW YORK

Andrew Nicholson
UNIVERSITY OF NEVADA, LAS VEGAS

Benedict Whalen
TEXAS A & M UNIVERSITY, CORPUS CHRISTI

With special thanks to Paula Berggren
BARUCH COLLEGE, CITY UNIVERSITY OF NEW YORK

A GUIDE FOR INSTRUCTORS

W. W. NORTON & COMPANY | New York · London

W. W. Norton & Company has been independent since its founding in 1923, when William Warder Norton and Mary D. Herter Norton first published lectures delivered at the People's Institute, the adult education division of New York City's Cooper Union. The firm soon expanded its program beyond the Institute, publishing books by celebrated academics from America and abroad. By mid-century, the two major pillars of Norton's publishing program—trade books and college texts—were firmly established. In the 1950s, the Norton family transferred control of the company to its employees, and today—with a staff of four hundred and a comparable number of trade, college, and professional titles published each year—W. W. Norton & Company stands as the largest and oldest publishing house owned wholly by its employees.

Ninth Edition.

Assistant Editor: Quynh Do
Project Editor: Rachel Mayer
Production Manager: Sean Mintus
Composition and project management: Westchester Publishing Services

ISBN 978-0-393-92345-2

W. W. Norton & Company Inc., 500 Fifth Avenue, New York, NY 10110
wwnorton.com
W. W. Norton & Company Ltd., Castle House 75/76 Wells Street, London W1T 3QT

Contents

USING THE INSTRUCTOR'S GUIDE / xi

Volume 1

I. ANCIENT MEDITERRANEAN AND NEAR EASTERN LITERATURE   1

Creation and the Cosmos / 3
The Epic of Gilgamesh / 8
The Hebrew Bible / 14
Homer / 21
Aesop / 29
Sappho / 34
Aeschylus / 39
Sophocles / 46
Euripides / 58
Aristophanes / 64
Plato / 69
Travel and Conquest / 74
Plautus / 79
Catullus / 84
Virgil / 89
Ovid / 95

II. CIRCLING THE MEDITERRANEAN: EUROPE AND THE ISLAMIC WORLD   101

The Christian Bible: The New Testament Gospels / 103
Apuleius / 109
Augustine / 113
The Qur'an / 117

Beowulf / 123
Abolqasem Ferdowsi / 129
From *Song of Roland* / 134
Petrus Alfonsi / 140
Marie de France / 145
Chrétien de Troyes / 150
"Thidrandi Whom the Goddesses Slew" / 155
"Authun the Bear" / 155
Medieval Lyrics / 160
Dante Alighieri / 166
The Thousand and One Nights / 172
Giovanni Boccaccio / 177
Geoffrey Chaucer / 182
Sir Gawain and the Green Knight / 190
Everyman / 195
Christine de Pizan / 200

III. EUROPE AND THE NEW WORLD: EARLY MODERNITY 205

Humanism and the Rediscovery of the Classical Past / 207
Petrarch and the Love Lyric / 212
Desiderius Erasmus / 218
Niccolò Machiavelli / 223
Ludovico Ariosto / 228
Sir Thomas More / 233
Baldassare Castiglione / 238
Marguerite de Navarre / 243
*The Life of Lazarillo de Tormes and of His Fortunes
   and Adversities* / 248
Michel de Montaigne / 253
Miguel de Cervantes / 258
The Encounter of Europe and the New World / 263
Lope de Vega / 269
William Shakespeare / 275
God, Church, and Self / 282
John Milton / 287

Volume 2

I. THE ENLIGHTENMENT IN EUROPE AND THE AMERICAS 293

What Is Enlightenment? / 295
Molière (Jean-Baptiste Poquelin) / 301
Marie de la Vergne de la Fayette / 307
Jean Racine / 312
Jean De La Fontaine / 317
Aphra Behn / 321
Sor Juana Inés de la Cruz / 326
Jonathan Swift / 331
Alexander Pope / 338
Voltaire (François-Marie Arouet) / 343
Samuel Johnson / 348

II. AN AGE OF REVOLUTIONS IN EUROPE AND THE AMERICAS 353

Revolutionary Contexts / 355
Jean-Jacques Rousseau / 361
Olaudah Equiano / 366
Johann Wolfgang von Goethe / 372
Alexander Sergeyevich Pushkin / 377
Nikolai Gogol / 382
Domingo Faustino Sarmiento / 387
Frederick Douglass / 392
Herman Melville / 398
Romantic Poets and Their Successors / 403

III. REALISM 413

Victor Hugo / 415
Fyodor Dostoyevsky / 420
Gustave Flaubert / 425
Leo Tolstoy / 431
Henrik Ibsen / 436
Giovanni Verga / 441

Guy de Maupassant / 445
Joaquim Maria Machado de Assis / 449
Anton Chekhov / 454
Perspectives on European Empire / 461
Orature / 465

IV. MODERNITY AND MODERNISM, 1900–1945   471

Joseph Conrad / 473
Thomas Mann / 479
Marcel Proust / 486
James Joyce / 492
Franz Kafka / 498
Luigi Pirandello / 503
Virginia Woolf / 508
William Faulkner / 515
Bertolt Brecht / 520
Jorge Luis Borges / 525
Modernist Poetry / 531
Manifestos / 537

V. POSTWAR AND POSTCOLONIAL LITERATURE, 1945–1968   543

Léopold Sédar Senghor / 545
Julio Cortázar / 549
Tadeusz Borowski / 554
Alain Robbe-Grillet / 559
Italo Calvino / 563
Paul Celan / 567
Doris Lessing / 571
James Baldwin / 576
Albert Camus / 582
Samuel Beckett / 587
Vladimir Nabokov / 591
Clarice Lispector / 597
Chinua Achebe / 600
Carlos Fuentes / 606
Alexander Solzhenitsyn / 611
Alice Munro / 616

VI. GLOBAL AND LOCAL IN CONTEMPORARY WORLD LITERATURE

621

Derek Walcott / 623
Seamus Heaney / 628
Ingeborg Bachmann / 632
Gabriel García Márquez / 636
V. S. Naipaul / 639
Leslie Marmon Silko / 643
Ngugi wa Thiong'o / 648
Wole Soyinka / 653
Bessie Head / 658
Salman Rushdie / 662
Jamaica Kincaid / 666
Toni Morrison / 672
Isabel Allende / 678
Junot Díaz / 684
Roberto Bolaño / 689
J. M. Coetzee / 694

INDEX / 701

Using the Instructor's Guide

Above all else, we have written about the texts in the *Norton Anthology of Western Literature* with our colleagues' time, or lack thereof, uppermost in mind. The full professor who chairs a department and serves on the faculty senate does not always have the time she would like to devote to the large lecture class that she volunteered to teach at the last minute when the budget line disappeared for the new hire. The tenure-track professor does not necessarily have any more time to prepare for that class, either, because he needs to finish his monograph, develop a prospectus for a new manuscript, and publish, publish, publish! Professors at liberal arts and teaching colleges and universities teach three or four classes every semester, and the variety of texts of western literature do not always fall within their subject specialties. The adjunct professor, whose office might be in a car and whose office hours might be held in Starbucks, shuttles between two, three, even four campuses each term. Time is scarce and at a premium for all of us!

This guide is the sort that we wish we'd had when we began teaching introductory and advanced western literature courses: compact, comprehensive, and useful. It addresses each text in outline form and limits discussion to an average of 1,500 words. Working in tandem with the expansive headnotes that precede each work in the anthology, the guide synthesizes the introductory material and takes a point of view designed to be stimulating, thoughtful, and provocative. The outlines stress plot construction and narrative, cultural context and history, and notable relationships between the texts; ask questions that relate to ideas for papers and class discussions; cite notable forms of electronic media related to the texts; and offer ideas for activities relevant to each work that can be performed in class. Each outline follows an identical template that could easily adapt to a single or several class lectures. The outlines function as a brief for the texts in the anthology, but they are also meant to supplement prior knowledge and to spur new lines of inquiry.

Each selection outline contains four sections:

1. **Topics for Lecture or Discussion.** This is the longest section of the outline and is divided and numbered in five parts on average, each part a paragraph headed by an action sentence presented in boldface type. Each lead sentence describes important aspects of the text, or presents

a thesis about the text. The supporting sentences of the paragraph elaborate the lead and provide examples from the text with an emphasis upon concrete evidence. Accompanying each topic is a suggestion for further reading regarding the critical context and history of the text, and a suggestion of online media resources and helpful search terms to find materials that complement the lecture or discussion.

2. **In-Class Activities.** A short series of exercises (usually three to five) that can be conducted within the classroom setting or institution library. Many of these are geared for group or team projects that can be integrated into a larger discussion of the text, and many encourage creative interaction with the texts in the anthology.

3. **Paper Topics.** A set of questions, generally 5–8, each one of which could spark a paper or essay. These questions frequently recast subjects from previous sections as well as broach new material.

4. **Resources.** A selection of resources with brief annotations, intended to complement the specific resources listed with each topic for lecture or discussion. These resources include articles and books that offer background and contextual information, as well as media resources including movies, websites, and audio recordings that are related to the text.

We did not design the above sections as discrete categories. Paper topics could become lecture topics and vice versa. Any of the "In-Class Activities" could also be lecture/discussion topics or paper topics. While the list of "Topics for Lecture or Discussion" is never meant to be exhaustive, it is quite possible that a single item could form the genesis of an entire class session. Indeed, the outline provides enough material for the teacher to read a provocative quote, make five or more points about the selection, show a short or long video clip, refer to one or two important aspects of cultural history, perform a couple of exercises, and provide a list of questions for papers, but all of this material might exceed a standard 50–75 minute period. The organizational structure invites the classroom teacher to pick and choose material with ease and according to personal tastes and predilections as well as time constraints. The instructor's guide complements the individual headnotes and responds to what the editors of each text have to say. Sometimes the guide makes direct reference to points made in the headnotes and repeats them for added emphasis; sometimes the guide runs parallel arguments to those laid down in the headnotes; and sometimes the guide veers off on its own tangent independent of the headnotes. Sandwiched between the headnotes and the guide is the meat of the matter, the texts. The guide tries to increase the pleasure of reading each work and encourages teachers to synthesize the competing, compelling, complementary, and sometimes contradictory arguments that exist between the introductory headnote, the text, and the teaching guide in order to enjoy a rich and full aesthetic and critical experience.

By no means, however, should this guide add to the burden that teachers face by becoming yet one more "crucial" document to read. Dialogue, synthesis, and questioning do require a lot of work, but the guide can also function as an academic cheat sheet to assist the working professional when the vagaries of life intervene: when sickness breaks out, when the pet misbehaves, when loved ones disappoint, when everything seems to fall apart, and yet tomorrow's class still looms as a foreboding constant. When such things happen, may this guide become a trusted companion to boost your preparedness and help pull you through a tough spot with aplomb.

Volume 1

I. Ancient Mediterranean and Near Eastern Literature

CREATION AND THE COSMOS

> Tell me, O Muses who dwell on Olympos, and
> observe proper order for each thing as it first
> came into being.
> —Hesiod, *Theogony*, 114–15

Topics for Lecture or Discussion

1. **A primary concern in these ancient cosmogonies is the relation of the god or gods to earth, not only with respect to creation but also to the dubious morality that the god (or gods) displays.** *The Great Hymn to the Aten* praises Aten as the source of life and the lord of all the Egyptian empire but also alludes to the dangers that Aten allows when he sets at night (lines 13–23). Similarly, Hesiod praises Zeus as he who "gives his verdict and with unerring firmness and wisdom brings some great strife to a swift end" (*Theogony*, 86–87), but Zeus is also designated as he who "devised sorrows and troubles for men" (*Works and Days*, 1). In which cosmogonies do the gods act evilly or well, and in which do they simply allow good and evil to happen? The different conceptions enunciated in these texts are indicative of the developing understanding of ethics and morality throughout the Mediterranean world. Lucretius most explicitly declares that religion is a major source of suffering and evil (80–100), but he too expresses the tension found in the aforementioned works through his literary invocation to and praise of the goddess Venus at the beginning of *On the Nature of Things* (lines 1–9).
    a. **Further Reading:** Collins, John J. "Cosmology: Time and History." In *Religions of the Ancient World*, edited by Sarah Iles Johnston, 59–70. Cambridge, MA: Harvard University Press, 2004.
    b. **Suggested Search:** A Google Images search for "Hesiod Theogony" results in several charts of the genealogy of the gods according to Hesiod, including the particularly helpful and clear chart at iwu.edu.

2. **Several of the works in this cluster illustrate at least a rudimentary conception of natural law theory, including reference to a binding, knowable moral code that humans are obliged to follow, or suffer divine retribution.** Hesiod makes reference to impious humans as "lawbreakers" who are ignorant of, or consciously ignoring, the dictum of the gods (*Theogony*, 137–41), with the possible implication that they ought to recognize and obey such laws. Similarly, the seventh tablet of *Enuma Elish* commands that humans ought to study and contemplate the laws of the gods and the story of the Creation, while it also threatens displeasure and punishment from Marduk if this is not done. The "Cannibal Spell for King Unis" offers a similar conception in indicating Unis's

power over and ordering of the world with the final threat of punishment for those who do evil deeds. How do humans come to know the laws of the gods, and is this ordering of nature merely punitive, or is there a final good toward which humans are directed? "The Great Hymn to the Aten" places all of creation under Aten's order but explicitly states that the god is also the proper order of human life: "Those on earth come from your hand as you made them, / When you have dawned they live, / When you set they die; / You yourself are lifetime, one lives by you" (111–14). These aspects of natural law and divine retribution might be fruitfully compared to passages in the Hebrew Bible, as for example in Genesis 4 (pp. 161–62), Cain kills Abel and is punished by God, though he had never been told not to kill. The implication is that there is a knowable, natural moral code which one is obliged to follow.

a. **Further Reading:** Fears, J. Rufus. "Natural Law: The Legacy of Greece and Rome." In *Common Truths: New Perspectives on Natural Law,* edited by Edward B. McLean, 19–56. Wilmington, DE: ISI Books, 2000.

b. **Suggested Searches:** A search for "Unis" within the "From A to Z" at ancient-egypt.org/ results in multiple resources in relation to the "Cannibal Spell for King Unis." Also, as an alternate spelling, search using "King Unas."

3. **Both Hesiod and Lucretius emphasize that suffering and toil are an essential aspect of the human condition, but Hesiod asserts that this is a fallen reflection of a better age, while Lucretius asserts that this is due to the cyclical and purposeless progression of nature.** The five ages of man that Hesiod describes in *Works and Days* express an understanding of the decay and corruption of humans and their world that progressively declines until virtue is no longer honored and Zeus destroys the human race (127–41). While deeply fatalistic, Hesiod does present an image of a past golden age that was without suffering, an image that is not to be found in Lucretius's presentation of a dooming cycle of suffering and death. Rather, Lucretius famously asserts that he can "prove that not for us and not by gods / Was this world made. There's too much wrong with it" (52–54). What are the ramifications of the differences between these similarly pessimistic but otherwise distinct accounts of the human condition? Philosophically, it is perhaps more important to note that both poets agree that the conditions of human life are not as they should be, and that by making this judgment, both Hesiod and Lucretius imply what their conception of the good life is. The Book of Job in the Hebrew Bible is an interesting counterpoint to these conceptions, as Job struggles with the question of theodicy, trying to reconcile a just God with the suffering and evil that Job endures (see especially Job's speech in sections 9–10, and God's reply in sections 38–42).

a. **Further Reading:** Bartlett, Robert C. "An Introduction to Hesiod's *Works and Days.*" *The Review of Politics* 68 (2006): 177–205.

b. **Suggested Search:** Search the JSTOR database at www.jstor.org for "Hesiod and the golden age."

4. **A common element in cosmogonies and foundational myths is the explanation or assertion of the authority of the work, and this invites, to varying degrees, scrutiny of the intended veracity of the work.** "The Great Hymn to the Aten" is spoken by "The Vizier, the Fan-bearer on the right of the King," and the hymn reveals that the king is the only one who knows Aten (107–10), thus revealing the authority of the source of the Vizier's knowledge. More emphatically, the seventh tablet of the *Enuma Elish* claims Marduk's imprimatur of the work and demands that it be studied and followed upon the gods' command. While both of these appear to make their assertions in all seriousness, Hesiod offers a slightly different source of authority by narrating his contact with the minor goddesses, the Helikonian Muses, who instruct him to "spread the fame of past and future, / and commanded me to hymn the race of the deathless gods, / but always begin and end my song with them" (32–34). The self-referential aspect of the Muses' narration, as well as their statement "we know how to tell many lies that pass for truth, / and when we wish, we know to tell the truth itself" (27–28), invites questions regarding Hesiod's religious sincerity in *Theogony.*

a. **Further Reading:** Burkert, Walter. "The Logic of Cosmogony." In *From Myth to Reason? Studies in the Development of Greek Thought,* edited by Richard Buxton, 87–106. Oxford: Oxford University Press, 1999.

b. **Suggested Search:** Perform a Google Images search for "great hymn to the aten hieroglyphs" and the first several results will present images of the original text of this work.

5. **The ontological emphasis of the readings in the section "Early Greek Philosophy" provides a provocative counterpart to Lucretius's question "For him who's never tasted the love of life—Never been on the roster—what harm, in not being born?" (34–35).** Aristotle's account of Thales's philosophy asserts a foundational substance from which all is formed, and Heraclitus maintained that this basic substance was eternal. Does this eternal being of the totality of substance have any implications for Lucretius's doubt about the essential good of being? Anaxagoras's elevation of the importance of the mind not only opens the door for metaphysics but also challenges Lucretius's doubts, implying a goodness to the being of mind, which is "infinite and self-controlling" (p. 50). Similarly, Empedocles's eternal dual actions of union and separation between love and strife have implications for whether or not it is good to be. Do these philosophers also address this

further question: *Why* is there being instead of nonbeing, and *why* is there something rather than nothing?

   a. **Further Reading:** Kahn, Charles H. "Religion and Natural Philosophy in Empedocless' Doctrine of the Soul." In *The Pre-Socratics: A Collection of Critical Essays,* edited by Alexander P. D. Mourelatos, 426–56. New York: Anchor Books, 1974.

   b. **Suggested Search:** Search for "Lucretius and being" for several pertinent and interesting results at Academic Search Premier (http://search.ebscohost.com/).

In-Class Activities

1. Compare the similarities and the dissimilarities between the attributes given to two of the gods. For instance, compile a list as a class of the similarities between Unis in "The Cannibal Spell for King Unis" and Aten in "The Great Hymn to the Aten." What insights can we gain from the congruencies and divergences in these descriptions?

2. Identify several important distinctions between the creation stories. Debate what the crucial issue is upon which they seem to differ. What is the most central aspect that is disagreed upon between these works? Then, as a class, read Genesis 1–3 in the Hebrew Bible (pp. 117–120), and compare that narrative to the creation stories in this cluster.

3. Ask students to write a journal entry in which they attempt to imitate the rhetorical encomium of the gods found in these works. Discuss the rhetorical effectiveness of such writing.

4. Ask students to write a thesis about which of the early Greek philosophers in this selection they find most compelling. Compare the responses and share them, sponsoring debate between opposing views.

Paper Topics/Suggestions for Writing

1. While there are obvious dissimilarities between these various religious traditions and writers, there are also salient points of contact and overlap between these cosmogonies. Identify the three most important unifying elements in these creation stories, and argue why they are significant.

2. Hesiod's *Works and Days* contains a deep pessimism about the human condition that leaves him wishing he had lived in a different age. Is this due to an inability to change circumstances? Is Hesiod's conception of human life entirely deterministic? Do humans have free will?

3. Lucretius begins *On the Nature of Things* with an invocation to Venus but then proceeds to argue in Book V that there the gods are entirely

separate from the human realm and cannot touch things of this world. Is this simply contradictory? How do these two points indicate some deeper implication? And how does Lucretius's conception of nature (Book V) correspond to this?

4. Consider the differences between the genres of the "Cannibal Spell for King Unis," "The Great Hymn to the Aten," and the *Enuma Elish*. What are the rhetorical differences between a spell, a hymn, and a creation epic? How do these generic differences influence the presentation of praise for the god or gods? What are the different purposes for these works, and how does this affect their material?

5. While Thales, Heraclitus, Empedocles, and Anaxagoras are pursuing philosophical questions, in what respects are their conclusions or thoughts similar to that which you find in Hesiod and Lucretius? Similarly, how do the poetically expressed ideas of Hesiod and Lucretius relate to the early Greek philosophers' thoughts? Is there a focal point of disagreement?

Resources

Gale, Monica R., ed. *Oxford Readings in Lucretius*. Oxford: Oxford University Press, 2007.

> This collection of essays covers a range of topics pertaining to Lucretius, including his poetic approach and philosophical background. Gale's collection should be helpful for a variety of approaches to Lucretius for students and instructors alike.

Gotshalk, Richard. *Homer and Hesiod: Myth and Philosophy*. Lanham, MD: University Press of America, 2000.

> Gotshalk makes an interesting argument about the development of the philosophical tradition in ancient Greece in relation to the great poetic myths of Homer and Hesiod. This should be helpful as further background and research and in linking this selection of Hesiod to the selection of Homer.

Hornung, Erik. *Akhenaten and the Religion of Light*. Ithaca, NY: Cornell University Press, 1999.

> This is a highly readable work that focuses on Akhenaten's development of his new religion centered upon Aten. This would be most helpful as an overview of many of the theories relating to Akhenaten and for gaining a general sense of this theological development.

Mourelatos, Alexander P. D., ed. *The Pre-Socratics: A Collection of Critical Essays*. New York: Anchor Books, 1974, 426–56.

> This helpful collection of essays covers a range of topics relating to early Greek philosophers. This work could be useful for any further research or discussion of this selection of philosophers.

THE EPIC OF GILGAMESH

> Enkidu, my friend whom I loved, is turned
>   into clay!
>   Shall I too not lie down like him,
>   And never get up, forever and ever?
> —Gilgamesh, *The Epic of Gilgamesh*, Tablet
>   10, 200–202

Topics for Lecture or Discussion

1. **At the very beginning of the work, Gilgamesh is described as one "who knew the ways, was wise in all things" (1.2), and this establishes the central role of knowledge and wisdom in *The Epic of Gilgamesh*.** When the narrative begins, Gilgamesh is not "wise in all things," leading the reader to understand that part of the development of the story will center upon his quest for and growth in knowledge. Gilgamesh seeks understanding in various forms throughout the work, and after Enkidu's death, all of his actions are governed by his final question about eternal life. In the course of the story, however, Gilgamesh also learns much about political philosophy, the structure of the earth, and the nature of the gods. The centrality of this quest for knowledge in the epic enables us to view the presentation of man as an intellectual creature whose nature inherently desires knowledge. Notably, this is true not only for Gilgamesh but for Enkidu as well, who "gained reason and expanded his understanding" (1.194) through the civilizing process that he undergoes with Shamhat.
   a. **Further Reading:** Jager, Bernd. "The Birth of Poetry and the Creation of a Human World: An Exploration of *The Epic of Gilgamesh*." *Journal of Phenomenological Psychology* 32:2 (2001): 131–54.
   b. **Suggested Search:** Go to flickr.com and search for "maps of Mesopotamia" for several helpful maps, including one of the locations of the ancient cities.

2. **The contrast between Enkidu and Gilgamesh establishes the dichotomy between human civilization and the wilderness that is a constant theme throughout the work.** While Gilgamesh is first introduced as the builder of Uruk and its walls, and thus, in a sense, civilization, Enkidu is entirely a being of the wilds until he is seduced by Shamhat. Their wrestling match can be understood as representative of the struggle between man and his environment, and their eventual unity and friendship are indicative of an ideal harmony between the two. At the conclusion of the epic, Gilgamesh is reconciled to his eventual death through his acknowledgment of the lasting achievement of having built Uruk,

but it is important to recognize that this contentment is realized through his journey in the wilds of the earth. Furthermore, the fact that both Gilgamesh and Enkidu are lonely before they meet one another indicates that man alone, whether in nature or in the city, is not sufficient unto himself. This indicates the essential aspect of human nature that Aristotle identifies: man is a political animal.

   a. **Further Reading:** Barron, Patrick. "The Separation of Wild Animal Nature and Human Nature in *Gilgamesh*: Roots of a Contemporary Theme." *Papers on Language & Literature* 38:4 (2002): 377–94.

   b. **Suggested Search:** Go to historyfiles.co.uk and search for "Gilgamesh" for interesting articles, images, and maps.

3. **Enkidu's important role in correcting the appalling tyranny of Gilgamesh at the opening of the story mirrors the fact that his death propels Gilgamesh to face the difficult reality of inescapable death, and to realize what it is about life that is really of value.** While Gilgamesh has dreams forecasting the advent of his friend, their initial meeting is a great struggle, and though Enkidu loses, he manages to curb Gilgamesh's tyrannical passions. This corrective and educative element is an important indication of the depth and value of their friendship. Similarly, though it is Gilgamesh who ignites the fury of Ishtar through his glib responses to her seductions, Enkidu is the one who must suffer the direct consequence of death. The sharing of another's suffering is another important aspect of their friendship. Finally, through death, Enkidu continues to teach Gilgamesh, leading him to seek answers to deeper issues than the simple glory quests with which he had been concerned before. It is through Enkidu's example and friendship that Gilgamesh moves beyond tyranny and ignorance.

   a. **Further Reading:** Orlin, Louis L. "On the Greatness of *Gilgamesh* as an Ancient Near East Epic." In *Life and Thought in the Ancient Near East,* 100–111. Ann Arbor: University of Michigan Press, 2007.

   b. **Suggested Search:** Go to the "Books" tab at aina.org to find a link to a rendering of *The Epic of Gilgamesh* that includes images of several ancient depictions of Enkidu and Gilgamesh.

4. **As is common in many ancient epics, women play an extremely important role in the development of the plot and in shaping the actions and understanding of the male characters.** Gilgamesh's mother, the goddess Ninsun, is an important character for guiding Gilgamesh and assisting him in the interpretation of his dreams. Similarly, Enkidu is created by the goddess Aruru, and his path to civilization is directly through Shamhat. Ishtar's role is the central pivot of the plot, for Gilgamesh's rejection of her advances leads to Enkidu's death and is thus the reason for his final quest for Utanapishtim. The goddess Siduri is important both for the assistance that she gives Gilgamesh

and for the wisdom that she demonstrates, and Utanapishtim's wife is similarly important for supporting Gilgamesh's cause in front of her husband. It can be useful to compare the role of women in *The Epic of Gilgamesh* to those in other epics, for example, Helen, Penelope, Athena, Dido, Aphrodite, and Lavinia.

   a. **Further Reading:** Harris, Rivkah. "Images of Women in the *Gilgamesh Epic*." In *Gender and Aging in Mesopotamia: The Gilgamesh Epic and Other Ancient Literature*, 119–28. Norman: University of Oklahoma Press, 2000.

   b. **Suggested Search:** Go to Oxford Art Online at www.oxfordart online.com/public and search for "Ishtar."

5. **Gilgamesh's voyage through the mountain (Tablet 9) and across the waters of death (Tablet 10) is indicative of his intellectual movement to inquire about the very nature of things and is reminiscent of the presentation of the land of the dead found in other epic literature.** Just as Homer's Odysseus crosses the ocean to the land of the dead to speak with Tiresias, and Virgil's Aeneas crosses the river Styx to speak with his father, so too Gilgamesh must journey through the darkness of the mountain and over the waters of death to gain the knowledge he seeks from Utanapishtim. In each of the cases the character seeks knowledge of some sort, and for Gilgamesh in particular, this is a different motivation from his earlier tyrannical and glory-seeking days. Though at first halted by the scorpion monster, his wife, and Siduri, the sincerity of Gilgamesh's desire to find Utanapishtim convinces them to give him advice. Similarly, in his overzealousness he destroys the Stone Charms that would have assisted in his crossing over the waters of death, and yet, despite this, he is sincere enough in his inquiry that Ur-Shanabi does decide to help him. It is this intellectual seriousness that Gilgamesh displays that enables him to move from the things of this world to inquire about those beyond death.

   a. **Further Reading:** Ataç, Mehmet-Ali. "'Angelology' in the *Epic of Gilgamesh*." *Journal of Ancient Near Eastern Religions* 4:1 (2004): 3–27.

   b. **Suggested Search:** Go to all-art.org and search for "Gilgamesh" for helpful background information, along with several images of the tablets, statues of gods and characters, and narrative engravings. The "History of Literature" section is the most helpful.

6. **After all of the great feats that Gilgamesh accomplishes, the seeming banality of Utanapishtim's challenge to stay awake for six days and seven nights serves as an important revelation of the limits of human nature.** Gilgamesh fails in his attempt to stay awake, and Utanapishtim's wife's recording time with the aging loaves of bread is similarly emphatic about the simple physical limitations that bar Gilgamesh

from becoming an immortal. These physical limitations are, moreover, joined to indications of intellectual limitations that separate man from the gods. Even after he is given directions and procures the plant that will return one to youth, Gilgamesh loses it through an absentminded carelessness while swimming. The limitations of human nature that Gilgamesh realizes are not without fruit, however, for upon his return to Uruk, he relishes the goodness of his city and civilization. Indeed, as is recounted at the beginning of *The Epic of Gilgamesh*, he writes down the story of his adventures and learning and preserves the story for future generations, indicating the final value that he places upon knowledge.

   a. **Further Reading:** Holland, Glenn S. "Mesopotamia: The World of Kings and Heroes." In *Gods in the Desert: Religions of the Ancient Near East,* 131–48. New York: Rowman & Littlefield, 2009.

   b. **Suggested Search:** Perform a Google Images search for "Gustave Dore the flood" for several excellent engravings depicting the flood of which Utanapishtim speaks.

7. **The gods in *The Epic of Gilgamesh* are, as is often the case in ancient literatures, immortal but anthropomorphized creatures with fickle minds and conflicting wills.** It is notable that Gilgamesh and Enkidu receive the aid of Shamash and Ninsun in their struggle with Humbaba, but when Ishtar falls in love with Gilgamesh and tempts him, they receive no supernatural aid or advice. Ishtar is initially presented as a vindictive character, as her fanatic anger when rebuffed by Gilgamesh is the direct cause of Enkidu's death. When Utanapishtim tells the story of the flood, however, Ishtar is a sympathetic character who weeps for the destruction of humanity. The various gods are similarly split in their opinions about the flood before it happened but are subsequently terrified by the force of the destructive weather. The god Enlil is likewise fickle, for though he planned the flood to destroy all of humanity, he quickly changes his mind when he finds Utanapishtim and his wife. It is helpful to compare the role of the gods here to those in other epics or ancient literatures, especially the Greek and Egyptian gods.

   a. **Further Reading:** Jacobsen, Thorkild. "Second Millennium Metaphors. 'And Death the Journey's End': The Gilgamesh Epic." In *The Treasures of Darkness: A History of Mesopotamian Religion,* 193–220. New Haven, CT: Yale University Press, 1976.

   b. **Suggested Search:** Search the JSTOR database at www.jstor.org for "Sumerian gods" for a variety of articles.

In-Class Activities

1. Ask each student to make a comparative list of the gods in *The Epic of Gilgamesh* and the gods in other cultures' ancient works (Egyptian,

Greek, Hebrew, etc.). Discuss the similarities and dissimilarities, and investigate what this might reveal about human nature.

2. As a class, catalog the various mistakes that Gilgamesh and Enkidu make, and pay particular attention to which character is primarily responsible for which mistake. Does this reveal any particularly illuminating understanding about their respective strengths and weaknesses?

3. Ask students to write a journal entry in which they expand upon the tension between death and the achievements of culture with which Gilgamesh struggles. What are other manifestations of this ancient fear of death and great cultural accomplishment?

4. Compare Utanapishtim's account of the great flood with the biblical account (Genesis, 6–9). Despite the amazing similarities between the accounts, there are also some crucial differences. Discuss what these are, and what significance they may hold.

5. Ask students to write down what they consider Gilgamesh's primary virtue and primary vice. Compare the responses, and organize a textual debate about the various answers.

Paper Topics/Suggestions for Writing

1. Consider the genre of *The Epic of Gilgamesh*. What about it makes it an epic? Are there aspects that are unusual to an epic? How does it compare to other epics?

2. What is the nature of the gods in *The Epic of Gilgamesh?* Are the gods good, or are they evil? Do the gods establish a good toward which humans should strive, or are they merely meddlers in the affairs of men? What does it mean for Gilgamesh to be two-thirds god and one-third man?

3. Examine Enkidu's curse of Shamhat when he is dying (7.58–86). Did Shamhat wrong him as he claims? Was it good that he became civilized? Why or why not? Why does he blame Shamhat more than Gilgamesh? Is this despair in the face of death?

4. Consider the etymology of the name "Gilgamesh" ("the old man is still a young man"). Is Gilgamesh's name significant, despite the fact that he loses the plant that would return him to his youth? In what ways is it a fitting name despite his failure in the quest for immortality? How, in fact, has he actually accomplished immortality?

5. Throughout *The Epic of Gilgamesh*, many dreams occur, and often their meaning is unclear, or at least inscrutable for the characters who

have them. Is there a general unity of the dreams? What is their purport? Do they come from the gods? Are they true? Are they good?

6. Is Gilgamesh a virtuous character? What is the crucial point for his transformation from a tyrant to one who seeks knowledge? Is Gilgamesh a man of action or a man of contemplation?

Resources

Dalley, Stephanie, et al. *The Legacy of Mesopotamia*. Oxford: Oxford University Press, 1998.

> Focused upon writing and reading and the impact that these developments had upon Mesopotamian and neighboring cultures, this is a fascinating historical account that provides substantial cultural material in its considerations.

Foster, Benjamin R., ed. *The Epic Of Gilgamesh*. Norton Critical Edition. New York: Norton, 2001.

> The historical and critical context that supplements the text in this edition is helpful in situating the reader properly, and it includes several of the other Gilgamesh stories and poems. The selected bibliography included is similarly helpful for further research and reading.

Maier, John, ed. *Gilgamesh: A Reader*. Wauconda, IL: Bolchazy-Carducci, 1997.

> This is a substantial collection of twenty-five essays on the *Epic of Gilgamesh*, and it addresses issues as various as the epic's influence on later literature, its poetic forms, and its cultural inheritance. This work also includes an excellent bibliography.

Tigay, Jeffrey H. *The Evolution of the Gilgamesh Epic*. Wauconda, IL: Bolchazy-Carducci, 2002.

> Tigay offers a textual study of the *Epic of Gilgamesh* that follows the development and evolution of the text through time, different peoples, and different schools of philosophy and theology. It is a serious work and is recommended for those interested in the textual history of the epic.

THE HEBREW BIBLE

And God created the human in his image,
in the image of God He created him,
    male and female He created them.
—Genesis 1

Topics for Lecture or Discussion

1. **In both creation stories in Genesis, God instills an order within all creation, but humanity has the singular exception of being able to choose whether to obey the order or not.** Genesis indicates that creation is good, and ordered toward the good, as God looks upon what he has created and "it was very good" (p. 118). The distinctly free human will, however, is indicated both in the fact that humans are made in God's image, and thus are capable of willing, as well as the fact that God gives man the command not to eat from the tree of knowledge of good and evil, indicating that humans have a choice concerning whether to obey or not. In the subsequent disobedience of man and woman, not only are they punished, but the inherent goodness of creation is in some measure corrupted, as is particularly evident in God's curse to the man: "Cursed be the soil for your sake, with pangs shall you eat from it all the days of your life" (120). Humanity's free will and the ability to choose good or evil are of central importance for the entirety of the Hebrew Bible.
   a. **Further Reading:** Augustine, Saint (Bishop of Hippo). "Book Eleven: The Sin of Adam and Eve and Their Expulsion from Paradise." In *The Literal Meaning of Genesis,* vol. II, translated by John Hammond Taylor, 133–77. New York: Newman Press, 1982.
   b. **Suggested Search:** Go to catholic-resources.org and search "Gustave Dore Old Testament" for a complete list of Dore's illustrations of Genesis, including the stories of the Creation and the Fall.

2. **The story of God asking Abraham to sacrifice his only son Isaac (Genesis 21, 22) is demonstrative not only of Abraham's faith but also of the nature of God's goodness.** It is notable that when God gives his command that Abraham should go and sacrifice Isaac, the Bible does not offer any details concerning Abraham's reaction short of his simple compliance. The reader must wonder if Abraham struggled with this command. Did he question either the source of the command, or his understanding of it? With poignant detail, however, the story does relate Isaac's question regarding where the sheep was that they would sacrifice, and Abraham's seemingly trusting response. In fact, God does provide the ram exactly as Abraham told Isaac he would, but not before Abraham demonstrated his willingness to be completely

obedient. This identification of God as one who does not demand human sacrifice and who values human life is significantly different than many ancient religious traditions and is an important facet of the uniqueness of the Hebrew tradition. Notably, Abraham's faith and obedience in this situation result in a profound blessing from God that passes on to Abraham's descendants. The potential and extent to which a good man might suffer foreshadows the story of, among others, Job.

a. **Further Reading:** Kass, Leon. "Inheriting the Way: From Father to Son." In *The Beginning of Wisdom: Reading Genesis*, 352–75. Chicago: University of Chicago Press, 2003.

b. **Suggested Search:** Go to caravaggio.com and search "sacrifice of Isaac" for a substantial selection of famous paintings and depictions of this scene.

3. **Part of the importance of Joseph's ability to interpret the Pharaoh's dream (Genesis, 37, 39–45) is that, from a cultural consideration, it illustrates the potential insight and understanding that one from outside a culture might have.** Joseph, who has dreams himself, is enabled by God to properly interpret the dreams of the chief cupbearer, the chief baker, and the Pharaoh. He is blessed with a particular prudence and ability, such that even while a slave "his master saw that the Lord was with him, and all that he did the Lord made succeed in his hand, and Joseph found favor in his eyes and he ministered to him, and he put him in charge of his house" (39). Joseph also understands the Egyptian culture with real insight and is able to properly direct the land in preparation for the coming famine. It is precisely this that finally reunites him with his brothers and father. Conversely, the inability of the Egyptians to understand their dreams implies a human difficulty in self-understanding and a fair evaluation of one's own culture.

a. **Further Reading:** Sacks, Robert. "The Lion and the Ass: A Commentary on the Book of Genesis. (Chapters 40–43)," *Interpretation* 12.1 (1984): 49–82.

b. **Suggested Search:** A Google Images search for "Joseph and Pharaoh dream" results in several interesting depictions that present Joseph, varyingly, as similar and dissimilar to the Egyptians.

4. **The question of theodicy is the central concern of the book of Job.** Despite the fact that Job is described as one who was "blameless and upright and feared God and shunned evil" (1), nevertheless he suffers a tremendous loss of his goods and family. Why should a good man suffer? And if God is just, why does he allow the adversary to inflict apparently undeserved torment upon Job? While these questions cannot be simply answered, a partial solution can be found in Job's refusal to follow his wife's advice to "Curse God and die" (2). Much like Abraham's willingness to sacrifice Isaac, Job laments his situation but does not

curse God. In God's testing of Job's faith and goodness, he must endure evils that are seemingly unwarranted. The deeper point of the text, however, is that despite the simplistic arguments of Job's friends—that the evil suffer and the good prosper—the justice of God is more inscrutable, and the proper course for a human is not to project one's conception of justice upon God but to willingly accept that which is ordained. God's final words to Job emphasize this distinction between limited human knowledge and understanding, and the depth of divine knowledge: "Where were you when I founded earth? Tell, if you know understanding. Who fixed its measures, do you know, or who stretched a line upon it?" (38).

a. **Further Reading:** Aquinas, Saint Thomas. *The Literal Exposition on Job: A Scriptural Commentary Concerning Providence.* Translated by Anthony Damico. Oxford: Oxford University Press, 1989.

b. **Suggested Search:** Search "Job" at blakearchive.org to find William Blake's engravings of the book of Job.

5. **Another important aspect of the book of Job is that through the suffering that Job endures, the Bible presents a compelling understanding of human nature and what constitutes happiness.** Many different schools of philosophy posit that happiness consists of interior virtue, pleasure, goods, or some combination of the three. Stoic philosophy, for example, would argue that a man of blameless virtue like Job should be happy, regardless of the condition of externalities such as his property or family. The book of Job, however, clearly asserts that the loss of such goods is a profound barrier to his happiness, and, as is made clear in Job's conversation with God at the conclusion of the book, true happiness—permanent happiness without fear—can only be had in perfect communion with God, and not in this life. And yet for human nature to achieve happiness in this life, the book of Job is clear in indicating the value of such things as personal possessions, family, friends, and interior virtue. The virtuous man, however, must rightly order such goods within the divine framework of created being, as God states in his rebuke of Job.

a. **Further Reading:** Ellis, Alice Thomas. "Forward." In *The Book of Job: Why Do the Innocent Suffer?*, edited by Lawrence Boadt, 7–10. New York: Lion Publishing, 1997.

b. **Suggested Search:** Search "Job" at the Web Gallery of Art (www .wga.hu) for several depictions of Job, including Georges de la Tour's wonderful "Job Mocked by His Wife" and Laurent de la Hire's more cheerful "Job Restored to Prosperity."

6. **The anthology's selection of the Psalms artfully combines aspects of adoration, propitiation, impetation, and thanksgiving in prayer.** These four aspects inform the motions of prayer throughout the Psalms,

with a different emphasis in each. Psalms 8 and 23 are particularly focused on encomium, as they do not request anything of God but praise him and enumerate his works. The repeated beginning and ending line of Psalm 8 is a clear example, simply offered up in adoration: "O Lord our Lord, how excellent is thy name in all the earth" (8.1). In contrast, Psalms 19 and 104 praise God throughout the beginning of the psalm, but they conclude with impetratory statements, as, for example, Psalm 19 concludes, "Let the words of my mouth, and the meditation of my heart, be acceptable in thy sight, O Lord, my strength, and my redeemer" (19.14). Psalm 137, however, is decidedly a prayer of propitiation and impetration, both contrite and expectant of God's coming deliverance. In contrast to the simpler praise of God in Psalm 8, Psalm 137 requests that God remember the enemies of Israel: "Remember, O Lord, the children of Edom . . . O daughter of Babylon, who art to be destroyed; happy shall he be, that rewardeth thee as thou hast served us" (137.7–8).

a. **Further Reading:** Chrysostom, Saint John. *Commentary on the Psalms.* Vol. 1. Translated by Robert Charles Hill. Brookline, MA: Holy Cross Orthodox Press, 2007.

b. **Suggested Search:** Go to youtube.com and search "Psalm 104 Anglican Cathedral" for choral performances of the psalm.

7. **While all are prayers addressed to God, the Psalms also serve as educative texts that inform the reader about the nature of God and his works.** Psalm 104, though it begins with an invocation for God's blessing, proceeds to enumerate and extol the extent of God's power and goodness, impressing the reader with an explanation of the origins of all the earth by describing God as he "Who laid the foundations of the earth, that it should not be removed for ever" (104.5). Similarly, Psalm 23 famously makes the impressive statement that the God of Israel does comfort his people beyond the power of death: "Yea, though I walk through the valley of the shadow of death, I will fear no evil: for thou art with me; thy rod and thy staff they comfort me" (23.4). Taken as a whole, the Psalms are not merely prayers of the Hebrew people but are catechetical and apologetical works. Indeed, insofar as they are sincere in their trust in God's power, the Psalms can also serve as threats to the enemies of the Hebrews, as Psalm 137 warns of the inevitable destruction of Babylon.

a. **Further Reading:** Lewis, C. S. "Introductory" and "'The Fair Beauty of the Lord.'" In *Reflections on the Psalms,* 1–8, 44–53. New York: Harcourt, Brace, and Company, 1958.

b. **Suggested Search:** Go to youtube.com and search "Allegri miserere Tallis Scholars" for a beautiful polyphonic composition of Psalm 51 by Gregorio Allegri.

In-Class Activities

1. Compare the creation story in Genesis to the other creation stories in this anthology. What are the similarities and differences?

2. Discuss the distinctions between approaching a text as a religious manifestation of divine revelation and as a literary work of art. Does this change how one reads the text? Does it offer different insights?

3. Compare a different translation of Genesis (or any other part here) to that included in the anthology (the King James Bible or the Douai-Rheims are recommended). Ask students to discuss the differences of interpretation or meaning that are available, depending upon which translation is used.

4. Ask students to write a journal entry in which they pick a character from this selection of the Hebrew Bible and discuss his strengths and weaknesses. Is it significant that his weaknesses are clearly shown? Who seems like the most noble character?

5. Ask students to memorize one of the Psalms and recite it to the class.

Paper Topics/Suggestions for Writing

1. Choose one of Job's friends' arguments and write an adequate summary of his points. Is he persuasive? What, in the perspective of the book of Job, is wrong with his argument? Why is Job not persuaded?

2. Compare the Hebrew Bible's presentation of dreams to another cultural tradition's understanding of dreams (ancient Egyptian, ancient Greek, etc.). Are they similar? What important distinctions are there? Why is such importance placed upon dreams?

3. Compare the Hebrew Bible's account of the Great Flood to Utanapishtim's in *The Epic of Gilgamesh*. What are the significant differences and similarities? How should they be interpreted? Is the Great Flood indicative of some deeper aspect of human nature?

4. What is the difference between the curse given to the first man and the curse given to the first woman? Why are they given different curses, and is this significant? Is there a fittingness to the punishments? Do the punishments correspond to the distinct manners in which the man and the woman fell into sin?

5. Ask students to write a poetic analysis of several of the Psalms. It might be useful to compare their various translations to find important differences. How are the Psalms not simply prayerful but truly poetic?

6. Consider the role of free will in any of these works from the Hebrew Bible. How is it important? What is the nature of its function, and how

do the characters understand their ability to choose good or evil? Is free will a good thing? In what manner is it most frequently exercised?

7. Consider the story of the Tower of Babel in comparison to Cain and Abel. In both cases people sin, but how does God deal with them differently? What is the significance of these sins, and their punishments? Can any important inferences be made concerning human nature or God's nature?

8. Joseph's preeminence in Egypt causes the Hebrew people to move there, and they eventually become enslaved and need Moses to save them. Why does this evil come out of the good of Joseph's success? What is significant about the children of Abraham abandoning their inherited land? How does this relate to the manner in which Moses saves his people?

Resources

Aquinas, Saint Thomas. *The Literal Exposition on Job: A Scriptural Commentary Concerning Providence.* Translated by Anthony Damico. Oxford: Oxford University Press, 1989.
>   An excellent, line-by-line commentary on the book of Job by one of the great thinkers of the medieval period, this work compares the book of Job to other biblical and philosophical writings.
Bede. *On Genesis.* Translated by Calvin Kendall. Liverpool: Liverpool University Press, 2008.
>   The Venerable Bede, a considerable commentator on the Old Testament, writes an interesting commentary on Genesis that seeks to relate the insights of the Church Fathers to his own students, coupled with his own reflections.
Kass, Leon R. *The Beginning of Wisdom: Reading Genesis.* Chicago: University of Chicago Press, 2003.
>   Kass's large work is a close and thoughtful reading of Genesis that rather than subscribing to a particular religious tradition seeks to approach the work through a philosophic reading. This is highly recommended for any reader or student of Genesis, and the thorough index will assist students in finding particular reflections on particular topics.
Lewis, C. S. *Reflections on the Psalms.* New York: Harcourt, Brace, and Company, 1958.
>   This work is an excellent resource for immediately accessible and general thoughts about the Psalms. It does not contain a particular discussion of each psalm but, rather, offers a general discussion on different themes, ranging from diverse issues such as death to allegorical readings and presentations of nature.

Reno, R. R. *Genesis*. Brazos Theological Commentary on the Bible. Grand Rapids, MI: Brazos Press, 2010.

> A thorough and thought-provoking commentary on Genesis, this work is an excellent resource for students or instructors who wish to gain an understanding of the theological and philosophical importance of this text. It contains helpful indexes based on subject and scriptural references.

HOMER

The Iliad
The Odyssey

Topics for Lecture or Discussion

1. **As is evident from the initial lines, Achilles's rage is the governing passion of *The Iliad*, but it is also representative of all of the passions without the guidance of prudence that are presented throughout the work.** Achilles's anger not only keeps him from the conflict with the Trojans at the beginning of *The Iliad* but is also that passion that leads to his slaughter of Hector after Patroclus's death. In brief moments of rational clarity, Achilles understands that he ought to control his rage and that his lack of ability to do so places certain blame upon his own head, as when he laments Patroclus, saying, "My friend is dead, Patroclus, my dearest friend of all. I loved him, and I killed him" (Bk. 18, 84–86). However much Achilles might "wish that all strife could stop" (18, 112), he does not control his rage, and as "fury incarnate" (18, 342–43) he kills Hector and then mutilates his body. Similarly uncontrolled passions and vices are Agamemnon's pride, Hector's vainglory, and Paris's lust. In each case the lack of prudence and temperance brings havoc and destruction as a necessary consequence.
   a. **Further Reading:** Routh, H. V. "The Heroes of *The Iliad*." In *God, Man, & Epic Poetry: A Study in Comparative Literature*, vol. I, 15–56. New York: Greenwood Press, 1968.
   b. **Suggested Search:** In the Web Gallery of Art (www.wga.hu), search "the wrath of Achilles" to find François-Léon Benouville's painting of the same name.

2. **The extended Homeric similes not only complement the vivid nature of the descriptions throughout *The Iliad* and *The Odyssey*, but they also anchor the depiction of what are otherwise often fantastic events firmly within the sphere of human experience and imagination.** In one of Homer's most gripping similes, Hector awaits the coming of Achilles "as a snake waits, / Tense and coiled / As a man approaches / Its lair in the mountains, / Venom in its fangs / And poison in its heart, / Glittering eyes / Glaring from the rocks" (Book 22, lines 103–110). Not only expressing the deadly intent, hatred, and tense expectation with which Hector waits, this simile also helps convey the depth of passion that such a superlative hero would have felt. Rather than simply record a description of the different, extraordinary aspects of Hector at this moment, the Homeric simile creates an entire likeness

that more succinctly and powerfully expresses the tension. In a similar manner, when Odysseus, finally home, strings his great bow, he is "like a musician stretching a string / Over a new peg on his lyre, and making / The twisted sheep-gut fast at either end" (21, 432–34). In contrast to the reader's understanding of the symbolic importance and precariousness of Odysseus's stringing of the bow, the simile compares the action to the commonplace and casual action of a musician, a comparison that at once conveys Odysseus's ease as well as the heightening of tension through situational understatement.

a. **Further Reading:** Beye, Charles Rowan. "Epic Technique." In *The Iliad, The Odyssey, and the Epic Tradition*, 75–110. New York: Anchor Books, 1966.

b. **Suggested Search:** Go to LION (Literature Online) at lion.chad wyck.com and search "epic simile" for various results, including critical and reference.

3. **The dissension in the Greek army between Achilles and Agamemnon is mirrored by dissension among the Trojans and the gods.** While the difficulties between Achilles and Agamemnon are most central to the plot because of the serious consequences of Achilles's anger, it is nevertheless important to understand that the Trojans have similar difficulties. Despite the fact that Troy is being besieged on account of Paris stealing Helen, the reader finds that Paris is not particularly devoted to the military defense of the city. Hector rebukes him for dawdling with Helen, saying, "We're dying out there defending the walls. / It's because of you the city is in this hellish war" (6, 343–44). Yet not only does Paris not become ashamed, but the very wife he stole rebukes him and praises Hector instead. The potential conflict of interest between all of the Greeks having to fight for Menelaus's wife is parallel to the problematic necessity of all of Troy having to defend Paris's theft. Differences between the gods concerning their favorite humans are similarly divisive, as the reader finds in the violent arguments between Hera and Zeus. Notably, the entire history of the Trojan War begins with Eris, the goddess of discord, and her legacy is a fundamental problem for all involved in *The Iliad*.

a. **Further Reading:** Weil, Simone. *The Iliad or The Poem of Force: A Critical Edition*. Translated by James P. Holoka. New York: Peter Lang, 2003.

b. **Suggested Search:** Search the JSTOR database (www.jstor.org) for "Eris and Troy" to find several articles addressing the role of discord in the Trojan War.

4. **A common feature of classical epics is that they begin *in medias res* (in the middle of things), and this not only creates a sophisticated narrative structure with the recounting of past events, but it also**

heightens the importance of time. When *The Iliad* begins, the Greeks have already been fighting at Troy for nine years, and the initial source of conflict between Agamemnon and Achilles is over plunder from battles that have already transpired. An essential question for the reader to ask, then, is why does the narrative begin where it does? *The Odyssey* begins in a parallel manner—Odysseus has been traveling home for nine years, since the sacking of Troy. While such a beginning allows Odysseus to show his own talents as a storyteller in recounting his journey to the Phaeacians, he too must ask "Where should I begin, where end my story?" (9, 15). Part of the importance of both epics beginning in medias res is that it reflects an understanding of man as a temporal, rational creature whose intellect can order and learn from past events and can look forward to future ones. Knowledge of placement in time, or in an understandable progression of events, is an important form of self-knowledge in these works.

    a. **Further Reading:** Wheeler, Graham. "Sing Muse . . . : The Introit from Homer to Apollonius." *The Classical Quarterly* 52:1 (2002): 33–49.

    b. **Suggested Search:** Go to Britannica online (www.britannica.com) and search "in medias res."

5. **Odysseus, identified as a "cunning hero" in the first line and constantly described as having a "teeming brain," must learn how to temper his wit and craftiness with the guidance of prudence over the course of his journey.** When Odysseus tells the Phaeacians what transpired since the fall of Troy, the reader learns that he made many imprudent choices, and that he did not display the marks of a great leader, losing all of the men under his command. For example, his decision to attack and pillage the Cicones cost him many men, and his curiosity regarding the Cyclopes ended in several gruesome deaths, nearly including his own. By the time Odysseus reaches Ithaca, however, he makes use of his craftiness in a manner entirely to his advantage, biding his time to return to his palace and carefully testing the loyalty of his servants. Indeed, Odysseus is prudent enough that, in contrast to the too-trusting nature of Agamemnon, who was murdered by his wife, Odysseus is even wary of the faithful Penelope. It can be helpful to compare this role of prudence in *The Odyssey* to the same virtue's role in *The Iliad*.

    a. **Further Reading:** Dimock Jr., George E. "The Name of Odysseus." In *Homer: A Collection of Critical Essays*. Twentieth Century Views Series, edited by George Steiner and Robert Fagles, 106–21. Englewood Cliffs, NJ: Prentice Hall, 1962.

    b. **Suggested Search:** Go to Academic Search Premier (www.ebscohost.com/academic) and search "Odysseus and Rhetoric" for a selection of pertinent articles.

6. **The large role that Telemachus plays, particularly at the beginning of *The Odyssey*, is in part a coming-of-age story that establishes an important contrast to Odysseus's role as the man of experience returning to his own.** While Odysseus is, without a doubt, the central character of this narrative, he is not presented until the fifth book. Rather, the plight of Ithaca and Penelope, especially the actions of Telemachus, is first narrated. The absence of Odysseus from the narrative conveys the sense of his absence from Ithaca, and Telemachus's assertive actions contrast with Odysseus's helplessness on Calypso's island. Telemachus's development from an uncertain youth into a decisive young man corresponds to Odysseus's return to Ithaca, and their unity in fighting the suitors at the conclusion of the story underscores significant similarities between their distinct developments. So, too, Telemachus's shorter journey reflects Odysseus's voyage, and the hospitality that Telemachus receives contrasts with the struggles that his father encounters.

   a. **Further Reading:** Austin, Norman. "The Power of the Word." In *Homer's The Odyssey*. Modern Critical Interpretations Series, edited by Harold Bloom, 69–85. New York: Chelsea House, 1988.

   b. **Suggested Search:** Search the Web Gallery of Art (www.wga.hu) for "Telemachus" for two artistic depictions of his situation and personality.

7. **Odysseus's journey is not only movement from one geographic location to another but is representative of the cosmological understanding of the Greeks, and more generally of the ancient world.** Not only can the understanding of the cosmos found in *The Odyssey* be related to that found in *The Epic of Gilgamesh*, on the shield of Achilles in *The Iliad*, and that shown in Hesiod, but it can also be related to the cosmology of the Egyptians (see the further reading selection). Odysseus's journey carries him from a god's island to a man's island, from the public sphere of war to the private sphere of family, and from the land of the living, through the underworld of his ancestors, to the accomplishments of his progeny. This movement not only includes a geographical transition from east to west but the entirety of the human experience of family, divinity, and time. In this respect, Odysseus's journey presents a thorough cosmological picture of existence and human experience.

   a. **Further Reading:** Marinatos, Nanno. "The Cosmic Journey of Odysseus." *Numen* 48:4 (2001): 381–416.

   b. **Suggested Search:** A Google Images search for "Odysseus journey" will bring up several maps that chart the movements of Odysseus during his ten-year voyage home.

8. **In his book *The Art of the Commonplace*, Wendell Berry describes "*The Odyssey's* understanding of marriage as the vital link that joins the human community and the earth" (122).** The amazing marriage between faithful Penelope and cunning Odysseus unifies the true community of faithful farmers and servants on Ithaca and stands in sharp contrast to the false, epicurean community of suitors that assails the marriage. Odysseus's slaughter of the suitors is not only fitting on the individual level due to their assault upon his family but is indicative of the centrality of the marriage as that essential bond within true human communities. Similarly, the immovable marriage bed, built into the trunk of a massive olive tree, illustrates the deep connection between the earth and marriage. That human bond between spouses and between members of a community is closely bound up with the importance of the place—in this case, Ithaca—in which that marriage and community live. Despite other enticing offers of marriage and immortality, Odysseus strives to return to his wife and land precisely because he is so deeply rooted to the place and community as essential elements for human happiness.

   a. **Further Reading**: Berry, Wendell. "The Body and the Earth." In *The Art of the Commonplace: The Agrarian Essays of Wendell Berry*, edited by Norman Wirzba, 93–134. Washington, DC: Counterpoint, 2002.

   b. **Suggested Search:** Search the Web Gallery of Art (www.wga.hu) for "Penelope" for several interesting depictions, including Leandro Bassano's portrayal of Penelope at the loom.

In-Class Activities

1. Provide students with a copy of W. H. Auden's poem "The Shield of Achilles." Compare the descriptions of Homer and Auden, and discuss the significance of the similarities and differences.

2. Similarly, provide students with a copy of Alfred Lord Tennyson's poem "Ulysses" and compare the character to Homer's Odysseus. Note the important reinterpretation of Odysseus's character into a restless man who does not appreciate living at peace on Ithaca.

3. Ask students to discuss the pervasive influence of *The Iliad* and *The Odyssey* in our culture, including art, film, and novels. Show or describe works such as *O Brother, Where Art Thou?* and James Joyce's *Ulysses* and discuss their pertinence and similarities to Homer's work.

4. Create a chart as a class that compares Odysseus's virtues and vices to Achilles's. Debate which character is more heroic, admirable, inspiring, and so on. A similarly profitable comparison would be to perform the

same exercise but with other epics, such as *Gilgamesh* or Virgil's *Aeneid*. Such distinctions will help clarify Homer's particular understanding of virtue and vice.

5. Ask students to write a journal entry in which they must identify the essential distinctive element between *The Iliad* and *The Odyssey*. Debate the question, focusing on both characters and the overall structure of the works.

Paper Topics/Suggestions for Writing

1. Is Achilles's anger a virtue or a vice, as presented in *The Iliad*? How is it made manifest in characters other than Achilles? Similarly, is Odysseus's cunning a virtue or a vice? How do other characters display a cunning similar to Odysseus's?

2. Consider the presentation of the gods in *The Iliad* and *The Odyssey*. What is the gods' role? Do they control humans? Do humans have free will? Are the gods simply fickle, or do they support some essential order? What does this presentation of the gods reveal about the ancient Greek understanding of the divine?

3. Does Odysseus change over the course of the epic? Does he learn anything? If so, what? How does this compare to Penelope? To Telemachus?

4. Compare either *The Iliad* or *The Odyssey* or both to *The Epic of Gilgamesh*. What is the essential, unifying feature of the epic as a genre? How do these works display that trait? In what important ways do the Greek epics differ from *Gilgamesh*?

5. In both *The Iliad* and *The Odyssey*, there are interactions and altercations between different cultures. From these clashes one can hope to find what it is that is most valued, most essential in the Greek culture from which these epics come. What are these central values? What is distinctively Greek, in contrast to the other cultures encountered? Why are these distinctions important?

6. What role does war play in *The Iliad*? Is it presented as a good thing or a bad thing? What understanding of war do the different characters have? What are the worthwhile causes for fighting a war?

7. Homer's epics both have important female characters who are tremendously influential in the development of the plots, including Athena, Helen, and Penelope. What role do women play within these works, and in what ways is this significant? In what respect, precisely, do women hold important positions? What is the manner in which they are accorded respect?

8. What is hospitality as it is presented in these works? Is it a virtue? Is it a duty? Is it a disposition? To what end is hospitality directed? Aside from Zeus's love of hospitality, what binds humans to be hospitable?

Resources

Empires—The Greeks: Crucible of Civilization. Dir. Cassian Harrison. Perf. Liam Neeson. PBS, 2000.
> This is a well-done documentary that focuses on the achievements of the Athenians in the ancient world and their development of Western culture.

Hanson, Victor Davis. *A War Like No Other*. New York: Random House, 2005.
> An excellent work focusing on the Peloponnesian War between the Spartans and Athenians, Hanson's book is valuable to the student and instructor of Homer for vividly realizing ancient military practices among the people who read and loved the Homeric epics.

In Search of the Trojan War. Dir. Bill Lyons. Perf. Michael Wood. BBC Warner, 1985. Film.
> An interesting documentary with Michael Wood, this film traces historical, literary, and geographical evidence for the historical existence of the Trojan War. While no certain conclusion is reached concerning the veracity of events in Homer, the presentation invites serious reflection.

Luce, J. V. *Celebrating Homer's Landscapes: Troy and Ithaca Revisited*. New Haven, CT: Yale University Press, 1998.
> This is an excellent resource for instructors seeking to show the students beautiful pictures of the landscapes Homer describes, while matching these images to maps and the text. The primary focus of the argument of this book is that Homer accurately describes the landscapes that he presents—a challenging element of realism in what is otherwise often dismissed as pure myth.

O Brother, Where Art Thou? Dir. Joel Coen. Perf. George Clooney, John Turturro, and Tim Blake Nelson. Touchstone Pictures, 2000.
> *O Brother, Where Art Thou?* offers an imaginative adaptation of *The Odyssey*, and should be particularly interesting for students who have just completed Homer's work, as they will be struck by resonances from Homer without finding entirely clear analogies between the works.

Rutherford, Richard. *Homer*. New Surveys in the Classics. Oxford: Oxford University Press, 1996.
> This is a helpful survey of critical and scholarly developments regarding Homer's epics without being laborious in accounting for critical fashions.

Troy. Dir. Peterson Wolfgang. Perf. Brad Pitt. Warner Home Video, 2004.
This is a loose adaptation of *The Iliad* that focuses on Achilles while ignoring the role of the gods. The film had a high production budget and broad release, though it adds little food for thought and has unremarkable acting. It is suggested here as an excellent example of the extent to which Homer's epics are commonplace in Western culture, and one might also address the degree to which a work of art can be properly adapted or reworked within another medium.

AESOP

Topics for Lecture or Discussion

1. **In many of the fables, the underlying assertion of authority based upon strength indicates a political warning that helps support the democratic institutions of the ancient Athenians.** In his article "Aesop, Aristotle, and Animals: The Role of Fables in Human Life," Edward Clayton argues that the fables can be understood to "actually point towards democracy, equality, and justice rather than hierarchy, power, and exploitation" (183). In our selection, fables such as "The Mice, the Cat, and the Bell" and "The Fox, the Lion, and the Footprints" create a contrast between the brute power of the cat and lion with the weakness of the other animals. This can not only serve as a warning about the dangers of the tyrannical tendencies of the powerful but can also help affirm the distinctly human institutions of democracy that animals cannot form. Similarly, the fable "The Stomach and the Body" supports democratic unity and cooperation, for as the parts of the body are to the whole body, so are individuals to the polis.
   a. **Further Reading:** Clayton, Edward. "Aesop, Aristotle, and Animals: The Role of Fables in Human Life." *Humanitas* 21:1 (2008): 179–200.
   b. **Suggested Searches:** Perform a Google Images search for "Francis Barlow cat mouse and bell" for an illustration that depicts the threatening power of the cat. Complete a Google News search for "bell the cat" for examples of how this idiom still speaks of the challenges that people and governments do not want to face.

2. **The simple form of the fable narrative as a means for conveying the moral of the story appeals to an innate human awareness of justice, wisdom, and goodness.** The fable, as a short prose narrative, does not persuade its reader of its moral through dialectical reasoning, as is done in philosophic works like Plato's. Rather, fables are persuasive because they appeal to basic human experience and correspond to an inherent desire for justice and happiness. As such, short narratives like fables might be said to appeal to common sense, but they also exert influence through their easy memorability, and this again stands in contrast to the difficult and detailed arguments of philosophy that can be difficult to remember. The fable, then, provides a persuasive and succinct guide for action—"a humble approach is always more effective" (587)—and one that can be adapted to various situations due to the pliability of the interpretation of the fable.
   a. **Further Reading:** Kurke, Leslie. "Plato, Aesop, and the Beginnings of Mimetic Prose." *Representations* 94:1 (2006): 6–52.

    b. **Suggested Search:** Go to aesopsfables.com for listings of the fables' titles along with their morals. Compare these morals to proverbs as a guide for action. A helpful resource for proverbs is Erasmus's massive collection, *Adagia* (in English, *The Adages*).

3. **G. K. Chesterton suggests that the essential truths and bits of wisdom in Aesop's fables are conveyed so clearly precisely because the characters of the story are not, typically, human.** He maintains that if they were human, the characters would necessarily have to be rendered more complex, and consequently the central clarity of the truth of each fable would be obscured. This highlights an important aspect of the fables, for while the fox always behaves like a fox in its characteristics and cunning (as is apparent in "The Fox, the Lion, and the Footprints"), it also speaks. One cannot say that the animals are entirely anthropomorphized, for their behavior still follows their animal natures, but their speech allows them to clearly present the essential truth of the story. Chesterton similarly emphasizes that the characters in Aesop's fables are impersonal—there is no pathos in "The Tortoise and the Hare"; there is, simply, a clear story with a decided point.

    a. **Further Reading:** Chesterton, G. K. "Introduction." *Æsop's Fables*. Translated by V. S. Vernon Jones. Illustrated by Arthur Rackham. New York: Doubleday, Page & Co., 1912.

    b. **Suggested Search:** Search youtube.com for the Walt Disney Productions 1934 cartoon *The Tortoise and the Hare* (8+ min.). Discuss the degree to which this cartoon may anthropomorphize the animals more than the fable does, especially in relation to Chesterton's argument.

4. **Fables, in part an explicitly didactic form of literature, can be profitably contrasted with other genres that do not contain such a clear moral.** For example, the fable "Jupiter and the Frogs" shares such themes as the interaction of terrestrial creatures with the gods with other works from ancient Greece, such as Homer's presentation of gods and humans in *The Odyssey* or Euripides's *Medea*. Yet while the fable presents the clear moral that one should try to be content with what one has, the proper relation of humans to the gods in Homer's epics is far more complex, and open to many differing positions. The fable's clarity, while perhaps less provocative of discussion than Homer's opacity, nevertheless fulfills the important role of teaching and conveying important lessons that could easily be misunderstood or contradicted in more complex works. A similar contrast might be made between the fable and the lyric, as Sappho's brilliance lies, in part, in a subtle, nuanced enunciation of love (see, for example, *Poem 31*), whereas "The Beauty Contest of the Animals" much more clearly asserts that love shapes the perception of beauty. It is also important to note, however, that the epic

and lyric certainly do contain didactic elements, though these are more open to disjunctive interpretations than the fable.

    a. **Further Reading:** Rose, H. J. *Outlines of Classical Literature.* New York: Meridian Books, 1959.

    b. **Suggested Search:** Search youtube.com for Walt Disney Productions' 1934 cartoon "The Grasshopper and the Ants" (8+ min.). The didactic nature of the fable clearly transfers to this film version.

5. **The various morals that might be drawn from a particular fable invite scrutiny and discussion but are rarely in disagreement with one another.** The fable "The Vegetables and the Weeds" concludes with the moral that "a mother's nurturing is stronger than a step-mother's attentions" (593), but one might also interpret the fable to suggest that human order requires constant care that natural things do not need. These various interpretations, however, are not contradictory, as they generally relate to the importance of nurturing or care, and the advantages of a natural union between things. Similarly, the fable "The Fox and the Raven" concludes with the moral "If you follow your enemies' advice, you will get hurt" (586), but the story might be understood to emphasize that vanity can make one lose the little one already has. In both cases, the emphasis is on the raven's need for prudence, both with respect to the fox's temptations and the raven's own susceptibility to flattery.

    a. **Further Reading:** Lewis, C. S. "On Three Ways of Writing for Children." In *On Stories and Other Essays on Literature,* edited by Walter Hooper, 31–43. New York: Harcourt, 1982.

    b. **Suggested Search:** Browse fables at aesop.pangyre.org by their moral, allowing a comparison of the possible differences of interpretation. This site also links to a collection of Grimm's fairy tales, allowing a comparison between the fable and the fairy tale, and what each might teach.

In-Class Activities

1. Ask students to write their own fable in imitation of the style and content of Aesop's. Ask them to exchange their fables to see if other students can properly infer the moral that they intended. Similarly, the teacher can provide students with a proverb for which students must then write a corresponding fable.

2. Choose one of the fables that does not include a written moral and ask students to write down what they understand the moral to be. Compare the various answers and discuss the differences and similarities in their morals.

3. Present to the students some illustrations of different fables (Arthur Rackham's illustrations in Vernon Jones's 1912 translation are

recommended) and discuss how these images do and do not correspond with the moral or theme of the fable. How might an illustration change the emphasis of the fable?

Paper Topics/Suggestions for Writing

1. Aesop's fables are now generally considered children's literature. Why is this the case? How is this classification inaccurate? Do these fables speak particularly to one age group?

2. Choose a fable that is not clear in its moral (for example, "The Two Men, the Eagle, and the Fox"), or that seems to contradict the moral that is attached to it (for example, "The Black Man in the River"), and write an analysis of the various interpretations that might be made concerning it.

3. To what degree are the animals anthropomorphized in these fables? Why? How does the attribute of speech change our perception of the animals? Does this affect the way that we enjoy the stories?

4. Compare the fables to the anecdotes of Odysseus on his journey home, and discuss in what manner they are similar or dissimilar from other short stories. For example, Odysseus's encounter with Polyphemus might be understood to have a clear didactic moral for Odysseus, and yet it is clearly not a fable. Why not? What is the generic difference?

5. What sort of wisdom is contained in the fables? Is there a particular type of knowledge conveyed in them? How does this relate to the manner in which they might be considered instructive or illustrative?

Resources

Aesop. *Æsop's Fables*. Translated by V. S. Vernon Jones. Illustrated by Arthur Rackham. New York: Doubleday, Page & Co., 1912.
> Arthur Rackham's classic illustrations of this work are excellent and are a valuable resource to present to the class as visual aids. G. K. Chesterton's "Introduction" is helpful both for its insights into the fables and its applicability to Rackham's depictions. Many of these illustrations are available online.

Aesop. *Aesop's Fables*. Illustrated by Jerry Pinkey. New York: Sea Star Books, 2000.
> Pinkey creates a contemporary presentation of Aesop's fables with many vivid and engaging illustrations. This is a good example of Aesop's continuing popularity both with children and adults.

Aesop. *Aesop's Fables with His Life*. Illustrated by Francis Barlow. London: Printed by William Godbid for Francis Barlow, 1666. EEBO.
> Available on the database Early English Books Online (EEBO), this Early Modern edition contains Barlow's illustrations of the fables,

which are, interestingly, presented in Latin, English, and French. This edition is not intended merely as children's literature.

Long, John R. *Aesop's Fables: Online Collection*. 1997. http://aesopfables.com. This is a large resource with over six hundred fables, some with audio recordings and illustrations. This site also includes fairy tales (including Hans Christian Andersen's), allowing comparison between genres. Two time lines of the centuries surrounding Aesop are also available.

Tolkien, J. R. R. "On Fairy-Stories." In *The Monsters and the Critics and Other Essays*, edited by Christopher Tolkien, 109–61. London: Harper Collins, 2006.

While not explicitly concerned with fables, many of the distinctions that Tolkien makes are useful when considering the importance of a fable and can clarify generic distinctions for students as well. This is an insightful, highly readable essay for students and instructors alike.

SAPPHO

Topics for Lecture or Discussion

1. **In his influential work "On Sublimity," Longinus praises Sappho's choice of detail and presentation of conflicting emotions as the source of sublimity in her work.** Longinus particularly refers to Poem 31 and states, "We see in her not a single emotion, but a complex of emotions. Lovers experience all this; Sappho's excellence, as I have said, lies in her adoption and combination of the most striking details" ("On Sublimity," 141). In Poem 31, for example, the speaker captures the seemingly incongruous elements of hot and cold feeling in the body: "fire is racing under skin . . . and cold sweat holds me" (lines 10–13). This complex of physical feeling corresponds to the varying emotions that rage within the speaker, from wings lifting the heart to the feeling of death. As Longinus indicates, not only does this capturing of the proper conflicting details correspond to the experiences of lovers, but it elevates the poem to the level of sublime expression that leads to the passion of wonder.
   a. **Further Reading:** Longinus. "On Sublimity." In *The Norton Anthology of Theory and Criticism,* edited by Vincent Leitch, 138–54. New York: Norton, 2001.
   b. **Suggested Search:** Go to classicpersuasion.org and follow the link to "The Divine Sappho" for a variety of resources, including H. T. Wharton's "Life of Sappho."

2. **Poem 94 contrasts the present existence of powerful desire with the delights of memory, and this tension expresses more than merely the despair of present separation.** While many readers interpret the poem as abandoned, hysteric sorrow, and though the lyric begins with the ominous "I simply want to be dead" (1), the subsequent lines do not simply despair in longing. Rather, in cherishing and calling to mind her memories of her beloved, Sappho's speaker creates a rich meditation on love. The speaker insists on recalling the "beautiful times we had" (11), and in following her memory through the richly sensual images of "many woven garlands / made of flowers / around your soft throat. / And with sweet oil / costly / you anointed yourself" (15–20), she does not simply yearn for what has passed. Rather, in what seems a moment of calm, poetic meditation, the speaker continues to love and reflect on the departed lover in a profound, grateful manner.
   a. **Further Reading:** Burnett, Anne. "Desire and Memory (Sappho Frag. 94)." *Classical Philology* 74.1 (1979), 16–27.

b. **Suggested Search:** Search the Web Gallery of Art (www.wga.hu) for "Sappho" to find several classic paintings of the poet.

3. **Sappho's "Poem," a prayer to Aphrodite, presents a difficult tension for the speaker with respect to the goddess of love, and this central struggle can be found in several of the fragments that remain.** Beginning with an invocation that is reminiscent of Homer's epic invocations, Sappho's speaker calls upon the goddess who embodies desire to satisfy her own passions. Aphrodite's response, however, is quixotic and challenging to the speaker, for she refers to past times when she has helped Sappho and then states, "For if she flees, soon she will pursue. / If she refuses gifts, rather will she give them. / If she does not love, soon she will love / even unwilling" (21–24). Aphrodite's ability to bend humans to her will, even against their own, is revealed not only here but in the very prayers of the speaker, who wishes another to be so influenced. Yet Aphrodite's power carries an ominous tone. Does the speaker really want Aphrodite's help? The potential for a possession by desire, a loss of will to Aphrodite, is at once wished for and troubling in this prayer to the goddess of love.

    a. **Further Reading:** Castle, Warren. "Observations on Sappho's *To Aphrodite*." *Transactions and Proceedings of the American Philological Association* 89 (1958): 66–76.

    b. **Suggested Search:** Go to Oxford Art Online (www.oxfordartonline .com/public) and do an image search for "Aphrodite," which will reveal pictures of several statues, including a Roman copy of Praxiteles's *Aphrodite of Arles*.

4. **In Plato's *Republic*, Socrates suggests that poets ought to be censored and that their material ought to portray the gods only as good and not as harmful or vicious.** Would Sappho's work fall under Socrates's censor? Sappho's Poem 16 elevates the beauty of the beloved over the political beauty of ordered military, declaring, "I would rather see her lovely step / and the motion of light on her face / than chariots of Lydians or ranks / of foot soldiers in arms (17–20). It might be argued that Sappho's emphasis on the personal, individual experience of love that shapes one's perception of things is a dangerous proposition for Socrates's republic, which relies on the utter dedication of its citizens to the political body. Sappho's recurring theme of the incapacitating nature of love is a similar challenge to Socrates's suggestions concerning the idea of poetry shaping the imaginations of the citizens. Finally, Sappho's attitude toward Aphrodite is a prayerful one, but it emphasizes the goddess's ability to coerce the will, and one cannot be sure that Sappho is consistently grateful for the powerful effect that Aphrodite has on her.

    a. **Further Reading:** Plato. *Republic.* In *Plato: Complete Works,* edited by John Cooper, 376a–383c. Indianapolis: Hackett, 1997.

    b. **Suggested Search:** Search the JSTOR database (www.jstor.org) for "Plato and poetry" for several helpful articles.

5. **The critical debate concerning Poem 31 centers on the question of the purpose of the man being described as "equal to gods" (1) and whether or not the speaker is filled with a jealous love or simply a deep love that celebrates the couple's union.** "Equal to gods" might be understood either to indicate that he is truly an exceptional man whom the girl is blessed to be with, or that he is an exceptionally lucky man, who by chance has happened to win the affections of the girl. This difference radically changes the understanding of the poem, as does the second question of jealousy. Sappho's speaker describes tremendous emotion at the sight of the couple, but it is debatable whether this is due to jealousy of the man's possession of the girl's attentions—in other words, the speaker herself wishing to replace the man—or whether she is delighted by their happiness and union. Indeed, some scholars suggest that rather than being a poem of jealous despair, it is a wedding poem that Sappho composed for the occasion.

    a. **Further Reading:** Furley, William D. "'Fearless, Bloodless . . . like the Gods': Sappho 31 and the Rhetoric of 'Godlike.'" *The Classical Quarterly* 50:1 (2000): 7–15.

    b. **Suggested Search:** A Google Images search of "vases with Sappho" reveals several ancient vases with depictions of Sappho reading and singing.

In-Class Activities

1. Ask students to break into small groups, in which they read the poetry aloud, trying to give a different intonation and emphasis on the parts of the poems. Discuss how certain poems are open to different interpretations, depending on the tone of voice and emphasis used.

2. Compare one of Sappho's lyrics to an ancient Egyptian love poem. In what ways are they similar and dissimilar? Discuss the universal elements of love poetry compared to those elements shaped by particular cultures.

3. Ask students to write a journal entry in which they write an analysis of one of the longer poems. Emphasize the need to be attentive to the phrasing and choice of expression and metaphor in crafting a compelling analysis.

Paper Topics/Suggestions for Writing

1. How does Sappho's presentation of love differ from Homer's? Compare the loving discourse between Odysseus and Penelope to that which Sappho writes. Are these differences significant? If so, how?

2. Choose three poetic tropes that Sappho makes use of and analyze their occurrences. What tropes are most common in her poetry? How does she employ them? What tropes are strikingly absent from her work?

3. Analyze the final poem given here, "The New Sappho," and compare it to the other works. Is it different? What is significant about its emphasis on age? Does Sappho speak about age with the same power that she expresses the passion of love?

4. What is Sappho's essential understanding of love as revealed in these works? To what degree is it a passion, and to what degree is it an intellectual state? Is love good or bad? What other passions are most commonly associated with love?

5. What is Sappho's conception of the gods? Are they active or passive? Are they good or bad? How does this conception of the gods compare to Homer, *Gilgamesh*, and the ancient Egyptians? Is there a central, unifying understanding?

Resources

Barnstone, Willis, trans. *The Complete Poems of Sappho*. Boston: Shambhala Publications, 2006.
> Barnstone's "Introduction" to his translation of Sappho's poems is informative, thoughtful, and readable and discusses both Sappho's historical situation and general aspects of her poetry.

Bowra, C. M. *Greek Lyric Poetry from Alcman to Simonides*. 2d ed. Oxford: Oxford University Press, 2001.
> This is a classic, influential study of the Greek lyric by Maurice Bowra, and this second edition (originally published in 1961) covers a substantial amount of material while focusing primarily on the poetry as literature. The "Introduction" is a helpful overview of the Greek lyric.

Budelmann, Felix. *The Cambridge Companion to Greek Lyric*. Cambridge: Cambridge University Press, 2009.
> This is a helpful collection of essays that will orient an unfamiliar reader to the major contexts, works, and poets of the Greek lyric. The volume contains significant considerations of Sappho, including a chapter that follows her in the nineteenth and twentieth centuries.

Roche, Paul, trans. *The Love Songs of Sappho.* New York: Prometheus Books, 1998.

> This is a valuable edition of Sappho's poetry because of the lucid introductory essay by Paul Roche, as well as the helpful, informative notes that accompany the poems.

AESCHYLUS

Agamemnon

> Zeus has led us on to know,
> the Helmsman lays it down as law
> that we must suffer, suffer into truth.
> —*Agamemnon*, 177–79

Topics for Lecture or Discussion

1. ***Agamemnon* is a revenge play in search of justice.** Clytaemnestra murders her husband because he sacrificed their daughter in order to fight the Trojan War. Clytaemnestra rationalizes her act to the chorus and claims that Agamemnon's death has brought an end to the cycle of killing in the House of Atreus (the history of which can be gleaned quickly from Edith Hamilton's *Mythology*). Yet Clytaemnestra's tone changes at the very end of the play as she expresses anxiety about the future. Does this reflect doubt in the righteousness of her act? Where does revenge inevitably lead? Can her actions be justified, and are her motives pure?
   a. **Further Reading:** Euben, J. Peter. "Justice and the Oresteia." *The American Political Science Review* 76:1 (March 1982): 22–33.
   b. **Suggested Searches:** Search for the following phrases in Google Images, Google Scholar, or an academic database to find images and additional resources: Dike Greek goddess of justice, sacrifice of Iphigenia, murder of Agamemnon, Trojan War, Helen of Troy.

2. ***The Oresteia*, the only remaining example of the Greek tragic trilogies conceived and performed as a unit, chronicles the move from a revenge society to one based on laws and trial by jury.** Clytaemnestra exacts revenge against her husband in *Agamemnon*. In the middle play, *The Libation Bearers*, Orestes, the returning son, avenges his father's murder by killing his mother. In the final play of the trilogy, *The Eumenides*, Orestes stands trial for the murder of his mother, Clytaemnestra, and the verdict among the twelve jurors ends in a deadlock, with half voting guilty and half voting not guilty. Athena, the goddess who oversees the trial, breaks the tie by voting in favor of Orestes, because, she says, she is always for the male and always on her father's side. Therefore, she seeks to limit the power of the Furies, who revenge matricide. As triumphant as the ending of the trilogy may seem, its establishment of justice is equivocal and not wholly satisfying. The

elevation of patriarchy compromises the nobility of justice and makes it seem arbitrary.

    a. **Further Reading:** Cohen, Michael. "The Victims and the Furies in American Courts. *The Humanist* 66:1 (January/February 2006): 19–23.

    b. **Suggested Searches:** Search for the following phrases in Google Images, Google Scholar, or an academic database to find images and additional resources: Temple of Athena Acropolis, Aeschylus Oresteia, vase painting Greek drama, Greek dramatic festivals, Greek trilogies.

3. **Aeschylus visualizes the gendered conflict between Agamemnon and Clytaemnestra brilliantly, theatrically, by minimal means in the form of the lone building, or *skene*, onstage.** At the outset, the Watchman sits on top of the building in the dark night, looking to the horizon for a burning fire that signals the end of the Trojan War, the capture of Ilium, and the imminent return home of Agamemnon. However, the light that shows the general the way home, even from a foreign war, also leads him to death in the dark interior of the very building that represents domestic safety. The presence and use of the skene, then, in relation to the rest of the theatrical space, create dramatic oppositions—masculine and feminine, inside and outside, dark and light, foreign and domestic—that fuel the intensity and interest of the drama.

    a. **Further Reading:** Taplin, Oliver. *The Stagecraft of Aeschylus.* New York: Oxford University Press, 1977.

    b. **Suggested Searches:** Search for the following phrases in Google Images, Google Scholar, or an academic database to find images and additional resources: Greek *skene*, Greek theater Epidaurus, theater of Dionysius.

4. **The door in the skene is the portal that connects all of the oppositions in the play.** It is the visual focus of the drama located in the prime position, upstage center in the theater space. Entrances and exits largely determine dramatic structure, and the spectator's eye always follows an onstage appearance. Thus Clytaemnestra attracts attention from the dominant speaking position (in front of the skene). The initial stage directions indicate that Clytaemnestra makes all her entrances through the central palace doors, while all the other characters make their entrances from the side wings. Clytaemnestra makes three entrances, the last of which reveals her standing over the bodies of her slain husband and his paramour, Cassandra, who were probably displayed upon an *ekkyklēma* that thrusts the bodies into the audience's view with quick and dramatic impact.

a. **Further Reading:** Aronson, Arnold. "Their Exits and Their Entrances: Getting a Handle on Doors." *New Theatre Quarterly* 20:4 (November 2004): 331–40.

b. **Suggested Searches:** Search for the following phrases in Google Images, Google Scholar, or an academic database to find images and additional resources: Greek skene, Greek theater Epidaurus, theater of Dionysius.

5. **The chorus, played in performance by Athenian citizens, links the audience to the dramatic characters onstage.** In this case a group of old men, perhaps too old to fight in the war and thus left at home to wait and ponder, comprises the chorus. One of the choral functions is to provide the needed exposition of the play and load the plot by discussing past events, mainly the story of the Trojan War, particularly its outbreak and the circumstances that led to Agamemnon's sacrifice of his daughter, Iphigenia, for trade winds to sail his ships. Hamilton's *Mythology* is a good source for further background on the Trojan War. Later in the play, after the murder of Agamemnon is revealed, the chorus challenges Clytaemnestra's authority and calls her a tyrant but then quickly retreats from such an aggressive stance of resistance. Why does the chorus fear Clytaemnestra, and what threat does she pose?

a. **Further Reading:** Goldhill, Simon. "Civic Ideology and the Problem of Difference: The Politics of Aeschylean Tragedy, Once Again." *Journal of Hellenic Studies* 120 (2000): 34–56.

b. **Suggested Searches:** Search for the following phrases in Google Images, Google Scholar, or an academic database to find images and additional resources: Greek chorus, Greek chorus masks, Greek chorus costume, ancient Greek chorus.

6. **The dramatic action ensnares all the characters in a complex cycle of violence and revenge from which none can escape.** In a particularly visceral, bloody image at the beginning of the play, the chorus describes two eagles, which represent the two brothers, Agamemnon and Menelaus, devouring a pregnant hare and ripping out the unborn young. This act, described by a seer, presages the Greek victory in Troy, but it also anticipates the blood sacrifice that Agamemnon will make of his own child. Moreover, the bloody image from nature, offensive to the goddess Artemis, recalls the blood crime that provoked the curse upon the House of Atreus—Atreus killed his brother's children and fed them to him in a dish. At the same time, the chorus describes the outbreak of the war as a result of one woman's promiscuity, which further coils the foreign/domestic opposition and foreshadows Clytaemnestra taking up with Aegisthus in the present play, as well as Agamemnon's return with his prize, Cassandra. From the outset, then, the play complicates the

notion that one action can be considered wholly good and another action wholly bad. Ambivalence, balance, and repetition are all seen as aspects that create the drama, in which no character can ever act wholly in the right.

    a. **Further Reading:** Krapp, John. "Ideology, Rhetoric and Blood-ties: From *The Oresteia* to *The Godfather.*" *Mosaic* 32:1 (March 1999): 1–16.

    b. **Suggested Searches:** Search for the following phrases in Google Images, Google Scholar, or an academic database to find images and additional resources: Eumenides, the Furies, Clytaemnestra kills Cassandra, dilemma of Orestes.

7. **Clytaemnestra lures her husband to his death by playing upon his vanity, or hubris.** The most dramatically powerful scene in the play is the confrontation between Agamemnon and Clytaemnestra outside the house, when the wife rolls out the red carpet for her husband as he enters and passes the threshold between the light of day and the dark interior of his house, with an unexpected death trap inside. She implores him to tread upon the rich tapestries not only to humiliate him but also to give him the choice of walking to his own death. Why does he submit to walking on the carpet when he knows it is wrong? Why doesn't Clytaemnestra's elaborate ceremony alert him to danger? How can he stand outside with his concubine, Cassandra, a spoil of war, and not think that his wife will take action against him? The elaborate spectacle onstage, in which Agamemnon ultimately descends from his chariot and crushes the flowers, allowing the juice to ooze from them, foreshadows his imminent death, an ignominious event marked by his offstage cries, in which his wife catches him in a net and slaughters him in his bath.

    a. **Further Reading:** Robertson, H. G. "The Hybristes in Aeschylus." *Transactions and Proceedings of the American Philological Association* 98 (1967): 373–82.

    b. **Suggested Searches:** Search for the following phrases in Google Images, Google Scholar, or an academic database to find images and additional resources: Clytaemnestra red carpet, death mask of Agamemnon, definition of hubris, examples of stichomythia.

In-Class Activities

1. Clytaemnestra brazenly takes responsibility for the murder of Agamemnon, defends the righteousness of her act to the chorus, and challenges its members to judge her. Pick a jury, with lawyers for each side, and stage a trial of Clytaemnestra. The trilogy itself ends with the trial of Orestes for the murder of his mother, so that case, too, is suitable for a retrial in class.

2. Aeschylus made dialogue possible by bringing a second actor onstage. Take a look at the dramatic scene (912–57) between Agamemnon and Clytaemnestra and read the short dialogue between the two where the latter convinces the king to walk on the red carpets. The dialogue, framed between two longer speeches by Agamemnon, creates a rhythmic, back-and-forth, stichomythic exchange that counters and balances the longer set speeches of characters and offsets the choral passages. In reading the scene, see if you can identify and create effective speech patterns and rhythms. Ask students to identify similar speech effects in other plays, such as *Antigone* and *Hamlet*.

3. Demonstrate the power of an entrance by having an actor play Clytaemnestra and enter through a classroom door. Observe how the door creates focus and suspense with the expectation of what will next happen. The manipulation of entrances and exits is one of the main ways that playwrights in any time period achieve focus and alter the rhythm between scenes. It functions analogously to the filmic cut, though of course the scene unit in theater is usually much longer than the shot in film.

4. Watch portions of the video version of Eugene O'Neill's twentieth-century adaptation of *The Oresteia, Mourning Becomes Electra*, which retells the classic myth in modern terms by replacing the gods with psychology and dramatizes family as fate. How does each create a sense of the tragic with respect to destiny and free will?

Paper Topics/Suggestions for Writing

1. *The Oresteia* is the only extant tragic trilogy, although we know that originally most tragedies were presented as trilogies at dramatic festivals. Is *Agamemnon* effective as an individual play apart from the subsequent two plays? Without considering the other plays of the cycle of which it is part, what is the dramatic message of *Agamemnon*?

2. Aristophanes lampooned the tragedians in *The Frogs* but ultimately picked Aeschylus as the best, heaviest dramatist. Based upon your reading of Aeschylus, Sophocles's *Oedipus the King*, and Euripides's *Medea*, how would you rate and rank the three playwrights?

3. Assuming *Agamemnon* is a revenge play, defend or attack Clytaemnestra's actions. What possible outcomes could represent justice? Consider also the aspect of revenge in Shakespeare's *Hamlet*. How are the characters' motivations and reactions similar and different? Are Hamlet and Clytaemnestra equally justified, or unjustified, in their revenge?

4. How does the following passage foreshadow the death of Agamemnon and carry the meanings of the play?

But Justice shines in sooty hovels,
   loves the decent life.
From proud halls crusted with gilt by filthy hands
   she turns her eyes to find the pure in spirit—
spurning the wealth stamped counterfeit with
      praise,
   she steers all things towards their destined end.
(761–66)

Resources

The Archive of Performance of Greek and Roman Drama. APGRD Database, University of Oxford. Edited by Amanda Wrigley. www.apgrd.ox.ac .uk/database.

This is an outstanding online database produced by the University of Oxford that lists over nine thousand productions and is constantly being updated. Here is a selection of influential works represented in the database:

- 2007. *The Oresteia.* Adapted by David Johnston. Dir. Stephen Speights. Access Theatre, New York.
- 2001. *Agamemnon and His Daughters.* Dir. Molly Smith. Arena Stage, Washington, D.C.
- 1990. *Les Atrides.* Dir. Ariane Mnouchkine. Théâtre du Soleil, France.
- 1983. *Oresteia.* Dir. Peter Hall. Royal National Theatre, United Kingdom.
- 1980. *The Greeks.* Dir. John Barton. Royal Shakespeare Company, United Kingdom.
- 1977. *Agamemnon.* Dir. Andrei Serban. Comp. Elizabeth Swados. New York Shakespeare Festival, New York.
- 1972. *Oresteia.* Dir. Luca Ronconi. Cooperativo Tusculano, Rome, Italy.
- 1966. *The House of Atreus.* Dir. Tyrone Guthrie. Minnesota Theatre Company, Minneapolis, Minnesota.

Aristotle. *Poetics.*

Translations of this work are available online at MIT's the Internet Classics Archive (http://classics.mit.edu/Aristotle/poetics.html) and Tufts's Perseus Digital Library (www.perseus.tufts.edu), among other sources.

Greek Drama: From Ritual to Theater. Films for the Humanities and Sciences, 2001, DVD/VHS.

This video includes key scenes from plays by Aeschylus, Sophocles, Euripides, and Aristophanes, as well as commentary from scholars Helene Foley, Jeffrey Henderson, Robert Fagles, and Aquila Theatre's Peter Meineck.

Greek Theater. Films for the Humanities and Sciences, 2001, DVD.
> This video provides an introduction to aspects of Greek drama and theatrical production.

Mourning Becomes Electra. By Eugene O'Neill. Dir. Nick Havinga. Perf. Roberta Maxwell and Josef Sommer. Broadway Theater Archive, 1979, DVD.

SOPHOCLES

Oedipus the King

[C]ount no man happy till he dies, free of pain
at last.
—*Oedipus the King*, 1686

Topics for Lecture or Discussion

1. **The riddle of the Sphinx, solved by the tragic hero to save Thebes from destruction prior to the beginning of the play, informs the action of *Oedipus the King*.** What walks on four legs in the morning, two in the afternoon, and three at night? Oedipus crawled as a baby, further hampered by pierced and pinioned ankles; he walked proudly as a grown man, the king of Thebes, the most powerful of men, the man we see in the action of the play; but, after the revelations of his true identity, he blinds himself and exits the stage in eternal darkness, hobbling along on three legs with only a stick to guide him. Ironically, while Oedipus knows the answer to the Sphinx's riddle, "mankind," he doesn't know the answer to the more fundamental question of his own identity. He has no idea of his true parentage, and in the action of the play he discovers that he is both son and husband to Jocasta, both father and brother to his two children.
   a. **Further Reading:** Hathorn, Richmond Y. "Existential Oedipus." *The Classical Journal* 53:5 (February 1958): 223–30.
   b. **Suggested Searches:** Search for the following phrases in Google Images, Google Scholar, or an academic database to find images and additional resources: ancient Greek art riddle of the sphinx, plague of Thebes, murder of Laius.

2. **The scene between Tiresias and Oedipus dramatizes the paradox of vision in the play.** The old prophet is blind but can see the truth; Oedipus has sight but does not know who he is or from where he comes. Having answered the riddle of the Sphinx, Oedipus does not hesitate to solve the present problem in the play of finding Laius's murderer and the cause of the pestilence. Oedipus's confidence leads him astray from reason. When Tiresias, the seer, formulates the riddles about Oedipus and the identity of the murderer, Oedipus does not even consider dropping his investigation and inquiry. Indeed, all the other characters in the play, including Creon, the Messenger, the Herdsman, and especially Jocasta, figure out the answer to the question Oedipus seeks to solve long before the king. Oedipus has a blind spot regarding his own identity and can only see outward in his steadfast quest for the murderer.

a. **Further Reading:** Lattimore, Steven. "Oedipus and Tiresias." *California Studies in Classical Antiquity* 8 (1975): 105–11.

b. **Suggested Searches:** Search for the following phrases in Google Images, Google Scholar, or an academic database to find images and additional resources: blind Tiresias, blindness in *Oedipus*, prophecy in *Oedipus*.

3. **Plot is the sequence of events and, according to Aristotle, the most essential aspect of tragedy because a tragedy is a representation of human action.** In his *Poetics*, Aristotle lists all the elements of theater in the following order: plot, character, thought, diction, music, and spectacle. What is the action in *Oedipus the King*? Ultimately, Oedipus discovers himself, but is that what he set out to do? How does the action of the play add stature to his character?

a. **Further Reading:** Fuchs, Elinor. "'Waiting for Recognition': An Aristotle for 'Non-Aristotelian' Drama." *Modern Drama* 50:4 (Winter 2007): 532–44.

b. **Suggested Searches:** Search for the following phrases in Google Images, Google Scholar, or an academic database to find images and additional resources: Aristotelian plot structure, Aristotle's *Poetics*, Aristotelian theory of drama. Also search the Internet Classics Archive (http://classics.mit.edu) and the Perseus Digital Library (www.perseus.tufts.edu) for English translations of *Poetics*.

4. **Aristotle claims that the best plots feature recognition (*anagnorisis*) and reversal (*peripeteia*) that occur close together and even simultaneously.** One example of recognition and reversal happens when the messenger arrives to tell Oedipus that Polybus of Corinth is dead and that Oedipus will be the new king. Good tidings quickly end when it is revealed that Polybus is not Oedipus's true father and that a herdsman gave the child to the messenger many years ago. The rapid juxtaposition of recognitions and reversals and the ebb and flow of the plot add dramatic intensity and build interest and suspense from beginning to end. Look for more examples of recognition and reversal and note the relationship between them. The structure of the entire play is built upon these dramatic principles. Oedipus's final recognition of his true identity precipitates an immediate and ultimate plot reversal. Oedipus, who was the greatest among men, now finds himself the lowest among men, the murderer of his father, husband of his mother, and father of his two sisters. In a stunning reversal brought on by a terrible insight, the most exalted among men becomes the most defiled. The king of Thebes is banished from the land and is thrown out as the cause of the pestilence that has sickened his country.

   a. **Further Reading:** Aristotle. "Simple and Complex Plots." In *Poetics,* translated by Gerald Else, 34–37. 1967. Ann Arbor: University of Michigan Press, 1986.

   b. **Suggested Searches:** Search for the following phrases in Google Images, Google Scholar, or an academic database to find images and additional resources: unity of action in *Oedipus,* Aristotle's *Poetics.* Also search the Internet Classics Archive (http://classics.mit.edu) and the Perseus Digital Library (www.perseus.tufts.edu) for English translations of *Poetics.*

5. **Oedipus is a tyrannical figure from the mythic past conceived by Sophocles in the age of democracy.** A very different leader than Oedipus, Creon is more reserved, deliberate, and smooth in speech. His character is consistent in subsequent plays such as *Antigone* and *Oedipus at Colonus.* Creon's reliance upon law and order leads to tragedy in *Antigone,* while his decency and fairness provide Oedipus a final haven in *Oedipus at Colonus.* While Oedipus displays many qualities of an arrogant despot, Creon seems specifically characterized as a democratic leader. Despite his flaws, however, Oedipus remains a much more sympathetic character than Creon. What does that suggest about government, human nature, and Athenian society?

   a. **Further Reading:** Knox, Bernard M. W. "Why Is Oedipus Called Tyrannos?" *The Classical Journal* 50:3 (December 1954): 97–102.

   b. **Suggested Searches:** Search for the following phrases in Google Images, Google Scholar, or an academic database to find images and additional resources: Oedipus tyrannos, golden age of Greece, fifth-century Athens, age of Pericles.

6. **The action scapegoats Oedipus for the crime of being born.** The change in fortune that Oedipus experiences in the course of the drama, from best to worst, begs the question, if it could happen to him, could it happen to anyone? The play reminds its audience that humans cannot control their destiny, that fate decreed by the gods cannot be altered, and that the meaning of life cannot be known until life has passed. In the case of Oedipus, his real story and the meaning of his life are not apparent until almost the end, and the revelations near the end change the entire arc and meaning of his life.

   a. **Further Reading:** Girard, René. "Oedipus and the Surrogate Victim." In *Violence and the Sacred,* translated by Patrick Gregory, 97–102. 1972. New York: Continuum, 2005.

   b. **Suggested Searches:** Search for the following phrases in Google Images, Google Scholar, or an academic database to find images and additional resources: House of Thebes, Gods of Olympus family tree, ritual theory of drama.

7. **Oedipus's greatest flaw is also his greatest strength.** He exhibits *hubris*, excessive pride or self-confidence, by reasoning that he alone can save the city of Thebes. Ironically, though, he is probably right in this estimation. While Oedipus is the cause of the present plague on Thebes, he is also the only cure. He is the only one capable of discovering the murderer and casting him out. This fact is borne out by the action of the play. Although the other characters may sense the danger of Oedipus's investigation and try to stop him, Oedipus refuses to halt his search and continues unabated until the truth surfaces at the end. If Oedipus were to listen to his family, friends, and advisers, he would save himself, perhaps, but he would doom Thebes to destruction. Thus the paradox of Oedipus: the cause of the plague is also the solution. When he saved the city the first time by solving the riddle of the Sphinx, he was a hero and became king, but when he saved the city a second time by discovering the murderer of Laius, the former king, he became an outcast, banished from his home, most defiled among men, and a scapegoat for the community and its ills. The early success and victory unwittingly set him up for a dramatic fall and tragic destiny. Yet that cruel destiny had been ordained from the very beginning. Oedipus stands as both savior and sinner, blameless and guilty, most heroic and most defiled, and greatest and worst among men. He is all these things not just over time and sequentially but immediately and simultaneously, and therefore most pitiably human of all the characters.

   a. **Further Reading:** Vernant, Jean-Pierre and Page duBois. "Ambiguity and Reversal: On the Enigmatic Structure of *Oedipus Rex*." *New Literary History* 9:3 (Spring 1978): 475–501.

   b. **Suggested Searches:** Search for the following phrases in Google Images, Google Scholar, or an academic database to find images and additional resources: myth of Oedipus family tree, Oedipus and knowledge, Oedipus and vision, hamartia in Greek tragedy, tragic flaw in Oedipus.

In-Class Activities

1. Perform the Second Messenger's speech, describing the death of Jocasta and the blinding of Oedipus. The descriptive imagery is richly graphic. What are the requirements for acting such a scene? What does the performer do to convey the intensity of the scene? How does the style of acting differ in this play from that of a contemporary play featuring naturalistic dialogue?

2. Think about casting a theatrical production of the play. What qualities do you need to consider when making decisions, and what do these qualities tell you about the play?

3. Discuss contemporary films and television shows in terms of narrative with an emphasis on plot. Drawing on Aristotle's *Poetics*, differentiate between story and plot. Give examples of how recognitions and reversals drive the plots of most programs.

4. Discuss *Oedipus the King* as a murder mystery. Why is mystery such a compelling (and addictive) genre? Why is the mystery plot the ultimate narrative?

Paper Topics/Suggestions for Writing

1. Freud's "Oedipus complex" is a staple of twentieth-century psychology. In the play, Jocasta dismisses Oedipus's spoken fears of his mother's bed. To what extent is psychology, as we know it today, relevant or irrelevant to an understanding of the tragedy written twenty-five hundred years ago? More bluntly, is it productive to ask, does Oedipus love his mother?

2. Reading Aristotle's *Poetics*, it is impossible not to see *Oedipus the King* as a perfect example of almost all of Aristotle's theories. As the most widely known and read Greek tragedy, *Oedipus the King* stands as a model, propped up by Aristotle, of what all Greek tragedies should be. How might Aristotle's view of tragedy, and our understanding of it, differ if he had chosen another play, for example, Euripides's *Medea*, as his favorite? Based on another Greek tragedy by Aeschylus or Euripides, devise a new poetics of tragedy.

3. Oedipus blames Apollo for bringing his sorrow to completion but claims that the act of putting his eyes out was his own. Certainly there is a sense that Oedipus does not deserve his fate, but what, then, is he responsible for, and what does the audience learn from the experience of the play?

4. At a point halfway through the play, Oedipus recognizes that he may well have been Laius's murderer. Instead of stopping, though, he accelerates his drive to find out the truth, which of course leads to his personal revelations and sufferings, as well as to the town's salvation. Oedipus's pride might be considered a tragic flaw, but does pride truly bring about his downfall? Looked at another way, could the pestilence afflicting Thebes be rooted out without Oedipus's single-minded determination to solve the latest riddle, regardless of the consequences? Does Oedipus's flaw make him blameworthy?

5. *The Gospel at Colonus,* created by avant-garde American artist Lee Breuer, with music by Bob Telson, retells the Oedipus story in the context of a Pentecostal church service. Obviously Greek tragedy has nothing to do with Christianity. Do universal qualities linking the modern and ancient works shed light on the original? Is it possible to stage a "straight" version of an old play? What insight does the modern version

shed on the Greek tragedies? In what ways do music and singing help the actors and singers meet the heightened physical, emotional, and performance demands required for a Greek tragedy?

Resources

The Archive of Performance of Greek and Roman Drama: APGRD Database, University of Oxford. www.apgrd.ox.ac.uk/database. Edited by Amanda Wrigley.

> An outstanding online database produced by the University of Oxford that lists over nine thousand productions and is constantly being updated.

Aristotle. *Poetics*.

> Translations of this work are available online at MIT's the Internet Classics Archive (http://classics.mit.edu/Aristotle/poetics.html) and Tufts's Perseus Digital Library (www.perseus.tufts.edu), among other sources.

The Gospel at Colonus. Adapted and directed by Lee Breuer. Comp. Bob Telson. 1988. Original Cast Recording. CD. Nonesuch, 1990.

New York Stories. Dir. Woody Allen. 1989. Walt Disney Video, 2003.

> Three short films, including *Oedipus Wrecks*.

Oedipus the King. Dir. Don Taylor. Perf. Michael Pennington, John Gielgud, and Claire Bloom. Language Arts and Literature Core Curriculum Video Library, the Cambridge Educational Core Curriculum Video Libraries, 1986.

> Part of the series Sophocles: The Theban Plays.

Oedipus Rex. Dir. Tyrone Guthrie. 1957. DVD. Image Entertainment, 2002.

> This famous production features actors wearing masks.

Oedipus Rex. Opera by Igor Stravinsky. Libretto Jean Cocteau. Dir. Julie Taymor. 1993. Perf. Jessye Norman and featuring Tokyo Opera Singers and Shinyou-Kai Chorus. DVD. Philips, 2005.

> Special features include a conversation with Julie Taymor.

Antigone

> . . . something has been bothering me:
> Suppose this business was inspired by the
> Gods?
> —*Antigone*, 309–10

Topics for Lecture or Discussion

1. **As indicated in the epigraph, and as is typical of Greek drama, the characters are not confident about the extent to which the gods interfere in human affairs.** Antigone asserts that her burying of and mourning for her brother Polyneikes will please the gods (93–94), and Tiresias's later dooming prophecy (1101–42) to Kreon seems to support her position. The recurring misfortune of Oedipus's family, however, is similarly attributed to the curse of the gods (946–49), and this is emphasized more extensively in *Oedipus the King*. To what extent do the gods control the characters? What, precisely, is the role of the gods in *Antigone*? Observe that no god actually appears in the play, and no explicitly miraculous or supernatural events occur. Tiresias is the character closest to the gods through his office as prophet, but even his efforts to determine the will of the gods are unsuccessful: "My attempt at prophecy failed; the signs I had sought never appeared" (1117–19). If the gods are so inscrutable, why do they seem to have such power and influence over the actions of the characters?
    a. **Further Reading**: Segal, Charles. "Lament and Closure in *Antigone*." In *Sophocles' Tragic World: Divinity, Nature, Society*. Cambridge, MA: Harvard University Press, 1995, 119–37.
    b. **Suggested Searches**: Google "Greek gods family tree," which results in numerous media presenting the relationships of the gods (see especially the family tree at ludios.org). "Encyclopedia Mythica" (at www.pantheon.org) provides a searchable collection of the myths and characters in mythological literature, including the stories of the gods' interferences in the lives of the various humans.

2. **Loyalty to family is a challenging and vexing issue throughout *Antigone*, particularly when in conflict with loyalty to the state.** Prior to the beginning of the play, the brothers Polyneikes and Eteokles killed one another, and their conflict is mirrored by both the difficulties that Antigone and Ismene face and the struggles between Kreon and Haimon. Antigone and Ismene disagree about whether or not to bury their brother Polyneikes, and in their following actions, the house of Oedipus is shown to split evenly in its loyalty to Thebes, with Antigone and Polyneikes rebelling and Eteokles and Ismene conforming.

Ismene later regrets her decision to abandon her brother and obey the law (581–82). What does this changing of the mind indicate or imply? Why, particularly, does she change her mind? Similarly, the disagreement between Kreon and Haimon is both familial and political, for the authority of the father is combined with the authority of the head of state. Haimon's rebellion from his current family and state is for the sake of future family, as he is engaged to Antigone. Is this important? Kreon later regrets his anger and decree, but it is too late, and Antigone, Haimon, and his wife, Eurydike, are all dead. The power of the state, used unjustly, has crushed even the ruler's family. Is there a parallel between the tyrant of the state and the tyrant of the family?

a. **Further Reading:** Sorum, Christina Elliott. "The Family in Sophocles' *Antigone* and *Electra*." *The Classical World* 75:4 (1982): 201–11.

b. **Suggested Searches:** Go to youtube.com: "Antigone 1961 argument for family" brings up multiple results, highlighting the parts of the work that debate the conflict between family and state. Go to the Academic Search Premier Database at www.ebscohost.com/academic/academic-search-premier and search for "Antigone and Family." Also search for Jean-Joseph Benjamin-Constant's painting "Antigone and Polynices."

3. **Questioning the usual association of wisdom and age, *Antigone* suggests that the prudent man will both guide youth and, at times, rely upon its insight.** This is most evident in the disagreement between Kreon and Haimon, for while Haimon states "I respect your wisdom" (707), he also understands that his father is, in this case, mistaken. Kreon betrays a narrow mind in rejecting his son's advice because of his age (805) and is then unable to save his son from a reckless suicide by having forfeited his claim upon authority and wisdom. Does this tragic failure of wisdom and age suggest any criteria for more prudent action, for the young as well as the old? Perhaps the answer is indicated in the figure of wise, blind Tiresias, who is led through Thebes by a youth. Even with respect to his art of prophecy, Tiresias relies upon the young man, saying "this I learned from my lad. He's my guide, just as I'm the guide for others" (1119–20). What does this play suggest about the nature of wisdom and its possessors, and how can one be guided by them?

a. **Further Reading:** Adams, S. M. "The *Antigone* of Sophocles." *Phoenix* 9:2 (1955): 47–62.

b. **Suggested Search:** Search the database JSTOR at www.jstor.org for "Sophocles and Wisdom."

4. **Aristotle states that moments of recognition and reversal are essential for a good tragedy. Where are these moments in *Antigone*, and who experiences them?** From the very beginning of Sophocles's play, Antigone knows what she will do and appears content to suffer the consequences, including death. Due to this consistent determination,

she does not seem to experience moments of recognition and reversal. It is notable that the titular character does not take part in this essential aspect of the work's genre. Kreon, however, clearly does endure recognition and reversal with respect to Polyneikes's body and Haimon's marriage, but the lateness of his recognition ushers in his share of the final aspect of Aristotle's understanding of tragedy: suffering. With the destruction of his entire family, it might be suggested that Kreon takes as large a part in the tragedy as Antigone does, and if this is the case, the work might be understood to suggest that suffering has a communal, and perhaps universal, human effect.

   a. **Further Reading:** Aristotle. *Poetics.* Translated by H. G. Apostle, E. A. Dobbs, and Morris A. Parslow. Grinnell: Peripatetic Press, 1990.

   b. **Suggested Searches:** Google "outline of Aristotle's theory of tragedy," which results in multiple outlines of various length; Barbara McManus's outline at cnr.edu is useful for hyperlinks to the original text of Aristotle's *Poetics*, and it includes a link to Freytag's triangle analysis of Aristotle's theory.

5. *Antigone* **is a politically serious play that raises questions concerning the foundations of political power and the extent to which the state can, in justice, interfere with individuals.** In Antigone's lines at the beginning of the play, she complains of the Theban government, as its new law "threatens our loved ones the same as our enemies" (14–15). The reader finds that the vindictive decree regarding Polyneikes's corpse is issued by the new ruler, Kreon, "who came to power abruptly" (187) and who reveals himself to be a strict proponent for the rule and authority of law. How did Kreon come to power, and is his authority just? What constitutes just authority in this work? The Leader of the Chorus tells Kreon, "You have all the authority you need to discipline the living and the dead" (246–47), but his rule is challenged not only by Antigone but also by his own son, who describes him as a tyrant. It seems, then, that Kreon is tyrannical in attempting to follow that which he perceives as best for his state. This, however, does not negate the fact that the state overreaches its proper boundaries and indicates the dangers of a well-meaning but misguided leader.

   a. **Further Reading:** Beer, Josh. *Sophocles and the Tragedy of Athenian Democracy.* Contributions in Drama and Theatre Studies: Lives of the Theatre series. Westport, CT: Praeger, 2004.

   b. **Suggested Searches:** Google "tyranny in Athens" to find several academic websites where the history and context of tyranny in Sophocles's city are discussed. Also see Open Yale Courses: Professor Donald Kagan's lectures (on video), "Introduction to Ancient Greek History," for further background (video no. 11 particularly addresses tyranny in Athens).

6. **Antigone is both admirable and troubling as a heroine, and despite characters' statements to the contrary, she reveals the power and influence that women in the Greek culture held.** Ismene attempts to caution Antigone's brash plan by advising, "Remember, we're women. How can we fight men. They're stronger. We must accept these things— and worse to come" (75–77). Despite this, however, Antigone defies Kreon, the guard, and the law of Thebes, and through her actions she gains the sympathy of the populace, her sister, Tiresias, and Haimon. Her influence is so great that Haimon kills himself, and Eurydike subsequently commits suicide as well. Yet while her determination and independence are admirable, Antigone's apparently self-destructive resignation lends a complexity to her character that is troubling. She does not try to escape her punishment or deny the charges that are made, and her apparent despair in the face of the law and the fate of the gods renders her a character that is at once a model for action and a cautionary tale against hopelessness.

    a. **Further Reading:** Johnston, Sarah Iles. "Antigone's Other Choice." Supplement, *Helios* 33 (2006t): 179–86.

    b. **Suggested Searches:** Search the database JSTOR at www.jstor.org for "Antigone and strength" and "Antigone and suicide." Also search for Lord Frederick Leighton's portrait "Antigone" (prompt students to interpret the painting as admirable or troubling).

In-Class Activities

1. Examine the argument between Kreon and Haimon (699–844). Debate about which character makes the better argument. If you ignore the impassioned comments, what is, precisely, the point of their disagreement?

2. Divide into two groups: one group must craft the best defense of Kreon's law about Polyneikes's burial, while the other group must attack that defense. Which arguments are most effective for and against this law? Are they both politically based? If not, what is the source of the best attack/defense?

3. Take some time for each student to write a comparison between Haimon and Antigone as a couple, as well as another famous couple from literature (Aeneas and Dido, Odysseus and Penelope, Romeo and Juliet, etc.). Discuss these comparisons, and consider how they are similar or distinct. Does Sophocles's couple fit within contemporary understandings of a romantic story?

4. Discuss whether or not Kreon will continue to rule Thebes after the conclusion of the play. Would he want to rule? Would he be a good ruler?

5. Write a journal entry considering the relation of the saying "the sins of the father visited upon the children" to the events in this play. Does this occur? How so? Is there a deeper understanding that can be gained from this idea of inherited guilt?

Paper Topics

1. Consider the different reactions of Antigone and Ismene to Kreon's law. Is one right and the other wrong? Why does Ismene change her mind? Is Antigone reckless, as she says? What deeper point can be made of the fact that these sisters act so differently?

2. Kreon makes the broad statement, "There's nothing worse than a man, while he's running a city, who fails to act on sound advice—but fears something so much his mouth clamps shut" (210–13). What does this illustrate about his understanding of a good ruler? Is he correct? How can this be misconstrued, and what are the problems with this statement?

3. What is the dramatic effect of the Chorus's laments and odes? How do these passages function in relation to the action of the play, both temporally and substantively? Does the audience or reader identify with the Chorus? Is the Chorus important?

4. The guard who is first threatened by Kreon and who subsequently catches Antigone makes the self-interested claim that whatever justification she had "matters much less to me than my own safety" (477). How are we to understand the guard in this light? Is he wrong? How is this statement similar or dissimilar to Ismene's refusal to assist Antigone?

5. Why does Eurydike die, and what is the point of her death? She does not enter the action until the end of the work, and her death might be construed as a meaningless suicide of a minor character. How can we understand Eurydike in a larger perspective, and does her role reveal an essential point of Sophocles's work?

6. Consider the tension between the laws of the gods and the laws of the state. What is the moral weight of each as presented in *Antigone*? How can these be reconciled when they are in conflict? Does the play suggest a deeper understanding of religion and the state?

7. In what ways is Kreon a tyrant, and in what ways is he simply attempting to follow what is best for his state? *Antigone* presents a conflict between the ruler's principle and the popular opinion, which Haimon states is sympathetic to Antigone and Polyneikes. Does this work suggest a proper course of action if popular opinion and ruling laws come

into conflict? Does popular opinion seem like a good guide for the actions of the state?

Resources

Anouilh, Jean. *Antigone*. New York: French & European Publications, 2006.
    This French play by Anouilh is an adaptation of Sophocles's original, with several substantive and provocative changes. It was, notably, first preformed in Nazi-occupied Paris in 1944, and it is thought to have undertones of the French Resistance and the occupying Nazis in the conflict between Antigone and Kreon. Geneviève Bujold starred in an American film production in 1974 (Image Entertainment).

Antigone. Dir. Don Taylor. Perf. Juliet Stevenson, John Shrapnel, and Sir John Gielgud. 1984. Part of the series Sophocles: The Theban Plays, Language Arts and Literature Core Curriculum Video Library, the Cambridge Educational Core Curriculum Video Libraries.
    This is a serious production of *Antigone* that is interesting for its use of the guard for comic relief and for its presentation of the brutality of Kreon. John Gielgud portrays an excellent Tiresias.

Antigone. Dir. George Tzavellas. Perf. Irene Papas. New York: Kino International Corp. [2004], 1961 (in Greek, with English subtitles).
    This is a faithful presentation and a classic film, with Irene Papas playing a powerful Antigone.

Griffith, Mark. *Sophocles: Antigone*. Cambridge: Cambridge University Press, 1999.
    This edition of Sophocles's play contains valuable notes and commentary and includes an extensive bibliography. Griffith also offers substantial linguistic notes and a useful, insightful introduction.

Knox, Bernard. *The Heroic Temper: Studies in Sophoclean Tragedy*. Berkeley: University of California Press, 1964.
    This book, a classic study of Sophoclean tragedies, with the third and fourth chapters devoted to *Antigone*, offers an accessible analysis that is clearly and closely reasoned. This is a useful complement to the discussion and paper topics outlined here.

Segal, Charles. *Sophocles' Tragic World: Divinity, Nature, Society*. Cambridge, MA: Harvard University Press, 1995.
    Segal offers a collection of nine essays on Sophocles's drama, including one on *Antigone*, "Lament and Closure in *Antigone*." He devotes particular attention to the cultural and social forces that influence and are captured in Sophocles's works.

EURIPIDES
Medea

Unexpected trouble has crushed my soul. It's
over now; I take no joy in life. My friends, I
want to die.
—*Medea*, 226–28

Topics for Lecture or Discussion

1. **As a work that is, in part, a revenge tragedy, it is notable that Medea's revenge upon Jason is not concerned with harming his person but with causing him immense intellectual and emotional suffering.** Whereas many revenge dramas culminate in the death of the avenger's enemy, Medea reveals herself to be particularly sensitive to the various ways in which she can harm people. Rather than slaughtering Jason, Medea revels in the thought of his suffering grief for his new wife and children. She seeks physical suffering for Creon and his daughter, telling the messenger, "If you can say / that they died horribly, I'll feel twice the pleasure" (1150–51), but when it comes to Jason, her desire is "to wound my husband the most deeply" (840). Medea is an astute observer of humanity, knowing it would be more grievous to Jason for his new wife and children to die, and for him to live on in mourning for them. If the instructor's syllabus includes later tragedies, especially revenge tragedies, Medea's particular form of revenge can be more clearly seen in comparison to these other works. For example, in Shakespeare's *Hamlet*, the titular character is more simply concerned with killing his uncle Claudius and rectifying the injustice of the throne. Unlike Medea, Hamlet does not seek to leave Claudius alive and suffering.
   a. **Further Reading:** Mills, S. P. "The Sorrows of Medea." *Classical Philology* 75:4 (1980): 289–96.
   b. **Suggested Search:** Go to the Web Gallery of Art (www.wqa.hu) and search "Medea" to find Eugène Delacroix's "Medea about to Kill Her Children."

2. **In his *Medea*, Euripides makes a particular point in presenting the Greek heroes as unheroic, weak, and selfish.** Jason, commonly hailed for his heroic journey with the Argonauts, is in this work a common opportunist who is untrustworthy and unlikable. In rewriting a heroic character with such typically human failings, Euripides presents a cynical view of those noble and honorable qualities typically hailed in ancient Greece. In making his hollow excuses to Medea, Jason is not only entirely

unconvincing about why he has married a new wife—"My motive was the best: so we'd live well / and not be poor" (575–76)—but his varying excuses allow for little respect of the man. Euripides's rewriting the character of this hero not only challenges the mythic understanding that the Athenians had but can also be viewed as a critique of the current opportunistic policies of the Athenian empire shortly before the Peloponnesian War.

   a. **Further Reading:** Tessitore, Aristide. "Euripides' 'Medea' and the Problem of Spiritedness." *The Review of Politics* 53:4 (1991): 587–601.

   b. **Suggested Search:** Perform a Google Images search for "Waterhouse Medea" for several images of John William Waterhouse's "Jason and Medea."

3. **In the *Poetics*, Aristotle praises Euripides as the playwright who "appears to be the most tragic of the poets" (1453a).** While Aristotle suggests that *Oedipus the King* was the perfect tragedy, his praise of Euripides in the *Poetics* is based on his choice of noble families as the subject, and the plays' conclusions in misfortune. Euripides's *Medea* also fulfills Aristotle's prescription for the unity of action, as there is only the single plot rather than a doubling of action. Notably, Aristotle emphasizes that the central difference between *Oedipus the King* and *Medea* is with respect to the knowledge of the central character as the action unfolds. As distinct from Oedipus's ignorance, Aristotle writes that another mode of tragedy is "making the agents know what they are doing and to whom they are doing it, e.g., as Euripides does in making Medea kill her children" (1453b). Part of the particularly horrifying force of Medea's actions is that they are done in full knowledge and consent of the will.

   a. **Further Reading:** Aristotle. *Poetics*. In *Aristotle: Selected Works*, translated by Hippocrates G. Apostle and Lloyd P. Gerson, 645–81. Des Moines, IA: Peripatetic Press, 1991.

   b. **Suggested Search:** Search youtube.com for "Medea 1959 Judith Anderson."

4. **Medea elicits differing responses both from the characters that she encounters and from the audience, for she arouses both sympathy and revulsion. This conflict mirrors the tension that Medea herself feels as she is torn between the love of her children and the desire to inflict great suffering on Jason.** While the chorus is initially sympathetic to Medea, and arrives to comfort her, their sympathy turns to horrified shock when she reveals her plan. The chorus warns her that her actions will only make her more miserable, but Medea's unbending fury refuses counsel. While pitying Medea's plight, the chorus condemns her actions and begs her to not kill her children. This

tension between horror and pity reflects the more central struggle that Medea endures in trying to decide her course of action. Famously, when in sight of her children, Medea falters in her resolve, and it is only with the messenger's gruesome recounting of Creon's and his daughter's death that Medea can summon the strength to kill her children. Central to *Medea*, then, is the resolution of conflicting sentiments or thoughts, as both Medea and the audience are challenged to formulate an understanding of the events that occur.

  a. **Further Reading:** Lawrence, Stuart. "Audience Uncertainty and Euripides' Medea." *Hermes* 125:1 (1997): 49–55.

  b. **Suggested Search:** Search youtube.com for "Medea 1983 Zoe Caldwell."

5. **Both in comments by Medea and by the chorus, Euripides's work demonstrates a thoughtful approach to the role of women in ancient Greek culture that is not androcentric.** While at various times Jason displays an arguably misogynistic attitude toward women and Medea, the work as a whole is far more complex. Medea, for example, argues that men "say that we lead safe, untroubled lives / at home while they do battle with the spear. / They're wrong. I'd rather take my stand behind / a shield three times than go through childbirth once" (251–54). In emphasizing the uniquely feminine suffering of childbirth, Medea suggests that women have their own distinct role in society that cannot be simply ignored or usurped by men. Indeed, Jason also acknowledges this when he dismissively states, "Men should really have some other method / for getting children. The whole female race / should not exist. It's nothing but a nuisance" (593–95). Jason's frustration stems in part from his recognition of the importance of women, as the chorus goes on to maintain as well. So, too, Medea's ability to complete her bloody plan reveals the true power that she does have, and her centrality to the plot and to the political orders within the play defies any simplistic, androcentric reading of Euripides's work.

  a. **Further Reading:** Fletcher, Judith. "Women and Oaths in Euripides." *Theatre Journal* 55:1 (2003): 29–44.

  b. **Suggested Search:** Search Academic Search Premier (http://search .ebscohost.com) for "Euripides Medea and women."

6. **The concept of time is an important issue throughout *Medea*, including not only family genealogy and time as an ordering force but also the often iterated desire to stop, reverse, or undo what has occurred in time.** Medea, as with many characters in ancient literature, is known in part by her genealogy, and her previous abandonment of her family for the sake of Jason is not only important because it was a serious and horrific action that foreshadows what occurs in Euripides's play, but because it is a severing of herself from an important aspect of

public and self-knowledge. This struggle with time is paralleled by the constant desire stated by several of the characters to go back and undo the past. Similarly, much of Medea's revenge is predicated on the expectation of future suffering on Jason's part. She mocks him at the conclusion of the work, stating, "Do you think that you're mourning them now? / Just wait till you're old" (147–48). It is also worth noting that in her struggle with the past, present, and future, Medea also kills people of all ages, from her children to the elder Creon.

    a. **Further Reading:** Allen, Danielle S. "The Flux of Time in Ancient Greece." *Daedalus* 132:2 (2003): 62–73.

    b. **Suggested Search:** Search the JSTOR database (www.jstor.org) for "time in ancient Greek drama" and "Euripides Medea and time."

In-Class Activities

1. Divide the students into two groups that will debate one another. One group must defend Medea's actions while attacking Jason, and the other must do the converse. Then discuss Euripides's manner of including both pitiable and repulsive aspects in both characters.

2. Divide students into small groups and ask them to read aloud certain passages from *Medea,* in dramatic context. Emphasize to the students that this work was initially meant to be performed, and that dramatic performance is necessary for appreciating certain tensions in the dialogue. It is preferable to assign them portions of dialogue that move quickly, from one character to another.

    Also ask students to write a journal entry in which they argue about which character is more miserable, Jason or Medea. Ask students to discuss what the most central element of this misery is, and whether Medea is, in the end, successful.

3. Present to students either certain artistic depictions of parts of *Medea* or portions of a film version, and discuss how the dramatic presentation is affected by such different media. How different would their experience of *Medea* be if they saw rather than read it first?

4. If the class has read any of the other ancient Greek tragedies included in this anthology, it will prove profitable to discuss the works in comparison. For example, Sophocles's *Oedipus the King* is also a tragedy, but it focuses on a man doomed by fate, rather than on a woman who is driven to seek revenge. A similarly profitable comparison might be made between the ancient genres of tragedy; a discussion comparing Aristophanes's *Lysistrata* to *Medea* should address the strong, active women at the center of each play, but the strikingly different tones and ends of the works.

Paper Topics/Suggestions for Writing

1. What is the nature of Medea's rage? Is there one specific thing that is the source of her anger? Is it a passion? Is it opposed to her intellect, or part of it? Compare her anger to Achilles's in *The Iliad*.

2. Medea states that Jason has left her because he tired of her as his wife. Jason states that he married Creon's daughter because he wanted to ensure the livelihood of Medea and their children. Is one of them right and the other wrong? Why does Jason leave Medea? What do their differing arguments reveal about their characters?

3. Consider Medea's final, startling escape on the flying chariot. What does it indicate or imply? Is Medea divinized at the conclusion of the play? Is this a final endorsement of Medea's actions, since she will not suffer punishment from the city?

4. Throughout *Medea*, many characters refer to the past exploits of Jason and Medea as important for understanding their current situation. How does this past inform the present? Do the characters vainly wish to turn back the clock, or is there a deeper meaning in these references to the past? Do their previous actions foreshadow their current predicament?

5. The closing statement of the play by the chorus is that the events occurred as they did because of the will of the gods. However, no god is explicitly present in the play. What is indicated in blaming the gods for the horrors that occurred? What role do the gods play? Keeping in mind Jason's and Medea's history, for how much might the gods be responsible? Do Jason and Medea have free will, and are they responsible for their actions or not?

6. The children in *Medea* are a vexed issue. Consider the fact that their only words in the work are offstage, before being slaughtered by their mother. Consider also that in contrast to Medea's killing of her children, Aegeus has just been to the Oracle in an effort to find a solution to his childlessness. What is the purpose of the role the children play here? Why are children so important to all of the characters? What is their relationship to society?

Resources

Ley, Gary. *A Short Introduction to Ancient Greek Theatre*. Chicago: University of Chicago Press, 2007.
> This is a useful volume that is easily accessible for new students of the ancient Greeks while being informative for all levels of familiarity. Ley considers various aspects of ancient Greek drama, from the writers to performers to the festivals in which they were produced.

Medea. Dir. Mark Cullingham. Perf. Zoe Caldwell and Mitch Ryan. John F. Kennedy Center for the Performing Arts, 1983.

> Zoe Caldwell plays an excellent Medea in this classic rendition, and she is supported by a very strong cast.

Medea. Dir. Pier Paolo Pasolini. Perf. Maria Callas and Giuseppe Gentile. Les Films Number 1, 1969.

> Maria Callas plays Medea, and the sparse dialogue, brilliant scenery, and certain deviations from the original make this a thought-provoking presentation of Euripides's work.

Segal, Erich, ed. *Euripides: A Collection of Critical Essays.* Twentieth Century Views Series. Englewood Cliffs, NJ: Prentice Hall, 1968.

> Segal presents a collection of essays about Euripides's work that addresses particular plays, including *Medea*, as well as larger issues. This work should be helpful for both students and instructors.

Taplin, Oliver. *Pots & Plays: Interactions between Tragedy and Greek Vase-painting of the Fourth Century B.C.* Los Angeles: J. Paul Getty Museum, 2007.

> *Pots & Plays* is a fascinating interdisciplinary study that contrasts the depictions painted on ancient pots to the drama that they might represent. In many cases, the argument is entirely compelling. Chapter 3 is titled "Vases That Might Be Related to Surviving Plays by Euripides."

ARISTOPHANES

Lysistrata

> Fine. So. Here goes. You need to know
> the plan.
> Yes, ladies. How we force the men to
> peace. . . .
> From now on, no more penises for
> you.
> —*Lysistrata*, Prologue, 119–20, 124

Topics for Lecture or Discussion

1. **Aristophanic comedy begins with a fantastic premise called the "happy idea."** In this case, Lysistrata proposes a female sex strike by Athenian and Spartan women that will quickly end the Peloponnesian War and bring their husbands back home to bed. Men, she reasons, need sex more than war. Thus the tension between domestic and foreign affairs visible in a tragedy such as *Agamemnon* plays out in comic terms in the comedy by Aristophanes. The war between wives and husbands at home complements the war of the Athenians and Spartans on the battlefield.
   a. **Further Reading:** Sofer, Andrew. "*Lysistrata* (review)." *Theatre Journal* 55:1 (March 2003): 137–38.
   b. **Suggested Searches:** Search for the following phrases in Google Images, Google Scholar, or an academic database to find images and additional resources: Germaine Greer sex strike *Lysistrata*, Norman Lindsay illustrations *Lysistrata*.

2. **The comic play poses a fanciful solution to a desperate situation.** Written in the aftermath of Athenian annihilation at Sicily in 413 B.C.E., a decisive turning point of the Peloponnesian War, *Lysistrata* posits that women, who had neither presence nor voice in Greek politics, could emerge to save the city-state. The audience would likely have been comprised almost exclusively of old men, given the wartime environment. It is as if Aristophanes comically and bitterly suggests by such an outrageous premise that all hope is lost and that only a sex strike could save the Athenians now, a kind of Swiftian modest proposal (see Volume 2, pp. 384–389). If this is the best solution, his play suggests, then the situation must be truly bad.
   a. **Further Reading:** Given, John. "When Gods Don't Appear: Divine Absence and Human Agency in Aristophanes." *Classical World* 102:2 (Winter 2009): 107–27.

b. **Suggested Searches:** Search for the following phrases in Google Images, Google Scholar, or an academic database to find images and additional resources: Project *Lysistrata*, peace plays Aristophanes, Golden Age Athens and the Peloponnesian War.

3. **A struggle over money and finances further increases the tension between men and women.** In addition to denying the men sexual access, the women also take over the Acropolis and the access to money that fuels the war effort. Visually, the *skene*, the lone building upstage in the theater, would represent the Acropolis. Once again an interesting parallel develops between the comedy and the tragic rendering in the *Oresteia*. In Aeschylus's *Agamemnon*, Clytaemnestra emerges from the center doors and begs her husband to come inside (where a death trap awaits him). In the comedy, however, Lysistrata emerges from the skene to prevent the men from entering; physical comedy, including beatings, ensues as the men try to gain access to the building. They cannot enter their women, and they cannot enter the temple to get their money either.

a. **Further Reading:** Stroup, Sarah Culpepper. "Designing Women: Aristophanes' *Lysistrata* and the 'Hetairization' of the Greek Wife." *Arethusa* 37:1 (Winter 2004): 37–73.

b. **Suggested Searches:** Search for the following phrases in Google Images, Google Scholar, or an academic database to find images and additional resources: battle of sexes in *Lysistrata*, men and women in *Lysistrata*.

4. **Aristophanes's characters, and Athenian Old Comedy in general, celebrate repeated combinations of jokes about male erections.** Frank candor, ribald humor, and sexual explicitness are refreshing aspects of Aristophanic comedy that suggest sexual attitudes quite different from our alternately pornographic and puritanical contemporary culture. There is no sense that sex is inherently shameful in Aristophanes. Male characters exploit a visual joke by wearing enormous phalluses that are meant to reflect the turgid state of prolonged sexual denial. The visual jokes also draw a humorous parallel to the war and the weapons of choice. At war, men pick up their spears to attack their enemy. At home, their male spears down below arise to battle with their women. It is as if they cannot raise both spears at the same time and must choose between war and sex. The action, comically, if optimistically, suggests that men would prefer to do battle at home. At the same time, the close relations between weaponry, war, masculinity, and sexuality are disturbing and provocative, insofar as sex with women becomes the preferred substitute or antidote for war against men.

a. **Further Reading:** Stehle, Eva. "The Body and Its Representations in Aristophanes' *Thesmophoriazousai*: Where Does the Costume End?" *American Journal of Philology* 123:3 (Fall 2002): 369–406.

b. **Suggested Searches:** Search for the following phrases in Google Images, Google Scholar, or an academic database to find images and additional resources: Greek fertility god, gender and sexuality Greek comedy, phallus in Greek comedy, phallus Greek vase painting.

5. **Classical comedy tends to be conservative, poking fun at societal ills and excesses, but ultimately reinforcing the dominant values of contemporary society.** Indeed, despite the abundant references to sex and sexuality, *Lysistrata* presents wives in monogamous and unchanging relationships with their husbands. And, too, given what we know about the roles of women in Greek society, coupled with the knowledge that men played the women's roles in drama, it is difficult to argue for the play as a feminist call to action. There is nothing to suggest that Aristophanes thought that women should achieve greater equality in society.

a. **Further Reading:** Silk, Michael. "Serious Issues and 'Serious Comedy.'" In *Aristophanes and the Definition of Comedy,* 301–49. New York: Oxford University Press, 2000.

b. **Suggested Searches:** Search for the following phrases in Google Images, Google Scholar, or an academic database to find images and additional resources: Aristophanes king of old comedy, Martin Revermann comic business, definitions of comedy, Aristophanes and Genre.

6. **The characterization of the Spartan women and men reveals much about how Athens, the home of the dramatic festivals, saw itself and its major city-state adversary.** English translations frequently present the Spartans as country hicks—physically beautiful, bodies almost perfect, but slow-witted and dumb—to contrast with the urban sophistication of the Athenians. Of course the characterizations of the intelligent, sophisticated and cultured urbanite and the stupid, slow, and illiterate hayseed exist as a shorthand stereotype, for both ancient and contemporary readers. Like all stereotypes, the characterizations are based on some partial truths that do not tell the entire story. We know that Spartan culture emphasized military training at the expense of the arts. We also know that Sparta eventually won the war against Athens. After all the laughter is done, what anxieties, then, does Aristophanes expose and try to mask?

a. **Further Reading:** Millender, E. G. "Spartan Literacy Revisited." *Classical Antiquity* 28:1 (April 2001): 121–64.

b. **Suggested Searches:** Search for the following phrases in Google Images, Google Scholar, or an academic database to find images and

additional resources: Peloponnesian War map, Thucydides and Peloponnesian War, history of Peloponnesian War.

In-Class Activities

1. Try staging the scenes with a variety of gender combinations: all male, all female, mixed according to specified gender, and mixed in opposition to specified gender. In what ways does the actor's gender play a role in the interpretation of the characters? How do masks affect the interpretation of gender?

2. Get a pack of multicolored balloons and blow them up in various sizes to wear in scene work for the play. How does the grotesque display of male sexuality simultaneously produce comic effects and reinforce the very serious issue of patriarchy? Female characters, too, can attach balloons to indicate enormous breasts. Does this produce the same sexual, comic response as phallic balloons? What are other ways of visually representing female sexuality?

3. Discuss how and why comedy draws heavily upon topical references and current events.

4. Concoct a "happy idea" for a contemporary comedy.

Paper Topics/Suggestions for Writing

1. What is the effect of all the vulgar language and graphic sex talk in the play? Is such crude language necessary? Why or why not?

2. How does "Old Comedy," the type of comedy in which Aristophanes wrote, differ from other types of comedy with which you are familiar? Compare it, for example, to a current television sitcom of your choice.

3. "Make love, not war" emerged as a slogan in the 1960s as a result of the prolonged and unpopular conflict in Vietnam. In what ways is such a slogan just as utopian, fanciful, and desperate a declaration now as it was in *Lysistrata* twenty-five hundred years ago or *in The Lysistrata Project* in 2003?

4. The emphasis on sex and celebration of the phallus in the play can be seen as a rite of spring with an emphasis on rebirth, renewal, and regeneration. Consider the ways in which the play might be considered a ritual, or an owing to ritual, and, as such, enacts a conservative ideology that reinforces the dominant patriarchy. How does the losing war effort counteract the rituals of rebirth?

Resources

The Archive of Performance of Greek and Roman Drama: APGRD Database, University of Oxford. www.apgrd.ox.ac.uk/database. Edited by Amanda Wrigley.

> An outstanding online database produced by the University of Oxford that lists over nine thousand productions and is constantly being updated.

The Gods Are Laughing: Aristophanes, His Life and Theatre. Films for the Humanities & Sciences, 1995, VHS/DVD.

> Aristophanes as the father of political comedy.

Operation Lysistrata. Dir. Michael Patrick Kelly. Perf. F. Murray Abraham, Kathleen Chalfant, Ellen McLaughlin, Keir Dullea, Mia Dillon, Viggo Mortensen, et al. Aquapio Films, 2006, DVD.

> This documentary traces how theater protested against war in Iraq in 2003 with readings and performances of Aristophanes's play in a worldwide movement started by two women.

Women in Classical Greek Drama. Films for the Humanities & Sciences, 2003, VHS/DVD.

PLATO

Symposium

> . . . the only thing I say I understand is the art
> of love.
> —Socrates, p. 872

Topics for Lecture or Discussion

1. **Repeatedly in the Platonic dialogues, Socrates describes himself as a lover of wisdom, and the *Symposium* clarifies what is meant by the word "lover."** Making important distinctions about love that the prior speakers had ignored or had been ignorant of, Socrates's Diotima stresses the point that love is between resource and need due to its genealogy. This general balance in the nature of love is found specifically in those who love wisdom, who are neither ignorant nor wise. Furthermore, the true lover of wisdom must begin in wonder, and Socrates demonstrates this passion in stating that several times Diotima's answers filled him with admiration and wonder and led him on toward truth. It is important to note, however, that Diotima also states that wonder is, in part, the conclusion of love, for "the man who has been thus far guided in matters of Love, who has beheld beautiful things in the right order and correctly, is coming now to the goal of Loving: all of a sudden he will catch sight of something wonderfully beautiful in its nature" (855). The sight of the truly beautiful fills the beholder anew with wonder, and thus with further love of wisdom, and Socrates attempts to convey this essential point as a prompting of wonder in his own audience in the *Symposium*.
   a. **Further Reading:** Quinn, Dennis. "Youthful Wonder: The Greeks." In *Iris Exiled: A Synoptic History of Wonder,* esp. 81–92. New York: University of America Press, 2002.
   b. **Suggested Search:** Go to the Web Gallery of Art (www.wga.hu) and search "The School of Athens" to find Raphael's painting of the same name.

2. **Socrates's eventual execution at the hands of the Athenians has been understood by some as a reaction of the polis to Socrates's apparent divorce from and disparagement of participation in the political life of the city, and this stems in part from his understanding of love.** However, Mary Nichols suggests that his enunciation of philosophy as a middle position between ignorance and wisdom indicates a political understanding that does not correspond to Alcibiades's imperialistic disregard for Athenian institutions. Rather, in seeking to answer his poet friends in the *Symposium*, Socrates suggests that love

is generative and reciprocal, and that the wonder of the true love of wisdom inspires one to share that wonder with others. In this context it is entirely fitting for Socrates to declare that the one thing he does know about is love (872), for it is precisely that love that makes him come in from the porch where he had been contemplating to share his wonder with those at the dinner party. This action is the fruit of that generative aspect of love that Diotima describes, and his participation in the city is the fulfillment of the other, non-self-sufficient part of love.

a. **Further Reading:** Nichols, Mary P. "Socrates' Contest with the Poets in Plato's *Symposium*." *Political Theory* 32:2 (2004): 186–206.

b. **Suggested Search:** Go to the Web Gallery of Art (www.wga.hu) and search "the death of Socrates" to find several famous paintings of Socrates's execution.

3. **Important to the setting of the *Symposium* is the fact that most of the interlocutors had been intemperate with wine the night before and were seeking a different course of action for the current evening.** Socrates had missed the prior party, which had seen such excesses, admitting to Aristodemus, "I really don't like crowds" (869). His avoidance of the truly bacchanalian celebration is important also because he is described several times as the one who "could drink the best of us under the table" (905). Socrates's preference for the more intimate dinner party is therefore due not simply to its more temperate atmosphere but also because in smaller groups one is able to carry on more serious conversations. These serious conversations, it turns out, are the generative product of love, for Diotima describes the lover of wisdom and beauty, stating, "When he makes contact with someone beautiful and keeps company with him, he conceives and gives birth to what he has been carrying inside him for ages" (896). Socrates's participation in a party where the members seek a temperate course of celebration, then, is his guidance of others in the fulfillment of this love.

a. **Further Reading:** Moors, Kent F. "Plato's Use of Dialogue." *The Classical World* 72:2 (1978): 77–93.

b. **Suggested Search:** Search the JSTOR database (www.jstor.org) for "Diotima" for several pertinent articles.

4. **The various types of praise and the definition of love in the *Symposium* indicate not only the richness of the topic addressed but also challenge simple generic understandings of comedy and tragedy, philosophy and literature, and so on.** While the great majority of Plato's works are presented in the form of interrogative dialogue, the *Symposium* presents a series of speeches with only a bit of Socrates's usual close questioning of the thoughts of his companions. Rather, the *Symposium* contains a series of basic rhetorical modes of speech: eulogy, legal discussion, medical diagnosis, mythical foundation, and

hymn (or dithyramb). Only after these does Socrates present his close reasoning, and that is followed by the startling interruption of the drunken Alcibiades and his mixed encomium and condemnation of Socrates. In blending the rhetorical and generic modes, Plato not only indicates the foundational importance of love—which Socrates affirms with his argument—but also argues that philosophy ought to inform those other pursuits. The doctor, lawyer, general, and poet ought to be supported by philosophy. And perhaps, as indicated in Socrates's final words about the unity of the tragic and comic poet, philosophy ought to be supported by poetry, a position that this dialogue might be said to exemplify in its diversity of rhetoric and poetry.

    a. **Further Reading:** Nelson Jr., Lowry. "Alcibiades' Intrusion in Plato's *Symposium.*" *The Sewanee Review* 94:2 (1986): 196–204.

    b. **Suggested Search:** Go to classics.mit.edu and search "Alcibiades" to find Dryden's translation of Plutarch's life of Alcibiades.

5. **Diotima's discussion of the "ladder of love"—a movement from the apparent, physically beautiful to the immortal, transcendent, and divine beauty—is embodied in the relationship between Alcibiades and Socrates.** Alcibiades declares in no uncertain terms that he was filled with, and still feels, a physical lust or an *eros* for Socrates. Yet as Alcibiades says, "In spite of all my efforts, this hopelessly arrogant, this unbelievably insolent man—he turned me down! He spurned my beauty" (904), and, instead, Socrates continued to converse with Alcibiades, drawing him beyond the merely physical. In this sense, then, Socrates becomes *eros* and is himself the "ladder of love" for Alcibiades as he endeavors to lead Alcibiades to the eternal beauties of truth and virtue. As Alcibiades admits, "I couldn't help admiring his natural character, his moderation, his fortitude—here was a man whose strength of character and wisdom went beyond my wildest dreams" (904). This movement of Alcibiades's love for Socrates from the physical to the spiritual is also important because Socrates was considered extraordinarily ugly, and it is, paradoxically, that ugliness that houses the greatest beauty.

    a. **Further Reading:** Bloom, Allan. "The Ladder of Love." In *Love and Friendship,* 431–546. New York: Simon and Schuster, 1993.

    b. **Suggested Search:** Go to the *Stanford Encyclopedia of Philosophy* (http://plato.stanford.edu) and search "Plato on Eros" for an article that addresses this issue; a helpful bibliography is included.

In-Class Activities

1. Ask students to attempt to write a definition of love in just one to three sentences. Compare their definitions, and emphasize the differences and difficulties in producing a definition. In relating their definitions to

those given in the *Symposium*, discuss the degree to which they agree with the various expositions of love that Plato presents.

2. As a class, reduce each character's definition of love to one to three sentences or major points. Discuss the central tenet of each formulation of love, and debate whether there is a central point on which most of the differences are based.

3. Ask students to pick two other authors or works in the anthology and try to write a definition of love for each that corresponds to the sentiments that they express. Sappho, Catullus, the ancient Egyptian love lyrics, and the *Ramayana of Valmiki* are particularly fruitful subjects. Once the students have completed this exercise, share these definitions as a class, and discuss how they compare to the definitions of love that Plato provides.

4. Ask students to choose a particular point in the conversation between Diotima and Socrates with which they disagree. Ask them to present their counterargument to the class, or to a smaller discussion group. Discuss with students which point they would least likely grant Diotima.

Paper Topics/Suggestions for Writing

1. What is the essential definition of love that Diotima gives? What is the essential point of disagreement between Socrates and the other speakers? Is this definition of love adequate? What might be the strongest objection that could be offered to Socrates?

2. Relate Alcibiades's entrance, drunkenness, and speech to that which happened in the earlier part of the *Symposium*. How is this fitting? What is the purpose of switching the dialogue from praise of love to praise of Socrates? Does Alcibiades have a wisdom of his own? How is this formulated? Does he disagree with Socrates?

3. Compare the dialogue in the *Symposium* with the dialogue in a drama that the class has read (e.g., *Oedipus the King*). How are these similar and dissimilar? Could the *Symposium* be performed? What are the dramatic elements in the *Symposium*, and what is the significance of these ideas being formulated in a dramatic dialogue?

4. The *Symposium* presents several different characters with distinct relationships with Socrates, ranging from the respectful and friendly to the "maniac" and the devoted. How is friendship presented in this work? Are there more proper attitudes toward Socrates than others? Which characters seem most inclined to learn from Socrates, and what is their relationship with him?

5. Compare Aristophanes's myths about the beginning of human beings to other foundational myths (Genesis, Hesiod, *The Epic of Gilgamesh*, etc.). What is significant about his formulation of this myth? Does it bear any similarities to any other creation stories? Is Aristophanes simply being farcical, or are there serious elements in this presentation of the creation of mankind? How profoundly does Aristophanes disagree with Socrates?

Resources

Hunter, Richard. *Plato's Symposium*. Oxford: Oxford University Press, 2004.
> This work is part of the series Oxford Approaches Classic Literature, and it serves as a helpful introduction to Plato's thought, works, and times. It is accessible and clear, with a helpful bibliography and suggestions for further reading.

Lesher, James H., Debra Nails, and Frisbee Sheffield, eds. *Plato's Symposium: Issues in Interpretation and Reception*. Cambridge, MA: Harvard University Press (Center for Hellenic Studies), 2006.
> A large collection of interesting essays, this volume addresses several different aspects of Plato's work, including literary considerations along with the philosophical.

Morrison, Donald R. *The Cambridge Companion to Socrates*. Cambridge: Cambridge University Press, 2011.
> This is a collection of essays about Socrates and his philosophy, including considerations of "Socratic Ignorance," the "Socratic Method," and Socrates's use of irony. While the essays vary in helpfulness, this work is recommended for both students and instructors.

Sheffield, Frisbee. *Plato's Symposium: The Ethics of Desire*. Oxford: Oxford University Press, 2006.
> Sheffield makes a compelling argument for the coherence of Plato's *Symposium* in relation to his other works, offering particularly detailed attention to Socrates's speech and Alcibiades's response. She suggests that this *eros* directed toward the good life is consistent with Plato's general philosophical questions.

Strauss, Leo. *Leo Strauss on Plato's Symposium*. Edited by Seth Bernardete. Chicago: University of Chicago Press, 2001.
> This work, published posthumously, contains an insightful close reading and analysis of Plato's *Symposium*, with an emphasis on the elements of political philosophy therein. It is based on a series of lectures that Strauss delivered in 1959, and thus the format should be particularly helpful for instructors.

TRAVEL AND CONQUEST

Show me a man who isn't a slave; one is a slave
to sex, another to money, another to ambition;
all are slaves to hope or fear.
—Seneca, Epistle 47

Topics for Lecture or Discussion

1. **While *Tale of the Shipwrecked Sailor* contains elements of a folk-tale, it also has religious elements of myth and didactic elements of the fable or moral story.** The theme of the shipwrecked sailor, or stranded traveler, who then warns the Count based on his experience, invokes the folktale genre. Woven into the story, however, are mythological elements of the gods, including an eschatological warning from the giant snake and a denial of the usefulness of sacrificing to the gods. The snake's instruction to the sailor to "Spread my renown in your city! Look, this is my due from you" (173) includes the explicitly didactic nature of the text and also explains why the experienced sailor would speak to the Count about his journey, and declare, "A man's utterance saves him" (19). The inclusion of such proverbs as a guide of action also complicates the narrative, as does the frame narrative that is not, finally, appreciated by its audience. The Count's final rebuke, "Don't act clever, my friend" (209), and response with a proverb of his own further invites the reader to question the degree to which the story is intended to be ironic.

    a. **Further Reading:** Baines, John. "Interpreting the Story of the Shipwrecked Sailor." *The Journal of Egyptian Archaeology* 76 (1990): 55–72.

    b. **Suggested Search:** Go to www.cs.st-andrews.ac.uk and search for "shipwrecked sailor" for a pdf in which the hieroglyphs tell the story.

2. **Both the "Semna Stela of Senwosret III" and Herodotus's *The Histories* are centrally concerned with preserving the memory of past events, and the influence of such memory on the actions of later readers.** "Semna Stela of Senwosret III" begins by extolling the greatness of Senwosret, including reference to Egyptian history before he was Pharaoh: "I have made my boundary, out-southing my forefathers. I have exceeded what was handed down to me" (10–11). Yet it concludes by enunciating the duty of those who come later, who must "make firm this boundary my Person made" (line 41). Not only does the stela look to history but to the future as well. So, too, Herodotus justifies his work in *The Histories* by stressing the importance of the past, giving the cause of his writing as "so that the actions of people shall not

fade with time, so that the great and admirable monuments produced by both Greeks and barbarians shall not go unrenowned" (920). Herodotus explains that since prosperity constantly changes, it is important to record the past, and the implication is that such memory will guide those in the future. This emphasis on time, and worry about the loss of memory in the future, is common in ancient cultures. Integral to this preservation of memory is the lasting nature of writing, for both of these works are effective insofar as they communicate through recorded language. Thus language and memory are closely united, and both of these works affirm that unity in their very nature.

 a. **Further Reading:** De Ste. Croix, G. E. M. "Herodotus." Second series, *Greece & Rome* 24:2 (1977): 130–48.

 b. **Suggested Search:** A Google Images search for "Semna Stela of Senwosret III" results in several images of Senwosret's stelae.

3. **The conflict between the Persians and Greeks clearly delineated the great cultural differences between the peoples, and both Herodotus's *Histories* and Aeschylus's *Persians* illustrate the Greek effort to capture and understand the root of such differences.** It is important to note that despite the recent Greco-Persian Wars and the suffering that they entailed for the Greeks, neither Aeschylus nor Herodotus attempts to demonize his previous enemy. Rather, Herodotus begins *The Histories* in seeking to find the beginning of the conflict, and in describing the Persian peoples and laws, he praises certain customs that they held, continually comparing them to those held by the Greeks. Aeschylus's *Persians* is similarly striking, for it portrays in a human, sympathetic manner the sorrows of the Persians in the loss of life at the battle of Salamis. Yet in understanding the differences between the cultures, Aeschylus has the messenger report that a Greek shouted "Set your country free! / Set free your sons, your wives, tombs of your ancestors" (137–38). This sense of freedom emphasizes an essential distinction between the Greeks and Persians, for all of the Persian soldiers were legally considered Xerxes's *bandaka* (or slaves). Both Herodotus and Aeschylus affirm the essential distinctions of citizenship and freedom as uniquely Greek in their development.

 a. **Further Reading:** Hanson, Victor Davis. "Why the West Has Won" and "Freedom—or 'To Live as You Please': Salamis." In *Carnage and Culture*, 1–59. New York: Anchor Books, 2001.

 b. **Suggested Search:** A Google Images search for "maps of Salamis" results in many maps that depict how the Greeks neutralized the Persian advantage in numbers.

4. **In emphasizing the deep relationship between humans, the land that they inhabit, and the culture that emerges, *Airs, Waters, Places* illustrates an understanding of human nature that incorporates**

all races, while attempting to account for the remarkable differences between peoples. *Airs, Waters, Places* does not consign foreign peoples and other races to a subhuman category but, in conjunction with Seneca, sees all as human beings. At the beginning of this selection, the author writes, "I now want to show how different in all respects are Asia and Europe, and why races are dissimilar, showing individual physical characteristics" (932). The differences between humans call for an explanation, but the work never alludes to a foundational, essential distinction between human beings; rather, it asserts that human beings and their culture adapt and respond to their physical environment. This universal understanding of human nature corresponds to the ancient Greek understanding of human nature, particularly that enunciated by Aristotle, which separates the essential aspects of human nature from the accidents that arise from geographic and cultural influences.

    a. **Further Reading:** Aristotle. "Book I." *Politics.* In *Aristotle: Selected Works,* translated by Hippocrates G. Apostle and Lloyd P. Gerson, 559–77. Des Moines, IA: The Peripatetic Press, 1991.

    b. **Suggested Search:** Search the JSTOR database (www.jstor.org) for "Airs, Waters, Places" for several helpful articles.

5. **Seneca's Epistle 47 understands slavery to be not only a material condition of one man's mastery over another but also an interior subjugation of the will to some vice, and in this he follows classical thinkers' concern for both material and spiritual freedom.** Much like Herodotus and *Airs, Waters, Places,* Seneca emphasizes that there is a universal human nature, and from this position he maintains that slaves must be viewed as human beings, writing, "The person you call your slave traces his origin back to the same stock as yourself, has the same good sky above him, breathes as you do, lives as you do, dies as you do" (937). Not only, then, is proper treatment of the slaves due to them through the dignity of their own being, but it is also necessary for the proper cultivation of virtue in the master. Indeed, Seneca then claims that all men are slaves, at least to hopes and fears, but often to other vices as well. The stoic philosophy that Seneca expounds maintains that only virtue can make one happy, and, as such, the master and slave alike should seek freedom from the tyranny of vice. Many classical thinkers maintained similar positions, as, for example, Plato states that "a real tyrant is really a slave, compelled to engage in the worst kind of fawning . . . he's full of fear, convulsions, and pains throughout his life" (*Republic* IX, 579d–e).

    a. **Further Reading:** Plato. "Book IX." *Republic.* In *Plato: Complete Works,* edited by John M. Cooper, 1180–99. Indianapolis, IN: Hackett, 1997.

b. **Suggested Search:** Search the Web Gallery of Art (www.wqa.hu) for "death of Seneca" for several classic paintings on Seneca's tragic death, including Luca Giordano's.

In-Class Activities

1. Review with the class the history of Cleopatra, and then examine Horace's *Nune est bibendum*. Ask students to discuss whether the poem's praise of Cleopatra is sincere and deserved and what it means. Is the work celebrating the fact that she is dead, or is it celebrating her courageous way of dying?

2. Ask students to discuss the comparison between the Greeks and other peoples in Herodotus and *Airs, Waters, Places*. Ask them to make a list of the essential distinctions, and, similarly, to try to catalog the similarities between the cultures.

3. Ask students to write a journal entry in which they compare, using one of these texts, the presentation of a different culture with an experience of their own interaction with a different culture. What sorts of things do they notice about new cultures that are similar to the descriptions in these texts?

Paper Topics/Suggestions for Writing

1. Compare the rhetorical goals of "Semna Stela of Senwosret III" and Seneca's Epistle 47. What are their audiences? What do these works aim to accomplish? In what ways are they similar in their didactic or imperative language? Is there a crucial rhetorical distinction between them?

2. Write an analysis of this selection of Aeschylus's *Persians*, and address the following questions: In what light are the Persians portrayed? Are they good or evil? Which elements or aspects of their culture can be understood from this selection? In what ways are they portrayed as different from the Greeks, and in what ways similar?

3. Compare the mythological and theological elements in "Tale of the Shipwrecked Sailor" to the scientific attitude taken in *Airs, Waters, Places*. Are there any similarities between these works? What is their understanding of human nature? What is their understanding of man's place in the world? How is this reflected in each work?

4. Seneca's Epistle 47 advocates good treatment of slaves based on their being human beings. Is this as far as Seneca goes? Does he suggest that slavery should not exist? If so, how does he convey this? If not, how does he reconcile a human being as being the possession of another?

5. Herodotus's *Histories* begins by trying to trace the source of the conflict between the Greeks and "barbarians." Why is this important? How would knowing the origins of the conflict be of use to Herodotus and the Greeks? Is it significant that he places the source of the conflict in their dealings with women?

6. What conception of human nature is contained in these texts? What essential traits of human beings do all of the texts agree upon, despite cultural differences? What essential differences do these texts imply? Given the variety of genres included here (poetry, drama, history, a boundary stela, etc.), is there a central question or concern that unifies these works? What did these authors seek to accomplish?

Resources

Casson, Lionel. *Travel in the Ancient World.* Baltimore, MD: Johns Hopkins University Press, 1994.

> Casson traces ancient sources and their accounts of travel through the ancient world, including fascinating sections on Egypt and Greece and a large section on Roman travel.

Dewald, Carolyn, and John Marincola. *The Cambridge Companion to Herodotus.* Cambridge: Cambridge University Press, 2006.

> This collection of essays is generally helpful for orienting and situating Herodotus's works within a historical context, and it includes essays such as Jasper Griffin's "Herodotus and Tragedy" that are not strictly generically bound.

Hanson, Victor Davis. *A War Like No Other: How the Athenians and Spartans Fought the Peloponnesian War.* New York: Random House, 2005.

> Hanson's excellent history of the Peloponnesian War is a military history that pays particular attention to the cultural strengths through which the Greeks triumphed. Recommended for both students and instructors, this volume vividly presents to the reader the historical and cultural situation.

Seneca. *Selected Letters.* Oxford World Classics. Translated by Elaine Fantham. Oxford: Oxford University Press, 2010.

> This edition is recommended for its excellent introduction, which discusses Seneca's life, works, and letters. This is a good selection of letters for the student who desires to continue with further reading of Seneca.

PLAUTUS

Pseudolus

1. **Plautus's *Pseudolus* is exemplary of the Roman adaptations of Greek "New Comedy," a dramatic tradition in which fictional plots feature complicated, fast-moving situations and stock characters that satirize elements of society.** New Comedy was popularized by the Greek playwright Menander (the best surviving example is his play *Dyskolos*); early Roman comic authors, including most prominently Plautus and Terence, wrote within this comic tradition. In contrast to Old Comedy, which often directly lampooned important public figures in ancient Athenian society and had pointed political messages (see, for example, Aristophanes's *Lysistrata*, in Volume 1 of this anthology), New Comedy typically depicted domestic or personal situations that require a cunning character (usually a clever slave) to outwit the antagonists. Hence, in *Pseudolus*, we find the titular character determined to assist his master's son in his love interest; he ends up making a fool of both his miserly master Simo and the pimp Ballio. Such stock characters, including forlorn lovers, quick-witted slaves, miserly or cruel parents, and braggarts, are common in New Comedy, and the gentle satire in these plays is intended to amuse and, perhaps, instruct the audience.

   a. **Further Reading:** Reiss, Timothy J. "Comedy." In *The New Princeton Encyclopedia of Poetry and Poetics*, edited by Alex Preminger and T.V.F. Brogan. Princeton, NJ: Princeton University Press, 1993. 224–28.

   b. **Suggested Search:** A search for "Plautus" at www.brittanica.com results in a helpful article that outlines his life and works, and includes a discussion of his dramatic techniques and a useful bibliography.

2. **Pseudolus is the stock character of the clever slave who outwits his master, but he is also notable for being partially representative of the playwright himself.** Throughout the play, Pseudolus arranges the course of action, and he is quick-witted enough that he never seems to be in danger of losing control. When he pledges his assistance to Calidorus despite the fact that he does not know how he will accomplish the feat of stealing Phoenicium, he displays a confidence that, as it turns out, is entirely well-founded. Pseudolus understands what motivates other people far more deeply than any other character in the play, and through that understanding he is able to manipulate and arrange things to fit his ends. Much like a playwright, Pseudolus directs the plot, characters, and even controls the conversations that take place when he is present.

The parallel nature between Pseudolus and the playwright is made explicit in the closing scene of the comedy, when he speaks, like a playwright would, directly to the audience: "But if you say / You liked our play, / And cheer our company before you go, / Then I'll invite you—to tomorrow's show" (5.2.75–78).

    a. **Further Reading:** Hallett, Judith P. "Plautine Ingredients in the Performance of the *Pseudolus*." *The Classical World* 87:1 (1993): 21–26.

    b. **Suggested Search:** A JSTOR search for "slaves of Plautus" results in several helpful articles.

3. **Although she is the cause and object of most of the action in *Pseudolus*, Phoenicium never utters a line, and only appears on the stage in two brief instances.** Phoenicium's silence is important for several reasons. On the one hand, it indicates the degree to which Roman society, and the "business" conducted within it, is dominated by men. On the other hand, it clarifies the parallel between Phoenicium and money that is made throughout the play. Both Phoenicium and money are spoken about at length, both are ardently sought after, and both are silently passed between characters as a means of exchange and as a means of gratifying desires. In this respect, Phoenicium is presented by Plautus as a commodity. Students should consider the degree to which Plautus is satirizing such treatment of women (and an important passage for this issue is the opening scene, in which Phoenicium's letter does reveal a certain degree of agency for an otherwise silent, passive character), and how the obsession with money throughout the play shapes the characters' abilities to interact meaningfully with one another (for example, consider the father-son relationship between Simo and Calidorus).

    a. **Further Reading:** Fantham, Elaine. "Sex, Status, and Survival in Hellenistic Athens: A Study of Women in New Comedy." *Phoenix* 29:1 (1975): 44–74.

    b. **Suggested Search:** A Google search for "women in Plautus's comedies" results in several helpful links.

4. **Despite the fact that there is significant competition and friction between the different characters in *Pseudolus*, Plautus is careful to emphasize elements of community and human cooperation as well.** The stage setting, with three adjacent houses, indicates that, however different, the characters in the play are neighbors. This communal sense persists throughout the play, even while the radically different characters struggle with one another in their pursuit of money and pleasure. The various encounters that take place in front of the houses further demonstrate the ways in which the community is necessarily formed by the close proximity of the living quarters. However, if this community is the source of both conflict and cooperation, it is also important as the basis for the comic situation and exchanges that occur. Plautus's comedy builds upon the famil-

iar problems that can arise between neighbors, and many of the witty jokes and comical wordplay depend upon the neighbors' familiarity with each other, as well as their ability to eavesdrop and spy upon their neighbors.

   a. **Further Reading:** Franko, George F. "Ensemble Scenes in Plautus." *The American Journal of Philology* 125:1 (2004): 27–59.

   b. **Suggested Search:** A YouTube search for "A Funny Thing Happened on the Way to the Forum" results in several clips of this adaptation of *Pseudolus*.

5. **Plautus's *Pseudolus* contains several interesting themes and dramatic elements that should be considered in relation to the satiric and comic nature of the play.** For example, the theme of food runs throughout the play, including the comic interlude with the cook (3.2), and it is related to the idea of festivity with Ballio's birthday. Food is, furthermore, deeply connected to the appetites, and stands as an important comment on the appetitive desires depicted in the play. In what ways does Plautus's presentation of food, the cook, festivity, and appetitive desire relate to the comedy and satire within the work? Students should also consider the extraordinary ways in which Plautus's characters break the "fourth wall" of the theatre by speaking directly to the audience. Similarly, the role of monologue is important to Plautus's comic craft, as it is through these solitary speeches and addresses to the audience that those watching the play are made party to Pseudolus's plots and find themselves rooting for his deceits and trickery.

   a. **Further Reading:** Hunter, R. L. *The New Comedy of Greece and Rome*. Cambridge: Cambridge University Press, 1985.

   b. **Suggested Search:** A search for "philosophy of humor" at the Stanford Encyclopedia of Philosophy website (http://plato.stanford.edu/) results in a helpful article that can supplement a discussion of Plautus' comic craft.

In-Class Activities

1. As a class, perform a dramatic reading of *Pseudolus*. To have each student participate more fully, rotate the roles at each act break. This exercise should facilitate a discussion of the differences between comedy that is read or performed.

2. Divide the students into two groups which must construct and present, respectively, a condemnation of and a defense of Pseudolus's manipulative and deceitful actions.

3. Break the students into small groups, each of which must imagine a variation of *Pseudolus* by changing the gender roles, financial attitudes, or historical context of the play. Ask the groups to share their ideas with the class.

Paper Topics/Suggestions for Writing

1. What role does money play in *Pseudolus*? What other things are equated to money in the play, and what other things are treated like money? Is there significance to the sum of twenty minas? If so, what?

2. Write an essay that contrasts Pseudolus and Ballio. In what significant ways are these characters similar and dissimilar? In what ways is Ballio a villain? Similarly, how might Pseudolus be considered a hero?

3. At one point, Pseudolus observes that "The plans of a hundred clever men / Can be overturned by a single goddess— / Luck" (2.3.23–25). How does luck feature in the play? Who benefits most from luck? In what ways is luck distinct (or not distinct) from clever planning?

4. In *Pseudolus*, a considerable amount of trickery, deceit, lying, and eavesdropping occurs. How does the play treat these things? Are they admirable? Helpful? Reprehensible? Which characters resort to duplicitous means, and what are the ends to which such deceptive actions are directed?

5. Write an essay that contrasts *Pseudolus* with Aristophanes's *Lysistrata* or Sophocles's *Antigone*. How does genre effect the respective plays? How is heroism treated in each? Are there clear villains and heroes in the plays? Consider the roles of wordplay, lying, anger, and references to the gods in each play.

Resources

A Funny Thing Happened on the Way to the Forum. Dir. Richard Lester. Perf. Zero Mostel, Phil Silvers, Buster Keaton. United Artists, 1966. DVD.
> This film, adapted from a Broadway musical of the same name, is a comic rendition of elements from several of Plautus's plays, including *Pseudolus* (which is also the name of the central character, played by Zero Mostel, in the film). The soundtrack of the musical is also available, although students of Plautus will probably appreciate the physical and situational humor in the film version.

Miola, Robert S. *Shakespeare and Classical Comedy: The Influence of Plautus and Terence.* Oxford: Clarendon Press, 1994.
> While this book is primarily concerned with Shakespeare's inheritance from Plautus and Terence, it is extremely helpful in showing the long-lasting and pervasive influence that Plautus has had upon the development of later Western drama. Miola is particularly clear in analyzing some of the comic tropes and themes in the Roman comedies, and this can prove a valuable supplement to a discussion or lecture about Plautus's artful comedies.

Moore, Timothy J. *The Theater of Plautus: Playing to the Audience.* Austin: University of Texas Press, 1998.

> Moore's volume offers a very informative background for understanding Plautus's plays, and he includes a section devoted to *Pseudolus.* Undergraduates should be encouraged to read *The Theater of Plautus* if they desire further information regarding the playwright's craft and historical context.

Slater, Niall W. *Plautus in Performance: The Theatre of the Mind.* Amsterdam: Harwood Academic Publishers, 2000.

> Slater provides a close reading of six of Plautus's comedies, including *Pseudolus*, and he focuses particularly on the figure of the slave who manipulates those around him. Both instructors and advanced students should find this work helpful.

CATULLUS

... who dared judge *me* on the basis of my
verses ...
—Catullus, Poem 16, line 3

Topics for Lecture or Discussion

1. **Several of Catullus's poems are carpe diem arguments, rhetorical works aimed at persuading the listener to give in to the speaker without delay, and thus "seize the day."** The carpe diem theme can be most clearly seen in poem 5, as the first line expresses both the exhortative nature and the loving desire common to such works: "Let's live, Lesbia mine, and love" (1). This persuasion is directed against the apparent objection that people will gossip or follow the course of their romance, and to overcome such an objection, the speaker urges the delight of thousands of kisses. Due to its attempt to be persuasive, it is proper to question the degree to which the argument is, or might be, successful. The emphasis on counting, as well as the line "Suns can rise and set ad infinitum" (4), also stresses the importance of time and making the most of what little one has. Catullus's influence with the carpe diem poem extended to other great Roman poets, including Virgil, Ovid, and Horace.

   a. **Further Reading:** "Carpe Diem." *The New Princeton Encyclopedia of Poetry and Poetics.* Edited by Alex Preminger and T. V. F. Brogan. Princeton, NJ: Princeton University Press, 1993.

   b. **Suggested Search:** Search LION (Literature Online) at lion.chad wyck.com for "carpe diem" for a variety of articles, poems, and reference entries that discuss such works.

2. **Catullus's poem 64 is a ring composition, and the detail of its structure reinforces the parallelism of much of its imagery. A ring composition is a work in which the structure follows a pattern of development through several images or ideas until the central, governing image is discussed. The work then continues by describing the previous ideas or images in reverse order. In effect, the central image is a pinnacle that the work builds up to and then descends from, touching upon the same points in both the ascent and descent.** As David Traill notes about Catullus's poem 64, "A basic pattern of ring-composition articulates the poem: prologue-guests-coverlet-Ariadne and Theseus-coverlet-guests-epilogue" ("Ring Composition in Catullus 64," 232). Understanding this structure helps clarify for the reader why, when the subject is purportedly the happy marriage of Thetis and Peleus, so much time is spent on the tragedy of Ariadne and Theseus.

As the center of the ring composition, this story governs the others, and rather than simply being a lengthy digression, it corresponds to the imagery in the rest of the work. The two couples are contrasted in their immediate happiness, and the coming birth of unhappy Achilles corresponds to the coming death of weeping Aegeus. Many such symmetries and parallels might be drawn, and it is important to note as well that Catullus reinforces these connections with specific words in the original Latin (see Traill).

a. **Further Reading:** Traill, David A. "Ring Composition in Catullus 64." *The Classical Journal* 76:3 (1981): 232–41.

b. **Suggested Search:** Searching the database JSTOR at www.jstor.org for "Catullus 64" provides a number of varying considerations of this work.

3. **Catullus's love poetry is not simply romantic immersion in the overwhelming emotion of the moment. Rather, it delicately presents reflective, controlled thought in conjunction with the immanent feelings of love.** The "passer" poems (2, 3) for example, powerfully present the sparrow and the speaker's love for the girl, but this love is fraught with worry in both poems. The speaker mentions "the spirit's black depression" (2.10), and in excoriating the deceased animal with various shades of irony, he shows himself to be more intellectually present than lost in emotion. Similarly, poem 8 is not simply a rant or personal exhortation but consciously contrasts the avowed effort not to think on precisely those things that the speaker is contemplating. In the semiparadoxical reflection on reason and will, Catullus's subject is not simply overcome with emotion. Rather, the human condition of intellect and passions simultaneously guiding or confusing the speaker is captured throughout these love poems. This is, perhaps, most clearly captured in the central paradox of poem 107, in which hopeless yearning is fulfilled and satisfied, yet now joyfully remembered and enunciated as that essential cause of current bliss.

a. **Further Reading:** Grimaldi, W. M. A. "The Lesbia Love Lyrics." *Classical Philology* 60:2 (1965): 87–95.

b. **Suggested Search:** A Google Images search for "Catullus and Lesbia" reveals several visual depictions of Catullus and his beloved, most notably Sir Lawrence Alma Tadema's "Catullus at Lesbia's."

4. **Catullus's poems contain a wariness toward his potential audience, and this caution emphasizes the public and private aspects of his lyric poetry.** Poem 1 identifies the dedicatee of the collection of poems and in this manner establishes the works as public in some degree. So too, as noted previously, the exhortative nature of some of the love poems similarly indicates a potential, identified audience: the beloved. Yet Catullus also appears to want to limit those who do read his works,

as his invectives against Furius and Aurelius in poem 16 indicate, and as is also shown in poem 42 when a mocking woman has stolen his writing tablets: "This vile slut seems under the impression / I'm a walking joke" (3–4). Catullus's speaker demands that his works be taken seriously, and in insisting upon this, he allows for profound irony in interpretation—perhaps the speaker protests too much? Finally, however, the speaker asserts that those who do not appreciate his work have no basis to judge it, and that even if the verses are bad, that is no ground upon which to judge the man himself: "Who dared judge *me* on the basis of my verses— / *they* mayn't be manly: does that make *me* indecent?" (16.3–4, emphases in original).

a. **Further Reading:** Sandy, Gerald N. "Catullus 16." *Phoenix* 25:1 (1971): 51–57.

b. **Suggested Search:** See the "Catullus" section at www.vroma.org for a valuable cross-listing of the "Social Set of Catullus," which identifies which people are mentioned in which poems.

5. **In both his love poetry and his moving lament for his brother in poem 101, Catullus ponders the challenge of the passing of time and human mortality in contrast to the human desire for eternity and happiness.** Poem 101 presents Catullus at his brother's grave, completing the Roman funeral rites while mourning the loss of his brother. Yet while offering "poor obsequies" (2), Catullus also acknowledges that his address to his brother is "all in vain" (3). The separation of death is, as the speaker sadly asserts, eternal, and in the face of such overbearing fortune and time, all he can do is "forever now hail and farewell" (10). The speaker's relationship with his beloved is similarly challenged by time, as poem 109 contrasts perpetual vows with the limitations of human life: "We can maintain, for the rest of our life together, / our hallowed friendship through this eternal pact" (5–6). Catullus's poetry continually presents the struggle between the human ability to conceive of the eternal, all the while being bound, even in moments of joy, to the passing of time and eventual loss of life.

a. **Further Reading:** Godwin, John, ed. and trans. "Commentary on 101." In *Catullus: Shorter Poems*. Warminster, England: Aris & Phillips, 1999, 102–103, 212–13.

b. **Suggested Search:** A Google search of "Catullus 101 read" renders several YouTube recordings of readings of the work that capture the rhyme and meter of the poetry in the original Latin.

In-Class Activities

1. Compare the presentation of love found in Catullus's poetry to that found in Sappho's (depending on what is included in one's syllabus, the Egyptian love lyrics, Ovid, and the Psalms in the Hebrew Bible are all

similarly excellent comparisons). Discuss whether one is more accessible to the students and the differences that these poets display in their discussion of the effects of the passions.

2. Ask students to memorize one of the love lyrics and recite the poem to the class.

3. Write a journal entry comparing the epic qualities of poem 64 to other epic works the class has read. Discuss the ways in which common tropes of epic poetry are changed by Catullus for this shorter work.

4. Read to the class one of Catullus's lyrics in Latin. Discuss the beauty of the language, rhythm, and meter of the original.

Paper Topics

1. Considering the fact that Catullus died as a young man, which indications of age can be found in his poetry? Which traits does his speaker usually exhibit, and is there anything distinctively young about them? How does he present age in these poems?

2. What is Catullus's essential conception of love as understood in these poems? To what degree is it a passion and to what degree is it intellectual? Is love a good thing? How powerful is love? Choose two other poets (or poems, if the author is anonymous) from different periods or traditions and compare the poetic approach of each to the subject of love. Do these works share any essential elements with Catullus's understanding of love? How do these different poets illustrate love as an essentially similar human experience regardless of country or culture?

3. Choose three of the short lyrics, analyze their language and structure, and then do the same with two of the love lyrics from Sappho. Is there a unifying element and are there certain tropes that Catullus and Sappho consistently make use of? Through close reading, demonstrate the essential features of this poetry and be sure to discuss the important differences between the love lyrics of these two great poets.

4. How does the central story of Ariadne and Theseus in poem 64 relate to the framing story of the marriage of Thetis and Peleus? In what ways does this story reflect positively or negatively on the coming nuptials? Is it important that this story is contained as a piece of artwork?

5. Comparing several of these poems, analyze the character of the speaker's beloved as shown through the language, rhetoric, and problems that are included in the poems. Is she a worthy object of devotion? What is her temperament, and to what degree does she hold affection for Catullus's speaker?

Resources

Garrison, Daniel H. *The Student's Catullus*. Norman: University of Oklahoma Press, 2004.

> This work presents the Latin original with substantial, helpful notes and is not weighed down with excessive attention to differing textual theories regarding the Latin.

The Latin Library. "Catullus." www.thelatinlibrary.com/catullus.shtml.

> This site presents all of the Catullus poems in their original Latin.

Putnam, Michael C. J. *Poetic Interplay: Catullus and Horace*. Martin Classical Lecture Series. Princeton, NJ: Princeton University Press, 2006.

> An important and accessible commentary on the relationship between these great masters of the Latin lyric, *Poetic Interplay* is helpful to both the student of Latin and the general student of literature.

Quinn, Kenneth. *The Catullan Revolution*. London: Cambridge University Press, 1959.

> This is a helpful work for understanding the breadth of influence that Catullus had upon the development of Western lyric poetry, and it provides substantial consideration to the literary situation in Rome before and during Catullus's life.

Wiseman, T. P. *Catullan Questions*. Leicester, UK: Leicester University Press, 1969.

> Wiseman's work is more particularly attentive to the textual history of Catullus's work, including the veracity and historical placement of the poems. He suggests that Catullus himself arranged the poems in the order in which we have received them.

VIRGIL

The Aeneid

> . . . buffeted left and right
> by storms of appeals, he takes the full force
> of love and suffering deep in his great heart.
> His will stands unmoved.
> —*Aeneid*, Book IV, lines 562–65

Topics for Lecture or Discussion

1. **Aeneas's powerful narration of Books II and III reveals him as being not only a great warrior but a speaker, or rhetor, of great skill.** Virgil describes great silence as all wait for Aeneas to begin speaking, and in his initial declaration "Sorrow, unspeakable sorrow, / my queen, you ask me to bring to life once more" (II.3–4), and in the course of his moving narrative, he does indeed bring the story to life. Aeneas's ability to speak so movingly and fluently not only allows the reader to doubt the veracity of certain details of his story—just as the reader can doubt parts of Odysseus's narration of his own history—but it also shows the depth of thought and feeling within Aeneas. This greatness of heart and mind elucidates the reader's understanding of such later trials that Aeneas undergoes, as leaving Dido and fighting in Italy are not simply the work of an unfeeling warrior. The psychological depth and pain that Aeneas endures are in part conveyed through his ability to so eloquently describe the suffering and fall of Troy.
   a. **Further Reading:** Lewis, C. S. "Virgil and the Subject of Secondary Epic." In *Virgil: A Collection of Critical Essays,* edited by Steele Commager, 62–67. Englewood Cliffs, NJ: Prentice Hall, 1966.
   b. **Suggested Search:** A Google Images search for "Aeneas telling his story" results in several paintings depicting Aeneas as orator or narrator.

2. **Despite the dooming influence of the gods in Dido's love for Aeneas, it is the depth of her passion, combined with the greatness of her character, that ennoble her suffering to the level of the truly tragic.** In writing about tragedy, Aristotle notes that it properly concerns people who are "better than average"; the depths of tragedy are only reached with the suffering of great people. With these criteria, the affecting situation of Dido's plight is in part understandable due to her superiority of position, beauty, and character. Dido is a noble queen, beloved by her people, and so impressive that honest Aeneas states, "What age has been so blest to give you birth? / What noble parents produced so fine a

daughter?" (I.725–26) when they first meet. Aeneas's commanding presence and active nobility are matched by Dido's, and the greatness of her character is apparent not only in her rule of Carthage but in the depth of love she felt for Aeneas and her loyalty to the memory of her first husband, Sychaeus, before the gods' interference.

    a. **Further Reading**: Aristotle. *Poetics*. In *Aristotle: Selected Works*, translated by Hippocrates G. Apostle and Lloyd P. Gerson, 645–81. Des Moines, IA: Peripatetic Press, 1991.

    b. **Suggested Search**: Go to the Web Gallery of Art (www.wga.hu) and search for "Dido death" for several depictions of her death, including Cavot's famous statue.

3. **The love between Aeneas and Dido is not only important as a tragic influence in the epic but because it most clearly depicts Aeneas's** *pietas*. While Aeneas's recounting of the fall of Troy is a story that does emphasize his *pietas* in relation to the city, gods, and his family and comrades, Dido most clearly challenges, or tempts, Aeneas to abandon this virtue. Mercury's warning to Aeneas that he must leave Dido emphasizes *pietas* and duty, and Aeneas suddenly conforms his mind to the will of the gods and his destiny, though he still loves Carthage and Dido: "Aeneas / was truly overwhelmed by the vision, stunned, / his hackles bristle with fear, his voice chokes in his throat. / He yearns to be gone, to desert this land he loves" (Book IV, lines 345–48). Similarly, when he is facing Dido's sorrowful anger at the news, "warned by Jupiter now, his gaze held steady, / fought to master the torment in his heart" (IV, 412–13). Fulfilling the demands of *pietas* is not easy for Aeneas, and while he does conform his will, he suffers tremendously. The deep enactment of the virtue of *pietas* in spite of his love for Dido is a crucial aspect of his heroic stature as the founder of Rome.

    a. **Further Reading**: McLeish, Kenneth. "Dido, Aeneas, and the Concept of 'Pietas.'" *Greece & Rome* 19:2 (1972): 127–35.

    b. **Suggested Search**: Go to the Web Gallery of Art (www.wga.hu) and search for "Bernini Aeneas" for a wonderful statue depicting Aeneas's *pietas*.

4. **Juno's enmity toward Aeneas and the Trojans is important for its emphasis of the historical continuity between the Greeks, Trojans, Romans, and Carthaginians, but it also serves as a potentially ominous warning about the future of Rome to Virgil's audience.** Juno's hatred for Aeneas is based on the old allegiances of the gods found in the Greek myths and Homer's epics, and Virgil's use of this anger as a primary force in *The Aeneid* emphasizes this historical unity. It also, obviously, explains the root of the enmity between the Carthaginians and Romans. However, while Virgil's audience would have proudly regarded the destruction of Carthage and the triumph of Rome, Juno's

anger at the conclusion of the work is ominously unabated. Despite her tentative, temporary accession to Jupiter's plan, her fury is worryingly similar to Aeneas's final, decisive anger in killing Turnus, despite pleas for mercy. If Aeneas is conclusively unmoved in his anger, might Juno similarly be finally unmoved in hers? The parallels between Aeneas and Juno at the conclusion of *The Aeneid* might be best understood, then, as a warning to Rome concerning overconfidence, complacency, or hubris in the face of a dedicated enemy or god.

   a. **Further Reading:** Feeney, D. C. "The Reconciliations of Juno." *The Classical Quarterly* 34:1 (1984): 179–94.

   b. **Suggested Search:** A Google Images search for "Juno and Aeolus" will result in many paintings of the scene when Juno asks Aeolus for a storm to wreck the Trojans.

5. **The description of Aeneas's shield is an instance of ekphrasis that not only prophesies greatness for the Romans but, through allusions to Achilles's shield in *The Iliad* and Pseudo-Hesiod's *Shield of Hercules*, it claims that *The Aeneid* itself is a great work of art.** Ekphrasis, as a verbal depiction or description of a visual work of art, is often laden with references to other works of visual and literary art, and this is the case with Aeneas's shield. Virgil's elaborate descriptions, which include verbal parallels to the descriptions in Homer and Pseudo-Hesiod, are important for presaging the coming struggles and triumphs of the Romans up to Virgil's own time. This depiction, which fills Aeneas with "wonder," illustrates that despite his prudence and *pietas*, Aeneas is acting for something far greater than even he understands— he becomes the founder of what is presented as the ordering principle of law in the world, the Roman Empire. However, in making allusions to prior literary works with similar ekphrastic moments, *The Aeneid* also claims that it is a great work of art worthy enough to be compared to Homer's epics and Pseudo-Hesiod's poetry (and one might think of Hesiod's cosmology as well).

   a. **Further Reading:** Vella, Horatio Caesar Roger. "Virgil's Aeneid VIII and the Shield of Aeneas: Recurrent Topics and Cyclic Structures." *Studia Humaniora Tartuensia* 5:A1 (2004): 1–7.

   b. **Suggested Search:** Go to the Web Gallery of Art (www.wga.hu) and search for "Batoni Aeneas" for Batoni's painting of Venus presenting Aeneas's armor to him.

6. **The parallel between Aeneas's narration of the fall of Troy at the beginning of *The Aeneid* and the concluding storming of the city of Latium emphasizes the importance of Turnus as a great but misguided warrior who, unlike Aeneas, attempts to resist the will of the gods.** The horrors of a besieged and eventually sacked city are narrated with considerable pathos by Aeneas in Books II and III, but when

he finally assaults Latium, Aeneas displays many traits of the erstwhile conquering Greeks. The chaos and terror that ran though Troy similarly fills Latium, and as Troy had burned, so burns the Latins' city. Important in both cases as well is the will of the gods that both cities fall, but whereas Aeneas is guided from Troy to his destiny of founding Rome, Turnus is fated to die in defense of the Latins—and in part because he sought to defy the will of the gods. Turnus's admirable courage in the face of fate and Aeneas's strength is not sufficient for victory, and his death at the conclusion of the work emphasizes the dangers of pursuing imprudent opposition to that which is fated.

   a. **Further Reading:** Otis, Brooks. "The Iliadic *Aeneid*." In *Virgil: A Study in Civilized Poetry*, 313–82. Oxford: Oxford University Press, 1964.

   b. **Suggested Search:** Perform a Google Images search for "Giordano Aeneas and Turnus" for images of Aeneas's defeat of Turnus, particularly Luca Giordano's famous painting.

7. **As the Roman epic,** *The Aeneid* **invites comparison to the great Homeric epics of Greece, while also attending to some of the critiques of poetry that Plato made with regard to Homer.** Through its epic scope, large battles, sieges, and catalogs of fallen warriors—and, needless to say, by beginning with the fall of Troy—*The Aeneid* refers and compares itself to *The Iliad*. So, too, through the lengthy voyages plagued by gods' ill wills, travel to the underworld, and frame narratives told by the central character, *The Aeneid* invokes *The Odyssey* and compares Aeneas to Odysseus in several explicit ways. However, in scenes such as Aeneas's settling with Dido and his sorrow in his hasty departure and in the description of his shield, Virgil also demonstrates a sensitivity to tensions between the demands of the political world and the personal or domestic or contemplative spheres. Rather than contemplative calm with Dido, Aeneas is called to political action in the founding of Rome. This tension between the political and philosophic modes of life is a central issue in Plato's works, and it is directly related to a critique of Homer's epics in *The Republic*.

   a. **Further Reading:** Shiffman, Mark G. "A Platonic Reading of Virgil's *Aeneid*." *Modern Age* 43:3 (2001): 211–22.

   b. **Suggested Search:** Search the JSTOR database (www.jstor.org) for "Plato and Virgil" for several interesting articles.

In-Class Activities

1. Read to the students the first twenty lines of *The Aeneid* in Latin, and discuss the poetic form and meter (dactylic hexameter) and the beauty and precision of Virgil's language and metrics.

2. Show the students Luca Giordano's painting *Aeneas and Turnus* (many other paintings could serve a similar purpose), and discuss the artist's interpretation and presentation of the text as compared to the students' imagining of the scene based on Virgil's description.

3. Show students an excerpt from Henry Purcell's opera *Dido and Aeneas* (I suggest "Dido's Lament" as a particularly powerful piece). Discuss the connections to Virgil's work and how the opera both captures and differs from the spirit in the text.

4. Ask students to divide into two groups that must debate between the conflicting claims of Turnus and Aeneas. Make sure they base their arguments on evidence from the text.

5. Ask students to write a journal entry comparing the sorrows of Dido to the sorrows of Turnus. In what ways are these characters similar and dissimilar, and who endures greater wrong and suffering at the hands of Aeneas?

Paper Topics/Suggestions for Writing

1. Compare Aeneas to Odysseus. What are the essential similarities and dissimilarities between the two characters? In what ways do they differ in their response to a god's enmity? To whom or what is their final loyalty given?

2. What is the role of the gods in *The Aeneid*? Do humans have free will? Are they doomed to a certain course of action? Are they able to change their fate? Are the gods capricious, or is there a principle that governs their actions, affections, and persecutions? How does this compare to other ancient epics' portrayal of the gods (Homer, Valmiki, the *Mahabharata*)?

3. What is Aeneas's greatest virtue? What is Turnus's greatest virtue? What are their greatest vices, or weaknesses? Is the essential difference between Aeneas and Turnus a virtue or a vice?

4. Write a paper that discusses the degree to which *The Aeneid* can be interpreted as a subtle critique of Roman customs and cultural tendencies. In what ways does Virgil seek to instruct his Roman readers, and how does he accomplish this?

5. What is the significance of the work concluding in a moment of ungranted pleas for mercy, and an unwavering rage in the hero of the story? What might this indicate about Rome? What might this imply in philosophical terms?

6. Does Aeneas change over the course of the work? In what important ways does he develop, or remain firm?

Resources

Farrell, Joseph, and Michael C. J. Putnam. *A Companion to Virgil's Aeneid and Its Tradition*. Malden, MA: Wiley-Blackwell, 2010.

> This work is a large collection of essays on a broad array of topics relating to *The Aeneid*. It is attentive to both antiquity and later centuries' reception of the work, and while one might desire more essays that deal directly with the text, this is a helpful collection.

Fratantuono, Lee. *Madness Unchained: A Reading of Virgil's Aeneid*. Lanham, MD: Lexington Books, 2007.

> Fratantuono's *Madness Unchained* is a lucid, detailed, and compelling reading of *The Aeneid*, and while it graces its readers by often examining passages line by line, it clearly presents a view of *The Aeneid* as an entire work as well. This volume also contains a helpful bibliography, which will be of great assistance to instructors when teaching *The Aeneid*.

Otis, Brooks. *Virgil: A Study in Civilized Poetry*. Oxford: Oxford University Press, 1964.

> This foundational work examines the poetic forms and culture of Virgil's works, including *The Aeneid, Georgics*, and *Bucolics*. Otis argues that Virgil is substantially different from, and departing from, the poetic tradition that he inherited, fashioning that inheritance into his new, civilized poetry.

Perkell, Christine G. *Reading Virgil's Aeneid: An Interpretive Guide*. Norman, OK: Oklahoma University Press, 1999.

> Perkell's collection of essays on *The Aeneid* is organized by having a different scholar write an analysis of each of the epic's books. This allows for a variety of perspectives and insights, while also providing detailed attention to each part of *The Aeneid*.

Purcell, Henry. *Dido and Aeneas*. Opera.

> Purcell's baroque opera *Dido and Aeneas* is important for the development of English opera as well as for the high tragedy with which it presents Dido—Aeneas is tricked into leaving her not because of the will of the gods but because of a sorceress.

OVID

Metamorphoses

> She spoke, and, moved by desire that struck
> without warning, loved without knowing what
> she was doing or feeling.
> —*Metamorphoses*, X.747–48

Topics for Lecture or Discussion

1. **Throughout *Metamorphoses*, Ovid includes many *aitia*, or stories of origins, that range in length from short asides to entire myths.** One example of a short *aition* occurs in the story "Ceres and Proserpina," when Ascalaphus reveals the fact that Proserpina did eat the fruit of the underworld, and as a consequence Ceres, in anger, changes his nature: "a filthy bird he's become, the grim announcer of mourning, / a slothful portent of evil to mortals—the owl" (V.724–25). The origins of the owl and its significance as a portentous symbol are here explained through the myth of Ascalaphus and Ceres, and in this change of one being into another, Ovid captures the sense of change in his title *Metamorphoses*. An example of a longer aition, in which an entire myth is used to explain the origins of something, is the story "Venus and Adonis" in Book X. Venus's love for Adonis was so great that she caused his death to be remembered by turning his blood into the anemone flower, explaining both the reason for its red variants and its delicacy in the face of nature. Attention to such aitia in *Metamorphoses* is important, for at one and the same time they capture the changes and shifts of nature and also offer foundational stories of the origin of continuing, permanent things with which Ovid's readers would be familiar.

   a. **Further Reading:** Myers, Sara K. "The Generic Question: Cosmogonic and Callimachean Aetiology." In *Ovid's Causes: Cosmogony and Aetiology in the Metamorphoses*, 1–26. Ann Arbor: University of Michigan Press, 1994.

   b. **Suggested Search:** A Google Images search for "Venus and Adonis" reveals many excellent paintings of this popular story.

2. **As is the case in many cosmological tales, Ovid's *Metamorphoses* begins with the existence of chaos (as does, for example, Hesiod's *Theogony*) and proceeds to the creation of humans, made in imitation of the gods.** Notably, the shifting of being that occurs at the beginning of *Metamorphoses* parallels the shifting ideas within Ovid's mind, as the invocation proem attributes his motivation for the work to the inspiration of the gods. It is also important to observe that Ovid allows

for a variety of theories concerning the beginning of creation, for he writes, "Some god (or kinder nature) . . ." (I.26) began to order chaos, and that man was made "either because the framer of all things, / the fabricator of this better world, / created man out of his own divine / substance—or else because Prometheus / took up a clod" (I.109–13). In juxtaposing the theory of human creation by the divine framer of order with the theory of the rebellious but well-meaning Prometheus, Ovid raises an essential question, returned to throughout the work, concerning the good and evil aspects of the gods but, more importantly, of human nature itself.

a. **Further Reading:** Graf, Fritz. "Myth in Ovid." In *The Cambridge Companion to Ovid,* edited by Philip Hardie, 108–21. Cambridge: Cambridge University Press, 2002.

b. **Suggested Search:** Search youtube.com for "Franz Liszt Prometheus," where you will find videos containing recordings of Liszt's symphonic poem, accompanied by art depicting Prometheus's suffering.

3. **While *Metamorphoses* is an epic, as indicated by the poetic form and the proem's stated intention of "epic sweep" (I.4), the continuous scenes of amorous intrigue, often presented in partial terms of elegiac attitudes, demonstrate the generic complexity of Ovid's work.** Ovid challenges literary conventions, especially those Roman expectations established by Virgil's epic *Aeneid* and various elegiac works, by blending and shifting between poetic presentations of the love-struck gods as predatory or sorrowful, aggressive or mourning. As Gottfried Mader argues, the famous story of Apollo and Daphne is one in which Apollo assumes different poses; initially he is presented as a hunter, then as a lamenting lover, and finally, again, as a hunter (I.628–783). These transformations are couched within appropriate imagery and poetic tropes that seemingly shift the genre, and they also correspond to the transformations that continually happen to characters within the work—Daphne (I.754–62), Pyramus's statue (X.353–63), Iphis (IX.1129–1138). Just as the characters change, they reflect the further metamorphoses of the literary genres themselves within this work.

a. **Further Reading:** Mader, Gottfried. "Programming Pursuit: Apollo and Daphne at Ovid, *Met.* 1.490–542." *Classical Bulletin* 84:1 (2008): 16–26.

b. **Suggested Search:** Go to galleriaborghese.it to view pictures of Bernini's *Apollo and Daphne* and *Pluto and Proserpina,* both of which are housed in the Borghese Gallery in Rome.

4. **In several of the selections included in this anthology, Ovid presents nature as the source and rule of human love and sexuality but com-**

plicates the situation through humanity's ability to desire that which is beyond the natural. In such cases, the result is either necessarily tragic or solved through supernatural interference. Iphis's story in Book IX of *Metamorphoses* presents a love between women that is "unnatural": "Nature, much more powerful than they are [her wishes], / wishes it not—sole source of all my woe!" (IX.1091–92). Iphis offers a lengthy consideration of the un- or anti-natural passion that she feels, noting that animals do not normally engage in homosexual activity, and the dilemma she faces is happily solved only by Isis transforming her into a boy. In a contrasting story, however, Myrrha's desire for her father, Cinyras, is understood as natural but against moral law, as she declares, "Human morality gives us such stifling precepts, / and makes indecent what Nature freely allows us!" (X.408–409). She observes that, in this case, animals are free to do what humans are not. This contrast is further emphasized by her tragic transformation into a myrrh tree, as she herself acknowledges that she belongs neither in the land of the living nor in the land of the dead.

a. **Further Reading:** Otis, Brooks. "The Pathos of Love: I." In *Ovid as an Epic Poet,* 2d ed., 166–230. Cambridge: Cambridge University Press, 1970.

b. **Suggested Search:** A Google Images search for "Poussin myrrha" results in several artistic presentations of Myrrha as a tree, and in Nicolas Poussin's, she is giving birth to Adonis.

5. **While these excerpts do not fully convey the complicated narrative structure of *Metamorphoses*, the frame narrative (a narrative contained or told within an overarching narrative) of Venus telling Adonis the story of Atalanta and Hippomenes is an excellent example of the layered stories, generations, and intertwined themes that permeate Ovid's work.** Atalanta's beauty is paralleled to Adonis's beauty, and so too is their mutual retirement to the woods. Adonis hunts animals, while Atalanta seeks to avoid marriage through living in the forest. In both cases, however, they are courted and won, and in both cases, they finally fall due to a lack of prudence: Atalanta fails to give thanks to Venus, and Adonis fails to follow Venus's warning. Notably, however, Atalanta falls in love with Hippomenes in the same manner that Venus, pricked by Cupid's bow, falls for Adonis, as neither woman has control: "moved by desire that struck without warning, / loved without knowing what she was doing or feeling" (X.747–48). Moreover, in the larger framework of *Metamorphoses*, both stories are told by Orpheus, who himself lost Eurydice because of a final, imprudent glance over his shoulder. Other frame narratives that might be discussed in comparison to *Metamorphoses* include the *Mahabharata*, Boccaccio's *Decameron*, *The Thousand and One Nights*, and Chaucer's *Canterbury Tales*.

    a. **Further Reading:** Otis, Brooks. "The Plan of Ovid's Epic." In *Ovid as an Epic Poet,* 2nd ed., 45–90. Cambridge: Cambridge University Press, 1970.

    b. **Suggested Search:** Go to youtube.com and search "John Blow Venus and Adonis" for videos of John Blow's opera *Venus and Adonis;* several videos present great paintings of Venus and Adonis, as the music plays.

In-Class Activities

1. As a class, read excerpts of Shakespeare's narrative poem *Venus and Adonis,* and compare Shakespeare's characters to Ovid's.

2. Show the class Bernini's *Apollo and Daphne* statue, and discuss the myth's and statue's presentation of Daphne's metamorphosis.

3. As a class, look at Giulio Bargolini's painting *Pygmalion and Galatea,* and discuss this interpretation of the myth as compared to Ovid's presentation. Be sure to note that Pygmalion is possibly terrified as his creation comes to life, and that the focus of the work is less upon the miraculous animation of stone than upon the human reaction to the miraculous.

4. Discuss the differences between the cosmological narrative here and those found in Hesiod and Genesis. What is similar and what is distinct in each?

5. Ask students to write a journal entry about the position of humans in relation to the gods, particularly as seen in the story of Jove and Io. Note that Io suffers innocently at the hands of both Jove and Juno.

Paper Topics/Suggestions for Writing

1. How are families presented in *Metamorphoses?* Consider familial relations between the gods, the humans, and their shared relations. What is good about family, and what is bad? Are human families similar to god families? What sort of loyalty does a family member have toward another member?

2. What are the consistent ways in which the gods interact with humans? Are they typically benevolent, antagonistic, or something else? Are the gods tyrannical, charitable? Are human prayers typically presented as efficacious?

3. Are the metamorphoses and changes that permeate the myths of this work typically beneficial or detrimental? Is change a good thing? Does it open one to new dangers, and, if so, what sorts of things are these

new dangers? In what context does Ovid indicate that change is bad or dangerous?

4. Consider the many characters that are described in these stories as beautiful. What is the nature of this beauty? Physical? Spiritual? Objective or subjective? Is beauty beneficial to its possessor? In what ways is beauty good and bad? Can humans control beauty?

5. Compare Ovid's aitia to Aesop's fables, Lucretius's *On the Nature of Things*, and Callimachus's *Aetia*. What are the essential attributes of Ovid's myths of origin compared to other explanatory works? Are Ovid's aitia didactic, and if so, what do they teach? How do such minor aitia compare to Ovid's (or others') major cosmological stories?

Resources

Hardie, Philip, ed. *The Cambridge Companion to Ovid*. Cambridge: Cambridge University Press, 2002.
> This collection of general essays introduces the student to Ovid's works and ideas. While some essays are more helpful than others, it is recommended for the student and instructor unfamiliar with these works.

Knox, Peter E., ed. *A Companion to Ovid*. Blackwell's Companions to the Ancient World. Malden, MA: Wiley-Blackwell, 2009.
> Knox presents a large collection of essays in which many issues of Ovid's time, literature, and influence are examined. While not as much time is spent specifically on the *Metamorphoses* as one might wish, this is still a helpful and informative volume for any study of Ovid.

Otis, Brooks. *Ovid as an Epic Poet*. 2d ed. Cambridge: Cambridge University Press, 1970.
> A major work in the field of Ovid studies, it is argued in this book that the *Metamorphoses* is a unified narrative poem in its movement through various themes, rather than through its succession of stories.

Volk, Katharina. *Ovid*. Malden, MA: Wiley-Blackwell, 2010.
> This volume is a thoughtful introduction to Ovid that includes a biography, sections addressing his works and the themes in his works, and his adaptations of myth. It is both highly accessible and readable, without sacrificing the quality of the substance.

II. Circling the Mediterranean: Europe and the Islamic World

The Christian Bible:
The New Testament Gospels

Topics for Lecture or Discussion

1. **The word "testament" (*testamentum*) is the Latin translation for the Greek word "covenant" (*diatheke*), which referred to a man's legal will bequeathing property and goods at his death.** The New Testament marks Jesus's establishment of a new pact between God and mankind, which would replace the Jewish alliance established through Moses in the Hebrew Bible (see Volume A, Exodus 19–20). It consists of twenty-seven books authored by eight writers but focuses on the synoptic Gospels (Matthew, Mark, and Luke) and a fourth, nonparallel Gospel (John), which together narrate Jesus's life and teachings and were composed about fifty years after his death. The New Testament adopts several religious doctrines from the Hebrew Bible: God's omniscience, omnipotence, and goodness; the emphasis of love for one's neighbor and practice of prayer, repentance, and charity to achieve closeness with God; validation of a messiah; and an afterlife and a resurrection based on messianic beliefs. It also creates new Christian doctrines that supersede the Hebrew Bible: the Trinity, the recognition of Jesus as Messiah, redeemer of mankind, the abolition of Mosaic law and substitution with new rites of baptism and the Eucharist, a church established by Jesus, an emphasis on poverty and charity, and a belief in eternal life after the Second Coming. Where do you see examples of a covenant, or of the Hebrew Bible and New Testament doctrines, represented in these excerpts?
   a. **Further Reading:** Elwell, Walter, and Robert Yarbrough. *Encountering the New Testament: A Historical and Theological Survey.* Grand Rapids, MI: Baker Academic, 2005
   b. **Suggested Search:** Durand, Alfred. "The New Testament." *The Catholic Encyclopedia*, vol. 14. New York: Robert Appleton Company, 1912. Available at www.newadvent.org/cathen/14530a.htm.

2. **The Four Gospels are canonized written records of Jesus's words and acts; they are considered the historical accounts of Jesus's life and comprise the three synoptic Gospels (Luke, Matthew, and Mark) and the fourth Gospel, John.** The synoptic works represent shared content and structure, suggesting that the writers all borrowed from the same source. Matthew is the first Gospel, and the writing style is marked by odd phrasing and citations from the Old Testament, repetition of words and expressions, and a firm position that Jesus's life and works fulfilled Hebrew Bible prophecies. Matthew's Gospel covers

Jesus's genealogy, birth, and presence of the Magi through the Passion and the Resurrection. Mark is the second Gospel (written in Rome for Roman Christians, between 50–67 C.E.); the writer is concerned with Christ's ministry and the events of Holy Week, with no mention of the birth or genealogy of Jesus. Unique to this Gospel is the writer's attention to Jesus's emotions, the crowd's reactions to his miracles, and the flaws of the apostles. Scholars view his writing style as direct and terse and note his overuse of adverbs and repetition to color the writing. Luke was a Greek physician living in Antioch (then capital of Syria) and may have been a Jewish proselyte who converted to Christianity and interacted with the apostles. Medical terminology appears throughout his writing, which is considered the most articulate of the Gospels and covers the following events: Jesus's infancy, ministry in Galilee, journey to Jerusalem, and events of Holy Week (preaching, Passion, Resurrection). His work accounts for parables not included in the other Gospels. John was likely a Palestinian Jew and may have been among Jesus's closest friends; the writing style suggests an eyewitness account or direct intercourse with Jesus. John's Gospel (written in Greek around 95 C.E. for third-generation Christians in Asia Minor) appears last, representing a life of Jesus from baptism to resurrection and appearance to the disciples; it follows a chronological framework and is comprised of a prologue, first part (life of Jesus from baptism to the Passion), second part (the history of the Passion and the Resurrection), and epilogue. The Gospel is less focused on Jesus's miracles than on the synoptic Gospels and more on Jesus as a redeemer; he explores Jesus as Divine Word and refers more to Jesus's discourses than to his acts to illustrate Jesus's Divinity. Because of its complexity of style and focus on discourse rather than on miracles and acts, many Christian theologians deny the historical genuineness of the Gospel of John. Discuss the importance of writing style and the intended audience in the Four Gospels. Which one do you most prefer as a modern reader?

a. **Further Reading:** *The Four Gospels: Webster's Timeline History, 172–2007.* Icon Group International, 2009.

b. **Suggested Search:** Search for "synoptic parallels" on the University of Toronto website (www.utoronto.ca/religion/synopsis). Compare the Four Gospels side by side with the corresponding passages.

3. **Luke 2: In this section of the Gospel, readers learn of Jewish childbirth rituals proscribed for a boy according to Jewish law: the Brit Milah, postpartum purification, the naming of the baby, and the exchange of the firstborn son at the temple.** During Jesus's time, a woman was considered ritually impure (*niddah*) for forty days after the birth of a male child (eight days for a female child), after which she

purified herself in a ritual immersion in water (*mikveh*) and returned to regular cohabitation with her husband. Female children were named upon the father's first call to read the Torah in synagogue, whereas males were named during the ritual circumcision (Brit Milah) after the eighth day of birth. According to Jewish doctrine, all Jewish males were obligated to be circumcised as part of the covenant established with their patriarch, Abraham, in the Old Testament; failure to circumcise resulted in spiritual excision, regardless of whether or not the male upheld all other tenets of the religion. Additionally, for all male children who were born by natural birth (not by Cesarean birth), and who were their parents' firstborn, the parents were obligated to present the child to the temple for ritual redemption, usually thirty-one days after birth. The child was redeemed for five silver coins, a lamb, or—in the case of poverty, as existed for Joseph and Mary, according to Luke's account—a sacrifice of a pair of doves or young pigeons. How do the rituals surrounding Jewish childbirth compare to those of your culture?

    a. **Further Reading:** Klein, Michele. *A Time to Be Born*. New York: Jewish Publication Society, 1998.

    b. **Suggested Search:** Search for "Birth and the First Month of Life" on the Judaism 101 website (www.jewfaq.org/birth.htm). An overview of birth, naming, circumcision, and redemption rituals, as well as adoption practices, is found on this site.

4. **The Sermon on the Mount (Matthew 5–7) represents the moral teachings of Jesus, including the Beatitudes, the Lord's Prayer, and the tenets of discipleship.** The Beatitudes originate in the Hebrew Bible but are newly presented with a focus on love and humility rather than on obligation. They represent eight blessings that consist of two parts—a condition and its result—and they begin with the phrase "Blessed are the": poor in spirit→kingdom of heaven, mourners→comforted, meek→inherit the earth, hungry for righteousness→filled, merciful→mercy, pure of heart→see God, peacemakers→children of God, persecuted for righteousness→kingdom of heaven. Matthew includes four Beatitudes that are not present in the other Gospels, introduces the metaphors of Salt and Light, establishes the ideas of "turning the cheek" and performing good works with pure intent, condemns judging others, and warns against false prophets. The Lord's Prayer appears in both Matthew and Luke, but its ending is different ("deliver us from evil" and "lead us not into temptation," respectively), reflecting some elements of Jewish prayer. How do the Beatitudes and Christian ethics compare to those of sibling monotheistic (Jewish and Muslim) counterparts?

    a. **Further Reading:** Beare, Francis Wright. *The Gospel According to Matthew*. Oxford: B. Blackwell, 1981.

b. **Suggested Search:** Search for "St. Augustine's commentary on the Sermon on the Mount" on the online Catholic Encyclopedia (www .newadvent.org/fathers/16011.htm).

5. **"The Word" is an important Christian concept that features in John 1, the "Parables," in Luke 15, and "Why Jesus Teaches in Parables," in Matthew 13.** "Word" (*logos*) is most often translated as "reason," "saying," "account," "meaning," "principle," "logic," and "path," among others, and it denotes God's essence or character rather than physical being; however, it should be noted that controversy surrounds the translation of John 1 as to whether or not the statement reflects a unified Jesus-God figure or two distinct Gods. Scholars have remarked on the cultural relevance of Platonic dualism and Hellenic Judaism in the context of John's description of Jesus's nature. Parables (meaning "comparison," "analogy") are short accounts or didactic works that, like fables, illustrate morals, principles, and lessons; they feature human characters, a prescriptive subtext (what "should" be done morally or socially but is not explicitly stated), and metaphors to represent complex ideas. Luke uses one parable with three illustrations—of the lost sheep (division of property among brothers), the piece of silver, and the prodigal son—to represent Jesus's purpose of coming to the world to save lost souls, to forgive those who have strayed, and to feel joy at those who repent and return; historically, it may have been Jesus's response to the Pharisees, who criticized him for interacting with those who appeared lazy or uninvolved in religious practice. Matthew uses the parable of sowing seeds in different soils to show mankind's reception to "The Word"; some theologians have argued that he represents three steps toward salvation. How does the use of parables clarify or cloud important lessons about Christian faith and practice?
a. **Further Reading:** Rausch, Thomas. *Who Is Jesus? An Introduction to Christology.* Collegeville, MN: Liturgical Press, 2003.
b. **Suggested Search:** Go to the following address on iTunes: http:// itunes.apple.com/us/album/haydn-seven-last-words-christ/id83169949.

6. **The Crucifixion, as represented in Matthew 27, can be divided into seven main sections: Pilate's trial, the death of Judas, the soldiers' mockery of Jesus, Simon of Cyrene's carrying of the cross, Jesus's Crucifixion, Jesus's entombment by Joseph of Arimathea, and the guarding of the tomb.** During the trial, the Jewish leaders brought three charges before the Romans: Jesus was corrupting the nation, blocking the payment of tribute, and committing seditious acts against the Roman Empire. Matthew's description of Judas's death states that Judas returned the blood money to the Sanhedrin (used to buy a potter's field) and then committed suicide as a fulfillment of an earlier-stated prophecy. Matthew's account also states that Jesus was beaten by sol-

diers with a staff and dressed in his own clothes (rather than royal garb) for the Crucifixion; Simon is mentioned in the synoptic Gospels as being compelled by the Romans to carry Jesus's cross. Matthew is the only Gospel account that mentions an earthquake and the presence of Roman soldiers to guard the tomb, while all agree upon the place of the Crucifixion, the presence of two thieves, the inscription "INRI" (Jesus of Nazareth, King of the Jews) at the Crucifixion site, the division of his clothes, and Joseph's request to entomb the body. As the primary figure of Christianity, how does Jesus's death compare to those of figures in other religions (e.g., Muhammad's death in his wife's lap, Moses's death at Pisgah after being forbidden to enter Israel, Buddha's Parinirvana, or Zoroaster's murder—as in the *Shahnameh* 5.92)?

    a. **Further Reading:** Parker, Rebecca. *Saving Paradise: How Christianity Traded Love of This World for Crucifixion and Empire.* New York: Beacon Press, 2009.

    b. **Suggested Search:** Go to http://oyc.yale.edu/religious-studies/rlst -152.

In-Class Activities

1. Film critique: In this activity, students will view one or more movie renditions of the Passion and do a write-up in which they compare the style and vision of the film with the New Testament Gospel accounts. (The following films are recommended: *The Passion of the Christ*, directed by Mel Gibson; *Jesus of Nazareth*, produced by Berard Kingham; and *The Greatest Story Ever Told*, directed by George Stevens.)

2. Musical appreciation: Students will watch *Jesus Christ Superstar* (musical by Andrew Lloyd Webber and Tim Rice), based loosely on the Gospel account of Holy Week. Students will then discuss the use of music, lyrics, and twentieth-century slang as compared to the New Testament Gospels.

3. Synoptic comparisons: Though not included in the Norton excerpts, the synoptic Gospels all offer an account of the Crucifixion and the Resurrection of Jesus. In this activity, students will compare three versions of the Crucifixion (Luke 23, Matthew 27, and Mark 15), looking at the language, description, and style.

4. Visual arts appreciation: In this activity, each student will bring a copy of a painting, drawing, or other visual representation of Jesus's Crucifixion (students might search "Crucifixion" through Google Images). How do the visual representations compare to the written descriptions of the events, and which representations do students most prefer and most dislike?

Paper Topics/Suggestions for Writing

1. In the section on why Jesus teaches in parables, Jesus explains to the disciples that "When a man has, he shall be given, and it will be more than he needs; but when he has not, even what he has shall be taken away from him." Do you agree with this statement? Explain the quote in your own words, and provide examples from other readings or current events to support your opinions.

2. Compare the use of parables in the New Testament to those of Petrus Alfonsi in *The Scholar's Guide*.

3. Compare and contrast the writing styles presented in at least two of the Gospels (Mark, Luke, Matthew, or John), paying particular attention to the vocabulary, the use of literary devices (e.g., metaphor, parable), and the intended audience.

4. How do the birth of Jesus and the role of the mother (and father) in the Gospels compare to the birth of a great leader and the role of his or her parents in other early texts? Compare the Gospel accounts of Jesus's birth and upbringing to one of the following: *The Epic of Gilgamesh* (Volume 1), Abolqasem Ferdowsi (this volume, "The Birth of Sekandar"), or the Hebrew Bible (Volume 1, chapters 21, 22).

Resources

The Catholic Encyclopedia. www.newadvent.org/cathen/14530a.htm.
This site contains extensive search terms, texts, links, a bibliography, and a commentary related to all things New Testament.

Haydn, Joseph. *The Seven Last Words of Jesus Christ, op. 51.* CD. Naxos, 1994.
Music compilation.

Jesus Christ Superstar. Musical by Andrew Lloyd Webber and Tim Rice. Universal Studios, 2004.
Broadway musical on New Testament theme.

The Life and Times of Jesus Christ. Dir. Diva AG. Create Space, 2009.
This film documents the history and culture of Jesus's period and provides a chronicle of his life.

University of Toronto. www.utoronto.ca/religion/synopsis.
This site offers a side-by-side comparison of the four Gospels and corresponding passages.

Yale University. "Introduction to the New Testament History and Literature." http://oyc.yale.edu/religious-studies/rlst-152.
This online course, offered by Professor Dale B. Martin, includes a syllabus, sessions, books, a survey, and audiovisual elements on YouTube and iTunes.

APULEIUS
The Golden Ass

Topics for Lecture or Discussion

1. *The Golden Ass* is appropriated as a novel based on the following
   elements: frame narratives, episodes, motifs (based largely on metamorphoses) and repeated themes, changes in setting, introduction of
   multiple characters, shifts in narrative voice (bathetic style, marked
   by abrupt shifts from exalted to vulgar language), and picaresque
   and bildungsroman. Picaresque works depict the world with caricatures, comic episodes, and graphic depictions of suffering; when coupled with "education," these novels tend to represent a young person
   adventuring and working in several capacities as he discovers his identity (see, for example, later works such as *Lazarillo de Tormes* and *Don
   Quixote*). As frame narrative, the novel is developed as a series of tales
   within tales. "The Tale of Aristomenes," for example, is used to segue
   into Lucius's experiences in Thessaly. James Svendsen notes that, characteristic of ancient novel form, "mirroring" is used to carry motifs and
   characters from the frame episodes into the extended stories (24); foreshadowing is regularly employed, and painterly description (as in the
   detailed and sensory description of Photis's hair) is prevalent. Readers
   find Lucius entrenched in a quest for knowledge, to the extent that
   (though warned), he endeavors on dangerous missions that blend reality with dream, which represents the picaresque elements of the work.
   As a young man, Lucius's misuse of Isis-based magic results in his
   metamorphosis into an ass, induction in the proper and respectful use
   of Isis magic, and return to human form with renewed spirit by the
   novel's end; this rite of passage and the desire to learn and improve
   himself both represent the themes of the education novel (bildungsroman). How does Apuleius's work differ from other long works that are
   considered collections of tales rather than novels (e.g., in this volume,
   The Thousand and One Nights and Giovanni Boccaccio's *Decameron*)?
   a. **Further Reading:** Svendsen, James. "Techniques in Apuleius' Golden
      Ass." *Pacific Coast Philology* 18:1–2 (1983): 23–29.
   b. **Suggested Search:** Do a Google Images Search for "Apuleius and
      metamorphoses" for drawings, paintings, manuscript miniatures,
      and illustrations based on the novel. See also http://platopagan.tripod
      .com/apuleius.htm.

2. **Lucius's exposure to magic marks his *curiositas*, which becomes a
   central theme of the first three books, evolving from induction and
   transformation into remedy and a return to human form following**

the proscribed instructions of Isis. Isis magic was considered benevolent during Apuleius's time; though he was an initiate in the Isis mysteries, he had been accused of using love magic in the form of a fish ritual to woo his wife, Pudentilla, by accessing the sinister magic of Hecate. Isis represents nature and fertility and was the most prominent deity of the Roman Empire; most of her mysteries are associated with the rescue of her brother/husband, Osiris, by his brother, Seth, and with the upbringing of Horus, their son. In *The Golden Ass*, Lucius stays at Pamphile and Milo's home while in Thessaly; Pamphile is reputed to be a seductress and specialist in necromancy, and Lucius's mother warns her son to avoid contact. Later in the story, Pamphile uses magic to disguise herself as a bird. According to several scholars, bad omens and problems stem from Lucius's *curiositas*, a quality of those who desire knowledge of most things or who worry too much. Joseph DeFilippo argues that Apuleius takes a Platonistic tradition to defining *curiositas* as "the daemonic, Typhonic or asinine condition of being under the control of one's appetites and the pleasures which motivate them" (491). Lucius himself notes that he was "already disposed to curiosity, as soon as I heard mention of the art of magic which I had always paid for" (section 6). The philosophy of dualism presents in Lucius's conflict between his chaotic physical self (Typhon) and his aspiration toward the Divine (Isis). Isis's intervention on Lucius's behalf is recounted in chapter 17 of the novel. In this and other texts, do you see *curiositas* as a positive or negative attribute?

a. **Further Reading:** DeFilippo, Joseph. "Curiositas and the Platonism of Apuleius' Golden Ass." *The American Journal of Philology* 111:4 (1990): 471–92.

b. **Suggested Search:** Go to The Golden Ass website at www.jnanam .net/golden-ass, developed by Benjamin Slade, where you will find images, information, hyperlinks, and a bibliography.

3. **The novel contains several autobiographical and cultural references related mainly to politics, law, and the treatment of slave women.** Apuleius studied in the highest learning centers of his time: he was likely a *duumvir* (Roman consul) in the city of Madaura before moving to Greece and then Rome, where he became an initiate of the Eleusinian and Isis mysteries. Wanderlust led him on a journey toward Alexandria, which ended abruptly in Carthage, where he was given the honorary title of *sacerdos provinciae*. In Carthage, he married the older widow, Pudentilla, for her fortune, though he was taken to court by her brother-in-law, who also sought her fortune. The case is interesting for readers because the court trial revolved around the practice of magic, which was considered a capital crime with heavy consequences (similar to the severe consequences Lucius pays in the novel due to magical practice). Lucius's

involvement with women tends to be associated with metamorphosis (whether physical transformation into an animal, emotional change, or a change of fortune), also reflecting the repeated changes that Apuleius encountered as a result of his initiation into goddess cults and the reverence of the divine female and marriage to Pudentilla and the mistreatment of human women. In the novel, Photis, as slave girl, encourages Lucius to physically punish her (through whipping and by putting his hands around her neck) for having put him in a difficult predicament. Historically, chattel slaves (slaves considered personal property) of ancient Greece could participate in all activities except politics and could be married and have children but had fewer judicial rights. New slaves were welcomed to the master's home with the same gifts as those bequeathed on a new wife and often partook in family religious practices and banquets. The female domestic slave cooked and made textiles for the home and was protected by law against rape. The issue of rape and slave sexuality is raised in the third book, when Photis urges Lucius to strangle and whip her: Lucius responds with loving and faithful respect for the slave girl, with whom he fornicates in "sweet orgy" throughout the night (section 23). Where else in the excerpt do you see references to transformation, initiation, slavery, and the treatment of women?

a. **Further Reading:** Franz, Marie-Louise von. *Golden Ass of Apuleius: The Liberation of the Feminine in Man.* New York: Shambhala, 2001.

b. **Suggested Search:** Search Fordham University's Ancient History Sourcebook for "documents on Greek slavery" at www.fordham.edu /halsall/ancient/greek-slaves.asp.

In-Class Activities

1. Literary history of the picaresque and bildungsroman: In this activity, students will compare an excerpt from a modern picaresque-education novel, looking at either *Lazarillo de Tormes* or *Don Quixote* (Volume 1). What characteristics are common in both Apuleius's and the later works, irrespective of their different cultures and time periods?

2. Understanding slavery: Slavery was widely practiced in ancient cultures yet differs from the slavery with which modern readers are familiar. In this activity, students will review the primary documents provided on Fordham University's website and compare the ancient lives of slaves to those depicted in Equiano's and Douglass's works (Volume 2).

3. Understanding ancient mysteries: In this activity, students will review the Smithsonian Channel episodes on ancient mysteries and rites (see Resources section). Students will first discuss how these rites present in Apuleius's work and then compare the practices to initiation practices in their own cultures.

Paper Topics/Suggestions for Writing

1. Compare Lucius's obsession with women's hair (sections 8–10, 23) to one of the following works: Attar's *Conference of the Birds* (lines 409–25, 432–37); Pope's *Rape of the Lock* (Volume 2); Baudelaire's "Her Hair" (Volume 2). What does hair represent for these writers, and how does it compare to contemporary views of a woman's hair and sensuality?

2. Discuss at least three characteristics that make Apuleius's work a novel, including a discussion of genre. Use examples from the work to support your claims.

3. Define the word *curiositas*, and discuss its role in Apuleius's work.

Resources

Argon Verlag GmbH, 2003.
A CD of the most celebrated section of Apuleius's novel, Barbara Becker sings the section on Cupid and Psyche: Music CD. Mia and Jonah. The Golden Ass. Mia and Jonah Records, 2011. Available on CD Baby, the work combines contemporary experience with Apuleius's tale.

The Lost Gods: Revealing the Mysteries of the Ancient Gods: The Egyptian Gods, the Greek Gods, Celts, Roman and Incas Gods and Goddesses. The Smithsonian Channel, TV series, 1984.
Included in this series are episodes on individual cultures. The series is also available for rent through Amazon Prime.

Schlam, Carl C. *The Metamorphoses of Apuleius: On Making an Ass of Oneself.* Chapel Hill: University of North Carolina Press, 1992.
Critical scholarship and analysis of Apuleius's work.

AUGUSTINE

Confessions

Topics for Lecture or Discussion

1. **Augustine exemplifies the nexus of the classical and medieval worlds. Liminal in the extreme, his writings bridge boundaries geographical, theological, philosophical, and literary.** *Confessions*, possibly the first autobiography, is formatively linked with Dante (*The Divine Comedy*) and Chaucer (*The Canterbury Tales*, particularly "The Wife of Bath's Prologue"). These unusually intimate narratives center on definitive events in a single life rather than the culturally or politically momentous movements of epic and the narrative distance and inevitability of scripture. The individual, rather than the collective, point of view becomes the locus of significance, and the merest personal discovery often takes on larger-than-life resonance. Recognizing that his life has been not only guided but "made" by his mother, Monica, his mentor, Bishop Ambrose, and, ultimately, God, is Augustine's pivotal epiphany. In the medieval sense, poets were secular "makers" as God was a divine creator, and Augustine admires each mentor's ability to understand him and make every choice his own. As comprehensive and absolute as his descriptions of belief can be, it is important to note that the language of Augustine's belief is Latin. When he complains about his Greek lessons and dismisses Homeric poetry, he ironically dismisses significant versions of the Old Testament as well as the New Testament in its original form. In contrast to the foundations of Islam—which would gain great strength among North Africans in the era to follow—language, for Augustine, is not a transmitter of faith.
   a. **Further Reading:** Mackey, Louis. *Faith Order Understanding: Natural Theology in the Augustinian Tradition*. Toronto: PIMS, 2011.
   b. **Suggested Search:** Go to Catholic Encyclopedia Online (www .newadvent.org/cathen/02084a.htm).

2. **Though a piece of devotional literature—perhaps the definitive work of devotion and conversion in the Christian tradition—Augustine's confession also provides a template for secular literary conceits.** Virgil, a pre-Christian (as Augustine seems to view himself in passages from his early life), bears the burden of Dante's spiritual enlightenment, while Beatrice represents only the saintly destination to which the pilgrim aspires. His tripartite mentorship (parent, teacher, literary authority) of Dante the pilgrim in *The Divine Comedy* seems strongly influenced by Augustine's relationship with Ambrosius. The narrative response to God in Augustine becomes for Dante and Chaucer an

interactive series of responses to the audience. Referring to his rejected Carthaginian mistress only as "The One," Augustine prefigures the intensely mystical poetic relationships of Dante with Beatrice and Petrarch with Laura, while his unwillingness to consider the sensual in terms of the divine establishes the very barrier that the *Dolce stil novo* aspired to transcend.

   a. **Further Reading:** Plumer, Eric Antone. *Augustine's Commentary on Galatians*. New York: Oxford University Press, 2003.

   b. **Suggested Search:** Search for "Christian mysticism," University of Central Florida, at http://pegasus.cc.ucf.edu/~janzb/mysticism.

3. **According to Augustine, conversion is rarely a conscious act or an act of will. Confession is an act of memory, while belief and faith are inherently sensory.** Augustine connects infancy with adulthood, suggesting that self-awareness and awareness of God begin at birth but are too overwhelmed by human instinct to take notice or responsibility. His memories of childhood lend themselves, as memories often do, to idealization. At their most extreme, Augustine reverse-engineers his remembered experience into divine foresight, establishing a tradition that continued at least through John Milton in the mid-seventeenth century. It is important to note that Augustine's "conversion" in the garden (revealed in VIII.xi) is not a conversion to Christianity. He was technically a Christian from the moment of birth, when his mother "salted" him against demons. As a catechumen, Augustine attended church services regularly; as an unbaptized member of the congregation, however, he had to leave prior to the Eucharistic portion of Mass. The major barrier between Augustine and the intensely serious sacrament of baptism was carnal desire. Though children were often baptized (and thereby sworn to perpetual chastity), Monica understood that baptism was a choice rooted mutually in faith and understanding. Baptism washed away the vast majority of sins, but once baptized, any sin Augustine committed would be damning in the extreme. His "conversion," then, is ultimately a cold-turkey rejection of the flesh illuminated by scripture, preparing him to accept the profound sacrament of baptism. The autobiographical narrative of *Confessions* emphasizes Augustine's liminal sense of self, ending as he and his mother await the ship that will return them to Carthage from Rome. The remaining books move directly into the enlightenment of conversion: situating his reborn consciousness at the beginnings of existence and Catholic belief, Augustine engages the book of Genesis in exegesis.

   a. **Further Reading:** Ayres, Lewis. *Augustine and the Trinity*. Cambridge: Cambridge University Press, 2010.

   b. **Suggested Search:** Search for "catechumen, early Christian baptism," at www.midwestaugustinians.org/saints/s_augconversion.html.

4. **Augustine's study of Greek and Latin (enforced and unpalatable as he presents it) ultimately enabled him to read, comprehend, and interpret far beyond his subjective perceptions of self, world, God, and universe.** His narrative of the self is rambling, repetitive, and nearly stream of consciousness, as if the truth can be deduced but never directly spoken. Though Augustine reverses Virgil, converting epic simile into the language of the pulpit, he rejects the intellectually sensuous along with the physical. He vividly embodies the conflict between two modes of creation, expecting us to be ever vigilant against emotional responses to literature because faith itself is primarily an emotional phenomenon. To feel God in the work of a poet, even in the sense of divine inspiration, seems to Augustine another of man's pathetic betrayals, none more complete or pathetic than his own. *Confessions* suggests that its author/subject achieved self-awareness before he gained awareness of God, and for this he cannot forgive himself, even in light of God's forgiveness. The accretion of experience and wisdom is the most direct, and certainly the most accessible, route to selfhood, but only the rarest individual comprehends that God is the maker (or poet) of that experience.

   a. **Further Reading:** von Heyking, John. *Augustine and Politics as Longing in the World*. Columbia: University of Missouri Press, 2001.

   b. **Suggested Search:** Search for "Virgil's Fourth Eclogue" at http://classics.mit.edu/Virgil/eclogue.4.iv.html.

5. **In Book IX, Augustine eulogizes his mother with a kind of moral biography verging on hagiography, adding further dimension to the record of his own life and prefiguring the spiritual near-perfection he discovered at her urging and persistent prayer.** He makes clear that the business of his life must wait or be subsumed into the recollection of Monica's life. Though he writes of her existence in miraculous terms and considers her a handmaid of God, he cites practical examples from her upbringing that many would dismiss as trivial in their own lives, such as the altercation with a servant over her wine consumption. Rather than merely putting her few, short-lived misbehaviors behind her, Monica learned lasting lessons from them and shared her personal narrative openly with her son. Augustine's recollection of the minutiae of his mother's saintly life both reflects and retroactively prefigures his own confession. In strong contrast to Augustine's brand of confessional autobiography, saints' lives morphed into a popular genre favoring the legendary or mythological aspects of their subjects over theological insights. Martyrs die in horrible ways, while beatific smiles mask their pain. Wanting to believe in the divine within themselves, medieval audiences were keen to find unwavering perfection in the souls and bodies of others.

    a. **Further Reading:** Ferguson, Everett. *Christianity in Relation to Jews, Greeks, and Romans.* New York: Taylor & Francis, 1999.

    b. **Suggested Search:** Search for "hagiography" on the Hagiography Society website (www.hagiographysociety.org/links.htl).

Paper Topics/Suggestions for Writing

1. If Augustine, or any artist, gives all credit to God, what is left of him? What does it mean to be faithful to God and yet still honor the God-given (certainly the case in Augustine's view, even when the thinker remains oblivious to gift or giver) gifts of language, poetry, and intellectual curiosity?

2. Confession, at least in the Catholic sense, is a sacrament. Even in the secular sense, the word implies confidentiality. Compose a short essay exploring Augustine's view of confession or one of his many "uses" of it, directly citing at least one example from the reading.

Resources

Augustinians of the Midwest Society. www.midwestaugustinians.org/saints /s_augconversion.html.

    Site includes background information on Augustine, his conversion, information on saints, the Order of St. Augustine, and links to vocations and missionary work for the Order of St. Augustine.

Hagiography Society. www.hagiographysociety.org/links.html.

    Links for resources, teaching on medieval saints, and background information on saints and their cults.

Portalié, Eugène. "Life of St. Augustine of Hippo." *The Catholic Encyclopedia*, Vol. 2. New York: Robert Appleton Company, 1907. www.newadvent .org/cathen/02084a.htm.

University of Central Florida. Pegasus Database. http://pegasus.cc.ucf.edu /~janzb/mysticism/

    Library resources and links for the study of Western Mysticism. Maintained by Professor Bruce Janz.

Yale University. RLST 152: "Introduction to the New Testament History and Literature." http://oyc.yale.edu/religious-studies/rlst-152.

    Open Course offered by Professor Dale B. Martin, including syllabus, sessions, books, survey, video and audio elements on YouTube and iTunes.

The Qur'an

Topics for Lecture or Discussion

1. **Islam ("obedience" or "voluntary submission to God") arose with Muhammad the Prophet in the seventh century c.e. as a sibling religion to the Abrahamic faiths of Judaism and Christianity; after Muhammad's death (632 c.e.), the religion split into two main groups—Sunni and Shia—based on who would succeed as leader for the faith.** Islamic theology is based on six articles for Sunni and five articles for Shia Muslims. For Sunni Muslims, the articles include belief in God and his oneness (Allah), angels, four books, messengers (prophets), Day of Judgment and Resurrection, and destiny. Sunnis also list five basic acts or "pillars" of Islam that are obligatory: daily prayer, charity, fasting, pilgrimage, and profession of the faith. Shia Muslims hold five articles, believing in God's oneness, justice, prophethood, Day of Judgment, and caliphate (leadership). Shia Muslims (of the Twelvers, which is the largest branch) hold additional "acts" in their ten ancillaries (practices) of faith: prayer, fasting, pilgrimage, charity, jihad, tribute, enjoining what is good (rules, according to the Qur'an and hadith), rejecting sin, loving the Ahl al-Bayt (people of Muhammad's house), and dissociating from enemies of the Ahl al-Bayt. Islamic law (Sharia) includes *fiqh* (jurisprudence), the practical rules for the religion. Where do the acts for Muslim believers appear throughout the provided excerpts?
   a. **Further Reading:** Nigosian, S. A. *Islam: Its History, Teaching and Practices*. Bloomington: Indiana University Press, 2004.
   b. **Suggested Search:** Go to http://islam.uga.edu.

2. **The Qur'an is divided into suras (chapters, sections) comprised of an unequal number of *ayat* (verses); each sura has a central *umud* (theme), recited during *salah* (prayer services) and generally titled after the characteristics or people represented within them.** Sura 112 (al-Ikhlas, "the purity") elucidates the declaration *tawhid* (God's oneness) and consists of four ayat (verses): Allah is the One and Only, Eternal and Absolute, does not beget nor is begotten, none are comparable to him. Tawhid is the foremost declaration of Muslim faith upon which all Islamic teaching is based—it asserts the Muslim belief in monotheism, in a unique and sole God. Sura 55 (ar-Rahman) is composed of 78 ayat with a refrain, "Which then of your Lord's blessings do you both deny?" This sura gives Allah's personal name (ar-Rahman) along with a list of signs and manifestations that prove his greatness but are denied by men and *djinn*. Allah's role as creator and omnipotent ruler, the goal-conflicting elements (e.g., the sun and moon) to work in

harmony for a higher purpose, Allah's immortality, and the rewards and punishments of the blessed and the sinful are outlined. How do the structure and division of the Qur'an compare to that used in other religious texts (e.g., the Hebrew Bible, the New Testament)?

    a. **Further Reading:** McAuliffe, Jane. *The Cambridge Companion to the Qur'an*. Cambridge: Cambridge University Press, 2006.

    b. **Suggested Search:** Search "Surah Rahman" on youtube.com for several recorded recitations (e.g., www.youtube.com/watch?v=riW4W 66ptqI).

3. **Sura 5 (al-Ma'ida) is comprised of 120 ayat and outlines the deeds of prophets. As a Medinan sura (revealed after Muhammad's journey to Mecca), it is concerned with establishing the social and moral principles for Islamic communities.** Laws of consumption are first established: hunting animals is forbidden in Sacred Precincts because they are sanctuaries for man and beast, as are animals that eat carrion. Muslims are also commanded not to enact violence upon the pagans who persecuted them ("Do not let your hatred for the people who barred you from the Sacred Mosque induce you to break the law"). Blessing food before eating is required. Jewish kosher food is acceptable for Muslims, and the text states that halal food is equally kosher for Jews; similarly, Muslims are permitted to take wives of the "People of the Book," provided they are chaste women and given a dowry rather than kept as mistresses. Stories from the Hebrew Bible are referenced as lessons to be learned from in Islam: the story of Cain and Abel, for example, illustrates that murder (unless for retribution or as punishment for corrupting the land) is equivalent to destroying the universe; it is suggested that the People of the Book are committing excesses, and that they "strive to spread corruption," thereby justifying punishments of death, crucifixion, amputation, and exile. According to this sura, each prophet delivered God's testament to the people, but only through Muhammad were all the scriptures validated with final authority. Here the rules for avoiding alcohol, gambling, idolatrous practices, and fortune-telling are outlined. The sura ends with a correction of Christian and Jewish dogma, stating that Jesus, as a prophet, would have denied that he and his mother were to be revered as divine beings. How do the social and moral principles for Islamic communities to live by compare to those established in other monotheistic religions?

    a. **Further Reading:** Mattson, Ingrid. *The Story of the Qur'an: Its History and Place in Muslim Life*. Oxford: Wiley-Blackwell, 2007.

    b. **Suggested Search:** Search YouTube for "UIUK lectures" to find four lectures on al-Ma'ida, with a PowerPoint and audio talk given at the Understanding Islam UK meeting in 2011 (e.g., www.youtube.com/watch?v=DchL5Ja7U_s).

4. **Suras 10, 12, and 19 bring lessons from the Hebrew and Christian prophets into the present Islamic revelation.** The sura on Jonah is structured to examine the Meccan rejection of Muhammad and to warn them of the tribulations they will face for this rejection on the Day of Judgment; it uses Moses's warning of the Egyptians (unheeded), Noah's warning of an impending flood (unheeded), and Jonah's warning to the people of Nineveh (who heeded his warning and were saved) to illustrate the consequences of denying a prophet. Joseph's is the lengthiest sura in the Qur'an and is more elaborate than the Hebrew original, likely because the original story (Joseph and Zuleika) had been adopted and built up in Persian literature. Joseph is extolled in Islam as a man completely committed to God: he inherits the powers of prophecy (dream interpretation) and is warned by his father not to reveal this gift to his brothers, who are jealous of their father's perceived favoritism for Joseph and Benjamin. Joseph suffers many injustices in the Islamic account yet still perseveres in his faith: his brothers abandon him in a well and announce his death to their father, women admire his beauty and he is imprisoned for refusing their offers, and he interprets dreams but receives no reward in spite of his supplication for help, but he still ends up an adviser to Egypt's king. That Joseph determines to help people return to the path of righteousness rather than to punish them is an important lesson in the Qur'an—proof that believers will be rewarded and disbelievers punished. While Joseph's story takes up an entire sura, Mary's is blended with accounts of John's birth and Abraham's rejection of idolatry and names the prophets Moses, Aaron, Ishmael (Abraham's first son, through Sarah's maidservant Hagar), and Idris. The overarching theme for Mary's sura is the Day of Resurrection. Vows of silence are emphasized in Mary's sura (Zachariah takes a three-day vow and Mary a single-day vow, related to the miraculous births of John and Jesus). What types of moral instruction and spiritual principles would you be able to derive from these stories provided you had no instruction or religious guidance on their background and intent?

   a. **Further Reading:** Al-Azami, Muhammad Mustafa. *The History of the Qur'anic Text: From Revelation to Compilation: A Comparative Study with the Old and New Testaments.* 2nd ed. London: UK Islamic Academy, 2011.

   b. **Suggested Search:** Go to www.renaissance.com.pk/index.html.

5. **The phrase "People of the Book" refers to all non-Muslim adherents of monotheistic faiths established through the patriarch Abraham, to whom scripture had previously been revealed incompletely (Jews, Christians, and Sabians).** The Qur'an is considered the synthesis of these peoples' scriptures and the sole fulfillment of God's message.

People of the Book were permitted to live in Islamic nations (as *dhim-mis*) under Sharia law (divine law comprised of Qur'anic precepts and Muhammad's example and character) and were permitted to practice their faith and receive state protection in exchange for *jizya* (a tribute or per-capita tax). The Sabians may have been nonconverts who observed tenets of Judaism or Christianity (known in Greek as "God-fearers), and some Islamic scholars derive the etymology of the word "Sabian" from the verb *"saba'a"* (defecting from one religion and joining another). Sabians are not mentioned in the Hebrew and Christian accounts, but (according to the Qur'an) followed a book of David (Zabur), which is one of the four scriptures revealed to God's messengers (Abraham, Moses, David, and Jesus) prior to Muhammad. Throughout the Qur'an, how do non-Muslim peoples living within Islamic jurisdiction appear to be described and treated?

   a. **Further Reading**: Ahlstrand, Kajsa, and Goran Gunner. *Non-Muslims in Muslim Majority Societies: With Focus on the Middle East and Pakistan*. Cambridge, UK: Lutterworth Press, 2011.

   b. **Suggested Search**: Search for "People of the Book" at www.oxford bibliographies.com.

In-Class Activities

1. Musical appreciation for the elocution (*tajwid*) of the Qur'an: Students will listen to selections from either youtube.com (www.youtube.com /watch?v=riW4W66ptqI) or CD compilations to understand how rules of elocution apply to the recitation of the sura, perhaps comparing enunciations to the prayer pronunciations in other religions. (Note: The professor might refer to the site Tajweed Podcast at http://tajweed podcast.libsyn.com, which includes information, videos, podcasts, and practice and readings of the suras)

2. Art appreciation: The Cambridge and Fihrist Digital Libraries make available several editions of the Qur'an. Students will visit the digital library to view the changes in visual presentation, images, and calligraphy from different editions. (Note: The professor might visit the Wordpress website "For One Islam: Path of a Shining Star," at http:// foroneislam.wordpress.com, which contains an archived collection of Qur'an calligraphy). This activity invites students not only to learn about calligraphy in Islam but also to study the scribal rules for the formation of Hebrew letters in Jewish documents, including Torah scrolls and mezuzahs.

3. The purpose of exegesis, hadith, parables, and dialogue to expand upon or reveal themes in the suras: In this activity, students will be divided

into three groups to examine Ibn Ishaq's "The Biography of the Prophet," Avicenna's *Mi'raj-nameh*, and Petrus Alfonsi's *The Scholar's Guide* in comparison to the Qur'an. How do these works incorporate the Qur'an, and how do they contribute to students' understanding of Muslim precepts?

Paper Topics/Suggestions for Writing

1. Compare the Qur'an and Hebrew Bible accounts on one of the following, noting the structural, contextual, and stylistic differences: account of Moses and the Exodus (Exodus 8–12) or Joseph (Volume 1, chapters 37, 39–45).

2. Define the phrase "People of the Book" according to Islam, and discuss the treatment of these peoples according to Muslim precepts established in the Qur'an.

3. Sura 112 outlines the four aspects of God (*tawhid*). List the four aspects, and provide at least three examples from different suras in which these aspects are illustrated.

4. Judeo-Christian prophets were considered to offer lessons that would later apply to guidelines for Muslims. Discuss the stories of at least two prophets as they are presented in the suras, as well as what lessons were derived from their acts and applied to Muslim principles.

5. Compare Ibn Ishaq's account of "The Beginning of the Sending Down of the Qur'an" to accounts of prophets receiving scripture in the Qur'an itself.

Resources

Al Islam: Official website of the Ahmadiyya Muslim community. www.alislam .org.
> This comprehensive site offers information on Islamic beliefs, Islamic texts, a library, a store, and hyperlinks.

Ereck, Hafiz Huseyin. *Music of Islam: Qur'an Recitation*. Vol. 10. Celestial Harmonies, 1997, CD.
> Multivolume set for Islamic music, with this volume focused on Qur'an recitations.

Fihrist: Islamic Manuscripts Catalogue Online, www.fihrist.org.uk.
> On this site, browse manuscripts with a searchable interface and works from collections in UK libraries.

Islam: Empire of Faith. Prod. Robert Gardner. PBS, 2005.
> Video series. See the PBS website at www.pbs.org/empires/islam, which offers five lesson plans, background on the Islamic faith,

culture, innovation, and profiles, and a link for teachers to purchase educational resources.

Qur'an Project. www.quranproject.org/portal.

Articles, miscellany, and biography of the Prophet Muhammad in addition to Qur'an studies and articles.

BEOWULF

The captain of evil discovered himself
in a handgrip harder than anything
he had ever encountered in any man
on the face of the earth. Every bone in his
    body
quailed and recoiled, but he could not
    escape.
He was desperate to flee to his den and hide
with the devil's litter, for in all his days
he had never been clamped or cornered like
    this.
Then Hygelac's trusty retainer recalled
his bedtime speech, sprang to his feet
and got a firm hold. Fingers were bursting,
the monster back-tracking, the man
    overpowering.
(lines 749–60)

Topics for Lecture or Discussion

1. ***Beowulf* is an epic at the collision of expansionist and missionary imperatives, seeking to stabilize heroes and kingdoms but ending in a prediction of chaos.** Fifth- through mid-eleventh-century Britain was a site of constant flux between absolute conquest and power vacuum. Abandoned as a Roman client-state, the island's factional territories lay open to Germanic invasion and Viking coastal raids until conquered utterly by the Normans, a cultural blend of Nordic aggression and French Christianity. Traditions of canonical and heretical Christianity (Pelagius) were well established on the island when the *Beowulf* narrative became part of Anglo-Saxon cultural currency. Grammatically similar to Latin, "Old English" was preserved in spoken form by Britons on the fringes of the realm when written Anglo-Saxon was overwritten by William the Conqueror. Besides the preservation of poetic narrative in *Beowulf* and a fragment of "The Battle of Maldon," a tradition of translation of Latin texts into Anglo-Saxon (such as the lost Greek novella *Apollonius of Tyre* and Alfred the Great's translation of Boethius's *The Consolation of Philosophy*) added further sophistication to the canon. Other surviving works in the language of *Beowulf* include hagiography, legal records, and chronicle history. *The Anglo-Saxon Chronicle* records many details of the raids, sieges, and conquests noted earlier.
   a. **Further Reading:** Rex, Peter. *1066: A New History of the Norman Conquest.* Gloucestershire, UK: Amberley Books, 2009.

    b. **Suggested Searches:** Search for *"Anglo-Saxon Chronicle*, Norman conquest,"* at Essential Norman Conquest Online (www.essential normanconquest.com).

2. ***Beowulf*, a Scandinavian story whose tribes and heroes hail from the lands known today as Denmark and Sweden, is also the foundation of British literature.** While it may have been related by travelers to Britain from these lands, its ultimate receivers were court scribes who "translated" its events and themes not only into a language and literary culture in flux but filtered it through Christian morality. This gives *Beowulf* (and many Western, pre-Christian works such as *The Aeneid*) a sense of preordination by the God of monotheism, suggesting that polytheism was merely a test and that even the staunchest unbeliever must someday recognize the Truth. Poets from Dante (*Divine Comedy*) through Milton (*Paradise Lost*) took full advantage of this concept. Their latter-day epics owe their particular brands of intertext, interfaith, and interculture to the poets and anonymous compilers of medieval epic and courtly romance. Like Dante and Milton, the *Beowulf* scribe never suggests that obsolete belief systems were fallacious for their adherents, but they become heretical upon revelation of the greater Truth. For example, the simple, almost human, nature of Grendel's anger—at his liminal status and Heorot's noisy joy—assumes the weight of divine retribution when the scribe claims the monster is one of "Cain's clan." This clear ideological tension between the old faith and the new permeates *Beowulf*, sometimes within the scope of poetic intent but most often in the uncomfortable crush of pagan polytheism against a monolithic, Old Testament Christianity.
    a. **Further Reading:** Orchard, Andy. *A Critical Companion to Beowulf.* Cambridge: D. S. Brewer, 2003.
    b. **Suggested Search:** Go to The British Library Online gallery (www .bl.uk/onlinegallery/onlineex/englit/beowulf).

3. **Poetically, *Beowulf* is a rare manifestation of a "sung" narrative that maintains much of its orality in writing, even when it does not feel especially musical.** The lines, of no fixed length or meter in the original Anglo-Saxon, are broken throughout into epic pronouncements and definitive phrases or clauses. This example corresponds to lines 749–53 of the epigraph:

> Sona þæt onfunde   fyrena hyrde
> þæt he ne mette   middan-geardes,
> eorþan sceatta   on elran men
> mund-gripe maran;   he on mode wearð
> forht on ferhðe;   no þy ær fram meahte.
> (lines 750–54)

Each caesura, while it may represent a singer's—or a scop's, in Anglo-Saxon—breath pause or tonal change, also suggests the space between ideas that demand declaration and elucidation in a violent and contrary world. Not easily translated for the modern ear, these midline breaks often cry out for punctuation in print, but in their oral form they are punctuation themselves. Rather than limiting the reading to pauses for breath and end stops, individual readers must determine the caesura's function in their vocal reproduction of the written text. Slightly less difficult to render effectively in modern English is the epic's driving alliteration, a feature of much medieval poetry. A sophisticated mnemonic device for auditor and poet, as well as the key weapon in the battle-singer's arsenal, the repetition of primary consonants (and occasional assonant vowels) gives the poem much of its epic character and archaic feel, even when modernized. Seamus Heaney's translation mediates the text on several levels: between Anglo-Saxon and modern English, between narrative expediency and poetic necessity, and perhaps, most significantly, between singer and audience.

a. **Further Reading:** Robinson, Fred C. *The Cambridge Companion to Beowulf*. Cambridge: Cambridge University Press, 2001.

b. **Suggested Search:** Go to The Electronic Beowulf (http://ebeowulf .uky.edu/studyingbeowulfs/overview).

4. **Though its verse form remains unique and archaic and defies traditional metrics, *Beowulf*'s deliberate, regimented lines support a schematic structure rooted in the poem's central themes.** Never keen to begin a narrative *ab ovo*, the epic form presumes foresight and relies heavily on central-character related flashbacks. Though the Homeric epics are not without embedded narratives—typically pitched as appeals to audience memory and thematic resonance—*Beowulf*'s narrative digressions are not as immediately accessible as, say, the tryst of Aphrodite and Ares, Aeneas's narrative of the Trojan Horse, or the fates of Francesco and Paolo in *Inferno*. Perhaps due to literary and mythological unfamiliarity of its peoples and environs (these are, after all, Spear-Danes and Geats divorced from Norse polytheism), the tales of Finn and Modthryth are unlikely to seem relevant to Beowulf's narrative until we recognize that the singer is appealing to a cultural consciousness more akin to classical tragedy than to the Homeric epic. Persistent and consistent throughout the poem, though, is an emphasis on elemental symbolism as palpable as the passage of time or the dependence of every narrative event upon the past. The natural world is tolerant but rarely comfortable as the civilized world expands, prone to rage against thoughtless encroachment and its inevitable by-product, stasis. Earth gives way to water as Beowulf embraces maturity and the certainty of

death. When that death ultimately materializes, it is an ancient winged serpent dominating the air and breathing fire.

a. **Further Reading:** Nicholson, Lewis E., ed. *An Anthology of Beowulf Criticism.* South Bend, IN: University of Notre Dame Press, 1963.

b. **Suggested Search:** Go to Beowulf on Steorarume (www.heorot.dk /beowulf-on-steorarume_front-page.html).

5. **Epic songs preserve legends, but not the collective sense of purpose that brought those legends into being. *Beowulf*, like *Gilgamesh* and many other narrative poems, comprehends its own ephemerality while attempting to construct an unassailable literary monument.** In addition to its emphasis on cultural memory, *Beowulf* foregrounds the mutability of human achievement, merging the heroic archetypes of *The Iliad* (Achilles and Hector) and casting the resultant hybrid as an underachiever. Beowulf exercises Achilles's hubristic self-glorification, but where the Greek warrior gives no thought to anything beyond the moment of glory, Beowulf follows Hector's example, ever aware of consequences and thankful to have subverted or diminished them. Likewise, Hrothgar's best days are well behind him. The great leader is utterly deflated by his own irrelevance, unaware that stasis is a degenerative condition akin to Arthur's immaculate but culturally stagnating court in *Sir Gawain and the Green Knight*. Beowulf's fatherlessness appears to have ostracized him from the Geatish court: by serving Hrothgar, he perpetuates past allegiances, honors his late father, Ecgtheow, and elevates himself to adoptive son and heir of his maternal uncle, Hygelac. Through no fault of Hrothgar's sons, Beowulf's deeds displace them temporarily from their father's legacy, much as Beowulf has been displaced from his own. As a surrogate father, the king of the Danes resembles a weary, jaded Priam in whom Beowulf's arrival inspires an Agamemnon-like sense of purpose. Like the classical Greek ideal exemplified in the Homeric epics and in Plato's *Republic*, masculinity and kingship in *Beowulf* hinge on the balance between physical dexterity and philosophical prowess and between tactile experience and ethereal knowledge. In this way, Hrothgar begins to resemble his *Iliad* antecedents more fully, at the halfway point between Agamemnon the conquering expansionist and Priam's hemmed-in wisdom under impossible pressure. Hrothgar understands that Beowulf's ultimate allegiance must be to Hygelac and his homeland, and yet the Geats and their leader have undervalued their greatest asset. Beowulf's threefold plan to serve a living legend, honor his own kinsmen, and attain legendary status himself is prideful to be sure, but it also demonstrates the young hero's growing wisdom by synthesizing multiple outcomes into a single, ever-evolving series of actions.

a. **Further Reading**: North, Richard. *Origins of Beowulf: From Vergil to Wiglaf.* Oxford: Oxford University Press, 2006.
b. **Suggested Search**: Go to Greene Hamlet, http://greenehamlet.com /beowulf-resources.

In-Class Activities

1. You and a partner are Grendel and his mother, the hell-dam. Consider a motive, other than simple revenge, that might justify your feelings and future actions against the court at Heorot. Compose a formal complaint against Hrothgar, seeking a diplomatic solution in spite of your urge to rip off men's limbs and drag the remains back to your swamp.

2. Committees of three to five students will work to adapt and transplant the *Beowulf* narrative to an alternate period and setting. Each group should consider how at least two significant scenes or events should be handled within this new context. Beyond determining that context, responsibilities include choosing an appropriate mode of delivery and an effective narrative voice, conforming characters to new environments and situations, and so on.

Paper Topics/Suggestions for Writing

1. Using *Beowulf* as a paradigm for the heroic epic, which three elements strike you as the most characteristic or vital? Which of these would be most effectively expressed through character consciousness and which through a poetic or narrative consciousness?

2. Many of the poem's defining features are derived from long-standing traditions of oral narrative. In contrast, what do you consider particularly "literary," "written," or "composed" about *Beowulf*?

3. Recall a challenge Beowulf faced that did not directly involve a monstrous enemy. How did this event, presented as part of the linear narrative or embedded within it, complement Beowulf's heroic progress?

Resources

Beowulf. Ubisoft, 2007, video game.
    Available for Xbox, PS3 and PSP.
Beowulf and Grendel. Dir. Sturla Gunnarsson. Truly Indie Films, 2006.
    Film rendition of *Beowulf.*
The British Library Online. Beowulf digital gallery. www.bl.uk/onlinegallery /onlineex/englit/beowulf.
    Images of the manuscript, video by curator Julian Harrison, podcast, related materials, and links.

The Electronic Beowulf. Chicago: University of Chicago Press, 2006. http://ebeowulf.uky.edu/studyingbeowulfs/overview.

Electronic edition with translation, glossary, critical editions, notes.

Essential Norman Conquest Online. Osprey Publishers. 2006. www.essentialnormanconquest.com.

Website with history, images, sounds, related links and information on the Norman Conquest.

Greene Hamlet. http://greenehamlet.com/beowulf-resources.

Resources for the study of Beowulf.

Slade, Benjamin, ed. Beowulf on Steorarume. www.heorot.dk/beowulf-on-steorarume_front-page.html.

Site contains translation, images, background information, links, and contemporary art work.

The York-Helsinki Parsed Corpus of Old English Poetry. www-users.york.ac.uk/~lang18/pcorpus.html.

Search lexical items and syntactic structure. Copyright to the Helsinki Corpus texts in their computerized form is retained by the Helsinki Corpus (© 1991); copyright to the annotated files is retained by Susan Pintzuk and Leendert Plug (© 2001); and copyright to the York Poetry Corpus Manual is retained by Ann Taylor and Leendert Plug (© 2001).

Abolqasem Ferdowsi

Shahnameh

Topics for Lecture or Discussion

1. ***Shahnameh* was written under the patronage of the Iranian Samanid rulers of Khorasan and represents a shift from Middle to New Persian language.** The Samanids comprised the first Persian dynasty after the Muslim Arab conquest, and though their founder converted to Islam (Sunni, see Ibn Ishaq in this volume) from Zoroastrianism, the dynasty revived Persian culture. Samanids modeled their society after the Abbasids, including a priority to advance the arts and sciences. With the decline of the Arab caliphate in Baghdad, Persian culture was revived; a New Persian language evolved in Khorasan, which remained Persia's cultural capital until the Mongol invasion (thirteenth century) and produced not only famous authors, including Abolqasem Ferdowsi and Rumi, but also scientists, including Avicenna, Khayyam, and important theological scholars and philosophers. New Persian arose during the eighth century under the Sassanid courts and reached fruition during the Samanid dynasty. Its influence is present in neighboring areas during the period, including in travel literature. The return of a Persian influence with Zoroastrian beginnings is reflected in Ferdowsi's epic, as is the influence of Middle Persian (Ferdowsi's work is partially based on the Middle Persian *Book of Kings*, as acknowledged in the sections about Zoroaster, and on the *Book of Deeds of Ardashir*, as represented in the historical chronicles). In what ways is Ferdowsi's epic a historiography?

   a. **Further Reading:** Meri, Josef. *Medieval Islamic Civilization: An Encyclopedia.* New York: Routledge, 2005.

   b. **Suggested Search:** Search "New Persian history" at www.cais-soas .com for suggested readings and links.

2. **Typical of epic poems, *Shahnameh* contains creation myths (first section) and genealogies and establishes a national identity based on Persian heroes (second section) and the history of kings (third section); stories interweave and include fanciful and supernatural elements.** Sekandar's birth is heralded by good omens, including a horse's birth and the sweet smell his flesh inherits from the sekandar plant used to cure his mother's breath. Sekandar is valiant and endowed by God with *farr* (God-given glory), which is similar to the Indian concept *kirti* (*kirtana*, fame and divine glory) but different than the Greek heroic concept *kleos* (renown, glory) precisely because it is God-given rather

than based on mortal fame. Plant and animal intervention drives parts of the epic, including Sekandar's solution to build large iron horses to combat Foor's exotic, divinely protected war elephants (1312). Sekandar defeats Foor in spite of his smaller stature, tired horse, and light armor (1314). Epithets are also used to describe the natural world (e.g., "the world's lamp" for sun and "glittering brocade" for the dewy, glowing landscape). Humanoids and enchanted objects often present in epic works: the corpse of a man-boar (1321) in a cursed castle, where premonitions arise from a fountain; the speaking tree, which (both male and female) warns him of impending death and urges him to abandon greed and war (1321); pillow-ears, the elephant-like man (1325); and the stillborn, chimera child in Babylon as an omen of Sekandar's death (1328). The epic ends with a short account of Sekandar's accomplishments, both military and civil, but not without imparting a moral lesson that applies equally to wealthy and poor: death is inevitable, and one should "act well, with valor and chivalry, eat well and rejoice" (1330). How does the Persian epic compare to those from others included in this volume (e.g., *Beowulf*)?

a. **Further Reading:** Hillenbrand, Robert. *Shahnama: The Visual Language of the Persian Book of Kings*. Edinburgh: Visual Arts Research Institute, 2004.

b. **Suggested Search:** Go to the Cambridge Shahnama Project (http://shahnama.caret.cam.ac.uk/new/jnama/page).

3. **Sekandar (Alexander the Great) acts as a transitional figure, linking the second (heroes) and third (kings) sections of the epic; Abolqasem Ferdowsi introduces him as both a Persian prince seeking enlightenment and as a Macedonian conqueror.** Dick Davis notes that this moral ambiguity largely reflects practices adopted by medieval Islamic historians, who presented several accounts of an incident in their work without taking a position. Older Iranian accounts portray Sekandar as an evil heretic who destroyed Iranian sovereignty, while Ferdowsi makes him the center of Iranian nationhood. He is an oxymoronic combination of *khwar* (God's glory, divine rulership, also known as "farr") and *ahriman* ("destructive spirit," a principle of evil from Zoroastrian mythology). Throughout the excerpt, Sekandar exhibits honorable acts toward his half brother, Dara (1309–11) the poor with Nasr (1315), and the peaceful resolution he makes with Arestalis (1326), as well as bellicose, destructive behaviors toward those he attempts to conquer, including Foor (1311–15), Queen Qaydafeh (1315–21), and the Chinese emperor (1323–25).

a. **Further Reading:** Davis, Dick. *Epic and Sedition: A Case of Ferdowsi's Shahnameh*. Waldorf, MD: Mage Publishers, 2006.

b. **Suggested Search:** Abstracts, introduction, and program are available online through the Iran Heritage site (www.iranheritage.org/Shahn ama_conference/default.htm).

4. **Women's rights, even those of royal women married to kings, are limited in ancient Persia, as illustrated in the opening tale "The Birth of Sekandar."** As noted by several scholars, only a handful of women appear in heroic or leadership roles in Abolqasem Ferdowsi's text, whereas almost seventy kings (some non-Iranian) are mentioned; female characters generally belong to the common public (as merchants and matchmakers) or feature as court ladies with domestic responsibilities. Heroic women appear with qualities of beauty, tolerance, wisdom, and chastity; broken or seditious women appear with negative physical features and commit depraved acts against their spouses. In this Norton excerpt, King Darius expels his wife, Nahid (Macedonian princess), because of her bad breath (*dēwānag*, "evil stench"). Women in distant lands rule with honor and prosperity; in this excerpt, the Egyptian King Qaytun comments on Queen Qaydafeh of Andalusia's dignity and eloquence, and on the wealth and military might of her nation, which only further incites Sekandar to attack. Nicknamed a "slayer of lions and conqueror of cities," Sekandar threatens the Andalusian Queen, Qaydafeh "the wise," who is little intimidated by his brute behavior or deceived by his attempts to disguise himself as a messenger, and who exhibits mercy and compassion for Sekandar in spite of his attempts to conquer her kingdom. How does the portrayal of royal and courtly Persian women compare to real women who held positions in other royal courts?

a. **Further Reading:** Anvari, Hassan. *Ancient Iran's Geographical Position in Shah-Nameh.* Iran Chamber Society, 2004.

b. **Suggested Search:** Search for "The Persian Lioness: Iranian Women in History" on the official website of Kaveh Farrokh, Ph.D. (www .kavehfarrokh.com).

In-Class Activities

1. Funeral rites in ancient cultures vary. Students might compare the visual description of Dara's funeral preparations (p. 188) and Sekandar's preparations (p. 205) to those of Scyld Scefing in the opening section of *Beowulf.*

2. Compare Sekandar's triumph over Foor to the tale of David and Goliath (see "The Hebrew Bible," Volume 1) and Odysseus and Cyclops (see *The Odyssey*, Volume 1). Why is nation-forming in early tales often linked to the triumph of the underdog over the fearsome enemy?

3. A lesson in journalism and objectivity: Abolqasem Ferdowsi, like many historians of the period, gladly presented contradictory versions of the same event in his work; in fact, a popular motto for historiographers of the period was that "Only God knows what is best." In this activity, students will be placed into groups of three to five and given a current event to research; each student in the group is responsible for finding two to three articles from sources that are different from those used by her or his peers (the articles might even come from foreign journals and newspapers). Each group will compile its articles and write an introduction or a prologue to its compendium, explaining what was learned about objectivity and whether "truth" can really be derived from a single document.

Paper Topics/Suggestions for Writing

1. Explain the following quote, providing examples from the reading to support your contentions: "Don't hide your gold away. Distribute and consume whatever comes to you, and put no faith in this passing world which sometimes favors Sekandar, sometimes Foor, and sometimes gives us pain and rage, sometimes joy and feasting."

2. Letters are exchanged several times throughout the epic and are often used to indicate a potential threat of invasion. Discuss at least two examples of letter exchanges, examining the role letter writing plays in forwarding the narrative.

3. Compare the roles that court and heroic women play in Abolqasem Ferdowsi's work and in at least two texts from other cultures.

4. Does Sekandar exhibit more *farr* (divine glory) or *ahriman* (destructive spirit) in this text? Provide examples to support your position.

Resources

Bahmani, Bruce. *Rostam: Tales from the Shahnameh*. Los Angeles: Hyperwerks, 2005–2010.
> This book series transposes Abolqasem Ferdowsi's text into American comic books. Slides and information are available online (search by title).

Cambridge University. The Shahnama Project. http://shahnama.caret.cam.ac.uk/new/jnama/page.
> This site has a large database of miniatures, background information, recent news events, and a bibliography.

Circle of Ancient Iranian Studies (CAIS). www.cais-soas.com.
> This site contains history, suggested readings, and links.

The Fitzwilliam Museum. www.fitzmuseum.cam.ac.uk/gallery/shahnameh /index.html.

> Audio gallery, online exhibition, interactive web resource, education resources.

The Heritage Institute. www.heritageinstitute.com/zoroastrianism/shahn ameh/index.htm.

> Background, analysis, images and manuscript collection, links to other resources. Maintained by K. E. Edujee.

Islam: Empire of Faith. Dir. Robert Gardner. PBS, 2000.

> This video covers the history of seventh-century Arabia through the Ottoman Empire.

FROM SONG OF ROLAND

Topics for Lecture or Discussion

1. ***Chanson de Geste*** **("songs of great deeds") and the** ***Geste du Roi*** **(heroic poem that takes Charlemagne as champion of Christianity as its theme) are epic poems dating from the medieval period. They are intended for oral performance and often recount the legendary (though often historical at their kernel) events of the eighth and ninth centuries in France.** These works particularly emphasize the wars with the Saracens but are embellished with anachronistic references to the medieval Crusades taking place at the time they were composed. The composers tended to use the same sets of stock characters (valiant hero, defiant traitor, cowardly traitor, Saracen goliath), incorporate fantasy elements, and utilize literary devices, including foil, epithet, hyperbole and conceit, and catalogs of deeds in their works. Structurally, the chansons were comprised of ten-syllable *laisses* (stanzas) that use *assonance* and *phrasal repetition* to link them. Repetition, for example, appears clearly in the following translated lines and was likely used as a *mnemonic* device: "It is better that they lose their heads than that we lose our" dignity and honors (1:45); beautiful Spain (1:59). Stanzas are also joined through repetition (e.g., "The Emperor . . . bows down his head," 9:137; "The Emperor held his head bowed down," 10:139; "When he heard that, Roland began to laugh," 21:302; "Ganelon sees: Roland laughing at him!," 22:303; "From what I hear, [Charlemagne] is past two hundred," 40:524–27; "He's two hundred years old," 41:539–41; and "over two hundred years, from what I hear," 42:551–54). *Hyperbole*, or exaggeration of deeds and punishments, is exercised throughout the text: Three men (Roland, Oliver, the Archbishop) alone killed more than four thousand men. Roland blows the *oliphant* so that it is heard 30 leagues away, causing blood to "leap" from his mouth and his temples to burst (134–35). Ganelon is brutally tortured by the king's cooks and imprisoned on a horse with an iron collar around his neck "as they would chain a bear" (137). *Epithets* and magical weaponry and animals include: (1) Roland's blade, Duredal (Roland attempts to destroy his sword on the rock of Cerritania to prevent the Saracens from taking it, yet it endures (172): a description of the sword's components includes holy relics—Saint Peter's tooth, the blood of Saint Basile, hair from Saint Denise, a shred of the Virgin Mary's robe (173); (2) Roland's horse, Veillantif; (3) Oliver's sword, Halteclere; and (4) Charlemagne's sword, Joiuse, which holds the iron point of the Spear of Destiny in its pommel and alone makes the French invincible (183:2511). Roland's similarity to Jesus as a heroic immortal is emphasized in *laisse* 160—he cannot be

killed in spite of the entire Saracen army hailing weapons upon him. With all of its richness in content and structure, what elements most appeal to you as a reader of this work?

   a. **Further Reading:** Malicote, Sandra. *Image and Imagination: Picturing the Old French Epic.* University Press of America, 2009.

   b. **Suggested Search:** Search for "The Digby 23 Project" at http:// timaeus.baylor.edu.

2. **Military ethos (chivalry) in medieval times played a central role in determining which knights had acted righteously and which were disloyal to their king and country; the narrator makes clear through several characters that duty means to die on behalf of one's king and country, and/or to defend the Christian faith (stanza 89), or to be marked a national traitor.** In this story, the Archbishop observes the battle, reminding them that they must all die fighting rather than have shameful songs sung about them after their deaths, and promising them Holy Paradise (stanza 113). Duty is also revealed in the Laments made for a dead fellow knight (stanza 151). Acts of disrespect become circumstances of treason: if a knight attacks another knight in the king's service, he is by default committing a wrongdoing against the king and his country. Both Roland and Ganelon are guilty of offending fellow knights, though neither Charlemagne nor the narrator recognizes Roland's sins of arrogance. For example, Roland both antagonizes and laughs at Ganelon, his stepfather, as he volunteers him to bring a message to King Marsilion. Roland later refuses to call Charlemagne back to battle, arguing that he "would lose [his] good name all through Sweet France"; his narcissism takes precedent to his duty, represented in the successive *laisses* that reveal his concerns for calling Charlemagne back: first, he will not lose his name to posterity; second, his kin will never bear his shame; and third, France will not lose its glory. Ganelon makes his defiance (lack of duty) clear to Charlemagne, not only by despising Roland but also those who love him (including the Twelve Peers); Ganelon shows disloyalty by dropping the emperor's right glove (stanza 25:333) and through the obvious conspiracy made with the Saracen king. Aude's death from "unrequited love" also bears chivalric tones ("May it never please God that I should go on living after Roland" [stanza 268]). The story ends with a trial for Ganelon, who argues that he has not committed treason but, rather, has sought revenge against one man, Roland. The men involved in the trial agree that he should go free because no retribution can be made ("Let this man live, for his family is great" [stanza 276]), whereas Tierri reminds readers of duty and military ethos: by waging revenge on a man in the king's service, Ganelon was attacking the king ("It's you he wronged when he perjured himself" [stanza 277]). Pinabel and Tierri duel to determine whether Ganelon should be

freed or executed: Tierri is wounded, but Pinabel is killed, meaning that Ganelon and all those who stood for him in court must be executed ("A traitor brings death on himself and others"). Compare the concepts of "duty" and "chivalry" in *Chanson de Roland* to that promoted in Christine de Pizan's *The Book of the City of Ladies* or to Bertran de Born's poem "In Praise of War" (see the "Medieval Lyrics" section in this volume). Can a universal description of chivalry and duty be ascertained from the reading of these works?

   a. **Further Reading:** Kaeuper, Richard W. *Chivalry and Violence in Medieval Europe*. Oxford: Oxford University Press, 2001.

   b. **Suggested Search:** Go to Base de Français Médiéval (http://bfm .ens-lyon.fr), which houses twenty-four complete Old and medieval French texts and links to associated projects.

3. **Dualism is an important aspect of the poem and particularly focuses on the "good" Christians and "evil" pagans (Muslims); characters often represent the thematic binaries, and through foil are paired with their opposite (good/evil, Christian/Muslim, bravery/ wisdom).** Blancandrin mirrors Ganelon: as chief warrior for King Marsilion, he urges the king to offer a payment of gifts and hostages to Charlemagne and even offers to convert to Christianity in France as an oath of friendship and service to Charlemagne to avoid war (compare this to Ganelon's advice and his later retraction of the same offer, making him a traitor and Blancandrin loyal). Roland is accused by his peers of being a man whose heart is "wild, spoils for a fight" (stanza 18:256); his foil is Oliver, the "voice of reason," who criticizes Roland for being led by madness rather than judgment, for lacking restraint, and for leading Frenchmen to death for his wildness. In this binary, Roland's prowess (*proz*) is both a heroic attribute and heroic flaw—it has led to unnecessary deaths that will ultimately shame France (stanza 131; note: students might compare this heroic flaw to those of other epic heroes, including Gilgamesh, Beowulf, and Odysseus). King Marsilion and Emperor Charlemagne mirror each other as Muslim-Christian rulers, and numerous binaries are associated with their leadership: just as Ganelon drops Charlemagne's glove and defies the Twelve Peers, Marsilion's nephew proudly holds his king's glove and wants to choose twelve men to fight the Twelve Companions (stanza 70). The list of Twelve Companions taking up arms is paralleled by the twelve volunteers who vouch to fight for Marsilion (stanza 71); the cutting off of Charlemagne's right arm (Roland) parallels the cutting off of Marsilion's right fist (Jurfaleu). In another binary, Algalife the Caliph (the Saracen spiritual leader) and Oliver (leader of conscience for the French) must kill each other to resolve their coupling. Finally, the duel between Pinabel and Tierri (substitutes for Ganelon and Roland) resolves the entire dualist conflict

established from the text's start: it first appears that Christianity prevails and the traitors are executed, but the story is left open-ended, with Charlemagne being urged to go back into battle with the Muslims. How does the theme of dualism add to or detract from your appreciation of the text and its numerous characters and events?

   a. **Further Reading:** Leverage, Paula. *Reception and Memory: A Cognitive Approach to the Chansons de Geste.* New York: Rodopi, 2010.

   b. **Suggested Search:** Search for "dualism" at http://plato.stanford.edu/entries/dualism.

4. **Time—both of past conquests and future portents—plays an important role in furthering the narratives of *chansons de geste*.** Foreshadowing, in the form of dream visions and visitations by angels, abounds in the text: "Now begins the council that went wrong," stanza 12:179; "Stand four great blocks of stone, all are of marble," stanza 168:2268–70; and "There stand four blocks of stone, gleaming of marble," stanza 169:2271–72; and has a Christian-Judas undertone as the twelve advisers (like twelve disciples for Jesus) convene to determine if the Saracen offer is sincere. Gabriel appears again at the story's end, urging him to go and fight in the land of Bire, where pagans have besieged the land. Charlemagne has several portentous dreams: First, he is at Cize, and Ganelon steals his great ashen lance. Second, he is in his chapel at Aix being attacked by both a boar and a leopard (stanza 56:717–36); he interprets his dream in *laisse* 67 ("France will be destroyed by Ganelon"). Later, the angel Gabriel appears and urges him to take vengeance for Roland's death on "that criminal race" (stanza 179). Finally, he has another vision of holding a bear by two chains as more bears attack him (stanza 186), which he predicts as foretelling the death of Marsilion and the defeat of his army. Further portents include the following: While the twelve companions are stuck in battle, an eclipse appears to overtake France (reference to darkness during Jesus's Crucifixion) and marks Roland's death. The characters introduce themselves, as in many heroic epics, with a list of conquests and noble deeds they accomplished (see Roland's introduction, stanza 14:198–200; Blancandrin's account of Charlemagne, stanza 28:370–73; Roland's lament for Oliver, stanza 163:2206–14; and the narrator's lament for Roland's deeds, stanza 176). How are past events, divine encounters, and future portents used in other early works, and do we see similar use in contemporary literature or film?

   a. **Further Reading:** Jean-Martin, Henri. *The History and Power of Writing.* Chicago: University of Chicago Press, 1995.

   b. **Suggested Search:** Go to www.vlib.us/medieval/lectures/roland.html.

In-Class Activities

1. The art of translation: In this activity, students will be divided into seven groups, and each group will examine one version of the final line in *Chanson de Roland*, determining how its wording affects the intention, lesson, and purpose of the entire work. Each group will then present its findings to the class.

2. Write a lament or an introduction of deeds: Each student will write four to six lines to introduce herself or himself to others based on deeds, beliefs, and qualities, similar to the introduction of characters in *Chanson de Roland* (Roland's introduction, 14:198–200; Blancandrin's account of Charlemagne, 28:370–73; Roland's lament for Oliver, 163:2206–14; the narrator's lament for Roland's deeds, 176).

3. Naming conventions: Throughout *Chanson de Roland*, objects take on personalities and heroic performances of their own. Students will first make a catalog of the named weapons and animals in the story, research the etymology of the names, and discuss the symbolism attached to each object and its name. As a second part to this activity, students might research the etymology and symbolism of their own names and create a short write-up discussing whether or not their name parallels their attributes and qualities.

Paper Topics/Suggestions for Writing

1. Compare in this text the trial and execution of Ganelon and the thirty men who supported him with the execution of the suitors and hanging of any maidservants who bedded them in *The Odyssey* (Book XXI, Volume 1). Do you believe the punishments were just, according to the evidence presented and legal conventions of the period regarding "loyalty"?

2. Is Roland a hero, or is he to blame for the death of so many valiant French warriors? Use evidence from the text to support your contentions.

3. Like many epic heroes, Roland possesses a heroic flaw, which is also perceived at times as a strength: his *proz* (prowess). Discuss this characteristic, citing evidence from the text in which the pros and cons of this quality are presented.

4. Seven possible translations are offered for the final line of this text. How does the change in that last line's meaning affect the purpose and meaning of the entire story?

5. Discuss dualism throughout the text, using at least four binaries (character, place, qualities) to support your claims.

6. Compare the content and purpose of Charlemagne's dreams and the appearance of the angel Gabriel to dreams and apparitions in two of the following: "Joseph" ("The Qur'an" section, this volume); "Jacob's Dream" ("The Hebrew Bible" section, chap. 28, Volume 1); the appearance of Lady Reason (Christine de Pizan, chap. 1, this volume).

7. Compare the concepts of "duty" and "chivalry" in *Chanson de Roland* to those promoted in Christine de Pizan's *The Book of the City of Ladies* or to Bertran de Born's poem "In Praise of War" ("Medieval Lyrics" section, this volume). Can a universal description of chivalry and duty be ascertained from the reading of these works?

Resources

Base de Français Médiéval. http://bfm.ens-lyon.fr.
> This database houses twenty-four complete Old and medieval French texts and the site provides links to associated projects.

The Digby 23 Project. http://timaeus.baylor.edu.
> Found on this site is the complete electronic archive of the Oxford Bodleian MS Digby 23, which contains Plato's *Timaeus*, as well as *Chanson de Roland*.

La Chanson de Roland. Perf. Madame Lucie de Vienne. Smithsonian Folkways, 2010, CD.
> Also see individual MP3s from this selection, as well as others on Amazon.com.

National Library of France. Online exhibition on *Chanson de Roland* and related exhibitions on the medieval period. http://expositions.bnf.fr/caro lingiens/antho/06.htm.
> This is a comprehensive digital collection of images, background information, texts, and links (available in English translation).

Nelson, Lynn H. "Lectures in Medieval History." www.vlib.us/medieval/lec tures.
> Numerous lectures on medieval culture including discovery of the New World and information about religion, culture, and the arts in Western Europe from the Roman through Renaissance periods.

United States Naval Academy. Medieval Chivalry. www.usna.edu/Users/his tory/abels/hh315/Chivalry.htm. Site maintained by Dr. Richard Abels.
> Comprehensive background information, the history of modern and medieval chivalry, definitions of terms, links, a bibliography, and citations from medieval sources are all found on this site.

PETRUS ALFONSI
The Scholar's Guide

Topics for Lecture or Discussion

1. Like the author of *The Thousand and One Nights* and *Pañcatantra* (and like European writers, including Marguerite de Navarre, Giovanni Boccaccio, and Geoffrey Chaucer), Petrus Alfonsi weaves stories into a larger framework in order to illustrate moral teachings using fanciful or supernatural tales. Characteristics of the frame narrative include flexibility of theme, length, and style; interpolation of stories from other contexts and periods; adaptability to different linguistic contexts; and a sense of incompleteness or perpetual storytelling that can be customized according to the audience and storyteller. Frame narrative appears in Alfonsi's work as a series of conversations held between teacher and student, in which the narrator (the teacher) integrates stories to elucidate his points; the work, therefore, falls into the genre of advice books known as "Mirrors for Princes" and follows a tighter framework due to the narrator's obligation to respond to student questions with a more limited choice of stories (30). The author combines parables, philosophy, and animal fables in order to make the content more accessible and retainable; the work's purpose is to discipline the scholar in spite of the writer's fallibility (287). Alfonsi occasionally uses Socratic dialogue ("On Hypocrisy") to establish his philosophy. Sections in didactic frame narratives rely upon a formula in which the student initiates the conversation with a question, and the teacher responds with a story, thereby creating more of an index or encyclopedic compendium with headings (e.g., "The Parable of the Half Friend," "On Hypocrisy"). Where do you find characteristics of the frame narrative in Alfonsi's work, and what morals and lessons does he seem most concerned with impressing upon the student?

   a. **Further Reading:** Irwin, Bonnie. "What's in a Frame? The Medieval Textualization of Traditional Storytelling." *Oral Tradition* 10:1 (1995): 27–53.

   b. **Suggested Search:** Search for "frame narrative" in the *Oral Tradition Journal* (online), a peer-reviewed journal with free access to digital scholarly articles (http://journal.oraltradition.org).

2. **Sufi influence may present in Petrus Alfonsi's use of a master-discipline framework, and in the prologue's opening with an invocation to God, which bears resemblance to the Sufi form of invocation (*dhikr*); in the invocation, Alfonsi thanks God, who has "deigned to endow me, although a sinner, with wide learning" (286).** Alfonsi

determines that mankind's purpose is to study "holy philosophy" and to live a virtuous life guided by continence in order to acquire knowledge of God and achieve perfection. Though he converted to Christianity and wrote anti-Judaic polemics, the seeds of Islam are also present in these statements; the concept of "pure intention" may stem from the Sufi belief that the ultimate source for one's intentions must be God (and pleasing God) rather than personal gain or pleasure. The concern with achieving perfection of character relates to divorcing oneself from the material world; for example, in "On Hypocrisy," the teacher warns that avoiding hypocrisy may only be achieved with pure intention, with no concern for glory or reward (stanza 288); Sufism, similarly, emphasizes material poverty and spiritual wealth. Alfonsi justifies his use of parables, fables, and fictional works from other cultures not only to illustrate morals on a simple level but also for purposes of reader retention (man's temperament is "delicate" and requires mnemonic devices to reduce boredom [stanza 287]). Where in the text do you see evidence of Jewish, Christian, and Sufi (or Muslim) influences?

a. **Further Reading:** Geoffroy, Eric. *Introduction to Sufism: The Inner Path of Islam.* Translated by Roger Gaetani. Bloomington, IN: World Wisdom, 2010.

b. **Suggested Search:** Go to The Sufi Way website (www.sufiway.org /home.php) for background on Sufism, documents, a glossary and articles, audio-visual resources, a list of conferences, related sites, and forums devoted to Sufi history and culture.

3. **Parables (meaning: comparison, analogy) are short accounts or didactic works that, like fables, illustrate morals, principles, and lessons. They feature human characters, a prescriptive subtext (what "should" be done morally or socially but is not explicitly stated), and metaphors to represent complex ideas.** "The Parable of the Half Friend" uses a fictional scenario of a murder cover-up to demonstrate that true friends are characterized as those who will assist when the world fails you (stanza 289). Whole friends are defined as those who will martyr themselves to save your life, to the extent that others in society are equally moved toward self-improvement and honorable action (stanza 291). Women are described as duplicitous creatures in Alfonsi's parables, no matter what their rank or purpose. In "The Parable of the Sword," a mother-in-law fabricates a story in which her daughter's lover is disguised as a refugee to prevent her daughter's husband from harming him (stanza 291). In "The Parable of the Weeping Bitch," women are punished with metamorphosis into animals (similar to the metamorphosis of Greek women into animals and plants) for fleeing from men as they attempt to maintain their chastity (stanza 292). How does "The Parable of the Weeping Bitch" compare to Ovid's story of

"Apollo and Daphne" (Volume 1), or to Jesus's parables (this volume, "The Christian Bible: The New Testament Gospels")?

    a. **Further Reading:** Taylor, Barry. "Medieval Proverb Collections: The West European Tradition." *Journal of the Warburg and Courtauld Institutes* 55 (1992): 19–35.

    b. **Suggested Search:** Go to the Fables for All website (www.fablesforall .org) for a database of fables, based on subjects, topics, and cultural origins.

4. **Petrus Alfonsi was exposed to and influenced by the three foremost monotheistic religions: he grew up a Jewish male in Al-Andalus (Muslim Spain) and later converted to Christianity.** The Iberian Peninsula was known simultaneously as Al-Andalus (Muslim), Sepharad (Jewish), and Hispania (Catholic) by people of the medieval period (now referred to as *convivencia* to represent this multicultural overlap); while Islamists developed science and medicine, Jews and Catholics focused on philosophical debates. The medieval period in Spain is marked by an attempt to resolve the conflict between scientific and religious truths, but it ended in violence, with the expulsion of both Jews and Muslims at the end of the sixteenth century. Scholars have described Alfonsi's work as an "anti-Judaic polemic," primarily based on the twelve dialogues he produced as a conversation between his Jewish persona (as Moses) and Christian identity (as Peter); interestingly, Alfonsi most criticized Judaism for following the Talmud (a secondary resource) rather than the Old Law and promoted Christian intolerance by suggesting that Jews had conspired against Jesus out of envy and were still a real threat to Christendom. Where in *The Scholar's Guide* do references to Islam, Judaism, and Christianity appear?

    a. **Further Reading:** Ben-Shalom, Ram. "Between Official and Private Dispute: The Case of Christian Spain and Provence in the Late Middle Ages." *AJS Review* 27:1 (2003): 23–71; Menocal, Maria. *The Ornament of the World: How Muslims, Jews and Christians Created a Culture of Tolerance in Medieval Spain.* Boston, MA: Back Bay Books, 2003.

    b. **Suggested Search:** Go to the Metropolitan Museum of Art's "Heilbrunn Timeline of Art History: Iberian Peninsula, 1000–1400 A.D." (www.metmuseum.org/toah/ht/?period=07&region=eusi).

In-Class Activities

1. Courtly love across cultures: In medieval and Renaissance courtly literature, young men often exhibit erratic emotions and become physically ill when they fall in love with an unobtainable woman. In this activity,

students will compare the feelings and reactions caused by love as they appear in Petrus Alfonsi and medieval lyrics (this volume).

2. Social networking and defining "friendship": The anthropologist Robin Dunbar theorized that there is a limit to the number of people with whom a person can maintain stable relationships (she estimates this number to be around 150). How does the lesson of "The Parable of the Half Friend" compare to issues people encounter on social networking sites in our time? Students may log into their Facebook accounts to determine which friends might be designated as "half friend," "whole friend," "enemy," or "other" based on the descriptions of friendship provided in Petrus Alfonsi's work.

Paper Topics/Suggestions for Writing

1. Petrus Alfonsi writes about fearing and obeying God as proof of love and devotion. Compare and contrast these two terms, using evidence from the work to prove your contentions. Be sure to include in your response a discussion of "pure intention."

2. Petrus Alfonsi discusses several types of hypocrisy, noting that the worst hypocrite is the anonymous person who hides his efforts in order to be even more revered by the people (288). Why does Alfonsi disdain this particular type of hypocrite above all others?

3. Compare Petrus Alfonsi's parables (of friends, of the sword) to Jesus's from the New Testament, to Aesop's fables, or to the *Jataka*, examining content, form, and cultural milieu.

4. Compare Petrus Alfonsi's depiction of women to the view of women presented in the opening of the story *The Thousand and One Nights,* or the theme of "metamorphosis of the maiden" with stories from Ovid's *Metamorphoses* (e.g., "Apollo and Daphne").

5. Discuss the influence of Christian, Jewish, and Muslim values and culture on Petrus Alfonsi, citing references from his text to support your claims.

Resources

Fordham University online archives. www.fordham.edu/halsall.
    Search: Internet Medieval Sourcebook; Selected Sources: Iberia. Links to documents, histories, timelines and primary resources on all aspects of medieval Spain.
Oral Tradition Journal. http://journal.oraltradition.org,
    A peer-reviewed journal with free access to digital scholarly articles related to orality in different cultures, historical periods, and art forms.

Tolan, John. *Petrus Alfonsi and His Medieval Readers.* Gainsville, FL: University Press of Florida, 1993.
This is an analysis of 170 Alfonsi texts, with a comparative approach to Alfonsi's influence on writers, including Chaucer and medieval literary history.

MARIE DE FRANCE

Lais

When the girl came through the gate
Lanval leapt, in one bound,
onto the palfrey, behind her.
With her he went to Avalun,
so the Bretons tell us,
to a very beautiful island;
there the youth was carried off.
No man heard of him again,
and I have no more to tell.
—"Lanval," lines 638–46

Topics for Lecture or Discussion

1. **Marie de France's plainspoken, pretense-free voice normalizes the fantastic and renders the everyday uncanny.** The work *Lais* operates on a mini-operatic scale, aware of the epic narratives and traditions from which they derive but preoccupied with the molehills out of which the epic singers built mountains. Her poetic style, influenced by the troubadour tradition, echoes this agenda and transforms her subject matter. Although alliteration dominated Anglo-Saxon poetry (with *Beowulf* as a prime example), Marie composed her *Lais* in lyrical octosyllabic couplets—a feature not only of the Breton *lais* she set out to preserve in writing but of many genres of medieval poetry. Yet those rhymes, which thrive upon and derive many of their effects from a nearly singsong melodic quality, create precisely the type of poetic artifice de France was keen to avoid when translating the work into modern English. What was fresh and highly esteemed in the twelfth century was ripe for parody two centuries later, as in Geoffrey Chaucer's "Tale of Sir Thopas." Considering that the poet's courtly audiences were so accustomed to rhyme that they could easily take it for granted, *Lais* ironically speaks truest to its modern audience in nonrhyming translation.
   a. **Further Reading:** Bloch, Howard. *The Anonymous Marie de France.* Chicago: University of Chicago Press, 2003.
   b. **Suggested Search:** Go to the Marie de France site (http://marie defrance.org) and listen to the MP3 by Lesl Harker.

2. **Though her inspirations are frequently Ovidian (Ovid was, for the majority of medieval poets, the ultimate authority on love and narrative), Marie de France explores psychological metamorphoses rather than physical ones.** She emphasizes subjectivity, especially

ironic when we consider that most of her characters have no control over their loves, wills, or worlds. She derives poetic and narrative authority not from the traditional name-dropping and citing of sources but from appropriating an extinct, oral form of poetic delivery that she will now preserve in writing. Though there is no indication that she knew these texts, her approach aligns her *Lais* with the traditions of *The Epic of Gilgamesh* and *The Aeneid*, which adopt techniques of oral narrative while remaining aware of their nature as written texts. The chain of being for *Lais* began with Celtic narratives, which were translated into Breton song (Breton being a Celtic language spoken in the northwest of modern-day France), ultimately appropriated by de France into "English" verse narrative in the court of King Henry II.

    a. **Further Reading:** Porter, Laurence. *Women's Vision in Western Literature: The Empathic Community.* Westport, CT: Praeger, 2005.

    b. **Suggested Search:** Go to "Life in the Middle Ages" at www.middle -ages.org.uk/life-in-middle-ages.htm.

3. **If Chretien de Troyes codified the substance of Arthurian—and medieval—romance for the late twelfth century, Marie de France established the genre's poetry.** She raises questions without easy answers in a narrative form that previously thrived on absolutes, harvesting Ovidian ambiguity not of shape or species (as so often in *The Thousand and One Nights*) but of attitude and situation. Like Dante Alighieri and Geoffrey Chaucer after her, de France strove to comprehend and express the tiny movements—like those of a clockwork—that ultimately result in major human actions, deconstructing the classical absolutes of Love, Faith, and Chastity into microcosmic elements no less epic in scope. Lanval is a knight of Arthur's court, but a knight apart, taken for granted by the king and envied into exile by his comrades; the lovers of "Laüstic" desire and admire one another not because Love in any of its forms has overwhelmed their reason (as it does Pyramus and Thisbe, Tristan and Isolde, Lancelot and Guinevere, or Francesca da Rimini and Paolo Malatesta), but because it is convenient. These characters become self-aware, if not self-actualized, through the trauma of being told "no." They attempt to reconcile the facts of their desires to the impossibility of pursuing them.

    a. **Further Reading:** Pearsall, Derek. *Arthurian Romance: A Short Introduction.* San Francisco: Wiley-Blackwell, 2003.

    b. **Suggested Search:** Search Georgetown University's site, The Labyrinth (www8.georgetown.edu/departments/medieval/labyrinth/labyrinth-home.html), for "special topics, medieval women."

4. **Lanval's journey to another, perfect existence inadvertently prods his rivals toward self-awareness, making the world left behind a less imperfect place.** The promise in "Lanval"—"You will have me and

everything you desire as long as I remain a secret"—echoes "The Tale of the Merchant and His Wife" from *The Thousand and One Nights*. Like the merchant, who understands the conversations of animals but may not reveal either this fact or what he learns to other human beings, Lanval's secret is also the proof that will release him from a death sentence. Faith—and its potential rewards and the punishments for its violation—is absolutely individual. No one can know, because no one can know, and yet the merchant's wife insists that her husband owes her an explanation, even if that explanation will cost him his life. This latter theme informs another of Marie de France's *lais*, "Bisclavret," in which a virtuous young knight's lycanthropy offends his wife's sense of gentilesse. When she demands to know where he will keep his clothes during the next full moon, he has no choice but to draw her a map. Lanval's acceptance by the fairy realm forces those who envied his perfections and inspired his exile to discover what he has that they lack.

   a. **Further Reading:** Irwin, Bonnie. "What's in a Frame? The Medieval Textualization of Traditional Storytelling." *Oral Tradition* 10.1 (1995): 27–53.

   b. **Suggested Search:** Go to the Lais Study Guide (http://public.wsu .edu/~brians/love-in-the-arts/marie.html).

5. **The sense of the modern in storytelling might be said to have originated when authors began to repurpose their sources rather than merely redact or rephrase them.** Marie de France presents "Laüstic" (The Nightingale) as an anti-fairy tale, appropriating the same narrative on which Giovanni Boccaccio would later build the tale of two Gugliemos in Day 4, Story 9, of *Decameron*, returning de France's nightingale to its original state: the folk version, taken from the *vida* of the troubadour Guillaume de Cabestaing, intensifies the defeat of passion and the punishment of adultery and criminalizes the actions of the wronged husband by making the unfaithful wife eat her murdered lover's heart. In de France's radical version, probably intended to contrast with *lais* such as "Lanval" and "Chevrefoil," where love is urged on by fate or blocked by social convention, the lady and her neighbor enjoy an infatuation of convenience. They can see each other from their bedroom windows and so begin gazing at each other at every opportunity. Almost admitting there is neither passion nor reason behind their pastime, both man and woman walk away with hardly a whimper when the lady's husband challenges it. The titular nightingale, however, experiences the consequences of their voyeurism differently. Since the merest deviation from marital chastity must be contained, this symbol of their love rots away in a pretty box. Even the "wronged" husband has it easy—rather than take up the gauntlet against his comrade in arms, he has simply to trap and kill a bird. But he does this with the excess (and

entire household staff) and violence (he wrenches the bird's neck, splattering the breast of his wife's gown with blood) one might reserve for his nemesis, not only defeating them with witnesses but destroying them utterly.

   a. **Further Reading:** Edwards, Robert. *Chaucer and Boccaccio: Antiquity and Modernity.* New York: Palgrave Macmillan, 1992.

   b. **Suggested Searches:** Go to Ravensgard Medieval Poetry and Literature (www.ravensgard.org/gerekr/liter.html).

In-Class Activities

1. Marie de France composed and read for a courtly audience, a socially and poetically complex relationship between author and audience with specific yet largely unwritten rules. In groups of three, establish a monarch, a poet, and a courtly intermediary. The lord or lady and the poet will each take five minutes to devise—in isolation—a list of three genres, three central characters, and three purely subjective expectations for this particular tale or storytelling in general. The courtly mediator will then reconcile the lists, balancing the royal edict against the artistic impulse to derive one choice each of genre, character, and delivery. The reconvened group should then work to produce a narrative based on these criteria that will best please the monarch.

2. As simple as they seem in concept and execution, Marie de France's *Lais* can be densely evocative. In a ten-minute freewriting session, have students elaborate on a "visual" environment presented in "Lanval." Suggestions include the riverside where Lanval takes his rest, the fairy queen's domicile, and Arthur's court, but perhaps the ultimate expression of this exercise would be to speculate on Lanval's ultimate destination, the fairy realm.

Paper Topics/Suggestions for Writing

1. Explain how the storytelling voice of *Lais* affects or directs your experience of its more fantastical content (e.g., imaginary lovers, or a love that is purely visual and hypothetical).

2. How does Marie de France present the concept of "knighthood" in "Lanval" and "Laüstic"? What does it mean to be "gentle"? Does her attitude toward chivalry in each *lai* complement or inform the other?

3. Using *The Lais of Marie de France* to inform your discussion, support or refute the following statement: Love and honor are simple concepts, inherent to humanity, which lovers and underlings make inordinately complicated for themselves.

4. Discuss the relationship between theme and structure (i.e., positive and negative lessons) as used in Marie de France's *Lais,* and in Chaucer and Boccaccio.

Resources

Brians, Paul. "The Lais of Marie de France: Study Guide." http://public.wsu .edu/~brians/love-in-the-arts/marie.html.
>   Washington State University faculty site with background information on Marie de France, links to other study guides on medieval and courtly writing created by Professor Brians.
Georgetown University. The Labyrinth: Resources for Medieval Studies. www8.georgetown.edu/departments/medieval/labyrinth/labyrinth-home .html.
>   Comprehensive site devoted to all aspects of medieval history.
"The Lais of Chevrefeuille." Perf. Boston Camerata. 1989. Available at www.youtube.com/watch?v=e2uDdwUQLqU.
>   YouTube video.
Ravensgard Medieval Poetry and Literature. www.ravensgard.org/gerekr/liter .html.
>   Divided by genre, location, period, and including weighty content on separate pages, devoted to cultures, arts and crafts, society and bibliographies.
Schwartz, Debra. "Courtly Love." California Polytechnic State University. http://cla.calpoly.edu/~dschwart/engl513/courtly/courtly.htm.
>   Links to Harvard Chaucer page, scholarly essays, university sites, images, handouts and lesson plans.

CHRÉTIEN DE TROYES

From *The Story of the Grail*

Topics for Lecture or Discussion

1. **When the young Perceval declares to the strange knight, "you're more beautiful than God" (line 179), he not only blasphemes, but he also expresses the tension that he will struggle with for the rest of the romance: the tension between his natural love of martial feats and worldly things, and his slow growth in knowing and loving things divine.** Perceval's confusion about whether the knights in the forest are devils or angels is also indicative of his spiritual immaturity, and is an important contrast with his confusion about whether he should inquire about the bleeding lance and the grail carried in the Fisher King's castle. In the prior case, his ignorance of the broader world leads him to erroneous conclusions, but in the latter case, the social customs of chivalry that he has learned lead him to error. In contrasting these two scenes, we can see that *The Story of the Grail* is critical of both isolated ignorance and worldly wisdom. Perceval's quest for the grail is a search for something that cannot be had (or at least understood) through either seclusion from or immersion in the affairs of the world. The grail, it might be said, can only be grasped by a Perceval who is attentive to both his worldly obligations and his spiritual growth, or in other words, who follows the mixed life of action and contemplation.

   a. **Further Reading:** Carey, Hilary M. "Devout Literate Laypeople and the Pursuit of the Mixed Life in Later Medieval England." *Journal of Religious History* 14:4 (1987): 361–381.

   b. **Suggested Search:** At "The Camelot Project," hosted by the University of Rochester (http://www.lib.rochester.edu/camelot/mainmenu .htm), there is a link for Perceval that includes many images depicting events from Chrétien de Troyes' tale.

2. **In Chrétien de Troyes' *Perceval*, women are presented in a contradictory light, as they are at times elevated objects of devotion and at other times they are subjected to abuse and their wishes are entirely ignored.** In a comically presented though troubling instance of this mistreatment of women, Perceval blithely disregards the weeping impetrations of the maiden whom he forcibly kisses and whose ring he seizes (lines 667–833). He does so because he misinterprets instructions that he had received from his mother, but he uses force to overcome a girl who "shook with fear" (line 687) and "struggled as hard as she could, / Trying to get away" (lines 704–705). Her subsequent treatment at the hands of her lover (the Haughty Knight) reinforces the theme of the

mistreatment of women, as she is forced to travel behind him without a change of clothes. On the other hand, women are also the principal motivations for many of the knights in the story, who seek to serve and protect their chosen ladies. Students should consider whether Perceval moves toward a more respectful attitude of women and their choices, or whether, despite his allegiances to some of them, he persists in his attitude of disrespect and obtuse self-centeredness. Does he differ from the other knights and men in his treatment of women?

   a. **Further Reading:** Duggan, Joseph J. "Knights and Ladies." In *The Romances of Chrétien de Troyes*, 311–327. New Haven, CT: Yale University Press, 2001.

   b. **Suggested Search:** Search LION (Literature Online) at lion.chadwyck .com for "women in medieval romances" for a variety of pertinent articles.

3. **As is the case in many medieval romances, Chrétien de Troyes' hero is motivated by a variety of things, including honor, love, chivalric devotion, and correcting past mistakes.** For example, when Perceval is at Blanchefleur's castle and learns of her situation, the narrator declares, "Ah, what an opportunity / For glory, if he's brave enough / To seize it" (lines 2038–2040). Yet even as Perceval strives for this glory, he is also motivated by his new love for Blanchefleur. As he comforts her and promises not to forsake her, he kisses her in his bed, combining honor and love in his promise to defend her. Perceval's chivalric duty is an obligation that he learns over the course of the story, but he is consistent in sending those he defeats to serve the woman that Kay struck in King Arthur's court. Similarly, as he realizes his mistake in remaining silent with the Fisher King, Perceval determines that his primary quest must be to find the King again, and understand the significance of the lance and grail (lines 4729–4740).

   a. **Further Reading:** *The Cambridge Companion to Medieval Romance.* Ed. Roberta L. Krueger. Cambridge: Cambridge University Press, 2000.

   b. **Suggested Search:** A Google Image search for "Perceval and the grail" results in several excellent paintings and some medieval depictions of the legend.

4. **When Perceval repents before the hermit, he is told that his failure with the Fisher King was due to a much older sin that he had committed, and this emphasizes an understanding of human nature in which a person's knowledge and actions are the result of earlier sins committed or virtues cultivated.** The hermit tells Perceval that when he left his mother, she collapsed on the ground and "there she died of her sorrow. / And that was the sin which caused you, / Later, to ask no questions / About the grail or the lance; / Everything followed from that"

(lines 6399–6403). This prior sin led to Percival's later significant failures, and mirrors the Christian conception of Original Sin, in which the first sin committed by human beings led to the many subsequent trials, sufferings, and sins of humanity. The course of repentance that the hermit prescribes is intended to counteract Percival's ruinous spiritual state after his original sin, as he must go to a church each morning, and he must charitably assist any that he meets who are in need. That is, he must be attentive to both his internal spiritual life and his standing within the Christian community.

    a. **Further Reading:** Lewis, C.S. *The Discarded Image: An Introduction to Medieval and Renaissance Literature.* Cambridge: Cambridge University Press, 1964.

    b. **Suggested Search:** Search for "medieval forms of penance" at Academic Search Premier (http://www.ebscohost.com/academic/academic-search-premier) for a selection of background articles that will clarify the penance that Perceval undergoes.

5. **Perceval's realization of his own name takes place at an important moment that marks a significant advance in his self-knowledge.** Perceval's name is not known by many in the story, including King Arthur, and the hero only realizes it as he is being questioned by his cousin after his failure with the Fisher King. The narrator recounts, "And then, not knowing his name, / He somehow knew, and said / He was Perceval from Wales, / Not knowing if he spoke the truth, / But he did, though he did not know it" (lines 3574–3578). Within the Christian tradition (stemming from Adam naming the animals), and in conjunction with Classical philosophy (which understood human beings' reason as a capacity that could name things by distinguishing characteristics between them), to name a thing was an important element in knowing the nature (or essence) of that thing. In this light, Percival's realization of his name at the critical moment after his failure with the Fisher King is deeply significant, and his cousin's revision of his name is equally meaningful; she replies, "You've just / Changed your name, my friend . . . You're Perceval / The Unhappy, the Miserable, the Unfortunate" (lines 3581–3584).

    a. **Further Reading:** Kass, Leon R. *The Beginning of Wisdom: Reading Genesis.* Chicago: University of Chicago Press, 2003. See especially pp. 54–97.

    b. **Suggested Search:** A YouTube search for "Hero and Quest Lectures" results in a series of lectures discussing literature and self-knowledge. Lecture 28 discusses Perceval.

In-Class Activities

1. Divide the class into small groups, and ask each group to write a dramatic retelling of a select passage from the story of Perceval. Ask the groups to share their results with the class.

2. Ask each student to write a journal entry in which they construct a conclusion for *The Story of The Holy Grail*. Encourage them to consider whether their conclusion seems to follow the direction that Chrétien de Troyes' plot takes before it abruptly ends.

3. To prompt a discussion, ask your students to write down a brief thesis in response to the question: "Is Perceval an admirable character?" Then ask your students to share their answers, and encourage discussion between differing theses.

4. Divide the class into several groups, all of which must prepare a research presentation concerning the extent of Chrétien de Troyes' influence upon later literature, and particularly the development of the Arthurian legend. Encourage each group to make use of resources in the library.

Paper Topics/Suggestions for Writing

1. Is there a turning point in our selection from *The Story of the Grail*? Is there a climax? Is there a moment of incomparable importance for Perceval? Defend your answers to these questions with substantial reference to the text.

2. What is the significance of the bleeding lance and the grail in *The Story of the Grail*? In what ways are these objects important for the plot of the story? What is the importance of them as images? Do they carry metaphorical significance? What characters are affected by the lance and the grail?

3. Write a paper in which you consider Perceval's initial ignorance and subsequent growth in knowledge over the course of the story. What sorts of things does Perceval learn? What does he come to value the most? Are certain forms of knowledge elevated above others?

4. Consider the role of women in *The Story of the Grail*. How are they treated? Does the story maintain a consistent perspective on the role of women in society? Who is the most admirable woman? Why? What aspects of the story might be read as a critique of the chivalrous culture? Conversely, what elements should be understood as reinforcing or endorsing chivalrous behavior?

5. Is Perceval really to blame for his mistakes throughout the story? Does his good will excuse him from culpability for the suffering he causes

others? How does his confession to the hermit relate to these questions? Is the hermit correct in his diagnosis of Perceval's failings?

6. Write a paper that analyzes the development of Perceval's character in *The Story of the Grail*. In what ways does the hero change? Is there a significant moment in which he changes his mind? How does his martial prowess relate to and shape his character? What things does Perceval understand well, and what must he still learn at the end of the story?

Resources

Hinton, Thomas. *The 'Conte du Graal' Cycle: Chrétien de Troyes's 'Perceval', the Continuations, and French Arthurian Romance*. Woodbridge, UK: D. S. Brewer, 2012.

> Instructors and students interested in the unfinished nature of *The Story of the Grail* can turn to Hinton's volume to find an interesting argument that Chrétien de Troyes' initial text was the foundation of a narrative cycle, of which the later continuations are a part. Hinton provides a helpful context for the larger influence of Chrétien de Troyes' story.

Krueger, Roberta L., ed. *The Cambridge Companion to Medieval Romance*. Cambridge: Cambridge University Press, 2000.

> This volume contains a variety of essays that should prove very helpful for contextualizing Chrétien de Troyes' work, especially for an instructor unfamiliar with medieval literary traditions.

Lacy, Norris J., and Joan Tasker Grimbert, eds. *A Companion to Chrétien de Troyes*. Cambridge, UK: D. S. Brewer, 2005.

> This collection of essays contains the general sections "Background," "Texts," and "Medieval Reception and Influence," and includes an essay by Rupert T. Pickens about our text: "*Le Conte du Graal*: Chrétien's Unfinished Last Romance" (pp. 169–187).

Stains, David. *The Complete Romances of Chrétien de Troyes*. Bloomington, IN: Indiana University Press, 1990.

> For further reading—which is especially helpful for understanding the different structures of Chrétien de Troyes' romances—this volume is helpful and easily accessible for students as well as instructors.

"Thidrandi Whom the Goddesses Slew"

and "Authun and the Bear"

> ". . . you had the opportunity to deprive me of both these things, the bear and my life too; yet you let me go in peace where others might not."
> —"Authun and the Bear"

Topics for Lecture or Discussion

1. ***Thaettir*, or the short narratives that take place within the larger Icelandic *sagas*, often tell of a character's travels, and in describing these travels, they often elucidate different aspects of the characters' strengths and weaknesses, or provide important details about different societies.** In our selections, "Athun and the Bear" is more concerned with travel than "Thidrandi Whom the Goddesses Slew," but both emphasize that travel is an important part of a young man's education. In "Thidrandi Whom the Goddesses Slew," for example, the narrator tells us that "Thidrandi went trafficking from land to land, and found lots of friends wherever he came" (1531), and we also learn that he does this travel before he turns eighteen years old. The number of friends that he makes is indicative of his admirable and genial character, a point that is further emphasized in the rest of the story. In "Authun and the Bear," Authun's travels not only lift him from poverty, but also prove to be spiritually salutary, as King Svein rebukes his courtiers by telling them that Authun "has provided for his soul better than you" (1535). Similarly, Authun gains several politically powerful friends through his travels, and his journeying is, like Thidrandi's, a means of demonstrating his excellent character.

   a. **Further Reading:** Andersson, Theodore M. *The Growth of the Medieval Icelandic Sagas (1180–1280)*. Ithaca, NY: Cornell University Press, 2006.

   b. **Suggested Search:** A YouTube search for "Iceland Ultimate Journeys" will result in a documentary about contemporary Iceland by the Discovery Channel. This will be most helpful for the footage of the terrain and geographical situation of Iceland, which can give students an idea of some of the difficult terrain that our heroes' travels entailed.

2. **In "Thidrandi Whom the Goddesses Slew," Thidrandi is killed while trying to be hospitable, and as in many ancient cultures, hospitality was held to be an important virtue.** Throughout the story, different moments of hospitality are referenced, and the friendship between

Hall and Thorhall is partially based upon their welcoming reception of each other: "Hall used to stay at Horgsland every summer on his way to the assembly, and Thorhall often went visiting out east and would spend long periods there" (1531). The narrator emphasizes the honor that Hall pays to Thorhall when he arrives, and Thidrandi is similarly well-treated when he reaches his father's house. This partially explains why, despite Thorhall's emphatic warning that everyone stay indoors and ignore whatever signs might occur outside the house, Thidrandi still opens the doors in the middle of the night. As he speculates, the sounds may come from more guests arriving (1532). This conflict between his desire to observe the virtue of hospitality and his need to obey the prophetic injunctions of Thorhall might reflect the coming conflict between the new religion of Christianity and the older faiths of the Icelandic people. Students should be encouraged to contrast the hospitality in "Thidrandi Whom the Goddesses Slew" to the hospitality presented in works such as *The Odyssey, The Aeneid*, and *Beowulf*.

  a. **Further Reading:** Clunies Ross, Margaret. *The Cambridge Introduction to the Old Norse–Icelandic Saga*. Cambridge: Cambridge University Press, 2010.

  b. **Suggested Search:** At http://sagadb.org, you will find the Icelandic Saga Database, which includes several helpful resources.

3. **The story "Authun and the Bear" illustrates in several ways the extensive power that kings held over their subjects in the medieval Nordic world.** When King Harald learns that Authun has a marvelous bear, he makes several serious offers to purchase the beast, yet Authun refuses each one. Authun does make a brief reference to the serious nature of their exchange when he admits, "'Sire . . . it is for you to command, yet I cannot willingly agree to anything except what I have already decide'" (1534). That is, the king certainly has the power to override Authun's desires, but only by using force; Authun himself will not agree to the king's proposals. The surprising extent of the king's power in this discussion is referenced again at the conclusion of the story, when Authun presents King Harald with the golden ring, declaring, "you had the opportunity to deprive me of both these things, the bear and my life too; yet you let me go in peace where others might not" (1537). The king could, then, have simply executed Authun and seized his bear, but he chose not to. Such arbitrary power over life and death is also apparent in Authun's encounter with King Svein, when the king decides not to execute his steward (for a trivial matter) but does banish him (1534–1535). Kings are also shown to have tremendous wealth, and some degree of spiritual and military authority.

  a. **Further Reading:** Vogt, Helle. *The Function of Kingship in Medieval Nordic Legislation*. Leiden, Netherlands: Brill, 2010.

b. **Suggested Search:** A Google Images search for "maps of medieval Iceland" results in some interesting maps, including some made in the same era as our stories were written.

4. **Both "Thidrandi Whom the Goddesses Slew" and "Authun and the Bear" make clear references to the profound influence that the advent of Christianity was having upon Nordic culture.** In "Thidrandi Whom the Goddesses Slew," the entire explanation for the tragic occurrence in the story is that the older pagan culture was being replaced by the Christian religion, and that such a change deeply affected the ways in which the culture would remember its dead. This change is presented as both good and bad: it is bad in so far as it requires Thidrandi's death at the hands of the old spirits, but it is good because, as Thorhall explains to Hall, "those of your family who are to adopt the unknown faith they foretell and follow will be helped by [the new spirits of Christianity]" (1532). Similar references to Christianity are made in "Authun and the Bear," as Authun makes a pilgrimage to Rome—indicating the new Christian practice of going on pilgrimages as well as the importance of Rome as the seat of the Pope—and King Svein speaks of the pilgrimage as a prudent measure that provides for one's soul.
   a. **Further Reading:** Carver, Martin, ed. *The Cross Goes North: Processes of Conversion in Northern Europe, AD 300–1300.* Woodbridge, UK: The Boydell Press, 2005.
   b. **Suggested Search:** A Google search for "Stave Church" will result in several helpful articles and images about these unique northern European churches that were built in the medieval period.

5. **In *thaettir*, fate or fortune is frequently alluded to, often with regard to things or events that are mostly out of human control.** In "Thidrandi Whom the Goddesses Slew," Thorhall has several forebodings of coming disaster, but when Hall proposes to delay the feast in order to avoid the coming tragedy, Thorhall declares, "what is fated must go forward" (1532). Thidrandi's death was not something that Hall or Thorhall could avoid, even by changing their plans. In this respect, fate governs human life even to the point of death, regardless of human choices or agency. "Authun and the Bear" presents a more complex picture, since Authun's choices do result in his final success. However, even in that story, fortune is referred to as an independent influence in human affairs. King Harald remarks to Authun that "it may be that you are a man of happy fortune" (1534) and King Svein tells Authun, "you will prove a man of happy fortune" (1536). In both cases, Authun's actions have led him to be recognized and aided by the two kings, but nevertheless, they refer to "happy fortune" as something that will happen to Authun, rather than being something entirely within his own hands.

    a. **Further Reading:** Miller, William Ian. *Audun and the Polar Bear: Luck, Law, and Largesse in a Medieval Tale of Risky Business*. Leiden, Netherlands: Brill, 2008.

    b. **Suggested Search:** At the website for the "Timeline of Art History" at the New York Metropolitan Museum of Art, selecting the "Medieval Art" link in the "Thematic Essays" section results in a wide variety of helpful resources, images, and brief essays.

In-class Activities

1. Ask the students to bring to class a fairy tale or fable that they read as children. Then divide the class into smaller discussion groups that share the fables, and compare them to the *thaettir* included in this anthology.

2. Ask each student to think of these stories as a fable, and to come up with a moral that might accompany each story. Share these morals with the class, and discuss their appropriateness in relation to the events that occur in the stories.

3. As a journal assignment, have each student write about a trip that he/she has taken in which something was learned or gained, and then contrast that personal experience with the travel that is described in "Thidrandi Whom the Goddesses Slew" and "Authun and the Bear."

4. As a research activity, ask your students to form small groups that must investigate certain topics in your institution's library. You can give the groups different research topics or let them perform general research on the background and context of these stories. Suggested topics include: the genre of sagas; sagas in comparison to ancient epics like the *Odyssey*; the political culture of medieval Scandinavia and Iceland; the religious culture of medieval Scandinavia and Iceland; the *Volsunga Saga*; the *Njáls Saga*; and the reception/preservation history of the sagas.

Paper Topics/Suggestions for Writing

1. Write an essay that analyzes travel in one of these stories, and in at least one other work that you have read this semester (for example, *The Odyssey*, *The Epic of Gilgamesh*, the "Travel and Conquest" section in our anthology, etc.). What special role does travel play in characters' lives? Is travel generally a good or bad thing? How does travel relate to the idea of home, or the idea of place? What does travel give to or take from characters?

2. What elements in these stories might be read with an allegorical or symbolic emphasis? Consider the possible symbolism associated with the following things: the bear, Authun's mother, the light and dark spirits, gold, travel, and the pilgrimage.

3. What do these stories reveal about Thidrandi's and Authun's characters? Are they admirable men? Heroes? Are they normal or exceptional individuals? What things do they hold to be most important, and what least important? What virtues and vices do they possess?

4. What are the social and political situations described in these stories? What do these societies value? Freedom? Courage? Wisdom? Life? What roles do the kings play in these societies?

5. Why does Authun want to give the bear to King Svein rather than King Harald? To what degree do you think Authun has a plan? Is his plan prudent? What are Authun's primary motivations in giving the bear to King Svein?

Resources

Andersson, Theodore M. *The Growth of the Medieval Icelandic Sagas (1180–1280)*. Ithaca, NY: Cornell University Press, 2006.

> Andersson's book offers an interesting analysis of the shift from an oral to a written medium in the literary tradition of the sagas, and provides a substantial amount of background information that should be of considerable use to instructors.

Clover, Carol J., and John Lindow, eds. *Old Norse-Icelandic Literature: A Critical Guide*. Toronto: University of Toronto Press, 2005.

> This collection of essays is a valuable resource for both instructors and students who want to understand critical approaches to Icelandic sagas, though certain parts may prove difficult for students not already familiar with Nordic literature.

Clunies Ross, Margaret. *The Cambridge Introduction to the Old Norse-Icelandic Saga*. Cambridge: Cambridge University Press, 2010.

> This brief book is an excellent introduction for students or instructors who do not have a background in medieval Norse literature. Students would profit from having passages assigned in accompaniment with the stories in our anthology.

McTurk, Rory, ed. *A Companion to Old Norse-Icelandic Literature and Culture*. Malden, MA: Blackwell, 2005.

> Included in this volume of essays are helpful entries about the literature, culture, and religion; see especially the essay "Short Prose Narrative" by Elizabeth Ashman Rowe and Joseph Harris (pp. 462–478).

MEDIEVAL LYRICS

Topics for Lecture or Discussion

1. **Lyric poetry during the medieval period was often accompanied by instruments and/or set to music; lyrical works included devotional poetry, philosophical treatises, and courtly songs.** Poets of the medieval lyric represented different social classes, religious and cultural backgrounds, and artistic capabilities. The one characteristic central to this collection is the "lyrical." In the ancient Western world, poetry, music, dance, and rhetoric had been disciplines gathered under a single term, "song" (*aoidos*); even ordinary speech possessed a basic melodic structure based on pitch variations indicated by accents, syllables, and vowel combinations. Increasingly, though, these disciplines became separate (artists no longer mastered several forms but instead specialized in one form due to changes in technology, patronage, and social collectives). Poetry was divided into types: lyric poetry, detached from dramatic and epic poetry, and poetry used for entertainment purposes. The troubadours (many represented in this collection), for example, were composers and performers of verse who were thought to hail from Occitania and who established their lyric traditions throughout Europe by the twelfth century C.E. (see the editor's introduction to "Medieval Lyrics"). Troubadour songs usually addressed chivalry and courtly love, and many lyrical poets of the period employed stylistic devices and structures that lent to the works performance, contest, musicality, and dance.
   a. **Further Reading:** Gaunt, Simon, and Sarah Kay. *The Troubadours: An Introduction.* Cambridge: Cambridge University Press, 1999.
   b. **Suggested Search:** Look for the CD compilation *From Byzantium to Andalusia: Medieval Music and Poetry* at http://itunes.apple.com /us/album/from byzantium-to-andalusia/id151214324.

2. **The rules of love were outlined in several treatises, including Ovid's *Ars Amoratia* and Andreas Capellanus's *Treatise on Courtly Love*; these works were purely philosophical and ludic and became part of the aesthetic established in the aristocratic and royal courts to entertain members, performers, and attendants rather than a real practice.** Capellanus describes love as an "inborn suffering proceeding from the sign and immoderate thought upon the beauty of the other sex" and notes that the etymological origin for "love" (*amor*) is the word *amar* (hook), which connotes that love captures and imprisons the lover. According to the treatises, true love has only ennobling effects: the ugly and rude become beautiful, the humble become noble, the proud become humble, and the greedy become generous. A single kiss represents the consummation of true love, more than courtship or sexual intercourse.

Rules for courtship were stipulated in treatises as well, defining not only the hallmarks of love (e.g., sweating, insomnia, jealousy, and obsession) but also stipulating guidelines for when a courtship should progress toward a first kiss or how long a lover was required to mourn the death of his beloved before seeking another. Ovid discusses the male's presentation: he should appear manly (i.e., not curling the hair or using a pumice stone) and must speak with eloquence to subdue the woman's heart. The rules of courtship and symptoms associated with true love and unrequited love or coquettishness on the beloved's part frequently appear in courtly lyric: Daniel pays masses, burns lights of wax and oil "so God give me good luck with her" (lines 15–20); Daniel's sole cure is a single kiss. In Bernart de Ventadorn's "When I see the lark stretch out," there are references to unrequited love: the woman has taken his heart and soul along with the entire world, with no reward in return (lines 10–15). Like a woman scorned, the poet vows to abandon love forever (lines 25–45), to become an exile, or to die and burn in the abyss of hell (as in "The Wound of Love," by Heinrich von Morungen). In "The Cult of Love," by Hadewijch of Brabant, love arises only through suffering and is prolonged only through the giving of love (section 4). "A Lover's Prize," by Beatrice of Dia, is a female response to unrequited love, more dominant and sexually daring than most male works; this sense of female independence and entitlement, so contrary to the reality of a woman's social and cultural obligations of the medieval period (when marriages were arranged for political or financial advantage, and when a lady's husband was often away at war or managing business and political affairs) appears again in Christine de Pizan's "All Alone Am I," in which a woman laments her husband's death but also realizes the benefit of a solitary life without marital obligation. Do you agree with the writers that love and suffering coexist? What rules for courtship or symptoms of lovesickness exist in your culture?

   a. **Further Reading:** Schultz, James. *Courtly Love, the Love of Courtliness and the History of Sexuality.* Chicago: University of Chicago Press, 2006.

   b. **Suggested Search:** Go to http://cla.calpoly.edu/~dschwart/engl513 /courtly/courtly.htm.

3. **Medieval lyrics are characterized not only as love poems or chivalric works but also as devotional and philosophical texts in which poets explore their relationship with God and within themselves; these works often make reference to ancient myths and gods and religious creeds and utilize jargon from academic disciplines or emulate themes and styles from earlier lyrical poets.** Boethius refers to Orphic myth in "The Consolation of Philosophy"; as the patriarch of lyric poetry, Orpheus also represents the loss of one's beloved at the

mercy of others' jealousy and revenge, as well as the consequences the artist suffers when love for his muse replaces love for his craft ("All that his unquelled grief bestowed And love, that doubles grief, Make his laments"). Readers find in Boethius a lesson similar to that presented in Farid Ud-Din Attar's "The Conference of the Birds": all is lost if one turns away from the light (a Platonic reference to truth; an Islamic reference to God/Islam) to look downward (for classical and Islamic writers both, the physical world of illusion). Similarly, in "Gentle Now, Doves," by Ibn 'Arabi, animal and natural pairings and references to real places along the Muslim pilgrimage to Mecca parallel the spiritual journey a Muslim has to make to achieve union with the divine ("I profess the religion of love. Wherever its caravan turns along the way, that is the belief, the faith I keep" [lines 57–60]). Devotional poetry often makes an erotic allusion to the marriage between church and Jesus or woman and God. In both of Hildegard of Bingen's "Responsory for the Virgin" ("bright was the rose that sprang from the maiden when the supernal father saw her virgin splendor and her mortal flesh spoke his word" [lines 11–14]; "the Holy One flooded her with warmth until a flower sprang in her womb" [lines 4–8]), and Jesus comes forth from her "secret chamber." What types of word choice, imagery, and structure seem most prevalent to the authors of medieval lyrics?

   a. **Further Reading:** Wilhelm, James, ed. *Lyrics of the Middle Ages: An Anthology.* New York: Garland, 1990.

   b. **Suggested Search:** Go to www.themiddleages.net/index.html.

4. **For the medieval writers, love is mirrored in nature; through metaphor and metonymy, physical love becomes intrinsically bound to physical beauty and health, to the extent that most works on love stipulate that a blind, excessively passionate, or aged person cannot experience true love.** Ovid, like Andreas Capellanus, had stated in his *Ars Amoratia* that "To find a fitting mistress, use your eyes," and he compares a man's search for a lover to the hunter's pursuit of the stag. Painterly writing that relies heavily on imagery and visual references characterizes many poets' methods for describing abstract concepts such as love, or for reimagining the woman's body in fragmented form. Natural references (birds' wings, bent trees, fragrant flowers, coiling waterways) parallel the poet's nostalgic emotions for a long-lost love in Ibn Zaydun's "Al-Zahra." In Yehuda Halevi's lyric "To Ibn al-Mu'allim," the woman's body parts are fashioned from flowers, gemstones, and textiles. This is echoed in Walther von der Vogelweide's "Dancing Girl," in which a girl's body parts reflect the natural world and gifts that her lover offers (e.g., red roses like her blushing cheeks). In "A Hymn to Holy Women," Notker Balbulus uses the metaphor of a

ladder to create a poetic diptych (medieval painting form) that contrasts physical love (Eve, represented by the odd, or "sinister," stanzas) with spiritual love (Mary, represented by the even stanzas). The anonymous poet of "The Ruin" uses the architectural remains from Roman ruins in the Anglo-Saxon countryside to construct a metaphor of the human condition, which itself is mortal and finite (lines 8–14). Alfonso X uses the metaphor of scorpions in "The Scorpions" to express his anguish and concern for dealing with the people of his nation and his desire to escape as a mariner, away from their poison. In Guido Guinizzelli's "Love Always Repairs to the Noble Heart," the transformation and resurfacing of stars, gemstones, or birds in flight back to their grove represent the changes required to heal a noble heart; real love and beauty are often hidden beneath an ugly or imperfect exterior, and one should not be deceived, on the surface, by a pretty face (lines 31–40, 60). In Jahan Khatun's "Heart, in His Beauty's Garden," the birds moan and the flowers disappear or wither, corresponding to the poet-as-student's lament that she cannot learn from her clever tutor's homilies (lines 10–20). How does the ideal beauty of medieval lyrics compare to your culture's appreciation for certain physical qualities and types?

  a. **Further Reading:** Dronke, Peter. *The Medieval Lyric*. 3rd ed. Boulder, CO: D. S. Brewer, 2002.

  b. **Suggested Search:** Go to http://public.wsu.edu/~delahoyd/medieval /index.html.

5. **Medieval lyricists often use terms or references from crafts, trades, and professions to establish a theme or set of images, all of which increase the ludic value of the poems.** In "The Art of Love," Arnaut Daniel uses a vocabulary of construction and craft involving the manipulation of wood, marble, and metal (plane, finish, file, polish: "so usurious is her demand, she gets craftsman and workshop together"). References to games (chess or gambling games with the dice) mirror the lover's pursuit and the competition established during courtship, as in The Archpoet's "His Confession" (lines 71–80). In Shem Tov Ardutiel's "The Battles of the Pen and Scissors," the scissors as object and representation of the frustrated poet want to cut (destroy) something, solely for the purpose of ending the division between the blades' halves. Guido Cavalcanti employs philosophical jargon in "A Lady Asks Me" (e.g., accidental quality, case and argument, physical demonstration, inner nature, possible intellect) and a lexicon based on optics (lines 64–70). In Charles d'Orleans's "If You Wish to Sell Your Kisses," the language of finance and mortgage appears (the heart as deposit, inheritance, price). Philosophical and artisans' professional styles and attributes are

also emulated in the structure and form of some works. Jalâloddin Rumi's "The Question" is presented as a student-teacher response, similar to the "Mirrors for Princes" format of Petrus Alfonsi's *The Scholar's Guide* (see Alfonsi in this volume). In Rumi's poem, the dervish asks his peer about a vision of God's presence, and the peer responds with a parable rather than a direct description (some people walk to the fire, others toward the water, and both end up in the opposite by guarding against that thing). Hafez makes references to Persian and Arabic myths in his poems; Jahan Khatun's poems also are *divans* that recall the practice of didactic relationships based on student-teacher learning (this poetic style influenced later European writers, including Goethe, who includes *divan* writing in his collections). Some poems recall the humor or satire of previous lyrics: Rumi's "An Empty Garlic" (in which he criticizes a friend for pursuing an old woman, comparing her to rotting garlic, withered flowers, and leathery black lizards) bears striking resemblance to some of the sordid love poems written by Catullus (see Volume 1). Does referencing other professions, trades, or established writers make a poem more understandable or accessible for a larger audience?

a. **Further Reading:** Cooper, Lisa. *Artisans and Narrative Craft in Late Medieval England.* Cambridge: Cambridge University Press, 2011.

b. **Suggested Search:** Go to www.ravensgard.org/gerekr/liter.html.

In-Class Activities

1. To better familiarize themselves with medieval culture and society, groups will take a virtual field trip to the medieval and Renaissance webring or the Ravensgard Medieval Poetry and Literature site; each group will then research a particular element of culture and present it to the class.

2. Music appreciation activity: Students will listen to a CD compilation (alternatively, music is also available at youtube.com if one searches by the poet's name) and either discuss or write about their reflections regarding their reactions and the merit of the works.

3. Students will try their hand at designing a medieval lyric using some of the rules established for different lyrical genres of the period. Alternatively, students might design a new "Treatise of Love," outlining modern rules for courtship and the symptoms and rewards of love.

Paper Topics/Suggestions for Writing

1. Compare Beatrice of Dia's lyrics to Christine de Pizan's "All alone am I, and alone I wish to stay," including a discussion of the woman's role as court official and wife during the period.

2. Examine and discuss the tendency toward fragmentation of the body in medieval lyrics.

3. How are nature and artisans' or craftsman's terms incorporated into medieval poetry, and what purpose do they serve? Reference at least five poems to support your position.

4. What were some rules established in courtly treatises on love, how did they differ from "real social mores," and how did both feature in poems of this period? Reference at least five poems to support your position.

5. Compare and contrast love poetry written during another period or culture with those found in the "Medieval Lyrics" selection, focusing on content, form, intent, and presentation.

Resources

California Polytechnic State University. http://cla.calpoly.edu/~dschwart /engl513/courtly/love2.htm.
> This site contains links to Harvard's Chaucer page, as well as scholarly essays, university sites, images, handouts, and lesson plans.

From Byzantium to Andalusia: Medieval Music and Poetry. Naxos, 2006, CD compilation.
> Music from the medieval world.

The Middle Ages. www.themiddleages.net/index.html.
> Links to sites on all things medieval—architecture and art, music, literature, people, history, etc.

Ravensgard Medieval Poetry and Literature. www.ravensgard.org/gerekr /liter.html.
> This site, divided by genre, location, and period, includes weighty content on separate pages, devoted to cultures, arts and crafts, society, and bibliographies.

Washington State University. http://public.wsu.edu/~delahoyd/medieval /index.html.
> This site contains background, images, examples, links, bibliographies, lesson plans, and documents on love writing in works from antiquity through modern times.

DANTE ALIGHIERI

The Divine Comedy

> O Muses! O high genius! Help me now!
> O memory that wrote down what I saw,
> here your true excellence shall be revealed!
> Then I began: "O poet come to guide me,
> tell me if you think my worth sufficient
> before you trust me to this arduous road.
> (2.1–12)

Topics for Lecture or Discussion

1. **The Divine Comedy is an epic, specifically a "tertiary" epic, following in the footsteps of Virgil's The Aeneid, which is itself based on the oral, Homeric epics The Odyssey and The Iliad.** The first part, *Inferno*, was published in 1314; the last cantos of *Paradiso* were published after Dante Alighieri's (hereafter, Dante) death in 1321. Significantly, Dante (1265–1321 C.E.) composed his epic in vernacular Italian—the vulgate, or lingua franca—rather than in Latin, medieval Europe's official language of literature, scholarship, and statecraft. Like Giovanni Boccaccio and Geoffrey Chaucer after him, Dante understood that neither his characters nor the majority of his audience experienced life in Latin. Unwilling to address only the educated and privileged, he included the nonreading Italian audience, who could still listen, understand, and experience his narrative of confession. The poet titled the greatest of his works simply *Commedia*, aligning it with the classical, Aristotelian notion that comedy is concerned with the restoration of order. The root of disorder in Dante's mind was mankind's increasing distance from God, beginning with the fall from grace in Eden and perpetuated by the spiritual disillusion that overwhelms the pilgrim in the forest. From Dante's point of view, any reunion of humanity with God must necessarily begin with his own understanding of divine intent, particularly the concepts of justice, charity, and salvation. Boccaccio later suggested adding "Divine" to the title to suggest not only the subject matter of the poem but its exalted qualities as well.

   a. **Further Reading:** Lewis, R. W. B. *Dante: A Life*. New York: Penguin, 2009.

   b. **Suggested Search:** Search for "vernacular poetry" at http://cla.cal poly.edu/~dschwart/engl203/vernacular.html.

2. **Virgil's reputation as a magician and philosopher, *The Aeneid*'s reputation as a holy book of prophecy, and much of Dante's inspi-**

ration for the underworld come from Book VI (itself derived from Book XI of Homer's *The Odyssey*). This vision of the underworld, approaching Judeo-Christian ideas of hell and the punishment of sinners, is one of the major shapers of Western cosmology. Combined with references to Roman religious ritual (such as the sprinkling of water on a person prior to entering a holy place), the poem predicts major tenets of Catholic ("universal") Christianity as it developed in the early centuries C.E. Virgil held a special place in the thinking of medieval Christendom. He lived in the first century B.C.E. and so of course was a pagan, but his fourth *Eclogue* is a poem that prophesies the birth of Augustus (Virgil's patron) as a savior of the world. The medieval West interpreted the poem as a prophecy of the coming of Christ and held Virgil in special esteem. If Christianity had not become the only legal Roman religion in 382, it is unlikely that it would have become the dominant Western belief system. Probably due to the evocative power of his poetry, Virgil was also considered a worker of magic. His status as epic poet, philosopher, and mystic makes him Dante the Pilgrim's ideal guide.

    a. **Further Reading:** Allan, Mowbray. "Does Dante Hope for Virgil's Salvation?" *Modern Language Notes* 104 (1989): 193–205.

    b. **Suggested Search:** Go to The World of Dante website (www .worldofdante.org).

3. **Dante was the leader of the *Dolce stil novo* ("sweet new style"), a poetic movement that explored the relations between earthly, secular love and Divine Love. The movement, which included Guido Cavalcanti, had tremendous influence on Francis Petrarch, who in turn influenced two centuries of European poetry.** Since Dante is presenting a confession by way of a dream vision (wherein truths are always revealed even if they elude the dreamer), his biography becomes unusually pertinent to *The Divine Comedy*. Beatrice—who, with St. Lucy and the Virgin Mary, recognizes Dante the Pilgrim's plight and sends Virgil to guide him—was a young woman of Dante's acquaintance (Beatrice Portinari), but she is also symbolic of the redeeming power of God's love. Her name, which translates to "she who brings happiness," suggests that she represents the gift of God's blessing on humanity. For Dante, salvation rests in the emotional embrace of God's loving goodness, but another of God's beatitudes to humankind is reason. Often contrary to emotion, human intellect is a necessary though insufficient means toward salvation, and we could say that the ultimate goal of the pilgrim's journey is to find balance between them. Virgil, a symbol of Reason, must guide Dante physically and interpretively through *Inferno* and *Purgatorio*. As a pre-Christian, however, he is forbidden to cross the threshold of *Paradiso*. There, Beatrice, a symbol of

overwhelming inspiration, romantic love, and divine adoration, becomes the pilgrim's guide.

    a. **Further Reading:** Dante. *Vita Nuova.* http://etcweb.princeton.edu /dante/pdp/vnuova.html.

    b. **Suggested Search:** Go to the Renaissance Dante in Print website (www.italnet.nd.edu/Dante/index.html).

4. **The *triune* (three-in-one) nature of Christian divinity—a single entity comprised of three aspects (Father, Son, Holy Spirit)—is the basis of structure and style in Dante's poem.** Many medieval poets considered such a conceit sufficient, but Dante was keen to instill echoes of the Trinity in every aspect of his poem. To achieve this ambitious confluence of substance and style, Dante created terza rima, a new type of versification. Medieval rhyme and metrics were generally unsubtle, encouraging deliberate and occasionally forced readings. Dante's iambic pentameter is highly refined, depending heavily on the elision of vowel sounds to create its unstressed/stressed effects. His *Divine Comedy* cantos consist of interlocking three-line units, following an ABA rhyme scheme with a BCB rhyme, followed by a CDC rhyme, and so on. The number of three-line units varies from canto to canto, but each canto closes out the current rhyme with a single line. In this way the structure of each canto expresses the triune theme of the entire work on a microcosmic level. Taking the epigraph as an example:

Lo giorno se n'andava, e l'aere bruno	(A)
toglieva li animai che sono in *terra*	(B)
da le fatiche loro; e io sol uno	(A)
m'apparecchiava a sostener la *guerra*	(B)
sì del cammino e sì de la pietate,	(C)
che ritrarrà la mente che non *erra.*	(B)
O muse, o alto ingegno, or m'aiutate;	(C)
o mente che scrivesti ciò ch'io vidi,	(D)
qui si parrà la tua nobilitate.	(C)
Io cominciai: «Poeta che mi guidi,	(D)
guarda la mia virtù s'ell'è possente,	(E)
prima ch'a l'alto passo tu mi fidi.	(D)

The interlocking rhyme continues to the end of the Latin alphabet and then resumes with the introduction of a new "A" rhyme:

Quando sarò dinanzi al segnor mio,	(Y)
di te mi loderò sovente a lui.	(Z)
Tacette allora, e poi comincia' io:	(Y)

> O donna di virtù, sola per cui . . .   (Z)
> l'umana spezie eccede ogne contento (A)
> di quel ciel c'ha minor li cerchi sui. (Z)
> (2.1–12; 73–78)

As in *The Thousand and One Nights*, mathematics and numerology play a significant role in *The Divine Comedy's* narrative and symbolic structure while enhancing theological and philosophical themes. Traditionally, the number nine (3×3) was significant (as in the Queen of Sheba's riddle and the title *The Thousand and One Nights*), as were ten ($9 + 1 =$ unity) and one hundred ($99 + 1$, a number representing completion and perfection). Dante extended the symbolism of three and one beyond these already intricate models. *The Divine Comedy* is comprised of one hundred cantos, thirty-three each in *Inferno, Purgatorio,* and *Paradiso,* supported by Canto 1, which introduces the work in its entirety. By arranging the poem and the geography of the afterlife according to rigid and schematic principles, Dante was better able to understand his spiritual disorder and convey it to readers on a universal scale.

  a. **Further Reading:** Abrams, Richard. "Illicit Pleasures: Dante among the Sensualists (Purgatorio XXVI)." *Modern Language Notes* 100 (1985): 1–41.

  b. **Suggested Search:** Go to the Princeton Dante Project website (http://etcweb.princeton.edu/dante/index.html).

5. **Like *The Thousand and One Nights* and *The Canterbury Tales*, one narrative trajectory of *The Divine Comedy* follows the embedded tales of characters, historical and legendary, who implore the narrator to report the truth to the living world.** Tailored to enhance the reader's experience of *Inferno* and *Purgatorio* by aligning past, present, and future, these brief, embedded narratives belong to several familiar genres: the tragedy of Francesca da Rimini and her brother-in-law, Paolo Malatesta, blamed upon their experience of Arthurian romance in Canto 5; the prophecy of one simonist pope of being replaced in Hell by the man who succeeded him; the beginnings of a *fabliau* of the social-climbing forger Gianni Schicchi in Canto 30; and the *de casibus virorum* ("falls of illustrious men") tragedy of Count Ugolino in Canto 33. But Dante's narrative strategy is more than a schematically arranged aggregation of genres and encounters intended to set the record straight. *The Divine Comedy* charts a triple narrative: In addition to the chronicle of Dante's world related through the souls he encounters, the poem presents an epic journey through the Christian afterlife and, perhaps most significantly for Western literature, Dante's own narrative of spiritual restoration, which fortifies the present by recalling and attempting to comprehend the traumatic past.

    a. **Further Reading:** Armour, Peter. "Words and the Drama of Death in *Purgatorio V.*" In *Word and Drama in Dante: Essays on the "Divina Commedia,"* edited by John C. Barnes and Jennifer Petrie, 93–122. Dublin: Irish Academic Press, 1993.

    b. **Suggested Search:** Go to the Danteworlds site (http://danteworlds.laits.utexas.edu).

6. ***The Divine Comedy*, particularly *Inferno*, is an act of memory, being recalled and written during the act of reading. The author is not only ever-present, he frequently reminds us that he feels now as he writes what he felt then, even if he cannot adequately describe what he saw.** The poem is an act of recollection closely related to the dream vision, a staple of medieval narrative poetry. The difference is that rather than literally falling asleep and dreaming the events and sensations of *The Divine Comedy,*

> How I entered there I cannot truly say,
> I had become so sleepy at the moment
> when I first strayed, leaving the path of truth.
> (lines 1.10–2)

Dante the Pilgrim is so spiritually and emotionally distraught that his inner strife becomes his outer life—a dream made manifest before his eyes. Despite the rare and irrefutable inseparability of Dante's biography and his poetry, students should make a clear distinction between Dante the Narrator and Dante the Pilgrim. Clear divisions in the poem between the remembering author and remembered subject remind us that they are not the same being.

    a. **Further Reading:** Armour, Peter. "Divining the Figures: Dante's Three Dreams in the *Purgatorio.*" In *Melbourne Essays in Italian Language and Literature in Memory of Colin McCormick*, edited by Tom O'Neill, 13–26. Dublin: Irish Academic Press, 1990.

    b. **Suggested Search:** Go to www.lib.rochester.edu/camelot/teams/sym0int.htm.

In-Class Activities

1. In groups of three, review and discuss Dante's ordering of sins, particularly the lower circles. How do the values he assigned to murder, suicide, and the various types of fraud and betrayal relate to twenty-first-century morality?

2. Compose a ten-minute personal narrative of what you consider the darkest moment in your life. Once time is called, review what you've written. How closely do your words evoke the tone and mood of events months, and even years, distant? Does the passage objectively narrate or engage your experience subjectively? Did you consciously or subcon-

sciously invoke hindsight? Now consider the changes you would have to make in order to provide readers outside of your own experience and imagination with a sense of what you went through. A continuation of this exercise might bring two to three students together to share and mediate their personal narratives.

Paper Topics/Suggestions for Writing

1. How is Virgil's presence vital to Dante's journey through Hell in *Inferno*?

2. Briefly discuss Dante's use of the numbers 3 and 1, and combinations of those numbers. Provide at least two examples of how these numbers function in the poem.

3. Select three circles (or sublevels) of *Inferno* and explain how the punishment fits the sin.

4. How would you describe Dante the Pilgrim's worldview at the beginning of the poem? What types of symbolism does he use to convey his situation to the reader?

5. Why is *The Divine Comedy* called a "comedy"?

Resources

Dartmouth University. Dante Project. http://dante.dartmouth.edu.
  Site contains seventy commentaries on Dante's work.
Institute for Advanced Technologies in the Humanities, University of Virginia. The World of Dante. www.worldofdante.org.
  Gallery, maps, music, timeline, teacher resources.
Princeton University. Princeton Dante Project. http://etcweb.princeton.edu/dante/index.html.
  Text, related works, audio recordings, notes, hyperlinks.
Schwartz, Deborah B. Medieval Attitudes Toward Vernacular Literature. http://cla.calpoly.edu/~dschwart/engl203/vernacular.html.
  ENGL 203 site.
Symons, Dana M. "Chaucerian Dream Visions and Complaints." Kalamazoo, MI: Medieval Institute Publications, 2004. www.lib.rochester.edu/camelot/teams/sym0int.htm.
University of Notre Dame. Renaissance Dante in Print. www.italnet.nd.edu/Dante/index.html.
  Exhibition of Renaissance editions of Dante's work from the John A. Zahm collection.
University of Texas–Austin. Danteworlds. http://danteworlds.laits.utexas.edu.
  Site described as "an integrated multimedia journey—combining artistic images, textual commentary, and audio recordings—through the three realms of the afterlife."

THE THOUSAND AND ONE NIGHTS
Prologue

> I would like you to marry me to King Shah-
> rayar, so that I may either succeed in saving
> the people or perish and die like the rest.
> —p. 562

Topics for Lecture or Discussion

1. ***The Thousand and One Nights* is a mixture of prose and poetry of anonymous authorship, compiled and edited over several centuries.** The many extant versions all derive their structure from the frame narrative of Shahrazad and Shahrayar, and this narrative frame encompasses a variety of stories of many different genres. Therefore, *The Thousand and One Nights* is not precisely one work of literature— there is no single, definitive text. The oldest fragment consists of a few pages and dates to the early ninth century C.E. The oldest significant manuscript dates to the fifteenth century C.E. and contains about 270 tales. The collection as we have it was composed in Arabia (in Arabic), although it borrows many tales and characters from the Persian, Indian, and Egyptian literary traditions. Though many of Shahrazad's tales are inherently fantastical or contain magical elements, their central characters tend to be marginalized or disenfranchised (women, fishermen, porters, victims of metamorphosis) rather than the powerful kings and magical beings likely to take the lead in Shahrayar's imagination.

   a. **Further Reading:** Irwin, Robert. *The Arabian Nights: A Companion.* New York: Tauris Parke Paperback, 2004.

   b. **Suggested Searches:** Search for Arabic literary genres at www .library.cornell.edu/colldev/mideast/arablit.htm.

2. ***The Thousand and One Nights* is an elaborate frame narrative, blending epic orality with the self-aware, self-referential qualities of the novella.** In contrast to Chaucer's constantly-in-motion *Canterbury Tales*, all tales, regardless of narrative voice, are ultimately told by Shahrazad (and at key junctures by her sister, Dinarzad) to Shahrayar at bedtime. Her novellas (short stories), a literary genre cultivated in Greece, Arabia, Persia, and, later, during the European Renaissance— take advantage of such calm and quiet, depending as they do, to a large extent, on the auditor's imagination. In spite of its relatively static narrative frame, the tales of *The Thousand and One Nights* are a wonder of narrative, cultural, and temporal variety. The contrasts Shahrazad

creates with her courtly storytelling ultimately reeducate the misogynist Shahrayar against a backdrop of social and political upheaval. Lyric poetry, significant in the Arabic and Islamic traditions, works within the tales as echo, comment, and counterpoint.

a. **Further Reading:** Gittes, Katherine. *Framing the Canterbury Tales: Chaucer and the Medieval Frame Narrative Tradition.* Santa Barbara, CA: Greenwood Press, 1991.

b. **Suggested Search:** Go to the "Tales from the 1001 Nights" art archive (www.mythfolklore.net/1001nights/pix/index.htm).

3. **The prologue of the frame tale "The Story of King Shahrayar and Shahrazad, His Vizier's Daughter" establishes the central theme of taking relief from the greater magnitude of another's suffering.** This is a kind of *schadenfreude* (there are few expressions as appropriate as the German and even fewer that express this complex and loaded concept in a single word). First Shahzaman regains his emotional and physical health after discovering that his sister-in-law's infidelity—and hence his brother's disgrace—is tenfold greater than his own. To be master of the world and yet powerless to discover flagrant infidelity in one's own household torments both kings. They embark on a pilgrimage, keen to find a being of power with troubles more woeful than their own, and they shortly discover a gigantic demon (an *ifrit*) so wary of his mistress's potential for infidelity that he keeps her locked in a chest on his head, but so proud to possess a woman of her sensuous beauty that the chest is made of glass. While the demon naps, the woman coerces the frightened kings to make love with her, then collects their rings to make her adulterous collection an even one hundred and the ifrit's misery ten times greater than Shahrayar's. The numerological angle takes on even greater significance in the context of the collection.

a. **Further Reading:** Heath, Peter. "Romance as Genre in *The Thousand and One Nights.*" In *The Arabian Nights Reader*, edited by Ulrich Marzolph. Detroit: Wayne State University Press, 2006.

b. **Suggested Search:** Go to the Harvard University Course Wiki (https://coursewikis.fas.harvard.edu/aiu18/1001_Nights).

4. **Passages such as the epigraph above and the repetitive interstices that mark Shahrazad's cliffhangers often lead students to believe that Shahrazad tells stories merely to keep herself alive.** In the broader contexts of the extended tales and the collection itself, however, she pursues a greater purpose, "to succeed in saving the people." She understands implicitly that Shahrayar's homicidal enforcement of marital chastity is murdering more than the women of court and kingdom. The king's lack of faith in women, one-half of God's creation, undermines the foundations of the kingdom and destroys the ability to create life. Her strategy relies on the epic tropes of invocation and repetition, as

well as the cliffhanger, but also depends on Shahrayar's willingness to connect embedded tales with their overall narratives as their tellers do (such as when something a demon says inspires a fisherman to cite an iconic, authoritative example of the last time someone said such a foolish thing). If these connections appear obvious to us, it is important to remember that Shahrayar may be the most self-absorbed literary character ever devised. Shahrazad must penetrate his vanity and captivate his interest before she can confront him, however subtly, with the consequences of his misogynistic and tyrannical behavior.

a. **Further Reading:** Menges, Jeff, ed. *Arabian Nights Illustrated: Art of Dulac, Folkard, Parrish and Others.* New York: Dover Publications, 2008.

b. **Suggested Search:** *1001 Nights.* Dir. Mike Smith. BS24 Studios, 1998.

5. ***The Thousand and One Nights* presents and depends heavily upon the vibrant literary culture of Baghdad, the capital of the Abbasid Empire.** Abbasid rulers such as Al Mansur (754–775 C.E.) and Harun al-Rashid (786–809 C.E.)—the first referred to consistently through the narrative and the second a character within it—fostered art and scholarship and maintained a peace in which art and science could flourish. Scholars and ideas from Persia and India made their way west, and Baghdad became the center of Arabic and Islamic scholarship. Poetry was highly valued under the Abbasids, as was Greek philosophy, which was avidly translated into Arabic during this period. Theologians began to develop an Islamic understanding of the problems of good and evil that is inherent to any monotheism. Religious understanding increasingly became rooted in the Qur'an and in an understanding of the customary practices (*sunna*) of Muhammad, codified as Sunnism. A widely prevalent notion—embraced by some Shiites as well—was that the proper Muslim ruler was not a dynastic caliph but an *imam*, a local community leader who held authority by virtue of his moral behavior. The community had an obligation to remove and replace an imam whose morality was perceived to lapse. Even though Shahrayar is a non-Islamic Persian ruler, he represents precisely a compromised imam in the context of frame narrative. Shahrazad takes on the responsibility, then, of not merely correcting the king's aberrant behavior toward women but restoring his integrity as a political and spiritual ruler.

a. **Further Reading:** Bennison, Amira. *The Great Caliphs: The Golden Age of the Abbasid Empire.* New Haven, CT: Yale University Press, 2010.

b. **Suggested Search:** Search for "Abbasids" on the Princeton University Islamic Timeline (Al-Khazina site) (www.princeton.edu/~batke/itl /scroll/scrollall.html).

6. **Arabic, the language in which Muhammad received the Qur'an, united Arabic and non-Arabic Muslim.** *The Thousand and One Nights* and the culture it presents valued craftsmanship and artistry in all its forms, from shoemaking and carpentry to sculpture and architecture. Naturally this aesthetic extended to language and poetry. The recording of Arabic became an art form, and calligraphy flourished, as it does in the Islamic world today. Regardless of the representations and ideas within, the work of art was only as beautiful and evocative as its physical presentation, a concept that recurs frequently throughout Shahrazad's narrative. The Arabic of the Qur'an reflected many features of pre-Islamic Arabic poetry and differed significantly from everyday Arabic. The Abbasid period saw the rise of "literary Arabic," with a style and vocabulary of composition very different from the vernacular Arabic of its day.

   a. **Further Reading:** Ja'far, Mustafa. *Arabic Calligraphy*. London: British Museum Press, 2002.

   b. **Suggested Search:** Search for "Arabic lyric poetry, Arabic calligraphy," on Felipe Quijano's Journey through Art History site (https://sites.google.com/site/journeythrougharthistory/arabiccalligraphy).

7. **The title of *The Thousand and One Nights* synthesizes the Arabic and Islamic literary traditions with mathematics and theology.** In the Islamic Shia tradition, at the end of a millennium the *mahdi* ("one who is guided," technically a descendant of Muhammad's nephew Ali) will return and an age of peace and justice will ensue. Extending her tales beyond the present time and into the next millennium, Shahrazad restores Shahrayar to himself and ends his tyranny. Further, medieval Arabic intellectuals were fascinated with numerology, and 1001 in binary is 9. The Queen of Sheba posed a famous riddle to King Solomon concerning the significance of the number 9, the answer being the human gestation period. During the course of the frame narrative, and without Shahrayar's knowledge, Shahrazad relegitimizes the king's rule and guarantees its future by bearing him three sons, whom she presents to him in the epilogue. Thus the title alludes to Shahrazad's life-giving force as superior to Shahrayar's ability to decree death.

   a. **Further Reading:** Martin, Richard C., ed. "Mahdi." In *Encyclopedia of Islam and the Muslim World*. Farmington Hills, MI: Gale Thomson, 2004.

   b. **Suggested Search:** Search for "*mahdi*, medieval numerology," on Encyclopedia Britannica Online (www.britannica.com/EBchecked/topic/358096/mahdi).

In-Class Activities

1. As a small group, set the scene for Shahrazad's storytelling by describing the nonstorytelling elements of her plan. Now that you have created the setting, what types of stories seem best suited for telling within it?

2. Freewrite a five-minute personal narrative with a specific genre or sub-genre in mind. Merging into groups of three, combine all three personal narratives into a ten-minute narrative with either logical or illogical transitions (do not mix and match). Define the single storyteller who could tell this tale, and invent the circumstances that lead to its telling.

Paper Topics/Suggestions for Writing

1. Consider the predicaments of Shahrayar and his brother, Shahzaman: How do they discover the truth and ultimately make themselves feel better about it?

2. Using two examples of narratives embedded in "The Story of the Fisherman and the Demon," explain Shahrazad's storytelling strategy (hint: genre, theme, character).

3. Why is Shahrazad telling stories? What does she hope to accomplish?

Resources

Cornell University Library. Middle East & Islamic Studies Collection: Arabic Literature. www.library.cornell.edu/colldev/mideast/arablit.htm.
> Digital bibliography site includes hyperlinks to websites related to Arabic literature of all historical periods and cultures.

Harvard University. AIU18: 1001 Nights. https://coursewikis.fas.harvard.edu /aiu18/1001_Nights.
> Course Wiki with cultural and historical background interpretations, plot summaries, hyperlinks, and images.

1001 Nights. Prod. Aly Jetha. Qatar Studios, 2010.
> Animated television series.

Tales from the 1001 Nights. www.mythfolklore.net/1001nights/pix/index .htm. Site maintained by Laura Gibbs.
> Art archive with images from Andrew Lang, Dulac, Europe, and objects from the Middle East.

GIOVANNI BOCCACCIO

Decameron

Topics for Lecture or Discussion

1. **Giovanni Boccaccio's first and one hundredth stories are each, in their way, hagiographies.** In strong contrast to the confessional autobiography of Augustine's *Confessions*, stories about saints' lives were a popular genre that tended to emphasize the legendary aspects of their subjects over philosophical meanings and theological insight. Characters such as St. Cecilia and St. Sebastian are martyred in horrible ways, while beatific smiles override grimaces of pain or injustice. Wanting to believe in the divine within themselves, medieval audiences were keen to find unwavering perfection in the souls and bodies of others. Intended to requite the moneylenders' hospitality, Ser Ceparello's deathbed confession results in the canonization of the worst human being in the world. Dioneo's telling of the famous "patient Griselda" story turns a cruelly tormented wife into a secular, domestic saint.
   a. **Further Reading:** Ricketts, Jill. *Visualizing Boccaccio: Studies on Illustrations of the Decameron, from Giotto to Pasolini.* Cambridge: Cambridge University Press, 2011.
   b. **Suggested Search:** Go to the Hagiography Society site (www.hagi ographysociety.org/links.html).

2. **Although its frame (much like that of *The Thousand and One Nights*) rarely becomes more than a frame, *Decameron* is the rare story collection that actually completes the cycle established in that narrative frame**. Beyond the fact of its centuries-spanning composition and cross-cultural accretion, the generally accepted master text of *The Thousand and One Nights* does not contain enough stories to fill nearly three years of bedtimes, no matter how finely Shahrazad dices them up. Chaucer's innkeeper, Harry Bailly, sets a goal of two stories per pilgrim en route to Canterbury and also on the return, and yet the pilgrimage has not reached the shrine of Thomas Becket in "The Parson's Tale" by the collection's end. Although Giovanni Boccaccio drew upon any number of extant folk tales and novellas from the Italian, Greek, and Arabic traditions, his is the work of a single author realizing a highly ambitious goal while invoking a massive and complex series of literary traditions, not least of which was his great predecessor in the Italian vernacular, Dante.
   a. **Further Reading:** Irwin, Bonnie. "What's in a Frame? The Medieval Textualization of Traditional Storytelling." *Oral Tradition* 10:1 (1995): 27–53.

b. **Suggested Search:** Search for "frame narrative" in the *Oral Tradition Journal* (online), a peer-reviewed journal with free access to digital scholarly articles (http://journal.oraltradition.org).

3. **Multigeneric diversity, themed days dictated by temporary "rulers," and storytellers derived from the most privileged of Florentines dictate structure, but almost anything goes when it comes to content.** Giovanni Boccaccio was much less concerned than Chaucer would be with regard to a teller's aptness to a particular tale. Certainly the most controversial (and bawdiest) tales originate with Dioneo, the youngest of the men, but none of the young women considers herself too chaste for a naughty story that ultimately brings joy to the group or emphasizes a moral theme. As long as the teller presents it "correctly," the most ribald fabliau can be contextually appropriate and socially acceptable within Boccaccio's frame. This frame is as unyielding and repetitive as that of *The Thousand and One Nights*—its young nobles, after all, are keen to maintain in the countryside a sense of order impossible in plague-ridden Florence—but its storytelling order predicts the structural and narrative instabilities of Chaucer's *Canterbury Tales*. Within the rigors of an objective frame, Boccaccio allows character subjectivities to occasionally present themselves as a natural feature of storytelling.
   a. **Further Reading:** Edwards, Robert. *Chaucer and Boccaccio: Antiquity and Modernity*. New York: Palgrave Macmillan, 1992.
   b. **Suggested Search:** See the entry on "action" in the *Stanford Encyclopedia of Philosophy* (http://plato.stanford.edu/entries/action).

4. **Though *Decameron* shares many features with *The Thousand and One Nights*, Giovanni Boccaccio's presentation (which may admittedly have much to do with the fact that his is a single-author omnibus) differs profoundly in its ideology of audience.** Unlike Shahrazad's deference to Shahrayar's wisdom and God's magnificence, *Decameron*'s narrators often instruct (directly, or by helpful analogy) their audiences how to listen to or what lesson to take from this particular telling. Voices embedded within characters in the Arabic collection (due in large part to the dramatic necessities of the frame tale) are enfranchised as narrators in *Decameron*. Boccaccio both criticizes and exalts the power of confession and the making of saints, often in the same breath. Panfilo's story of Ser Ciappelletto opens the collection with a treatise on deception, belief, and forgiveness, even as it elbows dramatic irony into the audience's ribs. The final tale, that of "Patient Griselda" (appropriated by Chaucer for "The Clerk's Tale"), applies fairy-tale features not out of place in a Breton lai to a book of Job-like narrative of whim and suffering, while criticizing a patriarchal system that allows a husband to dictate his wife's reality.

a. **Further Reading**: Grudin, Michaela Paasche, and Robert Grudin. *Boccaccio's Decameron and the Ciceronian Renaissance.* New York: Palgrave, 2012.

b. **Suggested Search**: *Il Decameron.* Dir. Pier Paolo Pasolini. 1971.

5. **Each of the other tales presented here displays interesting variations on "fairy-tale" narratives in the traditions of *The Thousand and One Nights* and the *Lais* of Marie de France.** In these semi-miraculous stories, Giovanni Boccaccio emphasizes the subjective perceptions upon which human belief is structured. "Day 2, Story 7" is a travelogue of Alatiel's misadventures in the Mediterranean world. The story has a strong kinship with the first half of *The Odyssey* as well as *Apollonius of Tyre*, a Greek novella widely translated—including one of the few surviving translations from Latin into Anglo-Saxon—and is a source for the Shakespearean collaboration *Pericles: Prince of Tyre.* As Alatiel passes through the hands of men who forget their faiths and allegiances when confronted with her beauty, she also crosses with ease the social, political, and religious borders that defined the Mediterranean world and its conflicts. It is that world's need (led by her father and soon-to-be husband, the Sultan of Algarve, who represent the Eastern and Western poles of that world) to see her as a heroic virgin rather than as a compromised victim of circumstance and masculine whim that allows her reversion to chastity. For "Day 4, Story 9" (Guglielmo Rossiglione and Guglielmo de Cabestaing), Boccaccio drew upon the same troubadour legend from which Marie de France derived her lai "Laustic," though he remains significantly truer to the details of the source. The collection's penultimate tale, of Messer Torello and Saladin (10.9), begins with an unpretentious contest of intercultural hospitality and then takes a detour into Christian fish in Islamic waters territory. Messer Torello has been driven so far off the path that only faith, abetted by magic, can restore him to his wife and preserve the sanctity of marriage.

a. **Further Reading**: Kinoshita, Sharon, and Jason Jacobs. "Ports of Call: Boccaccio's Alatiel in the Medieval Mediterranean." *Journal of Medieval and Early Modern Studies* 37:1 (2007).

b. **Suggested Search**: Go to Brown University's Decameron project (www.brown.edu/Departments/Italian_Studies/dweb/index.php).

In-Class Activity

1. Storytelling by committee is more common than we might think. The opening credits of recent films suggest that single authorship is a fading concept in popular entertainment. Even screenwriters with sole credit probably saw their work subjected to outside revision. Have students work in groups of three, with each student in a distinct role—one will dictate the theme of the story, the second will provide the narrative

genre, and the third will decide the central character. Each student should then draft a single-paragraph abstract and then combine elements from all three into a streamlined narrative for presentation to the class. Did the group choose the elements their treatments had in common or find that their differences were more compelling? Other useful questions include whether the end result conforms to the story committee's original parameters and whether the final narrative transmits those ideas to the audience.

2. Art Appreciation: Have students examine the visual works inspired by Boccaccio's text. How "true" are the artistic representations? What elements of the work are emphasized or portrayed, and how does each artist interpret those elements compared to their description and use in Boccaccio's text?

Paper Topics/Suggestions for Writing

1. Citing examples from two of the *Decameron* tales presented, consider how a desirable truth is often a mere construct of words.

2. Relate the style and substance of one of Giovanni Boccaccio's tales to that of another embedded narrative on the syllabus.

3. How are women represented in Boccaccio's stories? Consider issues of relationships, responsibility, and morality.

4. Discuss the themes of mercantilism and commerce in two of Boccaccio's stories.

5. Scholars have noted that some characters in Boccaccio's work (Guido Cavalcanti and Giotto di Bondone, for example) were real, historical persons. What relationship do you find between fiction and reality in the text? Does this lend credibility to the fictional versions, or does it diminish the real person's character and the historical milieu in which s/he lived?

Resources

"Action." *Stanford Encyclopedia of Philosophy.* http://plato.stanford.edu/entries /action.
    Background information on "agency," including its use in fiction.
Brown University. Decameron Web. www.brown.edu/Departments/Italian _Studies/dweb/index.php.
    Project, texts, background, related links, teaching materials, and visual aids related to Boccaccio and the Decameron.
Grand Valley State University. www4.gvsu.edu/wrightd/HNR215%20and %20216C/Decameron%20Images.htm.
    Paintings inspired by Boccaccio's Decameron.

Hagiography Society. www.hagiographysociety.org/links.html.

 Links for resources, teaching on medieval saints, and background information on saints and their cults.

Il Decameron. Dir. Pier Paolo Pasolini. 1971.

 Pasolini's film favors bawdier tales—and only ten in all—but his presentation of their deeper layers is highly evocative. His adaptation bypasses the frame narrative but gradually sets up Ceparello's backstory in interstitial segments before taking on *Decameron* 1.1 in full.

GEOFFREY CHAUCER
The Canterbury Tales

> But first I pray you, by your courtesy,
> That you not blame my own vulgarity,
> Although I might speak plainly in this matter,
> When I tell you their words and their
>   demeanor,
> Or if I speak their words, exact and true.
> For this you all know just as well as I do:
> Whoever tells a tale after a man,
> He must repeat, as closely as he can,
> Every last word, if that is his duty,
> Even if he has to speak quite rudely,
> Or otherwise, he makes his tale untrue
> Or makes things up, or finds words that are
>   new.
> —General Prologue, lines 724–36

Topics for Lecture or Discussion

1. *The Canterbury Tales* **is a frame narrative, a collision of the epic tradition and the novella of** *The Thousand and One Nights* **and Giovanni Boccaccio's** *Decameron.* In early spring, the poet encounters other pilgrims at the Tabard Inn of Southwark, where they are assembling for a trek to Canterbury—specifically the shrine of Thomas Becket, to whom they prayed during the winter months. Unlike the relatively static (yet bursting with narrative variety) frames of *The Thousand and One Nights* (Shahrazad's courtly storytelling reeducates the misogynist Shahrayar against a backdrop of social and political upheaval) and *Decameron* (young aristocrats entertain themselves and each other as they take refuge in the countryside during an outbreak of plague in Florence), Geoffrey Chaucer codifies and commodifies his frame narrative as a storytelling contest among socially and spiritually disparate storytellers. According to their presumptive master of ceremonies, Harry Bailly, the pilgrims will each tell tales of "*best sentence and most solas*"/"most meaning and delight" on the road to Canterbury. Among the many genres Chaucer embedded within this frame are confession ("The Wife of Bath's Prologue"), Arthurian romance ("The Wife of Bath's Tale"), sermons both sage ("The Parson's Tale") and ironic ("The Pardoner's Tale"), *roman d'antiquite* ("The Knight's Tale"), *fabliau* ("The Miller's Tale" and "The Reeve's Tale"), hagiography ("The Prioress's Tale" and "The Second Nun's Tale"), Breton *lai* ("The Franklin's Tale"),

de casibus tragedy ("The Monk's Tale"), and beast fable ("The Nun's Priest's Tale").

   a. **Further Reading:** Donaldson, E. Talbot. "Chaucer the Pilgrim." www.people.fas.harvard.edu/~chaucer/canttales/gp/pilgrim.html.

   b. **Suggested Search:** See "What's in a Frame? The Medieval Textualization of Traditional Storytelling" by Bonnie D. Irwin at http://journal.oraltradition.org/files/articles/10i/6_irwin.pdf.

2. **The variety of Geoffrey Chaucer's life experience—from child of the merchant class to court page, from customs collector to public works supervisor, from international ambassador to provincial member of Parliament—is unusually illuminative of his style and figure as a poet.** As a servant of three successive English kings, Chaucer was dispatched on a number of embassies—some of them secret—to Spain and Italy in particular. These missions apparently included peace negotiations and marriage arrangements. On one of his trips to Italy, Chaucer may have met Francis Petrarch and Giovanni Boccaccio, the underlying sources for much of his narrative output. Even if he did not, this would have been an invaluable opportunity to encounter their works in Italian editions. Unlike another major influence, Dante Alighieri, Chaucer tells the reader very little about himself or his times even when incorporating his persona into his narratives. Still we know more about Chaucer's life in the fourteenth century than we do of William Shakespeare's from the mid-sixteenth to the early seventeenth century. While French remained the language of his patrons Edward III and Richard II, Chaucer championed and popularized the London dialect of "English" as Dante and Boccaccio had vernacular Italian; the common tongue appropriate to so many of Chaucer's narrative voices became the standard of artistic expression.

   a. **Further Reading:** Pearsall, Derek. *The Life of Geoffrey Chaucer: A Critical Biography.* Wiley-Blackwell, 1994. This is a dense, comprehensive literary biography that avails itself of the most current biographical and historical source material.

   b. **Suggested Search:** Go to Harvard University's Chaucer site (www.people.fas.harvard.edu/~chaucer).

3. **Medieval narrative tended toward allegorical, didactic storytelling that emphasized monolithic truths over subjective experience and broad moral lessons over individual introspection.** In *Troilus and Criseyde*, Geoffrey Chaucer had begun to cautiously question the official, courtly version of events, while in *The Canterbury Tales* he began to reevaluate courtly authority from multiple points of view. "The General Prologue" presents its roster of pilgrims as a loose cross-section of the three estates (knights, priests, and peasants) with conflicting hierarchies and prebourgeois gray areas among the merchants and tradesmen.

Chaucer goes further than many of his predecessors, observing the storytellers-to-be and composing a detailed description (sometimes wittily critical) of them before finding himself invited into the pilgrims' fold and his own frame-narrative fabric. The presence of the poet on this presumably spiritual journey echoes Virgil's authoritative presence in Dante. The poet Chaucer's attempts to remain an observer backfire when he proves with "The Tale of Sir Thopas" that he is no Virgil. Before the Host (Harry Bailly) proposes the storytelling contest and defines its terms, the poet provides a diverse set of thematic and narrative expectations. That he subjects himself to the same scrutiny he reserves for the pilgrims affords *The Canterbury Tales* an unpretentious, freewheeling feel.

   a. **Further Reading:** Cooper, Helen. *The English Romance in Time: Transforming Motifs from Geoffrey of Monmouth to the Death of Shakespeare.* Oxford: Oxford University Press, 2004.

   b. **Suggested Search:** Go to the Chaucer Metapage (http://english complit.unc.edu/chaucer).

4. **Medieval readers placed a high value on *auctoritee*, sententiousness, and intertextuality. A work of literature might easily be considered valueless when its authors failed to acknowledge and position themselves within the hierarchy of authority observed by historians and philosophers or to produce quotable wise sayings.** This tradition extended from Homer and Hesiod, Virgil and Ovid, and Boccaccio and Dante, to name a few. In a sense, originality and innovation were beside the point if they did not serve the traditions that made them possible. This was neither plagiarism nor homage, as we might consider it today, but the mind-set of any serious poet. Readers habitually marked such passages in their personal copies, and many printed editions indicated sententiae with maniples. Geoffrey Chaucer occasionally refers readers to sources he has not lifted from entirely (the number of tales derived from Giovanni Boccaccio alone is staggering), usually in the "if you don't believe me, look at Livy" sense. Sometimes, however, he directs readers to alternate, preferred sources who deviate from the accepted masters. Beyond name-dropping and redacting famous narratives, Chaucer also employed sententiae, reinvented perennial genres, and assigned personalities to allegorical characters.

In "The General Prologue," the Host (innkeeper Harry Bailly) proposes a storytelling contest with specific rules and rewards: the pilgrims must tell stories "of best sentence and most solace," recalling Horace's "*dulce et utile*," and preferably drawing tales from their own experience. The tradesmen tend to observe the latter qualification, while those of higher rank typically do not. The poet aspires to a kind of social verite by insisting (and having the Host back him up) that the tales told on the Canterbury pilgrimage should also be appropriate to the storyteller.

Many disruptions occur when that subjective qualification is put to the test, as it is between the Miller and the Knight. Chaucer apparently composed what became "The Wife of Bath's Tale"—an Arthurian romance—for a masculine pilgrim. Though any account of his possible reasons remains apocryphal, he considered Alison the teller most appropriate to the tale. In the tradition of "quiting," discussed later, she is also reacting to the tale immediately preceding her prologue by appropriating classical exempla and scripture, which she frequently (and many scholars think willfully) misquotes and misinterprets. That the group, regardless of social class or position, agrees to the Host's rules suggests a social contract, further emphasizing Chaucer's pilgrims as a cross-section of fourteenth-century English society.

   a. **Further Reading:** Patterson, Lee. "'For the Wyves Love of Bathe': Feminine Rhetoric and Poetic Resolution in *The Roman de la Rose* and *The Canterbury Tales*." *Speculum* 58:3 (July 1983).

   b. **Suggested Search:** See the BBC 4 program *Chaucer*, discussed at www.bbc.co.uk/programmes/p003hycq.

5. **From Geoffrey Chaucer's knight down to the Wife of Bath's knight, the warrior class was supposed to uphold the values of chivalry (from *cheval*, French for "horse").** Writers of medieval romance, not to mention such political luminaries as Edward III of England, conflated moral duty and romance with the physical discipline of horsemanship. *The Roman de la Rose* (*The Romance of the Rose*), begun by Guillaume de Lorris (1230 C.E., 4,000 lines) and completed by Jean de Meun (c. 1275, 18,000 lines), was the classic courtly romance of idealized courtly love, combining Dantean and Petrarchan traditions with chivalric ideals and the structure of quest romance. Popular bedside reading during the High Middle Ages, *The Romance of the Rose* was a huge influence on "The Merchant's Tale," "The Squire's Tale," and, along with Giovanni Boccaccio's *Teseida*, "The Knight's Tale." The story is a dream vision, rife with classical and philosophical allegory. The young knight quests after "The Rose," his idealized lady love. Though romances remained popular reading for literate Europeans of all stations, by Chaucer's time stories and ideals of knights and ladies had also become material for satire and parody. The Old Woman of *The Roman de la Rose* may have inspired the character of Alison, the Wife of Bath, whose tale begins with a knight of Arthur's court raping a young woman. Though the tenets of courtly romance would see him executed immediately, the king is not the arbiter of justice that day. Instead, the queen, who understands a bit about illicit passion (see Dante's *Inferno*, Canto 5, and *Sir Gawain and the Green Knight*), offers the knight-rapist a quest for redemption. That quest, to answer the extremely subjective and rhetorical question "What do women most desire?," proves

fruitless until the knight encounters the Loathly Lady in the forest. His re-education comes at a price, but his marital misery becomes happily ever after when he learns to put the official answer (sovereignty in marriage) to practical use.

   a. **Further Reading:** *The Romance of the Rose*. Translated by Frances Horgan. Oxford: Oxford University Press, 1994, 2009.

   b. **Suggested Search:** See the British Library's digital editions of Caxton's Chaucer (www.bl.uk/treasures/caxton/homepage.html).

6. **A key theme of *The Canterbury Tales* as a whole—and at the center of many disputes on the road—is the notion of secular versus clerical authority.** Geoffrey Chaucer represents the ongoing battle between the Roman church and the English state in his intricate accounts of clashes between and within the three "estates" of English citizenry: Knights, Clerics, and Peasants. While misuse of social or church status tends toward comedy in the secular tales (Miller, Merchant) and saint-making in the clerical tales (Monk, Clerk), there are exceptions like "The Friar's Tale" (concerning a summoner's attempt to outfox Satan) and "The Nun's Priest's Tale" (a beast fable chock full of references to classical philosophy and medicine). In general, the closer two pilgrims are in social status, the more likely they are to quarrel. The encroachment of the merchant class upon economic and social privileges previously reserved for the knightly class makes matters all the more ambiguous.

   The Wife of Bath and the Pardoner straddle these social distinctions in a number of interesting ways. The Pardoner presents an unusual case. His profession—the selling of holy relics and papal indulgences—requires him to convince prospective clients of their sinfulness in evangelical terms. Yet the Pardoner (whom Chaucer portrays as a grotesque in "The General Prologue," down to a leather satchel of false relics in place of his manhood) is shameless about his own hypocrisy, preaching against iniquity for personal gain, making him iniquity's ultimate practitioner. It is also noteworthy that the Pardoner bears witness to the veracity of the Wife of Bath's claims, safeguarding her misappropriations of scripture against clerical protestation. His choice of vocation and high, castrato intonation, however, does her cause few favors with the Ecclesiasts of the group.

   a. **Further Reading:** Dinshaw, Carolyn. "'Eunuch Hermeneutics' and 'Glose/Bele Chose': The Wife of Bath and Her Glossators." In *Chaucer's Sexual Poetics*. Madison: University of Wisconsin Press, 1989.

   b. **Suggested Search:** Go to Dr. Debora B. Schwartz's university page on "The Three Estates" (http://cla.calpoly.edu/~dschwart/engl430/estates.html).

7. **Chaucer presents social relations as a series of verbal and thematic battles, a phenomenon known as "flyting" or "quiting" (from**

"**requite**"). While the Host is tickled when the drawing of straws establishes the highest-ranking secular authority as the lead story-teller, "The Knight's Tale"—a *roman d'antiquité*, or courtly romance, set in the age of Theseus—chafes the bum of at least one of its auditors. In spite of his drunkenness, the Miller is certain that love doesn't work in the real world as it does in *romans d'antiquite*. The natural order of things would allow the Monk—the highest-ranking member of the clergy among the Canterbury pilgrims—to follow the Knight. Instead of the sententious tale or a saint's life the Monk would have intoned, the Miller interrupts the storytelling hierarchy at its outset with a rollicking fabliau, a comic tale in verse. Fabliaux are always bawdy ("The Miller's Tale") and often on the dark side ("The Reeve's Tale"). In strong, deliberate contrast to "The Knight's Tale," the Miller includes himself in his tale as Robin, an adolescent eyewitness to its catalog of bad behaviors.

The requiting doesn't end there, perpetuated by Oswald the Reeve, a property manager whose duties included arbitrating disputes between tenant farmers and millers who were notorious for cheating their clients. The Reeve, formerly a carpenter, centers his fabliau on a miller to requite the Miller's treatment of John the Carpenter in his tale. Later, the Host, Harry Bailly, takes exception to the Pardoner's manipulation of honest, however superstitious, Christians. Most specifically, his diatribe against the Pardoner's sack of relics nearly turns violent, and the Knight intervenes. In another pointed example, Chaucer the Poet can't think on his feet when called upon for a "dainty tale of mirth" and recites instead a silly rhyme of knightly deeds ("The Tale of Sir Thopas") that goes nowhere. The Host chastises the poet, who comes back with a long, didactic, repetitive moral lesson in prose ("The Tale of Melibee"), which follows the Host's rules precisely and yet bores the entire party to tears. Though it may be incidental, Chaucer is the only traveler who tells more than one official tale. These requitings of wayward verisimilitude, personal affronts, poetic tastes, and excessive expectations further expand Chaucer's storytellers and their kaleidoscopic view of Englishness in the late fourteenth century.

By the time the Wife of Bath embarks on her prologue, the tone of quiting on the pilgrimage has moved from vengeful rhetoric to authoritative counter-tale and subtle intonation. Lest it appear that "quiting" in *The Canterbury Tales* is an exclusively retributive phenomenon, witness as the Pardoner, recognizing the Wife of Bath's preamble as just his brand of populist sermon, leaps to her aid in a supportive bit of audience participation. He claims, in a blast of full-blown hypocrisy only he could render sincere, that the Wife's revelations of "the tribulation that's in marriage" are sufficient to preclude his own unlikely nuptials. "The Wife of Bath's Prologue," though generically a confession (see

Augustine and Dante's *The Divine Comedy*), shares many features of the fabliau: domestic deception, sexual appetites paralleled with (or in place of) spiritual needs, and the comedic collision of a rigidly traditional older generation with a younger generation seeking knowledge and romantic freedom. Later, the Clerk (of the same calling as Dame Alison's fifth husband, Jenkin) sublimates a tasteful attack on the Wife of Bath into the tale of Patient Griselda, appropriated from the luminously authoritative Petrarch.

a. **Further Reading:** Kittredge, George Lyman. *Chaucer and His Poetry.* Cambridge, MA: Harvard University Press, 1915, 1970.

b. **Suggested Search:** Go to The Electronic Canterbury Tales (http://afdtk.uaa.alaska.edu/LBW_2_Trans.htm).

In-Class Activities

1. Given the poet's descriptions of the Canterbury pilgrims in "The General Prologue," ask students to determine which characters might be ideologically or thematically opposed to each other. What kinds of "flyting" relationships could develop from these oppositions? Divide the class into small groups or pairs and have each group choose a character pairing, and then compose a short, argumentative essay defending their adopted point of view. Present these as two sides of an in-class debate.

2. Though theatrical forms in Geoffrey Chaucer's England were dominated by the Mystery and Morality plays, how effective could the Wife of Bath's or Pardoner's tales be on stage? Choose a short scene to dramatize. Is it inherently dramatic? Is there enough for the characters to say, or would your audience require additional material? How would you stage the scene to most effectively convey the theme and feel of the tale it represents?

3. Consider a legendary episode from your experience and recreate it as either a courtly romance, a sermon, or a fabliau. You need not compose it in verse, but try to match the tone and voice with your experience of *The Canterbury Tales.*

Paper Topics/Suggestions for Writing

1. Consider three significant elements of Geoffrey Chaucer's frame narrative in *The Canterbury Tales.*

2. What are the relationships between the prologues and tales of the Wife of Bath and the Pardoner?

3. What is the function of "quiting" in *The Canterbury Tales?*

4. Consider three traits that distinguish the Wife of Bath from other fourteenth-century Englishwomen.

5. Considering the descriptions of "The General Prologue," how are the Wife of Bath's and Pardoner's tales appropriate for their tellers?

Resources

British Library. Caxton's Chaucer. www.bl.uk/treasures/caxton/homepage .html.
> Digital editions of the fifteenth-century originals of the British Library, with background on Caxton, links on Chaucer, timeline, and digital versions of the texts.

Chaucer. BBC 4 program. Broadcast February 9, 2006.
> Features Melvyn Brag; Carolyne Larrington, Tutor in Medieval English at St. John's College, Oxford; Helen Cooper, Professor of Medieval and Renaissance English at the University of Cambridge; Ardis Butterfield, Reader in English at University College London.

Harvard University. Chaucer. www.people.fas.harvard.edu/~chaucer.
> Chronology, biography, satires, translations, cultural background, bibliography, and links to related subjects.

Kline, Daniel T. The Electronic Canterbury Tales. University of Alaska Anchorage. http://afdtk.uaa.alaska.edu/LBW_2_Trans.htm.
> Digital project with compendium, papers, background, and hyper-links.

Schwartz, Debora B. California Polytechnic State University page. www .calpoly.edu/~dschwart.
> Links to online texts, images, bibliography, and extensive background information on medieval and Renaissance writing.

33rd International Congress of Medieval Studies. The Chaucer Metapage. http://englishcomplit.unc.edu/chaucer.
> Digitial project links to university-based scholarly digital projects and sites on Chaucer, works, bibliography, teaching suggestions, and background.

SIR GAWAIN AND THE GREEN KNIGHT

With head helmeted and lance in hand
he scrambled towards skylight in that strange
    abyss.
Then he heard on the hillside, from behind a
    hard rock
and beyond the brook, a blood-chilling noise.
What! It cannoned though the cliffs as if they
    might crack,
like the scream of a scythe being ground on a
    stone.
What! It whined and wailed, like a waterwheel.
What! It rasped and rang, raw on the ear.
"My God," cried Gawain, "that grinding is a
    greeting.
My arrival is honored with the honing of an
    axe."
(lines 2197–2206)

Topics for Lecture or Discussion

1. ***Sir Gawain and the Green Knight*** **is an Arthurian romance, a sub-
   genre that embodies countless characters and narratives beyond
   the Grail legends. Medieval romances tended toward the courtly,
   the chivalric, and the typical nexus of these behavioral prescriptions, the quest.** But Arthur is usually connected—as he is in *Sir
   Gawain*—with the Trojan diaspora, a tradition that finds Brutus, another
   of Priam's many sons, traversing the European continent to the island of
   Albion, defeating the race of giants there, and renaming the land "Britain." This long-standing desire to validate the founding of nation-states
   by connecting them with the Homeric past is perhaps best expressed in
   the legendary Brut's original name for the city of London: Troynovaunt,
   or "New Troy." This also connects the founding of Britain with that of
   Rome, realized by the descendants of Brut's brother-in-law, Aeneas.
   The poets of romance linked themselves with the epic tradition out of
   respect and to demonstrate their learning and classical erudition, but
   eventually they used the Greco-Roman legendary world as a kind of
   shorthand for their own mythologies. Unlike the tenuous relationship
   between pre-Christian culture and Christian belief in Beowulf, the
   God of Arthurian legend is Father, Son, and Spirit, inextricable from the
   Roman Catholic Church since the fourth century c.e. From the outside,
   Camelot is perfect, and from the inside, it is nearly so. The exalted status of Arthur's court among man-made things is unimpeachable. It has,

in fact, become "hypercivilized," a state also suggested in "Lanval" and in "The Wife of Bath's Tale." Only the natural world, tempered by the supernatural intervention of the "faerie" realm, can challenge it.

   a. **Further Reading:** Pearsall, Derek. *Arthurian Romance: A Short Introduction.* San Francisco: Wiley-Blackwell, 2003.

   b. **Suggested Search:** Go to "Life in the Middle Ages" (www.middle-ages.org.uk/life-in-middle-ages.htm).

2. **Sir Gawain is well intentioned and capable and is Arthur's nephew—in short, an ideal candidate to survive the Green Knight's "game" and glorify his uncle's kingdom—but his status as the Round Table's untested weakness is the reason he must answer the challenge.** Medieval romance, like Arthur's right to rule, is rooted in the oral epic. The genre's thematic juxtapositions and oppositions are about as monolithic as can be: the courtly world versus the liminal and primitive realms (the forest or wilderness, to which legends inappropriate in polite society have been banished; "the West," specifically Wales, where legend and superstition still thrive and may even claim their origins); the mythic past versus the preordained present; pagan versus Christian; natural production versus human manufacture; the chivalric ideal versus its manifestations; ritual versus pageant; and destiny versus happenstance. The construct of "chivalry" (the word's original meaning referred to a fighting man whose gear included a horse, while the word "knight" derives from the Anglo-Saxon word for "fellow") cannot rest—it must be constantly tested and improved.

   a. **Further Reading:** Cox, Catherine. "Genesis and Gender in Sir Gawain and the Green Knight." *The Chaucer Review* (2001) 35:4 (2001): 379–90.

   b. **Suggested Search:** Go to Ravensgard Medieval Poetry and Literature (www.ravensgard.org/gerekr/liter.html).

3. **In the fourteenth century, many poets on both sides of the English Channel were using romance as the stuff of satire or imposing Christian morality on the antique world;** *Sir Gawain and the Green Knight* **reincorporates several tropes of the quest romance.** While Sir Gawain's quest to meet the Green Knight is essentially a red herring designed to get him off the couch and into the wicked world, the actual meaning of his journey is always there to be discovered and pondered. Does the magical green girdle save Sir Gawain, or is it the Christian notion (emphasized in Dante) that a lesson unshared is a lesson unlearned? Whether he ends up beheaded because he remained true to his bargain with Bertilak and confessed taking the green girdle, or because he finds that the Green Knight wants to chop off his head in earnest, Sir Gawain's sin of faith-breaking can have no resonance if word of it fails to reach Arthur and his knights. The beheading game,

derived from Celtic legend, only completes its meaning when we consider all points of view. Each angle is comedic and waxes progressively sillier as hart hunt, boar hunt, and fox hunt are breathlessly described and then inexplicably requited with kisses. The season is also significant. Medieval romances typically open in and do their business in the spring, mating season for most species (not least of all Homo sapiens). Although Christmas and New Year's festivals look forward to the rebirth of the land and the human soul, winter in the temperate regions is a season of death. In spite of the cold and gray, the Green Knight remains green and vibrant—what dies for humanity, symbolically or otherwise, springs eternal and immortal.

    a. **Further Reading:** Cooper, Helen. *The English Romance in Time.* New York: Oxford University Press, 2008.

    b. **Suggested Search:** Go to www.lib.rochester.edu/camelot/gawmenu .htm.

4. **Sir Gawain represents chivalry and Arthur's court through acts of possession. By looking and behaving like a knight, he exemplifies knighthood to his beholders.** His shining armor brings the virtues of the Round Table to the world at large, imposing its glitter upon the green world. Bertilak's courtiers (likely unaware of the elaborate game their master and mistress have arranged) worship Sir Gawain based purely upon his gentilesse and sophisticated erudition. While Sir Gawain embodies many of the virtues they praise him for, he is master of none of them, save these elegant but largely impractical affectations. His humility is often overruled by a need to "represent." What is ultimately being tested, then, is the Arthurian ideal rather than Sir Gawain's ability to embody its myriad aspects in one body, soul, and mind. If the individual fails to uphold a superhuman value system, the system reveals itself as inherently flawed. But the game is unnecessarily rigged, since human frailty is guaranteed. Despite Dante's precedent of intense self-scrutiny on a universal scale and Chaucer's emphasis on psychological realism within and among communities, the Sir Gawain poet entrenches his romance and its lessons in the allegorical absolutism of *Beowulf* and the classical epics.

    a. **Further Reading:** Kittredge, George Lyman. *A Study of Sir Gawain and the Green Knight.* Cambridge, MA: Harvard University Press, 1960.

    b. **Suggested Search:** Search for "courtly behavior, Order of the Garter" at http://cla.calpoly.edu/~dschwart/engl513/courtly/courtly.htm.

5. **While it echoes other points of scriptural and philosophical reference, such as the Pentateuch, Psalms, and Aristotle's five classical elements, *Sir Gawain and the Green Knight* distinguishes itself— and helps create the seemingly closed world of the poem—with an**

arguably unique numerology. The year-and-a-day quest limitation is relatively commonplace in quest romance, as are permutations of the number 3 carried over from the epic tradition. If some traditions, including the Book of Revelations, view the number 6 as a signifier of temptation, fallen humanity, and dire, postlapsarian consequences, the Gawain poet appears to view manifestations of the number 5 as defenses against a second fall. Sir Gawain's own reliance on systems of five, especially in preparation for a journey into darkness, loneliness, the mythic West, and the icy North, suggests that his greatest fear, not to mention the fears of others for him, is that the civilized constructs on which chivalry, chastity, and the human imperative are based might crumble under the scrutiny of the eternal. Depending on the tradition, the "five joys of Mary" usually numbers 7–15. The five most likely invoked by her image inside Sir Gawain's shield are the Annunciation (which signifies a righteous call to pious duty), Christ's Nativity, Resurrection, and Ascension into Paradise (which reflect the expectations and, hopefully, milestones of a pious, Christian soul), and Mary's Assumption of the Crown of Heaven. Sir Gawain's detailed arming scene parallels many such in other works and yet sets its subject up to fall. He vows to follow the path of unreasonable expectation, giving his pure intentions and the Round Table's faith in him—and, by extension, itself and Arthur's legacy—the tragic inevitability of a Second Fall of Man.

a. **Further Reading:** Archibald, Elizabeth, and Ad Putter, eds. *The Cambridge Companion to the Arthurian Legend*. Cambridge, MA: Cambridge University Press, 2009.

b. **Suggested Search:** Search for "classical/medieval numerology" at http://web.cn.edu/kwheeler/documents/Numerology.pdf.

In-Class Activities

1. There are many ways of reading *Sir Gawain and the Green Knight* and what Sir Gawain represents in the context of the poem. In groups of three, locate two significant moments in the poem that do not directly involve the Green Knight. In a committee, compose a short prose narrative for each, filtered through the group's reading of Sir Gawain's character.

2. Compose a *Sir Gawain and the Green Knight*-style stanza, complete with bob-and-wheel. Students should choose either an object that needs describing, a moment of action in need of further definition, or perhaps a thought or an action unexplored by the Gawain poet. You might even go so far as to assign potential passages from a list and then have students work as a group to arrange them in an ideal running order, building transitions where appropriate.

3. In small groups, discuss and compile a list of contemporary alternatives to the "game" devised by Bertilak and Morgan le Fay.

Paper Topics/Suggestions for Writing

1. The Gawain poet blends a relatively informal narrative voice with a number of conspicuous literary devices. What do you consider "literary" or sententious about *Sir Gawain and the Green Knight*?

2. How does the theme of self-awareness, a major feature of epic poetry, figure in *Sir Gawain and the Green Knight*?

3. How does Sir Gawain's journey of self-discovery complement or complicate the greater scope of Arthurian legend?

Resources

Georgetown University. The Labyrinth: Resources for Medieval Studies. www8.georgetown.edu/departments/medieval/labyrinth/labyrinth-home.html.
   Comprehensive site devoted to all aspects of medieval history.
Ravensgard Medieval Poetry and Literature. www.ravensgard.org/gerekr/liter.html.
   Website divided by genre, location, and period, and including weighty content on separate pages devoted to cultures, arts and crafts, society, and bibliographies.
Schwartz, Debora. Courtly Love. California Polytechnic State University. http://cla.calpoly.edu/~dschwart/engl513/courtly/courtly.htm.
   Links to Harvard Chaucer page, scholarly essays, university sites, images, handouts, and lesson plans.
Sir Gawain and the Green Knight. New verse translation by Benedict Flynn. Naxos, 2008, CD.
University of Rochester. The Camelot Project. www.lib.rochester.edu/camelot/gawmenu.htm.
   Readings, symbols and motifs, and background information.

EVERYMAN

You think sin in the beginning full sweet,
Which in the end causeth the soul to weep,
When   the body lieth in clay.
—Messenger, *Everyman*

Topics for Lecture or Discussion

1. **As his name indicates, Everyman is an allegorical character who represents all human beings.** Everyman's allegorical character raises several interesting questions: Are Everyman's vices predicated of all humanity? Is Everyman's course to redemption a model that all human beings can or should follow? Are Everyman's sorrow and disillusionment with the world common aspects of human experience? In asking these questions, we can see both the advantages and limitations of allegorical depictions, for while on the one hand we can say that not all human beings believe in God—though Everyman does indeed—on the other hand his struggles with his conscience, his suffering, and his desire for and companionship with Knowledge are certainly typical aspects of human experience. So, too, all human beings must, like Everyman, encounter death and grapple with the fact of human mortality, and when Everyman sorrowfully pleads with Death to grant him more life, we can hear a sentiment that people often echo in their own experiences with death.
   a. **Further Reading:** Copeland, Rita, and Peter T. Struck, eds. *The Cambridge Companion to Allegory.* Cambridge: Cambridge University Press, 2010.
   b. **Suggested Search:** Search for "allegory" at LION Literature Online (lion.chadwyck.com) for several helpful articles and reference entries about the genre and techniques of allegory.

2. **As part of the tradition of morality plays, *Everyman* is meant to delight its audiences, but it also has a didactic or catechetical nature.** Through its humor, dialogue, clever contrasts, and allegorical references, *Everyman* has much to recommend it as a delightful, fun play to watch. However, the overarching story serves as a potent reminder to the audience that death and divine judgment are unavoidable facts of human existence, and consequently, the audience should try to live penitential and virtuous lives. In many particular lines of the play, a similar catechesis takes place. For example, when Death introduces himself as Death, Everyman responds, "O Death, thou comest when I had thee least in mind" (line 119). While this situation could be acted with great comical effect, Everyman's response exemplifies a lack of readiness for death

that was held to be a common and serious failing by the medieval Church. This instance serves to educate the members of the audience while amusing them, for it reminds them that they too should be prepared for death, since they know neither the day nor the hour.

a. **Further Reading:** Pineas, Rainer. "The English Morality Play as a Weapon of Religious Controversy." *Studies in English Literature, 1500–1900* 2.2 (1962): 157–180.

b. **Suggested Search:** At www.luminarium.org, a search for "Everyman" results in a helpful page with a collection of links, further reading suggestions, and pages discussion medieval drama in England.

3. **Penance, a central theme in *Everyman*, is necessary because of past sins and failings that have separated Everyman from God.** When Everyman learns that he is going to die, he admits that "all unready is my book of reckoning" (line 134), and his thoughts turn briefly to penance. Yet it is only after he is abandoned by Fellowship, Kindred, Cousin, and Goods that he realizes the extent to which he needs to perform penance. His previous life, focused upon the acquisition of goods and spending time in society, has not prepared him for his final judgment and has left him alone in his time of need. Good Deeds, who would accompany him, is bound to the ground by his sins, and she directs him to Knowledge, who begins Everyman's course of penance. Penance in *Everyman* is not only a necessary course of action for the play's hero with respect to his past sins, but is also important because it gives him access to other advantages: he is able to see through the limited benefits of Discretion, Strength, Five-Wits, and Beauty. Penance, then, is not only concerned with past sins, but also with future knowledge and growth in proper virtues.

a. **Further Reading:** Cunningham, John. "Comedic and Liturgical Restoration in *Everyman*." *Comparative Drama* 22.2 (1988): 162–173.

b. **Suggested Search:** At youtube.com, a search for "Everyman PCC Performing Arts Center" results in a recording of a stage performance of *Everyman* at Portland Community College.

4. **Everyman follows a course of penance that includes the three traditional Catholic parts of penance: contrition, confession, and satisfaction.** The late-medieval Church viewed penance as a sacrament that consisted of three separate parts or actions that the penitent must take. Contrition is the recognition of past sins and a resolve to correct one's life in the future; confession is the declaration of those sins to a priest who would then grant absolution and assign certain acts and prayers as the proper form of reparation for the wrongs done; finally, satisfaction is the performance of the penance enjoined by the confessor. In *Everyman*, we find all three elements in clear succession: filled with contrition for his past sins, Everyman approaches Confession and recounts his

failings, and finally performs the satisfaction of scourging himself and offering the pain up in reparation for his sins.

   a. **Further Reading**: Paulson, Julie. "Death's Arrival and Everyman's Separation." *Theatre Survey* 48 (2007): 121–141.

   b. **Suggested Search**: At Vimeo.com, a search for "Everyman part one" results in an adaptation of *Everyman* in a modern setting.

5. **While the fact that all people must die is at the heart of the plot in *Everyman*, nevertheless, the play is not a morbid or dark work, but one that celebrates life as an opportunity to live according to God's commands and to grow in virtue.** In the opening scene, the Messenger identifies the theme of death and states, "our lives and ending shows / How transitory we be all day" (lines 5–6). He stresses that human existence is a passing, transitory thing, and that this should remind each person to be attentive to the state of his or her soul. However, Everyman's subsequent encounter with death is comical, and even as he worries while his companions desert him, the play maintains a light and humorous tone. In fact, this lighter element in the play is in keeping with the Christian teleology in which life and death are understood: death is sorrowful since life is a good thing, but death is more importantly the joyful beginning of the just soul's enjoyment of God in heaven. As Knowledge states after Everyman descends into the grave, "Now hath he made ending, / Methinketh that I hear angels sing / And make great joy and melody / Where Everyman's soul received shall be" (lines 890–893). The joys of the hoped-for beatific vision surpasses the sorrow of death.

   a. **Further Reading**: Spinrad, Phoebe S. *The Summons of Death on the Medieval and Renaissance English Stage.* Columbus: Ohio State University Press, 1987. See esp. pp. 68–85.

   b. **Suggested Search**: A Google Images search for "medieval depictions of death" results in many interesting images of death speaking with people or taking them away.

In-Class Activities

1. Break the class into small groups, and assign a different passage of *Everyman* to each group. The group must study the passage and find some aspect that might be rendered comically when acted (this can include physical comedy that works in tandem with lines from the play). Discuss the relationship between the comedy and the educational/catechetical elements in *Everyman*.

2. Divide the students into several sections, each of which must perform a part of the play in front of the class (by dividing the class, you can ensure that all of the students participate, since there are only a limited number of roles in the play).

3. Assign a different morality or mystery cycle play to each student and ask each one to give a brief presentation to the class on the play's similarities and differences with *Everyman*. Discuss the ways in which Everyman is and is not representative of English medieval literature.

Paper Topics/Suggestions for Writing

1. Write an essay in which you identify and explain three different aspects of Everyman's character as generally representative of human beings.

2. Why is Everyman abandoned by nearly everyone? Consider the significance that not only Fellowship leaves him, but that Kindred does as well. What does this indicate about Everyman's situation? Does this comment in some way on all human beings?

3. Write an essay in which you contrast the allegorical elements in *Everyman* with another allegorical work that you have read (for example, Dante's *The Divine Comedy*). What are the hallmarks or generic traits of allegorical works? Where are those apparent in *Everyman*?

4. What sort of conflict takes place in *Everyman*? How is that conflict resolved? Is Everyman heroic in this conflict? Is there an antagonist in *Everyman*? Does Everyman triumph? If so, how? If not, why not?

5. Consider *Everyman* in comparison with another of the works of drama from the anthology (for example, *Oedipus the King*, *Hamlet*, or *Endgame*). Write an essay about the two works' presentation of human life and death. What is virtue and vice in these works? What is the teleological conception that informs these works?

Resources

Beadle, Richard, and Alan J. Fletcher, eds. *The Cambridge Companion to Medieval English Theatre*. 2nd ed. Cambridge: Cambridge University Press, 2008.

> This collection of essays includes a considerable amount of helpful background information on medieval drama and theatrical culture in England, and the essay "Morality Plays" by Pamela M. King (pp. 235–262) should be particularly helpful to students of *Everyman*.

Gray, Douglas. *Later Medieval English Literature*. Oxford: Oxford University Press, 2008.

> Gray's book serves as an excellent overview of the literature from the same period in which *Everyman* was written, and instructors seeking to gain an understanding of the larger context (especially concerning English prose and poetry as well as drama) should find this an informative and accessible volume.

Lester, G.A., ed. *Three Late Medieval Morality Plays*: Mankind, Everyman, Mundus et Infans. New York: W.W. Norton, 2006.

> This volume collects three morality plays, including *Everyman*, and is recommended for students or instructors who wish to read more primary texts in this tradition.

Paulson, Julie. "Death's Arrival and Everyman's Separation." *Theatre Survey* 48 (2007): 121–141.

> Julie Paulson's article is a clear argument about the relationship between penance and community in *Everyman*, and *Everyman's* place within the tradition of medieval English dramas. This article would be a good choice if you would like to assign additional critical reading to your students.

CHRISTINE DE PIZAN
The Book of the City of Ladies

Topics for Lecture or Discussion

1. **Christine de Pizan (ca. 1364–ca. 1431) is considered the first professional woman writer of the Western world, her career precipitated by her husband's death and the need to find a means of supporting her three children and other family members.** De Pizan describes her husband's death as having lost her dearest friend and the "captain" of her sunken ship (readers will find her grieving in the poem "All Alone Am I," in the "Medieval Lyrics" section in this volume). Her writings center on attacking misogyny, evident in her participation in the "Quarrel on the Romance of the Rose," for which she objected to vulgar terms and sexual references that the writer, Jean de Meun, had attached to noble women in the text. De Pizan was a prolix reader and acknowledged her habit to "engage in the pursuit of knowledge" in the work's opening; she explained what motivated her to write *The Book of the City of Ladies*: determined to put down difficult studies and instead read from Matheolus's work, she discovered that rather than offering "praise for women" it instead contained immoral language and slander. Interestingly, she is willing to consider Matheolus's and other men's arguments objectively; she reviews her life and those of fellow women yet determines that her reliance on personal experience and observation of her peers is flawed due to the overwhelming number of publications that corroborate this misogynist view of women ("My understanding was too crude and ill-informed to recognize the great flaws in myself and other women; these men had to be right"). How does the mixed tone of de Pizan's poem "All Alone Am I" parallel the mixed emotions she expresses in the book's opening chapter?
   a. **Further Reading:** Altmann, Barbara, and Deborah McGrady, eds. *Christine de Pizan: A Casebook.* New York: Routledge, 2003.
   b. **Suggested Search:** Go to www.themiddleages.net/people/christine _pisan.html.

2. **Though considered a medieval work, *The Book of the City of Ladies* prefigures humanist approaches to scholarship and social convention. Humanism did not reject Christian traditions but was more focused on the material world and human potential in this lifetime rather than a Christian afterlife.** Humanist writing included elements of satire that could be humorous or melancholy, featured utopian scenarios, and promoted the view that education using ludic (playful) activities, rather than rule by an authority or a study of rhetoric, could

guide civilians to a virtuous and civic life. In *The Book of the City of Ladies*, de Pizan uses allegory to construct a utopian, symbolic city that is ruled over by the ladies Reason, Justice, and Rectitude, who engage the writer in a witty, philosophical dialogue through which lessons are given on eliminating misogynist stereotypes. As an allegorical work, famous women of history physically form the building blocks of the city, thereby becoming foundations and participants of the entire construct (using the grammatical device *antiphrasis*, the women are presented in a positive light in spite of having been criticized and subordinated by men of earlier times). Lady Reason helps de Pizan lay the city's foundations with women who advanced science and made other contributions to human civilization (e.g., the leaders Dido and Semiramis), Lady Rectitude constructs the walls from women following God's will, and Lady Justice adds a roof composed of women saints and martyrs to reflect God's will. What advantages does de Pizan gain by presenting the work as an allegory (extended metaphor in which principles and concepts take human form) rather than as a nonfiction treatise?

    a. **Further Reading:** Brown-Grant, Rosalind. *Christine de Pizan and the Moral Defence of Women: Reading beyond Gender.* Cambridge: Cambridge University Press, 1999.

    b. **Suggested Search:** Go to www.bbc.co.uk/programmes/b00cnpkm.

3. **Chivalry as a code of conduct to be practiced by male knights is represented, interestingly, through the virtues of important women from history ("So much good has been brought into the world thanks to the intelligence of women" [chap. 37]).** Jean de Meun had translated *The Art of Chivalry* by Vegetius which, along with fourteenth-century writings, is later synthesized in Christine de Pizan's *The Book of Deeds of Arms and of Chivalry* (ca. 1410). *The Book of Deeds* discusses "Just War," a theme that she revisits under the guise of chivalry in *The Book of the City of Ladies.* Here the story of Minerva as a chaste inventress who is deified by the people of Athens offers a lesson on chivalry: Minerva's statue symbolizes the chivalric duty of a knight to enforce justice, the inscrutability of his thoughts, his unfailing courage, foresight, and self-protection from the vicissitudes of Fortune, his obligations as a diplomat of justice, his vigilance and cunning, and his preparation to defend his country "both day and night . . . to do what is right" (chap. 34). De Pizan also borrowed largely from Giovanni Boccaccio's *Famous Women*, which provided biographies of famous women from history and from the tales of *Decameron* (Day 4, stories 1 and 5); from his works she took ideas about the danger of forcing maidens into convents when they should instead be given a virtuous education and permitted to choose a religious or secular life of their own volition. Do the ideas of chivalry promoted in de Pizan's work compare to those

appearing in *Sir Gawain and the Green Knight, Song of Roland,* or
Marie de France's *Lais* (all in this volume)?

    a. **Further Reading:** Quilligan, Maureen. *The Allegory of Female
Authority: Christine de Pizan's "Cité des Dames."* Ithaca, NY: Cornell
University Press, 1991.

    b. **Suggested Search:** Go to http://cla.calpoly.edu/~dschwart/engl203
/christine1.html.

4. **Christine de Pizan employs complex rhetorical and literary devices,
including allegory, elements of fable, antiphrasis, and references to
philosophers, histories, and myths that will lend credibility to her
work.** Scholars identify four types of allegory during the medieval period:
literal (no underlying meaning), typological (connects Old and New Testament events), tropological (presents a "moral" or lesson to be applied to
present culture), and anagogical (prophetic or futuristic). De Pizan's
work, as allegory, introduces three concepts in flesh (Reason, Rectitude,
and Justice) to construct a divine city for women. In chapter 2, the three
goddesses visit (as fairy godmothers in medieval fairy tales), citing Aristotle, Plato, and the Church Doctors as proof that even the most educated writers are fallible and in discord with each other. They encourage
her to read texts using antiphrasis, to interpret fables and texts in the
opposite of their apparent or obvious meaning ("Turn them to your
advantage, no matter what the author's original intent"). The "goddesses"
are utilized in de Pizan's text to displace the fallible author from the writing and to place its authority in the hands of God, who commands the
three goddesses ("This has been decreed by God, who has chosen you to
do this with our help and guidance"). Symbolic objects appear, including
the first lady's shining mirror, in which a thing's true nature is reflected
and measured. There are classical references to Greek and Roman gods,
Troy and Thebes, and the Amazons as proof of cities and civilizations
that fell to ruin because they were earthly rather than divine constructs
to protect it from assault. Antiphrasis is also used in the philosophical
debates between de Pizan and the Ladies: Lady Reason and de Pizan
discuss women's strengths not as "fearful creatures with weak, frail bodies" but, rather, as stronger due to their physical beauty, kindness, and
generosity; Lady Reason cites the hideous deformity of Aristotle and the
sickliness of Alexander the Great as proof of their weaknesses and states
that their brute strength wins wars but does not allow them the divine
attributes of avoiding cruelty, murder, and violence; she also cites Semiramis and Thamiris, the Amazonian maidens Menalippe and Hippolyta
(female warriors with physical strength equal to that of men and even
able to defeat the strongest man and the heroes of antiquity—Hercules
and Theseus, respectively—with their strength and beauty), Dido (who
had the "virtue and valor of a man," chap. 46), and Penthesilea, a virgin

leader of the Amazons who was killed by Pyrrhus only after a horde of men encircled her (they "took a long time to do his bidding because . . . they were extremely afraid of approaching her," chap. 19). In sciences, Lady Reason credits Carmentis, for creating the alphabet, and Minerva, for her many inventions, including oil extraction, chariot design, and the forging of armor (Christine de Pizan cites Giovanni Boccaccio on Minerva as a flesh-and-blood girl revered as a goddess due to her extraordinary knowledge), and for her oath of chastity, which led to her deification as a goddess (chap. 34). Ceres and Isis advanced civilization from a hunter-gatherer to an agrarian society (chap. 38), and Lavinia saved her son and led a nation in spite of political upheaval. As a reader, do Christine de Pizan's references to historical figures and philosophers and her use of literary and grammatical devices further validate her position?

a. **Further Reading:** Brabant, Margaret. *Politics, Gender and Genre: The Political Thought of Christine de Pizan.* Boulder, CO: Westview Press, 1992.

b. **Suggested Search:** Go to the King's College website devoted to Christine de Pizan (http://departments.kings.edu/womens_history chrisdp.html), which includes background information, an annotated bibliography, and links.

In-Class Activities

1. Fictional cartography: Students will gather in groups and design maps that represent "the city of the ladies," based on details provided from the excerpts.

2. Famous women of modern times: In the excerpt provided, Christine de Pizan constructs her city's foundation of women who advanced human civilization with their inventions and technologies. In this activity, the class will construct the foundation for a new city, based on modern women (from the eighteenth century onward) who have promoted the sciences and industry in world civilizations. The purpose of this activity is to increase students' appreciation of modern women pioneers.

3. Writing a new code of chivalry: Students will examine the qualities promoted in Christine de Pizan's explication of chivalry and then design their own code, outlining a modern code of chivalry, or "just war."

Paper Topics/Suggestions for Writing

1. Discuss Christine de Pizan's use of allegory in *The Book of the City of Ladies*, making sure to define what type of medieval allegory is utilized.

2. Define the term *antiphrasis*, and cite at least three examples from the text in which de Pizan employs this device.

3. Compare de Pizan's writing style and content in the poem "All Alone Am I" to the ideas and structure presented in *The Book of the City of Ladies*.

4. How is de Pizan's book relevant to outlining the code of conduct for chivalry? Discuss the code of chivalry during her time, and provide two examples of specific heroines who exemplify chivalrous behaviors for men to emulate.

5. Compare de Pizan as a European aristocratic female writer to either of the following Japanese aristocratic female writers: Sei Shōnagon (*The Pillow Book*) or Murasaki Shikibu (*The Tale of Genji*).

Resources

"The Book of the City of Ladies." With Kathryn Hunt. BBC Radio 4 Extra Programme, Episode 5, 2011. www.bbc.co.uk/programmes/b00cnpkm. Scholarly discussion of Pizan's text.

King's College. http://departments.kings.edu/womens_history/chrisdp.html. This site is devoted to Christine de Pizan, with background information, an annotated bibliography, and links.

Schwartz, Debora B. A Woman's Voice: Christine de Pizan. California Polytechnic State University. http://cla.calpoly.edu/~dschwart/engl203/christine1.html.
This site contains background information on Christine de Pizan, questions, suggested assignments, links, and related readings.

United States Naval Academy. Medieval Chivalry. www.usna.edu/Users/history/abels/hh315/Chivalry.htm. Site maintained by Dr. Richard Abels.
This site offers comprehensive background information on medieval chivalry, a history of modern and medieval chivalry, definitions of terms, links, a bibliography, and citations from medieval sources.

III. Europe and the New World:
Early Modernity

HUMANISM AND THE REDISCOVERY
OF THE CLASSICAL PAST

Topics for Lecture or Discussion

1. **Humanists did not reject Christian traditions but were more focused on the material world and human potential in this lifetime rather than a Christian afterlife. Their primary motto was *ad fontes*, or "back to the sources."** Therefore, they researched and indulged more in the works of the ancient Greeks and Romans than their medieval predecessors, and they also sought more civic involvement and to inspire people, through mass education, to perform virtuous deeds. Practical professions and scientific inquiry were emphasized, and studies (*studia humanitatis*) would include rhetoric, history, and philosophy—all aimed at creating citizens that would engage their communities in virtuous action. In addition to mass printing using the printing press, the use of vernacular rather than Latin during the period increasingly allowed readership to expand. Two branches of Renaissance humanism (that often overlap) include Hermeticism and Neoplatonism, the former focusing on esoteric writings, the latter on works from classical antiquity. Many post-nineteenth-century scholars consider Petrarch the first early modern humanist, as he emphasized that the "age of Darkness" could be ended only through the study and imitation of the classics. What are some rumors you have heard about the medieval ages, and how do they relate to what you have learned about the evolution of knowledge and civic duty leading into the Renaissance?

   a. **Further Reading:** Kraye, Jill, ed. *The Cambridge Companion to Renaissance Humanism*. Cambridge: Cambridge University Press, 1996.

   b. **Suggested Search:** Go to the Library of Congress at www.loc.gov /exhibits/vatican/toc.html for images and objects, texts, and background information on Renaissance humanism.

2. **Humanism includes elements of satire that may be humorous or melancholy, depending on the writer's approach. Humanists believed that education through *ludic* (playful) activities, rather than rule by an authority or the study of rhetoric, will guide civilians to a virtuous and civic life.** Rabelais's Abbey of Thélème is a utopian humanist society based on education, civic engagement, and virtue, without an oppressive authority. The members engage in festivity and sport without the need for labor. In Machiavelli's "Letter to Francesco Vettori," the writer is clearly an agriculturalist, yet he carries books of poetry to read during his daily labors. After work, he plays

games with the local inn patrons and then returns home to study before bed. Rabelais and More create satirical utopias, whereas Machiavelli and Du Bellay write darker works. The debate between Panurge and Thaumaste is a deliberation on the value of vernacular and gestural communication versus Latin and rhetorical education, while the Abbey of Thélème mocks the traditional Catholic cloister. More's *Utopia* (see separate module) ridicules Westerners and introduces societies in which material wealth is irrelevant because of the infinite resources and lack of greed. On the other hand, Machiavelli mocks the Medici family and tyrannical rule in order to promote a republican form of government (see separate module). Du Bellay, in Sonnet 3 of "The Antiquities of Rome," warns that Rome's proud attempt to "vanquish all" led, ironically, to its own demise. For Du Bellay (Sonnet 5), Rome's beauty is also its failure—its art and culture are lifeless, and only its writings are worth safeguarding; similarly, it is remarked in Sonnet 13, after a long list of tragedies, that, in spite of all its natural disasters and destruction, people still admire and remember Rome's glory.

a. **Further Reading:** Huizinga, Johan. *Homo Ludens.* New York: Routledge, 2008.

b. **Suggested Search:** Go to the Allentown Art Museum's "The Renaissance Connection" site at www.renaissanceconnection.org, which contains activities for a broad range of Renaissance disciplines, including science, math, art, social studies, and language arts.

3. **The word "utopia" means "nowhere," because these societies are not only fictional but are also believed to be impossible to maintain.** Indeed, Rabelais's Abbey of Thélème appears to be a criticism of and response to Catholic monasteries and cloisters. Rabelais states that there are no protective walls and no sundials or regulation of tasks. Only good-looking and appealing people are permitted entry (rather than forced, as are ugly and disabled people) into convents, departure is permitted, and the Christian vows of "chastity, poverty, and obedience" are replaced with "honor, wealth, freedom." Rabelais, in humanist fashion, supports the contention that civic virtue is promoted by a humanist education rather than by Christian dogma. In Book I, Chapter 54, Rabelais provides an inscription listing the types of people not permitted, including hypocrites, bigots, impostors, lawyers, gouty judges, the greedy, and the aged. The people live in ornate and luxurious rooms, eventually conform to a uniform dress in a royal style, and lead a very hedonistic lifestyle, without a rigid schedule or responsibilities. They are, nevertheless, described as virtuous and engaged in their communities through the sharing of knowledge, sport, and pleasure. How does Rabelais's Abbey of Thélème compare to More's vision of a perfect society in *Utopia*?

a. **Further Reading:** Sargent, Lyman. *Utopianism: A Very Short Introduction.* Oxford and New York: Oxford University Press, 2010.

b. **Suggested Searches:** Google "Renaissance utopias" for several viable links (university, archive, scholarly blogs) on utopian philosophies and worlds outlined by thinkers of the period. Also go to www .gla.ac.uk/services/specialcollections/teachingandlearningmaterial /renaissanceliterature/utopia.

4. **As a member of the French Pléiade, Du Bellay (1522–60) wanted to reform literary and poetic principles.** The Pléiade poets included Jean-Antoine de Baïf, Joachim du Bellay, and Pierre Ronsard (among other minor participants). Their main concern was elevating French (then considered a vulgar language) to replace Latin and Greek as an appropriate literary language. Du Bellay's main contention was that contemporary French language lacked quality to serve in higher forms of poetry. His vision (thought by many to be extremist) was to improve French and to imitate the ancients rather than simply translate their works into French. Du Bellay and other Pléiade members had moved to rejuvenate poetry, but rhyme and the logic of form remained prerequisites for good writing. They added contextual requirements that made poetry aurally appealing from the listener's perspective: strong and convincing verses would be clear and concise and uniform and comprehensible to keep the reader from lolling off; vulgar topics and inappropriate language were to be avoided; and cadence and harmony were to be revered. How are Du Bellay's principles reflected in the modern evolution of your language? Are these changes considered acceptable in the academic world, or do they create a more popular, informal mode of expression?

a. **Further Reading:** Melehy, Hassan. *The Poetics of Literary Transfer in Early Modern France and England.* Surrey, UK: Ashgate, 2010.

b. **Suggested Search:** Go to the Gordon Library at the University of Virginia's page on Du Bellay at www2.lib.virginia.edu/rmds/port folio/gordon/literary/dubellay/index.html.

In-Class Activities

1. Divide students into small groups so that they can discuss their daily activities. Ask students to compare their activities to those described in the mundane lives of people living during the Renaissance. Examine in particular Machiavelli's "Letter to Francesco Vettori." What do the students' daily activities reveal about their social class as well as what our society values as important daily tasks? At the end of the group discussion, ask each student to compose a short journal entry (250 words) describing her or his daily tasks and then to analyze or assess them based on the group discussion.

2. Rabelais provides great detail about the structure and design of the Abbey of Thélème (Book I, Chapter 53). Ask students to look at images of different city spaces: How do the architecture, city plan, and decoration of the cultural centers (i.e., restaurants, window shops) define the city's feel? After comparing and discussing the images, ask students to move into small groups to design their own visuals of an ideal city.

3. Pantagruel receives a traditional humanist education. As a class, discuss the elements of humanist education, comparing it to the format and requirements of a traditional college education at your institution. Divide students into groups comprising three to five students and ask each group to design an "ideal college education" based on its own values. Ask each group to present its education to the class for further discussion and analysis.

4. After reading Book II, Chapter 19, of *Pantagruel*, ask students to debate the importance of nonverbal gestures for communication. Then ask them to research and perform gestures from different areas of the world and to discuss how gestures differ in international cultures.

Paper Topics/Suggestions for Writing

1. How did Pantagruel get his birth name, which means "all thirsty"?

2. Which elements of satire with regard to religion and living an upright lifestyle are presented in Rabelais's *Pantagruel*?

3. Of *homo ludens* (the playful man) the philosopher Huizinga writes that there are five characteristics of play: freedom, play not based on "ordinary" or "real life," play separate from real life with regard to form and duration, play based on order and creating order, and play disconnected from any profit or material benefit. Discuss examples of the "playful man" in two humanist works of your choice, looking particularly at the benefits and flaws of this approach.

4. In Sonnet 3 of "The Antiquities of Rome," Du Bellay writes, "Whatever stands firm is destroyed by time. And whatever flees resists time." Do you agree? Interpret this quote, using examples from Du Bellay's "Antiquities" and from modern times to support your contentions.

5. Rabelais, like many humanists, argues that free people born of noble lineage will be naturally inclined toward goodness and virtue and will possess "honor." Do you agree with this argument? Use examples from your humanist readings and current times to support your contentions.

Resources

The Allentown Art Museum. The Renaissance Connection. Samuel H. Kress Collection Online, 2000. www.renaissanceconnection.org.

> This site contains activities for a broad range of Renaissance disciplines, including science, math, art, social studies, and language arts. The activities appear to be designed for high school or freshman college students, but they can be easily adapted for a more challenging course.

Medici: Godfathers of the Renaissance. PBS television series, 2003. www.pbs.org/empires/medici.

> The PBS website includes not only information about the series but also a Medici gallery, lesson plans and activities for teachers, a reading list, and links to further resources.

"Joachim du Bellay." Gordon Library at University of Virginia. www2.lib.virginia.edu/rmds/portfolio/gordon/literary/dubellay/index.html.

> This site contains scanned images of published works, a biography and brief background on Du Bellay's works, sources for further reading, and hyperlinks to other Du Bellay sites.

Joseph, William A. Introduction to Political Science. Wellesley College, 2005. www.wellesley.edu/Polisci/wj/100/machsourc.html.

> This site provides a list of Machiavelli resources, including hyperlinked scholarly articles, images, Internet sources, and class notes.

Lenormant, Charles. *Reconstruction of the Theleme Abbey.* 1840, oil painting.

Roemer, Kenneth. *Utopian Audiences: How Readers Locate Nowhere.* Amherst: University of Massachusetts Press, 2003.

> This text examines how readers "manipulate imaginary worlds to gain new perceptions of their own worlds." Samples, questionnaires, and activities and resources are included.

PETRARCH AND THE LOVE LYRIC

Topics for Lecture or Discussion

1. **Rhyme and meter differ in the Petrarchan and Shakespearean variants of sonnet form.** Within the Petrarchan sonnet form, the sestet and octet often contrast formally or semantically, and rhymes in ABBA form are used to reinforce or contradict meanings—a problem is generally presented in the octet and resolved in the sestet. The Shakespearean sonnet form also comprises sixteen lines but uses an ABAB rhyme pattern and a different orientation—in Shakespeare's sonnets, three quatrains present a problem (often the third quatrain begins a partial resolution), which is then firmly resolved in the final couplet. Shakespearean sonnet form also relies heavily on enjambment (the content extends beyond one line's end, or it begins in the middle of a line). The translation for Petrarch's Sonnet 333 retains the original octet and sestet and the ABBA rhyme structure. The poem's octet represents the poet's attempt to woo his lover with poetry and to express his grief for unrequited love. The sestet contrasts it, focusing on the beloved's grace and his hope that she will be both immortalized in his poetry and honor him at his death. The rhyme reinforces the contrast between organic and lifeless or rough material (wild and harsh images of "stone" and "overgrown" [lines 1 and 4] are contrasted with tame and rounded "dear" and "sphere" [lines 2 and 3]; "blown" and "alone" [lines 5 and 8] represent distance and oppose the close and stable "steer" and "here" [lines 6 and 7]). Shakespeare's Sonnet 76 uses scientific allusions ("new-found methods," "compounds strange," line 4), textile imagery ("noted weed," line 6), and financial contexts ("Spending again what is already spent," line 12) to establish the problem (he thinks of her constantly, with no reward), while the terminal couplet neatly resolves the struggle: love endures and renews itself as the sun rises and sets. Shakespeare's Sonnet 116 uses nautical imagery: the first three quatrains refer to deliberation, a fixed star that acts as a guide for ships at sail, and Time (sickle), with a compass for direction. The final couplet resolves the poem with a statement that confirms the poem's opening lines (true love is firm and without impediment). How does the placement of a resolution affect the tenor and pace of the different sonnet forms?
   a. **Further Reading:** Brogan, Terry, and Alex Preminger, eds. *The New Princeton Handbook of Poetry and Poetics*. Princeton, NJ: Princeton University Press, 1994.
   b. **Suggested Search:** Go to the "Listening to Poetry: Sounds of the Sonnet" page of the National Endowment for the Humanities "Edsitement!" website at http://164.109.104.189/lesson-plan/listening-poetry-sounds-sonnet.

2. **In many humanist works, the contrast between the interior life and the exterior life often replaces the medievalist concern with the contemplative life versus the active life.** Contemplative persons included wanderers, hermits, and religious figures who were interested in exploring their inner selves rather than leading a public or physical life, and they often argued that too much focus on the present leads to impulsivity and temptation; the active person, on the other hand, may be more concerned with material issues involving business, family, and pleasure. Some poets, particularly Petrarch and Shakespeare, appear to blend both lifestyles in order to realize their aesthetic. Petrarch's sonnet sequence often describes Laura's physical appearance in extravagant depth, but only as a means for the poet to realize his own thoughts interiorly. In Sonnet 1, for example, Petrarch laments a "youthful error" for which he now seeks "repentance," having realized that physical pleasure is only a "brief dream"(line 10) compared to self-introspection. In Sonnet 3, Christian imagery contrasts with a lover's internal grief ("Maker" and "Lady" [lines 2–3], "defend" and "bound" [lines 2–3], "Love's blows" and "universal woe" [lines 4–6], "heart" and "tears" [lines 8–9], and Christian Crucifixion and cupid's arrows of love and hate). In Labé's Sonnet 18 the writer speaks about the pleasure in kissing, realizing that she has no identity or happiness without "some place outside myself." In Shakespeare's Sonnet 130 the poet takes painstaking efforts to point out his mistress's flaws: her eyes are not bright, her lips are pale, her breast is the color of manure, her hair is coarse, and her breath stinks. His mistress has a rough voice and a heavy gait, yet in the terminal couplet Shakespeare resolves that nobody compares to her. How are interiority and exteriority represented by the word choice and formation of the sonnet?

   a. **Further Reading:** Kreeft, Peter, ed. *A Summa of the Summa*. San Francisco: Ignatius Press, 1990.

   b. **Suggested Search:** Go to Stanford Encyclopedia Online's "Civic Humanism" entry at http://plato.stanford.edu/entries/humanism -civic, which addresses the importance of the active life versus the contemplative life during the Renaissance and early modern periods.

3. **Petrarch is considered the father of humanism, and references to classical societies, mores, and civic duty abound in several of his poems.** In Sonnet 62 Petrarch's love for Laura mirrors Apollo's love for Daphne—in the poet's life and in the Greek god's life, the greater reward is the laurel (the symbol of lyric poetry) rather than the fruition of romantic love that has been pursued by the poet and denied by his beloved. Sonnet 126 contains pastoral elements, in which nature and the Lady's body intertwine in a series of correspondences (i.e., sweet waters and lovely body, branch and column, grass and flowers and garments,

and air and breath). Sonnet 189 uses Odysseus's marine adventures as a metaphor for the trauma and turmoil that Petrarch experiences in unrequited love (i.e., ship and poet's soul, harsh sea and troubled relationship, Scylla and Charybdis and forgetfulness and sin, and sweet stars and Laura's eyes). Louise Labé's poetry makes numerous references to Greek gods and to pastoral settings. In Sonnet 1, Ulysses (Odysseus) parallels her beloved's beauty and honor, while Sonnet 10 creates a pastoral setting with lute music, a verdant landscape, and a man with blonde curls crowned by a laurel (representing Apollo). How does humanism differ from the values and activities represented in ancient or medieval works?

a. **Further Reading:** Schmitt, C. B., et al. *The Cambridge History of Renaissance Philosophy.* Cambridge: Cambridge University Press, 1991.

b. **Suggested Search:** Go to the "Petrarch" page of the Yale University Beinecke Rare Book and Manuscript Library at http://brbl-archive .library.yale.edu/exhibitions/petrarch/index.html.

4. **The humanist love lyric, inspired by Petrarch's poetry, often focuses on the beloved as a cause of deep grief, sorrow, and self-destruction for the poet; the lover is frequently accused of taking sadistic liberties with the poet's emotions.** Garcilaso de la Vega's Sonnet 1 uses imagery of losing one's path and wishing for death because he gave love to "one who could destroy and ruin me" (line 10). In Sonnet 10 he accuses the beloved of conspiring "to see my death" (line 4) and giving him joy for the express purpose "to see me die of memories filled with grief" (line 8). In Louise Labé's Sonnet 1, the beloved is accused of offering love that is compared to a scorpion sting or poison, and she begs the beloved to "kill the pain" (line 12). Veronica Franco's "Capitolo 13: A Challenge to a Lover Who Has Offended Her" uses battle imagery (battlefield, arms, challenge, duel) to evoke the sense of a war fought between two lovers, that she may free herself of "merciless mistreatment" (line 3). Franco's poem is more graphic than other poems in this cluster; it describes a sadistic and erotic scene, including bloodshed, cutting into her own breast for relief, with the bed as a place where, "stretched out in skirmishes with you" (line 80), she and her lover would die, "felled by the same blow" (line 85) by committing suicide ("end your agony with the same blade"—line 91). How do these poetic images compare to the real roles that women played in everyday life?

a. **Further Reading:** Jones, Ann Rosalind. *The Currency of Eros: Women's Love Lyric in Europe: 1540–1620.* Bloomington: Indiana University Press, 1990.

b. **Suggested Search:** Go to the "Petrarch at 700" digital exhibition of the University of Pennsylvania, Penn Libraries, at www.library .upenn.edu/exhibits/rbm/petrarch/petrarch.html.

5. **Shakespeare often confuses readers with his use of double entendre (a word or phrase having a double meaning), particularly in poems that appear addressed to an unidentified young boy (Will) or to a mysterious dark lady.** Of the 154 sonnets that Shakespeare wrote, the first 126 are devoted to an unidentified young man and deal with themes of marriage and family (Sonnets 1–17), and the ability of poetry to immortalize someone (Sonnet 18). Sonnets 127–54 are addressed to a "dark lady" whose suspect immorality and seductive behavior tempt the poet (she appears, also, in some earlier sonnets in which the young man and dark lady engage each other). Examine Sonnet 135, in which the word *will* means, among other things, "what you want," "sexual desire," Shakespeare's first name truncated, male and female genitalia, and "shall." How is meaning in the poem changed by substituting these varying ideas? (See the group activity below for interpretation options.)

   a. **Further Reading:** Schwartz, Robert. *Shakespeare's Parted Eye: Perception, Knowledge, and Meaning in the Sonnets and Plays.* New York: Peter Lang, 1990.

   b. **Suggested Search:** Go to the PBS website at pbs.org and search "In Search of Shakespeare" for a biography, a discussion, lesson plans, and media related to Shakespeare, including case studies on Shakespearean and Petrarchan sonnet forms. Students might also search "Shakespeare's language" for a discussion of word choice and double meaning in the poems and plays.

In-Class Activities

1. Divide students into small groups. Ask them to examine Shakespeare's Sonnet 135 using various definitions of the word *will*. Have each group use the provided definitions to decode the poem; groups then present their interpretation to the class. Additionally, students might be encouraged to look at urban slang in modern hip-hop lyrics and to bring into class a collection of urban slang or dialect terms to create their own coded poems.

2. In this sound experiment, the professor first orally demonstrates iambic pentameter through a reading of an assigned sonnet. The class should discuss how the professor's use of meter, rhyme, and form promotes context. Next, each student should give a performance of the same poem. Students should pay attention not only to gesture but also to the use of intonation and rhythm to emphasize their interpretation of the poem's structure. Discuss as a class the effects, successes, and failures. What new meanings arise as a result of different interpretations?

3. Ask students to bring in lyrics from their favorite song or a poem they enjoyed in childhood (e.g., works by Dr. Seuss or Shel Silverstein) and

to create mash-ups (pastiches) of their poem with a sonnet discussed in class. The mash-up should reflect some overlapping theme or structural style and should incorporate words from both texts. Ask students to then read aloud their pastiches and discuss the benefits of this learning activity. (See the Folger entry in the Resources for sample pastiches.)

Paper Topics/Suggestions for Writing

1. Petrarch's love lyrics are dedicated to a woman named Laura and reveal his struggle to renounce earthly joys for spiritual reward. Identify and analyze examples of this struggle in at least four sonnets of your choosing.

2. Many of Petrarch's poems rely on the devices of hyperbole, antithesis, and oxymoron, which also characterized secular poetry by the troubadours. Find examples of exaggeration and opposition in Petrarch's poems. Why are these devices important for the development of Western lyric?

3. Examine nature (one's fixed qualities, shaped by God) versus nurture (one's evolving qualities, shaped by history and culture) in Petrarch's poetry.

4. Discuss the formal characteristics of the Petrarchan sonnet, and use at least two examples to illustrate the rhetorical and stylistic devices.

5. Humanist poets often employ classical elements and themes in their works. Use one poem from at least three different poets to examine classical elements and themes.

6. How do the lover and beloved represent, respectively, the interior life versus the exterior life in humanist poems?

7. What purpose does sadomasochistic imagery serve in humanist poetry? Provide at least three examples to support your contentions.

Resources

Amazon.com.
> This site currently sells more than ninety individual MP3s for instant download, based on musical transpositions of Petrarch's sonnets. Composers include Liszt, Allanbrook, Monteverdi, and Schoenberg.

Folger Shakespeare Library. Washington, DC http://folger.edu.
> This site contains background information on Shakespeare, lesson plans with learning objectives, interactive activities, and multimedia resources.

"Listening to Poetry: Sounds of the Sonnet." National Endowment for the Humanities, "Edsitement!" website. http://164.109.104.189/lesson-plan /listening-poetry-sounds-sonnet.

> This site contains an overview of sonnet forms, lesson plans with detailed learning objectives, resources, and links to related lessons.

"Petrarch at 700." University of Pennsylvania, Penn Libraries. www.library .upenn.edu/exhibits/rbm/petrarch/petrarch.html.

> This digital exhibition contains images, an introduction, background history and culture, music, and translation information based on the original exhibition held in 2004.

Yale University Beinecke Rare Book and Manuscript Library. http://brbl -archive.library.yale.edu/exhibitions/petrarch/index.html. Fall 2004.

> This Petrarch exhibition site contains an introduction, a gallery, select works, with some facsimiles, a biography, and a bibliography.

DESIDERIUS ERASMUS

From *The Praise of Folly*

Topics for Lecture or Discussion

1. ***The Praise of Folly* assumes the tone and structure of a public oration, containing logical arguments and rhetorical questions, but the dramatic situation of the work—with the goddess Folly speaking— lends the arguments a satirical veneer that allows Erasmus to distance himself from some of the pointed mockery that the work contains.** The satire is readily apparent from the opening sentence of the work, in which Folly makes the claim that "I and I alone pour forth joy into the hearts of gods and men alike" (2083), mimicking grandiose claims often made by classical and medieval philosophers, poets, rhetoricians, and theologians. The satire continues with well-constructed arguments that are often built upon sound logic, though the premises and conclusions typically take absurd turns. Nevertheless, the satire is not simply silly or trivial; for instance, when Folly derides devotional practices that were common in Europe at the time (2097–2099), she targets features of medieval religious life that Erasmus did indeed find blameworthy, but because it is Folly and not Erasmus speaking, the author is able to keep the satire impersonal and less direct. After all, is Folly's mockery of these devotions foolish or wise?

   a. **Further Reading:** Griffin, Dustin. *Satire: A Critical Reintroduction.* Lexington: University Press of Kentucky, 1994.

   b. **Suggested Search:** A search for "satire" at LION (Literature Online) will result in several helpful articles and entries in works of reference.

2. **Folly begins her argument by recounting her genealogy and the companions that she keeps; this information is an implementation of classical rhetorical practices of the speaker establishing her authority and ethos, and it also serves as a clever introduction to the various things that will be associated with foolishness in Folly's speech.** Folly claims that her father was Plutus, the god of wealth, and that she was conceived by Neotes, a nymph who was representative of youth. She grew up on the Isles of the Blest, where things grow to abundance without effort, and she was nursed by Methe (Drunkenness) and Apaedia (Stupidity). By describing Folly as the offspring of youth and wealth, and emphasizing the ease with which foolishness grows to an abundance, Erasmus presents a character who, when she claims to rule over human life and to be the source of happiness, is quite surprising. She describes her companions, including Selflove, Pleasure, and Luxury (the full list

of companions can be found on page 2085), as "the loyal retinue which helps me to subject the whole world to my dominion, lording it over the greatest lords" (2085). Pleasure, luxury, drunkenness, and wealth all contribute to the subjugation of human beings to Folly's reign.

   a. **Further Reading:** Zatta, Claudia. "Democritus and Folly: The Two Wise Fools." *Bibliothèque d'Humanisme et Renaissance* 63.3 (2001): 533–549.

   b. **Suggested Search:** A search for "Desiderius Erasmus" at the Online Library of Liberty (oll.libertyfund.org) results in several helpful links to Erasmus's works, and includes a biography as well.

3. **Folly argues that she is the source of human life, since both procreation and marriage are silly enterprises.** In arguing that sex is foolish, Folly states, "the human race is propagated by the part [of the body] which is so foolish and funny that it cannot even be mentioned without a snicker" (2086). This passage is paradigmatic of Folly's combination of foolishness and wisdom; her argument about the funniness of the procreative act is juvenile, but it also points toward the absurdity of certain prudish or philosophically abstract positions regarding the human body, the passions, and procreation. Folly proceeds to make a similar argument about marriage, relying upon commonplace negative views of the married life: "would any man ever submit to the halter of matrimony if he followed the usual method of these wisemen and first considered the drawbacks of that state of life? Or what woman would ever yield to a man's advances if she either knew about or at least called to mind the perilous labor of childbirth, the trials and tribulations of raising children" (2086)? Because marriage is a foolish state and because sex is funny, so the argument goes, Folly is the primary source of life, including the lives of those stoic philosophers, monks, and kings whose seriousness and attention to ceremony would seem to scorn foolishness.

   a. **Further Reading:** Vredeveld, Harry. "'That Familiar Proverb': Folly as the Elixir of Youth in Erasmus's *Moraie Ecomium*." *Renaissance Quarterly* 42.1 (1989): 78–91.

   b. **Suggested Search:** A Google Images search for "the ship of fools" results in several images of the theme that Erasmus addresses (these images often depict some aspect of Sebastian Brant's fifteenth-century book *The Ship of Fools* which works within the same tradition as Erasmus's *The Praise of Folly*).

4. **In supporting her case, Folly makes many references to classical philosophy, mythology, and literature. While her use of these sources is often funny and frequently incorrect, she does nevertheless make some interesting and difficult philosophical points.** Perhaps the most striking example in *The Praise of Folly* is Folly's argument that the

foolish are at least as happy as the wise, and indeed, she proceeds to argue that they are happier than wise men. While making this argument, she refers to Plato's famous allegory of the cave, asking, "Surely you don't believe that there is any difference between those who sit in Plato's cave gazing in wonder at the images and likeness of various things—as long as they desire nothing more and are no less pleased— and that wiseman who left the cave and sees things as they really are" (2101). If all humans desire happiness, and someone is just as happy being deceived or incorrect as they would be if they knew the truth of things, why is it better to be wise than to be ignorant?

   a. **Further Reading:** Cooper, John M., ed. "The Republic." In *Plato: Complete Works*. Indianapolis, IN: Hackett Publishing Company, 1997. See esp. "Book VII," pp. 1132–1155.

   b. **Suggested Search:** At the Internet Classics Archive (http://classics .mit.edu), a search for "allegory of the cave" results in the text from Book VII of Plato's *Republic*. You can also perform a Google Images search for "allegory of the cave" for a variety of drawings that depict the situation that Socrates describes.

5. **Erasmus's *In Praise of Folly* is perhaps most pointed and challenging when Folly invokes Christian authorities, and particularly scripture, as endorsements of foolishness.** For example, Folly argues, "Christ always despises and condemns those savants who rely on their own wisdom. Paul testifies very clearly on this point when he says "What is foolish to the world, God has chosen," and when he says that "God was pleased to save the world through folly because it could not be redeemed by wisdom" (2103). While some might counter Folly's point with the serious objection that St. Paul and Folly are using the words "folly" and "foolish" in very different senses, this does not obviate Folly's point that Christ himself was born in poverty, associated with common tradespeople rather than scribes and philosophers, and died as a criminal rather than living in the courts of the powerful or the wise. The acts of Christ's incarnation and redemptive death on the cross are precisely what Folly calls foolish, and raise serious questions for those Christians who do pursue learning and worldly accomplishment.

   a. **Further Reading:** Saward, John. *Perfect Fools: Folly for Christ's Sake in Catholic and Orthodox Spirituality*. Oxford: Oxford University Press, 1980.

   b. **Suggested Search:** At the Stanford Encyclopedia of Philosophy (http://plato.stanford.edu), a search for "Desiderius Erasmus" results in a helpful article about Erasmus's life and works.

In-Class Activities

1. Ask your students to read different passages from *The Praise of Folly* aloud to the class, and follow these readings with a discussion of the ways in which Folly's argument works as a public oration.

2. Encourage your students to share aspects of their genealogy that shape their identities, and discuss the ways in which that is different from and similar to the claims that Folly makes.

3. Break your students into small research groups that must prepare presentations on some of the following topics: Erasmus as a humanist, Erasmus's adages, Erasmus and the Catholic Church, Erasmus and the Reformation, Erasmus and Thomas More, *The Praise of Folly* in relation to the *Utopia*, *The Praise of Folly* in relation to Sebastian Brant's *The Ship of Fools*.

Paper Topics/Suggestions for Writing

1. Write an essay in which you consider the uses of satire in *The Praise of Folly* and at least one other text that you have read in this class (for example, *Candide*). What are the objects of satire? How is satire used? In what ways does satire create an argument?

2. Consider Folly as a character. What is her personality? How does she speak? What are her primary points of reference? What does Folly consider to be the good, or what does Folly consider to be the *telos*, or end, of human existence? Does Folly embody or represent anything more than folly?

3. Contrast *The Praise of Folly* with Thomas More's *Utopia*. What are the important similarities between these two humanist texts? What are their methods of argument? How do they differ in their fictional situations? How are Folly and Raphael similar in their use of rhetoric?

4. What are some of the objects that Folly attacks that are also probably objects which Erasmus disapproved of? Can you identify an authorial voice in Folly's words? Does Folly offer any arguments that you suspect Erasmus would not agree with?

5. Is it significant that Folly is a woman? Or that she is presented as a goddess? Consider the different sorts of foolishness that are ascribed to men and women in Folly's discussion.

6. Is Folly persuasive? What is the strongest aspect of her argument? What is the weakest? At what point does Folly become most pointed, most satirical, or most aggressive?

Resources

Dolan, John P., ed. and trans. *The Essential Erasmus*. New York: Meridian, 1983.

> Students or instructors wishing to read more of Erasmus's works should turn to this volume, for it provides a manageable selection, a brief biography, and suggestions for further reading.

Kraye, Jill, ed. *The Cambridge Companion to Renaissance Humanism*. Cambridge: Cambridge University Press, 1996.

> This volume contains a collection of essays that should be very helpful for situating Erasmus and *The Praise of Folly* within the larger religious, political, and philosophical movements of his era.

Olin, John C. *Six Essays on Erasmus and a Translation of Erasmus' Letter to Carondelet*. New York: Fordham University Press, 1979.

> Olin's collection of essays includes several helpful entries, including "Interpreting Erasmus" and the fourth essay, which is devoted entirely to *The Praise of Folly*.

Thompson, Geraldine. *Under Pretext of Praise: Satiric Mode in Erasmus' Fiction*. Toronto: University of Toronto Press, 1974.

> This volume traces Erasmus's use of irony and satire as modes of education within the humanist tradition, and includes a discussion of *The Praise of Folly* in the second chapter.

NICCOLÒ MACHIAVELLI

The Prince

Topics for Lecture or Discussion

1. **Machiavelli argues that moral and righteous people make weak
   political leaders; the most important quality is the *virtù* of the
   Prince, which is better understood in Machiavelli's work as being
   "of flexible disposition" than of being virtuous.** Many medieval and
   Renaissance writers argued that upright character and virtuous behavior were essential characteristics for a ruler. Machiavelli moves away
   from traditional Christian advice for rulers and instead focuses on the
   concept that "the end justifies the means," even if this means resorting
   to immorality or violence in order to maintain power. Authority and
   power are linked, but neither is dependent upon nor requires moral
   (virtuous) behavior for effective rule. The ruler with *virtù* will be able
   to switch from good to evil conduct as necessary for each circumstance. His justification relies on the premise that man is inherently
   evil, and therefore cannot be led with morality or goodness ("If men
   were all good, this advice would not be good, but since men are wicked
   and do not keep their promises to you, you likewise do not have to keep
   yours to them"). *Virtù* is the second most important quality for achieving strong leadership and is attained by following three important steps
   to reclaim the Italian provinces from foreign influence (see discussion
   4). How does Machiavelli's use of the word "virtù" compare to your
   understanding of the word?
   a. **Further Reading:** Mansfield, H. C. *Machiavelli's Virtue*. Chicago:
      University of Chicago Press, 1996.
   b. **Suggested Search:** Go to the Wellesley College Political Science
      website at http://web.wellesley.edu/web/Acad/PoliticalScience and
      search for "Machiavelli."

2. **Machiavelli follows the early struggles and setbacks of Cesare Borgia as he attempted to gain power in Italy; as such, some scholars
   believe that *The Prince* is written as a political satire.** Borgia first
   relies on his father's status to gain power, which shows that he took
   small steps to acquire power before executing a full-blown plan. His
   father's intervention fails for two reasons: first, his father (as pope)
   already had enemies in parts of Italy who feared the pope (Venice,
   Milan); second, ill health (via "Fortune") overtook him. Borgia then
   acts independently but struggles on his own account as well: he believes
   his soldiers are disloyal, and he comes into conflict with the king of
   France and that country's intentions toward Italy. The duke succeeds

only after he resorts to "trickery" by enlisting French help, getting the Orsini to ally with him and wiping out disloyal generals. Jean-Jacques Rousseau wrote, "Machiavelli was a proper man and a good citizen; but, being attached to the court of the Medici, he could not help veiling his love of liberty in the midst of his country's oppression. The choice of his detestable hero, Caesar Borgia, clearly enough shows his hidden aim." Do you believe the text was written to promote democracy and ridicule tyranny?

a. **Further Reading:** Skinner, Q. *Visions of Politics, Volume II: Renaissance Virtues.* Cambridge: Cambridge University Press, 2002.

b. **Suggested Search:** Go to www.idehistuu.se/distans/ilmh/Ren/flor-mach-mattingly.htm for the article "Machiavelli's Prince: Political Science or Political Satire?" *The American Scholar* 27 (1958): 482–91.

3. **Fortuna (Fortune) is compared to a woman: she plays only half a role in a leader's success or failure, while the other half remains in the ruler's hands.** Fortune is compared to a "raging stream" that unleashes floods and destruction but is also capable of peace if she is "contained." Princes will fail if they are in constant strife with Fortune; instead, they must adapt to times and find the best method suited to overcome difficulty in that particular time (i.e., a leader who is naturally patient and cautious may find that certain situations call for rashness and recklessness). "Like a woman, Fortune is always the friend of young men because they are less cautious, more courageous, and command her with more boldness." Fortune is considered the opponent to political order, often leading to conflict and misery. Only through careful observation, preparation, and ability to adapt (*virtù*) may a leader avoid fortune's pitfalls. How would you translate the term *fortuna*—as fortune, fate, or another term? In your opinion, how does this concept feature in contemporary politics?

a. **Further Reading:** King, R. *Machiavelli: Philosopher of Power.* New York: HarperCollins, 2004.

b. **Suggested Search:** Go to the Humanistic Texts Organization website, http://humanistictexts.org.

4. **In "The Roman Dream" (chapter 26), Machiavelli compares the Italians' condition to that of the Hebrews being led out of bondage by Moses, receiving God's help but also needing to take some responsibility for their survival; the concept of Virtue (flexibility, manhood) is defined as the second quality (along with Fortune) for achieving leadership.** Relating back to discussion 3, two potential leaders (Sforza and Borgia, likely) failed to lead the Italians on account of Fortune. Continuing with the Moses-Hebrews comparison, Machiavelli speaks of apparent signs that show Italy is in God's favor—"manna

has fallen" and "the rock has given forth water" (both referring to the water and food provided by God while Moses and the Hebrews wandered the desert for forty years)—but it is time now for the Italians to contribute to their success. To accomplish this, Machiavelli advises that they (1) form and furnish their own army that is loyal to and honored by its leader, (2) use new military tactics for equipping the infantry in order to avoid making the mistake of the Spanish and Swiss armies in order to (3) throw foreigners out of the land ("he would be received in all those provinces that have suffered from those foreign deluges"). How do these tactics compare to actions used by modern governments to instigate change in their countries?

   a. **Further Reading:** Viroli, M. *From Politics to Reason of State: The Acquisition and Transformation of the Language of Politics 1250–1600.* Cambridge: Cambridge University Press, 1992.

   b. **Suggested Search:** Go to "Machiavelli, The Prince" at www.machiavelliblog.org/2009/03/online-compendium-of-machiavelli.html.

In-Class Activities

1. Ask students to research contemporary leaders in the world from various fields—political, spiritual, corporate CEOs, conductors, or athletic directors—and talk about the skills and characteristics required of leaders in different fields. On which positive and negative traits do leaders in different arenas rely to accomplish tasks? Ask students to prepare a visual diagram to represent the essential traits, desirable traits, and undesirable traits for different leaders and then compare their visuals.

2. Ask students to form small groups and list the attributes and virtues that represent their ideal leader. Ask each group to present its leader, and, using Machiavelli's text, ask the class to examine why the fictional leader might succeed or fail.

3. After dividing students into small groups of five to seven, according to Renaissance social groups, the professor will designate a Machiavellian leader. Groups will role-play based on descriptions provided in *The Prince* and class discussions of Renaissance Italy and humanist culture. Then ask each student to write a short reflection piece describing what she or he learned about Machiavelli's principles from the role-play experience.

4. Ask students to interview a local leader (perhaps a university administrator) to determine his or her attributes, leadership style, and qualifications. Then ask students to write a mock peer review (or audit), comparing and contrasting the local leader with Machiavelli's descriptions. Students might also hone their business writing skills by using a

template to write a professional evaluation that reviews the leader and offers advice for improvement based on Machiavelli's theories.

Paper Topics/Suggestions for Writing

1. Describe the relationship between *Virtù* and *Fortuna* in *The Prince*.

2. Sovereign power is a requisite element in Machiavelli's work, and it is contrasted with despotic power. Looking at chapter 7, how does Cesare Borgia qualify or fail as a leader with sovereign power?

3. Readers often feel that Machiavelli is writing with sincerity, while some scholars have claimed that he is writing satire. Which position do you support? Use examples from the text to support your contentions.

4. Machiavelli's work has often been blamed for tyrant rule in modern times. Read the following quote by Ernst Cassirer, and write a reflection essay that supports or refutes Cassirer's quote with examples from the text: "*The Prince* is neither a moral nor an immoral book: it is simply a technical book. In a technical book we do not seek for rules of ethical conduct, of good and evil. It is enough if we are told what is useful and useless. Every word in *The Prince* must be read and interpreted in this way. The book contains no moral prescripts for the ruler nor does it invite him to commit crimes and villainies. It is especially concerned with and destined for the 'new principalities.' It tries to give them all the advice necessary for protecting themselves from all danger" (Cassirer, *The Myth of the State*, p. 153).

5. Do beneficial ends justify immoral means? Use examples from *The Prince* to support your contentions.

Resources

Cassirer, Ernst. *The Myth of the State*. New Haven, CT: Yale University Press, 1961.

Humanistic Texts Organization. http://humanistictexts.org.
    This site hosts Machiavelli's writings and also provides a brief biography, background information, and links to other humanist writers.

Machiavelli. 2nd ed. Avalon Hill and Battleline, Reston, VA, 1995, board game.
    This game is for four to eight players and is suitable for young adults and older. Gamers recreate the shifting balance of power and political struggles among five major powers in Renaissance Italy, aiming for control of the peninsula.

Machiavelli and the Prince. Discovery Education, 2005, DVD.
    In this video Gary Hart and Henry Kissinger, among others, discuss how Machiavelli's text has influenced world leaders and world history.

"Machiavelli, The Prince." Video lecture by Professor Steven B. Smith, Yale University Open Course materials for Introduction to Political Philosophy, Lecture 10. www.machiavelliblog.org/2009/03/online-compendium -of-machiavelli.html.

> This video lecture is an introduction to Machiavelli and life in Renaissance Florence. It is stated in the presentation that "Machiavelli can be credited as the founder of the modern state."

Medici: Godfathers of the Renaissance. PBS, 2003.

> This television series is available for DVD rental on Netflix. The PBS website (www.pbs.org) includes not only information about the series but also a Medici gallery, lesson plans and activities for teachers, a reading list, and links to further resources.

Wellesley College Political Science. http://web.wellesley.edu/web/Acad/Politi calScience.

> This site provides a list of Machiavelli resources, including hyperlinked scholarly articles, images, Internet sources, and class notes.

LUDOVICO ARIOSTO
Orlando Furioso

Topics for Lecture or Discussion

1. ***Orlando Furioso* is inspired by Boiardo's popular romance *Orlando in Love* and largely influenced by the romance epic *Song of Roland*.** The romance as a literary genre originated in late medieval and early modern Europe; works usually contained elements of fantasy, fairy tale and legend, and quests by chivalrous heroes. Romances often emphasize adventure, include sensational or magical episodes, and show changes in aristocratic values and women's circumstances. They tend to end happily, mainly because the hero has a self-aggrandized view of his role in the world. Epics, on the other hand, tend to depict protagonists with human characteristics who are fighting for a community cause rather than a personal whim; the epic hero is governed by a heroic code, whereas the romance hero is led by a chivalric code. The Italian writers combined French and British legends (Roland and King Arthur, respectively) with classical sources and myths. However, Ariosto was determined to use humor, mixed genres (romance, pastoral, tragedy, satire, sublime, and grotesque), mixed geographies, and awkward settings of heroes in unexpected situations to surpass these and other romance epics. Do you think of Orlando as more of a romance hero or an epic hero?

   a. **Further Reading:** Marinelli, Peter. *Ariosto and Boiardo: The Origins of Orlando Furioso.* Columbia: University of Missouri Press, 1987.

   b. **Suggested Search:** Go to Professor Tucker's University of Virginia class site on "Epic, Romance, and the Love of God in Medieval France and England" at http://xroads.virginia.edu/~PUBLIC/tucker/medsyl.htm for activities, bibliographies, images, and links to other sites.

2. **The work contains numerous subplots that also explore taboo, forbidden, or betrayed love.** See Canto 25 (Fiordispina's love for Bradamant) on the tale of forbidden love between Fiordispina and Bradamant (a woman disguised as a male warrior, raising issues of transvestitism). The story reiterates the romance theme of "love versus duty and glory." Fiordispina, a Saracen, falls in love with Bradamant, who is disguised as a male knight. Bradamant reveals her identity as a member of the "gentle sex," and Fiordispina responds with shame ("Neither among humans nor among beasts have I ever come across a woman loving a woman; to a woman another woman does not seem beautiful") Ruggiero is distracted from his duty to Charlemagne as he saves the young

Richardet, whom he confuses for his beloved Bradamant ("You are not the first, nor the second to have mistaken us"). The introduction is used to segue into his account of duping Fiordispina into sex after pretending to be Bradamant. Richardet looks like his twin sister and tricks Fiordispina into a sexual interlude by convincing her that he has had a sex change ("She could not believe her eyes or fingers or herself . . . she needed solid proof to convince her that she was actually feeling what she thought she felt"). How do these relationships compare to those described in picaresque works such as *Don Quixote* and *Lazarillo de Tormes?* Do you believe the perception of relationships is linked to an author's culture?

    a. **Further Reading:** Stoppino, Eleonora. *Genealogies of Fiction: Women Warriors and the Medieval Imagination in Orlando Furioso.* New York: Fordham University Press, 2011.

    b. **Suggested Search:** Go to the Online Medieval and Classical Library (OMACL) page about Orlando Furioso at http://omacl.org/Orlando.

3. **Unlike previous romance epics, Ariosto is not interested in the medieval idea of a chivalric hero; instead, his protagonists possess humanist characteristics. Renaissance and early modern humanists also tend to mock the medieval focus on courtly love, instead writing satires on chivalry (see Miguel de Cervantes's *Don Quixote*) or relying more on classical epics by Homer and Virgil; nevertheless, they still tend to focus on the general theme of a hero torn between love and duty.** Orlando, under the influence of desire, becomes increasingly erratic. He neglects his duties to King Charlemagne and pursues the Chinese princess Angelica, who drives him mad due to her inconstancy and devotion to a Saracen soldier. In Cantos 23 and 24 ("Orlando's Great Madness"), Orlando discovers and obsesses over an inscription revealing that Angelica loves and has been physically intimate with Medor, and he has a psychotic break after learning that Angelica nursed her wounded lover back to health. His fury, however, mocks the medieval chivalric hero: rather than do his duty, he uses his superhuman strength for destructive purposes ("He now performed some truly astonishing feats: at one jerk he rooted up a tall pine, / after which he tore up several more as though they were so many celery-stalks . . . preying upon men and wild beasts, fighting with bears and boars"). Similarly, the Saracen Fiordispina masochistically punishes herself ("struck her face and tore her hair") when she discovers that her love for a woman has led her to sin against God ("You have done this to make an example of my aberration"). Fiordispina dresses Bradamant in women's clothing, dreams of her as a member of the opposite sex, and prays to Mahomet to release her of her desires. Does

Orlando uphold the humanist values and ideologies presented in the anthology (see "Humanism and the Rediscovery of the Classical Past")?

   a. **Further Reading:** Keller, H. E. *Romance Epic: Essays on a Medieval Literary Genre*. Kalamazoo, MI: Western Michigan University, 1987.

   b. **Suggested Search:** Greene, Robert. "The History of Orlando Furioso," *The Dramatic and Poetical Works of Robert Greene and George Peele*. London: Routledge, 1861, 89–118. Available at www .luminarium.org/editions/orlando.htm.

4. **Ariosto makes frequent reference to the Saracens, recalling the Islamic Arabs that Christians fought during the Crusades, often in the pejorative sense of Arab "tent dwellers" and fringe culture.** Historically, Christians associated the Saracens with the Bedouin living outside of the eastern Roman Empire; the Bedouin are pre-Islamic peoples from the Syrian-Arabian deserts, but they came to encompass a wider label as anyone (e.g., Turk, Arab) grouped with Muslims fighting against Christians during the Crusades. Scholars have found that Ariosto's and Boiardo's inclusion of the Saracens makes fewer distinctions between Christians and Muslims, showing no evidence that Western culture is superior to that of the Arabs and Turks, as found in earlier romances such as *Chanson de Roland (Song of Roland)*. During the humanist era, Christian Europe was dealing with a Turkish threat, yet romance epics of the period suggest that a knight's heroism is defined more by his glory in the trials of love than in his success in the war of religion. In Canto 25 Richardet narrates the story of Fiordispina, a Saracen who mistakenly falls in love with Bradamant (see the previous discussion 3): Fiordispina frequently prays to Mahomet and God to release her of sin and to turn Bradamant into a man. Historically, the text describes the Saracens at war with Charlemagne but also depicts the knights as being distracted from their duty by their attraction to the Saracen women. How does Ariosto's treatment toward the Saracens compare to the Spanish treatment of the Moors and Moriscos in *Don Quixote* and *Lazarillo de Tormes*? What do these descriptions tell you about the Arab-European relationship during the time period, particularly in comparison to current trends in Western-Arabic relations?

   a. **Further Reading:** Blanks, R. *Western Views of Islam in Medieval and Early Modern Europe: Perception of Other*. New York: St. Martin's Press, 1999.

   b. **Suggested Search:** Google "Saracen and Italy" for several academic sites and personal scholarly pages devoted to the topic (e.g., www .third-millennium-library.com/MedievalHistory/Cambridge/II/DOOR .html).

In-Class Activities

1. Ask students to work in pairs to create and play out scenarios in which they assume the role of a famous person and attempt to manipulate or deceive their peer based on the famous person's characteristics. The purpose of the game is to practice the art of uncovering artifice, as students guess their peer's masked identity.

2. Orlando exhibits extremely volatile and psychotic behavior during his episode. Ask students to diagnose elements of his mania and to devise a treatment plan to help him overcome his grief.

3. Ask students to create a short manifesto titled "The Art of Love in Our Times," influenced by the chivalrous and courtly love manifestos of Castiglione (*Book of the Courtier*) and Capellanus (*Art of Courtly Love*) (see Schultz in the Resources section). How have chivalry and the conflict of "duty versus desire" changed in our times?

Paper Topics/Suggestions for Writing

1. How do early modern romances differ from their medieval predecessors? Compare and contrast an excerpt from *Orlando Furioso* to *Song of Roland*.

2. Looking at an image from Dore's illustrations of *Orlando Furioso*, how do the text and illustration complement each other?

3. Discuss the conflict of duty versus desire in the text.

4. What purpose do the unconventional relationships and questions of transgenderism and homosexuality serve in this text?

Resources

Dore's Illustrations for Ariosto's "Orlando Furioso." Selection of 208 Illustrations. London: Dover, 1980.
    This collection includes sketches and finished works used as part of the German nineteenth-century edition of the text.
Orlando Furioso. Dir. Brian Large. Prod. Les Jarrett. San Francisco Opera, 2000.
    This 2000 performance of Vivaldi's opera by the San Francisco Opera is available as a DVD on amazon.com.
Orlando Furioso. Dir. Luca Ronconi. N.O.C. CIN.CA, 1975.
    This television series initially aired in Italy.
Panizzi, Antonio, ed. *Boiardo and Ariosto: With an Essay on the Romantic Narrative Poetry of the Italians*. London: Adamant Media, 2001.

Panizzi's edition, in addition to an essay on Italian romance epics, includes a facsimile of Pickering's 1830 edition.

Schultz, James. *Courtly Love, the Love of Courtliness, and the History of Sexuality.* 2nd ed. Chicago: University of Chicago Press, 2006.

This book examines the history and culture of courtly love in the context of medieval and Renaissance sexuality.

SIR THOMAS MORE

Utopia

Topics for Lecture or Discussion

1. **Social inequality in England is critiqued in More's *Utopia*, though slavery is permissible in utopia.** More disapproves of private property because ownership leads to inequality. In Book I, Raphael announces that he bequeathed all of his possessions to relatives and friends, prefers not to enslave himself to material things or a king, and lives a much happier life without possessions. Peter encourages Raphael to become civic-minded, as his service will "incite noble and just actions." The 1497 Cornish Rebellion against taxation is valorized ("There are a great many noblemen who live idly like drones off the labor of others, their tenants whom they bleed white by raising their rents," p. 2139). The dangers of ownership include exploitation of the poor, resulting in rising food prices, the inability to procure the wool, and decay in farming, as livestock are overpriced; in turn, this creates thieves, vagabonds, and lazy workers. Slaves are not abducted and oppressed or prisoners of war; rather, utopian citizens are made slaves either as a consequence of a crime, because they sought refuge from the death penalty in their native countries, on account of committing adultery, or voluntarily, as "low-wage" immigrants. How does More's vision of leadership compare to Machiavelli's description of leadership in *The Prince*?
   a. **Further Reading:** Yoran, Hanan. *Between Utopia and Dystopia: Erasmus, Thomas More, and the Humanist Republic of Letters.* Lanham, MD: Lexington Books, 2010.
   b. **Suggested Search:** Go to the Center for Thomas More Studies at www.thomasmorestudies.org for an art gallery and study materials.

2. **More's Utopia is founded primarily on principles from Plato's *Republic*, in which Plato describes the ideal commonwealth. The utopian government is formed of a syphogrant (phylarch), led by a tranibor.** The two hundred syphogrants elect a governor by secret ballot, listing four men nominated by people in four sections of each city; the governor holds office for life unless he exhibits characteristics of a tyrant, whereas tranibors are elected annually, with the option for reelection, and all other officials are elected for a single year, with no option for reelection. Rules are established for civic engagement, as well as for the process of introducing matters and making decisions for the public good. Few laws, no lawyers, and total transparency are emphasized as the sole method of achieving justice for all citizens. When (in Book I) Peter advises Raphael to engage civically, he adds, "A

people's welfare or misery flows in a stream from their prince" (2138). Raphael's lack of interest in material goods or self-promotion ("generous and philosophical nature," p. 2138) will benefit the commonwealth. The death penalty is not enacted for petty crimes ("It's altogether unjust to take someone's life for taking money," p. 2142), and not all crimes are considered equal. A king will distribute his "excess monies" (2150) to the people rather than hoard or waste it; this not only prevents extortion by the ruler but also "ensures an ample supply for the business transactions of the people" (2150). Gold and silver are abundant, but they are "scorned" (2167) to the extent that criminals are adorned with the metals to "mark their disgrace" (2167) and gemstones are collected as playthings by young children. The people are described as believing in God; in fact, their "first rule" is to "love and venerate the Divine Majesty," p. 2170, and their second rule is to seek pleasure by helping others and relieving them of their misery. The people are prolix readers and enjoy learning about crafts that promote progress (i.e., printing, papermaking). Compare More's principles to those promoted in the Protestant Reformation selections (*God, Church, and Self*)—More remained Catholic and was executed for his papist beliefs. Do you feel that his views were aligned with those promoted during the English Reformation?

    a. **Further Reading:** Claeys, Gregory. *The Cambridge Companion to Utopian Literature*. Cambridge: Cambridge University Press, 2010.

    b. **Suggested Search:** Go to the St. Thomas More Website at www .apostles.com/thomasmore.html.

3. **Though Utopia is presented by Thomas More as an ideal civilization, the people and land are often described as primitive and bestial.** In Book I the New World is described as a savage and primitive place ("As the sun moves, there lie vast empty deserts . . . desolate and squalid, grim and uncultivated, inhabited by wild beasts and serpents, and by men no less wild and dangerous," p. 2136). The people of the New World trade with other cultures, but they have not traveled due to the boats being made of inferior materials or the seamen's inability to navigate. The people do not use modern technologies for agriculture, instead avoiding horses and drinking lightly fermented drinks, and donating to their neighbors whatever surplus they produce. The city of Amaurot is built on rugged terrain but nevertheless profits from the land to capture and store fresh water. People produce their own clothes ("unpretentious garments of leather, that last seven years," p. 2161), and learn agriculture as their primary trade, plus a second craft; idleness is prohibited. Population is managed by limiting households to six thousand per city, with ten to sixteen adult family members to each household; people are transferred between large and small households

to maintain population standards. All are given free and extensive health care, and meals are taken communally (slaves "do all the particularly dirty and heavy work," p. 2164), with specific etiquette for men, women, and minors and their nurses. Suicide and euthanasia are acceptable, provided that the person first gets approval from the priests and senate. Premarital sex is strictly forbidden, because it makes marriage ("and all the petty annoyances it involves," p. 2178) pointless. How do More's writings about the New World compare to the ethnographies and letters written by explorers (see *New World and Europe*)? Students might also compare More's work to Montaigne's essay "Of Cannibals."

   a. **Further Reading:** Sargent, Lyman Tower. *Utopianism: A Very Short Introduction.* Oxford: Oxford University Press, 2010.

   b. **Suggested Search:** Search for "Sir Thomas More" at Luminarium: Anthology of English Literature (www.luminarium.org).

4. **Utopian religion is a combination of pantheism and monotheism.** The utopians recognize a single divine entity but worship their God through the contemplation of nature. There is an afterlife, and the most charitable citizens receive the greatest reward after death. Priests are elected by popular vote, are limited to thirteen priests per church, and also serve as army leaders in the event of war. Women are permitted to join the priesthood, and priests (even if accused of a crime) are not tried by law but, rather, are considered the most important citizens of the land; priestly garments are extravagant and are made from brightly colored bird feathers rather than gems and precious metals. Feasts occur bimonthly, and a lunar calendar is observed. How does More's description of a utopian religion compare to the religious views expressed by mystics, reformists, and fundamentalists of the period (see *Humanism and the Rediscovery of the Classical Past*)?

   a. **Further Reading:** Sullivan, E. D. S., ed. *The Utopian Vision: Seven Essays on the Quincentennial of Sir Thomas More.* San Diego, CA: San Diego State University Press, 1983.

   b. **Suggested Search:** Google "utopia and religion" for scholarly pages and student research sites devoted to the topic. Examples include the British Library overview at www.bl.uk/learning/histcitizen/21cc /utopia/more1/moral1/moral.html and John Boyle's article, "Theological Designs: Religion in Utopia," at www.thomasmorestudies.org /tmstudies/Boyle_Religion_in_Utopia.pdf.

In-Class Activities

1. Divide students into small groups and ask them to design their own utopian societies. The professor should establish some areas for design, which might include government, religion, education, economy, and family values.

2. Ask students to write a letter to a leader of their choosing, describing a fictional utopia that they have purportedly visited.

3. Is social inequality necessary on account of human nature? As a class, ask students to first share their ideas about where inequality exists in their own culture (gender, pay for various types of labor requiring the same number of hours and effort, and race are good places to start). Ask students to explain their ideas about how people are valued in society, and then, in small groups, to make a list of examples showing how different groups of people are treated as a result of stereotypes or general expectations of those people.

4. Distribute to students colored chips of unequal value (representing money, food, water, and computers). Assign tasks that force students to barter with each other. Once the tasks are completed, ask students to count their chips and then divide them into economic classes. The upper-class group now assumes leadership and assigns rules and tasks. After several play attempts, ask the class as a whole to evaluate ownership and exchange and think about their effect on social equality.

5. Ask each student to bring in an article or a description of a current event related to crime (robbery, murder, rape, embezzlement, etc.). Divide students into small groups and ask them to first discuss how the crimes would be punished by law in their cultures; then ask each group to designate an appropriate punishment according to the values dictated in More's text.

6. Over the course of two class periods, assign each student a partner. Students will then take turns providing service to their peers, with no opportunity to negotiate or determine guidelines for service requested. After the activity, ask students to define the words "community" and "equality," examining how service to others can improve or harm social relations.

Paper Topics/Suggestions for Writing

1. What social and economic systems does More describe as alternatives to private ownership? Do they guarantee social equality?

2. Discuss elements of the travel narrative genre in More's text.

3. Although More writes in favor of social equality, the book is written for an extremely elite readership. The average person of More's time was not literate and therefore could not appreciate or put these principles into practice. Do you feel that More is a hypocrite for writing a work that could be digested ("owned") by only an exclusive group of people?

4. Do the people of More's Utopia support the "eye for an eye" or "golden rule" philosophy of punishing a criminal? Support your opinion with examples from the text.

5. An important line in More's text states, "As long as money is the measure of all things, it is scarcely possible for a commonwealth to be just or happy." Do you agree with this contention? Use examples from current events to support your arguments.

6. Compare and contrast Utopia's religion and politics with the Protestant Reformation that Thomas More would have opposed in England.

7. More's work was written just a few years after Machiavelli's *The Prince*. How do the two texts compare with regard to political motivation and leadership?

Resources

Bruce, Susan, ed. *Three Early Modern Utopias: Thomas More: Utopia, Francis Bacon: New Atlantis, Henry Neville: The Isle of Pines*. Oxford: Oxford University Press, 2009.
>   This book includes the three utopian texts and an introduction to early modern utopias.

Center for Thomas More Studies. University of Dallas. www.thomasmorestudies.org.
>   This site includes online study materials, conference lists, a library with interactive maps/slide shows and travel guides, publications, an art gallery, and a historical and biographical overview.

Luminarium: Anthology of English Literature. www.luminarium.org.
>   This site includes links to other sites hosting biographies, bibliographies, utopian resources, More in foreign languages, and miscellaneous centers for research. It also links to related information on other literature and history of England.

Maxims, Monarchy and Sir Thomas More. Prod. Anna Marie. Perf. Graham Thatcher. Periaktos Productions, 1996.
>   This is a dramatic adaptation of More's ideas.

The St. Thomas More Website. www.apostles.com/thomasmore.html.
>   This site includes a biography, images, a bibliography, writings, and interactive studies.

Baldassare Castiglione
From *The Book of the Courtier*

Topics for Lecture or Discussion

1. ***The Book of the Courtier* takes the form of a dialogue, and as such, it invokes the philosophical tradition reaching back to Plato and Cicero, and resonates with contemporaneous Renaissance dialogues like Thomas More's *Utopia*.** Castiglione himself invokes the tradition of classical philosophy in his dedication of the book, writing, "I am content to have erred with Plato, Xenophon, and Marcus Tullius [Cicero]; and just as, according to these authors, there is the Idea of the perfect Republic, the perfect King, and the perfect Orator, so likewise there is that of the perfect Courtier" (2202). His point here is important: just as Plato's *Republic*, through the form of a dialogue, investigates the idea of a perfect republic, so too does Castiglione, through a dialogue, investigate the idea of the perfect courtier. Plato does not pretend that such an ideal actually exists, and neither does Castiglione, but in both cases, the investigation and discussion of the ideal might identify true goods or ends and direct people to pursue them. Thomas More's *Utopia* is another such philosophical dialogue, and it too consciously invokes Plato's *Republic* as an important precursor. It should be noted that *The Book of the Courtier*, functioning within this tradition, is much more than simply a book of manners; it is a work with philosophical aspirations of political and teleological import.
    a. **Further Reading:** Cooper, John M., ed. "The Republic." In *Plato: Complete Works*. Indianapolis, IN: Hackett Publishing Company, 1997.
    b. **Suggested Search:** A Google Images search for "Raphael's Castiglione" will result in images of Raphael's famous and influential painting of Castiglione.

2. **"Sprezzatura," a word that Castiglione coined, is one of the central qualities or arts of the ideal courtier.** Castiglione introduces the concept in the midst of the Count's discussion of the importance of grace, or graceful manners and appearance. The Count declares that the courtier must be able "to avoid affectation in every way possible as though it were some very rough and dangerous reef; and (to pronounce a new word perhaps) to practice in all things a certain *sprezzatura* [nonchalance], so as to conceal all art and make whatever is done or said appear to be without effort and almost without any thought about it" (2222). Sprezzatura is, then, somewhat paradoxical: it is the art of concealing all art; it is the studied practice of making anything done or said appear unstudied and easy. Notably, this concept immediately follows the Count's condemna-

tion of affectation, and the Count is not just against the appearance of affectation, but he is against affectation itself. Sprezzatura is not, as he sees it, an affectation, but an art that can be truly mastered. It is not so much a deception as it is a skill that frames one's action (and in this, he follows Cicero's discussion of the studied appearance of artlessness as an important quality for the orator in *De Oratore*). The Count himself identifies this almost paradoxical nature of sprezzatura by saying, "we may call that art true art which does not seem to be art" (2222).

   a. **Further Reading:** Richards, Jennifer. "Assumed Simplicity and the Critique of Nobility: Or, How Castiglione Read Cicero." *Renaissance Quarterly* 54.2 (2001): 460–486.

   b. **Suggested Search:** A JSTOR (http://www.jstor.org/) search for "sprezzatura" will result in several helpful articles, many of which show the later influence of this concept.

3. **Addressing some of the hotly debated philosophical and political questions of the day, Castiglione's discussion of the primary aim of the courtier serves as a contrast to the political ideas propounded in Machiavelli's *The Prince*.** In Book Four of *The Book of the Courtier*, Ottaviano Fregoso declares, "Therefore, I think that the aim of the perfect Courtier, which we have not spoken of up to now, is so to win for himself, by means of the accomplishments ascribed to him by these gentlemen, the favor and mind of the prince whom he serves that he may be able to tell him, and always will tell him, the truth about everything he needs to know, without fear or risk of displeasing him; and that when he sees the mind of his prince inclined to a wrong action, he may dare to oppose him and in a gentle manner avail himself of the favor acquired by his good accomplishments, so as to dissuade him of every evil intent and bring him to the path of virtue" (2238). Rather than simply enjoying courtly life, witty conversation, the arts, and contests of physical skill, the courtier puts all of his talents to use for the primary end of advising his ruler and guiding him toward virtue. The courtier, in this context, is far from a trivial character; rather than the foppish dilettante that we might imagine when thinking of a courtier, he is instead an important figure in the court who plays an instrumental role in the establishment of justice and other virtues in the state. This argument should be contrasted with Machiavelli's in *The Prince*, which rejected both classical and Christian conceptions of the virtues in favor of useful actions taken to maintain power.

   a. **Further Reading:** Machiavelli, Niccolò. *The Prince*. Trans. Leo Paul S. de Alvarez. Long Grove, IL: Waveland Press, 1989.

   b. **Suggested Search:** A search for "Machiavelli" at the Stanford Encyclopedia of Philosophy (http://plato.stanford.edu) results in a helpful summary and discussion of Machiavelli's thought.

4. **While the content of the dialogue discusses the attributes of the ideal courtier, the actual behavior of the interlocutors—particularly in the witty, polite exchanges between the men and women—serves as a practical example of proper behavior for the courtier.** It is worthwhile to observe that the people participating in the conversation in *The Book of the Courtier* are for the most part powerful, important people who had gathered for a visit from the Pope. Hence the setting in which the conversation occurs is a courtly, noble setting, and the behavior that is displayed is governed by many of the rules and qualities that are discussed as ideal. This is most readily apparent in the relationship between the men and women. The conversations take place in the rooms of the Duchess Elisabetta Gonzaga, and Emilia Pia acts as the moderator of the conversation. Pia's conversation displays both wit and prudence, and her guidance of the conversation, including the moments when she redirects the men's attention at awkward moments, is itself exemplary of behavior worthy of the ideal courtier.

   a. **Further Reading:** Rebhorn, Wayne A. *Courtly Performances: Masking and Festivity in Castiglione's* Book of the Courtier. Detroit, MI: Wayne State University Press, 1978.

   b. **Suggested Search:** A Google Images search for "Andrea Mantegna Court of Mantua" results in Mantegna's painting which depicts courtiers standing at court.

5. **Many of the ideal courtier's arts and skills are related to the art of rhetoric.** Classical thinkers, including Aristotle, Quintilian, and Cicero, conceived of rhetoric, or the arts of persuasion, as concerned with much more than simply correct logic or accurate reasoning. Logic (*logos*) alone often fails to persuade others, and hence a rhetor, or an orator, must be sensitive to the way that his character is perceived (*ethos*) and the ways in which he can arouse the passions of his listeners (*pathos*). Castiglione follows this sort of analysis of rhetoric when he discusses the courtier, since the courtier must be well-spoken, but he must also be attentive to his appearance, bearing, and the ways in which his manners affect those around him. Similarly, the courtier must be a master of understanding the passions, especially when it comes to guiding or rebuking a prince who is acting contrary to virtue. Only with attention to all of this would the courtier "be able to lead his prince by the austere path of virtue, adorning it with shady fronds and strewing it with pretty flowers to lessen the tedium of the toilsome journey for one whose strength is slight" (2241).

   a. **Further Reading:** Cicero. *De Oratore.* Trans. E.W. Sutton and H. Rackham. Loeb Classical Library. Cambridge, MA: Harvard University Press, 1942.

b. **Suggested Search:** A search at the Internet Classics Archive for "Aristotle's Rhetoric" results in the full text of this foundational work.

In-Class Activities

1. Discuss the differences and similarities between Castiglione's characterization of a courtier and the current aids, lobbyists, and auxiliaries that surround our government today.

2. Divide the class into groups, each of which must summarize a different speaker's ideas concerning the ideal courtier. Share these summaries and as a class try to discern the common elements that the different characters in the dialogue agree upon.

3. As a class, create lists of the attributes that one might find in the following roles: the courtier, the orator, the statesman, the philosopher, and the poet. Do these roles share any attributes? What different historical figures might fit within several of these categories?

Paper Topics/Suggestions for Writing

1. Why does Castiglione discuss his sorrow during the dedication of the work? How might this be related to the discussion of the ideal courtier?

2. Write an essay that contrasts Castiglione's presentation of the ideal courtier to Cicero's presentation of the ideal orator in *De Oratore*. What is the most significant difference between these ideal types?

3. Who makes the weakest argument in our selection of *The Book of the Courtier*? Why is it unpersuasive?

4. Imagine that you are seated in the room, partaking in the conversation described in *The Book of the Courtier*. Write a fictional presentation of the arguments that you would add to the discussion. Who would you disagree with? What attributes would you add to the catalogue ascribed to the idea orator?

5. Write an essay in which you consider the relationship between the men and women in *The Book of the Courtier*. Why is it mostly the men who describe the courtier? What are the significant statements made by the women? How do they reformulate or challenge the things that the men have said?

6. Consider the setting of *The Book of the Courtier*. Why does Castiglione choose to write a dialogue? Is he teaching us anything? Contrast the dialogue in Castiglione's work with the Plato's dialogues and the conversation that takes place in Thomas More's *Utopia*.

7. Write a research paper in which you contrast the ideals of the courtier (and the ruler) that we find in Castiglione's *The Book of the Courtier* with the ideal qualities of the ruler outlined in Machiavelli's *The Prince*. Be particularly attentive to the differences between Castiglione's and Machiavelli's uses of the word "virtue." What is the final end or purpose of action for Castiglione's courtier and Machiavelli's prince?

Resources

Burke, Peter. *The Fortunes of the Courtier: The European Reception of Castiglione's Cortegiano*. Malden, MA: Polity Press, 1995.

> In the work, Burke explores the reception history of *The Book of the Courtier* by examining the diffusion of the copies of Castiglione's book. Chapter 2, "The Courtier in its Time" should be of particular interest to an unfamiliar instructor.

Castiglione, Baldesar. *The Book of the Courtier: A Norton Critical Edition*. Daniel Javitch, ed. New York: Norton, 2002.

> This volume is recommended for students or instructors who wish to read the entire work. There are several helpful essays and a brief biography of Castiglione included in this edition.

Najemy, John M., ed. *Italy in the Age of the Renaissance 1300–1550*. The Short Oxford History of Italy. Oxford: Oxford University Press, 2004.

> While Castiglione is only quickly mentioned a few times, this volume is recommended for those seeking a brief but informative history of Renaissance Italy. See especially Chapter 1, "Education and the Emergence of a Literature Society" by Robert Black, and Chapter 2, "Humanism and the Lure of Antiquity" by Carol Everhart Quillen for pertinent background information for understanding *The Book of the Courtier*.

Rebhorn, Wayne A. *Courtly Performances: Masking and Festivity in Castiglione's* Book of the Courtier. Detroit, MI: Wayne State University Press, 1978.

> Rebhorn's book discusses the court and society presented in *The Book of the Courtier*, arguing that the festive and rhetorical situation is imperative for understanding Castiglione's argument.

Scaglione, Aldo. *Courtliness, Chivalry, & Courtesy from Ottonian Germany to the Italian Renaissance*. Berkeley: University of California Press, 1992.

> Part Four of this book, beginning with Chapter 7, discusses courtliness in Italy, and Castiglione is discussed extensively throughout the work.

MARGUERITE DE NAVARRE

The Heptameron

Topics for Lecture or Discussion

1. **Like Giovanni Boccaccio's *Decameron* and Geoffrey Chaucer's *Canterbury Tales*, Marguerite de Navarre's *The Heptameron* is presented as a collection of satirical and bawdy stories recounted by a broad range of people.** Structured as frame narratives, readers learn that the storytellers are often escaping from plague (*Canterbury Tales*), a flood and criminal activity (*The Heptameron*), or other tragedy and using storytelling to pass the time. The stories in this collection often emphasize corruption of religion and aristocracy, if told by someone from the middle class or the lower class but extol virtuous and chivalric behavior if recounted by someone of the upper class. *The Heptameron* comprises seventy-two stories, often dealing with romantic and sexual conflicts, and they are recounted in an abbey while the storytellers wait for a bridge to be built. Story 8 recounts a middle-class escapade gone wrong, while Story 10 relates the life of a pauper turned high knight of court aspiring to love a Lady. The stories are meant as a commentary on morality, love, and political intrigue, often revealing rich dramatic irony to illustrate the contradictions of human behavior, social class, and religious morals. How does Marguerite de Navarre's Reformation critique differ from those critiques proposed by later Protestant Reformation (and Spanish Counter-Reformation) writers?

    a. **Further Reading:** Lyons, John, and Mary B. McKinley. *New Studies of the Heptameron and Early Modern Culture*. Philadelphia: University of Pennsylvania Press, 1993.

    b. **Suggested Search:** Go to the University of Minnesota Digital Library at http://conservancy.umn.edu and search for "Early Modern French Women Writers: Secondary Studies."

2. **Marguerite de Navarre more often explores gender problems and stereotypes, looking at social class, religion, and financial corruption to the extent that they affect gender relations.** De Navarre herself was the queen consort of King Henry II and was sister to Francis I of France. Though de Navarre's brother ordered her to receive an extensive classical education, she also arranged her marriage with Charles IV, considered to be a "laggard and a dolt." The issue of arranged marriages and resulting liaisons is addressed throughout the tales. De Navarre later married Henry II and was considered a diplomat and great patron (like her brother) of humanists and reformers; scholars have conjectured that her mystic poems were direct influences

on the Reformation in England, and *The Heptameron* often includes critical attacks on the corrupt practices of Catholic clergyman as a call for reform. In Story 8, Bornet contrives to cheat on his wife with her chambermaid, with assistance from his neighbor. His wife, meanwhile, plots with the chambermaid to expose his intentions; she steals into the chambermaid's bed and both her husband and their neighbor are duped into an affair with her. Discovering the ruse, the wife then tries to teach her husband a lesson ("It's high time you were content with me for what I am—your own wife and an honest woman, and it's high time that you found that just as satisfying as when you thought I was a poor little erring chambermaid," p. 2250). The story concludes with the husband being publicly humiliated on account of his wife's trickery. In Story 10, Amador falls in love with Florida and plans to be closer to her by first courting Avanturada ("His marriage was no more than a cover, no more than a convenient excuse to enable him to visit her on whom his mind constantly dwelled," p. 2256); the story ends tragically with Amador's and Avanturada's deaths, and with Florida entering a convent and becoming a nun. Do you think comedy (as Molière would later argue) serves more in the correction of human vices than tragedy (as Aristotle argues)?

    a. **Further Reading:** Cholakian, Patricia, and Rouben C. Cholakian. *Marguerite de Navarre: Mother of the Renaissance.* New York: Columbia University Press, 2006.

    b. **Suggested Search:** Go to the Heptameron Information Society website, www.heptameron.info/author.html.

3. **Frame narratives are used in Marguerite de Navarre's story collection to link the narrators.** In "Prologue," the characters first debate about how they should pass the time. Oisille proposes reading the Holy Bible ("For, a person who knows God will find all things beautiful in Him, and without Him all things will seem ugly," p. 2246), while Hircan argues that something leisurely should be adopted to compensate for the loss of daily leisurely activities (e.g., fiber arts and singing for women, hunting and sporting for men). Each story enables the group of storytellers to examine the issues in their "real" lives. After Story 8 is recounted, Dagoucin remarks on marital fulfillment and the importance of finding one's soul mate, whereas the other male storytellers remark that Dagoucin is an idealist ("describing Plato's republic," p. 2251), and that passion and physical lust are requirements for a healthy relationship. After Story 10, the women argue that Florida was tested to the limits of endurance to remain virtuous, whereas the men argue that women need to have less faith in men to avoid being disappointed and creating misery for all. Story 10 creates a debate about men's "honor" and how it is proven in love and duty. How does the use of a frame narrative enrich storytelling?

a. **Further Reading:** Gittes, Katherine. *Framing the Canterbury Tales: Chaucer and the Medieval Frame Narrative Tradition*. Santa Barbara, CA: Greenwood Press, 1991.

b. **Suggested Search:** Go to Bonnie D. Irwin's article "What's in a Frame? The Medieval Textualization of Traditional Storytelling" at http://journal.oraltradition.org/files/articles/10i/6_irwin.pdf, available through the *Oral Tradition* journal.

4. **The Moors' battle with Christendom is detailed throughout *The Heptameron*.** In 1212 Christian kings began to push the Muslim Moors from Iberia and fully succeeded in 1492, when they overtook Granada. By 1502, all Moors (and Jews) were given the option of quitting Spain, converting to Catholicism, or being executed. During de Navarre's historical era, the Moors refer to these Islamic tribes that originated in northern and western Africa but were living as peasants in the Iberian territories, with wars taking place with the king of Granada. Story 10 of *The Heptameron* deals extensively with Amador in battle with the Moors, separated from his beloved Florida; he commits suicide rather than being taken by the Moors and forced to abjure Christianity. How does martyrdom in this story compare to events claimed as martyrdom in contemporary society? Students might also compare this text to *Lazarillo de Tormes*, published four years before *The Heptameron*.

a. **Further Reading:** Beik, William. *A Social and Cultural History of Early Modern France*. Cambridge: Cambridge University Press, 2009.

b. **Suggested Search:** Go to *Britannica Online Encyclopedia* at www.britannica.com/EBchecked/topic/391449/Moor for background information on the Moors.

In-Class Activities

1. Historically, people have traced a "map" of love, beginning with strong emotions and illness that develop into jealousy and suspicion, then tenderness, and finally commitment. Ask students to compare the "carte du tendre" (the seventeenth century in Madeleine de Scudery's novel *Clelie*; also see "Early Modern French Women Writers: Secondary Studies" in the Resources section) with the idea of love in their culture. Then ask students to design their own maps of love based on their ideas about a relationship's progress.

2. Divide students into groups and assign each group a social class. Each class will then create a short "tale" to illustrate a lesson on a given theme (love, war, family). Have the groups gather to share their stories with each other, and then have a designated student record the discussion that ensues (this is considered the "frame narrative"). Ask students

to collate the stories, record the class conversation in a digital book, and then publish the work under a collaborative title. (Note that numerous websites allow students to create and publish their digital books for free; students might also use PowerPoint.)

3. Ask students to compare and contrast illustrations from the 1698 and 1894 editions of *The Heptameron* (see the Resources section). Students should examine costumes, themes, and symbolism and how the illustrations contribute to or detract from the written story line. The professor might ask students to do a short write-up of their findings, reflecting on which of the illustrations they preferred, and why.

Paper Topics/Suggestions for Writing

1. Compare a tale by Chaucer or Boccaccio to one by Marguerite de Navarre. How do the earlier Estate Satire essays differ from de Navarre's writing style?

2. What do the frame narratives accomplish in de Navarre's work?

3. What is more important during de Navarre's period, honor and duty, or love?

4. Discuss de Navarre's criticisms of male-female romantic relationships, providing examples from the stories.

5. What is the role that the Moors, and historical references to war, play in de Navarre's work? Cite examples to support your statements.

6. The French philosopher Pierre Bayle argued that de Navarre is a queen who "grant[s] her protection to people persecuted for opinions which she believes to be false; to open a sanctuary to them; to preserve them from the flames prepared for them; to furnish them with a subsistence." Looking at the ways in which royalty treats its subjects in the tales, do you agree with this opinion?

Resources

Heptameron Information Society. www.heptameron.info/author.html.
> This site includes the 1894 illustrated version of *The Heptameron*, with biography and historical information about Marguerite de Navarre.

Portail Multimédia de Renaissance-France.org. www.renaissance-france.org /multimedia/pages/pagmultimedia.html. Site editor Rémi Morel.
> This site contains sound recordings of Stories 6, 11, 20, 40, and 60 of *The Heptameron*, playable in QuickTime, Real, and Windows Media layers, as well as audio for other authors who may be relevant

to the reading, including Michel de Montaigne, Louise Labé, François Rabelais, and Pierre de Ronsard.

University of Minnesota Digital Library. "Early Modern French Women Writers: Secondary Studies." Compiled for the EMFWW Project by Anne E. Duggan, Mary Skemp, and Michelle Miller (updated 2002). http://conservancy.umn.edu.

> This site contains a notable bibliography of books, articles, and essays related to three writers: Marie le Jars de Gournay, Louise Labé, and Marguerite de Navarre.

University of Provence. http://sites.univ-provence.fr.

> This site includes the 1698 Gallet illustrated version of *The Heptameron*. The site is in French, but the images can easily be explored.

University of Virginia. Gordon Collection. www2.lib.virginia.edu/rmds /portfolio/gordon.

> This site contains links to literary works of the period and images from two editions (1560 and 1547) of *The Heptameron*.

Williams, Hugh Noel. *The Pearl of Princesses: The Life of Marguerite D'Angouleme, Queen of Navarre*. London: Eveleigh Nash, 1916.

> This book is considered the definitive and most complete biography of Marguerite de Navarre.

The Life of Lazarillo de Tormes and
of His Fortunes and Adversities

Topics for Lecture or Discussion

1. **Lazaro is a *picaro* (rascal or rogue), and his narration through the account represents the picaresque genre.** Picaresque works largely differed from the more popular chivalric romance and pastoral works of the period, depicting the world more with caricatures, comic episodes, and graphic depictions of suffering. The picaro is often a member of the lower social classes and often relies on his cleverness to survive in a corrupt and morally bankrupt society. The picaresque genre emphasizes economic and social problems in blunt terms, often exposing hypocrisy; the protagonist is often a rogue adventurer who survives by outwitting the wealthy corrupt. Lazaro is inducted into the criminal world after his father (a thief) dies. His mother apprentices him with a blind beggar, and he later works for a priest, squire, friar, pardoner, chaplain, bailiff, and an archbishop; the story illustrates the abuse of power, regardless of social class, with which Lazaro must contend as he makes his way in the world. The genre is later adopted by Cervantes (*Don Quixote*) and expands into English novels by such writers as Defoe. Do you think the picaro is justified in his criminal behaviors, given that he is operating within a corrupt society?
   a. **Further Reading:** Cruz, Anne J., ed. *Approaches to Teaching Lazarillo de Tormes and the Picaresque Tradition.* New York: Modern Language Association, 2009.
   b. **Suggested Search:** Eisenberg, Daniel. "Does the Picaresque Novel Exist?" *Kentucky Romance Quarterly* 26 (1979): 203–19.

2. **The work also represents an early form of the *bildungsroman* (coming-of-age novel) from a picaresque standpoint, as Lazaro is trained in violence and corruption.** The "education novel" was so named only in 1819 and generally represented by German literature beginning with Goethe's *Apprenticeship of Wilhelm Meister*. Other eighteenth-century famous education novels include Rousseau's *Emile*, Laurence Sterne's *Tristram Shandy*, and Voltaire's *Candide*. American novels, including *Huckleberry Finn*, may be more aligned with the picaresque genre, as they detail a boy's life and education through criminal and lower-class cultures. They generally evolve from folkloric stories of a young son venturing out into the world to seek his fortune after a parent has died or in the absence of family provision. Aside from working as a beggar, Lazaro also seeks employment with a nobleman, a friar, an indulgences-seller chaplain, and a constable before he becomes pros-

perous. Each master exposes him to different trades, methods of earning money, and ways of treating people. How do experiences and book knowledge compare with each other, and how do they each contribute to a person's intelligence?

    a. **Further Reading:** Moretti, Franco. *The Way of the World: The Bildungsroman in European Culture.* London: Verso, 1987.

    b. **Suggested Search:** The Victorian Web (www.victorianweb.org/genre /bildung.html) contains several pages devoted to the history and development of the *bildungsroman* in Western Europe.

3. **Almost as a dystopian work, *Lazarillo* as satire calls for social reform, particularly of the corrupt clergy (greedy, debauched, and uncharitable).** As a predecessor to Weber's *The Protestant Ethic*, the writer remarks on the Spanish belief of that era: that social hierarchy was based on God's grace or condemnation (the wealthy and those of legitimate Christian birth were rewarded with wealth, while the Jewish and Moorish, as well as corrupt or condemned members of society, were rewarded with poverty). Even Lazaro's masters teach through their own wicked behavior: the first and blind master drinks and eats more than was rationed and recites prayers for lowly women. The third master, a nobleman, has moved to a different city and lives an impoverished life simply because he would not "doff his hat" for the higher-class knight that was his neighbor ("a nobleman owes nothing to anyone but God and the King, and it's wrong for a gentleman to derogate a jot from his self-respect"). Throughout the novel, religious figures (i.e., the friar, the archpriest) commit adultery, and the children of nobility are criticized for their gluttony and sloth. Do you find any heroic or honorable characters in the novel? What attributes do they possess?

    a. **Further Reading:** Benito-Vessels, Carmen, and Michael Zappala, eds. *The Picaresque: A Symposium on the Rogue's Tale.* Newark, NJ: University of Delaware Press, 1994.

    b. **Suggested Search:** Go to the SAAE (Spanish Arts Arte Espanol) website at www.spanisharts.com and search for "Lazarillo de Tormes."

4. **The book was published anonymously (and banned due to its anti-clerical content) during the Spanish Inquisition, at the outset of trials against the Lutherans.** Though not a direct attack on Christian principles and beliefs, because it mocked the Spanish Crown and the practices of the Inquisition, the book was censored and included in the *Index of Forbidden Books*, and it did not appear fully in print in Spain until the nineteenth century. Chapter 2 focuses on Lazaro's employment by a priest who uses church donations for personal gain. Nevertheless, at a funeral, the writer states his support for the prayers offered at funeral services and expresses his devotion to God ("I was in this

distress from which may the Lord deliver all faithful Christians"). His fourth master, a Mercedarian friar, is described as being too sociable and "a great enemy of prayers in the choir." His fifth master (chapter 5) is an indulgence seller who takes money in exchange for the faithful to be exempt from a sin committed. Throughout the novel, religious figures (i.e., the friar, the archpriest) commit adultery, and the children of nobility are criticized for their gluttony and sloth. The book appears to attack the Catholic Church but not necessarily Christian essential beliefs. Where do you see evidence of this in the novel?

a. **Further Reading:** Dunn, Peter N. *Spanish Picaresque Fiction: A New Literary History.* Ithaca, NY: Cornell University Press, 1993.

b. **Suggested Search:** Google "Spanish Inquisition" for numerous academic resources and images related to these historical proceedings (e.g., www.richeast.org/htwm/Inqui/inq.html).

5. **Taboo for its time, the subject of interracial love, between Lazaro's mother and a black stableman, is treated in this novel.** Historically, peoples of the Iberian Peninsula were more open to interracial marriage, particularly during the Muslim conquests of the eighth century; Islam permitted Muslim men to marry non-Muslim monotheists, and by the twelfth century this assimilated culture was known as the Moors. Christians recaptured the peninsula during the thirteenth century, during which time the Moors were exiled or forced to convert. Those who remained and converted were often discriminated against due to their "mixed blood," thereby ending the cultural practice of interracial marriage. Interracial problems are delineated in the story through the narrator's relationship with his stepfather. The narrator initially fears and dislikes the man due to his physical appearance but later likes him because he supports the family. Racial tensions are stereotyped when, after a child is born of the interracial union, the narrator recounts a story about his young brother calling his father the bogeyman, and also when it is revealed that the stepfather is stealing to support the family. How does the text's treatment of the Moors compare to the appearance of the Moors in Marguerite de Navarre's *Heptameron*, published only four years later?

a. **Further Reading:** Homza, Lu Ann, ed. *The Spanish Inquisition, 1478–1614: An Anthology of Sources.* Indianapolis, IN: Hackett, 2006.

b. **Suggested Search:** The Institute for Historical Review (IHR) website (www.ihr.org) contains several resources devoted to the history and development of the Spanish Inquisition.

In-Class Activities

1. Ask each student to create a digital time line (www.dipity.com, www.tiki-toki.com, and other websites host free time line development) for

Lazaro, representing important events in his education. Alternatively, each student might create a digital time line representing milestones in her or his personal growth and education.

2. Divide students into small groups. Ask each group to imagine a scenario in which Lazaro consigns himself to a new master. The scenario should illustrate a lesson or lifestyle not covered in the original text.

3. Ask each student to write a short letter to an imaginary leader justifying an example of his or her misbehavior or misdeed in a previous situation. An "Inquisition" is formed in class, and a decision in favor or not in favor of each student is made as the letters are read aloud. Alternatively, the class might convene as an Inquisition and assign one classmate to play the role of Lazaro, during which evidence from the story is examined to pronounce a judgment.

Paper Topics/Suggestions for Writing

1. Read Daniel Eisenberg's article "Does the Picaresque Novel Exist?" (see Resources section that follows). Do you agree with his contentions? Support your argument, using examples from the article and the *Lazarillo* text and class discussions on the picaresque genre.

2. Do you see more evidence that the writer disapproves of Christianity or merely of its hypocritical and corrupt leaders? Support your argument with examples from the work.

3. What is your response to reading a work narrated by a petty criminal? Do you believe he is justified, or should he be punished for his actions and statements?

4. Compare Lazaro's relationship with his masters to Candide's relationship with Panurge (Voltaire). What lessons do the two young men learn about life and human values?

5. What lessons does Lazaro learn about life and human behavior? Do you think he would be classified as a pessimist or an optimist?

6. Lazaro marries at the end of the text and gives his wife preferential treatment by overlooking her infidelity. What do you make of his behavior in light of his response to his masters' corrupt actions throughout the story?

Resources

Cruz, Anne J., ed. *Approaches to Teaching Lazarillo de Tormes and the Picaresque Tradition.* New York: Modern Language Association, 2009.
This volume of essays examines the materials, approaches, and methods of teaching this work, as well as the picaresque novel.

Dunn, Peter N. *Spanish Picaresque Fiction: A New Literary History.* New York: Cornell University Press, 1993.

> This work presents critical response and scholarship relating to the Picaresque genre.

Eisenberg, Daniel. "Does the Picaresque Novel Exist?" *Kentucky Romance Quarterly* 26 (1979): 203–19. Available at http://users.ipfw .edu/jehle/deisenbe/Other_Hispanic_Topics/does_the_picaresque.pdf.

> It is argued in this article that the word "picaresque" is a "convenient modern label," that the picaresque corpus is sparse, and that writers and critics since the sixteenth century have debated on the elements and examples of the picaresque style.

El lazarillo de Tormes. Dir. Cesar Fernandez Ardavin. 1959 (Spanish).

Lazaro de Tormes. Dir. Fernando Fernan Gomez. Theiapolis Cinema, 2001 (Spanish).

> This movie won the Goya award for best costume design and was nominated for three other awards.

SAAE (Spanish Arts Arte Español). www.spanisharts.com.

> This site includes a bibliography, images from four illustrated editions, plus information on those editions, and other background information, constituting more than twenty pages of text.

MICHEL DE MONTAIGNE
Essays

Topics for Lecture or Discussion

1. **The etymology for the word "essay" stems from the French word** ***essayer,*** **meaning "to attempt" or "try out."** As a style, Montaigne's essays represent exploratory and personal expositions on different topics and often include anecdotes or begin as a series of quotes, expanding into a study of the topic from an unbiased perspective. Throughout history, essays have been used to expound on daily life, outline a political or an artistic manifesto, share theory, and critique. Important essay collections include John Locke's *Essay Concerning Human Understanding,* Malthus's *Essay on the Principle of Population,* and Francis Bacon's *Essayes: Religious Meditations.* The essayist Aldous Huxley suggests that essays may be divided into three types: personal and autobiographical, objective and factual, and abstract-universal. Essays often use writing modes that include classification and division, cause and effect, descriptive, dialectic, exemplification, narrative, and critical—and the chosen modes generally pertain to the essay's purpose and intended audience. Montaigne's work comprises 107 essays, most often in didactic style to engage the reader. He relies upon citations from classical works and writes his collection to describe the human race, often examining the paradox of humankind's behavior. In the introduction "To the Reader," Montaigne warns the reader that his essays are written for a domestic and private purpose rather than for some public usefulness. Why would a didactic style appeal to readers of Montaigne's time period, and what might today's reader prefer?
   a. **Further Reading:** Kritzman, Lawrence. *The Fabulous Imagination: On Montaigne's Essays.* New York: Columbia University Press, 2009.
   b. **Suggested Search:** Go to the University of Chicago's Montaigne Project at www.lib.uchicago.edu/efts/ARTFL/projects/montaigne.

2. **Montaigne often reacts against the violent and corrupt behaviors of the French government of his period, both toward the French and in what he learned of European conquest and treatment of natives in the New World.** Students might begin by looking at the New World exploration literature, noting the observations of barbarism and primitive behavior described by Columbus, Caminha, and Cortés. Montaigne's works, though he never visited the New World, often oppose and criticize the European reaction and treatment of those peoples. His essays exhibit tolerance for others and loathing of dogma and also reveal his skepticism about human nature. European hypocrisy is

emphasized in the essays "Of Cannibals" and "Of the Inconsistency of Our Actions," both of which stress European inability to recognize barbaric or despotic behavior in its own culture. Montaigne criticizes European greed, desire to conquer and own to excess, the waste of natural resources, the development of artificial laws that are no better (and often worse) than natural laws, and following "the inclinations of appetite" (2335) rather than pursuing moderation and wisdom. Men, he argues, are fickle and inconstant, rarely exhibiting the same character and values in all situations across their entire lives. Therefore, we should not "judge men simply by their outward actions" (2339) but, rather, carefully examine their motivations and inclinations to determine their true nature. The essay "Of Coaches" also explores political corruption of the leaders, showing that kings of ancient and exotic places were more responsible and honorable than European leaders of his period ("We shall have greatly hastened the decline of this new world by our contagion" [2348]). Do you feel that Montaigne's views would have been more aligned with the explorers if he had traveled to the lands they describe as primitive and barbaric? How does reading about rather than visiting a culture bias your view of that place?

a. **Further Reading:** Langer, Ullrich. *The Cambridge Companion to Montaigne*. Cambridge: Cambridge University Press, 2005.

b. **Suggested Search:** Go to the University of Calgary's "The European Voyages of Exploration: Fifteenth and Sixteenth Centuries" site at www.ucalgary.ca/applied_history/tutor/eurvoya. This site contains information about Iberian pioneers, Portugal, and Spain, all related to adventurers and the cultural, political, and economic globalization of the period.

3. **Imagination, according to Montaigne, is responsible for miracles, visions, and extraordinary occurrences.** Though humanism is often considered a philosophy of pursuing knowledge, often that pursuit includes use of one's imagination and willingness to explore. Humanists valued reason and imagination equally as leading to human improvement and the development of morals. Imagination included one's thoughts, opinions, and mental pictures. In Montaigne's essay, imagination also appears to be linked to psychosomatic disorders. Montaigne describes a condition in which his friend suffers from physical impotence where no disease exists; his friend, he argues, can be duped (again by appealing to his imagination through quackery) into becoming healthy once more. Imagination represents the link between soul and body ("through which the experience of one is communicated to the other" [2323]), and Montaigne describes several historical instances in which the imagination acts against the physical body. Questionable "immoral" or "inappropriate" actions such as farting, erections, and

ecstatic delusions all arise from an overactive imagination overtaking the mind; humans are powerless regarding these behaviors because their imaginations are as powerful and important as Reason. How are these explanations both helpful and potentially dangerous for the justification of certain behaviors or actions that people commit?

a. **Further Reading:** Cave, Terrence. *How to Read Montaigne.* London: Granta Books, 2007.

b. **Suggested Search:** Go to the Imagination, Mental Imagery, Consciousness, and Cognition site at www.imagery-imagination.com /index.htm. This site includes a history, activities, and resources related to the theories of mind and consciousness. Conference papers, articles, and links also are included.

4. **Barbarism is a subjective term used to oppose whatever is different from one's own culture.** "Of Cannibals" makes an argument against colonists and discrimination of natives in the New World, arguing that what Europeans call "barbaric" is no more than behavior that is distinct from what a person recognizes as normal to his or her own culture ("Each man calls barbarism whatever is not his own practice" [2316]). Montaigne states that the people of New World culture are not "wild" but rather "naturalistic," whereas Europeans might be considered "wild" because they artificially produce things. If the nations being conquered appear barbarous, it is because they have not evolved as a result of human intervention and are still guided by natural law— their "purity" renders them "barbaric." Importantly, Montaigne remarks that his own culture is barbaric because European culture "eats man alive" (2319), whereas the New World cannibals eat dead carcasses with purpose. New World people wage noble and generous warfare, do not harshly punish their prisoners, use only what resources are needed (ownership and excess are superfluous), have a strong sense of community, and have healthier marriages without spousal jealousy; these qualities set them above Europeans, according to Montaigne. How do these issues compare to the treatment of prisoners of war, property, and marriage in your culture?

a. **Further Reading:** Bakewell, Sarah. *How to Live: Or, A Life of Montaigne.* New York: Other Press, 2011.

b. **Suggested Search:** Search the New World Encyclopedia Online (www.newworldencyclopedia.org) for information regarding the New World and European responses to New World explorations.

5. **Montaigne explores "natural law," often describing it in more positive terms than "positive law."** Positive laws are artificial and manmade, and they are applicable only to a specific culture. Positive laws assign privileges and rights to select groups and individuals. Natural law, on the other hand, is universal in that it represents "inherent"

rights conferred upon all peoples, cultures, and periods, and it cannot be manipulated by humans. Natural law would include a statement, for example, that "all men are created equal with the rights to life, liberty, and the pursuit of happiness" (thereby excluding slavery), whereas positive law would be focused on defining property rights (claiming to include a "slave" as property), privileges of citizens, and laws regarding crime and punishment. Montaigne's essays reveal that natural law is pure and infallible because humans cannot corrupt it. How do Montaigne's views of natural rights relate to government practices of democracy today?

a. **Further Reading:** Tierney, Brian. *The Idea of Natural Rights: Studies on Natural Rights, Natural Law, and Church Law, 1150–1625.* Grand Rapids, MI: Wm. B. Eerdmans Publishing Co., 1997.

b. **Suggested Search:** Google "natural versus positive law" for several university and academic websites that provide a foundation for this topic (e.g., http://web.nmsu.edu/~dscoccia/376web/376lpaust.pdf).

In-Class Activities

1. Ask students to explore the difference between positive and natural law, perhaps by examining an important issue such as slavery, abortion, or same-sex marriage. How is this issue interpreted according to both types of law? Do current judicial policies seem to reflect a tendency to support natural or positive leanings?

2. Groups of students are assigned a mundane topic and develop either an outline or a complete short essay using Montaigne's style (anecdotes, quotes, and exploratory reflections). Each group presents its essay and receives a critique from the class.

3. Students are put into small groups and assigned a "character." Each member is given a chance to explain why his or her culture is civilized and why the other cultures are barbaric.

4. Ask students to read the work "Body Ritual among the Nacirema," without being given any clues regarding its true intent (the essay is written as a faux-anthropological study of a "barbaric ritual" in a primitive, magic-obsessed culture and is actually an observation of the Western obsession with brushing one's teeth). Ask students to debate about whether or not this culture is truly barbaric. The instructor will then reveal the true meaning behind the essay, and the class will reflect upon the validity of Montaigne's definition of barbarism. (Note that the Nacirema essay can easily be located online as an e-text.)

5. Ask students to work in groups to determine whether Montaigne's definition of "imagination" is valid. Ask groups to make a list of examples

in which it appears that the mind and body affect each other by use of the imagination. Advertisement, subliminal messages, diet fads, and the placebo effect are good places to start.

Paper Topics/Suggestions for Writing

1. Do you agree with Montaigne that "barbarism" can best be defined as "whatever is not in one's own practice"? Argue your position by providing examples from a culture that you might define as barbaric relative to your own.

2. How do Montaigne's essays represent an "attempt" or a "trying out" of topics? Which elements render them "exploratory" and "personal" according to Montaigne?

3. How does Montaigne define imagination, and in what sense is it both a negative and a positive quality?

4. What evidence does Montaigne give against the European belief in "man-made progress" and "ownership"?

5. Montaigne often refers to "natural law" in his essays. Define this phrase, and compare it to positive law. What are the pros and cons of each form according to Montaigne?

Resources

Gordon Collection, University of Virginia Library. www2.lib.virginia.edu /rmds/portfolio/gordon/literary/montaigne/index.html.
> This collection includes a digital facsimile of the 1595 and 1588 publications of Montaigne's work, as well as background on the essays, a short biography, and links to other Internet resources.

The Montaigne Project, University of Chicago. www.lib.uchicago.edu/efts /ARTFL/projects/montaigne.
> This site contains e-texts, images, and a portrait gallery, as well as a list of conferences, and acts as the forum for the annual interdisciplinary journal *Montaigne Studies*.

Portail Multimédia de Renaissance-France.org. www.renaissance-france.org /multimedia/pages/pagmultimedia.html.
> Included on this site are audio recordings of excerpts from several Montaigne works, playable in QuickTime, Real, and Windows Media players.

Société des Amis de Montaigne. www.amisdemontaigne.fr.
> This site includes a biography, a Bordeaux copy of the *Essays*, a bibliography, and additional links to Montaigne-based websites.

MIGUEL DE CERVANTES
Don Quixote

Topics for Lecture or Discussion

1. **Quixote is a *picaro* (rascal or rogue), and his narration through the account represents the picaresque genre.** Picaresque works largely differed from the more popular chivalric romance and pastoral works of the period, depicting the world more with caricatures, comic episodes, and graphic depictions of suffering. The picaro is often a member of the lower social classes, and he often relies on his cleverness to survive in a corrupt and morally bankrupt society; though Don Quixote is a member of the aristocracy, his adventures exist only through his deluded view of self and through hallucination of low-status characters appearing as knights and damsels in distress. The picaresque genre emphasizes economic and social problems in blunt terms, often exposing hypocrisy; the protagonist is often a rogue adventurer who survives by outwitting the wealthy corrupt. The genre, initiated in *Lazarillo de Tormes*, was later adopted by Cervantes (*Don Quixote*) and expanded into English novels by writers such as Defoe. Cervantes's prologue states that the book is a real history to emphasize how out of touch the gentry is with reality. How are his views about the "deluded gentry" reflected in Quixote's delusions?
   a. **Further Reading:** Bjornson, Richard. *Approaches to Teaching Cervantes' Don Quixote.* New York: Modern Language Association, 1984.
   b. **Suggested Search:** Eisenberg, Daniel, "Does the Picaresque Novel Exist?" *Kentucky Romance Quarterly* 26 (1979): 203–19. Available at http://users.ipfw.edu/jehle/deisenbe/Other_Hispanic_Topics/does _the_picaresque.pdf.

2. **Quixote and Panza act as foils to each other to promote the narrative development.** As a literary device, the foil character contrasts with another character (usually the hero or protagonist) to emphasize, contrast, or complement the other persona. The foil or sidekick often acts as a confidant, offers contrasting views, completes minor but important tasks, or provides skills and services that the main character lacks or cannot offer. Idealistic morals such as "knowing thyself" and "righting all wrongs in the world" are promoted throughout Cervantes's text, as a thin and idealistic Quixote tries to impress his values upon his fat and skeptical sidekick, Panza. Scholars refer to the ironic Spanish proverbs as *sanchismos* (i.e., "He preaches well that lives well, quoth Sancho; that's all the divinity I understand"). Readers are more likely to sympathize with Quixote due to their identification with and appre-

ciation for Panza. Chapter 10 emphasizes the master-servant, crazy-witty dynamic between the two characters, illustrating Panza's ability to make rational suggestions that enable Quixote's success during his chivalric adventures. Which qualities do you admire in Panza, and how do his attributes contribute to your understanding and appreciation of Don Quixote's character?

    a. **Further Reading:** Cascardi, Anthony. *The Cambridge Companion to Cervantes*. Cambridge: Cambridge University Press, 2002.

    b. **Suggested Search:** Search for the "Don Quixote Iconography Digital Archive" in the Cushing Memorial Library's digital collection at http://cushing.library.tamu.edu/collections/digital-collections.

3. **Though romantic and chivalric love are glorified, amorous relationships in the text are more often resolved through trickery or inauspicious means.** Cervantes attempts to produce a parody of chivalric romances, focusing on knights completing valorous deeds, supernatural intervention and enchanted items, implausible adventures and tasks, and saving maidens in distress. The reading of chivalric tales drives Quixote insane ("his brain dried up and he went completely out of his mind"). Cervantes caricatures this lifestyle by placing Quixote into scenarios based on these fictional romances. Quixote's adventures are initiated as a result of his relationship with the plain farm girl, named "Dulcinea" to ennoble her status, who lives on his land and is unaware of the relationship of Quixote's chivalric activities. Upon their return from their adventure, Panza explains that this Dulcinea is living in a farmhouse and appears as a peasant because she has been enchanted; Quixote does not discover her true identity until the story's conclusion. In chapter 5 Quixote replies to a countryman using words and phrases from a story written by Jorge de Montemayor. Chapter 11 deals largely with pastoral settings and unrequited love among goatherds and shepherdesses and chapter 52 the resolution to satisfy a lady. How do Cervantes's depictions of relationships compare to those portrayed in *Lazarillo de Tormes*, another work of Spanish Golden Age fiction?

    a. **Further Reading:** Echevarria, Roberto. *Cervantes' Don Quixote: A Casebook*. Oxford: Oxford University Press, 2005.

    b. **Suggested Search:** Go to the Don Quixote page of the SAAE (Spanish Arts Arte Español) website at www.spanisharts.com/books/quijote/thequijote.htm.

4. **Dramatic irony is an important literary device in the text.** Dramatic irony occurs when the reader (or audience) has more knowledge about a situation than some characters in that situation; as a device, dramatic irony often emphasizes the limitations of human perception and the consequences of misunderstandings that result from that flawed perception. Dramatic irony serves to critique the problems

facing Spaniards during Cervantes's period, including poverty and unemployment, a corrupt landed gentry, a failed effort at empire, an obsession with "purity," and fears about political and religious practices. The windmills as giants (chapter 8), the sheep perceived as other soldiers (chapter 18), and Quixote's fortune to be born into a wealthy family while Panza suffers the consequences for his misdeeds all represent important examples of dramatic irony throughout the text. Though Panza is an intelligent person, he is more molded by social convention; Quixote manipulates these conventions when he promises to make Panza governor of an island for upholding his knightly duties. Panza consents, not realizing that Quixote has selected him as a squire only in his desire to emulate fictional knightly tales, which require the knight to have a sidekick. The reader is aware of Panza's stupidity yet unable to inform Panza of his misguided perception of this fictitious island (which he, in spite of its fantasy location, justly rules). What overall purpose does dramatic irony serve in this text, and why is it a necessary literary device for the picaresque genre?

a. **Further Reading:** Smith, Paul. *Writing in the Margin: Spanish Literature of the Golden Age.* Oxford: Oxford University Press, 1988.

b. **Suggested Search:** Go to Texas A and M University's Cervantes Project at http://cervantes.tamu.edu/english/biblio.html.

5. **Class conventions are upheld in the work based on feudalism.** The Spanish Golden Age (the fifteenth to seventeenth centuries) marks the "Age of Expansion" for Spain, under Habsburg rule. Though Spain expanded its empire, its government twice went bankrupt due to military campaigns, leading to increased taxes and mass inflation. The Spanish Inquisition began in 1516 and peaked during Philip II's reign, leading to (among other things) expulsion of the Jews, Moors, and Moriscos, which in turn directly affected the Spanish economy. The Moriscos lived through subsistence farming, and noblemen lost rents due to their expulsion; land was not redistributed, and the Church collected large percentages of the country's properties. The importation of silver from New World resources led to a price increase of 500 percent for wool, grain, and other goods, which in turn created hardship for the peasants. As a knight-errant, Quixote behaves according to feudal scenarios described in the stories he has read. He does not carry money on his person and therefore expects innkeepers and the poor to shelter and feed him, he collects income off of others' property, and he demands pay for a poor servant who has been abused and exploited by the farmer who employed him. Throughout the novel, Quixote often encounters and exploits or punishes farmers, whom he describes as good, but ignorant, and rustic, but helpful. In chapter 22 he fights to

free slaves from the galleys, believing the criminals to be wrongfully imprisoned. Does Cervantes appear to support or criticize feudal practices?

    a. **Further Reading:** Kamen, Henry. *Golden Age Spain.* New York: Palgrave, 2005.

    b. **Suggested Search:** Go to www.bbc.co.uk/programmes/p003hydl for information about the BBC's *In Our Time* radio program, "Don Quixote."

In-Class Activities

1. As a storyboard activity, ask students to design a farcical adventure that Don Quixote takes, to be added to the novel.

2. Ask students to design, in groups, a satirical epitaph to counter the epitaph that closes *Don Quixote.*

3. Ask students to research eccentric celebrities, political leaders, or wealthy people in modern times and compare their behaviors to Quixote's behavior. Do certain attributes become more prominent when money is no object?

4. Ask students to examine the "Banned Books List" (published online by the University of Pennsylvania at www.banned-books.com/bblist.html) and to try to identify themes or writing styles that are considered "dangerous." Have students compare these themes and styles to Quixote's experience of reading chivalric tales, which drove him insane. Ask students to discuss whether or not they think reading is dangerous.

Paper Topics/Suggestions for Writing

1. How accurate are Don Quixote's assumptions about knighthood and chivalric culture in comparison to the "real" history of medieval chivalry?

2. What important morals does Quixote glorify throughout the text? For example, based on the history you have learned about Cervantes's period, how does Quixote feel about property ownership, slavery, and marriage?

3. Do you believe Quixote was sane and really experienced the things he saw, or was he hallucinating and delusional? Use examples from the text to support your contentions.

4. How is social class addressed in the story?

5. Do you sympathize with Sanson's attempt to bring Quixote out of his delusions?

6. Is reading dangerous? What do you make of the conclusion when Quixote alters his will such that his niece will not inherit unless she renounces the reading of chivalric tales?

7. Explain how Quixote and Panza act as foils to each other throughout the story.

8. Examine in the novel the use of three picaresque elements.

9. Read an excerpt from the Carolingian or Arthurian romances as cited in *Don Quixote*. Compare and contrast the action, themes, and style of both texts. What purpose does the citation of one text serve within another text?

Resources

Cushing Memorial Library. http://cushing.library.tamu.edu/collections/digital-collections.html.

> Select "Don Quixote Iconography Digital Archive" for an NEH-sponsored digital iconography project created by the Cervantes Project that includes 1,231 iconography images through hyperlinked facsimiles of several editions.

Don Quixote. Original choreography by Marius Petipa and music by Ludwig Minkus, first performed by the Ballet of the Imperial Bolshoi Theater of Moscow, Russia, in 1869.

> Current productions of this ballet are more often based on the version staged by Alexander Gorsky in 1900.

"Don Quixote." *In Our Time*. Broadcast in March 2006 on BBC Radio 4. www.bbc.co.uk/programmes/p003hydl.

> During this program, Melvyn Bragg and guests discuss the novel, its history, and its relevance to contemporary society.

Texas A and M University. Cervantes Project. http://cervantes.tamu.edu/english/biblio.html. Edited by Eduardo Urbina.

> This site includes a biography, texts, a bibliography, an extensive image database, links to other digital collections and publications, and notes about the Cervantes Project.

THE ENCOUNTER OF EUROPE AND THE NEW WORLD

Topics for Lecture or Discussion

1. **Like traditional epic narratives that explore both myth and history, the Popol Vuh traces the Mayan creation myth through events at the time of writing (1530s) during the peak of Spanish conquest and the establishment of Christendom in Quiché, Guatemala.** Like oral epics that were recounted over centuries (i.e., Homer's *The Odyssey*), the Popol Vuh was written in the Quiché language but used the Roman alphabet and was likely based on a previous Mayan source. The blend of Christianity and Mayan myth is persistent throughout the work, particularly in the description of the tripartite Heart of Sky God (Thunderbolt Hurricane, Newborn Thunderbolt, Sudden Thunderbolt) being similar to the Christian trinity. God's speech brings the earth into formation from the waters, which parallels the Creation description in Genesis. Similar to the eating of forbidden fruit in the Garden of Eden, the false god Seven Macaw eats the fruit of the Nance tree. Competition and sport to demonstrate heroic valor and honor are important tributes in epic narratives. Part 3 of the Popol Vuh recounts the Mesoamerican ball game played between Seven Hunahpu, One, and the underworld deities. Similar to the Immaculate Conception, the Blood Gatherer's daughter (a virgin) is impregnated with Hunahpu and Xbalanque after the holy tree spits on her hand and "spreads the word." As with the Tower of Babel story, the gods fear that the humans will aspire to become gods; therefore, they blind them (in the story of Babel, the humans lose their ability to communicate with each other) to limit their foresight and wisdom. Notice the difference in blinding here compared to ancient Greek myth—the foreseer, Tiresias, and Oedipus and numerous other figures all gain the power of prophecy only after losing their physical eyesight. What does this difference tell us about Mayan culture?

   a. **Further Reading:** Coe, Michael. *The Maya*. 8th ed. New York: Thames and Hudson, 2011.

   b. **Suggested Search:** A Google search for "Mayan Civilization" will bring up numerous scholarly and personal sites devoted to the archaeology and exploration of ancient Mayan culture and practice (e.g., http://facstaff.gpc.edu/~shale/humanities/literature/world_literature/classprojects/mexico/maya.html).

2. **The Popol Vuh translates as "council book" and initially recounts the Creation story using many agricultural allusions and etiological myths.** The Creator, for example, carefully measures and stakes the earth just as a farmer would prepare a cornfield. Etiological myths

use divine and mystical explanations for natural occurrences; the myth of Seven Macaw losing his jeweled teeth and metal patches is used to explain why the scarlet macaw has white, featherless eye patches. In part 4 the animals bring news of the yellow and white corn from Split Place, which become the ingredients to manufacture human flesh. The goddess Xmucane grinds and prepares the corn with water before forming it into human shapes. In the opening song of part 5, the "green and yellow" drops refer both to semen and to plant growth to represent fertility and procreation. Etiological myths are often used to explain natural occurrences, such as the seasons (compare to the Persephone and Hades myth). Does this suggest that the ancients had a valid way of explaining the world, or do you find their explanations simplistic or unscientific compared to today's understanding of natural events?

a. **Further Reading:** Girard, Raphael. *Esotericism of the* Popol Vuh. Pasadena, CA: Theosophical University Press, 1987.

b. **Suggested Search:** Go to Authentic Maya (http://authenticmaya .com) for information on ancient Guatemala and on Mayan sites, culture and history, and nature.

3. **The Huarochiri manuscript details events from the Andean (Inca) conquest of the region through the arrival of the Spaniards and the end of the Paria Caca cult with the establishment of Christianity.** The editor of the manuscript was Andean, possibly a scribe, and thought by scholars to have been recruited by Father Francisco de Avila for several reasons: to document non-Christian rites and beliefs, to blackmail local parishioners, and to show a parallel between ancient and Christian beliefs (often deemphasizing the ancient cultic beliefs). The text recalls the lives of "the ancestors of the Huaro Cheri people" and credits the meeting of the female earth deity, Chaupi Ñamca, and the male water and mountain deity, Paria Caca, with the creation myth; according to the text, all of the Huaro Cheri peoples descended from a common forefather. Scholars argue that the union of earth and water (irrigation) myth parallels the political union between invaders and aborigines, showing the nuances and difficulties of coexisting societies. Cannibalism, difficulty initiating an agricultural society, and sacrifice were characteristics of the early huacas's culture, leading to the development of the Huaro Cheri civilization. Smaller communities within the society were sacrificed for revealing information about this sacred culture to the Spaniards (chapter 18, 224–27), particularly regarding gold and silver, which belong to the huacas. How does withholding sacred or cultural information compare to today's world, in which massive amounts of private information are publicly shared via the Internet?

a. **Further Reading:** Spalding, Karen. *Huarochirí: An Andean Society under Inca and Spanish Rule.* Stanford, CA: Stanford University Press, 1984.

b. **Suggested Search:** Go to the Wisconsin University Anthropology Department's site, "Huarochiri, a Peruvian Culture in Time" (www .anthropology.wisc.edu/salomon/Chaysimire).

4. **Letters written by Christopher Columbus and Vaz de Caminha describe the indigenous people as timid and generous, whereas Cortés's letter reaffirms the widespread assumption that these peoples were barbaric and deserving of punishment and oppression.** Christopher Columbus remarks on the absence of weaponry from their culture other than those weapons made of natural materials, such as reeds. The natives are described as timid, generous, and grateful to receive even the most lowly and broken items from the foreigners. Columbus and his men are viewed as deities visiting from heaven due to their color and stature. Caminha describes an exchange of a voyager's old hat for a worthless, green stone from the native's mouth piercing; the people dance and entertain themselves and become frightened when the foreigners kill a shark. Caminha, like Columbus, states that these are a "timid" people, though he ascribes it to their ignorance and primitive behavior ("bestial and of very little knowledge"). Cortés, on the other hand, acts as a police tyrant, shadowing the streets and, with other Spaniards, capturing a street and burning down several hundred homes and important towers in order to inspire terror in the people. What clues can readers use to determine what information is biased and what descriptions are objective, given the different travelers' viewpoints?

a. **Further Reading:** Mann, Charles. *1493: Uncovering the New World Columbus Created.* New York: Knopf, 2011.

b. **Suggested Search:** Go to the University of Calgary's site, "The European Voyages of Exploration: Fifteenth and Sixteenth Centuries" (www.ucalgary.ca/applied_history/tutor/eurvoya). This site contains information about Iberian pioneers, Portugal, and Spain, all related to adventurers and the cultural, political, and economic globalization of the period.

5. **The Florentine Codex and Jean de Léry's *History of a Voyage to the Land of Brazil* are both ethnographic research documents by foreigners, whereas Guaman Poma de Ayala's *First New Chronicle and Good Government* is an auto-ethnography (a description of a culture by one of its members).** Originally titled the "General History of the Things of New Spain," its writer, Franciscan friar Bernardino de Sahagun, gathered evidence for almost fifty years (1545 to 1590) and compiled 2,400 pages, with illustrations, to document the culture,

religion and ritual, economics, and history of the Aztec people. As an ethnographer, de Sahagun relied upon his work specifically to evangelize the Mesoamericans and uses a medical allusion to "curing" patients who suffer from the disease of idolatry. As an ethnographer, he uses the following methodology: adopts the native language, speaks to the authorities, immerses himself in Aztec culture to master its methods of recording and transmitting knowledge, objectively presents the Aztec culture without European bias, gathers information generally by using questionnaires, and evaluates information from multiple sources to verify their reliability. De Léry's account reports on the violence and savagery exhibited by the Tupinamba people; however, he acknowledges his role as an interpreter and emphasizes that personal experience is subjective and therefore no more credible than others' assumptions and observations (see in particular the closing line of his excerpt, which details the hypocrisy of the Europeans in comparison to the "humanity of these people, whom nonetheless we call 'barbarians'"). Guaman Poma condemns assimilation between Spaniards and Indians in order to prevent the extinction of his culture. His ethnography includes a letter written to a king to recommend rules that support colonization but that still preserve the local elite culture. He argues that the local Incas are unsuccessful precisely because the women are "taken" by the Spaniards and their servants, and the interracial relation creates an inferior mestizo accepted by neither the Indians nor the Spaniards. The resources in the Incan lands should be mined and used by the Spaniards; however, the local peoples should not be enslaved or mistreated as they labor to gather these resources. The locals, too, should pay income and property taxes to demonstrate their loyalty to the Catholic king, which in turn will make them more loyal to the king, Christianity, and European practices. How did these views later shape and/or compare to the economic and cultural conditions in the Americas?

a. **Further Reading:** Wolf, Gerhard. *Colors between Two Worlds: The Florentine Codex of Bernardino de Sahagún*. Florence: Villa I Tatti Series, 2012.

b. **Suggested Search:** Go to Latin American Studies' Florentine Codex site (www.latinamericanstudies.org/florentine-codex-1.htm), which contains images from the Codex.

In-Class Activities

1. Students can be divided into groups or they can complete individual projects in which they identify a group to study and then, over one to two weeks, adopt some of de Sahagun's ethnography methods to study

and write about that culture. A write-up and a presentation of each culture can then be given in class.

2. Ask students to study the history of different games in non-Western culture and compare them to Western games (i.e., the Mesoamerican ball game depicted in the Popol Vuh compared to soccer or basketball). Students may be put into groups to either role-play as game commentators or to design their own games. (See Authentic Maya in the Resources section.)

3. Ask students to write a letter to their "leader" (the professor) in which they describe a foreign place and people using the same style as Columbus or Caminha.

4. Ask students to examine illustrations from the Florentine Codex and the Popul Vuh and to compare and contrast narrative language with visual communication.

Paper Topics/Suggestions for Writing

1. Compare the Mayan description of creation in the Popul Vuh to the creation myth established in Genesis.

2. In the world of the huacas, the word "camay" refers to endowing with power, essence, and force. The huaca is a superhuman or deity, inhabiting the world within a shrine, or is a holy and powerful object or natural place. Discuss these concepts as they appear in the Huarochiri manuscript.

3. How is ownership of land, gold, and silver treated in the Huarochiri manuscript?

4. Is it possible to maintain indigenous spiritual beliefs when ritual practices are forbidden and a new language system is adopted? Use examples from the readings and your knowledge of the Spanish conquest of the New World to support your argument.

5. How do Columbus and de Caminha's letters debunk and/or confirm stereotypes that the Europeans held about the native Indians in the New World?

6. What are the pitfalls of ethnographic study? Compare and contrast the studies of de Sahagun (the Florentine Codex) and de Léry (*History of a Voyage to the Land of Brazil*) in your discussion of the elements of ethical and improper ethnography.

7. According to Inca Garcilaso de la Vega, how did "Peru" get its name?

Resources

Authentic Maya. http://authenticmaya.com.
    This site contains information on ancient Guatemala and on Mayan sites, culture and history, and nature. The images and videos reenact the Mesoamerican ball game and other references in the Popol Vuh.
Christopher Columbus: Explorer of the New World. A&E Home Video. 1995.
    This documentary explores Columbus's life and travels.
Latin American Studies: Florentine Codex. www.latinamericanstudies.org /florentine-codex-2.htm. Website created by Antonio Rafael de la Cova.
    This site contains images from the Florentine Codex.
Lost Treasures of the Ancient World: Mayans and Aztecs. Dir. Chris Gormlie. Horizon Pictures, 1999.
    This documentary includes on-location footage and historical recreations.
Ohio State University. http://library.osu.edu/projects/popolwuj.
    Manuscript editions are available, with transcriptions in K'iche' and Spanish, as well as notes and bibliography and some images.
Peru Cultural Society. www.discover-peru.org.
    Links on Inca civilization can be found on this site, with extensive categories, including history, geography, biodiversity, travel, and myth. Images and hyperlinks, as well as links to further resources, also are included.
Wisconsin University Anthropology Department. "Huarochiri, a Peruvian Culture in Time." www.anthropology.wisc.edu/salomon/Chaysimire. Maintained by Frank Salomon.
    This site contains background on the Huarochiri manuscript and culture, a photo gallery, overviews of khipus, Tupicocha, and rural Huarochiri, and an extended list of relevant literature.

LOPE DE VEGA
Fuenteovejuna

Have you no honor left as men?
Have I no kinsmen here, no sire?
How has my sorry plight not left
Your likes contorted with the pain
Of seeing me so cruelly pained?
You're lambs, the sheep from which our town's
Old sheep well takes its timid name!
. . . .
By God above, I'll see to it
That only womenfolk respond
To tyrants who'd leave honor stained
By seeking their perfidious blood!
—*Fuenteovejuna*, 3.1.102–108, 123–32

Topics for Lecture or Discussion

1. **The Commander challenges the young Master to attack a provincial town (Ciudad Real) and prove his worthiness as a leader.** The first scene establishes the very tricky political situation of feudal society in which power is a function of patronage and landownership. The family of the Master is allied with the king of Portugal, who lays disputed claim to Castile against King Ferdinand and his Queen Isabel. The Commander urges the Master to take Ciudad Real as a strategic maneuver to control the frontier around Castile. More importantly, the scene shows the Commander's lack of loyalty to Ferdinand and manipulation of the young Master to do the Commander's bidding. The Commander goads him into battle by suggesting, in no uncertain terms, that his manhood and future as a leader are at stake. His advice, though, provides an excuse to unleash his own bellicose instincts. The Commander, a war hero, plans to lead the charge.
   a. **Further Reading**: Fiore, Robert. "Natural Law in the Central Ideological Theme of *Fuenteovejuna*." *Hispania* 49:1 (March 1966): 75–80.
   b. **Suggested Searches**: Search Google Images, Google Scholar, or an academic database for "Laurence Boswell adaptation *Fuenteovejuna* (video)" to find images and additional resources. See also www.youtube.com/watch?v=jmyRyraB390.

2. **Frondoso and Laurencia joust verbally to debate the existence and merits of love.** In lengthy, witty passages, both cite the discrepancies

between words and the things or meanings that such words signify. After parrying back and forth in a way that establishes each character as a perfect match for the other, the supporting characters take over, and Mengo, Frondoso's friend, seemingly wins the argument with his claim that "only self-love rules the day" (1.2.230). He concludes: "There / Can be no love but of the kind / That everybody seeks to find / By courting pleasure everywhere" (1.2.245–48). The action in the rest of the play determines the nature of love as self-sacrifice in the service of another. What is true on a personal level is true on a political level as well: the realm of state prospers through loyalty to the king and queen.

   a. **Further Reading**: Spitzer, Leo. "A Central Theme and Its Structural Equivalent in Lope's *Fuenteovejuna*." *Hispanic Review* 23 (October 1955): 274–92, esp. 275–77.

   b. **Suggested Searches**: Search Google Images, Google Scholar, or an academic database for "Nylon Fusion Collective *Fuenteovejuna*" to find images and additional resources. See also http://offbroadway.broad wayworld.com/article/Nylon_Fusion_Collective_Presents_Lope_De _Vegas_FUENTE_OVEJUNA_61773_20100608.

3. **The Commander, a notorious seducer of women, returns home to Fuenteovejuna after victory at Ciudad Real in pursuit of Laurencia.** His intentions are well known and expected. In the second scene Laurencia articulates the abuse of power by the Commander and other tyrants like him: "When, worn down, we give up the fight, / They take their pleasure in the night / And leave us wretched on the morn" (1.2.74–76). Later, in act 2, the Commander confirms this judgment when he speaks of his pleasures with women and how he quickly becomes tired of the women after sexual conquest. He despises them to the degree that they capitulate to his advances. He philosophizes: "The surest course for love to run / Once all delight had been bestowed / Is down oblivion's well-worn road / Of favors far too easily won" (2.1.240–43). Accordingly, then, both his ardor for and his hatred of Laurencia increase greatly as she eludes his grasp.

   a. **Further Reading**: Pring-Mill, R. D. F. "Sententiousness in *Fuente Ovejuna*." *Tulane Drama Review* 7:1 (Autumn 1962): 5–37.

   b. **Suggested Searches**: Search Google Images, Google Scholar, or an academic database for the following images and additional resources: *Fuenteovejuna* at Stratford, Ontario, *Fuenteovejuna* in Washington, D.C., Lope de Vega Festival in Washington.

4. **Frondoso prevents the Commander from raping Laurencia and puts his own life in peril.** In an open field, Laurencia and Frondoso continue to flirt, but she will not consent to marry him just yet. Their witty, verbal flirtation contrasts with the Commander's reputation for

immediate physical, sexual gratification with women. Indeed, his two retainers, Flores and Ortuño, procure women for his insatiable lust. On a hunt for deer, the Commander surprises Laurencia and Frondoso in the field and prepares to take advantage of a chance meeting. Paying no heed at all to the presence of Frondoso, and angered by Laurencia's repeated insults, the Commander advances on her as if to rape and kill her. Frondoso violates all codes of behavior by picking up the Commander's crossbow and aiming it at his lord in order to defend his love. Laurencia escapes, but the Commander suffers shame and vows vengeance.

a. **Further Reading**: Gillespie, Gerald. "The Rebel in Seventeenth-Century Tragedy." *Comparative Literature* 18:4 (Autumn 1966): 324–36.

b. **Suggested Searches**: Search Google Images, Google Scholar, or an academic database for the following to find images and additional resources: Laurencia and Frondoso *Fuenteovejuna* (video). See also www.youtube.com/watch?v=gl0x_mWh8yQ.

5. **Laurencia shames the men of Fuenteovejuna into rebellion against the tyrants.** At the end of act 2, the Commander interrupts the wedding of Laurencia and Frondoso and sends them both to prison. "The wedding has become a wake!" one character exclaims, strengthening the close ties in the play between love and marriage and death and war (2.3.170). At the start of the third and final act, Laurencia returns, having escaped from prison and once again having repelled the sexual advances of the Commander. Angrily, she upbraids the townspeople, on behalf of all women who have suffered similar abuse, for not defending her honor and failing to intervene in her abduction. She claims that the Commander plans to execute Frondoso, and she challenges the town to do something to prevent such tyrannical behavior. She concludes that the town must take action before the Commander exploits all of them. At the end of this long speech, first the men and then the women agree to take the law into their own hands and turn against their lords and masters. Rallying the women, Laurencia concludes, "Who needs / El Cid or Rodomonte when / It's I who'll lead with gallantry?" (3.1.194–96).

a. **Further Reading**: Swietlicki, Catherine. "Close Cultural Encounters: Speech and Writing in *Fuenteovejuna*." *Hispanic Review* 60:1 (Winter 1992): 33–53.

b. **Suggested Searches**: Search Google Images, Google Scholar, or an academic database for the following to find images and additional resources: Vakhtang Chabukiani ballet *Laurencia*, tyranny and rebellion in *Fuenteovejuna*. See also www.theballetbag.com/2010/07/30/laurencia.

6. **The townsfolk hunt down the Commander and his lackeys and kill them savagely and mercilessly.** Hearing the approaching mob, Frondoso comments, "It's love that made their passion wake" (3.2.18). Once again, the play-off of love as war takes a decisive turn this time on the side of righteous vengeance. The love that spurs the town to action is not self-love, which Mengo suggested earlier as the only kind of love, but love for others (e.g., Frondoso and Laurencia) and love of freedom and justice. The vigilantism of the crowd is swift and violent. Flores describes the attack in graphic language, noting that the mob impaled the Commander, dragged his body through the streets, plucked his face and beard, and sliced up his face to the extent that, when they finished, only his ears remained intact. Celebrating after the event, the town recognizes the reign of their Catholic monarchs, Ferdinand and his Isabel, but repeats again and again in scene 3.4, "Death to tyrants all!"
   a. **Further Reading**: Fischer, Susan L. "*Fuente Ovejuna* on the Rack: Interrogation of a Carnivalesque Theatre of Terror." *Hispanic Review* 65:1 (Winter 1997): 61–92.
   b. **Suggested Searches**: Search Google Images, Google Scholar, or an academic database for the following to find images and additional resources: tyranny and rebellion in *Fuenteovejuna*. See also Linda L. Elman's "None Dare Call It Rape: The Case of Laurencia," available at http://tell.fll.purdue.edu/RLA-Archive/1996/Spanish-html/Elman ,Linda.htm.

7. **The townsfolk defend themselves in the subsequent investigation by claiming that "Fuenteovejuna" killed the Commander.** Despite torture upon the rack, the judge can force no confessions and can make no inroads on the town's solidarity. Just as the young Master begs forgiveness from Ferdinand and Isabel for his insurrection against the crown, the townsfolk appeal for clemency to the king and queen and pledge future and enduring loyalty. In both cases the wise royal rulers grant the pleas, and new order is restored at the conclusion. The monarchy is unthreatened, with the understood proviso that tyranny will not be tolerated.
   a. **Further Reading**: Casalduero, Joaquin, and Ruth Whittredge. "*Fuenteovejuna*: Form and Meaning." *Tulane Drama Review* 4:2 (December 1959): 83–107.
   b. **Suggested Searches**: Search Google Images, Google Scholar, or an academic database for the following to find images and additional resources: historical truth town Fuenteovejuna, Plaza Lope de Vega, Fuente Obejuna. See also www.youtube.com/watch?v=CzEgWm fhwZ0.

8. **Love's concern is not for the self but for the beloved.** Laurencia reveals the true nature of love near the end of the play in act 3 when

she enters alone to declare that the test of true love is caring more for what happens to the beloved than for one's own self (3.6.1–14). Her statement rejects both the cynicism of Mengo, who argued for self-love as the only love in existence, and the lust of the Commander, who seduces women as an inexhaustible matter of habit only to immediately discard them without further thought after the sexual conquest. Frondoso and Laurencia deliver the coda on the subject in the scene where he asks, "And how did I slay you, dear girl?" She answers: "By loving me so tenderly" (3.6.129–30). The thematic tie between love and war gets an ironic twist as Laurencia admits that Frondoso won her heart not through any martial display of arms but by treating her with consistent care and regard over a long period of time. Once again, the personal relationship provides a model for the proper political relationship between subject and sovereign.

   a. **Further Reading**: McCrary, William C. "*Fuenteovejuna*: Its Platonic Vision and Execution." *Studies in Philology* 58:2 (April 1961): 179–92.

   b. **Suggested Searches**: Search Google Images, Google Scholar, or an academic database for the following to find images and additional resources: Antonio Gades Company *Fuenteovejuna* flamenco dance. See also www.theartsdesk.com/dance/fuenteovejuna-antonio-gades -company-sadlers-wells.

In-Class Activities

1. See lines 1.2.118–87 for the first exchange between Laurencia and Frondoso. How do they use language to convey their thoughts and feelings about one another?

2. How does the action of the play both confirm and subvert stereotypical and traditional patterns and attitudes concerning gender in the Spanish Golden Age?

3. Discuss the role of honor as an important value. What does it mean to various characters? What does it mean to you as an interpreter of the drama?

4. How do you respond to the town's rebellion against its lord and the subsequent bloody murder of the Commander? The defense against the crime is clever, but is it just?

5. How would you perform Laurencia's big speech in act 3 (3.1.72–142)? What is the assembled crowd doing while she berates the group? How can the group help the actress play the scene?

Paper Topics/Suggestions for Writing

1. Regarding the overthrow of the tyrant, do the ends justify the means?

2. What conclusions can you draw concerning the relationship in the play between community and nation?

3. Discuss the code of honor as it develops in the play. What does it signify?

4. How does the young Master function at the beginning and the end of the play?

5. What is the chivalric code, and to what extent does the Commander uphold its values? Do the code and its obligations lead him astray of moral behavior?

6. It is easy to see the Commander as the antagonist in the play, but write an essay that advances your choice for protagonist(s). Laurencia? Frondoso? Both? Others?

Resources

Fuenteovejuna. Films for the Humanities and Sciences, 1980, DVD.
  This film features a group of Spain's finest actors (in Spanish).
Lope Félix de Vega Carpio. Films for the Humanities and Sciences, 2004, VHS/DVD.
  This film includes scenes from selected performances (in Spanish, with English subtitles).

WILLIAM SHAKESPEARE
Hamlet, Prince of Denmark

> We defy augury. There's a special providence in
> the fall of a sparrow. If it be now, 'tis not to
> come. If it be not to come, it will be now. If it
> be not now, yet it will come. The readiness is
> all. Since no man has aught of what he leaves,
> what is't to leave betimes?
> —*Hamlet*, 5.2.166–71

Topics for Lecture or Discussion

1. **The ghost of King Hamlet incites the action.** "Stand and unfold yourself," demands Francisco in the second line. The ghostly presence is a sign that "something is rotten in the state of Denmark," but exactly what? The ghost does not respond to any of the men in the opening scene, but Horatio reasons that it will speak to Prince Hamlet. Indeed, the ghost lures Hamlet later in act 1 to a private scene in which he informs him of his father's violent murder at the hands of his Uncle Claudius. The ghost demands that Hamlet remember him and avenge his father's death. Hamlet agrees but does not act immediately because he doubts the validity of the ghost's claims and seeks empirical evidence against his uncle. At the ghost of act 2, he reasons: "The spirit that I have seen / May be the devil, and the devil hath power / T'assume a pleasing shape; yea, and perhaps, / Out of my weakness and my melancholy—/ As he is very potent with such spirits—/ Abuses me to damn me" (2.2.592–97). In search of proof, Hamlet instructs Horatio to observe Claudius during the performance of a play that somewhat reenacts the murder of Hamlet and thereby to "catch the conscience of the king" (2.2.599). This tactic proves successful, but a visit to his mother's bedroom almost sidetracks his bloody revenge. In the midst of his argument with Gertrude, the ghost appears to him again to remind him of his almost "blunted purpose" (3.4.105). While the ghost appears but does not speak to all of Hamlet's friends at the start of the play, in the ghost's final appearance it is present to Hamlet alone. Gertrude neither sees it nor hears it. Thus the scene (3.4) confirms Hamlet's madness from her point of view but strengthens his own resolve for bloody revenge, which continues unabated until the end of the play.

   a. **Further Reading**: Ackerman, Alan L. "Visualizing Hamlet's Ghost: The Spirit of Modern Subjectivity." *Theatre Journal* 53:1 (March 2001): 119–44.

b. **Suggested Searches**: Search Google Images, Google Scholar, or an academic database for the following to find images and additional resources: Hamlet's ghost, Freytag's pyramid, supernatural in Hamlet, *Hamlet* act 1, scene 4. See also www.imdb.com/title/tt0116477/mediaindex for images from the film *Hamlet*, directed by Kenneth Branagh (Warner Brothers, 1996).

2. **Gertrude's hasty marriage to her late husband's brother, Claudius, disturbs Hamlet.** Before Hamlet even learns of his father's murder, the timing of the wedding on the heels of the funeral upsets him. "I came to see your father's funeral," says Horatio, a friend from school at Wittenberg. "I think it was to see my mother's wedding," Hamlet quips in response (1.2.175, 177). His first soliloquy in the play ("O that this too too solid flesh would melt" [1.2.129–59]) laments the passing of his father, certainly, but it draws ire from the fact that his mother, who seemed to love his father dearly, quickly thereafter married his brother, Hamlet's uncle. "O most wicked speed, to post / With such dexterity to incestuous sheets!" (1.2.156–57). Hamlet loved his father and cannot understand how his mother could so quickly marry another man who, at least to him, is much less a man. Beyond an unbalanced comparison between two brothers, however, Hamlet later accosts his mother for her loose sexuality and tells her that she, who once hung upon the neck of her former husband, is too old for love. He accuses her of living in the "rank sweat of an enseamèd bed" (3.4.85) and leaves her with the final injunction: "Go not to mine uncle's bed. / Assume a virtue if you have it not" (3.4.154–55). For Hamlet, then, the two events, the death of his father and the subsequent marriage of his mother to his uncle, are almost interchangeable and simultaneous. Initially, in his first soliloquy, he says that his father had been dead two months, but he then amends that statement to something less ("not so much, not two" [1.2.138]). In the same speech a few lines later, near the end, he claims that Gertrude remarried within a month. Later, to Ophelia, he remarks that his mother remarried within two hours of his father's death. The ghost's report of his father's murder at the hands of Claudius leads Hamlet to revenge, but the fact of his mother's remarriage to Claudius had already put dark and bloody thoughts into his head.

a. **Further Reading**: Levin, Richard. "Gertrude's Elusive Libido and Shakespeare's Unreliable Narrators." *SEL Studies in English Literature 1500–1900* 48:2 (Spring 2008): 305–26.

b. **Suggested Searches**: Search Google Images, Google Scholar, or an academic database for the following to find images and additional resources: BBC Hamlet, Hamlet chair Edwin Booth, Hamlet's first line, first soliloquy *Hamlet*, Hamlet and Gertrude, Hamlet and Oedipal complex. See also www.bbc.co.uk/programmes/b00pk71s.

3. **Hamlet tries to reconcile outward appearance and stated resolve with inner feeling and decisive action.** Initially, in mourning his father's death, Hamlet appears dressed entirely in black and plays the part of a grieving son. He is aware that his outward behavior is both excessive and conventional but claims that he has "that within which passeth show— / These but the trappings and the suits of woe" (1.2.85–86). The depth and intensity of his inner feelings, he suggests, cannot receive adequate representation on the surface of appearance. This crisis of identity haunts Hamlet throughout the play. The player, for example, tears a passion to tatters when he performs a written scene from antiquity. "What's Hecuba to him, or he to Hecuba?" Hamlet soliloquizes about the nature of acting and the phenomenon of creating an emotional display over nothing, remote events in which one has no vested personal interest (2.2.553). He lambastes himself because, in contrast, he has every reason to carry out his revenge, suffering the real death of his father, but he can do nothing yet. Beyond the player, though, Hamlet also sees a resemblance of his cause in Laertes, whose father has also been murdered. Unlike Hamlet, Laertes returns from France willing and eager to avenge his father's death immediately. Hamlet envies Laertes's conviction and readiness for action, but, ironically, Laertes's impetuous desire for vengeance allows Claudius to use him as a foil for his own devious purposes. The model for action seems to be Fortinbras, the son of the Norwegian king, who has marched across Denmark to defeat a Polish army and arrives at Elsinore at the end to take the crown.
   a. **Further Reading**: Halpern, Richard. "Eclipse of Action: *Hamlet* and the Political Economy of Playing." *Shakespeare Quarterly* 59:4 (Winter 2008): 450–82.
   b. **Suggested Searches**: Search Google Images, Google Scholar, or an academic database for the following to find images and additional resources: Hamlet and the player, Hamlet's revenge of father's death, Hamlet and Laertes, Hamlet and metadrama. See also Emory University's list of *Hamlet* performances across the ages, with images, at http://shakespeare.emory.edu/playdisplay.cfm?playid=7.

4. **Revenge demands both good timing and certain proof.** After seeing Claudius's guilty reaction to the play, Hamlet catches him alone soon thereafter and prepares to kill him (3.3). Drawing out his sword, though, he realizes that Claudius is kneeling to recite his prayers, thus Hamlet aborts his revenge for the moment. He is afraid that if he kills Claudius during prayer, the king's soul will travel straight to heaven. Hamlet fears that he will actually reward Claudius by killing him. In contrast, Hamlet's father, according to the ghost in act 1, died without atonement: "Cut off even in the blossom of my sin, / Unhouseled, disappointed, unaneled, / No reck'ning made, but sent to my account / With all my imperfections

on my head" (1.5.76–79). Likewise, Hamlet vows to kill Claudius during some act that "has no relish of salvation in't" (3.3.92) in order to send him to hell: drinking, gambling, swearing. Recollecting his lament from the start against his mother, he hopes to catch his uncle in the "incestuous pleasure of his bed" (3.3.90). With better timing and a little luck, then, Hamlet would have gotten his revenge at the ghost of his father's behest in the third act and little more than halfway through the play. Ironically, Hamlet could have carried out his impulsive desires against Claudius with impunity when he first stumbled upon him when he was reciting his prayers. Filled with guilt, Claudius confesses after Hamlet departs for his mother's chamber: "My words fly up, my thoughts remain below. / Words without thoughts to heaven never go" (3.3.97–98).

   a. **Further Reading**: Garber, Marjorie. "A Tale of Three *Hamlets* or Repetition and Revenge." *Shakespeare Quarterly* 61:1 (Spring 2010): 28–55.

   b. **Suggested Searches**: Search Google Images, Google Scholar, or an academic database for the following to find images and additional resources: Hamlet and revenge, Hamlet poised to kill Claudius, murder of Gonzago. See also www.theatrehistory.com/british/art_of _hamlet.html.

5. **Hamlet impulsively kills Polonius in an act of madness.** In order to stall for time to effect his revenge, Hamlet puts on a seeming "antic disposition" (1.5.173) to mask his true thoughts and inclinations. Polonius advises the king that the prince is madly in love with Ophelia, Polonius's daughter, although Claudius always suspects that Hamlet's madness has its roots in another cause. Indeed, Hamlet feigns madness in order to find the right moment to carry out his plot against Claudius. After failing to kill his uncle in the scene described earlier (3.3), Hamlet moves on to his mother's bedroom, where he violently confronts her about her behavior. Thinking that the sound he hears in her room might be coming from his uncle, although he did just see him in another part of the castle, he thrusts his sword through the arras and unwittingly kills Polonius, who has been spying on him. Hamlet expresses little remorse over this killing initially, even though Polonius might have become his father-in-law and even though his rash action leads directly to Ophelia's breakdown and insanity. This reaction raises the question, is Hamlet really mad? Has the madness he once adopted as a role to play become his reality? After all, now he is the only one who can see and hear the ghost. What is more, his feigned behavior is indistinguishable from the true madness displayed in the following scenes by Ophelia. The intensity of his mad "performance" takes over and does not subside until he travels to England and later returns to announce himself as "I / Hamlet the Dane" (5.1.254–55), jumping into Ophelia's grave alongside

her brother, Laertes, to proclaim his love and devotion to her. Apologizing to Laertes later, Hamlet distances himself from his madness by reasoning that his identity and his madness are two separate entities, brought about by his thus far failed revenge against Claudius. Referring to his accidental killing of Polonius, Hamlet indicates Claudius as the missed target when he admits, "That I have shot mine arrow o'er the house / and hurt my brother" (5.2.191–92). With the final goal of his revenge in sight, that madness of Hamlet also subsides.

   a. **Further Reading**: Bynum, W. F., and Michael Neve. "Hamlet on the Couch: Hamlet Is a Kind of Touchstone by Which to Measure Changing Opinion—Psychiatric and Otherwise—about Madness." *American Scientist* 74:4 (July–August 1986): 390–96.

   b. **Suggested Searches**: Search Google Images, Google Scholar, or an academic database for the following to find images and additional resources: Polonius behind an arras, murder of Polonius, action in *Hamlet* Polonius. See also Hannah and Wolf Tompkins's Shakespeare Art Museum at http://shakespeare-art-museum.com/index.html.

6. **The clown in the grave digger scene humorously presents the certainty, equanimity, and naturalness of death.** From the beginning, Claudius and Gertrude question Hamlet's belabored mourning of his father's death, and both point out that everyone loses a father, and that even "your father lost a father" (1.2.89). At the other end of the play, the grave diggers offer none of the solemnity of the royal crowd that will soon come bearing Ophelia for her funeral. Instead, they joke and knock about the skulls and bones of former courtiers and commoners alike. When Hamlet discovers the remains of Yorick, a man of "infinite jest" from his childhood, the prince reflects on the passing of time and the mortality of human life (5.1.180–81). This humorous, ultimately poignant scene is followed by the theatrics of Ophelia's burial and the challenge of a competition with swords between Laertes and Hamlet. Tonally, the play undergoes a radical shift at this point to quiet contemplation and expectation. Horatio warns his friend that the contest might be a trap, but Hamlet responds: "If it [death] be now, 'tis not to come. If it be not to come, it will be now. If it be not now, yet it will come. The readiness is all. Since no man has aught of what he leaves, what is't to leave betimes?" (5.2.167–71). Acknowledging the limits and inevitability of his own mortality, Hamlet relaxes going forward and, although he also dies, he exacts his revenge against his uncle.

   a. **Further Reading**: Stevenson, Ruth. "Hamlet's Mice, Motes, Moles and Minching Malecho." *New Literary History* 33:3 (Summer 2002): 435–59.

   b. **Suggested Searches**: Search Google Images, Google Scholar, or an academic database for the following to find images and additional resources: grave digger scene in *Hamlet*, alas poor Yorick. See also http://pages.unibas.ch/shine/linkstraghamletwf3.html, a German site providing links to images, editions, and criticism on *Hamlet*.

In-Class Activities

1. How should the ghost scenes be staged in the first act and later in Gertrude's closet? How can modern staging practices and new technologies solve potential staging problems?

2. Read aloud the first part of the grave digger scene (5.1). Is it funny? Can you find the rhythms of the joke structure embedded in the lines?

3. Examine Hamlet's "To be or not to be" soliloquy (3.1.59–92), and identify the problem that the speech considers. The thesis or action statement comes near the end. After locating it, see if a similar structural pattern holds true in other soliloquies.

4. What is the dramatic climax of the play? How do you justify this choice? What remains after this moment in the final resolution or denouement?

5. Discuss Polonius's parenting techniques. How does he help create ripe circumstances for tragedy? You might also ask students to compare/contrast this role to parents in other tragedies, such as *Oedipus the King* or *Agamemnon*.

Paper Topics/Suggestions for Writing

1. Discuss the place of religion with the play's dramatic action. Would the play make sense in an atheistic society?

2. Laurence Olivier's famous film of the play stated overtly that *Hamlet* was about a man who could not make up his mind. Is this a reasonable or a reductive interpretation of the play?

3. Starting with Hamlet's advice to the players, discuss the art of acting on a stage with respect to action in the world of human affairs. How does the artifice of theater reveal truth?

4. Discuss the role and impact of madness in the play. Is Hamlet culpable for the death of Polonius? In playing madness, does Hamlet, in fact, become mad?

5. Discuss the role of Rosencrantz and Guildenstern. To what extent does their goal to pluck out Hamlet's mystery equate to the aims of literary criticism?

6. What language do Hamlet and other characters use to establish the world of Elsinore in the play's opening three scenes?

Resources

Hamlet. Dir. Bill Colleran. Perf. Richard Burton. 1964. DVD: Image Entertainment, 1999.

    This is a film of the notable stage production directed by John Gielgud.

Hamlet. Dir. Kenneth Branagh. Perf. Kenneth Branagh. Castle Rock, 1996, DVD.

    A special edition of this film adaptation was released in 2007.

Hamlet. Dir. Laurence Olivier. Perf. Laurence Olivier. 1948. DVD: Criterion, 2000.

    This is a notable film adaptation of *Hamlet*.

Hamlet. Dir. Franco Zeffirelli. Perf. Mel Gibson. 1990. DVD: Warner Home Video, 2004.

Hamlet: A Critical Guide (with key scenes and commentary). Films for the Humanities and Sciences, 1998, DVD.

    Scholars Russell Jackson and Stanley Wells of Stratford-upon-Avon offer analysis and insight into the play.

Hamlet—Stage Scenes: Breathing Life into Text. Insight Media, 2001, DVD.

    This is a presentation of two different interpretations of key scenes.

Shakespeare. Insight Media, 2001, DVD.

    The life and works of the playwright, including *Hamlet* and several other plays, are discussed here.

Shakespeare's Globe. Insight Media, 2005, DVD.

    This DVD explores the planning and reconstruction of Shakespeare's theater, tours the facility, and includes footage of the production *Romeo and Juliet*.

Shakespeare on the Silver Screen. Films for the Humanities and Sciences, 2000, DVD.

    This DVD combines clips and interviews to show Shakespearean imagination on film, with productions from Julie Taymor, Kenneth Branagh, Laurence Olivier, Baz Luhrmann, Peter Brook, and *Othello*, with Laurence Fishburne.

The Shakespeare Sessions. Insight Media, 2003, DVD.

    Noted director John Barton teaches actors how to handle Shakespearean language. This DVD features Kevin Kline, Dustin Hoffman, Cynthia Nixon, Peter O'Toole, Ian McKellen, and Judi Dench.

GOD, CHURCH, AND SELF

Topics for Lecture or Discussion

1. **The Protestant Reformation largely shaped political and artistic development during the sixteenth century.** Initiated by Martin Luther's Ninety-Five Theses (1517), hints of the Reformation first began when Erasmus and humanists demanded Church reforms that would remove hierarchy and corruption (especially for selling indulgences and clerical offices). Tragic events of mass death and religious doubt (i.e., the Black Plague, the Western Schism) in part led to the Reformation, which emphasized personal devotion over public ritual, and the accessibility of the Bible in a vulgar language rather than in Latin. Luther took these ideas further, emphasizing a break with Rome (and Romanists), as well as marriage for priests and nuns and arguing that only grace (no reward or punishment deemed by the Church leaders) could save a sinner. Numerous advances were made as a result of the Protestant Reformation, including: the development of the printing press and the mass publication of Luther's translation of the Bible in German; the nascent growth of "individualism" and the middle-class spread of the "work ethic"; and the rise of the Thirty Years' War (which led, in turn, to the Peace of Westphalia: the end of the pope's universal dominion in Europe, a prince's guaranteed right to name his nation's religious affiliation, and the right of Christians not of that affiliation to practice their beliefs in private). Luther's primary documents (journals, letters) reveal that he later regretted some of the effects of the Reformation, primarily that morality was on the wane, the poor were neglected, support for schools and clergy was diminished, and princes who replaced bishops tended to be even more corrupt than their religious counterparts. Where do you see evidence in the modern world of the Reformation's influence on modern culture?
   a. **Further Reading:** Hillerbrand, Hans. *The Protestant Reformation.* New York: Harper Perennial, 2009.
   b. **Suggested Search:** Go to Tyndale Seminary's "16th Century Reformation Reading Room" page at www.tyndale.ca/seminary/mtsmodu lar/reading-rooms/history/16th-century for texts, collections, and resources.

2. **Women play an increasing role in guiding religious conviction and social values during the period.** Reformers within the Church include Teresa of Ávila, who called for a reformed convent and was a Spanish mystic of the Counter-Reformation (Catholic revivalists responding to the Protestant Reformation); Ávila described a mystical communion with Christ, and she and other mystics of the period were

influential in the evolution of the Spanish language and the beginning of Golden Age literature, as well as the establishment of multiple convents and monasteries that required absolute poverty and abandonment of property. Teresa experienced sadomasochistic visions during which she tortured herself and envisioned angels and Jesus visiting her; she developed a mystical practice based on the soul's ascent in four stages: mental prayer, prayer of quiet, devotion of union, and devotion of ecstasy or rapture (these stages are not dissimilar to the stages of enlightenment practiced in yogic meditation). The aristocrat Arcangela Tarabotti called for an end to the patriarchal culture created by church and political rule. Tarabotti received an education at the local Benedictine convent and was later forced by her parents to take vows (being the oldest of nine children and female, she was considered a liability). Scholars describe some convents as being more secular in nature, forming more of a salon environment; Tarabotti was known to receive visitors from the Academy, as well as news and books from the secular world. Ávila describes her childhood as already inspired to commit acts of devotion to God based on her desire to emulate the saints. As an adult, Ávila describes the delusions that led her to found the Monastery of St. Joseph (where she now lives) as a burning hell, in which she has visions of lurking spirits, the wicked being punished, and living in a dark prison. Tarabotti argues that a convent is "hell" for women without a vocation, that fathers should make provisions according to their individual daughters' needs, and that religious devotion must be freely chosen rather than impressed upon a woman. What are some perceptions of women's rights and their roles in Christian sects today?

   a. **Further Reading:** Weber, Alison. *Approaches to Teaching Teresa of Ávila and the Spanish Mystics.* New York: Modern Language Association, 2009.

   b. **Suggested Search:** Go to www.poetseers.org/spiritual_and_devo tional_poets/christian/teresa_of_avila.

3. **Devotional poetry flourishes during this period. The genre often examines religious upheaval, skepticism, mysticism, and personal acts of faith.** Elements of the devotional poem include conceits (exaggerated or hyperbolic comparisons and metaphors), standard metaphors, and turns of phrase. San Juan de la Cruz (a major figure of the Counter-Reformation, who formed the Discalced Carmelites with Teresa of Ávila) uses erotic language to describe his soul's longing for Christ. Written in the spirit of the biblical *Song of Songs*, each of his "songs" recounts an intimate setting with a "beloved" (God). In Song II, "The Dark Night," an evening interlude is recounted ("on fire with the passions of love," blazing heart, "joined lover with beloved," "with love

I caressed him"). The poem (and the phrase "dark night of the soul") relates a spiritual crisis—a journey of the soul as it detaches from the material world and rejoins God in the light; the "dark night" is considered rock bottom for the soul, in which it is most depraved but also at the turning point back toward a true love and unification with the Creator (one might compare the steps that San Juan's "soul" takes in this poem to the four steps of the soul's ascent as described by Teresa of Ávila). Song III, "Flame of Living Love," recounts the intimate communion with God using sadomasochistic language ("wounds with tenderness," "rend the fabric of this sweet encounter," "gentle the searing," "soft the blow"), in which God "delicately" shows his love to the writer through acts that are described as physically painful. John Donne experienced severe illness, financial strain, and the loss of loved ones (particularly his wife and stillborn infant) that resulted in more pious writings later in life; he publicly aligns with Protestantism, but his works reveal a conflicted theological orientation. Donne is known as the master of the metaphysical conceit, in which two completely unrelated objects are compared; in Donne's sonnets, conceits are taken to an extreme (the soul compared to a thief and pilgrim in Sonnet 4; the four elements of water, wind, earth, and air in Sonnet 5; and the usurped town in Sonnet 14). Early works were more secular and erotic, while later works increasingly became more pious and personal, and this is reflected in his poetic meter through the use of varied rhythms to resemble casual articulation. How do devotional poems differ from secular lyrics of the period? (Students might compare the devotional writing to secular poems of the period.)

a. **Further Reading:** Papazia, Mary, ed. *John Donne and the Protestant Reformation: New Perspectives.* Detroit, MI: Wayne State University Press, 2003.

b. **Suggested Search:** Go to Luminarium's John Donne site at www .luminarium.org/sevenlit/donne. This site contains a biography, works (written and audio MP3s), essays, a bibliography, and links to metaphysical poets and other writers of the Renaissance devotional and seventeenth-century periods.

In-Class Activities

1. Ask each student to write a devotional poem, not necessarily to a divinity but, rather, to something or someone they honor and glorify. The poem should maintain elements typical of devotional poetry.

2. Divide the class into two groups representing members of the Protestant Reformation and members of the Roman Catholic Church. Ask each group to present its ideology, citing examples from contemporary culture to support its position for or against change.

3. Ask students to brainstorm and then share examples of the depiction of hell in contemporary film, television, and music. How do these examples compare to Ávila's description of hell? (Note: Students might also compare Ávila's description to Dante's depiction of hell.)

4. Ask students to take turns improvising conceits for different topics presented by the audience.

5. Ask students to compare Christian devotional poems from this selection to those by devotional poets of non-Western origin (see the "Poet Seers" entry in the Resources section).

Paper Topics/Suggestions for Writing

1. Define and discuss Martin Luther's use of the word "grace."

2. Ávila describes several scenarios that she and her younger brother created to demonstrate their devotion. Describe the scenarios and whether or not their outcomes were successful according to Ávila.

3. What purpose (or flaw) does erotic language serve in the writing of devotional poetry? Use examples from our readings to support your contentions.

4. What arguments does Arcangela Tarabotti make against the placement of women into convents?

5. John Donne is considered a master of the conceit. Define this literary term, explain its relevance, and provide several examples from Donne's poetry.

Resources

Empires: Martin Luther. Dir. James Hawes. PBS, 2002.
    This documentary offers a historical overview of Martin Luther and the sixteenth-century church.
Images of St. Teresa of Ávila.
    Images include *St. Teresa of Ávila,* by Peter Paul Rubens; the *St. Teresa* statue in the Church of St. Marin Bled (Slovenia); a church stained-glass window at the Convent of St. Teresa; *Teresa of Ávila,* by Francois Gerard; a St. Teresa sculpture in St. Peter's Basilica, by Bernini; and a 1576 painting, artist unknown.
John Donne. Luminarium. www.luminarium.org/sevenlit/donne.
    This site contains a biography, works (written and audio MP3s), essays, a bibliography, and links to metaphysical poets and other writers of the Renaissance devotional and seventeenth-century periods, as well as links to other sites that provide images, biographies, time lines, and e-texts of the poets' works.

Poet Seers. www.poetseers.org/spiritual_and_devotional_poets/christian
/teresa_of_avila.

> This site features poetry by Christian, Buddhist, Hindu, and Sufi mystics, as well as spiritual and devotional writings from ancient to modern times.

The Sor Juana Ines de la Cruz Project. Dartmouth University. www.dart
mouth.edu/~sorjuana.

> This site includes a biography, exegeses, digital files, a bibliography, and links to other influential figures of the period.

University of Cambridge Center of Latin American Studies. www.latin
-american.cam.ac.uk.

> Resources on this site pertaining to Sor Juana Ines de la Cruz include video clips from a film on the author's life (directed by Maria Bemberg), a biography, and a detailed lecture and bibliography.

JOHN MILTON

Paradise Lost

Topics for Lecture or Discussion

1. **Epic poems contain several conventions, including an opening invocation to a muse or God ("Sing in me Muse"), an epic hero who possesses a serious character flaw or physical weakness and must overcome several trials and tribulations, and a moral or cultural lesson to be learned (*prepositio*).** The poems often open *in medias res* (in the middle of the action), contain long lists and long speeches, and involve relationships between humans and supernatural or divine creatures. They usually take place in multiple locations, occur in several episodes, and may include long, formal speeches by main characters. Epic poems deal with important historical, religious, or legendary events that relate to the development or identity of a nation. Milton's work uses several of these conventions, opening with the purpose to "justify the ways of God to men," beginning in the middle of things (Satan and fellow rebels reside in hell after their Fall), using long catalogs (Satan recounts the war in great detail), and including several locations (hell, heaven, and Eden), and over several events, recounted in twelve books. Satan and other primary characters use long-winded rhetorical arguments to recount the Angelic War and to debate about how to destroy mankind. How does Milton's work differ from earlier Western epic poems you may have read, such as Homer's *Iliad* or *Odyssey*, Virgil's *Aeneid*, or Ovid's *Metamorphoses*? How does it compare to contemporary epics of the period, such as Ariosto's *Orlando Furioso*?

   a. **Further Reading:** Crump, Galbraith, ed. *Approaches to Teaching Milton's Paradise Lost*. New York: Modern Language Association, 1986.

   b. **Suggested Search:** Go to the National Endowment for the Humanities' "A Story of Epic Proportions: What Makes a Poem Epic?" page at http://edsitement.neh.gov/lesson-plan/story-epic-proportions-what-makes-poem-epic.

2. **Satan is often considered the poem's epic hero.** Hell is Satan's prison, where he is sent for attempting to oust God from his seat in heaven. Hell is described as a sulfurous place where fires burn and peace does not exist. Satan is presented not as an evil character but, rather, as one who has no option but to go to war because peace is unobtainable and submission is the only alternative. As a leader, Satan calls for "union, faith and accord" to achieve prosperity (Book 2, lines 35–50). He argues that it is better to be free and living in "hard liberty" than to submit to

God and his requirement of worship and "servile pomp." Throughout
the text, God is described as a tyrant, whereas Satan is a compassionate leader of the underdog. Satan is described as regretting his actions
(Book 4, lines 22–32: "conscience wakes despair"), and he feels ashamed
of his vain boast to subdue God (Book 4, lines 80–99). He laments that
Adam and Eve have found bliss in Eden, while he remains unfulfilled
(Book 4, lines 506–15). Circling the earth in Book 9, he laments that he
cannot appreciate its beauty ("all good to me becomes Bane"). Throughout Book 9 he envies the joy and beauty experienced in the Garden of
Eden but struggles internally with the realization that it is not "pleasure
for him ordained" (Book 9, lines 465–92). Throughout the text Satan's
evil intentions result from his resentment of exclusion rather than callous apathy; he therefore appears emotional and less conniving than the
Satan of biblical renown. Satan assumes a heroic position in early modern works, mainly because he encourages creativity and individuality
and because people could identify with his conflicted desires and personality flaws. What characteristics does Satan possess in this work that
parallel the character flaws possessed by heroes and heroines in other
works of the period?

   a. **Further Reading:** Wray, T. J., and Gregory Mobley. *The Birth of
Satan: Tracing the Devil's Biblical Roots.* New York: Palgrave, 2005.

   b. **Suggested Search:** Go to the New Arts Library Paradise Lost Study
Guide at www.paradiselost.org.

3. **Milton's description of man and the Garden of Eden is more reminiscent of classical and pastoral settings than of the original biblical
description.** Adam and Eve are described as noble creatures modeled
after God, and Adam is granted "absolute rule" as the first king on earth;
readers later note that this "divine right" fails, because, in Milton's opinion, it is linked to idol worship. Physically, though, Milton's description
resembles that of the Greek heroes (hyacinthine locks and broad shoulders for Adam, golden ringlets and a virginal flirtatiousness for Eve), as
the Old Testament reveals very little about their physical appearance.
The Garden of Eden is a place in which the wind god, Zephyr, assists
Adam and Eve in retrieving food, and in which the landscape is depicted
as a pastoral setting with fountains and green banks. In the Old Testament account, nature is not personified, and animals remain subordinate to man. In Milton's epic, man's behavior is mirthful, and animals
reside nearby in play and contentment, just as featured in pastoral
paintings. After committing sin, Adam and Eve intentionally seek out
God to confess their sins; this differs from the biblical tale, in which
Adam and Eve hide from God and initially deny any misdeeds. Milton
focuses on the symbiotic dependence that Adam and Eve share and
emphasizes a natural landscape because (as a Protestant) he believed

that man-made temples and altars (which Adam attempts to build) inevitably led to idol worship. How does Milton's definition of "idol worship" relate to his use of a pastoral setting in the epic?

  a. **Further Reading:** Frye, Northrop. *The Return of Eden: Five Essays on Milton's Epics.* Toronto, Canada: University of Toronto Press, 1965.

  b. **Suggested Search:** Go to www.theartofpainting.be/AOT-Eden.htm for an analysis of Jan Brueghel the Elder's painting and a list of other paintings of the Garden of Eden.

4. **Gender issues are addressed throughout the poem. Solitude, like submission, is presented with negative and positive attributes in Milton's text, and it is linked to gender issues.** Adam asks the angel how to love without physical desire; the angel explains that there is a higher love that leads to happiness, contingent upon purity and inner joy "without outward aid," and to obey rather than to let passion sway judgment (Book 8, lines 620–40). Adam is advised to consider self-esteem and to treat Eve as an equal. Adam initially complains that Eve appears to be inferior in mind, feeling first passion toward her and not "all enjoyments superior and unmoved" (Book 8, lines 530–60). He initially refers to Eve as an ornament who is able to attract him by her physical beauty but who has a less elaborate interior. The angel reminds Adam to use his reason, thereby treating Eve honorably and coming to love her through honor. Eve proposes that they should divide labor in caring for the Garden of Eden in separate areas so that they are not distracted by conversation: she will devote herself to the cultivation of flowers, while Adam will work in the wilderness; at this point Adam's personal growth is demonstrated, as he states that "solitude sometimes is best society" (Book 9, lines 220–50). The fear of solitude returns in Book 9, when Adam eats the fruit to avoid separation from Eve; the two resolve that separation would be worse than death (Book 9, lines 960–93). Eve blames Adam for the sin, arguing that voluntary separation permitted the serpent to beguile them (Book 9, lines 1140–88) and that they should unite against the serpent rather than unite with each other. Adam asks God for a companion, stating that there is no contentment in solitude (Book 8, lines 365–410). God argues that he lives with no equal, and therefore he must find pleasure in created life that submits to his will without contempt; similarly, Adam should find joy in the past time spent with animals (Book 8, lines 370–76). Adam argues, and God later acknowledges, that animal life cannot content man because he has "good reason" and is not a "brute." By Book 9, Adam iterates that goodness and happiness can be achieved only by obedience, which he defines as "free will obeying reason." Milton was one of the first writers to promote gender equality and to argue that divorce was a viable option for couples. Nevertheless, do you feel (as some scholars do) that his treatment of Eve is anti-feminist?

   a. **Further Reading:** Mikics, D. "Miltonic Marriage and the Challenge to History in Paradise Lost." *Texas Studies in Literature and Language* 46:1 (2004): 20–48.

   b. **Suggested Search:** A Google search for "Adam and Eve and feminism" will bring up several websites hosted by academic sites and scholarly pages devoted to the topic.

5. **Free will is defined as that which "obeys reason."** Reason by nature is good, so Adam argues that it is reasonable for man and woman to unite in order to prevent temptation by "the foe suborned" (Book 9, lines 351–60). In the eating of the fruit, both Eve and Adam are guided by temptation rather than by reason. Adam is driven to eat the fruit so that he may remain united with Eve, regardless of the consequences. Eve eats the fruit, convinced that there would be no major consequences (the serpent consumed the fruit without apparent penalty). Through faulty reasoning, Adam also becomes convinced that God will not destroy his "prime creatures, dignified so high" but, rather, will revise his work (Book 9, lines 935–60). Flawed logic also results in their decision to engage in "amorous play" after committing the sin (Book 9, lines 1015–45); they do not feel shame or remorse until they have slept. Christianity and Judaism often describe the Fall (original sin) as an abomination, but some scholars see it as a necessary event to prove that free will was more than a theoretical possibility. Does Milton appear to glorify or criticize Adam and Eve's decisions surrounding temptation and the Fall?

   a. **Further Reading:** Featheringill, Ron. *The Tension between Divine Will and Human Free Will in Milton and the Classical Epic Tradition.* New York: Peter Lang, 1990.

   b. **Suggested Search:** Go to the Stanford Encyclopedia Online (http:// plato.stanford.edu) and search for "free will." The site provides an extended overview of free will philosophy across the ages, a bibliography, and links to other Internet resources.

In-Class Activities

1. Ask students to identify and compare Milton's work to another epic poem (e.g., *The Odyssey, Beowulf, The Ramayana*).

2. Divide students into groups comprising no more than five students to design an outline for a modern epic poem on a contemporary event.

3. Have students watch a film from the series *Lord of the Rings* or *Harry Potter* and then ask them to write a movie review that analyzes the epic conventions used in the film.

4. Have students create a trial and appoint lawyers, a judge, and a jury to try three accused characters (Adam, Eve, Serpent/Satan). Evidence

from the text should be presented, logical fallacies examined and refuted, and a final judgment made according to the class opinion of each character.

Paper Topics/Suggestions for Writing

1. Do you consider Satan the poem's hero? Use examples to support your argument.

2. Discuss three literary elements of an epic poem as they appear in Milton's work.

3. Compare the Adam and Eve in Genesis to the Adam and Eve in Milton's text, both before and after the Fall.

Resources

Luminarium: Anthology of English Literature. www.luminarium.org.
> Resources pertaining to John Milton include his life, works, essays, additional links, and bibliography, as well as links to other authors of the period.

The Morgan Library and Museum. John Milton's Paradise Lost. October 2008–January 2009. www.themorgan.org/exhibitions/exhibition.asp?id=12.
> This exhibition includes background, interpretations, and images from several editions in the special collections of the Golda Meir Library.

New Arts Library. Paradise Lost Study Guide. www.paradiselost.org.
> Resources include an overview, an e-text, a biogeography, essays, illustrations, and a compendium of biblical references in the text.

Rutgers Library. John Milton and the Cultures of Print. www.libraries.rutgers.edu/rul/exhibits/milton. Exhibition curated by Thomas Fulton and Fernanda Perrone, 2011.
> This site includes lesson plans, with activities, resources, background information, and images.

Volume 2

I. The Enlightenment in Europe and the Americas

What Is Enlightenment?

1. **While their ideas are diverse, Enlightenment thinkers are united by their rejection of the old authority of church and state and their belief in the power of human reason.** The writers included in this cluster differ on many issues: the intelligence of other races, the morality of slavery, the rights of women, the existence and nature of God, and the proper function of government. However, all of these writers are identified as Enlightenment thinkers because they are rejecting the accepted way of thinking and subjecting those accepted ways of thinking to critical inquiry. These Enlightenment ideas underpin much of modern thought, including the U.S. Constitution, which is based on the idea that rational people can govern themselves better than a king or God, and modern education, which is based on teaching critical thinking, the ability to examine a subject critically and reach one's own conclusions about it.
   a. **Further Reading:** Kramnick, Isaac. "Introduction." In *The Portable Enlightenment Reader*, edited by Isaac Kramnick, v–xxxii. New York: Penguin Books, 1995.
   b. **Suggested Search:** Search the web for "Enlightenment."

2. **Immanuel Kant argues in "What Is Enlightenment?" that "enlightenment is man's emergence from his self-incurred immaturity." He states that the immaturity is self-incurred because it is not due to lack of intellect but lack of courage.** Like many Enlightenment thinkers, Kant defines "enlightenment" as man's recognition of his own reason and intellect and rejection of church-and-state authorities that attempt to limit man's ability to think for himself. Kant's idea rejects traditional hierarchical ways of thinking, which held that certain men, such as kings and priests, were naturally imbued with greater reasoning abilities than others and that these men must lead society, lest it descend into chaos. Kant's essay is also notable for distinguishing between an "age of enlightenment" and an "enlightened age." Like many Enlightenment thinkers, he does see a fully "enlightened age" as possible and on the horizon, though he argues that it has not yet arrived. Later critics of Enlightenment thinking would find fault with this utopian idea of a fully enlightened age.
   a. **Further Reading:** Wood, Allen W., ed. "Introduction." In *The Basic Writings of Kant*, iii–xxv. New York: Modern Library, 2001.
   b. **Suggested Search:** Search the web for "Kant and Enlightenment."

3. **René Descartes's famous maxim *cogito ergo sum* ("I think, therefore I am") is a commonplace phrase today, but it represented a radical new direction in philosophy and highlights the Enlightenment's focus on individual reason and rationality.** Descartes begins by both rejecting what we often refer to as "common sense" and anything he could not prove to be true. While most of us will accept that the shirt we are wearing is red by looking at it, Descartes would reject this on the grounds that he cannot fully trust his eyesight. Following this logic, he determines that the only thing he can say with certainty is that he is thinking. While he cannot say with certainty that his shirt is red, he can say with certainty that he *thinks* his shirt is red. Due to this certainty, and the lack of certainty in all physical and sensual experience, Descartes concluded that the mind and body are separate, and that the mind is superior to the body. "Cartesian dualism," as this mind-body separation is called, has been a staple of Western philosophy ever since, as philosophers have debated its implications.

   a. **Further Reading:** Sorell, Tom. *Descartes: A Very Short Introduction.* Oxford: Oxford University Press, 2000.

   b. **Suggested Search:** Search the web for "Descartes and Enlightenment."

4. **Denis Diderot and Jean le Rond D'Alembert's *The Encyclopédie* represents the Enlightenment idea that all human knowledge can be organized and classified. It also demonstrates that the creation and dissemination of knowledge is an inherently political act.** The eighteenth century saw the creation of many modern storehouses of knowledge: encyclopedias, dictionaries, and museums. Today we often think of encyclopedias and museums as being rhetorically "neutral," providing "unbiased" facts and information. However, *The Encyclopédie* demonstrates that the creation of knowledge is never completely neutral and unbiased. Many of the entries challenge traditional ideas, such as the entry on political authority, which declares "No man has received from nature the right to command others" (33). This idea of political authority, which was central to Enlightenment thinking, challenged traditional ideas such as the Divine Right of Kings. Other entries, such as the one on "Beast, Animal, Brute" (26), reject traditional and dogmatic religious definitions of these terms and attempt to come to a definition using reason and logic. All of these definitions, just like definitions in modern encyclopedias, are not definitive but are part of an ongoing, often contentious, debate about what these concepts actually mean.

   a. **Further Reading:** Brewer, Daniel, and Julie Candler Hayes, eds. *Using the Encyclopedie: Ways of Knowing, Ways of Reading.* Oxford: Voltaire Foundation, 2002.

   b. **Suggested Search:** Search the web for "Encylopedie."

5. **Both David Hume's and James Beattie's debates over racial inferiority and slavery are important, for two reasons: (1) They demonstrate the difficulty Enlightenment thinkers had in dealing with this issue. (2) They demonstrate the rational, logical form of debate that is one of the legacies of the Enlightenment.** The question of slavery and racial inferiority was an issue that vexed many Enlightenment thinkers, and the apparent hypocrisy that many thinkers displayed on this issue is unsettling to many modern readers. In perhaps the most famous example of this hypocrisy, Thomas Jefferson could write that "all men are created equal" (a classic Enlightenment idea) while also owning slaves. Beattie's refutation of Hume highlights this hypocrisy. Beattie's refutation is a classic example of the Enlightenment style of debate, as he systematically illustrates how the conclusions Hume draws from his evidence are flawed. He points out that Hume uses absolutist terms such as "There *never* was a civilized nation of any complexion other than white" (43, emphasis in the original) and then provides counterexamples to disprove this statement. This style of systematic argumentation and counterargumentation will probably be familiar to those students who have been taught to use it in their composition classes.

   a. **Further Reading:** Bodeker, Hans Erich. "Reconstruction of the Discourse on Tolerance and Intolerance in the Age of Enlightenment." In *Discourses of Tolerance and Intolerance in the European Enlightenment*, edited by Han Erich Bodeker, Clorinda Donato, and Peter Hans Reill, 3–23. Toronto: University of Toronto Press, 2009.

   b. **Suggested Search:** Search the web for "Enlightenment and race."

6. **Mary Wollstonecraft's extension of the Enlightenment ideas of equality to women was too radical even for many of the most radical thinkers of this time.** While the extension of the Enlightenment's ideas about the equality of man to both people of other races and women may seem commonsensical to us today, both were radical ideas even for the time. And while the extension to other races was a topic of controversy, as the Hume-Beattie debate demonstrates, the extension to women was considered almost beyond the pale. While writers such as Beattie could recognize that differences in perceived intelligence and achievement among the races were due to historical circumstances, Enlightenment thinkers did not realize the same with women. And while Wollstonecraft is respected today, many of her ideas, such as equating marriage to slavery, are still considered radical. Many modern women believe in Wollstonecraft's basic argument about equality but still choose to get married. Is this a violation of Wollstonecraft's ideas, or can an effective counterargument be made against her on this topic?

    a. **Further Reading:** Jones, Chris. "Mary Wollstonecraft's Vindications and Their Political Tradition." In *The Cambridge Companion to Mary Wollstonecraft*, 42–58. Cambridge: Cambridge University Press, 2002.

    b. **Suggested Search:** Search the web for "Mary Wollstonecraft."

7. **Benjamin Franklin's optimism about the unlimited potential of scientific progress represents the optimistic, practical American strain of the Enlightenment.** It is often said that the American Revolution and the establishment of the American democratic republic represent the theory of the Enlightenment put into action. The American Founding Fathers, especially Franklin and Thomas Jefferson, were heavily influenced by Enlightenment ideas, which led to such hallmarks of the American system of government as the Bill of Rights, which explicitly limited the power of government of citizens' private affairs. Franklin and Jefferson were also scientists, and the optimism Franklin demonstrates represents the promise and the downfall of Enlightenment thinking. While many of Franklin's predictions have come true, others, such as overcoming death, still seem ridiculous. In addition, Franklin's belief that scientific progress is always a social good seems naive in the wake of inventions such as the atomic bomb.

    a. **Further Reading:** Isaacson, Walter. "Introduction." In *A Benjamin Franklin Reader*, 1–8. New York: Simon & Schuster, 2003.

    b. **Suggested Search:** Search the web for "Benjamin Franklin."

8. **The Marquis de Sade represents the dark underbelly of Enlightenment thought. He argues that, at their core, men are still animals and, freed of societal constraints, men will be free to indulge in their darkest, most base instincts.** De Sade, who spent nearly half his life in prison or in an insane asylum, is an odd contradiction who demonstrates the dangerous edge of Enlightenment thinking. Like Enlightenment thinkers, he believed in complete individual freedom and hated all forms of religious and governmental control. However, de Sade saw the removal of these controls as giving license for men to engage in the unrestrained pursuit of pleasure, which for de Sade and the libertine heroes of his novels came about by mixing sex and violence. In *Philosophy in the Bedroom* the speaker makes the argument, using Enlightenment logic, that murder should not be considered a crime. Ironically, though he hated religion, de Sade ends up making the same argument that religious critics of the Enlightenment would make: that without constraints, men would act like animals and revert to their base instincts. The difference is that de Sade argues that this would be a good thing.

    a. **Further Reading:** Phillips, John. *The Marquis de Sade: A Very Short Introduction.* Oxford: Oxford University Press, 2005.

    b. **Suggested Search:** Search the web for "Marquis de Sade."

In-Class Activities

1. Divide the class into eight groups and assign each group one of the writers from this section. Ask each group to prepare a short speech, in the voice of its author, in reply to the question "What is enlightenment?" You can either do this as a one-day activity and have students base their responses strictly on the texts in the book, or as a multiday project and have them do outside research.

2. Assign students, either individually or in groups, a term from *The Encyclopédie,* and ask them to look up the term on the Wikipedia website (wikipedia.org). Ask students to prepare a short presentation to the class on the similarities and differences between the entries and what these similarities and differences say about how knowledge is classified.

3. Gather examples of contemporary political speeches or newspaper op-ed pieces. Distribute them to the class and discuss how the author's thinking either does or does not reflect Enlightenment thinking.

4. Discuss what the various writers' opinions would be of contemporary social and political issues, for example, same-sex marriage, stem cell research, or censorship of the Internet. Remind students to ground their opinions based on the writers' texts.

Paper Topics/Suggestions for Writing

1. Compare and contrast Denis Diderot and Jean le Rond D'Alembert's definition of "wife" with Wollstonecraft's. What Enlightenment ideas do the two definitions share, and where does Wollstonecraft part from Diderot and D'Alembert?

2. Do you agree with Marquis de Sade's vision of human nature? If you do not, do you believe that complete freedom is possible or desirable? If you do, what limits should be placed on freedom?

3. Read carefully Denis Diderot and Jean le Rond D'Alembert's definition of education. How has your own educational experience resembled and/or differed from this definition?

4. Choose one of the ten amendments that make up the U.S. Bill of Rights and explain how it reflects Enlightenment ideas.

5. What does Immanuel Kant mean when he writes that we do not live in an "enlightened age" but in an "age of enlightenment"? What is the difference between the two?

6. How does René Descartes's method of reaching his famous maxim, "I think, therefore I am," demonstrate the principles of the Enlightenment?

7. Some of Benjamin Franklin's predictions, such as the ability to "deprive large masses of gravity," have come true, while others, such as overcoming death, have not. Do you agree with Franklin that science has the capacity to solve all problems?

Resources

Fordham University Enlightenment Sourcebook. www.fordham.edu/halsall /mod/modsbook10.asp.
> This is an online overview of the Enlightenment, primarily from a historical outlook. The overview is easy to understand and geared toward undergraduates.

Kors, Alan Charles. *Oxford Encyclopedia of the Enlightenment.* New York: Oxford University Press, 2003. www.oxford-enlightenment.com.
> This comprehensive encyclopedia is available both in hard copy and online with a library subscription to the Oxford Encyclopedias. The information is useful and easy-to-read but aimed more for teachers and scholars than undergraduates.

Rutgers Eighteenth-Century Resources. http://andromeda.rutgers.edu /~jlynch/18th/lit.html.
> This comprehensive list of links to online resources about the eighteenth century would make a good starting point for a student research project.

MOLIÈRE (JEAN-BAPTISTE POQUELIN)
Tartuffe

> You judge a man as good without real proof.
> Appearances can lie—witness: Tartuffe.
> If your respect is something to be prized,
> Don't give it away to those disguised
> In a cloak of piety and virtue.
> Don't you see how deeply they can hurt you?
> —Molière, *Tartuffe*

Topics for Lecture or Discussion

1. **Cléante, Elmire's brother, functions as the voice of reason (*raison-neur*).** Since Orgon is quite unreasonable in his fanatical devotion to Tartuffe, Cléante attempts to balance the action by preaching modera-tion and the rational consideration of events. Orgon turns his household upside-down with his newfound religious fervor; Cléante tries to bal-ance his brother-in-law's radical position: "It's as if you think you'd never find / Reason and the sacred intertwined" (1.5.90–91). Typically, the *raisonneur* appears at the beginning of the play to assist with the play's exposition. Before opposing Orgon, Cléante serves as a foil to Madame Pernelle, Orgon's mother, who also holds idealistic and, as it turns out, naïve opinions concerning Tartuffe. Although as an advocate of reason Cléante's character is not particularly vibrant, one aspect that does make him more interesting is that the character is something of a know-it-all, and insufferable as all such know-it-alls are.

   a. **Further Reading:** Peacock, N. A. "The Comic Role of the 'Raison-neur' in Moliere's Theatre." *Modern Language Review* 76:2 (April 1981): 298–310.

   b. **Suggested Searches:** Search for the following phrases in Google Images, Google Scholar, or an academic database to find images and additional resources: raisonneur; voice of reason; French neoclassi-cal drama.

2. **Orgon transfers all of his money, power, authority, and love to the religious hypocrite Tartuffe.** At the start of the play, the family mem-bers discuss the growing influence Tartuffe exerts in the household after having been taken in off the streets by Orgon. Comments by Orgon later confirm that the impostor has usurped the dominant posi-tion of trusted friend and family adviser. The most pressing matter is daughter Mariane's betrothal to Valère, a match that will also allow son Damis to wed Valère's sister. Irritated by his family's objections to

Tartuffe, Orgon decides to arrange a marriage between his new best friend and Mariane. This plan inspires family rebellion and a counter-plot to expose Tartuffe as a fraud. In the meantime, though, Orgon disinherits his own son and then signs over the deed of his house and property to Tartuffe, also giving him access to politically sensitive documents. Adamant to prove his love for a stranger as well as to assert his role as head of the family, Orgon completely dispossesses himself in favor of Tartuffe.

a. **Further Reading:** Crisp, Roger, and Christopher Cowton. "Hypocrisy and Moral Seriousness." *American Philosophical Quarterly* 31:4 (October 1994): 343–49.

b. **Suggested Searches:** Search for the following phrases in Google Images, Google Scholar, or an academic database to find images and additional resources: Orgon in *Tartuffe*; fool in *Tartuffe*; religious hypocrisy in *Tartuffe*.

3. **Religious fanaticism nearly ruins Orgon.** Several factors contribute to Orgon making a fool of himself and almost losing everything to Tartuffe. An older man with a second marriage and a much younger, very attractive wife, Orgon also has a domineering mother, two children who are about to marry and leave the household, a saucy maid who bosses him around and makes him feel incompetent and out of control, and a know-it-all brother-in-law who also makes him feel inferior. Add to this his penchant to allow his volatile emotions to rule his actions and Orgon becomes ripe for Tartuffe to pick as a fool. Tartuffe enters Orgon's world at the precise moment that Orgon feels his age and his life spinning out of control. Under Tartuffe's tutelage, Orgon learns that none of his family concerns really matter: "Everything that's written, all that's sung, / The world, and you and me, well, it's all dung! Yes, it's crap! And isn't that a wonder! / The real world—It's just some spell we're under! / He's taught me to love nothing and no one! / Mother, father, wife, or daughter, son— / They could die right now, I'd feel no pain" (1.5.22–28). Tartuffe convinces Orgon that religion, Catholicism, holds singular importance and significance. By focusing exclusively on heaven and the sky above, Orgon loses sight of his family and finances and nearly turns them both over to the "religious" man he once called his best friend.

a. **Further Reading:** Chill, Emanuel S. "*Tartuffe*, Religion and Courtly Culture." *French Historical Studies* 3:2 (Autumn 1963): 151–83.

b. **Suggested Searches:** Search for the following phrases in Google Images, Google Scholar, or an academic database to find images and additional resources: satire in *Tartuffe*; Catholics and Huguenots; French Wars of Religion.

4. **The action critiques the custom of arranged marriages.** Orgon and Tartuffe, middle-aged men, try to block the young love between Mariane

and Valère. Orgon's selfish opposition to Valère in favor of Tartuffe has nothing to do with what is best for his daughter's future happiness, only his own desire to keep Tartuffe in the family. The proposed union of an old man and a young woman is viewed as unnatural and necessarily comic. Mariane remains torn between her heart's desire and her perceived obligation to please her father. Ultimately, though, nature wins over duty. Dorine, the maid, paints a creepy portrait of what life would be like for Mariane to be married to such a man as Tartuffe. This loathsome image pertains not just to Tartuffe in particular, who has not appeared in the play as yet, but to old men in general. At root, though unspoken, is the presumed sexual incompatibility between an old man and a young woman. As such, Orgon's marriage to beautiful Elmire appears as another source of tension in the play.

a. **Further Reading:** Gutwirth, Marcel. "*Tartuffe* and the Mysteries." *PMLA* 92:1 (January 1977): 33–40.

b. **Suggested Searches:** Search for the following phrases in Google Images, Google Scholar, or an academic database to find images and additional resources: arranged marriage of Louis XIV and Marie Therese of Austria; seventeenth-century women France; late seventeenth-century French history.

5. **The delayed entrance by Tartuffe builds anticipation and spotlights a brilliant theatrical character.** The title character does not enter until the start of Act 3. Prior to that, other characters discuss almost every aspect of his character. On the positive side, Madame Pernelle and her son, Orgon, praise him incessantly, but he is described by the rest of the family members—including Cléante, Elmire, Damis, Mariane, and especially Dorine, the maid—as a complete hypocrite. Other characters firmly establish Tartuffe in the mind of an audience before his first entrance. Furthermore, the long wait before the first entrance builds theatrical suspense for the actor playing the role: Will the performance be equal to or surpass the preceding colorful descriptions? Not only do the other characters establish the character of Tartuffe, but they also do all the heavy lifting required to get the drama moving. Much of the first part of the play involves detailing what Tartuffe has already done. When Tartuffe enters, he does not have to talk about what he thinks so much as he has to do things that reveal his character. Much has been spoken about his piety, for example, but almost immediately after he appears he actively tries to seduce Orgon's wife. The perceived disparity between who he is (a lecher) and who he pretends to be (a solemn religious man of God) is apparent immediately and is outrageously comic. After other characters get the play started, Tartuffe drives three comic scenes in the second half in which he tries to seduce Elmire twice, the second instance more outrageously than the first, and feigns

the part of best friend to her husband in the third. Tartuffe is a dream role for an actor.

    a. **Further Reading:** LePage, Raymond. "Brian Bedford's *Tartuffe*: The Erotic Violence of Hypocrisy." *Theatre Journal* 34:3 (October 1982): 389–96.

    b. **Suggested Searches:** Search for the following phrases in Google Images, Google Scholar, or an academic database to find images and additional resources: entrance of Tartuffe; Antony Sher as Tartuffe; Brian Bedford as Tartuffe; Tartuffe as hypocrite.

6. **Elmire exposes Tartuffe's lechery and finally convinces her husband to see the truth.** The playwright positions his most comic scene near the end of the fourth act, in which Elmire hides her husband under a table and gives Tartuffe the opportunity to reveal himself as a scoundrel. The scene breeds suspense because Elmire must first encourage Tartuffe to make his move and then ward him off before he goes too far. Her intent is to show her husband that Tartuffe is interested in her, but Orgon does not want to acknowledge that he has been greatly mistaken about his friend. As the scene progresses, the question persists: How long will the scene continue, and where will it end? Just before an imminent rape, Orgon emerges from under the table to confront Tartuffe. Like his son before him, Orgon stomps his feet and bellows his anger at Tartuffe's transgression. Orgon orders Tartuffe out of the house, but Tartuffe responds in kind by saying that the house now belongs to him. In contrast to male anger and indignation, Elmire remains very calm and rational (like her brother). She assumes that if she is not physically hurt, then no real harm has been done. She certainly does not mind that Tartuffe flirts and pursues her. When she is allowed to handle the situation, she demonstrates an ability to diffuse hostilities and avoid confrontations. Her serenity provides a welcome, if not always an observed, antidote to her husband's bluster.

    a. **Further Reading:** Cholakian, Patricia Francis. "The Itinerary of Desire in Moliere's *Le Tartuffe*." *Theatre Journal* 38:2 (May 1986): 164–79.

    b. **Suggested Searches:** Search for the following phrases in Google Images, Google Scholar, or an academic database to find images and additional resources: table scene in *Tartuffe*; Tartuffe's lechery; Le Tartuffe.

7. **The king's omnipotent intervention at the last moment, a stunning *deus ex machina*, saves Orgon and his family from total ruin.** Tartuffe appears in the final scene as a smiling, cocky villain on the verge of defeating Orgon. The reversal of fortune that comes with his arrest and Orgon's redemption provides a dramatically satisfying and tidy ending. The revelation that the wise king has been watching Tartuffe from

the very beginning and just now swoops in to lock him up flatters the royal powers but stretches dramatic credulity beyond belief. The tacked-on ending shows how close the family came to losing everything. But for the grace of Molière and gratitude of a monarch, Tartuffe would not survive as a comedy at all. Despite the laughs, it is a very serious play.

   a. **Further Reading:** Simonds, P. Muñoz. "Molière's Satiric Use of the *Deus Ex Machina* in *Tartuffe*." *Educational Theatre Journal* 29:1 (March 1977): 85–93.

   b. **Suggested Searches:** Search for the following phrases in Google Images, Google Scholar, or an academic database to find images and additional resources: Louis XIV and Molière; *deus ex machina* in drama.

In-Class Activities

1. Discuss Tartuffe as an archetypal confidence man. Why do such villains make such popular dramatic characters?

2. Molière, influenced heavily by *commedia dell'arte*, truly comes alive in performance. Discuss the desirability of particular roles in terms of what they allow performers to do on the stage.

3. What makes the play funny? What is the best, most comic scene in the play?

4. Examine the love quarrel between Mariane and Valère in scene 2.4, especially the section in which he continually threatens to leave, but then he returns. Explore how movement creates a comic rhythm. When and where have you seen such scenes on television or film?

5. Take a look at any scene of choice. Read the text aloud and try to enjoy the rhymed couplets without falling into a predictable and repetitive singsong pattern. Which elements in the text, implied or explicit, help the actor create variety and aural interest?

Paper Topics/Suggestions for Writing

1. Why is hypocrisy a fruitful theatrical subject?

2. This play explores ideas about false piety or religious fanaticism. What might prompt some individuals to gravitate toward extremism, while others retain more balanced beliefs?

3. Defend Orgon as the protagonist of the play. What argument does he advocate?

4. How does the play view marriage and relations between men and women?

5. Why does Orgon trust Tartuffe, a complete stranger, more than any member of his own family?

6. What is the relationship in the play between the spiritual and the secular?

Resources

Molière. Dir. Laurent Tirard. Perf. Romain Duris. 2007. DVD. Sony Pictures, 2008, in French with English subtitles.
> This fictional account, comparable to *Shakespeare in Love*, traces the playwright's life between his release from prison in 1645 (for failure to pay his theater's debts) and his triumphant return to Paris thirteen years later.

Molière and the Comédie Française. Insight Media, 1982, DVD.
> This overview of the Comédie Française features selections from *Tartuffe* and *The Misanthrope*.

Molière's Tartuffe: An Analysis. Insight Media, 1994, DVD.
> This video considers the significance of the *deus ex machina* ending.

Tartuffe. Dir. Bill Alexander. Perf. Antony Sher, Nigel Hawthorne. RKO Home Video, 1984, VHS.
> This Royal Shakespeare Company version, after the acclaimed stage production, stars Antony Sher as Tartuffe and Nigel Hawthorne as Orgon.

Tartuffe. Dir. Kirk Browning. Perf. Donald Moffat, Stephan Gierasch. Broadway Theatre Archive, 1978, DVD.
> This Broadway production stars Donald Moffat as Tartuffe and Stephan Gierasch as Orgon.

MARIE DE LA VERGNE DE LA FAYETTE
The Princess of Clèves

Her life, which was not long, furnished examples of the loftiest virtue.
—*The Princess of Clèves*

Topics for Lecture or Discussion

1. **As a central object of attention in the court of Henri II, the princess is a complicated character who is both master of courtly forms and unable to completely control her appearance or to effectively dissimulate.** Despite the fact that the narrator announces at the beginning of the story, "At no court had there ever been gathered together so many lovely women and brave men" (113), Madame de Clèves earns considerable attention, as she is an active character in the society and conversation of the court. Yet despite her grace, beauty, and facility with courtly manners, the princess does not follow the more deceptive and unfaithful practices common to the court; moreover, she is also unable to entirely control herself. For example, as Leah Chang has observed, the princess is the only character in *The Princess of Clèves* who blushes, and doing so is a significant revelation of personal responses in a world where the ability to maintain a polite and dissimulating façade is paramount.
   a. **Further Reading:** Chang, Leah. "Blushing and Legibility in *La Princesse de Clèves*." *Romance Studies* 30.1(2012): 14–24.
   b. **Suggested Search:** A Google Images search for "tomb of Henry II and Catherine de Medici" will result in images of the remarkable burial statues on these rulers' graves.

2. ***The Princess of Clèves* is a fictional story, but it integrates a considerable degree of the historical context of its setting as a motivation for different characters' actions and as a means of authorial comment.** *The Princess of Clèves* was first published in 1678, but its fictional setting is more than a century before that, during the reign of Henry II, in the midst of the turmoil caused by the Reformation and protracted enmity between various early modern European states. The novel begins by offering the reader a catalogue of the brightest characters of Henry's court, and in recounting their historical strengths or interests, de la Fayette anchors the milieu of her fictional characters in a court that she attempts to recreate with historical accuracy. Similarly, the historical anecdotes and tales within the story are important for raising questions about historical certainty, in addition to serving as a means of

understanding different characters (see, for instance, the story of Mme. de Tournon, pages 136–140).

   a. **Further Reading:** Singerman, Alan J. "History as Metaphor in Mme. De Lafayette's *La Princesse de Clèves.*" *Modern Language Quarterly* 36.3 (1975): 261–271.

   b. **Suggested Search:** A search at Literature Online (LION, http://lion .chadwyck.co.uk) for "Marie de la Vergne de la Fayette" brings up several helpful resources.

3. **Despite the great importance of historical details for de la Fayette's craft, *The Princess of Clèves* is most notably a psychological novel, and it is this psychological element that makes the novel particularly unusual for its time.** Students should be able to sense the differences between the narrative style of *The Princess of Clèves* and more contemporary novels, part of this having to do with de la Fayette's compression of the passages that narrate action (in contrast to the longer passages of conversation and introspection). *The Princess of Clèves*, however, also shares the discussion and presentation of interiority and psychological states with later developments in the tradition of the novel. Over the course of de la Fayette's work, readers are presented with gradual developments in the princess' psychological states: she moves from premarital doubts and constrictions to unhappiness and temptation in a marital state, to her final state of regret and penitence after the prince dies. This progression is presented in a psychologically sensitive manner and acts as a complementary counterbalance to the historical emphasis of *The Princess of Clèves*.

   a. **Further Reading:** de Lafayette, Marie-Madeleine. *The Princess of Clèves.* Norton Critical Edition. Ed. John D. Lyons. New York: Norton, 1993.

   b. **Suggested Search:** A Google search for "Study Guide for Madame de Lafayette: *The Princess de Clèves* (1678)" results in a helpful outline and discussion of *The Princess of Clèves* put together by Paul Brians from Washington State University.

4. **Central to the conflict in *The Princess of Clèves* is the tension between the impulses of the passions and the requirements of duty.** The princess is clearly cognizant of her responsibilities toward her husband; it is even clear that she wishes that she could love her husband more than she does. Her struggle with her passionate love for Monsieur de Nemours is not presented as simply a situation of the repression of desires, but as the turmoil caused by a person's ability to recognize rival but exclusive goods that each call upon the person for action. Notably, at the end of her short life, the princess' long illness and familiarity with death teaches her to reevaluate the things that she perceives as

good. As the narrator tells us, "This long and near view of death enabled Madame de Clèves to judge mundane matters in a very different spirit from that of health. Her imminent peril taught her indifference to everything, and the length of her illness enforced this upon her" (200). While she still must resist Monsieur de Nemours, the manner of her recovery fundamentally shifted the ways in which she understood things and encountered her passions.

   a. **Further Reading:** Allentuch, Harriet Ray. "The Will to Refuse in the *Princesse de Clèves*." *University of Toronto Quarterly* 44.3 (1975): 185–198.

   b. **Suggested Search:** A YouTube search for "La Lettre 1999" will result in the trailer for the 1999 award-winning movie adaptation of *The Princess of Clèves*.

5. **One of the scenes that is most talked about by scholars and general readers alike is the confession scene, in which the princess admits to her husband that she is in love with another man.** The purpose of her confession is to get her husband's help in resisting her passions, and while this is unusual enough for a novel principally concerned with romantic relationships, it is even more odd because the object of her affection, Monsieur de Nemours, is eavesdropping on the conversation. The scene is both passionate and somewhat comical, as both the husband and lover are provoked by the confession: "Monsieur de Nemours lost not a single word of this conversation, and Madame de Clèves' last remark made him quite as jealous as it made her husband" (167). Yet despite this comic aspect, the confession scene is most notable for its profound presentation of the princess' own psychological struggle, and her lack of clarity in the actions that she takes. As the narrator recounts after the confession scene, when the princess "was alone and began to think of what she had done, she was so amazed that she could scarcely believe it true . . . She asked herself why she had done this perilous thing, and saw that she had stumbled into it without intention. The strangeness of such a confession, for which she knew no precedent, showed her all her danger" (167–168). It is striking that both readers (historically) and the characters themselves find the confession strange.

   a. **Further Reading:** Beasley, Faith E., and Katharine A. Jensen, eds. *Approaches to Teaching Lafayette's* The Princess of Clèves. New York: MLA, 1998.

   b. **Suggested Search:** A Google search for "La Princesse de Clèves: the heroine" results in a helpful page hosted at http://d-barfield.co .uk that outlines important aspects of the princess' character.

In-Class Activities

1. Divide the students into discussion groups, and ask each group to consider the significance of the fact that the author was a woman and that the novel was first published anonymously. Encourage them to consider whether these facts influence our understanding or interpretation of the text. How might this novel be different if it were written by a man? Ask the groups to share the main points of their conversation with the rest of the class at the end of the period.

2. Ask the students to complete research projects in the library about the development of psychology and its relationship to fiction and narratives. These projects should culminate in five-minute presentations to the rest of the class about what the students found.

3. Divide the class into two parts, and hold a debate in which the two parts must either defend and praise or condemn and revile the conclusion of *The Princess of Clèves*. As a class, make a list of the best arguments for each position.

Paper Topics/Suggestions for Writing

1. Write an essay in which you consider the importance of propriety in *The Princess of Clèves*. When is propriety ignored/observed? Does propriety have good as well as bad consequences?

2. What are the essential factors that motivate the princess? What is it that she most desires? What is it that she most fears? Is the princess a consistent person in seeking and following these motivations?

3. While the princess is an interesting and complicated figure, the prince is also difficult to understand. Write an essay about the prince's character in which you identify his three greatest strengths and two greatest failings. Defend your assertions with evidence from the text.

4. What is your response to the conclusion of *The Princess of Clèves*? Is it a happy or unhappy ending? What does the princess learn? Is there a possible moral to the story?

5. How important is the princess' relationship with her mother? To what degree does this relationship shape her character?

6. Write an essay in which you consider the relationship between the historical and psychological elements in *The Princess of Clèves*. Is one aspect more important than the other? How are they related? How do they complement each other? Do they also detract from the emphasis or force of the other? If so, give a particular example from the text.

Resources

Beasley, Faith E., and Katharine A. Jensen, eds. *Approaches to Teaching Lafayette's* The Princess of Clèves. New York: MLA, 1998.

> This volume is recommended for instructors, as it has several helpful essays that address both the historical and critical contexts for understanding the novel, as well as essays that consider different themes that are good points to discuss in class.

Fidelity. Dir. Andrzej Żuławski. Perf. Sophie Marceau. Gemini Films, 2000. Film.

> *Fidelity* is an adaptation (in French) of *The Princess of Clèves*, and it won several awards at the Cabourg Romantic Film Festival.

Goldsmith, Elizabeth C., and Dena Goodman, eds. *Going Public: Women and Publishing in Early Modern France.* Ithaca, NY: Cornell University Press, 1995.

> This collection of essays provides an informative view of women's place in society in early modern France, and their complex relationship to publishing. This volume will likely prove difficult for underclassmen, but should be a substantial help for instructors.

Haig, Sterling. *Madame de Lafayette.* New York: Twayne, 1970.

> While dated, this volume should prove helpful as an introduction to instructors who are not familiar with de la Fayette's life and works.

Jean Racine

Phèdre

Topics for Lecture or Discussion

1. ***Phèdre* is consciously modeled after classical drama in both its formal elements and in the themes and questions raised.** Perhaps most obviously, the family of Theseus is drawn from Greek mythology, and the location of the play in Athens allows it to straddle the historical and the mythological, just as many of the ancient Greek dramas do. However, following conventions ascribed to classical drama and derived from Aristotle's *Poetics*, Racine also constricts the action to one day, and limits the location to only one place. Yet the degree to which Racine included a tragic flaw (or *hamartia*, as Aristotle expresses it) that leads to the conclusion is an interesting question: what precisely causes the tragedy? Themes of fate, doom, suffering, and family conflict resonate in Racine's *Phèdre* just as they do in its classical ancestors. It can be helpful in class to actively contrast *Phèdre* with either *Oedipus the King* or *Medea*, and to examine the central character's responsibility in each play.
   a. **Further Reading:** Storey, Ian C., and Arlene Allan. *A Guide to Ancient Greek Drama*. Malden, MA: Blackwell Publishing, 2005.
   b. **Suggested Search:** A search for "Aristotle" at the Stanford Encyclopedia of Philosophy (http://plato.stanford.edu) results in an article that discusses the philosopher's *Poetics* in Section 13: Rhetoric and the Arts.

2. **The beginning of *Phèdre* echoes the beginning of the Greek epic poem *The Odyssey*.** Often referred to as the epic most concerned with domestic matters, *The Odyssey* begins with Telemachus wondering whether his father Odysseus is alive or dead, after which he becomes determined to search for his father. The complicated situation, with Penelope (Odysseus's wife) being pursued by suitors who consume and destroy the goods of Odysseus's household, shows the family under assault from the outside; this lends a real urgency to the problem of the absent father. In *Phèdre*, Hippolytus begins the play in much the same manner as Telemachus, wondering where his father is and also determining to find him. So, too, *Phèdre* finds herself struggling with marital issues, and the unlooked-for return of Theseus is reminiscent of Odysseus's reappearance after so many years. Because of these similarities, the particular points at which Racine diverges from Homer's earlier story are important; for example, in *The Odyssey*, the family is under assault from without, but in *Phèdre*, the family itself is the source of its prob-

lems. This is a fundamental reorientation of some of the domestic questions which are raised in the Greek epic, and should direct the reader's attention to the intensely personal struggles which Racine investigates in his works.

  a. **Further Reading:** Fagles, Robert, trans. *The Odyssey*. New York: Penguin, 1996. See esp. Book I.

  b. **Suggested Search:** A search at the Education Portal website (http://education-portal.com) for "The Odyssey" brings up a short animated summary of the epic that may be helpful if your students are unfamiliar with Homer's poem.

3. **In *Phèdre*, Racine refers back to the classical world in his dramatic structure and echoes of *The Odyssey*, but he is also influenced by the classical world in his presentation of the family as a microcosm of the whole social and political order.** The most famous ancient enunciation of this type of conception occurs in Plato's *Republic*, in which Socrates treats a republic or city-state as a much enlarged representation of the parts of the soul. Socrates proposes this comparison as a way to facilitate an understanding of the place and role of the virtue of justice in the soul. In *Phèdre*, Racine condenses many large, political questions to the microscopic level of the family, inverting Plato's comparison. For example, we find that Theseus is both rash and tyrannical in his dealings with his family, and that this ultimately destroys the people he loves. Writ large, one can see the outcome of such imprudent and passionate actions undertaken by a ruler who has authority in both the natural and supernatural world. The family, in this case, destroys itself, and the gnawing sense of despair and destruction in the face of these un-checkable but contradicting passions paints a bleak picture for the larger political and social reflections of Theseus's family.

  a. **Further Reading:** Plato. *The Republic*. Trans. C. D. C. Reeve. Indianapolis, IN: Hackett Publishing Company, 2004. See esp. Book II.

  b. **Suggested Search:** At the Internet Encyclopedia of Philosophy (http://www.iep.utm.edu), a search for "Plato: The Republic" results in an informative summary and discussion of Plato's work. It may be worthwhile to ask students to read this article prior to class, so that they might more easily understand a comparison to Racine's work.

4. **The passions in Racine's *Phèdre* are presented as in constant tension with reason, and as they appear to triumph over reason, they also appear to lead to tragedy and destruction.** As the editors of the anthology observe when introducing the play, there is no villain in *Phèdre* (and you might contrast this with other works that contain memorable villains, like Claudius in *Hamlet* or Satan in *Paradise Lost*). Instead, the central characters all struggle inwardly: Hippolytus struggles with his senses of loyalty to his father and love for Aricia; Phèdre struggles with

her love for Hippolytus and her shame at not being able to conquer those feelings; and Theseus struggles with a wide range of unruly passions that are all imprudently dealt with. It is important to note that while students sometimes see Theseus as a villain, he is quite different from characters such as Iago or Satan, who actively seek to destroy things. Theseus does cause considerable harm, but it is because of his lack of prudence and ability to control his passions, not because of a deeply seated desire to destroy either Hippolytus, Phèdre, or Athens.

    a. **Further Reading:** Pocock, Gordon. *Corneille and Racine: Problems of Tragic Form.* Cambridge: Cambridge University Press, 1973. See esp. "Phèdre," pp. 237–278.

    b. **Suggested Search:** A Google Images search for "Rubens's Death of Hippolytus" will result in several images of this famous painting by Peter Paul Rubens.

5. **One of the central themes addressed in Racine's *Phèdre* is the way in which one's failings and evil deeds transcend the particular, and have lasting consequences even beyond one's life.** This is perhaps most clear in Theseus's closing words over Phèdre's body, as he declares, "If only / The results of her evil could die with her. / Come. Now my error of judgment / Is so monumental and plain / Let us go weep at my son's body. / Let us embrace the little of him that's left / And expiate the madness of my prayer" (V.485–491). Theseus recognizes that Phèdre's improper passion will have ramifications that reach far beyond her own death, just as her own situation is blamed upon her cursed ancestry. It is odd, however, that in this context, Theseus believes he can expiate the guilt of having cursed his innocent son to death. Nevertheless, the sense of the lasting indebtedness for evil acts and curses persists throughout the play (for another example, see Phèdre's curse of the nurse Oenone, IV.448–480).

    a. **Further Reading:** Lino Costa, Jeanine Luciana. "Myth Making and Un-Making in Euripides *Hippolytus*, Racine's *Phaedre*, and Villaurrutia's *La Hiedra.*" *Romance Notes* 46.2 (2006): 195–204.

    b. **Suggested Search:** A search for "Jean Racine" at the Encyclopedia Britannica website (http://www.britannica.com) results in a helpful article discussing his life and works, and includes a portrait of the playwright.

In-Class Activities

1. Divide your students into several groups, each of which must dramatically present a part of the play to the class. Encourage your students to think outside the box in the manner of their presentations, and discourage them from simply reading or reciting the text.

2. Divide the class into two different debate teams. The first team must prosecute Theseus as a murderer in a mock trial, and the second must act as his defense. Be sure that your students prepare arguments that use citations from the text as their proof of guilt or innocence.

3. Ask your students to prepare media presentations (PowerPoint, flash animations, filmed documentary reports, etc.) on some of the following topics: Phèdre's family history; the classical myths references in the play; Phèdre's character; the reason why the play is named after her; Racine's divergence from his sources; the similarities of the play to *The Odyssey*; Hippolytus's character; Theseus's character; etc.

4. Perform a YouTube search for "Benjamin Britten Phaedra" to find several performances of Britten's dramatic cantata which draws its libretto from Racine's play. Play the cantata to the class (recordings are usually around 15 minutes long), and then hold a discussion about the ways in which Britten's music and characterization do or do not capture the sentiments of Racine's play.

Paper Topics/Suggestions for Writing

1. Write a journal entry in which you compare Racine's narrative style with that of another playwright whom you have read this semester. In what different ways do the authors develop the action in their stories, and how quickly does the narrative move?

2. Consider culpability in relation to Racine's *Phèdre*. Is one character particularly responsible for the outcome of the play? If so, why? If not, what is to blame, or how is the blame shared? Is it pertinent that the play is named *Phèdre*? Is Racine making a comment with this title?

3. Write a paper that analyzes Phèdre's character. Does she understand herself? What is her greatest weakness and strength? Why does she think that death is necessary? Does she love Theseus? What is her relationship with Athens?

4. By using the resources in your library and online, write a research paper that discusses the background of at least four of the classical references that Racine includes in his *Phèdre*. What traditions does he include, and why? Does he modify any of the traditions or myths? Is Racine interested in the same questions that we find in classical Greek literature?

5. Theseus makes many mistakes in *Phèdre*. What is his greatest mistake? What is his greatest weakness or vice? Are there any redeeming qualities in Theseus? In what ways is Theseus referred to by other characters? You might want to compare him with the Theseus in Shakespeare's *A Mid-Summer Night's Dream* or the Theseus in Chaucer's "The Knight's

Tale." How does Racine's Theseus differ from Shakespeare's and Chaucer's presentation of the character?

Resources

Gossip. C. J. *An Introduction to French Classical Tragedy.* Totowa, NJ: Barnes & Noble, 1981.

>Gossip's book is a very helpful introduction to the general tradition and context in which Racine wrote, and it primarily discusses Corneille and Racine. Both instructors and students should find this a helpful volume.

James, Edward, and Gillian Jondorf. *Racine: Phèdre.* Cambridge: Cambridge University Press, 1994.

>This is a short volume that discusses the context, structure, and themes of Racine's *Phèdre*. Students in particular should find this a helpful introduction to the play, and instructors may wish to structure discussions around some of its chapters (see particularly "Principles of French Classical Tragedy," pp. 6–12).

Racine, Jean. *Brittanicus, Pheadra, Athaliah.* Trans. C.H. Sisson. Oxford: Oxford University Press, 1987.

>Students and instructors who wish to read further in Racine's works should turn to this volume, which includes two additional tragedies which number among Racine's more commonly read works. The introduction to this text is brief but informative.

Sayer, John. *Jean Racine: Life and Legend.* Bern: Peter Lang, 2006.

>This is an informative biography of Racine, and the ninth chapter discusses *Phèdre* and Racine's abandonment of the theater. The final chapter might also be of interest, as it discusses Racine's reputation and reception in the centuries following his death.

JEAN DE LA FONTAINE

Topics for Lecture or Discussion

1. **Insofar as they are ostensibly didactic, brief narratives that include speaking animals, La Fontaine's fables stand well within the generic traditions associated with fables.** Your students will probably be familiar with some of the stories (particularly "The Cicada and the Ant") through Aesop and other adaptations, and this can be a helpful point for beginning discussion about the fable as a genre. Typically, the stories attempt to teach or reinforce a particular view, and this view is sometimes expressed as a written moral before or after the fables. At other times, however, the stories do not explicitly state what they are teaching (see "The Oak and the Reed"). In both cases, readers should question what it is that the story is illustrating, including whether or not they agree with the stated moral. Another hallmark of fables is that the stories often include animals that share certain important human attributes, including the ability to speak, and animals that are susceptible to certain vices (for example, pride) or trickery. Readers should consider the ways in which these anthropomorphized animals are used to make pointed comments about human nature and society.
   a. **Further Reading:** Chesterton, G.K. "Introduction." *Aesop's Fables*. Translated by V.S. Vernon Jones. Illustrated by Arthur Rackham. New York: Doubleday, Page & Co., 1912.
   b. **Suggested Search:** At www.la-fontaine-ch-thierry.net/fables.htm, you can find La Fontaine's stories in the original French, along with many of their traditional illustrations.

2. **La Fontaine's fables are also clearly products of the early Enlightenment era.** Part of this is evident in the very fact that La Fontaine adopts the plots of Aesop and writers from antiquity in his tales, following the neoclassical movement to turn back to the ancients as inspiration for the moderns. It is important to observe, however, that La Fontaine does not simply translate or copy the older fables; rather, he recasts them in his own terse style, and crafts many of his own morals. La Fontaine uses the fables to assert certain truisms, but he also adds a particularly satiric edge to some of the fables that renders them more pointed than Classical fables tend to be (for example, "The Fox and the Grapes" presents its moral in the form of a question, which hints at the fable's satiric tone). Many Enlightenment thinkers were often deeply interested in developing a new philosophy of education, and by rewriting ancient didactic tales, La Fontaine plays an early role in this movement.

a. **Further Reading:** Goodman, Deena. *The Republic of Letters: A Cultural History of the French Enlightenment.* Ithaca, NY: Cornell University Press, 1994.

b. **Suggested Search:** A search for "the Enlightenment" at the Stanford Encyclopedia of Philosophy (http://plato.stanford.edu) results in a helpful, lengthy article about the period.

3. **One of the most commonly noted aspects of Jean De La Fontaine's fables is the power of his short, direct language and poetic style.** While we are reading La Fontaine in translation and consequently lose some of our basis for studying his exact style, the translation included in our anthology does a good job of representing the ways in which La Fontaine employs language in his fables. For example, in "The Wolf and the Lamb," La Fontaine uses short, crisp sentences to state the moral at the beginning of the story, "Might is right: the verdict goes to the strong" (line 1), and he uses the same approach to reemphasize this moral at the conclusion: "There was no right of appeal" (29). These short, direct statements stand in a poignant contrast with the lack of justice that we observe in the fable, and through their very brevity they invite us to question whether might actually is right.

a. **Further Reading:** Pensom, Roger. "Sense and Rhythm in La Fontaine's Fables." *French Studies* 64.4 (2010): 395–409.

b. **Suggested Search:** A Google Images search for "Jean De La Fontaine" results in several portraits of the poet.

4. **While fables are often regarded as works appropriate for children, Jean De La Fontaine's fables are intended for both immature and mature audiences.** One of the aspects of these fables that indicates their appropriateness for adults as well as children is the prevalence of satire as a literary technique. Satire was commonly used in works of the Enlightenment, and La Fontaine makes pointed use of it in his fables. One example in our selection occurs in "The Two Pigeons." The story that La Fontaine recounts clearly shows the propriety and safety of staying at home with one's beloved rather than traveling in search of adventure, and after the story about the pigeons is complete, the narrator confirms this point, saying, "O lovers, happy lovers, must you fly the nest? / Fly, then, but never far away" (65–66). However, in the narrator's following comments, he reflects upon the fact that his own love life has been unhappy and unsteady, and he wonders "Can love perhaps have passed me by?" (83). La Fontaine here gently satirizes those who, unhappy in their own love, still offer advice and moralizing sentiments about how others should love.

a. **Further Reading:** Birberick. Anne L. *Reading Undercover: Audience and Authority in Jean De La Fontaine.* Cranbury, NJ: Associated University Presses, 1998.

b. **Suggested Search:** At www.nndb.com, a search for "Jean De La Fontaine" results in a helpful article that contains both bibliographic information and a discussion of La Fontaine's works.

In-Class Activities

1. As a class, read "The Crow and the Fox" aloud together, and ask each student to write down a different moral for the story. Share the morals with the class, and discuss which is most fitting for the fable.

2. Ask each student to bring a fable to class (either a fable that the student recalls from childhood, or a random one that the student finds from works of Aesop and other writers). Divide the students into groups and ask them to share their fables with the groups, and to discuss how these fables relate to Jean De La Fontaine's fables.

3. Ask each of your students to pair up with another member of the class, and have each pair write a fable in imitation of Jean De La Fontaine. Then, redistribute each pair's fable to another pair of students, and ask the pairs to write constructive criticism about the ways in which they did and did not capture La Fontaine's style.

Paper Topics/Suggestions for Writing

1. Write a brief essay that discusses the relationship between art and work in "The Cicada and the Ant." Are the tensions between art and work reconcilable in the terms of the story?

2. Which of La Fontaine's fables represent pride or aspects of pride? Is there a similarity between the stories regarding what happens to the proud? Is pride ever a good thing in our selection of La Fontaine's fables?

3. Write an essay in which you consider the morals that La Fontaine attaches to his fables. Are they the morals that you would draw from the stories? Where would you agree and disagree with La Fontaine's morals? What does this agreement and disagreement imply about the ways human beings react to and understand stories?

4. Write an essay in which you evaluate the story of "The Lion and the Rat." Be sure to address not only the contrast between the size of the animals, but also the anthropomorphized adjectives that we commonly attribute to the animals (lion=kingly; rat=untrustworthy).

5. In a research paper that incorporates background resources from your institution's library, consider the role of the narrator in La Fontaine's fables. When does the narrator intrude himself into the story? What opinions does the narrator seem to hold? Do you regard the narrator as a character of the story?

Resources

Danner, Richard. *Patters of Irony in the Fables of La Fontaine*. Athens, OH: Ohio University Press, 1985.

    Danner's volume offers a helpful examination of La Fontaine's fables that includes both close analysis and broader perspectives. It is particularly helpful in demonstrating the unity and coherence of the fables taken as a whole.

La Fontaine, Jean De. *The Complete Fables of La Fontaine: A New Translation in Verse*. Trans. Craig Hill. New York: Arcade Publishing, 2008.

    If the students or instructor wishes to compare one of the translations in the anthology with a different rendering of the fable, this is a helpful and accessible volume by another translator, Craig Hill.

Rubin, David Lee. *A Pact With Silence: Art and Thought in the fables of Jean De La Fontiane*. Columbus, OH: Ohio State University Press, 1991.

    This is a short, accessible reflection on La Fontaine's thought and artistry in his fables, and is recommended for both students and instructors.

APHRA BEHN

Oroonoko; or, The Royal Slave

Topics for Lecture or Discussion

1. ***Oroonoko; or, The Royal Slave* is divided into four parts: the narrator's introduction to Surinam, the flashback to Coramantien, the peace and adventures of Oroonoko, and Oroonoko leading the slave rebellion.** Like many early novels, *Oroonoko*'s plot is episodic, which can make it difficult for first-time readers. Dividing the novel into these four sections can make it easier to follow the plot and see the novel's underlying structure. Each of the four parts can be read and analyzed as an individual episode. The first section highlights the clash between European civilization and the primitive culture of Surinam. The second section focuses on the narrator's approving view of Coramantien, which is portrayed as retaining the courtly virtues England has lost. The third section establishes Oroonoko's noble character. The fourth section's drama is driven by the contrast between Oroonoko's nobility and his role as a slave.

    a. **Further Reading:** Warner, William. "Lecture: Behn's *Oroonoko*: Ethnography, Romance, and History." University of California, Santa Barbara. Available at www.english.ucsb.edu/faculty/warner/courses /w00/engl30/Oroon1.html.

    b. **Suggested Search:** Search the web for "Oroonoko."

2. **The novel's three locations—England, Coramantien, and Surinam— represent the clash between European civilization and "pure" primitive cultures. Oroonoko is the hero because he combines the best of both cultures.** Aphra Behn portrays England as both enlightened and corrupt. Surinam, in contrast, is portrayed as a prelapsarian paradise full of primitive yet noble savages. Oroonoko's home of Coramantien sits between the two, retaining some of the innocence of the noble savage and also practicing the old forms of honor and virtue that Europe has lost. Courtly romance and exotic locations were hallmarks of Restoration literature, but Behn uses these elements to create a pointed critique of contemporary Europe, where old virtues have been pushed aside and "enlightenment" has led to the creation of the slave trade.

    a. **Further Reading:** Gallagher, Catherine. "Introduction: Cultural and Historical Backgrounds." In *Oroonoko; or, The Royal Slave: A Bedford Cultural Edition*, edited by Catherine Gallagher and Simon Stern, 1–35. New York: Bedford St. Martin's, 2000.

    b. **Suggested Search:** Search the web for "Oroonoko and background."

3. ***Oroonoko* presents a complicated view of the slave trade in the eighteenth century. It demonstrates the horrors of slavery but also argues that these horrors are only notable because of Oroonoko's status.** Slavery was a contentious issue through much of the eighteenth century, and the personal views on slavery of both Aphra Behn and her narrator (who should not be assumed to be one and the same) have been frequently debated by the novel's critics. On the one hand, the novel is one of the first in English to demonstrate the horrors of slavery, detailing Oroonoko's savage beatings and showing him being torn away from his homeland. However, at the same time, we as the audience are made to feel sympathy for Oroonoko because he is a prince who has been wrongfully enslaved. It could be argued that Behn is not highlighting the horrors of slavery as much as using them as a device to create sympathy for her noble hero.

   a. **Further Reading:** Brown, Laura. "The Romance of Empire: *Oroonoko* and the Trade in Slaves." In *New Casebooks: Aphra Behn*, edited by Janet Todd, 180–208. New York: St. Martin's Press, 1999.

   b. **Suggested Search:** Search the web for "Oroonoko and slave trade."

4. **The narrator's description of Oroonoko's beauty negotiates English stereotypes about race and beauty in a very complex way. Othello's beauty defies typical stereotypes, but he is also clearly marked as unique, meaning his exception does not disprove the stereotype.** In England, and in English literature in particular, beauty was traditionally associated with being white and fair, while being dark-skinned was thought of as being ugly. For example, see Shakespeare's Sonnet 130 (Volume 1, p. 2079), in which he describes the famous "dark lady," associating her darkness with ugliness, or *Othello,* in which many characters, including Othello himself, comment on Othello's ugliness. Oroonoko, however, is both beautiful and black. The narrator's description highlights these contradictions: "His face was not of that brown rusty black which most of that nation are, but of perfect ebony, or polished jet. His eyes were the most awful that could be seen, and very piercing; the white of 'em being like snow, as were his teeth. His nose was rising and Roman, instead of African and flat" (271). In his beauty, as in many other ways, Oroonoko is a contradiction, both defying English stereotypes about Africans and, with his clearly exceptional nature, reinforcing them.

   a. **Further Reading:** Ferguson, Margaret. "Juggling the Categories of Race, Class and Gender: Aphra Behn's *Oroonoko*." In *New Casebooks: Aphra Behn*, edited by Janet Todd, 209–33. New York: St. Martin's Press, 1999.

   b. **Suggested Search:** Search the web for "Oroonoko and race."

5. *Oroonoko* **raises important questions about the nature of kingship, which was an important question in Restoration England. Aphra Behn, an ardent monarchist, makes a strong argument for the inherent nobility of kings but also extends that nobility by making her king an African.** The Restoration period, which followed the restoration of monarchy in England after a decade of parliamentary rule, was a time in which the divine sanction and inherent nobility of kings were strongly reasserted, though still controversial. As an ardent supporter of the monarchy, Behn believed in the inherent nobility of kings and Oroonoko's inherent nobility, and the tragedy of his fall into slavery illustrates this. However, Behn is unique in putting this nobility in an African character. Instead of dividing the world into inherently superior Europeans and inherently inferior Africans, as many writers of the time do, Behn instead divides the world into the inherently noble and the inherently ignoble, regardless of origin. Oroonoko's noble nature remains intact, even when he is reduced to being a slave.

   a. **Further Reading:** Gallagher, Catherine. "Introduction: Cultural and Historical Backgrounds." In *Oroonoko; or, The Royal Slave: A Bedford Cultural Edition*, edited by Catherine Gallagher and Simon Stern, 1–35. New York: Bedford St. Martin's, 2000.

   b. **Suggested Search:** Search the web for "Oroonoko and kingship."

6. *Oroonoko* **is significant for being one of the first works of English fiction written by a woman. In addition, the work gives specific attention to its female characters and is told from a female point of view.** Aphra Behn is generally thought to be the first woman in English literature to earn her living as a writer. Though *Oroonoko* is her most well-known work today, she was also a successful playwright, most famous for her comedy *The Rover*. *Oroonoko* has received attention from feminist scholars not only for being the earliest English novel written by a woman but also because the female characters and female subjectivity play a large role in the novel. Oroonoko is in many ways a classic example of the masculine virtues of chivalry, nobility, and martial strength, but our impression of him is filtered entirely through the perspective of the female narrator.

   a. **Further Reading:** Pearson, Jacqueline. "Gender and Narrative in the Fiction of Aphra Behn." In *New Casebooks: Aphra Behn*, edited by Janet Todd, 111–42. New York: St. Martin's Press, 1999.

   b. **Suggested Search:** Search the web for "Oroonoko and gender."

In-Class Activities

1. Ask students to act out scenes from Thomas Southerne's adaptation of *Oroonoko*. Key scenes could include Oroonoko's murder of Inoinda and the torture of Oroonoko. After the students' performances, discuss the

changes that Southerne makes to the story and the significance of these changes.

2. Show the final scene of *Braveheart* and compare and contrast it with Oroonoko's torture and death in *Oroonoko*. What are the similarities and differences in these portrayals of torture? What do they say about the works' ideas of masculinity?

3. Ask students to create an ideological map of the novel. Give students a map that includes the novel's three locations and ask them to write on the map the words and phrases that are associated with each location, as presented in the novel. This activity can be done in small groups or as a class, using a large map on the projector, and can be expanded upon by applying terms to the three places from the perspective of other characters, such as Oroonoko and Tuscan.

Paper Topics/Suggestions for Writing

1. Is Aphra Behn's narrator for or against slavery?

2. Does Rousseau's concept of the "noble savage" properly describe Oroonoko? Why or why not?

3. Compare and contrast Aphra Behn's portrayal of Africans and slavery with Hume's and Beattie's. Does *Oroonoko* agree with the worldview of either of these thinkers more strongly?

4. What does *Oroonoko* say about the nature of nobility and kingship? According to the novel, what makes a "true" king?

5. How does the narrator's position as a European woman affect the narrative? How would the novel be different if told from the perspective of a man or a native of Africa or Surinam?

Resources

"Aphra Behn." Luminarium. www.luminarium.org/eightlit/behn.
    This is another useful compendium of resources, including links to scholarly articles available online and a bibliography.
The Aphra Behn Page. www.lit-arts.net/Behn.
    This is a useful compendium of online information about Behn, including essays on Behn's background and place in English literature.
Aphra Behn Society. www.aphrabehn.org.
    This scholarly society is dedicated to research on women in literature and the arts in the eighteenth century.
Braveheart. Dir. Mel Gibson. 1995.
    Use this film with In-Class Activity 2.

Gallagher, Catherine, and Simon Stern. *Oroonoko; or, The Royal Slave: A Bedford Cultural Edition.* New York: Bedford St. Martin's, 2000.

> This is a useful edition of *Oroonoko* which includes documents and essays about the social, political, and cultural background of the text. It is useful for lessons that focus on the racial or gender issues in the text.

Southerne, Thomas. *Oroonoko.* Cambridge: Chadwyck Healey, 1994.

> Use this Restoration adaptation of the novel with In-Class Activity 1.

Todd, Janet, ed. *New Casebooks: Aphra Behn.* New York: St. Martin's Press, 1999.

> This is a collection of essays about Behn, useful both for background information and for possibly assigning in class.

SOR JUANA INÉS DE LA CRUZ

Topics for Lecture or Discussion

1. **In *The Poet's Answer to the Most Illustrious Sor Filotea de la Cruz*, Sor Juana Inés de la Cruz (hereafter, Sor Juana) makes an argument for women's learning by arguing that learning in the arts and sciences could not be disconnected from theological and spiritual learning, countering the church-sanctioned misogyny of many male priests.** Both the civil authority and the church authority in Spain and New Spain (modern-day Mexico) were heavily patriarchal, and male church leaders made biblical arguments for the subjugation of women, drawing primarily on the writings of St. Paul. However, Sor Juana was one of many well-educated nuns who devoted her life to religious and academic study and whose existence challenged these sexist assumptions. Mexican nuns were typically well-educated and hailed from wealthy families and in relatively liberal orders, such as Sor Juana's Convent of Santa Paula, where they were able to educate themselves in the arts and sciences as well as in theology. Sor Juana, a voracious reader and an autodidact, makes the argument that all forms of learning are connected, and that to deny women learning in the arts and sciences is to impede their spiritual growth.

   a. **Further Reading:** Eich, Jennifer L. "Women's Spiritual Lives: The History, Politics, and Culture of Religious Women and Their Institutions in Colonial Society." In *Approaches to Teaching the Works of Sor Juana Ines de la Cruz*, edited by Emilie L. Bergman and Stacey Schlau, 55–64. New York: Modern Language Association, 2007.

   b. **Suggested Search:** Search the web for "Sor Juana Ines de la Cruz."

2. **In *The Poet's Answer*, Sor Juana combines two rhetorical modes—the forensic oration and the familiar letter—in order to present her argument. The choice of these two modes is important, enabling her to present her controversial argument in a manner that would be most acceptable to its audience.** *The Poet's Answer* takes the form of a letter to the nun Sor Filotea de la Cruz, but this is largely a construct, as Sor Filotea was the pseudonym of the male bishop Manuel Fernandez de la Cruz, which Sor Juana would have known, and *The Poet's Answer* was clearly written with the expectation that a larger audience than de la Cruz would read it. In addition to the form of the familiar letter, *The Poet's Answer* also takes the form of the forensic oration. One of the three types of classical oration, the forensic oration is concerned with accusation or defense in the courts. This places Sor

Juana in the position of someone who has been put on trial for a punishable offense, and thus she must defend herself. *The Poet's Answer* follows the four-part division of a classical oration: exordium, (introduction, pp. 314–315); narration (statement of facts, pp. 315–320), proof (the affirmative proof of the speaker's case and refutation of opposing opinions, pp. 320–325); and the peroration (conclusion, pp. 325–327).

    a. **Further Reading:** Perelmuter, Rosa. "*The Answer to Sor Filotea*: A Rhetorical Approach." In *Approaches to Teaching the Works of Sor Juana Ines de la Cruz*, edited by Emilie L. Bergman and Stacey Schlau, 186–92. New York: Modern Language Association, 2007.

    b. **Suggested Search:** Search the web for "Sor Juana and rhetoric."

3. **Unlike Mary Wollstonecraft, Sor Juana makes an argument for women's equality that does not call for an overthrow of the established patriarchal system. This has led to her being one of the most-read female writers of all time.** Wollstonecraft's *A Vindication of the Rights of Woman*, which condemned marriage, among other radical pronouncements, was met with derision and caused Wollstonecraft to be nearly forgotten until she was rediscovered by feminist writers and scholars in the 1960s and 1970s. Sor Juana, in contrast, was a celebrity in her own time and has been widely read and beloved, particularly in Latin America, continuously since her death. *The Poet's Answer* was prized for its focus on spiritual matters before being identified as a key feminist text in the twentieth century. It argues that women are as rational and intelligent as men, but it does so within the confines of the Catholic Church, and it also argues that women should be respected in the church. Sor Juana believes that women can be respected and given equal rights without radically overthrowing the existing societal structure, thus making her argument much more palatable to a large audience than Wollstonecraft's more radical message.

    a. **Further Reading:** Arenal, Electa. "Sor Juana and Company: Intellectuals and Early Feminists." In *Approaches to Teaching the Works of Sor Juana Ines de la Cruz*, edited by Emilie L. Bergman and Stacey Schlau, 37–46. New York: Modern Language Association, 2007.

    b. **Suggested Search:** Search the web for "Sor Juana and feminism."

4. **Sor Juana highlights the conflict between Enlightenment thinking and religion. Unlike many other Enlightenment writers, she is able to reconcile her scientific rationalism with her religion.** The Enlightenment represents the beginning of the modern conflict between science and religion, as new scientific discoveries were beginning to undermine religious assumptions about the universe, and many Enlightenment thinkers prized the rational pursuit of truth through science over the supposedly irrational pursuit of truth through religion. Sor

Juana represents this conflict. Though she was a devoted Catholic, her Enlightenment rationalism caused her to question many tenets of the church, chief among them the subjugation of women. However, Sor Juana, unlike many other Enlightenment writers, was able to reconcile her religion and her scientific inquiry and began to see all modes of knowing and learning as essentially spiritual.

  a. **Further Reading:** Eich, Jennifer L. "Women's Spiritual Lives: The History, Politics, and Culture of Religious Women and Their Institutions in Colonial Society." In *Approaches to Teaching the Works of Sor Juana Ines de la Cruz*, edited by Emilie L. Bergman and Stacey Schlau, 55–64. New York: Modern Language Association, 2007.

  b. **Suggested Search:** Search the web for "Sor Juana and religion."

5. **Sor Juana's sonnets often invert typical subject matter for sonnets, as is illustrated in poem 145 and in "Philosophical Satire."** The sonnet tradition, following in the form created by Petrarch, features themes such as unrequited love and the praise of youth and beauty. Sor Juana's sonnets frequently invert this tradition, particularly the praise of beauty. Poem 145 is a perfect example of this, as she calls a portrait of herself a "painted snare" intended to trap and deceive the person to whom she is speaking, presumably a suitor. While the idea of a woman's beauty being a malicious force that traps a man is common in Petrarchan sonnets, in this poem Sor Juana puts the blame not on the woman herself, as is common in sonnets, but on the portrait, presumably painted by a man. In doing this, Sor Juana exposes the folly of the male pursuit of beauty and argues that it is the fault of men, not women. This theme is repeated in "Philosophical Satire."

  a. **Further Reading:** Rabin, Lisa. "Sor Juana's Petrarchan Poetics." In *Approaches to Teaching the Works of Sor Juana Ines de la Cruz*, edited by Emilie L. Bergman and Stacey Schlau, 170–77. New York: Modern Language Association, 2007.

  b. **Suggested Search:** Search the web for "Sor Juana and Petrarch."

6. **Sor Juana's writing and persona continue to have a large influence on modern Chicana and Latina writers. Her preeminence as the first major female writer of Latin America means that almost all modern Latin American women writers must respond to her legacy in some way.** Many current Chicana and Latina writers explicitly invoke Sor Juana in their own work, including Mexican feminist writer Rosario Castellanos, who has written two essays about Sor Juana: "Sor Juana Besieged" and "Sor Juana, Once Again." Meanwhile, writer Pat Mora has written a novel entitled *A Library for Sor Juana: The World of Sor Juana Ines*, about the young Sor Juana's love of books. These writers and others use Sor Juana as a touchstone for dealing with issues of gender and Latin American identity. Many of the writers were raised in

Latin American cultures that are still highly patriarchal and in which women are not expected to be educated. These writers use Sor Juana's struggle with the same issues as a way of dealing with their own.

    a. **Further Reading:** Poot-Herrera, Sara. "Traces of Sor Juana in Contemporary Mexicana and Chicana/Latina Writers: *The Answer to Sor Filotea*: A Rhetorical Approach." In *Approaches to Teaching the Works of Sor Juana Ines de la Cruz*, edited by Emilie L. Bergman and Stacey Schlau, 256–64. New York: Modern Language Association, 2007.

    b. **Suggested Search:** Search the web for "Sor Juana and influence."

In-Class Activities

1. Ask students to read Petrarch's Sonnet 90 alongside Sor Juana's poem 145. How does Sor Juana invert the typical sonnet imagery and ideas of beauty?

2. Divide students into six groups and assign each group one of the six portraits of Sor Juana (available through a Google Images search). Ask each group to analyze its portrait, paying attention to how Sor Juana's figure is portrayed, the objects that surround her, and the elements from *The Poet's Answer* that are present in the portrait. Ask each group to present its analysis to the class and then to compare and contrast the six portraits. For more information, see Mariselle Melendez's article, "Visual Technologies as Pedagogical Artifacts: Teaching Sor Juana in a Virtual World," in *Approaches to Teaching the Works of Sor Juana Ines de la Cruz*.

3. Show students the film *Yo, la peor de todas* ("I, the Worst of All"). Compare and contrast the construction of Sor Juana that appears in the film with that in the *Reply* and the poems and, if you choose, with those in the portraits. See Mariselle Melendez's essay in *Approaches* for more information.

4. Ask students to read passages from works by contemporary Chicana and Latina writers that reference Sor Juana, such as Rosario Castellanos's essays "Sor Juana Besieged" and "Sor Juana, Once Again." Discuss how Castellanos uses Sor Juana to handle contemporary issues. For more information, see Sara Poot-Herrera's essay, "Traces of Sor Juana in Contemporary Mexicana and Chicana/Latina Writers," in *Approaches*.

Paper Topics/Suggestions for Writing

1. What is Sor Juana's opinion of beauty? Do you agree or disagree with her views?

2. What are Sor Juana's views on education? How do they compare to Denis Diderot and Jean le Rond D'Alembert's ideas on education?

3. How do Sor Juana's views on female equality compare to Mary Wollstonecraft's?

4. In the *Reply*, how does Sor Juana reinterpret Christian doctrine to support her arguments?

5. What is Sor Juana's opinion of tradition?

Resources

Bergman, Emile L., and Stacey Schlau, eds. *Approaches to Teaching the Works of Sor Juana Ines de la Cruz*. New York: Modern Language Association, 2007.

> This is a very useful collection of essays on teaching Sor Juana's works. It features several essays that expand on the In-Class Activities above.

The Sor Juana Ines De La Cruz Project. www.dartmouth.edu/~sorjuana.

> This is a primary online resource of Sor Juana scholars. It features a frequently updated bibliography of primary and secondary material and links to the resources when available.

Yo, la peor de todas ("I, the Worst of All"). Dir. Maria Luisa Bemberg. Perf. Assumpta Serna. GEA Cinematografica, 1990. Film.

JONATHAN SWIFT
Gulliver's Travels
A Modest Proposal
A Letter from Captain Gulliver
to His Cousin Sympson
The Publisher to the Reader

Topics for Lecture or Discussion

1. **Jonathan Swift is generally considered one of the greatest satirists in the English language.** Satire is a form in which vices, folly, and abuse are held up for ridicule, with the intent of changing behavior. There are two types of satire: Horatian, which tends to be good-natured and gentle (Alexander Pope's *The Rape of the Lock* is a good example), and Juvenalian, which is darker and more biting. Both part 4 of *Gulliver's Travels* and *A Modest Proposal* are examples of Juvenalian satire. Swift satirizes human weaknesses and evil by exaggerating them and presenting them in their most extreme, grotesque form. In *Gulliver's Travels* the Yahoos represent humans' unrestrained animal instincts, and the Houyhnhnms represent perfect reason, divorced from emotion. In *A Modest Proposal*, Swift takes to its extreme the English idea that the Irish are somehow less than human by suggesting that they be used for food. Swift's satire relies frequently on scatological humor and on highlighting the thin division between humans and animals. As a result, his satire has frequently inspired revulsion and outrage. Many contemporary readers took seriously *A Modest Proposal*'s suggestion to eat Irish children, and critics have called Swift a misanthrope because of part 4 of *Gulliver's Travels*.
   a. **Further Reading:** Suarez, Michael. "Swift's Satire and Parody." In *The Cambridge Companion to Jonathan Swift*, edited by Christopher Fox, 47–63. Cambridge: Cambridge University Press, 2003.
   b. **Suggested Search:** Search the web for "Swift and satire."

2. **In a letter to Alexander Pope, Jonathan Swift said his goal with *Gulliver's Travels* was "to vex the world, not divert it."** Though *Gulliver's Travels* takes the form of an adventure story, filled with magical creatures, it conceals a dark satire on human nature. The satire becomes darker and more biting through each of the four voyages, culminating in part 4, which is the most disturbing and controversial part of the

book. Swift raises disturbing questions here about the nature of human beings but provides no easy answers to the problems he raises. The Yahoos and the Houyhnhnms are both extreme caricatures of the two poles of human nature, but both contain enough truth in them that they haunt the reader and are hard to dismiss simply as caricatures. The vexing and disturbing nature of part 4 is why it is frequently left out of children's and film versions of the book.

  a. **Further Reading:** Corman, Brian. "'In What Ordure Hast Thou Dipped Thy Pencil': Problems in Teaching Part 4." In *Approaches to Teaching Swift's* Gulliver's Travels, edited by Edward J. Rielly, 63–68. New York: Modern Language Association, 1988.

  b. **Suggested Search:** Search the web for "Gulliver's Travels Part 4."

3. **In both the "Letter from Captain Gulliver to His Cousin Sympson" and in "The Publisher to the Reader," Swift heavily emphasizes claims of veracity, and in doing so, he prepares the reader to be attentive to instances of satire that, while absurd on the surface, may contain pointed critiques.** In "The Publisher to the Reader," the publisher recounts the author's family connections and genealogy in order to lend plausibility to Gulliver's character. He also claims to have eliminated many of the specific seafaring references for the sake of brevity, but this too functions as a defense of the work in case there were any factual errors. Gulliver's letter to his cousin performs the same function, although it does so with the absurd much more obviously incorporated (as, for example, his regular references to Yahoos and Houyhnhnms would be incomprehensible to a first-time reader, and are clearly absurd to someone who has read Part IV). By having his fictive author and publisher insist upon the veracity of Gulliver's account, the reader is prepared to watch for those instances that might not be entirely believable, and consequently alerted to the possibility of satire. Thomas More employed a similar strategy of insisting upon the veracity of his fanciful account by including his letter to Peter Giles at the beginning of the *Utopia*. Swift's imitation of More's *Utopia* is itself significant, as it indicates that while the general narrative in *Gulliver's Travels* will be absurd, the text will also present important philosophical questions.

  a. **Further Reading:** Stanlis, Peter. "Jonathan Swift: The Satirist as Philosopher." In *Gulliver's Travels (Ignatius Critical Editions)*, edited by Dutton Kearney, 413–432. San Francisco: Ignatius Press, 2010.

  b. **Suggested Search:** A search on Schmoop (www.shmoop.com) for "Gulliver's Travels" results in several study aids for the work, including brief discussions of the genre, quizzes, and a summary that students usually find helpful.

4. **The Yahoos demonstrate Jonathan Swift's fascination with the thin line between humans and animals.** Throughout his career, Swift was fascinated by humans' animal nature. While Enlightenment thinkers were praising the rationality and boundless capacity of humans, Swift preferred to highlight the fact that we humans are in many ways closer to animals than we would like to admit. He frequently used scatological humor and grotesque descriptions of the human body to accomplish this. Gulliver describes the human-like Yahoos' bodies in the most unattractive language possible in order to deflate any ideals about human beauty. The Yahoos' behavior, such as digging up pretty stones, represents other undesirable human traits, such as materialism. Though Gulliver's inability to distinguish between humans and Yahoos when he returns to England is often read as a sign of madness, his attitude in many ways mirrors Swift's own, making it hard to completely dismiss.

   a. **Further Reading:** Fussell, Paul. "The Paradox of Man." In *Jonathan Swift: Modern Critical Views*, edited by Harold Bloom, 73–82. New York: Chelsea House, 1986.

   b. **Suggested Search:** Search the web for "Swift and Yahoos."

5. **The Houyhnhnms represent the Enlightenment ideal of complete rationality. Swift's attitude toward the Houyhnhnms has been a source of great controversy.** The Houyhnhnms' complete rationality and lack of passion, and Gulliver's response to them, have been read very differently by critics. Many read them as a satire on the limits of Enlightenment rationality and as an affirmation that humans must find a middle ground between the lifeless Houyhnhnms and the savage Yahoos. In this reading, Gulliver's inability to readapt to life in England, and his end living in the stables, makes him the butt of the satire. However, other critics argue that this reading is too easy and reassuring and goes against Swift's stated intention to "vex" his readers. These critics argue that the Houyhnhnms, for all of their flaws, do represent a better alternative to the savage Yahoos and that Swift leaves his reader to grapple with the consequences of this.

   a. **Further Reading:** Rodino, Richard. "*Gulliver's Travels* and Controversy." In *Approaches to Teaching Swift's* Gulliver's Travels, edited by Edward J. Rielly, 19–24. New York: Modern Language Association, 1988.

   b. **Suggested Search:** Search the web for "Swift and Houyhnhnms."

6. ***A Modest Proposal* represents Jonathan Swift's complex views on Ireland and satirizes both the English exploiters and the exploited Irish.** Swift was dean of the Anglican St. Patrick's Cathedral in Dublin and a member of the Anglo-Irish, the Anglican, English-born minority that controlled Ireland. The native Irish were primarily Catholic, and

most lived in poverty. Swift was angered by both the exploitation of the English and the passivity of the Irish, whom Swift felt refused to take steps to change their situation. Swift had made many serious proposals to improve the plight of the Irish, which the Irish Parliament had rejected, which led him to lash out using satire in *A Modest Proposal*. *A Modest Proposal* proposes a solution that takes the English dehumanizing of the Irish to its logical conclusion and also does not require the Irish to actually do any work.

a. **Further Reading:** Cody, David. "'A Modest Proposal': An Introduction." The Victorian Web. Brown University. July 2000. Available at www.victorianweb.org/previctorian/swift/proposal1.html.

b. **Suggested Search:** Search the web for "A Modest Proposal."

7. **Jonathan Swift forces the reader to both reject and accept his premise.** *A Modest Proposal* is disconcerting to readers because its proposal is so horrifying but also logical. The Proposer argues that the difference between selling a child for food and letting him starve to death on the street is not a question of kind but of degree. By the Proposer's logic, the English already treat the Irish as less than human, so the idea of eating them should be no more offensive than the idea of eating animals. Swift paints his readers into a rhetorical corner: either admit the Irish have the right to be treated with human dignity and protected from starvation, or accept the Proposer's conclusion that they are acceptable as food.

a. **Further Reading:** Cody, David. "'A Modest Proposal': An Introduction." The Victorian Web. Brown University. July 2000. Available at www.victorianweb.org/previctorian/swift/proposal1.html.

b. **Suggested Search:** Search the web for "A Modest Proposal."

8. *A Modest Proposal* **is a perfect example of classical rhetorical arrangement.** The essay is written in the classical arrangement that was the model for rhetoric in Jonathan Swift's day: *exordium* (paragraphs 1–7), *narratio* (8–19), *confirmatio* (20–28), *refutatio* (29–30), and *peroratio* (31–33). The narrator's emotionless logic is contrasted with the vivid descriptions of Irish poverty to create in the reader sympathy for the Irish and revulsion toward the narrator. According to Charles Kay Smith, this disconnect forces the reader "to consider just what perverted values and assumptions would allow such a diligent, thoughtful, and intelligent man to propose so perverse a plan" (139). The use of this classical, logical argumentation style also once again demonstrates Swift's frustration with the scientific Enlightenment thinking of his day, which he saw as completely sublimating emotion and morals in favor of rationality and reason.

a. **Further Reading:** Smith, Charles Kay. "Toward a 'Participatory Rhetoric': Teaching Swift's *Modest Proposal*." *College English* 30:2 (1968): 135–49. "Arrangement." Silvae Rhetoricae. Brigham Young University. Available at http://rhetoric.byu.edu/canons/arrangement.htm.

Jonathan Swift | 335

b. **Suggested Searches:** Search the web for "a modest proposal and rhetoric" and "classical rhetoric."

In-Class Activities

1. Play the recording of Alec Guinness reading from part 4 of *Gulliver's Travels* (see the Resources section). Discuss how Guinness's reading highlights Jonathan Swift's satire by shifting from rational to ranting, undercutting Gulliver's ostensible happiness in the land of the Houyhnhnms. Assign students passages to read aloud in a similar fashion, with their performances highlighting the disconnect between Gulliver's words and what is actually happening in the story. Some good passages for this exercise are as follows:
   • chapter 1, paragraph 4
   • chapter 4, final two paragraphs
   • chapter 8, paragraphs 9–10
   • chapter 12, final two paragraphs

2. Ask students to read the selection of negative reactions to part 4 in Brian Corman's work (see Resources). Ask students if they agree or disagree with any of these opinions, and discuss whether the authors are missing the point of Jonathan Swift's satire, or if their complaints are legitimate.

3. Divide the class into five groups, and assign each group a section of *A Modest Proposal* based on its classical arrangement (see *Topics for Lecture or Discussion*, point 8). Either provide an entry or ask students to look up an entry in *Silvae Rhetoricae* in their section and prepare to explain to the class how their section demonstrates the qualities of the corresponding section of classical arrangement and how Jonathan Swift uses those qualities for satirical purposes.

4. Show students the clip in Resources from *The Colbert Report* (search terms: Stephen Colbert; modest proposal). Ask them to discuss how and why Stephen Colbert appropriates Jonathan Swift's form for his satire; the advantages and disadvantages of adopting a satiric persona to get one's message across; and other contemporary topics that could similarly be satirized in the style of *A Modest Proposal*.

Paper Topics/Suggestions for Writing

1. Based on part 4 of *Gulliver's Travels*, would you characterize Jonathan Swift as a misanthrope? Why or why not?

2. Following Jonathan Swift's model, write your own satire on a contemporary topic that you are outraged by. Like Swift's satires, yours should adopt a familiar genre and use exaggeration and irony to attack a particular

topic. Start by closely reading *A Modest Proposal* and *Gulliver's Travels*, focusing on how Swift uses exaggeration and irony to make his point.

3. Do you believe the Houyhnhnms represent an ideal for Jonathan Swift?

4. Compare and contrast part 4 of *Gulliver's Travels* with one of the selections from the "What Is Enlightenment?" cluster. How does Jonathan Swift represent Enlightenment ideas?

5. Compare and contrast *A Modest Proposal* and Alexander Pope's *The Rape of the Lock*. Which satirical qualities do they share? How do their satires differ?

Resources

Alec Guinness Reads Passages from Jonathan Swift's Gulliver's Travels. Salad Publishing, 2008, CD.

> On this CD, Alec Guinness reads selections from parts 1 and 4 of *Gulliver's Travels*. He also reads from *A Modest Proposal* and from other works by Jonathan Swift, including *Meditation on a Broomstick* and "Verses on the Death of Dr. Swift." This is also available as a download from audible.com and iTunes.

Bloom, Harold, ed. *Jonathan Swift: Modern Critical Views*. New York: Chelsea House, 1986.

> This collection is largely dated now, but it does contain many classic twentieth-century essays on Jonathan Swift, including Paul Fussell's "The Paradox of Man," which does an excellent job of placing Swift's views on man in the context of Enlightenment thought.

Corman, Brian. "'In What Ordure Hast Thou Dipped Thy Pencil': Problems in Teaching Part 4." In *Approaches to Teaching Swift's* Gulliver's Travels, edited by Edward J. Rielly, 63–68. New York: Modern Language Association, 1988.

> Use this for In-Class Activities 2.

Fox, Jonathan, ed. *The Cambridge Companion to Jonathan Swift*. Cambridge: Cambridge University Press, 2003.

> The chapters in this work provide concise introductions to various aspects of Jonathan Swift's life and work: his satirical style, religious and political views, and relationship with contemporaries such as Alexander Pope.

"Jonathan Swift." The Victorian Web. Brown University. www.victorianweb.org/previctorian/swift/swiftov.html.

> This website provides excellent background material on Jonathan Swift and links to other resources, including online editions of his works. Due to the nature of the website, it is focused primarily on placing Swift in his social and intellectual context in England and demonstrating his influence on later writers, particularly Jane Austen.

"A Modest Proposal." *Colbert Nation.* July 24, 2007. Available at www
.colbertnation.com/the-colbert-report-videos/183164/july-24-2007/the
-word—modest-porpoisal.

> Use this for In-Class Activities 4.

Murray, Douglas. "Writing a Satire: Or, Everyone His or Her Own Swift."
In *Approaches to Teaching Swift's* Gulliver's Travels, edited by Edward J.
Rielly, 126–28. New York: Modern Language Association, 1988.

> Use this for Paper Topics 2.

Rawson, Claude, and Ian Higgins, eds. *The Essential Writings of Jonathan
Swift.* Norton Critical Edition. New York: W. W. Norton, 2009.

> This work contains both *Gulliver's Travels* and *A Modest Proposal,*
> plus Jonathan Swift's other major writings. It provides a generous
> selection of contemporary criticism, focusing primarily on *Gulliver's
> Travels* and *A Tale of a Tub.*

Rielly, Edward J. *Approaches to Teaching Swift's* Gulliver's Travels. New
York: Modern Language Association, 1988.

> Though dated, this book provides several excellent writing topics
> and in-class activities on *Gulliver's Travels.* It is especially useful in
> dealing with how to teach the difficult part 4 to undergraduates.

Rivero, Albert, ed. *Gulliver's Travels.* Norton Critical Edition. New York:
W. W. Norton, 2002.

> This volume contains a deeper selection of *Gulliver*-only material
> than the *Essential Writings* volume and also contains extended
> excerpts from many of the most famous pieces condemning part 4.

Schakel, Peter. *Critical Approaches to Teaching Swift.* New York: AMS Press,
1992.

> This book focuses on postmodern and critical pedagogy approaches
> to Jonathan Swift.

Smith, Charles Kay. "Toward a 'Participatory Rhetoric': Teaching Swift's
Modest Proposal." *College English* 30:2 (1968): 135–49.

> This piece is very dated but provides a useful primer on the rhetori-
> cal structure of *A Modest Proposal.*

ALEXANDER POPE
The Rape of the Lock
An Essay on Man

Topics for Lecture or Discussion

1. **Alexander Pope's highly formal, learned style is representative of the neoclassical movement in eighteenth-century England. Neoclassicism is marked by the influence of ancient Greek and Roman models and its emphasis on order, logic, and decorum.** Neoclassicism, which began with the Restoration in 1660 and was predominant in England throughout the eighteenth century, was a response to the literature of Renaissance writers such as Shakespeare, John Donne, and Ben Jonson. Renaissance literature was emotional and experimental, and it was influenced by the belief that man contained an infinite capacity for intellectual and spiritual growth. Renaissance writers were influenced by classical models but frequently broke the classical rules of order and form, as in Shakespeare's *The Winter's Tale*, which mixes the classical genres of tragedy and comedy. Neoclassical writers saw man as limited and imperfect, and they emphasized order, reason, and restraint. They also emphasized the order of classical genres and closely followed classical models. They saw art as being primarily useful by providing models of reason and restraint.
   a. **Further Reading:** "Neoclassicism: An Introduction." Victorian Web. Brown University. www.victorianweb.org/previctorian/nc/ncintro.html.
   b. **Suggested Searches:** Search the web for "Alexander Pope and Neoclassicism," "Neoclassicism," and "Neoclassicism and literature."

2. ***The Rape of the Lock* is a classic example of a mock epic. Alexander Pope creates humor by using the inflated language and standard set pieces of the classical epics to describe the trivial event of the theft of the lock of Belinda's hair.** Pope was incredibly well versed in all classical forms, including the epic, and he published incredibly popular English translations of Homer's The *Iliad* and *The Odyssey*. The many formal elements of a classical epic first appear in Homer's epics and were imitated by Virgil in *The Aeneid*. The mock-epic form, with its many conventional elements, such as the invocation of the muse, arming of the heroes, intervention of the gods, and visit to the underworld, highlights the triviality of the society Pope is satirizing. The upper-class society where the poem takes place is highly ritualized, but the rituals have largely been emptied of meaning, as they no longer

govern the behavior of heroes on the battlefield but, instead, young socialites at parties.

a. **Further Reading:** Morris, David B. "Wit, Rhyme, and Couplet: Style as Content in Pope's Art." In *Approaches to Teaching Pope's Poetry*, edited by Wallace Jackson, 25–32. New York: Modern Language Association, 1993.

b. **Suggested Searches:** Search the web for "The Rape of the Lock and Mock epic" and "Mock epic."

3. ***The Rape of the Lock* and *An Essay on Man* are written entirely in heroic couplets. Alexander Pope's use of the heroic couplet demonstrates his neoclassical focus on form and restraint and allows him to display his wit.** The heroic couplet is an extremely formal and confining form. It consists of units of two rhyming lines in iambic pentameter. Pope's rhyming couplets compress language, which has a subversive effect on its meaning. Though Pope's poetry seems clearer and more accessible than that of other poets, the surface clarity hides all of the things that have been left out by the compression of words. The rhyming couplets also bring together disparate ideas, such as in this famous couplet: "Know further yet; Whoever fair and chaste / Rejects Mankind, is by some *Sylph* embrac'd" (Canto I, lines 67–68). By rhyming the opposing concepts of the words "chaste" and "embrac'd," Pope highlights the dichotomy between human and celestial love.

a. **Further Reading:** Morris, David. "Wit, Rhyme, and Couplet: Style as Content in Pope's Art." In *Approaches to Teaching Pope's Poetry*, edited by Wallace Jackson, 25–32. New York: Modern Language Association, 1993.

b. **Suggested Search:** Search the web for "Pope and Rhyming couplets."

4. ***The Rape of the Lock* is an example of Horatian satire, which gently pokes fun at a society's excesses in order to bring about change.** Satire is a literary mode in which follies, abuses, and vices are held up to ridicule with the goal of bringing about change. There are two main types of satire, Horatian and Juvenalian, named after their classical inventor, Horace and Juvenal. Juvenalian satire is brutal and contemptuous and often takes on serious evils such as social inequality and bigotry. *Gulliver's Travels* is probably the best-known example of Juvenalian satire in English literature. Horatian satire is more gentle and lighthearted and usually tackles follies such as vanity and pomposity. Alexander Pope was a member of the upper-class Catholic society in which *The Rape of the Lock* takes place, therefore, the poem does not express complete disdain for the society and its people but instead mocks its excessive pretension and triviality.

> a. **Further Reading:** Brown, M. Elaine Dolan. "The Horatian View of the Poet." In *Approaches to Teaching Pope's Poetry*, edited by Wallace Jackson, 96–101. New York: Modern Language Association, 1993.
>
> b. **Suggested Searches:** Search the web for "Pope and satire" and "Juvenalian and Horatian satire."

5. **Alexander Pope's comic juxtaposition of epic poetry and trivial plot also allows him to explore philosophical concepts such as the nature of beauty.** For both Renaissance and neoclassical writers, the nature of beauty was a vexing concept that highlighted the conflict between the Greco-Roman and Christian value systems. Christianity taught that physical beauty was a superficial distraction and that attempts to make oneself more beautiful, through clothing or makeup, for example, were deceptive and evil. However, classical writers praised beauty as an ideal that, like art, could lead the viewer to new spiritual heights.

> a. **Further Reading:** Cody, David. "*The Rape of the Lock*: An Introduction." Victorian Web. Brown University. www.victorianweb.org/previc torian/nc/ncintro.html.
>
> b. **Suggested Searches:** Search the web for "The Rape of the Lock" and "Pope and Beauty."

6. ***An Essay on Man* demonstrates Alexander Pope's mistrust of Enlightenment thinking. Instead of situating man at the center of the universe and infinitely improvable, Pope highlights the limited perception of mankind and argues that the overall design of the universe is beneficent.** Enlightenment thinkers had challenged traditional Christian views of the world as divinely ordered while simultaneously arguing that humans have an unlimited potential for intellectual improvement and that the only truth is that truth come to by rational thinking. Pope, a devoted Catholic, argues in *An Essay on Man* that man's perception is limited. Anti-religious Enlightenment writers such as Voltaire (421) pointed to the prevalence of evil and destruction in the world as evidence against the Christian idea of God as loving and all-powerful. Pope, however, argues that the existence of violence and destruction is not proof against God's existence but of man's limited perception. The divine plan for the universe, Pope argues, is ultimately good and beneficent, but man lacks the ability to perceive this plan in its totality, leading us to believe that the universe is evil and lacks order.

> a. **Further Reading:** Cody, David. "Alexander Pope's *An Essay on Man*: An Introduction." Victorian Web. Brown University. www.victorian web.org/previctorian/pope/man.html.
>
> b. **Suggested Search:** Search the web for "Essay on Man."

7. **The religious argument of *An Essay on Man* is underlined by the medieval idea of the Great Chain of Being.** Developed by medieval

theologians, the Great Chain of Being is the hierarchical organization of the Christian universe, which sees all beings as part of a vertical organization, going from the most spiritual beings at the top to the least spiritual at the bottom. In one of the most common organizations of the Great Chain of Being, God is on top, followed by angelic beings, humanity, animals, plants, and minerals. In the Great Chain of Being, there is a contrast between spirituality and materiality, as beings become less spiritual and more material as they go down the chain. Humanity, importantly, is placed in the center of the chain, and a common Christian idea is that man is constantly being pulled between the spiritual world and the material world. Alexander Pope references the Great Chain of Being, and the fact that God alone created it and can fully comprehend it, when he asks, "Is the great chain, that draws all to agree, / And draws support, upheld by God or thee?" (415).

    a. **Further Reading:** Cody, David. "Alexander Pope's *An Essay on Man: An Introduction*." Victorian Web. Brown University. www.victorianweb .org/previctorian/pope/man.html.

    b. **Suggested Searches:** Search the web for "Pope and Great Chain of Being" and "Great Chain of Being."

In-Class Activities

1. Divide the class into five groups. Assign each group one of the following sections: The Morning Dream, The Barge, The Rape of the Lock, The Cave of the Spleen, and The Battle of the Belles and Beaux. Using the list of illustrations, by tableaux, on *The Rape of the Lock* home page (see Resources section), ask students to compare and contrast the different illustrations from each section. What does each illustration say about the artist's interpretation of the scene? Which illustration best captures the content and tone of the scene?

2. Compare mock-heroic sections from *Rape of the Lock* with selections from Homer and Virgil.

3. Ask students to read Alexander Pope's "A Key to the Lock" (which can be found by searching the title in a web browser). What does this humorous interpretation tell us about the poem and about attempts to interpret it? Does it enhance or lessen the impact of the poem?

4. Before reading the full version of the poem, assign students Alexander Pope's original 1712 version of the poem (which can be found by searching "Rape of the Lock 1712 version" in Google). After reading both, ask students how Pope's additions, particularly the mythological allusions and the sylphs, enhance the poem. For more information, see John Sitter's essay, "What the Sylphs Do," in *Approaches to Teaching Pope's Poetry* (see Resources).

5. Ask students to write and share their own heroic couplets, either in small groups or with the whole class. After students have read their couplets, discuss the difficulty of expressing an idea in such a confined space.

Paper Topics/Suggestions for Writing

1. How does Alexander Pope portray manhood in the poem? What is the poem saying about the role of manhood in the society he portrays?

2. What is the function of Clarissa's speech?

3. Compare and contrast the 1712 and 1717 editions of the poem. How do Alexander Pope's additions alter the meaning of the poem?

4. Compare and contrast *An Essay on Man* with part 4 of *Gulliver's Travels*. How do both works illustrate the writers' belief in the capacity of man?

5. How does *An Essay on Man* reconcile the belief in a divinely ordered universe with the existence of evil and seeming disorder in the world? Do you find these arguments believable? Why or why not?

Resources

Jackson, Wallace, ed. *Approaches to Teaching Pope's Poetry.* New York: Modern Language Association, 1993.
> This work contains useful essays on teaching Pope in a variety of classroom situations, including lesson plans and ideas for incorporating Pope into the curriculum. It includes John Sitter's essay on comparing the two versions of the poem (In-Class Activity 4).

Rape of the Lock. http://people.umass.edu/sconstan.
> This site contains a hypertext version of the poem and brief essays on important elements of the poem. It also contains illustrations of the poem and other resources.

Victorian Web. www.victorianweb.org.
> This site contains a brief essay on Pope and his major works, as well as essays on Pope's contemporaries and time period.

VOLTAIRE (FRANÇOIS-MARIE AROUET)
Candide, or Optimism

Topics for Lecture or Discussion

1. ***Candide* is a refutation of the optimistic philosophy of German philosopher Wilhelm Leibniz, who argued that we live in the best of all possible worlds. *Candide* presents the reader with repeated examples of evil and injustice in order to argue against this proposition.** Leibniz's philosophy was developed as an answer to the problem of *theodicy*: the reconciliation of the existence of evil in the world with the belief in a God that is all-good, all-powerful, and all-knowing. For centuries, this problem has been resolved by the Christian belief in original sin: that people are responsible for evil in the world due to their disobedience. However, Enlightenment philosophers questioned this idea and looked for more rational explanations to this problem. Leibniz put forth a philosophy that came to be known as "optimism," the belief that, despite the existence of evil, we live in the best of all possible worlds because the good in the world outweighs the evil. In *Candide*, Pangloss represents the Leibnizian worldview and instructs Candide in it. Candide starts out believing in the optimistic philosophy, but the parade of human evils he encounters throughout the story leads to his refuting Pangloss at the end of the novel and arguing that "we must cultivate our garden" (482).

   a. **Further Reading:** Brooks, Richard. "Some Aspects of the Philosophical Background of *Candide*." In *Approaches to Teaching Voltaire's* Candide, edited by Renee Waldinger, 158–65. New York: Modern Language Association, 1987.

   b. **Suggested Search:** Search the web for "Voltaire and philosophy."

2. ***Candide*'s fractured narrative structure, in which multiple characters interrupt the main narrative in order to tell their own story, reinforces its content, presenting a world in which intellectual authority and totalizing systems, such as Leibniz's philosophy of optimism, are brought into question.** The primary narrator is frequently interrupted by other characters who take over the novel to tell their story, a technique known as "diegesis." The first of these characters is Cunegonde, in chapter 8, followed by the Old Woman, in chapter 11 and the beginning of chapter 12. Other characters who take over the narrative include Cunegonde's brother, the Negro, in Surinam, Martin, Paquette, Brother Giroflee, the six dethroned kings, and Cacambo. The content of all of these stories challenges Pangloss's Leibnizian optimism, as the characters tell tales of misfortune and injustice. However, the

form of these diagetic incursions also reinforces this challenge to Leibniz by presenting a world in which personal, subjective experience overpowers absolute truth. Candide's narrator is unable to fully tell of the experiences of all of the characters and therefore must cede control of the narrative to them, just as Leibniz's totalizing philosophy is unable to account for the specifics of human experience, and Candide's belief that everything works out for the best is replaced by his belief that everyone must tend their own garden.

    a. **Further Reading:** O'Neal. John C. "Interpolated Narrative in Voltaire's *Candide*." In *Approaches to Teaching Voltaire's* Candide, edited by Renee Waldinger , 45–51. New York: Modern Language Association, 1987.

    b. **Suggested Search:** Search the web for "Candide and narrative structure."

3. **Voltaire's Eldorado follows in the tradition of utopian literature started by Thomas More and popular with Enlightenment writers.** The idea of a utopia comes from Renaissance writer Thomas More's novel *Utopia* (Volume 1), which presents a supposedly perfect society governed by reason. Many Enlightenment writers borrowed More's idea to create their own supposedly perfect societies. Voltaire's Eldorado and Jonathan Swift's Land of the Houyhnhms in Book 4 of *Gulliver's Travels* (Volume 2, p. 338) are the two most notable examples. In all utopian societies, there is always a question of how seriously the reader should take the utopia. Is the writer really suggesting that this is a perfect society, or is he parodying the very idea that there can be a perfect society? Voltaire's Eldorado seems to be perfect in that it is serene and peaceful, unlike all of the other places to which Candide travels, and some readers do agree with the king that Candide is foolish to leave. However, other readers have argued that the serenity of Eldorado, like the serenity of More's Utopia and Swift's Land of Houyhnhms, marks a stasis and lack of feeling that would make the place ultimately unbearable.

    a. **Further Reading:** Haac, Oscar. "*Candide*: or, Comedy in Utopia." In *Approaches to Teaching Voltaire's* Candide, edited by Renee Waldinger , 172–75. New York: Modern Language Association, 1987.

    b. **Suggested Search:** Search the web for "Candide and Utopia."

4. *Candide* **uses one of the most popular forms of narrative—the voyage tale—to tell the story of Candide's philosophical voyage.** The story of a voyage is one of the most persistent in literature, going back to ancient texts such as *The Epic of Gilgamesh* and *The Odyssey*. Candide's physical voyage takes him from Europe to South America and back again, with many stops in between. Voltaire uses the voyage tale to show the disjunction between Pangloss and Candide's cloistered view

of the world and the world itself. Candide goes out into the world with the idea that Pangloss's naive optimistic theories, developed in isolated context of the chateau, will hold true for the rest of the world. The reader quickly sees that these theories do not hold up to the test of real-world experience, though it takes Candide much longer to realize this. In most voyage tales, the hero learns something from the journey. For example, Gilgamesh learns that it is futile to try to achieve immortality. However, unlike other heroes of voyage tales, Candide seems for most of the novel to learn nothing from his journeys and encounters, and even when he does, he backslides into naivete once again. As late as chapter 27, he is approvingly referencing Pangloss's theories, though he does eventually come to reject them.

   a. **Further Reading:** Weinreb, Ruth Plant. "The Voyage in *Candide*: Interpolated Narrative in Voltaire's *Candide*." In *Approaches to Teaching Voltaire's* Candide, edited by Renee Waldinger, 64–68. New York: Modern Language Association, 1987.

   b. **Suggested Search:** Search the web for "Candide and voyage narrative."

5. **Voltaire frequently uses incongruity, obscenity, and accumulation of realistic detail, among other devices, to create his dense satire, as can be illustrated by the scene in chapter 4 in which Pangloss discusses his syphilis.** The brief exchange between Candide and Pangloss about Pangloss's syphilis is an excellent introduction into Voltaire's satirical techniques. The passage (429–430) uses many of Voltaire's techniques, such as incongruously contrasting high-minded philosophical musings and obscenity. This begins with Pangloss's academic description of the genealogy of the disease, tracing it back to Christopher Columbus: "He had it from an elderly countess, who picked it up from a captain of cavalry, who acquired it from a marquise" (429), and so on. Pangloss then goes on to argue that the existence of such a horrible disease is not evidence against his belief that this is the "best of all possible worlds," since if Columbus had not brought this disease back from the New World, Europe also would not have had chocolate or cochineal. Voltaire uses these devices of incongruity throughout the novel to show the encroachment of the real world into Pangloss and Candide's optimistic philosophy.

   a. **Further Reading:** Mabe, Cassandra. "On Teaching the Ironical Satire of *Candide*." In *Approaches to Teaching Voltaire's* Candide, edited by Renee Waldinger, 83–87. New York: Modern Language Association, 1987.

   b. **Suggested Search:** Search the web for "Candide and Satire."

6. **Gardens recur frequently throughout the novel, as Candide begins the story in the garden at the castle of the Baron and ends the novel**

in a garden of his own making with Cunegonde. The garden at the castle of the Baron is frequently interpreted as an Eden-like paradise, with Candide and Cunegonde's expulsion paralleling Adam and Eve's. It is only in this Eden that Pangloss's optimistic philosophy makes sense, as Candide frequently encounters evil after being expelled and has his optimistic philosophy challenged. El Dorado is another type of Eden-like garden, and the El Dorado episode notably presents a brief respite from the parade of evils and misfortunes that make up most of the book. Cyclically, the novel ends with Candide and Cunegonde making their own garden and Candide refuting Pangloss's philosophy by arguing that each man should tend his own garden. Gardens can be read as an example of human industry and self-reliance, disconnected from society, which is the only way to escape the evil and misfortunes of the world. The gardens also have been read as representing *The Encyclopédie,* as Voltaire elsewhere compared the creation of *The Encyclopédie* to gardening and encouraged his companions to retire from society to complete it.

a. **Further Reading:** Bottiglia, William F. "Candide's Garden." *PMLA* 66:5 (September 1951): 718–33.

b. **Suggested Search:** Search the web for "Candide and Garden."

In-Class Activities

1. Ask students to listen to Leonard Bernstein's operetta adaptation of *Candide.* Discuss which elements Bernstein chose to keep and which he chose to cut, as well as his reasons for doing so. Why did he choose to focus on these elements in 1956? Which elements would a modern-day adaptation most likely focus on?

2. Ask students to debate the "inside-outside" controversy. Ask them to read excerpts from critics on one of the two sides of the debate (see Braun in Resources) and, using these critics as their basis, to present their assigned side of the argument. The class can be divided into two groups, or, in larger classes, into four, six, or eight groups, with each group assigned a different critic and paired off for the debate.

Paper Topics/Suggestions for Writing

1. Compare and contrast Voltaire's Eldorado and Jonathan Swift's land of Houyhnhms in *Gulliver's Travels.*

2. Is Voltaire's portrait of Eldorado optimistic or pessimistic?

3. Compare and contrast Voltaire's portrayal of colonialism and slavery with that of Aphra Behn's in *Oroonoko.*

4. Is Voltaire advocating retreat from society or active engagement in it?

5. How do the experiences of the women in *Candide* differ from those of the men?

6. Compare and contrast *Candide* and another voyage narrative you have read, for example, *Gulliver's Travels, Journey to the West,* or *The Narrow Road to the Deep North.*

Resources

"Bernstein's *Candide.*" *Great Performances.* www.pbs.org/wnet/gperf/shows /candide.

> This is the website for the PBS production of Bernstein's *Candide,* featuring videos of the performance and other educational resources. The performance is also available as a DVD.

Braun, Theodore E. D. "Interpreting *Candide*: The Anvil of Controversy." In *Approaches to Teaching Voltaire's* Candide, edited by Renee Waldinger, 69–75. New York: Modern Language Association, 1987.

> Use this for In-Class Activities 2.

"Voltaire." Lucid Cafe. www.lucidcafe.com/library/95nov/voltaire.html.

> This is a brief, useful overview of Voltaire's life and philosophical positions.

"Voltaire." *Stanford Encyclopedia of Philosophy.* http://plato.stanford.edu /entries/voltaire.

> This is an in-depth description of Voltaire as a philosopher, with links to related philosophers and an extensive bibliography.

Voltaire Foundation. www.voltaire.ox.ac.uk/www_vf/default.ssi.

> This scholarly society is dedicated to the study of Voltaire. The website provides many links to useful resources.

Waldinger, Renee. *Approaches to Teaching Voltaire's* Candide. New York: Modern Language Association, 1987.

> This is a useful collection of essays on teaching *Candide,* with a focus on practical in-class activities.

Samuel Johnson

From *The History of Rasselas, Prince of Abissinia*

Topics for Lecture or Discussion

1. ***The History of Rasselas, Prince of Abissinia* is remarkable in part because it was written in only one week, as Johnson needed to raise money for his mother's funeral.** Because of the sorrow-filled historical context of its composition, we might be inclined to dismiss or explain away some of the claims about happiness, human experience, and the intellect that are made in *The History of Rasselas*. However, Johnson treats these themes and others with a serious mind and capacious imagination, and even when discussing death—a subject that must have been a tender one for Johnson—he is sophisticated and balanced. For example, when speaking with the philosopher in Chapter XVIII, Rasselas claims, "mortality is an event by which a wise man can never be surprised: we know that death is always near, and it should therefore always be expected" (502). This dispassionate claim is countered by the philosopher, who rebukes Rasselas with the words, "you speak like one that has never felt the pangs of separation" (502). Such a debate in *The History of Rasselas* assumes a particular poignancy when read in light of its composition history.

    a. **Further Reading:** Nokes, David. *Samuel Johnson: A Life*. New York: Henry Holt and Company, 2010.

    b. **Suggested Search:** A Google Images search for "Joshua Reynolds Samuel Jonson" will result in images of several of Reynolds's famous portraits of Johnson.

2. **It is frequently observed that *The History of Rasselas, Prince of Abissinia* is remarkably similar to Voltaire's *Candide*.** Even if your class is not reading both *Candide* and *The History of Rasselas*, it is helpful to inform students about the similarities between these works in order to facilitate a discussion about the intellectual developments and philosophical questions that were debated in Europe in the eighteenth century. First published in the same year, both works use a journey, undertaken by a young man, as the fictional setting for exploring some difficult questions, especially those related to the causes of human happiness and suffering. *Candide* satirically examines claims of happiness and mocks many political, social, and religious aspects of society, and *The History of Rasselas*, while more serious, examines many similar issues. Both works contain critiques of idealism, as well as illustrations

of some absurdities of sentimentalism. It is also notable that both works are short novels but that neither is particularly gripping as a work of fiction; rather, the success of the works comes from their use of the novel as a vehicle for exploring the philosophical issues of the day.

a. **Further Reading:** Temmer, Mark. *Samuel Johnson and Three Infidels: Rousseau, Voltaire, Diderot.* Athens, GA: University of Georgia Press, 1988.

b. **Suggested Search:** A search at Harper's Magazine (http://harpers .org) for "Johnson and Voltaire cultivating our garden" results in an informative article by Scott Horton that you might give to students if the class is not going to read *Candide*.

3. **Samuel Johnson's *The History of Rasselas, Prince of Abissinia* levels a serious critique against philosophical idealism and political utopianism.** Rasselas and his companions Nekayah, Pekuah, and Imlac begin the story in an idyllic setting in which the valley "supplied its inhabitants with the necessaries of life" (486). Nevertheless, Rasselas is unhappy, and it becomes clear that simply fulfilling physical needs is wholly insufficient for leading a happy and meaningful life. Recognizing a fundamental difference between human beings and other animals, Rasselas determines to undertake a quest for knowledge. However, over the course of his journey, his youthful idealism is undermined and revised as he encounters more and more forms of suffering, and realizes that happiness, as he has conceived of it, is not a state that can be permanently attained in this life. Both philosophical and political efforts at finding the ideal way of life fail, as varied human experience cannot be systematically solved.

a. **Further Reading:** Pahl, Chance David. "Teleology in Samuel Johnson's *Rasselas*." *Renascence* 64:3 (2012): 221–232.

b. **Suggested Search:** At www.samueljohnson.com, you will find a wealth of Johnson's quotes, a discussion of his politics, and a helpful timeline of his life and works.

4. **One of the conclusions that *The History of Rasselas, Prince of Abissinia* points toward is the importance of community for intellectual growth and happiness.** The closing chapter of *The History of Rasselas* finds the travelers confined together in a house during a storm, and the narrator tells us, "being well supplied with materials for talk, they diverted themselves with comparisons of the different forms of life which they had observed, and with various schemes of happiness which each of them had formed" (528). Each of the companions has formed a different conception of happiness over the course of the story, but the fundamental point is that, while they are trapped by this storm, they are able to divert themselves with pleasing, beneficial conversation. Indeed, each of the ideals of happiness that the characters have gained

are recognized as ideals: "Of these wishes that they had formed they knew well that none could be obtained. They deliberated awhile what was to be done, and resolved, when the inundation should cease, to return to Abissinia" (529). Without being able to live an ideal happy life, this small community agrees about where they should go and what they should do, and with the expectation of further delights of companionship and conversation, they have not entirely abandoned the pursuit of the happy life.

a. **Further Reading:** Parker, Fred. "The Skepticism of Johnson's Rasselas." In *The Cambridge Companion to Samuel Johnson*, edited by Greg Clingham, pp. 127–142. Cambridge: Cambridge University Press, 1997.

b. **Suggested Search:** A Google Images search for "John Opie Samuel Johnson" will result in Opie's famous portrait of Johnson.

5. **The journey and exploration of foreign cultures that occurs in *The History of Rasselas, Prince of Abissinia* reflects the growing ease with which travel occurred and cultures interacted over the course of the eighteenth century.** Technological advances had made sea travel safer and faster than it had been in previous centuries, and consequently, there was a considerable increase in the communication and trade between dramatically different cultures. *The History of Rasselas* presents aspects of these developments. For example, when the travelers arrive in Cairo, Rasselas is told that the city is "the place where travelers and merchants assemble from all the corners of the earth. You will here find men of every character, and every occupation. Commerce is here honorable: I will act as a merchant, and you shall live as strangers, who have no other end of travel than curiosity; it will soon be observed that we are rich; our reputation will procure us access to all whom we shall desire to know; you will see all the conditions of humanity" (499). Commerce, variety, and the growing importance of wealth as the decisive factor in determining one's status is all as common to Johnson's London as it was to Rasselas's Cairo.

a. **Further Reading:** Blanning, T. C. W., ed. *The Eighteenth Century*. Short Oxford History of Europe. Oxford: Oxford University Press, 2000.

b. **Suggested Search:** At the Great Writers Inspire website (http://writersinspire.org) a search for "A history of the dictionary: Dr Johnson, I presume?" results in an interesting video of a lecture by Henry Hitchings about Johnson's work in London on his dictionary.

In-Class Activities

1. Ask your students to prepare some sort of creative presentation (animation, illustrations, poster, mock documentary, poem, etc.) to the class

in which they imagine further aspects of the "Happy Valley." After these presentations are made, discuss with the class the shortcomings of imagining a utopia (you might also discuss Thomas More or Karl Marx).

2. Divide the class into four sections, each of which must defend the form of happiness endorsed by one of the four characters in the final chapter (528–529). Encourage them to use evidence from the text as well as creative arguments in support of that position.

3. Ask each student to write a journal entry in which he/she must contrast Rasselas's journey and the things he learned with a journey that the student has taken and the things that he/she learned. Share some of these journal entries with the class.

Paper Topics/Suggestions for Writing

1. Does *The History of Rasselas* contain arguments against the pursuit of happiness? What are they? Which is the strongest argument or critique? What is proposed in the place of the pursuit of happiness?

2. Consider Rasselas's character and his philosophical positions at the beginning and end of the story. In what ways does he change? What is the most important, or most fundamental, change that Rasselas undergoes? In what ways does he remain constant throughout the story?

3. Write an essay in which you contrast *The History of Rasselas* with Voltaire's *Candide*. What is the essential or most important difference between the two books? Why? Which book is darker in tone? Which of the two works is more interesting as a work of fiction?

4. Consider the importance of place in the narrative. How are characters affected by place? Contrast Cairo to the Happy Valley. What is the role of the pyramids in the plot? What is the significance of the fact that the characters decide to return to Abissinia at the conclusion of the story?

5. What is the strongest argument against idealism in *The History of Rasselas*? Why is that the strongest argument? Be sure to support your claim with substantial use of quotations from the text.

6. Choose another work that you have read for this class that straddles the boundaries between fiction and philosophy. In what ways is that work like *The History of Rasselas*? In what ways are they different? What distinguishes a work of philosophy from a work of fiction?

7. Is *The History of Rasselas* successful as a work of fiction? If so, why? If not, where are its primary weaknesses or failings?

Resources

Anderson, David Ray, and Gwin J. Kolb, eds. *Approaches to Teaching the Works of Samuel Johnson*. New York: Modern Language Association, 1993. While this volume addresses all of Samuel Johnson's works, instructors should still find it a valuable resource for its information about his life and historical context.

Boswell, James. *Life of Johnson*. Oxford World Classics. Edited by R. W. Chapman. Oxford: Oxford University Press, 1998. This is an accessible edition of Boswell's famous biography, and students should be encouraged to read part of it in conjunction with Johnson's works.

Clingham, Greg, ed. *The Cambridge Companion to Samuel Johnson*. Cambridge: Cambridge University Press, 1997. This collection of essays contains several excellent pieces, and an essay that discusses skepticism and *The History of Rasselas* by Fred Parker.

Johnson, Samuel. *Samuel Johnson: The Major Works*. Edited by Donald Greene. Oxford: Oxford University Press, 1984. Students and instructors who wish to read further in Johnson's corpus should turn to this volume, which includes selections of Johnson's poems, essays, excerpts from his dictionary, and some of his works on the English poets.

Nokes, David. *Samuel Johnson: A Life*. New York: Henry Holt and Company, 2010. Nokes's biography of Johnson is a helpful resource for students and instructors alike, but it ought to be supplemented with parts of Boswell's great biography as well, since it does not consistently convey Johnson's genius and influence.

II. An Age of Revolutions
in Europe and the Americas

REVOLUTIONARY CONTEXTS

Topics for Lecture or Discussion

1. **Edmund Burke's objections to the French Revolution show him to have a fundamentally different view of humanity's natural state than the revolutionary followers of Jean-Jacques Rousseau.** Rousseau believed humanity to be naturally good—it was a corrupt society and its social institutions that changed this natural state in humanity. Some of these views can be gleaned from the selection from *Confessions,* later in this anthology, but it would have been his novel *Émile* that would have most commonly been read by revolutionaries. To Rousseau's followers, a revolution would improve government, giving humanity a chance to govern itself and to break free of existing institutions' corrupting influence and create the opportunity for a government that would bring citizens closer to their natural state. Burke, though, does not share Rousseau's views and believes that instead of institutions corrupting individuals, those very institutions hold humanity's dark impulses in check. Burke can agree to many of the revolutionaries' claims to the rights of human beings, but, from his viewpoint, revolutionary activity will push humans away from achieving those rights they are fighting to receive.

   a. **Further Reading:** Stanlis, Peter J. "Burke, Rousseau, and the French Revolution." In *Burke and the French Revolution,* edited by Steven Blakemore, 97–119. Athens, GA: University of Georgia Press, 1992.

   b. **Suggested Search:** Search for "Edmund Burke" at the *Stanford Encyclopedia of Philosophy* (plato.stanford.edu).

2. **Simón Bolívar's letter from Jamaica displays a fundamental tension of revolutionary documents: revolutionary documents had to be both philosophical in their claims for human rights and had to pragmatically further the revolution's goals.** Bolívar admired both the American Revolution and French Revolution and saw Latin America's revolution as a similar rejection of tyranny. It is as a Europeanized Latin American that Bolívar claims his rights in "Reply," writing, "though Americans by birth we derive our rights from Europe" (576). It is by those rights that Bolívar claims the right to self-rule, and yet in that same passage he describes indigenous Latin Americans as "the legitimate proprietors of this country" and sees a necessity to assert his rights "against the rights of the natives" (576). Bolívar follows a belief in inalienable human rights, to a point, but he admits that in his position between Spain and indigenous Latin Americans, he ultimately takes a self-interested, pragmatic position. While Bolívar discusses this tension in his "Reply," a similar tension is common to the period's revolutions. Olympe de Gouges's "The Rights of Woman," "Declaration of

Sentiments," and Frederick Douglass's *Narrative* all exist as evidence of revolutionaries not following to its end point the philosophic argument of inalienable rights.

   a. **Further Reading:** Racine, Karen. "Simón Bolívar and Andrés Bello: The Republican Ideal." In *Simón Bolívar: Essays on the Life and Legacy of the Liberator*, edited by David Bushnell and Lester D. Langley, 55–72. Lanham, MD: Rowman and Littlefield, 2008.

   b. **Suggested Search:** The Library of Congress website has a large number of reproductions of Simón Bolívar portraits in the "Prints & Photographs Online Catalogue" at www.loc.gov/pictures, which can be found by searching for "Simón Bolívar" at the site.

3. **Olympe de Gouges's "The Rights of Woman" is not only a document that asks the French Revolution to extend rights to women, but it also exists in an attempt to bridge between genders the gap in power that grew following the revolution.** De Gouges references the influence women had at court in order to denounce the "perverted" way in which women could have formerly achieved power. This renunciation of the women of the Ancien Régime serves as a platform for de Gouges to demand that direct political power be given to women, but it is also an acknowledgment, with the loss of the court, that (privileged) women lost their sole means to political power. De Gouges's "The Rights of Woman" fell on deaf ears, and following the French Revolution, it became increasingly excluded from the public sphere.

   a. **Further Reading:** Landes, Joan B. *Women and the Public Sphere in the Age of the French Revolution*. Ithaca, NY: Cornell University Press, 1988.

   b. **Suggested Search:** A search for "Liberty Leading the People" at the Louvre website (www.louvre.fr/en) leads to the famous painting by Eugène Delacroix.

4. **The philosophical differences between the American Revolution and the French Revolution are born from the different contexts and goals of both.** The American colonies were, on the whole, financially successful. The complaints in the Declaration of Independence list the ways in which King George curtailed the colonies' economic growth and freedom and the ways in which the colonies were refused full legal rights. The complaints of the French citizens were more extreme, stemming from an economic inequality that left the poorest citizens struggling for subsistence. The aftermath of the two revolutions can be understood from this viewpoint. The American Revolution, having argued for the colonies' right to self-rule, maintained the American economic and social situation after the revolution. The French Revolution, dealing with France's severe economic gap, worked to disenfranchise (often killing) members of the First and Second Estate of the clergy

and aristocracy, in order to improve the rights and living conditions of the Third Estate, which was the average French citizen.

a. **Further Reading:** Tonsor, Stephen J. "Equality as a Factor in the American and French Revolutions." *Reflections on the French Revolution: A Hillsdale Symposium,* edited by Stephen J. Tonsor, 114–37. Washington, DC: Regnery Gateway, 1990.

b. **Suggested Search:** The Library of Congress's online exhibit "John Bull & Uncle Sam" at www.loc.gov/exhibits/british includes a page on the American Revolution. This page features images of stamps from the famous Stamp Act, political cartoons, and other documents from the American Revolution.

5. **Two revolutions began in the eighteenth century, one industrial and the other political. The first revolution created the context in which the second revolution occurred.** The Industrial Revolution resulted in a rapid development in England, and the resulting economic realignment set the American colonies in a potentially lucrative position of providing much-sought-after cotton to English entrepreneurs. Hampering the potential wealth of the American colonists was their subordinate position in a mercantile system, which was aimed at increasing the wealth of England before that of any colonies. England's need to keep its colonies in a subordinate position pushed American colonists toward revolution. The American Revolution can be understood both as a revolution putting forward a new claim toward self-rule and, through its position as one colony among many, as a major moment in the global history of the Industrial Revolution.

a. **Further Reading:** Stearns, Peter N. *The Industrial Revolution in World History.* 2nd ed. Boulder, CO: Westview Press, 1998.

b. **Suggested Search:** Charlie Chaplin's film *Modern Times* contains humorous twentieth-century responses to industrialization. A search for "Modern Times" and "factory" at youtube.com leads to a number of available and appropriate clips from this film.

6. **The struggle for women's right to vote grew out of the abolitionist movement. Although the founders of the movement were abolitionists, the limits of the abolitionist movement were what sparked the Seneca Falls Convention.** Women made up a significant portion of this movement. While the movement sought to expand the rights of Americans by abolishing slavery, it was limited in its imagination of that expansion, and women abolitionists found themselves restricted within the movement itself. The World Anti-Slavery Convention's refusal to allow Lucretia Mott and Elizabeth Cady Stanton to speak sparked the convention at Seneca Falls. Frederick Douglass's participation in the Women's Rights Convention, where he spoke out in favor of women's suffrage, speaks to the desire of some to broaden the political representation of all,

not just select, groups. Douglass himself had felt limited by the abolitionist movement, whose white organizers wanted him to speak only about his experiences as a slave and to not engage in public philosophic or political discussions regarding slavery.

a. **Further Reading:** Stanton, Elizabeth Cady, Susan B. Anthony, and Matilda Josyln Cage, eds. *History of Woman Suffrage.* Vol. 3. Rochester, NY: Charles Mann, 1887.

b. **Suggested Search:** A search for "Seneca Falls" on the American Treasures of the Library of Congress website at www.loc.gov/exhibits /treasures leads to images of a number of documents from the convention and newspaper clippings in which remarks are made about the event.

In-Class Activities

1. In *Reflections on the Revolution in France*, Edmund Burke writes, "Far is my heart from withholding in practice . . . the *real* rights of men" (31, author's emphasis). Does the document lead you to believe in Burke's concern for the rights of common citizens, or are you led to believe his statement to be a purely rhetorical move? What, according to Burke, are the *real* rights of men?

2. Both "The Rights of Woman" and "Declaration of Sentiments" satirize existing revolutionary documents as part of a sincere demand to extend full legal rights to women. How might this satiric tactic persuade audiences and how might it dissuade them? How might this satire function differently during a revolutionary period, as Olympe de Gouges uses it, than years after a revolutionary conflict, as is the case with "Declaration of Sentiments"?

3. The "U.S. Declaration of Independence" and "Declaration of the Rights of Man and of the Citizen" are both major early revolutionary documents. What similar claims do the documents make for human rights, and what different demands are insisted upon in the documents? Do the two documents take similar attitudes toward the aristocracy? In what ways are their attitudes different?

4. One major shift from the neoclassical mind-set of the eighteenth century to the romantic mind-set of the nineteenth century is away from valuing the logical to valuing the passionate. Are the revolutionary documents in the "Revolutionary Contexts" section more neoclassical or more romantic? Which documents are more neoclassical and which are more romantic?

5. Simón Bolívar's "Reply" is the only revolutionary document included that is addressed to an individual, although Bolívar intended the letter

to be widely read. Why might Bolívar choose this rhetorical strategy, and why might it be a rare strategy among revolutionary documents?

Paper Topics/Suggestions for Writing

1. Jean-Jacques Dessalines's "Liberty or Death" is harsher and more violent in its rhetoric than Thomas Jefferson's "U.S. Declaration of Independence." Explain why the rhetoric of these two revolutionary documents is so different, and account for the different political and philosophical goals you can identify in the texts.

2. The selection from William Wordsworth's *The Prelude* reflects on a period when Wordsworth turned away from his younger revolutionary political views and became more conservative in his views. After reading the Wordsworth poems later in the anthology, explain what Wordsworth might value in a society or a citizen, and then show which of these values are and are not met by the French Revolution.

3. In his "Reply," Simón Bolívar mentions the complex racial situation in Latin America, which includes Europeans, indigenous Latin Americans, and a variety of mixed-raced Latin Americans. Latin America's racial makeup will be discussed again in Domingo Faustino Sarmiento's *Facundo*. Describe the similarities and differences in how race functions in the two documents. How might the political goals of the two documents create differences in how the authors deal with race?

4. William Wordsworth's poem "To Toussaint L'Ouverture" is written to the Haitian leader prior to Jean-Jacques Dessalines's rule. Looking at the poem and at Dessalines's "Liberty or Death," describe the differences between the earlier Haitian leader as presented by Wordsworth and the later Haitian leader as he presents himself. How is the tone of the poet, removed from violent revolution, different from the tone of the military and political leader, amid violent revolution?

5. From the "U.S. Declaration of Independence" to "Declaration of the Rights of Man and of the Citizen" to "Reply," most of the documents in the "Revolutionary Contexts" section make concise cases for basic human rights. Both Olaudah Equiano's *The Interesting Narrative* and Frederick Douglass's *Narrative* give more expansive cases for human rights, centered on the experience of individuals. Choose one document from this section and one of the slave narratives, and detail the different rhetorical strategies the authors use for their arguments, giving the reasoning behind each strategy.

6. Edmund Burke's *Reflections on the Revolution in France* and the selection from William Wordsworth's *The Prelude* are both English responses to the French Revolution. Describe the different reactions you see in

these two responses, and explain whether the genre choices of philosophical essay and autobiographical poem aid their respective responses.

Resources

Giele, Janet Zolinger. *Two Paths to Women's Equality: Temperance, Suffrage, and the Origins of Modern Feminism*. New York: Twayne Publishers, 1995.
This book examines both the period leading up to the Seneca Falls Convention and its aftermath in the twentieth century. It focuses on the ongoing concern with social issues in the developing women's movement.

Ginzberg, Lori D. *Elizabeth Cady Stanton: An American Life*. New York: Hill and Wang, 2009.
This is a critical biography of Elizabeth Cady Stanton, one of the authors of "Declaration of Sentiments."

Jones, Peter, ed. *The French Revolution in Social and Political Perspective*. New York: Arnold, 1996.
This selection of essays offers a wide range of historical perspectives on the French Revolution.

Lynch, John. *Latin America: Between Colony and Nation*. New York: Palgrave, 2001.
This collection of essays examines the time up to and during the revolutionary period in Latin America. It includes several essays on Simón Bolívar.

Melton, James Van Horn. *The Rise of the Public in Enlightenment Europe*. Cambridge: Cambridge University Press, 2001.
This study provides the social context in which the American Revolution and French Revolution occurred.

Swenson, James. *On Jean-Jacques Rousseau: Considered as One of the First Authors of the Revolution*. Stanford: Stanford University Press, 2000.
This work examines the complex relationship between Jean-Jacques Rousseau and revolutionary thought and looks at the often-made claim that Rousseau was an important predecessor of the revolutionaries.

JEAN-JACQUES ROUSSEAU
Confessions

Topics for Lecture or Discussion

1. **In his *Confessions*, Jean-Jacques Rousseau depicts himself as a unique individual whose childhood experiences and strong passions are often not in line with the dictates of logic. Traits such as these set him up as a precursor to and an influence on romanticism.** Discussed in the early sections of Rousseau's *Confessions* are his early childhood experiences, including the great value Rousseau puts on living in the countryside when in the care of his uncle Bernard. These values of childhood, nature, and the individual's development would all become hallmarks of romanticism. William Wordsworth's "Ode on Intimations of Immortality" and Samuel Taylor Coleridge's "Frost at Midnight" show two different treatments of these themes. The sense of affinity and difference that each poet had with the other signifies both Rousseau's broad influence and the new ground he broke, with his writing inaugurating the conversation that romantic artists would later have.
   a. **Further Reading:** McFarland, Thomas. *Romanticism and the Heritage of Rousseau.* Oxford: Oxford University Press, 1995.
   b. **Suggested Search:** A search for "Thomas Cole" and "childhood" at the National Gallery of Art's website (www.nga.gov) will lead to Cole's famous painting in his *The Voyage of Life Series*.

2. **While Jean-Jacques Rousseau's *Confessions* may have literary precedents, the secular analysis of a flawed individual points to an important moment in the history of biography and autobiography—it points to the modern autobiography.** The most famous autobiographical work before Rousseau's *Confessions* is the autobiographical writings of Augustine, whose book shares its name with Rousseau's. The titling of Rousseau's book draws a link to Augustine, and Rousseau draws another link with biography, explicitly in the body of his text, naming Plutarch's *Lives* as an important formative influence. Augustine and Plutarch point to the major forms of autobiography and biography that existed before Rousseau. Augustine's text details his own spiritual life, his sins, and his conversion to Christianity. Plutarch's text describes the lives of major historical figures. Rousseau modernizes the autobiography by writing about his life (his historical importance not yet being assured) and by writing about the development of his personality and ideas instead of a spiritual development.
   a. **Further Reading:** Olney, James. *Memory and Narrative: The Weave of Life-Writing.* Chicago: University of Chicago Press, 1998.

    b. **Suggested Search:** The special exhibits page of Villanova University's library links to its special exhibit titled "Tolle lege." The website for this exhibit, http://exhibits.library.villanova.edu/tolle-lege-the-confessions-of-st-augustine, has a number of highlights from its display of manuscripts of Augustine's *Confessions*.

3. **Jean-Jacques Rousseau believes his autobiographical work to be of value not because he believes himself to be a virtuous role model or because of any great act he has done to change civilization but because of how deeply his work examines an individual, and in doing so, Rousseau sets up modern notions of self.** One difference that Rousseau sees between himself and the average human is a greater sensitivity. This claim to a heightened sensitivity sets up much of *Confessions,* as Rousseau focuses much of the text on his self-examination of emotional and psychological states as well as analyzes the thought processes that lead him to actions. A similar self-analysis will later be seen in poems such as William Wordsworth's "Lines Composed a Few Miles above Tintern Abbey" and Samuel Taylor Coleridge's "Frost at Midnight." These concepts of a changing individual whose emotions and psychological states are not necessarily logical but can be analyzed and understood open up a modern concept of self.

    a. **Further Reading:** Damrosch, Leo. "The Past Relived." In *Jean-Jacques Rousseau: Restless Genius*, 434–46. Boston: Houghton Mifflin, 2005.

    b. **Suggested Search:** Caspar David Friedrich's "Wanderer above a Sea of Fog" is the most famous romantic image of an individual in contemplation. The painting can be found at the *Caspar David Friedrich— The Complete Works* website at www.caspardavidfriedrich.org, often on the front page but otherwise as a search on the site.

4. **Jean-Jacques Rousseau holds up his experiences as a child as formative and as a subject important enough to write about, and among these experiences, he examines his sexual desires as a child. This sense of childhood desire is later advanced by Sigmund Freud, whose psychoanalytic practice is in large part indebted to *Confessions*.** In opposition to the prevailing notions of his time, Rousseau placed a high value on childhood experience, detailing his own formative experiences in *Confessions* and developing theories of education centered on childhood experience. His examination of the effect of Mademoiselle de Lambercier's corporal punishment on his adult sexuality is especially notable. Both the idea that children have sexual desires and that those early experiences affect adult sexuality form the backbone upon which Freud develops his theories of sexuality. Rousseau's analysis of the meaning of these experiences and their effect is both a practice Freud used in his own writing, describing his childhood

experiences as examples, and turned into the analyst-analysand relationship of psychoanalysis.

    a. **Further Reading:** Szajnberg, Nathan M. "Psychoanalysis as an Extension of the Autobiographical Genre: Poetry and Truth, Fiction and Reality." *International Review of Psycho-Analysis* 19 (1992): 375–87.

    b. **Suggested Search:** The Freud Museum London website (freud.org.uk) has a large photo library of images related to Sigmund Freud. A large number of images of Sigmund Freud can be found through the site's "Photo Library," linked as "Freud Portraits."

5. **Jean-Jacques Rousseau's own childhood experience points the reader toward a philosophy of education.** Among Rousseau's major works is *Émile, or On Education,* his book on childhood education. Rousseau demonstrates his interest in childhood education and development in *Confessions* through his description of his own childhood. He presents his childhood experiences as important, formative experiences at a time when a child's experience was rarely valued. Rousseau's understanding of his childhood includes generally good moral character when first living with his father, Rousseau's worry about the effects of books on a child, and the positive effects of living in the countryside under the care of his uncle Bernard. These themes—the inherently good moral character of children, the danger of introducing reading too soon, and the connection between nature and children—are all major ones for Rousseau's philosophy of childhood education.

    a. **Further Reading:** Parry, Geraint. "*Émile:* Learning to Be Men, Women, and Citizens." In *The Cambridge Companion to Rousseau,* edited by Patrick Riley, 247–71. Cambridge: Cambridge University Press, 2001.

    b. **Suggested Searches:** The artist Jean-Michel Moreau etched images for Émile. While no single website contains all of these etchings, a Google Images search for "Jean-Michel Moreau" and "Émile" will generate a number of these etchings.

6. **Paradox and supplements are central to *Confessions*, and they structure Jean-Jacques Rousseau's actions in the text.** One of the most influential works of late twentieth-century French philosophy is Jacques Derrida's *Of Grammatology.* In that text he writes on Rousseau and the logic of the supplement. Rousseau describes writing as a substitute for speech; when a person reads a book, the writer is absent, and when one hears a person speak, the speaker is present. Presence being preferable to absence, speech becomes preferable to writing. Derrida, though, sees the existence of a supplement as telling—it is supposedly an artificial addition to the original, natural whole, yet its existence shows nature as not being whole. If a supplement exists, then what it

supplements is flawed, and if the natural is flawed, then the supplement is not artificial but a logical extension of nature. Derrida's reading of the supplement shows a complex relationship between what is supplemented and what supplements. Corporal punishment in Rousseau's *Confessions* shows how complicated this relationship can be. Rousseau sets up his punishment as a supplement to procreative sexual relationships. His sexuality is founded on this supplement. He learns about other sexual relationships after the supplement has been established, and even into adulthood he requires the supplement for a successful sexual relationship. Rousseau's sexuality exists as the paradox of the supplement founding his sexuality and his preference for the "artificial" supplement to sexuality over "natural" sexuality.

   a. **Further Reading:** Derrida, Jacques. *Of Grammatology.* Translated by Gayatri Chakravorty Spivak. Baltimore, MD: Johns Hopkins University Press, 1974.

   b. **Suggested Search:** The *Stanford Encyclopedia of Philosophy* at plato. stanford.edu has a good introduction to Jacques Derrida. Videos of his lectures and interviews, as well as clips from the biographical film *Derrida*, can easily be found by searching for "Jacques Derrida."

In-Class Activities

1. Literacy in France increased dramatically in Jean-Jacques Rousseau's lifetime. What in Rousseau's *Confessions* might have been found distasteful or unappealing to an earlier aristocratic audience? What in *Confessions* might have been easier to write with an imagined populist audience in mind?

2. "This is the only portrait of a man, painted exactly according to nature and in all its truth, that exists and will probably ever exist" (585). Do you believe that Jean-Jacques Rousseau's opening to *Confessions* remains accurate now that the modern autobiography and memoir exist? What are the traits that Rousseau's book shares with recent autobiographies, and what in his book continues to be strange or unusual for an autobiography?

3. Jean-Jacques Rousseau's work is often cited as a major predecessor to romanticism. What similarities do you see between Rousseau's treatment of self in *Confessions* and the treatment of self in poems from "Romantic Poets and Their Successors"?

Paper Topics/Suggestions for Writing

1. Compare Jean-Jacques Rousseau's *Confessions* with Douglass's *Narrative.* Douglass writes his autobiography with the goal of furthering the abolitionist movement. What reasons might Rousseau have had for writ-

ing his autobiography? Examine both texts, and explain which traits of each work further each author's goal.

2. Jean-Jacques Rousseau's political philosophy was a major influence on the revolutions that occurred at the end of the eighteenth century. Compare *Confessions* with the "U.S. Declaration of Independence," the "Declaration of the Rights of Man and of the Citizen," or "The Rights of Woman," which appear in the "Revolutionary Contexts" section of this anthology. What depictions of the individual, human nature, and positive relationships in *Confession* can also be found in the document you chose? (It may also be useful to give selections from Jean-Jacques Rousseau's most famous work of political philosophy, *The Social Contract,* to students writing about this topic.)

3. Major critics of Jean-Jacques Rousseau, such as Paul de Man, see *Confessions* as a work of self-aware textual performativity. Describe the value of text in *Confessions*: identify the qualities that Rousseau gives writing in his book, and examine any moments where Rousseau points to his own act of writing.

4. Compare Jean-Jacques Rousseau's life with his father to his life with his uncle Bernard. For each situation, discuss what Rousseau finds valuable to a child's development and what Rousseau finds detrimental.

5. In Book Two of *Confessions,* Jean-Jacques Rousseau steals a ribbon and blames Marion for the theft. Explain the value of the ribbon in this scene, and argue for whether or not Rousseau is speaking in good faith when he claims, "I have never been less motivated by malice than at this cruel moment" (599).

Resources

Crocker, Lester G. *Jean-Jacques Rousseau.* 2 vols. New York: Macmillan, 1963.
     This work, in two volumes, is an exhaustive yet perceptive treatment of Jean-Jacques Rousseau's life and works.
France, Peter. *Rousseau,* Confessions. Cambridge: Cambridge University Press, 1987.
     This critical study focuses entirely on *Confessions.*
Gremsley, Ronald. *Jean-Jacques Rousseau: A Study in Self-Awareness.* Cardiff: University of Wales Press, 1961.
     This work provides a psychological analysis of Jean-Jacques Rousseau's personality.

OLAUDAH EQUIANO

From *The Interesting Narrative of the Life of Olaudah Equiano, or Gustavus Vassa, the African, Written by Himself*

Topics for Lecture or Discussion

1. In addition to his early narrative, Olaudah Equiano's book tour following *The Interesting Narrative's* publication was groundbreaking. His use of both book publication and public appearance would serve as a model that would be followed throughout the abolitionist movement. In addition to being one of the first freed slaves to write an autobiography, Equiano launched the first modern book tour. His tour of Britain was extremely popular, and both the slave narrative and the freed slaves' public speech would be used for their political effectiveness by the abolitionist movement, throughout its existence. Both the autobiography and the book tour were created as part of Equiano's self-conscious understanding of how to use publicity for political advantage. As these models became standard to the abolitionist movement, they would become limitations with which later freed slaves would struggle. Frederick Douglass, wishing to discuss his views on the ethics of slavery and his political philosophy, found that the white-run publishing presses only wanted him to write as a witness of slavery, and that white-organized abolitionist meetings only wanted him to speak about his experiences as a former slave.

   a. **Further Reading:** Bugg, John. "The Other Interesting Narrative: Olaudah Equiano's Public Book Tour." *PMLA: Publications of the Modern Language Association of America* 121:5 (October 2006): 1424–42.

   b. **Suggested Search:** The Equiano Project website at www.equiano .org has a limited number of images relating to Olaudah Equiano and lists any news regarding Equiano traveling exhibits. While the site may be of limited interest as a resource, the project itself may be of interest, as it allows discussion of Equiano's public touring to be set beside the ongoing public exhibition of Equiano at the Birmingham Museum.

2. **Olaudah Equiano's attempt to listen to a book talk is a recurring event in slave narratives, which can be read as emblematic of the issues surrounding subjectivity and published writing.** The image of the young Equiano trying to get a book to talk to him is a striking one,

and Equiano is not the first to use the image. Ukawsaw Gronniosaw's earlier narrative included a similar image, and later slave narratives would reuse the image of the biographical subject listening or speaking to a book. The critic Henry Louis Gates Jr. reads the recurring image as an image of subjectivity: the illiterate, enslaved figure is denied his subjectivity by the European culture that has produced the book. The freed slave must learn the white speech of European literary culture in order to write the autobiography and become publicly recognized.

a. **Further Reading:** Gates, Henry Louis, Jr. "The Trope of the Talking Book." In *The Signifying Monkey: A Theory of Afro-American Literary Criticism*, 127–69. Oxford: Oxford University Press, 1988.

b. **Suggested Search:** The Open Yale website at oyc.yale.edu includes the course "Introduction to Theory of Literature" by Paul H. Fry, found through the English Department tab under "Courses." The twenty-first of these lectures is on African American criticism and deals extensively with the thought of Henry Louis Gates Jr.

3. **One of the major contemporary debates regarding Olaudah Equiano's *The Interesting Narrative* is its historical accuracy. The issues regarding *The Interesting Narrative*'s accuracy demonstrate the wider question of truthfulness in an autobiographical narrative.** While in Equiano's lifetime there was doubt that a freed slave had written *The Interesting Narrative,* contemporary debate centers on whether or not Equiano was truly from Africa, and while the earlier debate was racially charged, the contemporary debate deals with Equiano as brilliantly self-aware as he presents himself to the reading public. Regardless of the accuracy of Equiano's narrative, his successful marketing of *The Interesting Narrative* and his successful book tour show him to be tactfully aware of himself as a public figure. All the autobiographical works in "An Age of Revolutions in Europe and the Americas" have been questioned for their accuracy at some point in their reception, and especially in a political work such as Equiano's *The Interesting Narrative,* the distance between truth and efficacy can often be wide.

a. **Further Reading:** Lovejoy, Paul E. "Autobiography and Memory: Gustavas Vassa, alias Olaudah Equiano, the African." *Slavery and Abolition* 27:3 (December 2006): 317–47.

b. **Suggested Search:** The Trans-Atlantic Slave Trade database at www.slavevoyages.org/tast/index.faces contains a large number of resources related to the transatlantic slave trade. Under "Resources" you will find a link for "Images" that leads to a large number of images related to the slave trade.

4. **Olaudah Equiano makes a point of the similarities between Ibo traditions and Judaic traditions. His treatment of Judaism speaks to his aim to write his autobiography as a Christian narrative for a**

Christian audience. At several points, Equiano notes the similarities between the African culture in which he grew up and the Jewish culture, to the extent that he writes that he is led "to think that the one people had sprung from the other" (613). Equiano has a political stake in drawing an affinity between his culture and Judaism: despite the anti-Semitism endured by eighteenth-century Jews, a comparison with ancient biblical culture could show the Eboe people as existing in an Edenic, nascent Christianity. Equiano's own status as a Christian and his desire to move a widely Christian audience into recognizing the humanity of Africans attest to the high stakes of the comparison. If people in Africa already have some awareness of God, then it could be argued to a Christian audience that the people of Africa are spiritual, thinking, and human.

    a. **Further Reading:** Schamp, Jutta. "Transfiguring Black and Jewish Relations: From Ignatius Sacho's *Letters* and Olaudah Equiano's *Interesting Narrative* to David Dabydeen's *A Harlot's Progress*." *Ariel* 40:4 (October 2009): 19–46.

    b. **Suggested Search:** A search for "Igbo wedding" on the BBC News website at www.bbc.com/news leads to a set of journalistic photographs of a contemporary Igbo wedding in Nigeria.

5. **In his *The Interesting Narrative*, Olaudah Equiano shows a slave economy functioning within Africa as well as among Europeans and the colonies. By spending time discussing his experience with these forms of slavery, Equiano is able to discuss other societal constructions of slavery and is able to complicate his discussion of race relations.** Equiano's presentation of his original Eboe culture is predominantly idyllic, relating a Rousseau-like notion of humanity in its natural state and living in an almost Edenic relationship with nature. Even this ideal community is not free from slavery, though, as Equiano admits that this culture occasionally sold slaves to Europeans, qualified as "only prisoners of war, or such among us as we had been convicted of kidnapping, or adultery, and some other crimes, which we esteemed heinous" (609). From this use of slavery as a punishment for crimes, Equiano gives an account of Africa that includes some groups treating slaves as members of the family and some groups that engage in the slave trade purely for their own profit. One advantage to describing these different cultural arrangements is to show a European audience different, and often more humane, ways in which slavery can be imagined. Another advantage is that this more complicated discussion of race relations keeps Equiano's text from vilifying white, slave-owning Europe, an important move in order for the narrative to be politically effective with an eighteenth-century white audience.

a. **Further Reading:** Rolingher, Louise. "A Metaphor for Freedom: Olaudah Equiano and Slavery in Africa." *Canadian Journal of African Studies* 38:1 (2004): 88–122.

b. **Suggested Search:** The William Blake Archive at www.blakearchive .org/blake includes Blake's depictions of slavery. A search for "slave" in the site's "image search" leads to the Blake images "A Coromantyn Free Negro, or Ranger, armed," "A Negro hung alive by the Ribs to a Gallows," and "Slave Owner."

In-Class Activities

1. Olaudah Equiano's description of his idealized home and the strangeness of European artifacts was written with a European audience in mind. To what degree do you read the text as a genuine remembrance, and to what degree might these passages be written to move an audience?

2. Olaudah Equiano's *The Interesting Narrative* gives an account of the infamous Middle Passage. What details in his description of it make the horrible experience vivid for his readers?

3. A contemporary debate has ensued as to whether or not Olaudah Equiano was actually from Africa. To what degree does it matter whether Equiano's narrative was factual? How would you read the narrative differently if you thought Equiano was relating stories he had been told rather than relating his own history?

Paper Topics/Suggestions for Writing

1. Olaudah Equiano's narrative is one of two slave narratives in the anthology. Compare and contrast his *The Interesting Narrative* with Frederick Douglass's *Narrative*. Describe which features of the slave narrative and rhetorical strategies are maintained between Equiano's earlier narrative and Douglass's later narrative and which features and strategies change between the texts.

2. Olaudah Equiano describes a variety of ways in which he is treated as a slave within Africa. Explain what advantages there might be for Equiano to provide a detailed account of slavery within Africa to eighteenth-century European readers.

3. Olaudah Equiano's *The Interesting Narrative* works with two different consciousnesses: the younger Equiano as he first encounters European culture and the older Equiano who has a commanding grasp of European thought and manners. Examine one of the moments when there is a significant difference between these two consciousnesses, such as

the younger Equiano's youthful belief that the first white men he sees are spirits and not human beings versus his mature understanding that they were ordinary men. Detail how the older Equiano presents the younger Equiano, whether that presentation of himself is naive, comical, wise, or some other mode.

4. William Blake's "The Little Black Boy" is told as a first-person account by an African child but is written by an antislavery Englishman. Olaudah Equiano, writing to an English audience, gives his autobiographical account of being a child in Africa. Describe the similarities between the two authors' understanding of the thoughts of an African child and the differences between their understanding. Give an account of the different rhetorical strategies employed in the two texts as both are writing with the aim to convince European audiences about the humanity of Africans.

5. Both Olaudah Equiano's *The Interesting Narrative* and Domingo Faustino Sarmiento's *Facundo* detail a culture's way of life and the landscape in which those cultures exist. Explain how the two authors make use of the exotic, giving an account as to the ways in which the exotic might entice readers and the ways in which it might emphasize cultural difference for a reader.

Resources

Davis, David Brion. *The Problem of Slavery in the Age of Revolution: 1770–1823.* Ithaca, NY: Cornell University Press, 1975.
> This is a historical study of slavery during the revolutionary period, focusing on English and American slavery.

Gronniosaw, James Albert Ukawsaw. *A Narrative of the Most Remarkable Particulars in the Life of James Albert Ukawsaw Gronniosaw, an African Prince.* Newport: Electronic Text Center, University of Virginia Library, 1774. http://etext.lib.virginia.edu/etcbin/toccer-new2?id=GroGron.sgm&images =images/modeng&data=/texts/english/modeng/parsed&tag=public &part=all.
> Another early slave narrative, Gronniosaw's work predates Olaudah Equiano's and makes earlier use of the trope of the "talking book."

Korieh, Chima J., ed. *Olaudah Equiano and the Igbo World: History, Society, and Atlantic Diaspora Connections.* Trenton, NJ: Africa World Press, 2009.
> This collection of essays covers a range of Equiano-related issues, such as Igbo culture, African encounters with Europeans, and the Atlantic Diaspora.

Schorsch, Jonathan. *Jews and Blacks in the Early Modern World.* Cambridge: Cambridge University Press, 2004.
> Although it does not mention Olaudah Equiano's rhetorical links between Jewish and Igbo cultures, this study does examine the relationship between Jewish and African relations at the height of the transatlantic slave trade.

JOHANN WOLFGANG VON GOETHE

Faust

Still as man strives, he still must err.
—Johann Wolfgang von Goethe, *Faust*

Topics for Lecture or Discussion

1. **As stated in the headnote, Mephistopheles steals the show.** His first scene after the "Prologue in Heaven," anticipated by Faust's declarations and then the appearance of a poodle, focuses on his entrance in disguise as an itinerant student. The prime evilness of the devil figure allows him a theatricality and leeway for robust action that is denied to the "good" characters. Also pointed out in the headnote is that Mephistopheles functions as Faust's critic and proffers a critique of the age as well. If Faust embodies boundless human aspiration, Mephistopheles comments on the extreme hubris of man and the destruction that results from such arrogance. Consider the following speech by Mephistopheles (disguised) in his first exchange with Faust:

> Man in his world of self 's a fool,
> He likes to think he's all in all.
> I'm part of the part which was all at first,
> A part of the dark from which light burst forth,
> Arrogant light which now usurps the air
> And seeks to thrust Night from her ancient chair,
> [. . .]
> When by degrees all matter's burnt up and no more,
> Why, then light shall not matter any more.
>
> (lines 1138–49)

Mephistopheles observes the importance of the dark forces to balance the light and says that light, if unchecked, will destroy the world. This viewpoint contrasts nicely with the traditional contest of good (light) versus evil (dark). For a historical, scholarly interpretation of the devil figure, consult Jeffrey Burton Russell's *Mephistopheles: The Devil in the Modern World* (1986), the fourth in a series of books by the author and one that extensively discusses the character in Johann Wolfgang von Goethe's *Faust*.

   a. **Further Reading:** Colvin, Sarah. "Mephistopheles, Metaphors, and the Problem of Meaning in *Faust*." *Publications of the English Goethe Society* 79:3 (November 2010): 159–71.

   b. **Suggested Searches:** Search for the following phrases in Google Images, Google Scholar, or an academic database to find images and

additional resources: Faust and Mephistopheles; devil in *Faust*; evil on stage; Faust light versus dark.

2. **Faust desires knowledge of the universe as well as sensual experience in the world.** These twin drives often work at cross-purposes; as Faust notes early on: "The noblest conceptions our minds ever attained / Are watered down more and more, corrupted, profaned" (lines 410–11). Since Johann Wolfgang von Goethe has no way to resolve the mysteries of the world, except through fantasy, the second half of Part 1 concentrates on Faust's seduction of Gretchen. This pursuit, unlike the desire for knowledge, can be shown in all its complexity and carnality. Consequently, the "arrogant light" of Faust seems directed primarily to fulfill his sexual appetite more than to enhance his intellectual understanding of the world. On the one hand, Faust slakes his sexual thirst because it is a primary drive that can readily and easily be satisfied. On the other hand, from the perspective of a playwright dramatizing the Faust story, sexual desire can be easily represented onstage and therefore stands, metaphorically, for the desire for attaining all things in the world.

   a. **Further Reading:** Phillips, D. Z. "Knowledge, Patience and Faust." *Yale Review* 69:3 (1980): 321–41.

   b. **Suggested Searches:** Search for the following phrases in Google Images, Google Scholar, or an academic database to find images and additional resources: Delacroix Faust; Faust seduction of Gretchen.

3. **Designated by locale, the individual scene titles give the play an epic scope.** *Faust* violates the formal principles of Aristotelian drama, including the famed neoclassical unities of time and place. The scenes sweep from place to place over an extended time interval, spanning the meeting, seduction, and ultimate destruction of Gretchen. Significantly, Johann Wolfgang von Goethe's dramaturgy favors Shakespearean models far more than continental European ones. The episodic construction moves from private to public spaces, beginning with long scenes in Faust's study and concluding wildly with the penultimate scene, "Walpurgis Night." The shift from private to public space mirrors the trajectory of Faust's journey from intellectual thinker to worldly wanderer and explorer. Overall, the loose, episodic scene structure, saturated with Faust's desire to know and to do more, worked and reworked throughout the second half of Goethe's lifetime, encapsulates a vision of humanity that refused to be constrained by neoclassical ideals. Nevertheless, there is only one action in the play: "Impelled in this direction, then in that one, / A good man still knows which way is the right one" ("Prologue in Heaven," lines 88–89).

    a. **Further Reading:** Littlejohns, Richard. "The Discussion between Goethe and Schiller on the Epic and Dramatic and Its Relevance to *Faust*." *Neophilologus* 71:3 (July 1987): 388–401.

    b. **Suggested Searches:** Search for the following phrases in Google Images, Google Scholar, or an academic database to find images and additional resources: cinematic scope of *Faust*; Murnau's *Faust*; *The Damnation of Faust* by Hector Berlioz; Robert Lepage *Faust*; *Faust* and opera.

4. **The sad plight of Gretchen reads as a morality tale that Faust ultimately transcends.** In the "Prologue in Heaven," the Lord bets on Faust against Mephistopheles to find the right course of human action. At the end of Part 1, Faust vanishes with Mephistopheles, having ruined Gretchen. In other versions of the *Faust* story and legend, the central character loses his soul to the devil. In Christopher Marlowe's *The Tragical History of Dr. Faustus*, for example, the final scene shows Faust carried off to hell. In a significant departure from the primary text, Johann Wolfgang von Goethe redeems the title character in Part 2 by presenting Faust's unyielding curiosity and thirst for knowledge. It may be tragic, but it is also heroic and, ultimately, according to the playwright, laudable. The valorization of Faust comes at the expense of Gretchen: he devotes himself to doing great deeds (in Part 2) to make up for Gretchen's death. Her destruction, then, results from her interactions with a great man and is the unfortunate but perhaps inevitable collateral damage incurred. This interpretation of what transpires between them is quite provocative and perhaps further suggests that the "light" of Faust might enlighten others but it might also burn and destroy them.

    a. **Further Reading:** Anchor, Robert. "Motherhood and Family in Goethe's *Faust*: Gretchen's Mother and the Gretchen Tragedy." *Historical Reflections/Reflexions Historiques* 23:1 (Winter 1997): 29–48.

    b. **Suggested Searches:** Search for the following phrases in Google Images, Google Scholar, or an academic database to find images and additional resources: *Faust* as morality play; Marlowe's *Dr. Faustus*; Dante Gabriel Rossetti and *Faust*; Goethe's romantic vision of *Faust*.

In-Class Activities

1. Speculate what it will require for Faust to redeem himself in Part 2. Do you think redemption is possible?

2. The play is wildly theatrical; at the same time, it is very difficult to stage. How do you reconcile these two statements? Would the dramatic text fare better in production as a cinematic screenplay?

3. Take a look at the "Garden" scene beginning at line 2873. How does the staging of the couples strolling reinforce and amplify the act of seduction?

Paper Topics/Suggestions for Writing

1. Faust is both relentless and indefatigable. How does the dramatic structure of events simultaneously reveal important aspects of character?

2. Mephistopheles is a great role and one with which audiences can relate and identify. Why do you think this is so? Is this character a modern antihero?

3. Identify the cinematic qualities of the dramatic text. How might this play make a good film?

4. Given that the action ultimately redeems Faust, does the play deserve its subtitle as a tragedy? Why or why not?

5. Gretchen clearly does not deserve her fate. Justify or condemn the victimization of Gretchen at the hands of Faust. What does your evaluation and judgment of their relationship say about the roles of men and women in the world?

6. Compare and contrast Christopher Marlowe's *The Tragical History of Dr. Faustus*—or twentieth-century adaptations such as Gertrude Stein's *Dr. Faustus Lights the Lights* or Václav Havel's *Temptation*—with Johann Wolfgang von Goethe's *Faust*. What do the different versions say about the respective epochs?

Resources

Faust. Dir. F. W. Murnau. 1926. DVD. Kino on Video, 2001.
    This is a great silent film adaptation of the Faust tradition.
Faust (Opera). Dir. Ken Russell. 1985. DVD. Universal Classics, 2006.
    This Vienna State Opera production of *Faust* is based on Charles Gounod's five-act opera.
From Weimar to Rome: 1775–1789. Insight Media, 1997, DVD.
    This video chronicles the middle period of Johann Wolfgang von Goethe's career.
Into a New Century: 1789–1832. Insight Media, 1997, DVD.
    This video covers the last phase of Johann Wolfgang von Goethe's career, including his life's project, *Faust*.
Russell, Jeffrey Burton. *Mephistopheles: The Devil in the Modern World.* Ithaca, NY: Cornell University Press, 1986.
    This is a scholarly interpretation of the devil figure in Johann Wolfgang von Goethe's *Faust*.

The Young Goethe: 1749–1775. Insight Media, 1997, DVD.
This video covers Johann Wolfgang von Goethe's early years and experiences, including his education, legal training, and love affairs.

Alexander Sergeyevich Pushkin
The Queen of Spades

Topics for Lecture or Discussion

1. **In its several references to Paris, *The Queen of Spades* reflects the tremendous influence on style, manners, and literary tastes that France, and Paris in particular, had upon Europe in the nineteenth century.** Russia in particular was enamored with French styles, and educated Russians in the period would typically be fluent in French (evidence of this trend is apparent in Pushkin's use of French words for polite conversation and for the quotes at the beginning of each chapter). Similarly, when Tomsky tells the story of the Countess's gambling debt while on a trip to Paris, he tells of a fairly common journey and pastime for the fashionable and wealthy. The popularity of Paris and all things French might be contrasted with the lack of knowledge of German; Lisaveta Ivanovna does not know the German language nor German literature (746), and hence her vulnerability to being taken in by the scheming German Hermann. The extensive influence of the French in Russian society is similarly apparent in the fiction of other great Russian writers, including Leo Tolstoy (see *The Death of Ivan Ilyich* in this volume) and Fyodor Dostoevsky (see *Notes from the Underground* in this volume).

    a. **Further Reading:** Figes, Orlando. *Natasha's Dance: A Cultural History of Russia*. New York: Picador, 2002.

    b. **Suggested Search:** A YouTube search for "Russia: Empire to Revolution" results in a lecture series from Vanderbilt University given by Dr. Frank Wcislo that discusses the cultural and political history of Russia.

2. **The centrality of gambling in *The Queen of Spades* not only reflects the great popularity of gambling during this period, particularly among the members of the Russian military, but it also demonstrates the degree to which society, at least in Pushkin's story, is obsessed with money.** Hermann is the character most obviously driven by the desire to accumulate wealth; when he excuses himself from gambling at the beginning of the story by saying, "I am not in the position to sacrifice the essentials of life in the hope of acquiring the luxuries" (739), we might think that that is a prudent attitude until we find that Hermann is excessively thrifty, penny-pinching, and motivated solely by money. His gambling at the conclusion of the story, when he thinks that he is assured of winning, further emphasizes the point that these characters desire to win money by gaining an unfair advantage. Gambling

represents the ways in which a gentlemanly and fashionable occupation that involves both honor and serious financial issues can be caught up in a juvenile, trite obsession.

　　a. **Further Reading:** Helfant, Ian M. "Pushkin's Ironic Performances as a Gambler." *Slavic Review* 58.2 (1999): 371–392.

　　b. **Suggested Search:** At http://alexanderpushkin.com, there are a variety of resources available, including Pushkin's poems, drawings, and a biography,

3. **While *The Queen of Spades* can be properly categorized as a ghost story, it does not attempt to scare the reader. In fact, the aim of the narrative appears to be far more didactic than chilling.** By having Hermann accidentally kill the Countess and then having her appear to him, Pushkin incorporates situations that are commonplace in ghost stories and scary tales; these situations by Pushkin, however, are used with much less terrifying effect than by Edgar Allan Poe, for example. In *The Queen of Spades*, the situations are almost comical; rather than scaring the reader, they satirize the money-chasing character of Hermann as he desperately attempts to become rich. Indeed, after the ghost appears to Hermann, the narrator tells us, "Two fixed ideas can no more exist in one mind than, in the physical sense, two bodies can occupy one and the same place. 'Three, seven, ace' soon eclipsed from Hermann's mind the form of the dead old lady" (755). Hermann himself forgets that he has seen a ghost in his excitement at having a supposed advantage in gambling. By minimizing the impression that the ghost makes, Pushkin breaks from the tradition of ghostly tales and instead turns to satire.

　　a. **Further Reading:** Briggs, A. D. P. *Alexander Pushkin: A Critical Study*. London: Bristol Classical Press, 1991.

　　b. **Suggested Search:** A YouTube search for "Tchaikovsky The Queen of Spades" results in clips from a lovely opera that Tchaikovsky based upon Pushkin's story.

4. **In *The Queen of Spades*, Pushkin complicates Hermann's character by emphasizing the fact that he still encounters twinges of conscience and moments of feeling.** In certain respects, Hermann is a stock character: he is a miser so obsessed with money that he is immensely interested in gambling but too afraid of losing to join in the game. Similarly, Hermann fulfils the stock role of the deceptive lover, whose amorous advances are made for a wholly different reason than affection for the woman he pays court to. Yet despite these characteristics, Pushkin makes a point of describing Hermann as not wholly lacking any better sentiments. For example, when Hermann is hiding in the Countess's closet and hears Lisaveta hurry to her room in excitement, the narrator write, "In his heart there echoed something like the voice

of conscience, but it grew silent, and his heart once more turned to stone" (749). Similarly, Hermann attends the Countess' funeral for feelings of superstitious fear but also because his conscience still echoes thoughts of guilt in his head (753). These are important details, as they render Hermann a much more human character who has a conscience but has squelched it. His pursuit of money is not the action of an automaton, but of a man who had consistently and decidedly devoted himself to the vice of acquisitiveness.

   a. **Further Reading:** Rosenshield, Gary. "Gambling and Passion: Pushkin's *The Queen of Spades* and Dostoevsky's *The Gambler*." *Slavic & East European Journal* 55:2 (2011): 205–228.

   b. **Suggested Search:** A YouTube search for "The Queen of Spades (1949 film)" will result in a famous adaptation of Pushkin's story for the screen, directed by Thorold Dickinson.

5. ***The Queen of Spades* can be interpreted as having no supernatural occurrences; instead, the appearance of the ghost can be explained by the fact that the usually abstemious and scrimping Hermann was drunk, and having been so fixated upon the lost secret of the cards, he imagined the fantastic appearance of the Countess.** This interpretation is attractive in part because Hermann does go mad at the end of the story, demonstrating the degree to which his fevered mind was susceptible to being imbalanced. If the story is to be interpreted in this manner, however, one must still explain not only the way that Hermann knew of the winning cards, but also of the reputation of the secret that, it would seem, the Countess really did possess. The Countess herself, directly before she dies, explains that it was a joke (750), but she is also disconcerted by Hermann's mention of Chaplitsky.

   a. **Further Reading:** Rosen, Nathan. "The Magic Cards in *The Queen of Spades*." *The Slavic and East European Journal* 19:3 (1975): 255–275.

   b. **Suggested Search:** A YouTube search for "Favorite Story The Queen of Spades" results in a 1940s radio dramatization of Pushkin's story (listening to part of this in class might serve as a good way to illustrate the popularity of this story).

In-Class Activities

1. Turn off the lights of the classroom (while ensuring that safety standards are met), and read a few passages from *The Queen of Spades* aloud to your students in as scary a manner you can muster. Then do the same with another, scarier story (you might turn to Edgar Allan Poe for inspiration). Use the contrast between the two works as a means of holding a discussion about what makes a scary story, or a ghost story, or a suspense story.

2. On youtube.com, find a 1940s radio dramatization of Pushkin's *The Queen of Spades* by searching for "Favorite Story The Queen of Spades." Play part of this adaptation to the class to promote discussion about the tone and genre of the story. For example, you might ask the students about how scary, comical, or odd the dramatization is, and the degree to which it accurately represents Pushkin's story.

3. Divide the class into two sections and hold a formal debate. One part of the class must defend the thesis that Hermann really did see a ghost, and the other part of the class must try to refute that thesis, insisting that Hermann imagined the whole thing.

4. Either read aloud or hand out to the class passages from Pushkin's great poem *Eugene Onegin* (Vladimir Nabokov's translation is recommended). Ask your students to compare the style of the two works. What does Pushkin do differently when dealing with the supernatural as opposed to passionate love?

Paper Topics/Suggestions for Writing

1. Is *The Queen of Spades* a ghost story? A scary story? A suspense story? A mystery story? How would you characterize *The Queen of Spades* in terms of genre, tone, and plot?

2. Write a brief character sketch of Hermann, and be sure to address the following three questions: What does Hermann feel for Elisaveta? Why, exactly, does he go insane? Is Hermann admirable in *any* respect?

3. Write an essay that contrasts Pushkin's *The Queen of Spades* with Nikolai Gogol's *The Overcoat*. What do these great Russian writers share? In what respects do they differ? In what instances can you discern Pushkin's and Gogol's senses of humor?

4. Does Hermann see a ghost? Regardless of how you answer this question, be sure to address the three strongest arguments against your position, as well as presenting your own argument with thorough evidence from the text.

5. Given the extensive French influence upon Russia apparent in Pushkin's references and use of French, write an essay in which you compare *The Queen of Spades* with a work by a French author from the anthology (for example, Voltaire's *Candide*, Molière's *Tartuffe*, or Flaubert's *Madame Bovary*). What narrative techniques do these writers share? In what techniques do they differ? Are there stylistic or thematic similarities between the works?

Resources

Bethea, David M. *Realizing Metaphors: Alexander Pushkin and the Life of the Poet.* Madison, WI: University of Wisconsin Press, 1998.
> Pushkin is often known for his dramatic, explosive life story, and this volume is an interesting analysis of the relationship between Pushkin's life and his craft. Students as well as instructors would profit from reading this argument about Pushkin's life as a poet.

Binyon, T. J. *Pushkin: A Biography.* New York: Random House, 2004.
> This biography has the advantage of being well-written and accessible to students, without sacrificing interest or insight. Binyon is provocative and stimulating in his presentation of the passionate and poetic life that Pushkin led.

Pushkin, Alexander. *Eugene Onegin.* Trans. Vladimir Nabokov. Vols. 1 and 2. Princeton: Princeton University Press, 1975.
> Pushkin is best remembered for *Eugene Onegin*, and Nabokov's translation captures the poetry and passion of the original. This poetic narrative is accessible and delightful to students as well as their instructors.

Pushkin, Alexander. *Alexander Pushkin: Complete Prose Fiction.* Trans. Paul Debreczeny. Stanford: Stanford University Press, 1983.
> This is an excellent volume for students and instructors wishing to read further in Pushkin's prose works. Works such as "Roslavlev" and "Egyptian Nights" might prove of interest to instructors seeking further familiarity with Pushkin's works.

The Queen of Spades. Dir. Thorold Dickinson. Perf. Anton Walbrook and Edith Evans. De Grunwald Productions, 1949. Film.
> This critically recognized film is still considered a great work, and it is well worth watching with your students. It adds a considerable degree of dark and frightening elements to Pushkin's story.

Nikolai Gogol

The Overcoat

Topics for Lecture or Discussion

1. **One of the central themes of *The Overcoat* is the presentation of government as incompetent and caught up in insignificant things.** *The Overcoat* discusses aspects of government and bureaucracies in many different respects, but it never appears in a good light. For example, the community of clerks who do the government's business are petty and often mean-spirited. Similarly, the more important people in the government, and particularly the Person of Consequence at the end of the story, are full of pride and care more about rank and appearances than about the actual human troubles that they encounter. So, too, the policemen in *The Overcoat* are shown to be ineffective in reducing or solving crimes and cowardly in investigating odd occurrences. Furthermore, as the second sentence of the story declares, "There is nothing in the world more touchy than a department, a regiment, a government office, and, in fact, any sort of official body" (761). With all of these negative presentations of the persons in government and the government services, Gogol presents his readers with a profound skepticism regarding the people and programs of the government.

   a. **Further Reading:** Gogol, Nikolai. *Plays and Petersburg Tales: Petersburg Tales, Marriage, The Government Inspector.* Translated by Christopher English. Oxford: Oxford University Press, 2008. See especially *The Government Inspector.*

   b. **Suggested Search:** A YouTube search for "Gogol The Government Inspector" results in several recordings of performances of Gogol's play, which satirizes government and local officials.

2. **All, or almost all, of Akaky Akakievich's identity is derived from his job as a "titular councilor."** The narrator tells us that at the same time he received his name at his baptism, Akaky's future career was foreshadowed: "The baby was christened and cried and made sour faces during the ceremony, as though he foresaw that he would be a titular councilor" (762). Baptism is a fundamental action in the identity of a Christian, and Akaky's career is linked, at least metaphorically, to this moment. When introducing Akaky, the narrator also tells us that "among us a man's rank is what must be established first" (761), and that even among the government officials who can't remember who hired him or how long he had worked as a clerk, "they used to declare that he must have been born a copying clerk, uniform, bald patch, and all" (762). Akaky's identity is so bound up with his job that his only

social companions are the same fellows who harass him at work, and the only form of real enjoyment that he knows prior to his idea of an overcoat is the activity that he performs in his official capacity.

   a. **Further Reading:** Bernheimer, Charles C. "Cloaking the Self: The Literary Space of Gogol's *Overcoat*." *PMLA* 90.1 (1975): 53–61.

   b. **Suggested Search:** A YouTube search for "Nikolai Gogol (1809–1852)" results in a clip from a Soviet propaganda/documentary movie that extols the virtues of Gogol's works. This clip is helpful for demonstrating the extent of Gogol's reputation, and the ways in which he was appropriated by communists as an advocate for the common man (despite his profound skepticism of government).

3. **Nikolai Gogol is well known for his unusual narrative style—a style in which he shifts tones, moods, and genres quickly and effortlessly—and the traits of this style are readily apparent in *The Overcoat*.** For example, the narrator intrudes himself as an obvious character when he tells readers, "Of this tailor I ought not, of course, say much, but since it is now the rule that the character of every person in a novel must be completely described, well, there's nothing I can do but describe Petrovich too" (765). At multiple points in the following story, the narrator alludes to the choices he makes in what information he gives to the readers; he also mentions his failing memory. The narrative style is also interesting in its shifts from the direct narration to indirect discourse; for example, when the police officer responds to Akaky after he is robbed, the narrator writes, "The policeman answered that he had seen nothing, that he had only seen him stopped in the middle of the square by two men, and supposed that they were his friends, and that, instead of abusing him for nothing, he had better go the next day to the police inspector, who would certainly find out who had taken the overcoat" (774). Gogol also mixes moments of tragedy and comedy, and quickly shifts from elevated rhetoric to common, staccato-like language.

   a. **Further Reading:** Shapiro, Gavriel. *Nikolai Gogol and the Baroque Cultural Heritage.* University Park, PA: Pennsylvania State University Press, 1993.

   b. **Suggested Search:** At the PBS website (www.pbs.org) a search for "Nikolai Gogol timeline" results in an interesting page with clips of movies from several of Gogol's works.

4. **Akaky Akakievich is a complicated character in that he finds such deep fulfillment in his mundane pursuits while also being transformed by the relatively mundane process of acquiring a new overcoat.** Readers should not underestimate or ignore the depth of Akaky's satisfaction in his work prior to his new overcoat. Gogol writes, "After working to his heart's content, he would go to bed, smiling at the thought of the next day and wondering what God would send him to

copy. So flowed on the peaceful life of a man who knew how to be content with his fate" (764–765). Though the cause of this satisfaction is his mundane work as a copy clerk, nevertheless, the depth of contentment and pleasure that Akaky takes in doing a good job is far from trivial. The distraction of his new coat, however, represents a fundamental challenge to his peace: "His whole existence had in a sense become fuller, as though he had married, as though some other person were present with him, as though he were no longer alone but an agreeable companion had consented to walk the path of life hand in hand with him, and that companion was none other than the new overcoat" (770). Akaky's new devotion to his overcoat not only removes the possibility that he could continue to take such deep satisfaction in his work, but it also makes it poetically fitting that the loss of the overcoat would lead to his death.

   a. **Further Reading:** Brombert, Victor. "Meanings and Indeterminacy in Gogol's *The Overcoat.*" *Proceedings of the American Philosophical Society* 135:4 (1991): 569–575.

   b. **Suggested Search:** A Google Images search for "Nikolai Gogol" results in several portraits of the author.

5. **Gogol presents St. Petersburg as a city that is dark, intimidating, and beyond a reasonable human scale; this presentation reflects a larger movement of thought in the nineteenth century concerned with the explosive growth of cities, the rise of industrialism, and the detachment from the land and the means of production in the poor.** The most obvious critique of St. Petersburg occurs when Akaky crosses the city square that is so massive that he is robbed while a policeman, unaware, sits on the far side. Indeed, in the heart of this heavily populated city, Akaky feels that he "seemed to be at the end of the world" (774). Gogol describes the contrast between the impoverished, poorly lit sections of the city and the wealthy, brighter parts (772); throughout the city, the police are utterly ineffective even in the midst of apparent crime and rumors of supernatural thefts.

   a. **Further Reading:** Lees, Andrew, and Lynn Hollen Lees. *Cities and the Making of Modern Europe, 1750–1914.* Cambridge: Cambridge University Press, 2007.

   b. **Suggested Search:** A Google Images search for "19th century St. Petersburg" results in several interesting pictures of the city from this era.

In-Class Activities

1. Divide the class into three or four groups, each of which must work together to write, act, film, and edit an adaptation of *The Overcoat* (smaller groups are recommended; because there are so few active characters in the story, too many students in a group will lead to lower partici-

pation rates). Ask each group to present their film to the class, and use the differences between them as a means of speaking about the themes and scenes that different groups found more important than others.

2. As a class, spend part of the period in the library, and ask all of the students to find at least three facts about Gogol and his historical and national context and to write those facts down on an index card. Then gather the index cards and share with the class all of the details that the students found. Use these findings to supplement the class's discussion of *The Overcoat*.

3. Divide the class into two groups, one of which must act as prosecutor, accusing Akaky of being absurd, and the other group must defend him, arguing that he is reasonable to be content with his situation and work. Require each side to make use of citations from the text as proof of their arguments.

Paper Topics/Suggestions for Writing

1. How does *The Overcoat* compare to any other Russian works that you have read for this class? Are there ways in which the author's nationality are apparent? How do the authors treat the Russian government and city life?

2. Write an essay in which you evaluate the change of character that Akaky undergoes in *The Overcoat* in relation to the character of Emma Bovary in Flaubert's *Madame Bovary*. In what important ways do material goods impact Akaky's and Emma's characters? How do they change over the course of their stories? In what ways are they unaffected by their surroundings?

3. Write a journal entry in which you compare yourself to Akaky. You must think of some accoutrement or article of clothing that plays an important role in the formation of your identity, and use this as a means of comparison with Akaky's identity and his overcoat.

4. Why does Akaky change so much when designing and wearing his new coat? If we grant that he is not a complete eccentric, what explains his sudden transformation? How does this explain his reaction after he is robbed of the overcoat?

5. Choose another author that has a distinctive style and that you have read for this course, and write an essay that compares him/her with Gogol. What aspects of each author's style makes for a successful story? How does style contribute to the overall effect of these works?

6. Write a brief reflective piece on the ways in which Gogol's critique of his government still applies or does not apply to your government.

Resources

Gogol, Nickolai. *The Diary of a Madman, The Government Inspector, and Selected Stories.* Trans. Ronald Wilks. New York: Penguin, 2005.

> This volume contains *The Overcoat*, but it also includes several other of Gogol's best known shorter works. Instructors are particularly recommended to read *The Government Inspector* to get a better understanding of Gogol's political critiques and his comical/satirical tone.

Hosking, Geoffrey. *Russian History: A Very Short Introduction.* Oxford: Oxford University Press, 2012.

> This brief work is both insightful and accessible, and instructors as well as students should turn to this volume if they are seeking a manageable work that provides a context for Gogol's thought.

McGuire, Robert A. *Gogol from the Twentieth Century.* Princeton: Princeton University Press, 1974.

> This collection of essays is a well-balanced and informative volume, and it contains two recommended essays (by Boris Eichenbaum and Dmitri Chizhevsky) about *The Overcoat*.

Shapiro, Gavriel. *Nikolai Gogol and the Baroque Cultural Heritage.* University Park, PA: Pennsylvania State University Press, 1993.

> For instructors generally unfamiliar with Gogol's works and his influences, this is a helpful and informative volume. Shapiro sets many of Gogol's works in context in an interdisciplinary manner that is attentive to many of the historical and cultural symbols and traditions that he inherited.

DOMINGO FAUSTINO SARMIENTO

From *Facundo*

Topics for Lecture or Discussion

1. **Despite favoring the urban to the rural and democratic government to dictators, Domingo Faustino Sarmiento's romantic sensibilities created an ambivalent portrait of those he meant to criticize.** Sarmiento's political goals included moving Argentina toward a European model, a model that he viewed as enlightened, urban, and democratic. One of the major surprises of *Facundo* is how romantic Sarmiento's portraits are of the gauchos and anti-democratic Facundo. Like the English romantics, Sarmiento seems drawn to rural life and the wilderness. Unlike Wordsworth, whose little cottage girl in "We Are Seven" has a deeper spiritual insight than the poem's educated speaker, Sarmiento did not see wisdom in rural life and wilderness but rather a dangerous barbarism. This ambivalence, between his attraction to the wild and the danger he sees in the wild, forms a major tension in *Facundo* and gives the book its larger-than-life characters, while complicating them with accusations of cruelty, violence, and dictatorial rule.

   a. **Further Reading:** Shumway, Nicolas. *The Invention of Argentina.* Berkeley: University of California Press, 1991.

   b. **Suggested Search:** Another major, early Argentine literary work is *Martin Fierro.* A translation of the work can be found on the Sparrow Thorn Press website at http://sparrowthorn.com/MartinFierro_INTRODUCTION.pdf. *Martin Fierro* can be especially interesting in a discussion of Sarmiento's treatment of the gaucho, as it is an epic about a gaucho character written by José Hernandez, who politically opposed Sarmiento and who published his epic gaucho poem during Sarmiento's presidency.

2. **Domingo Sarmiento regularly uses a sociological perspective to examine the connection between the people of Argentina and their landscape. Through its connection between citizens and their land, *Facundo* became a major text in how Argentina envisioned itself.** The initial widespread embrace of *Facundo* can be seen in Sarmiento's increasing political power, winning the presidency a couple decades after the publication of his major literary work. It was not, though, just Sarmiento's intended aims that were embraced by the Argentine people. His romantic portrait of the gauchos turned the very culture he attacked into an important symbol of Argentine culture. Additionally, the mixture of genres in *Facundo* made the text an important step toward modernism in literature. With *Facundo* as a keystone text, Latin American

authors could envision themselves as part of a cosmopolitan, experimental tradition.

   a. **Further Reading:** Bunkley, Allison Williams. *The Life of Sarmiento.* New York: Greenwood Press, 1952.

   b. **Suggested Search:** See National Geographic's Argentina Guide at http://travel.nationalgeographic.com/travel/countries/argentina -guide. This guide includes a photo section with numerous photographs of the Argentine landscape.

3. **Although *Facundo* received numerous positive literary reviews, the intellectual and political group with which Domingo Sarmiento allied himself had mixed and often negative responses to the work.** Sarmiento was connected to the "Generation of 1837," a group of writers and activists who opposed Argentine dictator Juan Manuel de Rosas. The writers desired a European model for Argentina, favoring democracy to Argentina's dictatorship and favoring urban, cosmopolitan cities to rural life. While Sarmiento's *Facundo* was written in opposition to de Rosas, the book contains exaggerations and inaccuracies about gauchos and about the text's biographical subject, Facundo, and other members of the Generation of 1837 worried that Sarmiento's distortions would keep the group's opposition to de Rosas from being taken seriously.

   a. **Further Reading:** Katra, William H. "Exile: A New Set of Priorities." In *The Argentine Generation of 1837: Echeverría, Alberdi, Sarmiento, Mitre,* 66–143. Madison, NJ: Fairleigh Dickinson University Press, 1996.

   b. **Suggested Search:** See the exhibit from the University of Notre Dame's library on rare books related to the Generation of 1837 at www.library.nd.edu/rarebooks/exhibits/riverplate/07-critics/index .shtml.

4. **Politically, Domingo Sarmiento admired the United States and sought to have Argentina follow its example. Sarmiento's opposition between civilization and barbarism created an opposition that allowed him to follow both American ideals and America's failure to reach those ideals.** Like the United States' policy toward Native Americans, as president Sarmiento would pursue an aggressive and a largely violent policy against indigenous Argentines. The opposition between civilization and barbarism that Sarmiento sets up in *Facundo* would be followed through in his policy toward indigenous Argentines. Racial categories had largely defined which category an individual would fall under in *Facundo,* but by the time he became president in late 1868, Sarmiento's policies were even more strongly decided along racial lines. The barbaric elements of Argentina (which Sarmiento identified as non-European Argentines) needed to either be civilized or exterminated to protect the civilized elements of Argentina. Earlier in this anthology is an example

from the Seneca Falls Convention of a group enlarging the category of "men" in the "all men are created equal" of the Declaration of Independence. It is through his barbarian-civilization axis that Sarmiento would narrow the category of humanity.

a. **Further Reading:** Jones, Kristine L. "Civilization and Barbarism and Sarmiento's Indian Policy." In *Sarmiento and His Argentina*, edited by Joseph T. Criscenti, 35–44. Boulder, CO: Lynne Rienner, 1993.

b. **Suggested Search:** A military reaction to attitudes toward indigenous people in Argentina can be seen in the Conquest of the Desert. See the illustrated article on the military campaign by Professor Andermann of Birkbeck University at www.bbk.ac.uk/ibamuseum /texts/Andermann02.htm.

5. *Facundo's* **mixed genre creates a new kind of book to match the newness of the Argentinean landscape and people. But by mixing genres, it also becomes unclear how this new kind of book should be understood.** Critic Diana Sorensen Goodrich has noted that *Facundo* has been received "as history, as a pamphlet . . . as a sociogeographical study, as a biography, as a novel" and "even as epic" (42). *Facundo* has been read from each of these generic perspectives because it participates in all of these genres. The radical experimentation of the text places Sarmiento as an extension of the recent romantic movement and as a forerunner of the coming modernist movement. Domingo Sarmiento's experiments are, like Whitman's in the United States, grounded in an interest as to how to best represent a landscape and a population that have yet to be represented on their own terms, outside of a European literary model. By mixing genres, Sarmiento creates this new kind of book, which becomes a foundational text in Argentine literature, but, as with any kind of literary experiment, this new form of writing requires a new way to read it, which none of the older literary genres entirely provides.

a. **Further Reading:** Goodrich, Diana Sorensen. "The Risks of Fiction: *Facundo* and the Parameters of Historical Writing." In *Facundo and the Construction of Argentine Culture*, 41–66. Austin: University of Texas Press, 1996.

b. **Suggested Search:** A search for "Facundo" at Project Gutenberg's website (www.gutenberg.org) will lead to a complete copy of the text.

In-Class Activities

1. Domingo Sarmiento believes gauchos and political figures like Facundo are bad for Argentina because they are barbaric, violent, and often cruel. At the same time, he makes these characters thrilling and romantic. How do you reconcile these opposing stances within the text?

2. Domingo Sarmiento claims dictatorial rule to stem from gaucho culture and claims gaucho culture to result from the environment in which the gauchos are raised. By connecting an individual's outlook to landscape, is Sarmiento excusing the cruel acts of Facundo? Is Facundo responsible for his actions if his way of life stems from the landscape in which he was born?

3. Do these selections from the first and second section of *Facundo* work as political activism? Based on what you read, what do you think the political aims of the author were? Do the political aims you find in the text differ from the political aims you saw in the introduction to *Facundo*? If so, how do you reconcile these differences?

4. In what ways is *Facundo* a racist text? Which traits does Domingo Sarmiento directly ascribe to race? Does his aim to connect society to landscape inherently lead to stereotyping? How do the romantic portraits of those he deems barbaric affect his stereotyping?

Paper Topics/Suggestions for Writing

1. Both Domingo Sarmiento and Olaudah Equiano describe groups of people living outside a European-model style of life while writing for Westernized audiences. Examine the similarities and differences between their two presentations of non-European cultures. Explain these similarities and differences based on the authors' political aims, audiences, and real differences between the cultures being presented.

2. This selection from *Facundo* includes a portrait of an Argentine landscape, a sociological examination of the people of Argentina, and a biography of a contemporary historical figure. Look at these very different modes of writing and see what other modes of writing you can find in the text. Describe how you understand the mixture of genres to work in *Facundo*, and consider to what degree *Facundo* should be read as historical truth and to what degree it should be read as a work of fiction.

3. In *Facundo*, Domingo Sarmiento sets up an opposition between civilization and barbarism. This opposition is similar to the opposition set up by Jean-Jacques Rousseau, but whereas Sarmiento favors civilization, Rousseau favors humanity in an original, uncivilized state. Looking at both *Facundo* and *Confessions*, explain why the two authors take different sides on a mutually agreed-upon opposition. Explain what civilization and barbarism might mean for each author and what each author's text says about his views on humanity in its precivilized state.

4. Domingo Sarmiento denied claims that he was a romantic, wishing his writing to function toward pragmatic, political goals. After looking at the authors included in "Romantic Poets and Their Successors," give

your own opinion: describe which values you see Sarmiento having in common with romantic poets, and argue how politically useful you believe *Facundo* to be.

5. Domingo Sarmiento makes generalizations about Argentine groups based on their racial makeup, clearly believing white Argentines to have superior traits and arguing for Argentina to become more European. Explain how you believe a historical text containing racist claims should be read. Consider to what degree *Facundo* is ethically unrecoverable, to what degree it should be read based on its historical significance, and what values or features of the text might be admirable today.

Resources

Alonso, Carlos J. "Reading Sarmiento: Once More, with Passion." *Hispanic Review* 62:1 (Winter 1994): 35–52.
> This is a sensitive reading of the contradictions within *Facundo* that seeks neither to explain away *Facundo's* contradictions nor to simply recognize them but to understand them through a sophisticated mix of theory and culture context.

Luiggi, Alice Houston. "Some Letters of Sarmiento and Mary Mann 1865–1876, Part I." *The Hispanic American Historical Review* 32:2 (May 1952): 187–211.
> This is the first of three selections of Domingo Sarmiento and his first English translator, Mary Mann, published in *The Hispanic American Historical Review*.

Waisman, Sergio Gabriel. "Argentina and Translation: Delineating a Culture Context." In *Borges and Translation: The Irreverence of the Periphery*, 19–40. Cranbury, NJ: Associated University Presses, 2005.
> Discussed in this chapter, which is from a larger critical work on Borges, is the influence of Domingo Sarmiento's cosmopolitan and literary side on the later, Nobel Prize–winning Argentine.

FREDERICK DOUGLASS

Narrative of the Life of Frederick Douglass, an American Slave

Topics for Lecture or Discussion

1. **In his *Narrative*, Frederick Douglass struggles with a generic problem of slave narratives: the problem of writing about self in the context of a political situation.** Douglass's rhetorical situation is a complex one: on the one hand, as an autobiographical narrative, his text is supposed to give a true account of the author's life; on the other hand, this account of the truth is presented for a white audience and in the context of continuing slavery. The effects of writing in the context of slavery are most noticeable in Douglass's omission of his escape from slavery. Douglass must omit the details of this major event in the narrative in order to keep future runaway slaves safe. His narrative is affected by that political reality and by the desire to move his primarily white audience toward the abolitionist cause. Toward this end, Douglass keeps his narrative focused on his experiences with slavery and leaves out any experience—such as the romance between himself and his wife—that does not fit his political focus.

    a. **Further Reading:** Gibson, Donald B. "Reconciling the Public and Private in Frederick Douglass' Narrative." *American Literature* 57:4 (December 1985): 549–69.

    b. **Suggested Search:** Search for Harriet Jacobs's *Incidents in the Life of a Slave Girl* at www.gutenberg.org for another major slave narrative.

2. **While Frederick Douglass's *Narrative* specifically details the horrors of slavery, the complexity of the power relationships depicted opens up the text to other human rights issues. Douglass's belief in other human rights issues was demonstrated in his political action, including his participation in women's suffrage.** In Douglass's *Narrative*, power relationships in Southern society are more complex than one blanket slave-master relationship. Both black and white characters in the text often have a more powerful white character to whom they must answer, such as the first master in the text, Captain Anthony, whose position as farm clerk and superintendent is described as "overseer of the overseers" (813). The power of slavery is also shown to have negatively impacted not only the enslaved black population but also the enslaving white population, with Sophia Auld turning away from her originally kind disposition under the influence of owning her first slave. This complexity of unbalanced power relationships and mutual

harm caused to both participants in the master-slave relationship allows for a universalizing of the "irresponsible power" inherent in slavery. After gaining his freedom, Douglass publically argued not only for the abolition of slavery but also for women's rights. His involvement in the women's rights movement included his participation in the famous women's rights convention at the Seneca Falls Convention (see "Declaration of Sentiments" in "Revolutionary Contexts" in this anthology).

a. **Further Reading:** Douglass, Frederick. *Frederick Douglass on Women's Rights*. Edited by Philip Sheldon Foner. Westport, CT: Greenwood Press, 1976.

b. **Suggested Search:** Search *Women and Social Movements in the United States* at asp6new.alexanderstreet.com/wam2/wam2.index.map.aspx, a database that includes documents detailing the relationship between abolition and the women's rights movement.

3. **Written language is shown to be a powerful force in Frederick Douglass's *Narrative*. Literacy is powerful both as a tool to fight slavery and as a power that creates and destroys communities in which the literate participate.** In his text Douglass credits his literacy with strengthening his desire for freedom, citing *The Columbian Orator* as an early, major influence and writing about the same time, "The more I read, the more I was led to abhor and detest my enslavers" (827). Later, in his first escape attempt, Douglass's literacy gives him the power to create documents that should increase the likelihood of safety for him and his fellow escapees. Douglass's literacy does, however, separate him from his highly illiterate community. While literacy fuels his interest in escape, the community around him is encouraged to engage in "vicious dissipation" during its free time and tricked by slave owners into believing "there was little to choose between liberty and slavery" (844). Literacy also literally separates Douglass from his community as it fuels his desire to escape, and by escaping, he leaves behind the majority of his relationships in Baltimore. Complicating the power of literacy is the ability to engage with new communities through writing, such as the class Douglass teaches on Sundays and his written participation in the public sphere, placing his *Narrative* alongside the quoted texts of Whittier and Shakespeare.

a. **Further Reading:** Royer, Daniel J. "The Process of Literacy as Communal Involvement in the Narratives of Frederick Douglass." *African American Review* 28:3 (Autumn 1994): 363–74.

b. **Suggested Searches:** Search for *The Columbian Orator* on the website 19th Century Schoolbooks at http://digital.library.pitt.edu/nietz, and for John Greenleaf Whittier, "The Farewell of a Virginia Slave Mother to Her Daughters Sold into Southern Bondage," at www.bartleby.com/248/213.html. For a twentieth-century response to

Douglass, see Robert Hayden, "Frederick Douglass," the Poetry Foundation, at www.poetryfoundation.org/poem/175757, which includes an audio file of the poet reading his poem.

4. **Structurally, Frederick Douglass's *Narrative* begins with a series of oppositions that Douglass immediately subverts.** The famous literary critic Henry Louis Gates Jr. reads the first chapter of Douglass's text through the lens of structuralism and poststructuralism. He notes that Douglass sets up a series of binaries on which Southern society relies, such as the binaries of white and black, master and slave, knowledge and ignorance, and civilization and barbarism. Douglass, though, does not fit into this structure. He is neither purely black nor white but of mixed race, and he writes that the increase in mixed-race slaves upsets the black-and-white binary upon which the pro-slavery "God cursed Ham" argument is based (841). Jean-Jacques Rousseau's *Confessions*, an autobiography found earlier in this volume, is the text considered in some of the most famous poststructuralist readings by Jacques Derrida and Paul de Man. The binaries set up by the two autobiographers, however, begin in very different contexts. Rousseau begins his text with what he knows about himself and his personality as a free, European child, while Douglass begins with what he does not know—his father, his true date of birth, and his age—due to being born into slavery.

   a. **Further Reading:** Gates, Henry Louis, Jr. "Binary Oppositions in Chapter One of *Narrative of the Life of Frederick Douglass, an American Slave, Written by Himself.*" In *Afro-American Literature: The Reconstruction of Instruction*, edited by Dexter Fisher and Robert B. Stepto, 212–32. New York: Modern Language Association, 1979. Also reproduced in *Frederick Douglass' Narrative of the Life of Frederick Douglass* (1988) and *Critical Essays on Frederick Douglass* (1991).

   b. **Suggested Search:** The critical strategy employed by Henry Louis Gates Jr. was pioneered by Jacques Derrida. An introduction to this form of criticism can be found under "Deconstructive Strategy" in the "Jacques Derrida" entry of the Internet Encyclopdia of Philosophy at www.iep.utm.edu/derrida.

5. **In its account and through its publication, Frederick Douglass's *Narrative* shows Douglass fighting for the abolitionist cause through his book publication and career as an orator. Douglass also had a career as a newspaper editor, which gave him a public platform that allowed greater freedom than did autobiography or oratory.** By starting his first newspaper, *The North Star*, Douglass became his own publisher. The newspaper allowed him to engage in the issues surrounding slavery in a manner he saw fit. This was a great freedom compared to his work as an orator at white-run abolitionist meetings or publishing

his autobiography through the white-controlled book industry. Douglass was frustrated by these early experiences, since many white abolitionists expected him to give his account of slavery but not voice his opinions regarding the philosophy or politics of abolitionism. Douglass's newspapers allowed him to engage with a range of issues in the slavery debate and to use a variety of rhetorical techniques, including journalism, fiction, and open letters.

a. **Further Reading:** Fishkin, Shelly Fisher, and Carla L. Peterson. "'We Hold These Truths to be Self-Evident': The Rhetoric of Frederick Douglass' Journalism." In *Frederick Douglass: New Literary and Historical Essays*, edited by Eric J. Sundquist, 189–204. Cambridge: Cambridge University Press, 1990.

b. **Suggested Searches:** The Frederick Douglass Project at www.lib .rochester.edu/index.cfm?page=2494 includes the text of some of Douglass's newspaper writing; also search for "*North Star* documents" at the Library of Congress's website, www.loc.gov/index.html.

In-Class Activities

1. Frederick Douglass's writing style changes during his apostrophe in chapter 10. Why does he choose to change his style so dramatically? Does this change in style heighten the dramatic situation for the contemporary reader? Do you believe it heightened the situation for the original nineteenth-century reader?

2. While Frederick Douglass emphasizes the power of written language throughout his *Narrative,* he mentions language as song in chapter 2. After listening to a few nineteenth-century spirituals (or reading the lyrics from contemporary documents such as *Slave Songs of the United States*), consider the following: How do the style and language of the songs differ from the style and language of Douglass's document? Who is the intended audience of the spirituals, and who is the intended audience of the written *Narrative?*

3. The *Narrative's* appendix breaks from the linear story of the narrative to comment on the text. How does the position of the appendix at the end of the text affect your reading? Why might this appendix exist at the back of the book instead of Frederick Douglass clarifying his comments about Christianity within the main body of the *Narrative* itself? If the appendix did exist in the main body of the text, instead of at the end, how would it change your experience of the *Narrative?*

4. At the end of the *Narrative* Frederick Douglass speaks before a predominantly white audience at an anti-slavery convention. Why would Douglass choose this moment to end his text? What does it say about

his relationship with white Americans? How does this public address reflect on the public address that is the *Narrative* itself?

Paper Topics/Suggestions for Writing

1. Frederick Douglass emphasizes the power of written language throughout his *Narrative*. Examine the status and value of written language as depicted in the text, looking at moments such as the forged documents during Douglass's first escape attempt and Douglass ending the text with the signature of his new name.

2. Frederick Douglass quotes or alludes to a number of written sources, from the Bible to John Greenleaf Whittier to William Shakespeare. Write about the relationship between Douglass's text and one or more of the referenced texts. Is the relationship between Douglass's text and each outside source identical, or does it change depending on the referenced source?

3. Frederick Douglass describes his fight with Covey as a "turning-point" in his life (842). Examine how this physical struggle affects Douglass psychologically and spiritually. What is the relationship between the physical and the psychological or spiritual throughout the rest of the text?

4. Frederick Douglass frequently describes how well or poorly fed he is by the various slave owners. Examine the value of food in the text, looking at its value beyond literal nourishment. It may be helpful to compare and contrast hunger with other horrors, such as the whippings that numerous characters endure.

5. The main body of Frederick Douglass's *Narrative* ends with him speaking at an antislavery convention. Write about how Douglass's story provides him with both the education and the authority to effectively address this subject. Consider how Douglass presents in his text the relationship between outside knowledge (such as literacy) and self-knowledge.

Resources

Chander, Harish. "Frederick Douglass." In *African American Autobiographies: A Sourcebook*, edited by Emmanuel S. Nelson, 95–109. Westport, CT: Greenwood Press, 2002.
    This is a brief introduction to Frederick Douglass and his work, including a biography, themes, critical reception, and extensive bibliography.
de Man, Paul. "Excuses (*Confessions*)." In *Allegories of Reading: Figural Language in Rousseau, Nietzsche, Rilke, and Proust*, 278–301. New Haven, CT: Yale University Press, 1979.

This work contains Paul de Man's famous reading of Jean-Jacques Rousseau, as mentioned earlier in the fourth point in the section *Topics for Lecture or Discussion.*

Fisch, Audrey, ed. *The Cambridge Companion to the African American Slave Narrative.* Cambridge: Cambridge University Press, 2007.

This work includes essays on the genre, including essays specifically on Frederick Douglass.

Frederick Douglass: When the Lion Wrote History. Dir. Orlando Bagwell. PBS Home Video, 1994. Turner Home Entertainment, VHS.

This video, a biography of Frederick Douglass, includes interviews with Douglass historians.

Lawson, Bill E., and Frank M. Kirkland, eds. *Frederick Douglass: A Critical Reader.* Malden, MA: Blackwell, 1999.

This work contains essays that examine the philosophic aspects of Frederick Douglass's work.

Presenting Mr. Frederick Douglass: "The Lesson of the Hour." Dir. Joseph Camp. Perf. Fred Morsell. Films for the Humanities & Sciences, 2003, DVD.

Fred Morsell reads Frederick Douglass's last speech in character as Douglass.

Rawick, George P., ed. *The American Slave: A Composite Autobiography.* Westwood, CT: Greenwood Publishing Group, 1972.

This book contains transcripts of numerous slave narratives gathered by the Federal Writers' Project.

HERMAN MELVILLE
Bartleby, the Scrivener

Topics for Lecture or Discussion

1. **"Bartleby, the Scrivener" can be read as a parable in which Herman Melville writes about his own experience around the period when he was writing *Moby Dick*.** After his initial success with conventional novels about the South Seas, Melville was increasingly drawn to the unconventional writing that would result in *Moby Dick*. He wrote to Nathanial Hawthorne, "What I feel most moved to write, that is banned,—it will not pay. Yet, altogether, write the *other* way I cannot" (868, emphasis in original). "Bartleby" reflects Melville's situation. Like Melville, Bartleby is, initially, a successful writer. Whereas Melville's critics wished to see him continue to write in his original style, Bartleby is required to literally copy texts. Both writers eventually refuse to copy. Melville's sense that contemporary literary expectations were impeding him from the writing and reception of his most ambitious works is echoed by the impediments in Bartleby's world: Bartleby is walled behind a screen in a walled building whose windows all look out onto further walls.
   a. **Further Reading:** Marx, Leo. "Melville's Parable of the Walls." *The Sewanee Review* 61:4 (Autumn 1953): 602–27.
   b. **Suggested Search:** Herman Melville's home, Arrowhead, where he wrote his fiction, including *Moby Dick* and "Bartleby," can be viewed on the website for Melville's Arrowhead, www.mobydick.org. Search the site for "Herman Melville" and "Arrowhead."

2. **Bartleby's noncompliance echoes the passive resistance of Henry David Thoreau, Herman Melville's contemporary.** By refusing to work, Bartleby resists social expectations, the power of his employer, and, most importantly, he refuses to be obligated to participate in the economics of his society. All of these themes and ideas are dealt with in Thoreau's essay "Civil Disobedience." While Bartleby passively refuses to work with his polite "I would prefer not to," Thoreau allows himself to be put in jail, passively resisting the Mexican-American War of the 1840s by refusing to pay his taxes. Thoreau's actions are based on the government's fight to extend slavery and his own abolitionist views, but Bartleby's actions are never understood by the employer he resists. Bartleby's inscrutability and extreme resistance, resulting in his death as he refuses the prison food, depict the character's noncompliance as an absurd form of resistance and mark Bartleby as an ironic or a parodic version of Thoreau.

a. **Further Reading:** Rogin, Michael Paul. "Class Struggles in America." In *Subversive Genealogy: The Politics and Art of Herman Melville*, 187–220. New York: Knopf, 1983.

b. **Suggested Search:** A search for the "Walden Woods Project" results in the website for The Walden Woods Project at www.walden.org, which is devoted to Thoreau and the preservation of the forest near the famous pond in *Walden*, Thoreau's book. The "Explore" tab leads to a series of pages that contain photographs of the area around Walden Pond. The "Thoreau" tab leads to an introduction to Thoreau, including a link to "Civil Disobedience," which gives a brief introduction to the famous essay and a link to its text.

3. **"Bartleby's" depiction of a power struggle between an employer and a worker on Wall Street reflects the power struggles occurring at that time between employers and workers during a resurgence of the labor movement.** A lawyer's office is a difficult place to work in "Bartleby." The hours are long, and the employees are shown as lacking a life outside of their workplace. The characters have not fared well in this work, as Turkey has become an alcoholic after years of this work and Nippers has already endured ulcers. Into this environment comes Bartleby, a worker who refuses to work and who maintains an ongoing protest throughout the text, answering "I would prefer not to" whenever he is asked to work. Among the references to the American economy and the resulting labor movement are Herman Melville's placement of his story in Wall Street, already a financial center that influenced the conditions and need for workers, and the narrator's explicit admiration for the "late John Jacob Astor" (871), a prominent and controversial New York businessman.

a. **Further Reading:** Foley, Barbara. "From Wall Street to Astor Place: Historicizing Melville's 'Bartleby.'" *American Literature* 72:1 (March 2000): 87–116.

b. **Suggested Search:** A search for "The Rise of Wall Street" leads to an exhibit of the same name held at the Skyscraper Museum website, www.skyscraper.org. The introduction to the exhibit includes images of Wall Street architecture over the years, beginning with the 1850s, when "Bartleby" was written. The video on the page includes a panorama of Wall Street in the 1850s, with successive architecture later layered atop the panorama.

4. **Like Walt Whitman, in "Bartleby" Herman Melville highlights the setting of New York, using the reality of its location to ground metaphysical concerns.** Melville is specific about New York locations in "Bartleby," setting the story on Wall Street, having his narrator visit real New York locations, such as Trinity Church, Jersey City, Hoboken, and Astoria, and having Bartleby himself die in Manhattan's jail, nicknamed

"The Tombs." The specificity and realism of the story's setting exist in opposition to the unreality of the story's strange, enigmatic main character. The real setting grounds Bartleby, a character who seems to exist outside of reality, and thereby grounds the metaphysical themes that arise from him, such as questions of free will and limits on an individual's ability to refuse the drudgery of modern life. Whitman uses a similar tactic. He highlights New York and the surrounding area in many of his poems, locating "Crossing Brooklyn Ferry" on New York's East River and "Out of the Cradle Endlessly Rocking" at Paumanok, the Native American name for Long Island. In these and many other of his poems, Whitman uses real places to ground the metaphysical concerns of his poetry, including his concern with democracy, which he places across the American landscape. This similar tactic of highlighting a setting to ground metaphysical concerns connects two writers who were otherwise linked by their New York home and their shared pro-democracy, antislavery views.

    a. **Further Reading**: Thomas, M. Wynn. "Walt Whitman and Mannahatta-New York." *American Quarterly* 34:4 (Autumn 1982): 362–78.

    b. **Suggested Searches**: Victor Prevost is one of the best-known, early photographers of nineteenth-century New York City. A Google Images search at google.com for "Victor Prevost" and "New York" will generate a variety of these images. A search for "Victor Prevost" at the George Eastman House website, www.eastmanhouse.org, will link to a series of Prevost's pictures of Central Park.

5. **Herman Melville has been read as a proto-absurdist writer. "Bartleby" is a prime example of Melville's absurdist mode, as the narrator is in an absurd struggle with an unchangeable force.** The great theorist and author of mid-twentieth-century absurdist literature, Albert Camus, admired the writings of Melville. While he recognized a form of absurdity in *Moby Dick* and *Billy Budd,* he, strangely enough, did not set "Bartleby" in the tradition of absurdist literature. This should be surprising, considering Camus's writing on the myth of Sisyphus, the Greek king who is doomed to repeat the absurd, eternal task of rolling a stone up a hill, only to have it roll back to the bottom once he has completed his task. The narrator essentially is working at a Sisyphean task throughout the narrative, determined to understand the unfathomable Bartleby and continually trying to alter the course of this unalterable character.

    a. **Further Reading**: Spector, Robert Donald. "Melville's 'Bartleby' and the Absurd." *Nineteenth-Century Fiction* 16:2 (September 1961): 175–77.

    b. **Suggested Search**: UbuWeb's Film site, www.ubu.com, includes a number of videos by the most famous playwright who employed absurd themes, Samuel Beckett. These can be found by searching for the playwright's name.

In-Class Activities

1. While Bartleby is the story's titular character, it is the narrator whose thoughts and feelings we get, instead of the inscrutable Bartleby. Who do you think is the story's main character? Does "Bartleby" play with or frustrate what you expect from a protagonist?

2. In addition to Bartleby and the narrator, Turkey, Nippers, and Ginger Nut work at the law office. What do these secondary characters add to a story so centered on two primary characters? Are these secondary characters flatter or more well rounded than Bartleby?

3. Is "Bartleby" a tragic short story or a comedy? How does humor work in "Bartleby"?

Paper Topics/Suggestions for Writing

1. Compare the narrator of "Bartleby" with the narrator of "Notes from Underground." Discuss how the extreme respectability of the "Bartleby" narrator undercuts his reliability. Compare and contrast the ways in which each author signals that his narrator is unreliable.

2. "Bartleby" is an early absurdist short story. Examine what it is about "Bartleby" that is absurd, and make your case for what the story's absurdity is meant to show about society.

3. Throughout the story, the narrator continually tries to understand Bartleby's actions. Based on the narrator's inability to understand the character, consider whether or not it is possible for readers to understand Bartleby. If Bartleby can be understood, argue for what the character represents. If Bartleby cannot be understood, explain how the story makes use of a character who refuses to be a symbol.

4. Jean-Jacques Rousseau's *Confessions* details the development of an individual. Look at *Confessions* and related poems in "Romantic Poets and Their Successors" for literature that insists on the importance of individuality. Compare this previous assessment of the individual to the status of the individual in "Bartleby."

5. Bartleby repeatedly replies "I would prefer not to" in response to his boss's requests. Write about whether this stock phrase shows Bartleby to have free will or not.

Resources

Bartleby. Dir. Anthony Friedman. Perf. Paul Scofield and John McEnery. Maron Films, 1972. DVD.
> This film is a mostly faithful adaptation of "Bartleby" that sets the story in London in the early '70s.

Bartleby. Dir. Jonathan Parker. Perf. Crispin Glover and David Paymer. Parker Film Company, 2001. DVD.
> This film is a less faithful adaptation of "Bartleby" that includes a number of additional subplots.

Miller, Edwin Haviland. *Melville.* New York: G. Braziller, 1997.
> This work is both biographical and critical, stressing Freudian interpretation.

Newman, Lea Bertani Vozar. "Bartleby, the Scrivener." In *A Reader's Guide to the Short Stories of Herman Melville*, 19–78. Boston: G. K. Hall, 1986.
> This work is an introduction that covers a wide variety of interpretations and critical approaches to "Bartleby."

ROMANTIC POETS AND THEIR SUCCESSORS

Topics for Lecture or Discussion

1. **Many of the values of the romantics and symbolists would be maintained in future avant-garde movements.** The avant-garde modernists in America and France that followed the romantics and symbolists in the twentieth century would frequently distance themselves from their predecessors. The avant-garde's insistence on breaking with tradition was, however, a tactic previously used by the romantics and symbolists. A number of other values would continue into twentieth-century movements, including the romantics' interest in natural speech and experimenting with form and the symbolists' experiments with creating reality through perceptual breaks and Stéphane Mallarmé's explorations of page layout. Percy Shelley's claim, that "Poets are the unacknowledged legislators of the world," was itself a claim that poets imagined new forms of life and influenced society through those imaginings. A similar mind-set would guide movements like surrealism, which sought to explore the subconscious and how imaginative life could influence and even dominate the more logical, normative waking life.

   a. **Further Reading:** Poggioli, Renato. *The Theory of the Avant-Garde.* New York: Harper & Row, 1971.

   b. **Suggested Searches:** UbuWeb's (www.ubu.com) page on Stéphane Mallarmé contains two translations of Mallarmé's famous visual poem "A Throw of the Dice Will Never Abolish Chance." A search for "Marcel Broodthaers" and "Un Coup des Dés" at the Museum of Modern Art's website, moma.org, will give an image of the artist Broodthaers's transformation of the poem into pure visual art. A search for "Max Ernst" and "retrospective" on the Metropolitan Museum of Art's site, www.metmuseum.org, will generate a number of results, including a former exhibit of the works of this major surrealist painter.

2. **A new, larger reading public came into existence around the birth of romanticism. This change in reading audiences would influence the writers of the nineteenth century.** While previous generations could, at best, hope their writing would amuse the aristocracy, the success of Rousseau illustrates the new hopes of aspiring writers: literary celebrity and inspiration for political revolutionaries. This imagination of a genius who gains populist support for radical new thought did not always successfully play out in a writer's lifetime. The politically radical Percy Shelley was not widely read in his lifetime, and Charles Baudelaire was similarly not accepted by the general reading public. Some of the writers in our selection, such as Elizabeth Barrett Browning, did

manage to attract public interest, and Walt Whitman famously used Ralph Waldo Emerson's praise for *Leaves of Grass* in an attempt to further promote the book. Stéphane Mallarmé's career and literary salon illustrate the new imagination of the radical artist by the end of the century: an artist who never achieved popular success in his life. Mallarmé was influential for artists of a younger generation and only received widespread public acclaim after his death.

   a. **Further Reading:** Jarvis, Robin. *The Romantic Period: The Intellectual and Cultural Context of English Literature, 1789–1830.* Harlow, UK: Pearson/Longman, 2004.

   b. **Suggested Search:** The European Library's "Reading Europe" online exhibit at www.theeuropeanlibrary.org/exhibition-reading-europe, collects images and information for a large number of books throughout the history of European publishing. Examples of book publishing practices of the period can be found under the link "Timeline," or publishing examples can be specifically examined by region through the link "Countries."

3. **Walt Whitman's forceful American poetry would become very influential among Latin American poets, and José Martí and Rubén Darío were among his early admirers.** As colonies broke away from their former European colonizers, writers in the United States and Latin America sought to create a uniquely American literature. Whitman was viewed as one of the first major poets to achieve this, creating poetry about the American landscape, and his achievement found influence in other poets writing about American landscapes, including Martí and Darío. Martí in particular was interested in Whitman's rhetoric of brotherhood, pointing to a kind of nationalist poetry. In counterpoint to Whitman's nationalism, the development of poetry in the Americas would also look toward the French avant-garde, including poets Charles Baudelaire and Paul Verlaine, as it took on an international side. Brazilian modernist poets, for example, would famously develop their tendency toward the international through the influence of and personal interactions with French-language poet Blaise Cendrars in the early twentieth century.

   a. **Further Reading:** Englekirk, John E. "Notes on Whitman in Spanish America." *Hispanic Review* 6:2 (April 1938): 133–38.

   b. **Suggested Searches:** Several of the twentieth-century Chilean poet Pablo Neruda's poems referencing Walt Whitman can be found in editor Ilan Stavans's *The Poetry of Pablo Neruda*. Large selections from this book can be found on Google Books, and a search for "Whitman" will quickly lead to these poems. A search for "Blaise Cendrars" and "Sonia Delaunay" on the Museum of Modern Art's website, moma .org, will lead to an image of Cendrars's famous collaborative illustrated poem with Sonia Delaunay, *Le Prose du Transsibérien et de la petit Jehanne de France.*

4. **The growth of cities in industrializing Europe and America pushed poets to reformulate their understanding of the countryside and the city. Two major trends were a valorizing of rural experience and the democratization of the city street.** As England became industrialized, romantic poets looked to nature for an alternative way of life, apart from the overcrowding and industrialization. Poems like William Wordsworth's "Lines Composed a Few Miles above Tintern Abbey" and John Keats's "Ode to a Nightingale" show the poets putting forward the value of a psychological experience of nature. William Blake's "The Chimney Sweeper" poems and "London" show the harsh, wretched conditions of the city that pushed poets to reimagine the experience of nature. Cities did, however, place people of various economic positions in the same physical position, and this democratizing power of the city street would be worked through by French poets like Charles Baudelaire, especially in *Paris Spleen*, his book of prose poems that followed *The Flowers of Evil.*

   a. **Further Reading:** Krober, Karl. *Ecological Literary Criticism: Romantic Imagining and the Biology of Mind.* New York: Columbia University Press, 1994.

   b. **Suggested Searches:** The landscape paintings of Caspar David Friedrich are among the most important of romanticism as a visual arts movement. These paintings can easily be found on the Caspar David Friedrich—The Complete Works website at www.caspardavid friedrich.org. The artist Constantin Guy represented city life later in the nineteenth century and was the subject of Charles Baudelaire's famous essay *The Painter of Modern Life.* Guy's work remains underappreciated, but a Google Images search for "Constantin Guy" will generate a number of his works, while a brief, English-language introduction to the artist can be found by searching for "Constantin Guy" and "the painter of modern life."

5. **Both John Keats and Charles Baudelaire expand the poetic vocabularies of their languages. Understanding how subsequent poets responded to their achievements demonstrates how two different poetic traditions understood language.** While Keats expanded poetic vocabulary by transforming words into other parts of speech, and Baudelaire used words previously considered too coarse for poetry, each expanded poetic vocabulary in his own cultural context. French poet, critic, and translator of William Shakespeare, Yves Bonnefoy has written on these cultural differences, noticing the effects of the larger, English poetic vocabulary and the smaller, French poetic vocabulary. According to Bonnefoy, French poetic convention pushes its poets to

treat language as universal, as an almost Platonic sense of language, while English-language poetic convention pushes its poets toward the particular. The central difference can be seen in the keystone writers for each tradition: Jean Racine, the keystone writer of the French tradition, who uses a vocabulary that numbers only in the hundreds throughout his entire career, and William Shakespeare, the keystone writer of the English tradition, who uses a vocabulary so large that many English words make their first appearance in his plays. Stéphane Mallarmé can be read as renewing the French tradition, reducing his vocabulary and giving his images the feel of Plato's forms, while William Carlos Williams might be seen continuing the English-language tradition, seeking to write a poetry closer to American speech.

a. **Further Reading:** Bonnefoy, Yves. "Shakespeare and the French Poet." In *Shakespeare and the French Poet*, translated by John Naughton, 10–20. Chicago: University of Chicago Press, 2004.

b. **Suggested Searches:** While students will have some knowledge of Shakespearean language, a knowledge of Jean Racine is far less likely. The Theatre in Video database (ativ.alexanderstreet.com) includes full productions of Racine's *Phèdre* and *Bérénice*, although both are in the original French. An alternative introduction to Racine would be Gabriel Fauré's composition *Cantique de Jean Racine*, performances of which can easily be found as a video search.

6. **William Wordsworth and Samuel Taylor Coleridge work toward a modern sense of self in their poems, breaking new ground in their descriptions of psychological experience.** They positioned the visionary individual outside the confines of common, urban life. If, however, the speaker of worth speaks from outside of society, then the worth of what that individual says might not be immediately obvious—the speaker's outside position excludes a repetition of society's common adage. Wordsworth and Coleridge chose to examine psychological states in poems like "Lines Composed a Few Miles above Tintern Abbey" and "Frost at Midnight," giving a history of the individual and showing how the individual became himself or herself or developed his or her beliefs. This examination of an individual's mental state would reappear later in the nineteenth century as psychoanalysis, and Coleridge's experience of soot generating a childhood memory would find new expression in French novelist Marcel Proust's psychological claim of "involuntary memory."

a. **Further Reading:** Wilson, Douglas B. "Psychological Approaches." In *A Companion to Romanticism*, edited by Duncan Wu, 420–30. Oxford: Blackwell, 1998.

b. **Suggested Searches:** A search for "Tintern Abbey" on the Castles of Wales website at www.castlewales.com produces large images of

Tintern Abbey. Images of the Lake District, where Wordsworth and Coleridge wrote a number of their poems, may also be viewed, and images of the region can be seen at the Lake District National Park website at www.lakedistrict.gov.uk.

7. **Friedrich Hölderlin's belief that the gods have departed is not just a theocratic statement but a statement about his experience of the world. Understanding "the gods" as experiencing divinity in the world or shared being, Hölderlin's poetry influenced subsequent German philosophy.** The philosopher Martin Heidegger would become one of the most famous readers and interpreters of Hölderlin in the twentieth century. Heidegger would interpret Hölderlin's claims about the gods as claims about Being, which shares an existence that grounds and surrounds all our experience, but which we do not notice in everyday experience. In Hölderlin's "The Half of Life," for example, a Heideggerian interpretation would understand the fullness of ripe pears and blossoming roses as pointing to an experience of the fullness of being, while the anticipation of the coming winter would point to the inevitable modern self-consciousness that distances the individual from the world. Hölderlin would become important to later philosophers like Michel Foucault and Jacques Derrida, but, in part, later philosophical struggles with Hölderlin would also be struggles with the thinking of the influential Heidegger.

   a. **Further Reading:** Gosetti-Ferencei, Jennifer Anna. *Heidegger, Hölderlin, and the Subject of Poetic Language: Toward a New Poetics of Dasein.* New York: Fordham University Press, 2004.

   b. **Suggested Search:** An introduction to Heidegger can be found in the "Martin Heidegger" article on the *Internet Encyclopedia of Philosophy* website at www.iep.utm.edu/heidegge.

8. **The enduring legacy and radical experiments of Walt Whitman and Emily Dickinson hold a special significance for American poetry, as Whitman and Dickinson broke away from British models.** While Edgar Allan Poe would gain influence in France and Latin America, few American poets of the nineteenth century would maintain their influence among American poets throughout the twentieth century. Whitman and Dickinson would become the most influential American nineteenth-century poets in twentieth-century America. Among the poets who would share an affinity for one or both of these poets were Wallace Stevens, Allen Ginsberg, and Susan Howe. Even poets who disliked their predecessors, such as Ezra Pound, in his harsh reaction to Whitman in "A Pact," often found themselves having to respond to the American tradition. The reason for Whitman's and Dickinson's lasting influence can be understood as their willingness to break from British models of poetry. Both wrote in experimental new forms, anticipating

the formal experiments of twentieth-century American poetry, and even while Whitman's poetry contains romantic characteristics, his focus on the American landscape and people kept his poetry separate from romanticism in Britain.

   a. **Further Reading:** Salska, Agnieszka. *Walt Whitman and Emily Dickinson: Poetry of the Central Consciousness.* Philadelphia: University of Pennsylvania Press, 1985.

   b. **Suggested Searches:** Extensive Walt Whitman resources can be found in the Walt Whitman Archive at www.whitmanarchive.org. Of particular interest is the audio page, which contains a recording of what is believed to be Whitman reading a few lines of his poem "America." The Emily Dickinson Museum website at www.emilydick insonmuseum.org contains images and information about the family home in which Dickinson lived. Responses to Whitman, including Allen Ginsberg's "A Supermarket in California," Jack Spicer's "Ode for Walt Whitman," and Ronald Johnson's "Letters to Walt Whitman," can be found by searching for the poems at The Poetry Foundation website, www.poetryfoundation.org. Responses to Emily Dickinson, including William Carlos Williams's "Dedication for a Plot of Ground," Yvor Winters's "To Emily Dickinson," and selections from Susan Howe's *My Emily Dickinson*, can also be found on this website.

In-Class Activities

1. The poets collected in "Romantic Poets and Their Successors" have all, at some point, been read as participating in or responding to romanticism. What common traits do you see that you would label "romantic"? Are there contradictory traits you see within this category?

2. Both Elizabeth Barrett Browning, in her *The Cry of the Children,* and William Blake, in his "The Chimney Sweeper" poems, use the voices of child workers in response to the terrible, dangerous child labor practices of the nineteenth century. How do the two poets use children's voices differently? How effective is the use of children's voices in these poems?

3. Alfred, Lord Tennyson's "Ulysses" and Robert Browning's "Porphyria's Lover" and "My Last Duchess" are all poems written as dramatic monologues. What does each poem tell us about the individual—about how individuals present themselves and what makes up an individual's psychology? Based on the choice of characters for these monologues, what kind of individuals do you see the poets promoting in their poems?

4. In her poem beginning "As I composed this little book," Rosalía de Castro writes, "Although my songs may never bring me fame . . . / they can be sure-fixed in memory / As are the prayers of rituals of belief" (1079). If her poems will not make her famous and will not be fixed in the mem-

ory of a large readership, then in whose memory does she hope these poems will be "sure-fixed"? A select group of readers? Her own mind? What in the poetry leads you to your choice of readership, and how does the audience affect how these poems should be read?

5. Like Domingo Sarmiento, Andrés Bello writes about the South American landscape. What is similar and what is different about the ways in which the two deal with landscape?

Paper Topics/Suggestions for Writing

1. The "Romantic Poets and Their Successors" section contains a number of overtly political poems, including Anna Barbauld's "Eighteen Hundred and Eleven," William Blake's "The Chimney Sweeper" poems, Anna Bunina's "Conversation between Me and the Women," Percy Shelley's "England in 1819," and Rubén Darío's "To Roosevelt." Select two or three of these poems, and describe who the audience is for each poem, what the poet hopes to gain from the audience, and what rhetorical strategies are used to affect the audience.

2. Romanticism brought back to poetry an interest in the exotic and the fantastic that continued through the nineteenth century. Samuel Taylor Coleridge's "The Rime of the Ancient Mariner," John Keats's "La Belle Dame sans Merci," and Christina Rossetti's "Goblin Market" are all poems that participate in this trend. Examine one of them, looking for a theme that is brought out by the exotic or the fantastic elements of the poem. Explain why this theme either could not be presented in a realistic depiction of the world, or explain how the fantastic elements aid the presentation of the theme.

3. Anna Bunina's "Conversation between Me and the Women" is one of a number of instances of gender issues being written about satirically, but while the authors of "The Rights of Woman" and "Declaration of Sentiments" used satire to argue for the rights all women, Bunina seems to distance herself from women's demands. Explain how humor functions in "Conversation between Me and the Women" and how it functions in one of the other previously mentioned documents, arguing whether or not Bunina's claims should be taken at face value.

4. Both Charles Baudelaire and Arthur Rimbaud work with new techniques in an attempt to represent the new speed, new energy, and crowding cities of industrializing Europe. Choose a poem from one of these poets, and describe what techniques you see in the poem that might relate the energetic experience of modernizing Paris.

5. Both Emily Dickinson and Giacomo Leopardi spent most of their lives at their family homes, writing personal, contemplative poetry. Choose a

poem from each poet and compare and contrast their thoughts on shared themes in the poems, such as spirituality, the nature of existence, and life and death.

6. The poetry of Anna Barbauld influenced both William Wordsworth and Samuel Taylor Coleridge and was an important step in the creation of the romantic movement. Looking at the poetry of Barbauld and the poetry of either Wordsworth or Coleridge, explain what similar themes and techniques you see between Barbauld and the later poets.

7. While many poems selected here are personal lyrics, presented as if the poet were writing to himself or herself, Robert Browning's dramatic monologues are often presented as a character talking to an audience. Look at "My Last Duchess" and explain why Browning might have made this choice, showing what the Duke's public speech teaches us about him that we might not have learned if his speech were interior.

8. Look at Percy Shelley's "A Defence of Poetry" and give an account of what Shelley claims happens in the composition of a poem, what experiences go into the composition of a poem, and what traits a poet has. Then look through the poetry selected here and choose one or two poets who embodied these values, providing examples that show how each poet meets Shelley's claims about poetry.

Resources

Baudelaire, Charles. *Paris Spleen.* Translated by Louise Varèse. New York: New Directions, 1947.
    This is an accurate and exciting translation of Charles Baudelaire's book of prose poems, many of which more fully demonstrate how the *flâneur* functions as a figure in French poetry.
Bewell, Alan. *Wordsworth and the Enlightenment.* New Haven, CT: Yale University Press, 1989.
    This work is an anthropological approach to William Wordsworth and his historical context.
Bloom, Harold, and Adrienne Munich, eds. *Robert Browning: A Collection of Critical Essays.* Englewood Cliffs, NJ: Prentice Hall, 1979.
    This collection is useful for suggesting varied critical approaches.
Bonnefly, Yves. *Rimbaud.* Translated by Paul Schmidt. New York: Harper & Row, 1973.
    This is a classic biography of Arthur Rimbaud that offers a psychological reading of his poetry.
Constantine, David. *Hölderlin.* Oxford: Oxford University Press, 1988.
    This work is an excellent introduction for the English-speaking reader, written by a veteran teacher who knows how to present mat-

ters relating to rhythm and form. David Constantine's analysis of the odes is particularly worth reading.

Frye, Northrup. *Fearful Symmetry*. Princeton, NJ: Princeton University Press, 1947.

> The author of this work views Blake as developing a unified myth through his poetry.

Grennan, Eamon, trans. *Leopardi: Selected Poems*. Princeton, NJ: Princeton University Press, 1997.

> See in this work the helpful introduction by John C. Barnes and the translator's comments. Like the translations in Ottavio Casale's *A Leopardi Reader,* these translations are accompanied by the Italian originals.

Howe, Susan. *My Emily Dickinson*. Berkeley, CA: North Atlantic Books, 1985.

> This book, with meditations on, responses to, and selections from Emily Dickinson by Susan Howe, revitalized Dickinson's influence on contemporary American poetry in the late twentieth century.

Mallarmé, Stephane. *Collected Poems*. Translated by Henry Weinfield. Berkeley: University of California Press, 1994.

> The full book of Henry Weinfield's translations includes some very useful commentary on Stéphane Mallarmé's often difficult poetry.

Rimbaud, Arthur. *Illuminations*. Translated by Donald Revell. Richmond, CA: Omnidawn, 2009.

> This work is a sensitive and lively translation of Arthur Rimbaud's prose poems.

Vendler, Helen. *The Odes of John Keats*. Cambridge, MA: Harvard University Press, 1983.

> This book offers brilliant, exhaustive interpretations of all the odes of John Keats.

III. Realism

VICTOR HUGO
From *Les Misérables*

Topics for Lecture or Discussion

1. **In our selection of *Les Misérables*, Hugo goes to great lengths to demonstrate that a human being's character can be fundamentally transformed by pressures and situations that are forced upon his or her person.** Jean Valjean is, at the beginning of *Les Misérables*, a thoughtful, uneducated, industrious man. He is dutiful in fulfilling his responsibilities, and although he is "brusque and gruff" (1119), he is also generous (for example, he secretly pays for his nieces' and nephews' extra milk). However, Valjean's character becomes radically different over the course of his imprisonment; instead of love, Valjean nurtures his hate: "The beginning and end of all his thoughts was the same: hatred of human law, the hatred that, if it is not nipped in the bud by some miraculous event, turns, within a certain time frame, into hatred of society, then hatred of the human race, then hatred of creation" (1127). When he finally becomes free, hatred is his guiding principle; in terms of his character, he is as far from the love that motivated his stealing the bread as he is close to murdering the bishop. Valjean moves from being a character who loves to one who hates, and in this, Hugo depicts the degree to which a person's character and temperament can be manipulated and transformed by the pressures and events of society.
   a. **Further Reading:** Roche, Isabel. *Character and Meaning in the Novels of Victor Hugo*. West Lafayette, IN: Purdue University Press, 2007.
   b. **Suggested Search:** A JSTOR search (www.jstor.org) for "Jean Valjean's character" results in several interesting articles.

2. **A central theme throughout all of *Les Misérables* is that society's responsible for much of the evil and suffering that occurs, most especially among the impoverished classes.** Hugo emphasizes that Valjean is not a vicious or law-breaking man by nature, and that he was more than willing to work. He writes that it was "a serious matter to start with that he, who was a worker, lacked work; that he, who was industrious, lacked bread" (1123). Yet further, it was society's overbearing and disproportionate punishment that created a man driven by hate instead of love, and who was more criminally inclined than otherwise at the end of his sentence. As Valjean ruminates, "human society had only ever done him harm. Never had he seen anything of it but this wrathful face that it calls Justice and that it shows to those it strikes. People had only ever touched him to wound him. All contact with them had been, for him, a blow" (1123). Society itself, through its brutality

and inhuman blindness to the plight of the poor, is responsible for many of the evils that readers find in Hugo's book.

   a. **Further Reading:** Brombert, Victor. *Victor Hugo and the Visionary Novel*. Cambridge, MA: Harvard University Press, 1984.

   b. **Suggested Search:** A Google Images search for "Émile Bayard Les Misérables" results in several images of Bayard's famous illustrations of characters from Hugo's novel. His illustration of young Cosette is most famous.

3. **While *Les Misérables* indicts society as a whole for the injustices that Jean Valjean endures, Hugo's novel is particularly critical of cities as the central focus point and breeding ground for the evil workings of corrupt societies.** Many examples of this critique of cities are apparent in later sections of the novel, but the excerpts included in our anthology clearly introduce this theme. For example, when discussing the difference between a poacher and a thief, Hugo writes, "there is still a gulf between this species of men [i.e. poachers and smugglers] and the murderous city-dwelling criminal. The poacher lives in the forest; the smuggler lives in the mountains or by the sea. Cities turn out ferocious men because they make men corrupt. The mountains, the sea, the forest, make men wild. They bring out the fierce side of human nature but often without destroying the human side" (1120). Without idealizing the characters of men who live closer to nature, Hugo argues that cities present a profound danger in that they can actually eradicate the human, or humane, part of one's being.

   a. **Further Reading:** Grossman, Kathryn M. *Figuring Transcendence in* Les Misérables. Carbondale, IL: Southern Illinois University Press, 1994.

   b. **Suggested Search:** A search on the Britannica Encyclopedia Academic Edition website for "Victor Hugo" results in a helpful entry with many interesting links.

4. **In our selection from *Les Misérables*, Jean Valjean's reaction to the tremendous injustices he endures is to reject the idea of a benevolent God.** Hugo writes that Valjean did acknowledge that he was not an innocent man, and that he did deserve punishment, but that he also understood quite clearly that his punishment did not fit his crime, and that society's conspicuous lack of justice was a greater problem than his having stolen a loaf of bread. The absence of justice in a social system with such immense coercive force led Valjean to conclude that not only was society to blame, but that God, too, must be responsible. Hugo writes, "He passed judgment on the Providence that had brought about that society. He condemned it, too" (1124). Notably, the effective theodicy that he encounters is the charitable and forgiving attitude of the bishop, and while the outcome of this encounter is not included in our

selection of the text, Valjean's opinion about God's nature is changed once more by the goodness of the bishop.

    a. **Further Reading:** Gasbarrone, Lisa. "Restoring the Sacred in *Les Misérables*." *Religion & Literature* 40:2 (2008): 1–24.

    b. **Suggested Search:** A YouTube search for "Les Misérables bishop" results in several clips and a soundtrack recording of the scenes between Valjean and the bishop from the musical adaptation of Hugo's novel, *Les Misérables*.

5. **As an extended metaphor, "Book VIII: The Dark and the Deep" is an excellent example of Hugo's typical variation of style and mode of progression and digression throughout *Les Misérables*.** The chapter begins by grabbing the reader's attention with the urgent phrases, "Man overboard! Who cares! The ship does not stop" (1127). The ship is representative of society, and the man who has fallen off is likened to Valjean. Hugo's comparison is particularly striking because ships are, for the most part, under human control, and by implication, society is as well. But just as this ship does not turn back for the man who fell off, neither does society help a man who falls. As the man gradually loses strength and drowns, Hugo elaborates upon the desperation and loneliness of the man condemned to an unjust sentence and left without recourse when released. The full rhetorical pathos of Hugo's prose is evident at the conclusion of the chapter, as he declares, "O relentless march of human society! All the men and souls lost along the way, written off! Ocean into which all those that the law drops, fall! Vile withdrawal of all help! O moral death!" (1128).

    a. **Further Reading:** Masters-Wicks, Karen. *Victor Hugo's Les Misérables and the Novels of the Grotesque*. Bern: Peter Lang Publishing, 1994.

    b. **Suggested Search:** A search for "Victor Hugo Timeline" at the BBC website (www.bbc.co.uk) results in a helpful timeline detailing important evens in Hugo's life.

In-Class Activities

1. Play a film clip of the musical *Les Misérables* that corresponds with the selection in our anthology to the class. Use this to begin a discussion of the ways in which Hugo's novel is followed by the musical, and if the differences between the two are important.

2. Ask your students to write their own character sketches of Jean Valjean, and to share what they have written with a partner. Then as a class discuss the ways in which Hugo carefully delineates the changes that Valjean undergoes.

3. Find a student who can read French if you are not able to, and ask him/her to read a selection of Hugo's original to the class. Take this opportunity

to emphasize the remarkable differences in Hugo's sentence structures and the unusual rhythm of his language.

Paper Topics/Suggestions for Writing

1. Write a journal entry in which you consider Hugo's use of time in his narrative. At what points does he compress time, and when does he expand it? How does time relate to his characters, especially Jean Valjean?

2. Using the library resources that you are given access to, write a research paper that investigates the political and social situation of France during the time period that Hugo writes about (*note*: do not research the time when Hugo lived, but the historical period in which the story takes place, 1815–1832).

3. Write a paper in which you evaluate Hugo's critique of society and penal systems in *Les Misérables*. What is his strongest point? At which point is his rhetoric or condemnation most powerful? What is his weakest point? Is he, finally, convincing? What is the essence of the problem that he is attacking?

4. In a reflective essay that builds upon your reaction to the events in *Les Misérables*, discuss justice and its relationship to law, criminals, and society. Be sure to formulate a definition of justice that would correspond with the sentiments expressed in Hugo's novel.

5. Write a comparative essay in which you identify a central theme that is in both Hugo's novel and the musical adaptation of *Les Misérables*. How does the musical/movie change or develop the theme what we also find in the novel? What are the limitations and advantages of both mediums in relation to this theme?

6. Compare Hugo's *Les Misérables* to either Voltaire's *Candide* or Gustave Flaubert's *Madame Bovary*. What important ideas or themes do these French writers share? In what important ways do they differ? Is their common nationality apparent in these works?

Resources

Blackmore, E. H., and A. M. Blackmore, trans. *The Essential Victor Hugo*. Oxford: Oxford University Press, 2004.
> This volume offers a good and wide-ranging selection from Hugo's many other works, and is a helpful resource for students and instructors wishing to read further.

Les Misérables. Dir. Tom Hooper. Perf. Hugh Jackman, Russell Crowe, Anne Hathaway. Universal, 2012. Film.

A recent hit that many of your students have probably seen, this rendition of the musical is a fine substitute if your students are not able to find a stage production to watch.

Robb, Graham. *Victor Hugo: A Biography.* New York: W. W. Norton, 1998.
This is an accessible and informative biography of Hugo, and while it is lengthy (more than 600 pages with the notes), it has a helpful index and manageable chapter sizes, so students and instructors should be able to find information with ease.

Roche, Isabel. *Character and Meaning in the Novels of Victor Hugo.* West Lafayette, IN: Purdue University Press, 2007.
While this volume might prove difficult for some students, it is especially recommended for instructors because it not only considers Hugo's characters with respect to the general thought of his works, but it also situates them within the larger tradition and developments of the French novel.

FYODOR DOSTOYEVSKY
Notes from Underground

Topics for Lecture or Discussion

1. In *Notes from Underground*, Fyodor Dostoyevsky's narrator is critical of Jean-Jacques Rousseau's *Confessions*. The narrator attempts to avoid the problems he sees with Rousseau's *Confessions* only to highlight those same problems with autobiography that he tried to move beyond. Near the end of part one of *Notes from Underground*, the narrator mentions Heinrich Heine's critique of Rousseau's *Confessions*. Heine critiqued Rousseau for being unable to be truthful about either his actions or his character, claiming that vanity would ultimately influence any public confession. The narrator of *Notes from Underground* claims to get around this problem with confessions because his narrative is for himself, with his audience being a purely imaginary construction. Rousseau's audience, though, was also an imaginary construction, as is the audience of any book, since the audience is absent during the writing of the text. The distinction between these two imaginary audiences is, then, a rhetorical distinction. The rhetorical distinction between audiences is set up by the author to combat the problematic rhetoric of the confession, and critic Barbara F. Howard notes that this forms the "central paradox of the *Notes*" where the use of rhetoric to combat rhetoric threatens to deprive Underground Man's experiment of its validity, transforming it into the very thing he wishes to reject" (484). Instead of the narrator's honesty being reinforced, the novel's paradox emphasizes how questionable his account is as part of a caricature of the narrator of Rousseau's *Confessions*.

   a. **Further Reading:** Howard, Barbara F. "The Rhetoric of Confession: Dostoevskij's *Notes from Underground* and Rousseau's *Confessions*." In *Critical Essays on Dostoevsky*, edited by Robin Feuer Miller, 64–72. Boston: G. K. Hall and Co., 1986.

   b. **Suggested Search:** The website www.fyodordostoevsky.com has numerous resources related to Fyodor Dostoyevsky, including a selection of images, selections from Dostoyevsky's work, and additional links to other Dostoyevsky-related websites.

2. While the narrator of *Notes from Underground* reacts viciously and negatively toward other characters in the narrative, the style and structure of the short novel are influenced by the narrator's antagonistic relationship with his imagined audience. The narrator of *Notes from Underground* relates his story with the awareness that his actions will be viewed negatively by his society. Since a text about an

individual, an individual's psychological makeup, and an individual's unpleasant actions is most often a confession, the narrator feels the need to insist that his text is not a confession. The critic Mikhail Bakhtin writes about the narrator: "More than anything else he fears that people will think that he is repenting before another person, that he is asking someone's forgiveness, that he is submitting to someone's judgment or assessment, that his self-affirmation is in need of confirmation and recognition by another person. And it is in this direction that he anticipates the other person's reply" (192). By stating his actions without the intent of confessing them, the narrator ignores his audience's ethical response, but by claiming that he is ignoring that response, the narrator is simultaneously anticipating what he must ignore. The narrator's aggressive posture, claim to ignore his audience, and ongoing anticipation all create the novel's distinctive style and illustrate his extreme psychology.

   a. **Further Reading:** Bakhtin, Mikhail. *Problems of Dostoevsky's Poetics.* Translated by R. W. Rotsel. Ann Arbor, MI: Ardis, 1973.

   b. **Suggested Search:** Mikhail Bakhtin is one of the most important literary critics of the twentieth century, and Fyodor Dostoyevsky's fiction was of central importance to him. For a good introduction to Bakhtin, see the "Mikhail Bakhtin" entry at the *Internet Encyclopedia of Philosophy*, www.iep.utm.edu/bakhtin.

3. **Throughout part two of *Notes from Underground*, the narrator attempts to gain freedom through willful antisocial actions but instead is faced with a social reality that he cannot escape.** From his attempt to be recognized by the officer he bumps into to the billiard player he attempts to get into a fight with, part two of *Notes from Underground* begins with a series of actions where the narrator attempts to will those around him into acting in accordance with his own desires. This begins the narrator's continual failure throughout the novel's second section to gain freedom by willing society to change its course. As the narrative progresses, it also becomes clear that the narrator has no freedom over his own actions either: he is compelled to act against the societal norm with his consistent negations being as predictable as any societal norm.

   a. **Further Reading:** Jackson, Robert Louis. "Aristotelian Movement and Design in Part Two of *Notes from Underground*." In *Dostoyevsky: New Perspectives*, 66–81. Englewood Cliffs, NJ: Prentice Hall, 1984.

   b. **Suggested Search:** The Museum of Russian Art at tmora.org has a number of visual resources, including an exhibit of photographs of St. Petersburg, the city in which the action of *Notes from Underground* occurs. This exhibit is titled "Imperial St. Petersburg: Architectural Visions" and can be found under the "Online Exhibits" subheading of the "Exhibitions" tab on the main page.

4. **By choosing *Notes from Underground* to be narrated in the first person by an unreliable narrator, Fyodor Dostoyevsky foregrounds his story as a monologue.** While even an omniscient, third-person narration demonstrates the narrator's bias, based on aspects of the narrative such as word choice and which details are chosen or left out, the narrator's inevitable biases can be foregrounded by an unreliable narrator. Among the aspects that are foregrounded by Dostoyevsky's narrator are some aspects often foregrounded in a spoken dramatic monologue: the narrator's desires and stylistic speech. By being unreliable, the *Notes from Underground* narrator's word choices and style of speech increase in importance, showing how the narrator interprets the world, transforming the word and his desires on the world into the language of his narrative.

   a. **Further Reading:** Erlich, Victor. "Uses of Monologue in Artistic Prose." In *Notes from Underground*, edited by Michael R. Katz, 178–85. New York: W. W. Norton & Company, 1998.

   b. **Suggested Search:** To emphasize the ways in which *Notes from Underground* functions as a monologue, hearing the selections of the story as an audiobook may be useful. A free audio recording of *Notes from Underground* can be found by doing a search for the title on the LibriVox website at librivox.org.

5. **Fyodor Dostoyevsky's *Notes from Underground* satirizes Nikolai Chernyshevsky's novel *What Is to Be Done?*, rewriting Chernyshevsky's hope for a "new man" in society to usher in a new age as the warped, self-conscious Underground Man.** Chernyshevsky's novel responds to the turmoil of nineteenth-century Russia with a call to revolution through his idealized characters, imagining a new kind of man and woman is coming into existence in society. The Underground Man is a satire of this new man whom Chernyshevsky envisions. Critic Jane Barstow writes of the novel's narrator, "He is intelligent, he is logical, he likes to talk about himself, he is self-indulgent, and he desires freedom; these are all characteristics of Chernyshevsky's 'new men'" (25). While Chernyshevsky sees society moving toward positive progress, the thoroughly contemporary narrator of *Notes from Underground* shows society to have moved toward sickly self-consciousness and an inability to act effectively in the world.

   a. **Further Reading:** Barstow, Jane. "Dostoyevsky's *Notes from Underground* versus Chernyshevsky's *What Is to Be Done?*" *College Literature* 5:1 (1978): 24–33.

   b. **Suggested Search:** Scanned images of the entirety of Nikolai Chernyshevsky's *What Is to Be Done?* can be found online at the Internet Archive's website, archive.org. A search for "What Is to Be Done?" (in quotations) and the author's name will lead to the online copy of the novel, titled *A Vital Question: What Is to Be Done?*

In-Class Activities

1. How does Fyodor Dostoyevsky use a demented character to comment on the nature of modern humanity?

2. *Notes from Underground* was written after Fyodor Dostoyevsky turned toward conservative politics and became critical of the influence of Western European philosophy in Russia. What in *Notes from Underground* reflects Dostoyevsky's views? How might the story have been different if written by Dostoyevsky earlier in his life?

3. Why might Fyodor Dostoyevsky choose to not name his narrator in *Notes from Underground*? How did this choice affect your reading of the story?

Paper Topics/Suggestions for Writing

1. Compare and contrast Fyodor Dostoyevsky's *Notes from Underground* with Leo Tolstoy's *The Death of Ivan Ilyich*. In what ways are the two authors' critiques of Russian society similar, and in what ways are they different?

2. Write an essay on the Underground Man's relationship with his audience in *Notes from Underground*. Why is it necessary for such an antisocial character to imagine an audience in order to write? How does his erratic behavior affect his credibility with an audience?

3. Both the Underground Man of *Notes from Underground* and Jean-Jacques Rousseau in his *Confessions* are highly self-conscious narrators. Compare and contrast the narrators of the two works, focusing on how each narrator's self-conscious nature affects his ability to take action.

4. While Gustave Flaubert strove toward an impersonal style in works like *A Simple Heart*, Fyodor Dostoyevsky took an entirely different tactic in *Notes from Underground* and wrote from the viewpoint of a character whose strong opinions affect every moment in the text. Write a paper that examines how the viewpoint affects each work. What does each choice allow the audience to see, and what does each choice withhold from the audience?

5. The narrator's attempt to follow his old classmates led him to the brothel where he meets the prostitute Liza. Write a paper on the effect of the juxtaposed scenes of the narrator with his classmates and the narrator with Liza. Examine the contrasts between these scenes, including the public interactions with his classmates and the private interactions with Liza.

Resources

Gide, André. *Dostoyevsky.* New York: New Directions, 1961.
>This work contains critical writings on Fyodor Dostoyevsky by one of France's major twentieth-century novelists.

Murry, John Middleton. *Fyodor Dostoyevsky: A Critical Study.* New York: Russell & Russell, 1966.
>This work contains critical writings on Fyodor Dostoyevsky by an influential, early twentieth-century English critic.

Paris, Bernard J. *Dostoyevsky's Greatest Characters: A New Approach to* Notes from Underground, Crime and Punishment, *and* The Brothers Karamazov. New York: Palgrave Macmillan, 2008.
>This is a critical examination of Fyodor Dostoyevsky's memorable characters, covering not only the narrator of *Notes from Underground* but also the character Liza.

GUSTAVE FLAUBERT

Madame Bovary

Topics for Lecture or Discussion

1. ***Madame Bovary* is an important, foundational text in the development of literary realism in fiction, and one of the ways that Flaubert's realism is most apparent is his choice and depiction of the characters in the novel.** To demonstrate the striking difference between Flaubert's realism and early forms of romanticism, it is often helpful to draw students' attention back to the medieval romance of *The Story of the Grail* by Chrétien de Troyes (which is included in Volume 1 of this anthology). Chrétien's characters are kings, lords, knights, and ladies, and his central character Percival is a man of superlative martial ability and strength, despite the fact that he is found living in obscurity and ignorance at the beginning of the story. In *Madame Bovary*, however, Flaubert intentionally focuses upon realistic characters that live in a small provincial town, who do not rise from their obscurity, and who are not superlative in any way. Indeed, even Emma's adulterous affair is local and unremarkable (at least compared to the tumult caused by affairs like that between Guinevere and Lancelot). Almost paradoxically, Flaubert's characters are interesting because they are *not* superlative or exceptional.

   a. **Further Reading:** Tilby, Michael. "Flaubert's Place in Literary History." In *The Cambridge Companion to Flaubert*, edited by Timothy Unwin, 14–33. Cambridge: Cambridge University Press, 2004.

   b. **Suggested Search:** A search for "realism" at "The Literature Network" (http://www.online-literature.com) results in a helpful discussion of realism and several links describing the works of major realist authors, including Flaubert.

2. **Another aspect of Flaubert's realism in *Madame Bovary* is the detached, observant tone of the narrator in describing the story's events and the passions that the characters feel.** One striking example is during Emma's funeral. While Charles is sorrowful, and many of the other townspeople are being critical or inconsiderate, the narrator withholds any tones of sympathy or judgment. In language that is beautiful and precise but more diagnostic than sympathetic, the narrator describes Justin's sorrow over Emma's grave, writing, "On the grave, among the pines, a boy was kneeling and crying, and his heart, broken with sobbing, throbbed in the darkness under the pressure of an immense regret, sweeter than the moon and deeper than the night" (1430). Justin, who had inadvertently provided the means of his beloved's death, is

simply described, and nothing in the narrator's tone indicates appro-
bation or commiseration. This should be held in contrast to the passionate, evaluative expressions and descriptions in such works as
Henry Fielding's *Tom Jones*, Victor Hugo's *Les Misérables*, (excerpted
in Volume 2 of this anthology) or more subtly, Jane Austen's *Pride and
Prejudice*.

   a. **Further Reading:** Culler, Jonathan D. "The Realism of Madame
Bovary." *Modern Language Notes* 122:4 (2007): 683–696.

   b. **Suggested Search:** At www.schmoop.com, a search for "Madame
Bovary" will result in a helpful page with a series of links, including
interactive quizzes and study flashcards for the students.

3. **As a character whose imagination and understanding is profoundly
turned by the books that she reads, Emma Bovary's most famous
literary ancestor is Don Quixote, the hero of Cervantes's famous
novel of the same name.** In both *Don Quixote* and *Madame Bovary*, the
central characters become swept away by the works of the literature
that they read, and in both cases, the characters respond to the literature
by dramatically changing the ways in which they live. Despite these
similarities, however, there are several important differences as well.
For example, Don Quixote's mind is turned by reading romances (c.f.
Chrétien de Troyes' *The Story of the Grail* in this anthology), but Emma's
mind is turned by, among other things, Balzac, who was an important
figure in the development of realism. As Flaubert writes, "she read Balzac
and George Sand, seeking in their books the vicarious satisfaction of
her own desires. She took her book with her even to the table, and she
would turn the pages while Charles ate and talked to her" (1253). The
final sentence of this quotation points toward one more fundamental
difference between Don Quixote and Emma Bovary: while Don Quixote's reading renders him desirous of helping others and of living by an
honorable and charitable code, Emma's reading makes her progressively more selfish and focused upon accomplishing her own pleasure
and will.

   a. **Further Reading:** Fox, Soledad. *Flaubert and Don Quixote: The
Influence of Cervantes on* Madame Bovary. Eastbourne, UK: Sussex
Academic Press, 2008.

   b. **Suggested Search:** At YouTube, search for "Madame Bovary 1949"
to find the full film of Vincente Minnelli's adaptation of the book.
Jennifer Jones plays Emma Bovary.

4. **When Flaubert was on trial for the morally dubious nature of
Madame Bovary, his defense argued that the story serves as a warning against adulterers; after all, Emma dies in the end. The moral
ambiguity of the narrator's tone, however, belies such a simple
reading.** For example, when Emma begins to be disillusioned about her

affair with Rudolphe, and as she realizes that their relationship was not the profound union of two people perfectly in love with each other, the narrator's detached tone withholds any moral commentary. He writes, "She didn't know whether she regretted having yielded to him or whether, on the contrary, she wanted only to love him more. The humiliation of sensing her own weakness turned into a resentment that was only tempered by voluptuous pleasures. This was not an attachment; it was more like a continuous seduction. It subjugated her. She was almost afraid of it" (1323). Conspicuously absent is any authorial comment that such disillusionment is the way of all adulterers, or that Emma's devotion to voluptuous pleasures was reprehensible. In simply describing her changing attitudes toward her lover, Flaubert withholds language that might indicate his opinion regarding her behavior, thereby making ambiguous his position on its morality.

    a. **Further Reading:** Porter, Laurence M. "The Art of Characterization in Flaubert's Fiction." In *The Cambridge Companion to Flaubert*, edited by Timothy Unwin, 122–144. Cambridge: Cambridge University Press, 2004.

    b. **Suggested Search:** Search for "Madame Bovary" at LibriVox (http://librivox.org) results in a link to listen to Flaubert's novel read in French (this is suggested so that students might hear the flow of Flaubert's original language).

5. **Despite her best efforts, nearly everything that Emma Bovary plans and does comes to a different conclusion than that which she had intended.** While Emma's marriage, her love affairs, and her exaggerated ideas about romance and money are spectacular disasters, even her suicide is a pathetic attempt to take control of things that do not go as she planned. After eating the arsenic, Emma thinks, "Ah! Death isn't such a difficult thing! . . . I'm going to go to sleep, and it will all be over!" (1414). In contrast to this pleasant thought of a quiet death, Emma's screams wake the whole neighborhood, and she undergoes tremendous suffering while being an object of public attention as she slowly and miserably dies. Even her suicide note is read long before she is dead, but after she is beyond help. Emma's final moments encapsulate in miniature many of the aspects of her whole life: her selfish behavior is mistaken and absurd, causes great suffering for others including especially her family, and is a public spectacle. Her lack of control over most things in part reflects the limitations that were placed upon women in this period, but it also demonstrates Flaubert's skepticism regarding sentimentality and intentionality.

    a. **Further Reading:** Vargas Llosa, Mario. *The Perpetual Orgy: Flaubert and Madame Bovary.* Trans. Helen Lane. New York: Farrar, Straus, Giroux, 1986.

b. **Suggested Search:** A YouTube search for "An Evening of Madame Bovary with Lydia Davis" results in a reading and discussion with Lydia Davis, who has recently translated *Madame Bovary* and who speaks of the difficulties of rendering Flaubert's precise language in a different tongue.

6. **Part of the reason for Emma's ongoing unhappiness in the first half of the novel is due to her discontent with having to live in a small country town; her unhappiness with the country reflects the growing influence of the wealth, goods, and styles of cities in the nineteenth century.** Emma's active imagination and her continual reading make her well aware of the advantages of living in a city, though as she does with her romantic encounters, she idealizes the city and demonizes the country life. In presenting Emma thus, Flaubert captures an attention to, and envy of, city dwellers that was growing throughout the European countryside during and after the Industrial Revolution. Similarly, Emma's acquisitiveness and imitation of urban fashions demonstrates the extent to which a person in an excellent position in a small town could, nevertheless, be restless and feel deprived of common goods.

a. **Further Reading:** Merriman, John M. *The Margins of City Life: Explorations on the French Urban Frontier, 1815–1851.* Oxford: Oxford University Press, 1991.

b. **Suggested Search:** A Google Images search for "Gustave Flaubert" results in several paintings and photographs of the author.

In-Class Activities

1. Watch one of the film versions of *Madame Bovary* and ask each student to write a review of the movie. Each student must evaluate the film in terms of its own artistic qualities and in the ways it is successful or not at adapting Flaubert's novel.

2. Ask each student to write on an index card a list of the four most important adjectives that describe Emma Bovary. Collect these cards, shuffle them, and then redistribute them randomly to the class. Ask the students to read the new adjectives that they have been given, and to share with the class which adjective they disagree with most, giving a reasoned argument that is based upon passages from the text. Then, as a class, try to come to an agreement about the four most accurate adjectives from those that were written.

3. Read a passage of the original French to the class (or ask a student or colleague if you are unable) while your students follow along in their English translations. Use this as an opening for a discussion about the limitations (and advantages?) of reading works in translation.

4. After dividing your class into two groups, hold a formal debate in which one side must contend that Victor Hugo's *Les Misérables* is superior to Flaubert's *Madame Bovary*, and the other side must contend the opposite. Use this debate as an opportunity to emphasize the tremendous difference of tone in the narratives of the two works.

Paper Topics/Suggestions for Writing

1. Write a character analysis of Emma Bovary. What is her greatest strength/virtue? What is her greatest weakness/vice? In what things is she successful and in what things does she fail? Is she an admirable character? Pitiable? Likable? How does she change over the course of the novel?

2. Write a character analysis of Charles Bovary. What is his greatest strength/virtue? What is his greatest weakness/vice? In what things is he successful and in what things does he fail? Is he an admirable character? Pitiable? Likable? How does he change over the course of the novel?

3. Construct a definition of love, drawing upon characters and events in *Madame Bovary*. Which characters love, and what or who do they love? Is love a good thing? Is it the cause of good things? Or is it a burden, and the cause of sorrow? What is the role of love in the society that we find in *Madame Bovary*?

4. Using resources in your library and online, write a research essay about the culture of France during the historical period in which *Madame Bovary* is set. What is the relationship between the major cities and the surrounding towns and countryside? What impact did the Industrial Revolution have upon French culture, society, and fashions? In what ways are the changes that occur during this period reflected in *Madame Bovary*?

5. Write an essay in which you compare Emma Bovary to at least one other significant woman character in another work that you have read for this class. How do these characters represent women's roles in society during those times? In what ways are these women admirable? In what ways are they similar to one another? Are there significant differences in their roles?

6. Consider the shifting perspective of the narrator in *Madame Bovary*, and write an essay in which you identify at least three different moments when the narrative perspective is both important and unusual. How does the narrator's tone, distance, and moral ambiguity affect one's reading of *Madame Bovary*?

7. Write an essay in which you analyze *Madame Bovary* as a foundational work within the tradition of literary realism. What are the primary ways in which this text exhibits realism? In what ways does this text not correspond with the prescriptions of later theorists and authors of realism?

Resources

Flaubert, Gustave. *Three Tales*. Trans. A.J. Krailsheimer. Oxford: Oxford University Press, 1991.

> This short volume contains three of Flaubert's shorter works, including his historical story "Herodias," and students as well as instructors are encouraged to read this to gain a further appreciation for Flaubert's range and style as a writer.

Madame Bovary. Dir. Vincente Minnelli. Perf. Jennifer Jones. MGM, 1949. Film.

> This is an excellent, black-and-white adaptation of Flaubert's novel, though at almost two hours in length, it will usually take two class periods to watch the complete film.

Steegmuller, Francis. *Flaubert and Madame Bovary: A Double Portrait*. Introduction by Victor Brombert. New York: New York Review of Books, 2004.

> This is a reprinting of Steegmuller's classic biography of Flaubert that situates the artist in relation to *Madame Bovary*. Steegmuller is particularly helpful for demonstrating the ways in which Flaubert used real, historical situations as inspirations and models for parts of his book.

Unwin, Timothy. *The Cambridge Companion to Flaubert*. Cambridge: Cambridge University Press, 2004.

> This collection of essays provides a good overview of Flaubert's writing, style, thought, and historical context. It also contains essays that examine his influence and reception following his death.

Vargas Llosa, Mario. *The Perpetual Orgy: Flaubert and* Madame Bovary. Trans. Helen Lane. New York: Farrar, Straus, Giroux, 1986.

> This classic essay is an interesting and provocative consideration of *Madame Bovary* taken by itself and within the context of its literary tradition. Students interested in Emma Bovary as an antihero should begin with Vargas Llosa's work.

LEO TOLSTOY

The Death of Ivan Ilyich

Topics for Lecture or Discussion

1. **The theme of death is treated in many different ways throughout *The Death of Ivan Ilyich*.** At the beginning of the story, death is treated as a distant event that is important because of the changes it can cause in other people's careers (1441). It is also treated as an opportunity for gain for the family (1445–1446) and a reassuring event for those that didn't die and are in good health (1442). However, at the end of the first chapter, Gerasim describes death as a universal fact, saying, "It's God's will. We'll all be there" (1446), and this more serious understanding of death—as something that all must endure—is explored in great detail in the remainder of the story. Death is, paradoxically, the most effective way for a person to understand his life, since it forces Ivan to look back at his past, rather than forward toward his ambitions.

    a. **Further Reading:** Pachmuss, Temira. "The Theme of Love and Death in Tolstoy's *The Death of Ivan Ilyich*." *American Slavic and East European Review*. 20.1 (1961): 72–83.

    b. **Suggested Search:** A YouTube search for "The Death of Ivan Ilyich Andrew Kaufman" results in a short talk by Dr. Kaufman about Tolstoy's story, encouraging people to read more Tolstoy.

2. ***The Death of Ivan Ilyich* carefully depicts the way in which Ivan's coming death gives him the opportunity to realize finally that he has not led a good life, and that despite the propriety which he has always followed, he has not been a good person.** Notably, Ivan's reflections upon his past life are one of the positive effects of his slow death. Initially, Ivan meditates upon his life with an urgent desire to live, but as his condition worsens, even the memories that he had cherished become tarnished. Yet, as Tolstoy writes, "And when there came to him the thought, as it did often, that all this was happening because he had lived wrongly, he at once remembered all the correctness of his life and rejected this strange thought" (1474). Convinced of his own rectitude at the beginning of his illness, he refuses even to consider whether he had been a good person. However, because his death lingers, because he suffers greatly, and because Gerasim's charity is so overwhelming, Ivan eventually does realize his own culpability, and he dies with the recognition that he had been wrong.

    a. **Further Reading:** Shepherd, David. "Conversion, Reversion and Subversion in Tolstoi's *The Death of Ivan Il'ich*." *The Slavonic and East European Review* 71.3 (1993): 401–416.

b. **Suggested Search:** A search for "The last days of Leo Tolstoy" at Open Culture (http://www.openculture.com) results in a page with several links and an excerpt from a documentary that shows film of Tolstoy shortly before he died.

3. **By the time he wrote *The Death of Ivan Ilyich*, Tolstoy firmly held the idea that Russia's peasants (or serfs) were both more virtuous and happier than the wealthier classes, and this belief is readily apparent in the story.** On the one hand, everyone in the story who belongs to the wealthier classes is depicted as unsatisfied and always seeking promotion or some further personal advantage. Until late in his illness, Ivan clearly belongs to this group, and he is restless and preoccupied by a selfish focus on his own desires. Gerasim, a peasant, stands in contrast to the unhappiness and self-serving ways of Ivan, his family, and his colleagues. Gerasim is always described as cheerful and good-natured, and he is so genuine that he even wins Ivan's goodwill. For example, Tolstoy writes, "From that day Ivan Ilyich started sometimes to call Gerasim in to him and made him hold up his legs on his shoulders and he liked to talk to him. Gerasim did this easily, willingly, simply, and with a goodness of heart which touched Ivan Ilyich. In all other people Ivan Ilyich was offended by health, strength, high spirits; only Gerasim's strength and high spirits didn't depress but calmed Ivan Ilyich" (1467). Ivan's gradual realization about Gerasim's fidelity and happiness mirrors Tolstoy's own growing conviction about the virtue of the serfs, and through the contrast of the selfishness and vice of the other characters in the story, the reader is encouraged to reach a similar conclusion.

a. **Further Reading:** Tolstoy, Alexandra. "Tolstoy and the Russian Peasant." *Russian Review* 19.2 (1960): 150–156.

b. **Suggested Search:** At Open Yale Courses (http://oyc.yale.edu), a search for "Shelly Kagan Lecture 16 Dying Alone" results in an interesting lecture about death, and it includes many references to Tolstoy's story.

4. **In conjunction with Tolstoy's praise of the peasants, he was also an outspoken critic of government; this, too, is apparent in *The Death of Ivan Ilyich*.** Ivan is himself a government man, and his ambition, self-centeredness, and disregard even for the happiness of his own family are all elements that are indicative of the sort of government for which he works. His colleagues, moreover, are not distraught by the news of Ivan's death; rather, as Tolstoy writes, "on hearing of Ivan Ilyich's death the first thought of each of the gentlemen meeting in the room was of the significance the death might have for the transfer or promotion of the members themselves or their friends" (1441). Other negative aspects of the government include many references to the fact that promotions are gained through friendship and connections, not through merit, and that

the pension system is corrupted and manipulated by the greed of the government officials' families as well as their own.

   a. **Further Reading:** Moss, Walter G. *Russia in the Age of Alexander II, Tolstoy, and Dostoevsky.* London: Anthem Press, 2002.

   b. **Suggested Search:** A YouTube search for "The Trouble with Leo Tolstoy 1: At War with Himself" results in an interesting documentary discussing the development of Tolstoy's political and religious ideas.

5. **Ivan Ilyich's attention to the proper appearance of things rather than their moral worth prevents him from leading a life of meaningful actions.** While this is apparent in his earlier life, it is particularly striking when Ivan lies on his deathbed. Preparing to die but not reconciled with death, Ivan goes through the proper motion of receiving the sacraments of confession and communion. These sacraments do not demarcate a significant change in his attitude, however; and while he is briefly comforted, as soon as he sees his wife, he is filled with hatred: "Her clothes, her body, the expression of her face, the sound of her voice—everything said to him one thing: 'Wrong. Everything by which you have lived and are living is a lie, a fraud, concealing life and death from you.' And as soon as he thought that, hatred rose up in him" (1477). Ivan despises his wife because she does not have the same understanding of life and death that he does, and his self-centered attitude works against his religious preparations for death. Rather than receiving the sacraments in a sincere, meaningful manner that would render him charitably disposed, he only performs the outward show of religious action, and returns to his hatred nearly at once.

   a. **Further Reading:** Medzhibovskaya, Inessa. *Tolstoy and the Religious Culture of His Time: A Biography of a Long Conversion, 1845–1885.* Lanham, MD: Lexington Books, 2008.

   b. **Suggested Search:** A Google Images search for "Leo Tolstoy" results in many photographs and paintings of the author.

In-Class Activities

1. Ask each student to choose another work in which a death occurs from among the works that he or she has read for this class, and to make a small chart that denotes the similarities and differences in the ways in which death is treated.

2. Divide the students into small research groups, and assign them topics that they must research, followed by a brief presentation. Some possible topics include: *War and Peace*; *Anna Karenina*; Tolstoy and government; Tolstoy and religion; Tolstoy and war; Tolstoy and the serfs; nineteenth-century Russian politics; Tolstoy and Dostoevsky; Tolstoy and French authors, etc.

3. As a creative exercise, ask your students to rewrite the conclusion of the story in such a way that Ivan recovers. Share some of these rewrites with the class, and promote a discussion of whether or not Ivan would be a different person after his recovery.

Paper Topics/Suggestions for Writing

1. Write a journal entry that identifies at least three different ways that death is mentioned in *The Death of Ivan Ilyich*, and discuss the significance of each.

2. Why does Ivan Ilyich become distant from his family? What are the character flaws that make him so unloving toward his family? Does he redeem his relationship or attitude toward his family before he dies?

3. Write a research essay about Tolstoy's attitude toward government, and connect this discussion to aspects of *The Death of Ivan Ilyich*. You might also incorporate discussion of Tolstoy's fellow writers and their skepticism of government as well.

4. Write an essay that compares Tolstoy's Ivan Ilyich to the unnamed narrator in Dostoevsky's *Notes from Underground*. What are the relative strengths and weaknesses of the two characters? In what respects do they change over the course of their respective stories?

5. Consider the role of time in *The Death of Ivan Ilyich*. How does it function in relation to the narrative? How does it function in relation to Ivan?

6. Write a paper that compares Tolstoy's *The Death of Ivan Ilyich* to Melville's *Bartleby, the Scrivener* (in Volume 2 of this anthology). Both are stories that depict work and death, and both stories raise questions about social propriety and responsibility. How does Melville's narration of death differ from Tolstoy's? What important similarities and differences are there in the two accounts about people and the work that they do?

Resources

Bartlett, Rosamund. *Tolstoy: A Russian Life*. New York: Houghton Mifflin Harcourt Publishing, 2011.
> While this biography is over five hundred pages long, and thus cannot be easily read for class preparation, the later chapters that cover the period when Tolstoy wrote *The Death of Ivan Ilyich* are recommended. There is also a helpful and recent bibliography in the back of the book.

Medzhibovskaya, Inessa. *Tolstoy and the Religious Culture of His Time: A Biography of a Long Conversion, 1845–1885*. Lanham, MD: Lexington Books, 2008.

This volume is extremely helpful in demonstrating the ways in which *The Death of Ivan Ilyich* fits within Tolstoy's evolving religious ideas.

Moss, Walter G. *Russia in the Age of Alexander II, Tolstoy, and Dostoevsky.* London: Anthem Press, 2002.

Moss' work does a good job of introducing readers to the historical and political contexts in which Tolstoy wrote, and enables readers to understand some of the pointed critiques made in *The Death of Ivan Ilyich*.

Tolstoy, Leo. *Tolstoy's Short Fiction.* Norton Critical Edition. Edited by Michael R. Katz. New York: W. W. Norton, 2008.

This is an excellent collection of Tolstoy's shorter works (his larger works of *Anna Karenina* and *War and Peace* are too long to be recommended as supplemental reading for a class), and it also provides many excellent essays, including several that analyze *The Death of Ivan Ilyich*.

HENRIK IBSEN
Hedda Gabler

All I ask is an intimate circle of good friends,
friends I can be of service to in any way necessary.
Places where I am allowed to come and go as a
trusted friend.[...] That kind of triangular
arrangement is really a magnificent convenience
for everyone concerned.
—Henrik Ibsen, *Hedda Gabler*, Act 2

Topics for Lecture or Discussion

1. **Henrik Ibsen adapts the well-made play formula to rework the past in the present.** Typical intrigue drama features a buried secret in the past that comes to light during the course of a plot-driven narrative that reverses direction several times to increase suspense and postpones an ultimate resolution until the end. Such plays require a great deal of exposition in order to get the dramaturgical machinery in working order. Ibsen frequently innovates by folding the exposition into the forward drive of the drama. He introduces background material not as information that is past and long dead but that recurs in the stultifying atmosphere of middle-class Norway. The Act 2 scene in which Hedda Gabler and Eilert Løvborg look at the photo album from Hedda's honeymoon re-creates the same dynamic that Hedda and Eilert enjoyed years earlier when they were both much younger. This scene fills in the past, even as the two re-create the same sexual tension that ultimately drove them apart years earlier. This use of dramatic technique advances the plot and shows the audience what is happening without resorting to narrative description to fill in details about the unseen past. Thematically, Eilert represents Hedda's opportunity for love and a chance to escape the boredom of her mundane, provincial life. Eilert is a brilliant scholar who has just written a manuscript that projects the future of civilization. In contrast, George Tesman is a competent, dry academic who rummages in the past and whose specialty is domestic crafts in the Middle Ages. Hedda chose Tesman as a husband because she thought that he represented a safe choice and that he would earn a decent living as a university professor. Eilert appeared to be too unstable.
   a. **Further Reading:** Sofer, Andrew. "Killing Time: Guns and the Play of Predictability on the Modern Stage." In *The Stage Life of Props*, 167–202. Ann Arbor, MI: University of Michigan Press, 2003.
   b. **Suggested Searches:** Search for the following phrases in Google Images, Google Scholar, or an academic database to find images and

additional resources: well-made play; *piece bien faite*; Hedda and Løvborg; General Gabler's pistols.

2. **The language rips the polite veneer off bourgeois life.** Eilert Løvborg is a true genius who cannot live within the acceptable boundaries of society: he drinks too much, he chases women, and he cannot modify his excessive modes of behavior to fit the prevailing standards of decency. By the end of the play, Judge Brack observes, all the doors of polite society are shut to Løvborg, yet Løvborg is hardly the worst citizen imaginable, only the most overt in his nocturnal revelry. Judge Brack, a leading citizen of the community, is thoroughly morally corrupt. His bacchanal leads Løvborg astray, and it is at such a drinking party that the gentlemen visit Mistress Diana, the "redheaded singer" who operates a kind of brothel. More insidiously, Judge Brack plots from the beginning of the play to get power over Hedda Gabler that will allow him to visit her regularly through the "back way" and enjoy sexual privileges. Throughout the play, Judge Brack veils his sexual machinations with innocent discourse, and the split between what he says and what he intends gives drive and nuance to the drama. The deep corruption in Judge Brack signifies the moral fissure in society at large.
   a. **Further Reading:** Moi, Toril. "Rethinking Literary History: Idealism, Realism, and the Birth of Modernism." In *Henrik Ibsen and the Birth of Modernism*, 67–104. New York: Oxford University Press, 2006.
   b. **Suggested Searches:** Search for the following phrases in Google Images, Google Scholar, or an academic database to find images and additional resources: subtext in Ibsen; Shaw *Quintessence of Ibsenism*; Emma Goldman on drama; *The Social Significance of Modern Drama*.

3. **The dramaturgy sports a series of triangles to achieve and sustain dramatic tension.** Drama's dependence on dialogue usually dictates the majority of scenes between two characters. Here, though, triangular relationships govern the action. Scenes may still consist of dialogue between only two characters, but there is often a third character watching or listening or attempting to break the intimate bond of the other two. A primary triangle exists between Judge Brack, Hedda Gabler, and George Tesman, in which Brack wants to intrude upon Hedda's marriage and enjoy intimacy with her. Another sexual triangle exists between Hedda, Eilert Løvborg, and Mrs. Thea Elvsted, in which Hedda is jealous of the intimacy between the other two and tries to destroy that bond. With the death of Eilert, the triangle shifts at the end to include Thea, George, and Hedda, in which the working relationship between the first two threatens to become personal and exclude Hedda completely. In a nonsexual arena, the opening of the play presents a familial triangle of George, Aunt Julie, and the maid,

Berta, in which their mutual history and love and understanding resist outside penetration from the caustic and critical Hedda.

   a. **Further Reading:** Blair, Rhonda. "Acting, Embodiment, and Text: *Hedda Gabler* and Possible Uses of Cognitive Science." *Theatre Topics* 20:1 (March 2010): 11–21.

   b. **Suggested Searches:** Search for the following phrases in Google Images, Google Scholar, or an academic database to find images and additional resources: staging *Hedda Gabler*; Edvard Munch on Ibsen.

4. **Hedda Gabler manipulates others, but she lacks the courage to control her own life.** Most of what she actually does is mean, as stated in the headnote, but it is also petty and largely inconsequential. She makes fun of Aunt Julie's hat, she pretends to be Mrs. Thea Elvsted's friend, she goads Eilert Løvborg into drinking and bad behavior, and she withholds his manuscript. Only the last act is truly despicable, and even her eventual decision to burn the manuscript is the product of mixed motives. To an extent, she ensures her own financial future and her husband's career by eliminating Eilert as his rival. Her decision to protect her husband masks her jealousy of Thea, who inspired and helped Eilert write his masterpiece. Hedda cannot tolerate her former classmate's influence over Eilert, and since she cannot rival Thea as inspiration, she elects to destroy instead. She convinces herself that this act of violence serves the greater purpose of motivating Eilert to commit suicide "beautifully" (Act 3), but even this twisted and misguided act goes awry. Ironically, Hedda tries to manipulate others to do what she wants, when she lacks the ability or conviction to act on her own will and interests. She claims to love freedom above all else, but she is afraid to do as she pleases for fear of public censure and scandal. Such cowardice prevents her from claiming Eilert as her lover; her love of at least an illusion of freedom, though, prevents her from striking a bargain with Judge Brack and allowing him easy access to her house. The prospect of submitting to someone else or to enduring any public scandal drives her to take her own life.

   a. **Further Reading:** Thresher, Tanya. "'Vinløv i håret': The Relationship between Women, Language, and Power in Ibsen's *Hedda Gabler*." *Modern Drama* 51:1 (Spring 2008): 73–83.

   b. **Suggested Searches:** Search for the following phrases in Google Images, Google Scholar, or an academic database to find images and additional resources: Cate Blanchett as Hedda; Kate Burton as Hedda; Mary-Louise Parker as Hedda; Elizabeth Marvel as Hedda; Diana Rigg as Hedda; Richard Gilman *The Making of Modern Drama*.

5. **George Tesman does not love his wife.** It would be wrong to see him as a victim of his marriage, a dupe, because he alone gets everything at

the end. He regards her as his trophy wife, but he never displays any affection for her. He spent the majority of his honeymoon doing meticulous research in dusty archives. Back home, he seems far more concerned about his dying elderly aunt than about meeting any of his wife's needs. Worst of all, when Hedda Gabler informs him that she burned Eilert Løvborg's manuscript, he thinks about that action only insofar as it applies to him. He is thrilled that this gesture represents a sign of her love for him, but he quickly assuages his guilt by vowing to resurrect Eilert's manuscript by going through all the notes with Mrs. Thea Elvsted. After turning to the other woman, George forgets completely about Hedda, and he and Thea actually displace Hedda's position on the stage with the burgeoning notes that Thea had kept. The alliance between them makes Hedda a distant onlooker and pushes her toward death. At the end of the drama, it is clear that George will enjoy the role of bereaved husband only as long as social customs demand, and that Thea is poised to become the next Mrs. Tesman. With her devotion and will to help others, Thea fits in perfectly with the entire Tesman clan.

    a. **Further Reading:** Barstow, Susan Torrey. "'Hedda Is All of Us': Late-Victorian Women at the Matinee." *Victorian Studies* 43:3 (Spring 2001): 387–411.

    b. **Suggested Searches:** Search for the following phrases in Google Images, Google Scholar, or an academic database to find images and additional resources: Bergman's production *Hedda Gabler*; Ivo van Hove directing *Hedda Gabler*; *Hedda Gabler* interpretation.

In-Class Activities

1. Read the scene between Hedda Gabler and Mrs. Thea Elvsted in Act 1 or the scene between Hedda and Eilert Løvborg sharing the photo album in Act 2. Determine the differences between what the characters say and what they mean. It is the actors' job to get the right meanings across. How would you play these scenes?

2. The high point of the play is the burning of the manuscript at the end of Act 3. Take a sheet of paper and perform the act-ending gesture. What attitudes toward the papers can you take as Hedda Gabler? What can an actor do to convey meanings? Why does she do it?

3. Examine the opening stage directions. Why does the playwright use so much detail, and why is it so important? How does the wealth of information delivered apart from speech or dialogue contribute to an appreciation of the play? Why is the particular locale so important to the action, and why does the playwright take such care to describe it?

Paper Topics/Suggestions for Writing

1. Costume and properties are important theatrical elements that reveal character in this realistic play. How do Aunt Julie's hat and the flowers that she brings, along with Hedda Gabler's loose-fitting dressing gown in the opening scene, convey information that would be impossible or awkward to deliver in dialogue alone?

2. Which strategies or techniques does the playwright employ to handle the challenges of expository information? What is the "buried secret" in the play, and how does it come to light?

3. Mrs. Thea Elvsted appears timid and is very much afraid of Hedda Gabler—for very good reasons. How does she shock Hedda and emerge as the stronger character of the two? How does this revelation fit with Henrik Ibsen's critique of contemporary society?

4. Dishonest characters such as Hedda Gabler and Judge Brack frequently say one thing when they mean something else entirely. How does language serve as a veil for private or subversive thoughts and actions?

5. Hedda Gabler speaks of her desire several times to see Eilert Løvborg with vine leaves in his hair. Discuss the symbolism of vine leaves in relation to the themes of the play. What is the importance of this ideal, romantic image?

6. The role of Hedda Gabler has been a favorite of actresses ever since it was first produced. One reason is the complexity of the character and the challenges and possibilities of bringing out a range of qualities in performance. Hedda can be seen as evil incarnate or as helpless and misunderstood. Do you think that she is a victim of society, the scourge of society, or perhaps something else?

Resources

Hedda Gabler. Adapted by John Osborne. Dir. David Cunliffe. Perf. Diana Rigg, Dennis Lill, Philip Bond. 1981. DVD. Koch Vision, 2007.
> This is a TV movie adaptation of Ibsen's play, starring Diana Rigg as Hedda Gabler.

Hedda Gabler. Dir. Alex Segal. Perf. Ingrid Bergman, Michael Redgrave. 1963. DVD. BBC Warner, 2007.
> Also included in this video is *The Lady from the Sea*, starring Eileen Atkins and Denholm Elliott.

Henrik Ibsen: The Master Playwright. Insight Media, 1987, DVD.
> This program traces the playwright's development through all four phases of his career—early failures, epic dramas, realistic prose plays, and final plays.

GIOVANNI VERGA
Freedom

Topics for Lecture or Discussion

1. **Giovanni Verga's story *Freedom* exhibits elements of literary realism (or, as it is called in Italian, *verismo*), including verisimilitude in detail and plot, dispassionate narration, and protagonists who are common or typical people.** Reacting against the emotional emphasis of literary philosophies that can be loosely labeled as Romantic, Verga and the *verismo* movement sought to render life realistically, and to withdraw indications of authorial opinion or emotion from the telling of their stories. However, while *Freedom* is a work within this movement, Verga is not wholly successful in removing authorial predispositions and opinions from his narrative (or, at least, from his narrator's telling of the story). For example, readers find that the narrator announces that "the worst moment of all" (1542) was the slaughter of the notary's son, though other moments might be considered equally horrific. Similarly, the narrator tells of the trial by claiming, "The judges were dropping off to sleep so often behind their spectacle lenses that your heart absolutely froze" (1545), which demonstrates an authorial presupposition that one would care about the judges' behavior or the fairness of the trail. Yet in allowing his narrator to intrude certain important judgments in the story, Verga himself might be pointing to the limitations inherent in some of the objectivist principles inherent in the claims of literary realism.

   a. **Further Reading:** Lucente, Gregory L. "Critical Treatments of Verga and Verismo: Movements and Trends (1950–1980)." *MLN* 98:1 (1983): 129–138.

   b. **Suggested Search:** A Google search for "Giovanni Verga's verismo New Criterion" results in a helpful article by Martin Greenburg about Verga's realism.

2. **A central theme in many of Giovanni Verga's stories, including *Freedom*, is the contrast between the country and the city.** In discussing this contrast, however, it is important to note that Verga does not idealize life spent in the country, as many of his Romantic literary predecessors had done. Instead, he produces bleak and seemingly critical pictures of life in both places. In *Freedom*, the country is clearly a scene of social inequities, danger, minimal justice, and ineffective amendments. However, in the city too we find extreme poverty, justice abused, and a dislocation from human ties that finally leads to forgetfulness. In fact, while in certain details there are important differences between the city and country, Verga is careful to draw many parallels

between the two places, to demonstrate that the problems that arise are not simply the result of one's location, but are something that human nature carries with it.

a. **Further Reading:** Verga, Giovanni. *Little Novels of Sicily.* Trans. D. H. Lawrence. New York: Grove Press, 1953.

b. **Suggested Searches:** At Think Sicily (http://www.thinksicily.com) under the "Guide to Sicily" tab, you can find a timeline about Sicily's history with several pictures and links to further information.

3. **Verga's story uses the word "freedom" with several different implications and associations.** The initial use of the word associates it with brutal murder as the mob slaughters the town's wealthy citizens, and the mob evidently has no clear idea what "freedom" means; it becomes a vacuous rallying cry. This association is quickly replaced by one of material sufficiency, as the next morning, the townspeople declare, "Freedom meant there was going to be enough for everyone" (1544)! Yet the practical results of this work for freedom result in a complete loss of freedom for those found responsible for the rebellion—an ironic reversal of the intentions of those imprisoned. These various implications of "freedom" are united in the closing statement of the story. As the charcoal-burner is shackled with a sentence that permanently strips him of freedom, he declares, "Where are you taking me? To prison? What for? I never even got a square meter of land out of it! They told me it was all in the cause of freedom" (1545).

a. **Further Reading:** Guida, George. "Giovanni Verga and the Roots of Italian America." *Italian Americana* 21:2 (2003): 150–163.

b. **Suggested Search:** A Google Images search for "Giovanni Verga" results in several images and photographs of Verga.

4. **In *Freedom*, Verga emphasizes that justice is completely lacking on both sides of the conflict.** Quite clearly, the rabid mob that indiscriminately and brutally slaughters people does so without regard to justice. Verga emphasizes this point through his graphic descriptions of the painful murder of several innocent children. However, the government and the wealthy are just as blind to justice. The general who arrives at the town orders the random execution of half a dozen citizens, "whoever happened to come within reach" (1544), and the judges that arrive and preside over the trial are uninterested and repeatedly fall asleep. Indeed, even the families and friends of those who are condemned are shown to be unjust and ungrateful towards those who were punished with life in prison, since "nobody gave them a second thought any more" (1545). In presenting the poor as well as the rich as profoundly unjust, Verga calls into question simplistic socialist idealizations of the working classes while also critiquing the upper class's accumulation of wealth and power.

a. **Further Reading:** Moretti, Franco. *The Bourgeois: Between History and Literature.* Brooklyn, NY: Verso, 2013.

b. **Suggested Search:** A YouTube search for "Cavalleria Rusticana" results in several clips of Pietro Mascagni's famous operatic adaptation of a play by Giovanni Verga.

5. **In many of his stories, including *Freedom*, Giovanni Verga demonstrates a sensitivity to the different, unjust ways that men and women are treated by late nineteenth-century Italian society.** One striking example of the injustice of these differences is, surprisingly, the fact that men are prosecuted for the crimes of the rebellion, but women are not punished. In his description of the violent riot, Verga writes, "The women were even more ferocious, waving their skinny arms, shrieking with anger in high-pitched voices, their tender flesh showing beneath the rags they were wearing" (1542). Despite the fact that the women were more aggressive and violent than the men, it is only men who are sent to prison. Verga also adds dispassionate details that depict the plight of women as well. For example, when the women go to the city following their convicted men, Verga writes, "One fine-looking young woman disappeared in the city and was never heard of again" (1545), and Pirru's wife was "stolen" by the chemist's son as an act of revenge (1545).

a. **Further Reading:** Duggan, Christopher. *A Concise History of Italy.* Updated Edition. Cambridge: Cambridge University Press, 2002.

b. **Suggested Search:** A Google Images search for "Bronte Italy" results in several pictures of the town where the uprising historically took place.

In-Class Exercises

1. Ask your class to spend some time reviewing the other works that they have read in your course, identifying other moments in which violent action is described. As a class, contrast several of these moments with Verga's striking and graphic description, and hold a class discussion about the ways that violence is represented in literature.

2. Divide your students into several groups, each of which must rewrite part of *Freedom* as a stage play, and then have the groups enact their adaptations.

3. Assign a "Further Reading" project in which each student must choose and read two more of Verga's stories and give a brief presentation to the class about the similarities and differences between those works and *Freedom.*

Paper Topics/Suggestions for Writing

1. What does the word "freedom" mean in the context of this story? How is this different from or similar to the ways that we speak of freedom today? Why is freedom invoked for such a bloody cause?

2. Write a brief essay in which you contrast the two types of people that Verga presents: the peasants and the "bigwigs." What are the problematic aspects of each group, and what can be said in praise of each group?

3. Write a creative essay in which you consider the fate of the village twenty years after the uprising. How do the townspeople remember the event? What is their relationship with the moneyed, powerful class? Did the uprising accomplish anything?

4. For a comparative research essay, contrast Verga's style of realism with at least two other realist writers in this volume. What are their distinctive characteristics? In what ways do these writers represent a school or literary movement?

5. Consider the narrative style of *Freedom*. What unusual details does the narrator offer the reader? What expected details does the narrator withhold from the reader? At what points does the narrator offer commentary, and when does he betray emotions or passions?

Resources

Carsaniga, Giovanni. "Literary realism in Italy: Verga, Capuana, and Verismo." In *The Cambridge Companion to the Italian Novel*, eds. Peter Bondanella and Andrea Ciccanelli, pp. 61–74. Cambridge: Cambridge University Press, 2003.

> This is a helpful and accessible essay, and might serve well as required reading for students in conjunction with Verga's *Freedom*.

Pagano, Tullio. *Experimental Fictions: From Emile Zola's Naturalism to Giovanni Verga's Verism*. Cranbury, NJ: Associated University Presses, 1999.

> Pagano's work situates Verga's efforts at *verismo* within the larger context of the development of literary traditions and philosophies in the nineteenth century.

Verga, Giovanni. *Little Novels of Sicily*. Trans. D. H. Lawrence. New York: Grove Press, 1953.

> This volume, artfully translated by D. H. Lawrence, includes a wide selection of Verga's short stories, and should serve as a good place to begin further reading in Verga's works.

GUY DE MAUPASSANT

Hautot and His Son

Topics for Lecture or Discussion

1. ***Hautot and His Son* focuses upon boundaries between upper and lower classes, between what is acceptable and what is unacceptable, and between what is right and wrong.** The older Hautot is described as "half peasant, half gentleman" (1548) because he is both wealthy and a working-class farmer. Hautot's son also straddles cultural boundaries, as he is half educated but he still works the farm, and his interest is in farming despite his great wealth. Similarly, the acceptable and unacceptable is addressed in the person of Caroline, since having a mistress was publicly and morally condemned, but widely disregarded. The younger Hautot is sensitive to the fact that Caroline plays several different roles; he is initially uneasy with meeting her when he regards her as his father's mistress, but when he views her as the mother of his brother, his perspective shifts.

   a. **Further Reading:** Schehr, Lawrence R. *Figures of Alterity: French Realism and Its Others*. Stanford: Stanford University Press, 2003.

   b. **Suggested Search:** A YouTube search for "Hautot Père et Fils" results in a video that presents the first several minutes of a 2007 French adaptation of Maupassant's story.

2. **The idea of family, including both its social roles and the natural relationships that constitute family, is explored in *Hautot and His Son*.** On the one hand, Guy de Maupassant's story depicts the importance of the family as a cultural institution: the younger Hautot is well provided for by his father, and he is legally entitled to his father's property even though his father never made a will. Similarly, the younger Hautot steps in to fill his father's role when the elder Hautot dies. These social roles and elements of family necessarily entail limits about what is properly called family, however, and consequently we find that Emile, though also the child of the elder Hautot, would not be entitled to any of his father's property. In contrast to these social, legal aspects of family, Maupassant depicts the natural bond that forms between the younger Hautot and Caroline, which is based primarily upon their shared love for the elder Hautot. Similarly, as the younger Hautot finds, the bonds of natural family are strong, and he feels a growing affection for his half-brother Emile.

   a. **Further Reading:** Counter, Andrew J. *Inheritance in Nineteenth-Century French Culture. Wealth, Knowledge and the Family*. London: Legenda, 2010.

b. **Suggested Search:** At the Elsevier website (http://www.elsevier
.com), a search for "History of the Family" results in a journal of
the same name, which contains several relevant articles concerning
these issues.

3. **In both their style and content, Guy de Maupassant's stories reveal
the influence of Gustave Flaubert.** Flaubert's realism, with its dispassionate narrative voice, its focus upon the common rather than the
exceptional, and its restraint regarding moral judgment, was a great
model for Maupassant, and Flaubert also met with the young Maupassant regularly to give him advice and critique drafts of his stories. Even
if your students have not read *Madame Bovary*, it is helpful to read a
brief passage aloud and to compare its narrative tone to that in Maupassant's stories. Maupassant was not, however, simply an imitator of
Flaubert, and his stories exhibit a mastery and development of the
short story as a genre for realism in a distinctive and influential way.
   a. **Further Reading:** Lyons, John D. *French Literature: A Very Short
   Introduction.* Oxford: Oxford University Press, 2010.
   b. **Suggested Search:** The website Maupassantiana (http://www.mau
   passantiana.fr) is in Frnech, but has many informative links, including a filmography and biography among others.

4. **The character of Old Hautot embodies some of the changes that
were occurring in French culture and society over the course of
the nineteenth century.** One of these changes was the growth of "new"
money, or people who were not nobles or aristocrats, but who were
financially successful enough to enjoy some of the advantages traditionally reserved for the upper class. Hunting for sport, which occurs at the
beginning of the story, is an example of this, as is having the affluence
to support a mistress who lives secretly and apart from the home. Changes
in traditional morality are also apparent; Hautot does not seriously
engage with the sacraments that are administered to him, and he does
not have any moral concerns regarding his sexual actions. A final indication of the cultural shift is Hautot's attitude toward education, which
is seen as a good thing in so far as it is useful (in this case, it legitimates
the Hautots' influential, wealthy lifestyle), but it is not desired as a good
in itself (evident in the fact that he stops educating his son when he
fears that it will make him uninterested in the farm).
   a. **Further Reading:** Price, Roger. *A Concise History of France.* 2nd
   Edition. Cambridge: Cambridge University Press, 2005.
   b. **Suggested Search:** A Google Images search for "Guy de Maupassant" results in several photographs of the author.

5. **Leo Tolstoy and Guy de Maupassant admired each other's works,
and in *Hautot and His Son* readers find a treatment of death that**

echoes aspects of the treatment of mortality in *The Death of Ivan Ilyich*. Maupassant's *Hautot and His Son* was published three years after Tolstoy's novella, and of the two, it is Tolstoy's work that more deliberately and thoroughly explores death as an incident and idea. Nevertheless, Maupassant presents death as an event that forces a man to review his past life and to evaluate the situation of the family that he is leaving behind. Both Ivan and the older Hautot find that they have left things in a more problematic situation than they had intended. Similarly, both characters receive the last sacraments that are administered to them in a cursory fashion, without serious attention to the states of their souls. Upon the point of death, Ivan must realize, finally, his own shortcomings, and the older Hautot must ensure that he has properly provided for his mistress and son. For both Tolstoy and Maupassant, death leads to a final realization or action, and the dying men's hearts are moved by the desire to set things right.

   a. **Further Reading**: Tolstoy, Leo. "Introduction to the Works of Guy de Maupassant." 1894.

   b. **Suggested Search**: At the Literature Network (http://www.online-literature.com) a search for "Guy de Maupassant" results in a brief biography with links to the full text of many of his stories.

In-Class activities

1. Divide the students into small groups, each of which must scour the anthology for other stories about fathers and sons, making a list of the interesting father-son relationships in Western literature. Share these lists with the class, and discuss the significance of this theme.

2. After dividing your students into several small groups of three, ask each group to discuss and identify what the most important moment of the story is. Then have each group pair up with another group, and ask them to share their thoughts and offer constructive criticism to the new group.

3. As a class, make two lists on the board that contain adjectives describing the older and younger Hautots respectively. Try to be precise, and use good textual evidence to support the descriptions.

Paper Topics/Suggestions for Writing

1. Write a creative essay that describes the relationship between Caroline and the younger Hautot ten years after the end of the story.

2. How is death presented in *Hautot and His Son*? What impact does it have upon the different characters in the story? How does Maupassant's presentation of death contrast with other authors' discussions of death in this anthology?

3. Is there a climax in *Hautot and His Son*? If so, where? If not, how does the story move from beginning to end?

4. Write a descriptive essay that examines the three main characters of the story. Is one character more noble, just, wise, or virtuous than the others? Is one character more low, dishonest, vicious, or foolish than the others?

5. What conception of family is presented in *Hautot and His Son*? How does this presentation of family challenge cultural norms? How does it reinforce those norms? Is family a good thing? If so, why? If not, in what respects is it a bad thing?

Resources

James, Henry. *Literary Criticism French Writers; Other European Writers; The Prefaces to the New York Edition*. New York: Literary Classics, 1984.
> Included in this volume are two essays (pp. 521–554) by James about Guy de Maupassant that are highly recommended. This work also does a helpful job of providing cultural context for readers.

Kay, Sarah; Terence Cave; and Malcolm Bowie. *A Short History of French Literature*. Oxford: Oxford University Press, 2003.
> This volume has many virtues to recommend it, including its brevity, accessibility, and thoughtfulness. It should be an excellent introduction for any instructor or student unfamiliar with French literature.

Maupassant, Guy de. *Bel-Ami*. Translated by Margaret Mauldon. Oxford: Oxford University Press, 2001.
> *Bel-Ami* is Maupassant's best known novel, and while it is longer than many of Maupassant's short stories, it is recommended as a fine example of Maupassant's use of realism in the form of a novel.

JOAQUIM MARIA MACHADO DE ASSIS
The Rod of Justice

Topics for Lecture or Discussion

1. **Although Joaquim Maria Machado de Assis (hereafter "Machado") also wrote poetry and plays, his reputation rests on his fiction. "The Rod of Justice" demonstrates many of the characteristics for which Machado's short stories are known.** Throughout his lifetime, Machado published seven collections that contained hundreds of short stories. Many of the stories from the latter period of his life share similar characteristics, and "The Rod of Justice" is an excellent representation of many of Machado's central concerns. These characteristics of Machado's mature short fiction include urban settings, self-conscious narrators, notable use of irony, and satire of the bourgeoisie. Additionally, Machado favored writing about contemporary Brazil. "The Rod of Justice" not only presents a Brazil that would have looked familiar to nineteenth-century Brazilians, but it marks an important date by noting that the story happens before 1850. With "The Rod of Justice" having been written in 1891, this places the events of the story in the near past. The importance, though, of 1850 is that it is the year in which the slave trade was abolished, however, slavery continued to be practiced until 1888, although new slaves could not legally be brought into Brazil. Machado's concern with writing about the contemporary can be seen in the use of these dates, as "The Rod of Justice" links the contemporary abolition of slavery with the recent abolition of the slave trade—two dates that legally fought slavery but did little to reduce the power of Brazil's class structure.

   a. **Further Reading:** Fitz, Earl E. "The Short Story Collections." In *Machado de Assis*, 61–71. Boston, MA: Twayne Publishers, 1989.

   b. **Suggested Search:** First editions of Machado's books can be found at the website Brasiliana USP (www.brasiliana.usp.br) by selecting the *"autor"* tab near the search bar and searching for the author's name, "Machado de Assis."

2. **Damião's difficulties with his father reflect Machado's broader concern with the difficulties men face within a patriarchy.** "The Rod of Justice" is one of Machado's numerous works of fiction that deals with these difficulties. Machado's concerns often center on the expectations placed on men by the patriarchal Brazilian society and the trouble that Brazilian men face when trying to meet or reject these expectations. In "The Rod of Justice," Damião struggles with his father's expectation that he become a priest. Damião wishes to reject

449

this socially acceptable career path. While he is a man in a patriarchal society, his role as a son keeps him from being able to reject the path his father wishes for him. Paradoxically, the societal expectation is for Damião to accept power in a patriarchal society by becoming a priest, yet he lacks the power to reject this career path. His power in society and in his family is so weak that he is even unable to directly argue against his father but can only hope to use the intermediary of his father's mistress to change the mind of the man who has power over him.

a. **Further Reading:** Valente, Luiz Fernando. "Machado's Wounded Males." *Hispania* 84:1 (March): 11–19.

b. **Suggested Search:** Machado made his home in Rio de Janeiro, and many buildings that existed in the nineteenth century are still standing. To see some of these notable landmarks, conduct a Google Images search for "Theatro Municipal," "'Our Lady of Mount Carmel' Cathedral 'Rio de Janeiro,'" and "Castelo da Povoa."

3. **In "The Rod of Justice," Damião's inability to leave the priesthood exists because he has no financial security and remains under the control of his father. The tension between economics and freedom, presented in Damião's case, mirrored the tension between economics and freedom in Brazilian slavery.** As Brazil abolished slavery years after most countries in Europe and the Americas had already ended the practice, the justification for slavery changed in the latter half of the nineteenth century. While earlier justifications tended to universalize a necessity for slavery, appealing to sources such as the Bible, pro-slavery advocates had a difficult time arguing that slavery was a universal necessity, as former slave-owning countries abolished the practice. Critic Roberto Schwarz argues that Brazil altered its justification for slavery by discussing slavery in particularly Brazilian terms. The new justification emphasized Brazil's growing economy and credited slavery as an economic practice that uniquely empowered the nation. Damião struggles with the tension between economics and freedom: he wishes to act freely and to keep Sínhá Rita from harming Lucretia. He is, though, pressured by his economic situation not to anger Sínhá Rita, and it is this pressure that keeps him from standing up to her cruel treatment of a slave.

a. **Further Reading:** Schwarz, Roberto. "The Practical Matrix." In *A Master on the Periphery of Capitalism: Machado de Assis*, translated by Roberto Schwarz, 20–28. Durham, NC: Duke University Press, 2001.

b. **Suggested Search:** The Trans-Atlantic Slave Trade Database website (www.slavevoyages.org) has numerous resources on the transatlantic slave trade. While the site is not exclusive to Brazilian slavery, the "Introductory Maps" section, located under "Assessing the Slave Trade," on the home page, puts Brazilian slavery in the wider context of the slave trade. The time line of the slave trade, linked as "Estimates" under "Assessing the Slave Trade," can give a sense of the impact that Brazil's 1850 suppression of the slave trade had on ending the transatlantic slave trade.

4. **While "The Rod of Justice" centers on the evils of slavery, Machado complicates the issue by keeping slavery on the margins of his story and by rendering the relationship between his characters and audience ambiguous.** Damião's uncertainty about interceding on behalf of the enslaved Lucretia serves as a major conflict for Damião, and his decision to not intercede serves as the great denial of justice at the end of the story. Machado, though, does not choose to create any strong enslaved characters in his text. Instead of drawing on his readers' empathy by fleshing out the character of Lucretia, Machado allows his story to marginalize Sínhá Rita's slaves in a manner similar to Brazil's attempts to push to the margins the social issue of slavery and race. As race was a central issue that Brazil's ruling class wished to ignore, so the overwhelming problem of slavery in "The Rod of Justice" is all the more palpable because it is the one issue that Damião cannot discuss with Sínhá Rita. As critic Renata Mautner Wasserman writes, "The realism of Machado de Assis is . . . deconstructive, depending on playing narrative and plot, tone and subject against each other" (97). Machado's indirect and complex handling of realism can also be seen in his critique of Damião. While Damião's final failure to act is clearly unethical, the close third-person narration highlights the pain of Damião's inner conflict. The tone of narration neither ultimately condemns Damião, nor does it absolve him because of his circumstances. The ambiguity in the narrator's tone is important when considering that Machado's audience contained many readers who continued to benefit from the class structure that was originally created by Brazilian slavery. Machado does not allow his readers an easily dismissed condemnation of their own culpability, nor does he absolve them. Instead, the reader's own struggle with race and slavery in Brazil is laid bare in Damião's inner turmoil.
   a. **Further Reading:** Mautner Wasserman, Renata R. "Race, Nation, Representation: Machado de Assis and Lima Barreto." *Luso-Brazilian Review* 45:2 (2008): 84–106.
   b. **Suggested Search:** The Atlantic Slave Trade and Slave Life in the Americas: A Visual Record website at http://hitchcock.itc.virginia.edu/Slavery contains over a thousand images related to the slave trade. Click on "Explore the Collection," which will lead to a search bar. Search there for "Brazil" for images specifically related to slavery in Brazil.

5. **"The Rod of Justice" demonstrates a paradoxical feature of Machado's realistic stories: frequently commenting on or satirizing Bra-**

zilian society while aiming for a universality that moves beyond Brazilian society. Slavery, patriarchy, and the power of the Catholic Church are all features of Brazilian society that are dealt with in "The Rod of Justice." At the same time, the story meets critic Donald Decker's description of Machado's fiction: "He constantly eschews descriptions of settings and elements of local color. The interpersonal problems which he deals with occur principally among members of the middle or upper classes of Rio de Janeiro and could easily be applicable to life in any large city of the Occident" (78). In "The Rod of Justice," Machado writes against slavery not by detailing the particularities of the life of a Brazilian slave but instead focuses on the interpersonal relationships between well-off Brazilians, keeping Sinhá Rita's treatment of Lucretia constantly at the periphery.

a. **Further Reading:** Decker, Donald M. "Machado de Assis: Short Story Craftsman." *Hispania* 48:1 (March): 76–81.

b. **Suggested Search:** Despite its rich literary culture, Brazilian literature has received little recognition in the United States. To get a sense of how Brazilian literature continued to grow and develop in the twentieth century, explore the internationally renowned visual poetry of Augusto de Campos and Haraldo de Campos on the website UbuWeb (www.ubu.com). Both authors can be found under the "Historical" link.

In-Class Activities

1. Damião first notices Lucretia because she is being beaten for being distracted from her work by Damião himself. Is his disgust toward Sinhá Rita's treatment of Lucretia based more on disgust with slavery or on vanity?

2. To what degree is "The Rod of Justice" a story about the evils of slavery, and to what degree is it making a claim about justice that goes beyond a single issue?

3. Why does Machado choose to make Damião a reluctant priest? How does the Catholic Church factor into "The Rod of Justice"?

4. Is it essential that the story is set in Brazil? Does Machado show Brazilian slavery to be different than slavery in Olaudah Equiano's *The Interesting Narrative* or Frederick Douglass's *Narrative* (both in this volume)?

Paper Topics/Suggestions for Writing

1. Trying to win his freedom from his father, Damião tries to win over his father's mistress through flattery. At her house, Damião's vanity is flattered when Lucretia is distracted by him, and he wishes to keep her

from being harmed by Sinhá Rita. Examine how freedom and vanity are related in "The Rod of Justice," paying special attention to the characters of Damião and Lucretia.

2. Both Machado's "The Rod of Justice" and Leo Tolstoy's *The Death of Ivan Ilyich* (in this volume) center on characters who are dealing with inner turmoil: Damião wishes to act justly and to be free, while Ivan Ilyich struggles with his relationship with death. Write a paper that examines how each author handles the inner turmoil of a character and that discusses how each character's inner state relates to outward acts. What does Damião wish to do, and what does he actually do? What actions in Ivan Ilyich's life were frivolous, and what actions could he have taken to have a meaningful life?

3. Gender is a major component of the relationships in "The Rod of Justice." Write a paper that examines how gender relates to power in the story.

4. Both Olaudah Equiano and Frederick Douglass discuss the evils of slavery in their autobiographies. While Equiano and Douglass are both the main characters of their narratives and are enslaved, "The Rod of Justice"'s central characters, Damião and Sinhá Rita, are both free. Write a paper that discusses how making an enslaved character a narrative's main character or placing enslaved characters at the margin of a narrative changes how slavery is treated within the text itself.

5. Damião wishes to be free from his father's influence, and he also wishes to be able to act justly and to protect Lucretia from Sinhá Rita's abuse. Examine both freedom and justice in "The Rod of Justice," and show how they are related in the story.

Resources

Machado de Assis, Joaquim Maria. *Dom Casmurro*. Trans. Helen Caldwell. New York: Noonday Press, 1991.
>This is Machado's most famous novel.

Machado de Assis, Joaquim Maria. *The Psychiatrist and Other Stories*. Translated by William L. Grossman and Helen Caldwell. Berkeley: University of California Press, 1963.
>This collection of short stories is from Machado's later phase.

Neto, José Raimundo Maia. *Machado De Assis, The Brazilian Pyrrhonian*. West Lafayette, IN: Purdue University Press, 1994.
>This study of Machado's writings is broken up into two major phases in his career.

ANTON CHEKHOV

The Lady with the Dog
The Cherry Orchard

> Oh, why didn't you listen to me? You dear
> woman, you dear good woman, you can't ever
> go back to the past. [. . .] Oh, if only we could
> change things, if only life were different, this
> unhappy, messy life.
> —Anton Chekhov, *The Cherry Orchard*, Act 3

Topics for Lecture or Discussion

1. **One of the most striking features of Chekhov's short fiction is his tendency to avoid resolution.** The most obvious example of this in *The Lady with the Dog* is at the conclusion of the story, a conclusion that often bothers students because of its indecisive and uncertain nature. Throughout the fourth part of the story, Chekhov builds tension, as if leading to a climactic scene or decision. Instead of such a scene, however, Chekhov leaves both his characters and readers suspended in indecision, writing, "they both realized that the end was still far, far away, and that the hardest, the most complicated part was only just beginning" (1580). Chekhov's descriptive techniques often function in a manner similar to this narrative style, as he will allow an allusive description to imply things without spelling them out for the reader. One example occurs at the end of the first section; after meeting Anna, Gurov returns to his room, and Chekhov writes, "He recalled her slender, delicate neck, her fine gray eyes. 'And yet there's something pathetic about her,' he thought to himself as he fell asleep" (1571). Instead of elaborating on Gurov's typically calloused attitude towards women, and the way in which that was changing with respect to Anna, Chekhov allows a few words and a lingering thought to convey both Gurov's insensitivity and his interest.
   a. **Further Reading:** Bykov, Dmitrii. "The Two Chekhovs." *Russian Studies in Literature* 47.1 (2010–11): 30–47.
   b. **Suggested Search:** A YouTube search for "The Lady with the Dog" results in a variety of videos, including several of stage adaptations of Chekhov's story.

2. **Following certain ideals of literary realism in his fiction, Chekhov tends to focus upon regular people in typical situations rather than exceptional heroes completing extraordinary feats.** In *The Lady with*

the Dog, even the mundane, common nouns of the title hint at the unexceptional nature of the characters involved. The affair between Gurov and Anna is not the stuff of a dramatic tragedy or epic love story; while illicit, their affair is more pitiful than grand, and more common than notable. The interest of the story comes not from the events, passions, or characters themselves, but from the deft artistry of the narration, which unfolds a sophisticated depiction of real human passions, desires, and situations. For example, instead of a story of overwhelming, all-consuming love, it is the verisimilitude of Gurov's conflicted thoughts as he drops his daughter off at school on the way to a tryst with Anna that makes the story so striking (1579).

    a. **Further Reading:** Gottleib, Vera, and Paul Allain, eds. *The Cambridge Companion to Chekhov.* Cambridge: Cambridge University Press, 2000.

    b. **Suggested Search:** At the Literature Network (http://www.online-literature.com), a search for "Anton Chekhov" results in a brief biography, as well as links to many of his short stories.

3. **Liubóv Andréyevna hosts a ball on the day that the cherry orchard is to be sold at auction.** Spending her last pennies on a frivolous party to bide the time while waiting to find out who bought the orchard, Liubóv seems incapable of decisive action. Why didn't she listen to Yermolái Lopákhin? Why was his sensible plan to save the estate unreasonable to her? Despite Lopákhin's persistent warnings and pleas, Liubóv does nothing to prevent the sale of land to someone else on August 22. She does not want to preserve the estate. She longs to return to her lover in Paris, and she voices her desire, in Act 3, to go back even before the buyer of the estate is revealed. She arrives from France at the start of the drama with no intention of rescinding the foreclosure on the property. Instead, she leaves Paris in order to escape from her philandering lover and, more importantly, to make him jealous and arouse his neediness. Liubóv flaunts a number of telegrams from her lover in the first three acts, prompting her, ultimately, to return to him. Despite losing the cherry orchard, Liubóv gets exactly what she wants in the course of the action.

    a. **Further Reading:** Evdoklmova, Svetlana. "What's So Funny about Losing One's Estate, or Infantilism in *The Cherry Orchard*." *Slavic and East European Journal* 44:4 (Winter 2000): 623–48.

    b. **Suggested Searches:** Search for the following phrases in Google Images, Google Scholar, or an academic database to find images and additional resources: Act 3 *Cherry Orchard*; Madame Ranevskaya; Liubóv Andréyevna.

4. **The future happiness that Pétya Trofímov foresees is an abstract concept in comparison to the cutting down of the orchard for**

summer cottages that Yermolái plans and executes. Trofímov, the perpetual student, critiques the sins of the past and says that only hard work can guarantee a better future. Alone with Ánya, he says: "[I] f there's one thing that's clear to me, it's this: if we want to have any real life in the present, we have to do something to make up for our past, we have to get over it, and the only way to do that is to make sacrifices, get down to work, and work harder than we've ever worked before" (1602). Trofímov believes these words but does nothing to further his stated goals for humanity. He cannot even complete his degree. Lopákhin's plan, conversely, is one that will produce real changes in the world. The sound of the ax thudding against the trees at the end of the play is meant to be devastating. Subdivisions and summer cottages are not the stuff of Trofímov's dreams, but they represent, from one point of view, progress that is measurable.

a. **Further Reading:** Baehr, Stephen L. "The Machine in Chekhov's Garden: Progress and Pastoral in *The Cherry Orchard.*" *Slavic and East European Journal* 43:1 (Spring 1999): 99–121.

b. **Suggested Searches:** Search for the following phrases in Google Images, Google Scholar, or an academic database to find images and additional resources: Ethan Hawke as Trofímov; Sam Mendes directs *The Cherry Orchard*; conclusion *The Cherry Orchard*; conflict Trofímov and Lopákhin.

5. **Failed or lacking love and romance indicate the immense challenge of embracing everyday life as it occurs.** Liubóv Andréyevna may be involved in an abusive relationship as a result of her guilt over past events, but two other relationships stand out in the play as central to the playwright's message. Liubóv tells Pétya that she would welcome him as her son-in-law, but that he must graduate from university and get on with life. Responding indignantly, he claims that he is "above love" (1606). All his talk to Ánya about the future, however, can also be read as a flirtation, in which his words and visions of the future completely mesmerize her. Trofímov as much as admits his love for her at the end of Act 1, but his cowardice prevents him from acknowledging the truth and allowing personal growth and progress. Even more painful to witness, however, is the relationship between Lopákhin and Várya. Liubóv and others assume that they will marry because they are well suited for one another. Lopákhin, however, never gets over his childhood memories and romantic crush on Liubóv. His speech, dress, and comportment in the opening scene provide ample evidence that he very much retains his love for the mistress of the estate. His illusion of love for her might even explain, in part, his decision to buy the estate. Várya cannot compete against the charisma and beauty of Liubóv in his mind, and Lopákhin overlooks his chance at marriage by holding onto an unrealistic, fanciful pipe dream.

a. **Further Reading:** Reid, John McKellor. "Polemic as Parting Advice: The 'Argument' of *The Cherry Orchard*." *Modern Drama: World Drama from 1850 to the Present* 48:1 (Spring 2005): 30–54.

b. **Suggested Searches:** Search for the following phrases in Google Images, Google Scholar, or an academic database to find images and additional resources: Várya and Lopákhin; Trofímov and Ánya; Chekhovian worldview; Chekhovian dramaturgy.

6. **The estate is an untenable refuge from the world. Liubóv Andréyevna returns to her childhood home because she wants to teach her lover in Paris a lesson.** She cannot stay at the family home, though, because it is the site where her little boy drowned years ago. The cherry orchard no longer produces enough to provide an income. Firs, the ancient family servant, recalls a time when the serfs picked fruit by the wagonload. He also remembers when the czar freed the serfs in 1861. Trofímov, too, speaks eloquently about the history of the family estate and the fact that slaves once worked the land and that penance for such crimes needed to be served. The loss of cheap labor is tied inextricably to the demise of the family estate. It became impossible to manage such a property. Fittingly (if ironically, given the family's earlier fuss about remembering him), Firs is accidentally left behind and locked inside the house at the end of the play. Lying down, he mutters, "No strength left, nothing left, not a thing" (1619). Change has come, the future is now, and the estate will be demolished. For more historical context on Russian life, see Frances Nethercott, *Russian Legal Culture Before and After Communism: Criminal Justice, Politics, and the Public Sphere* (New York: Routledge, 2007), and Werner Eugen Mosse, *Alexander II and the Modernization of Russia* (New York: Collier, 1962).

a. **Further Reading:** Mamet, David. "Notes on *The Cherry Orchard*." In *Writing in Restaurants*, 118–125. New York: Penguin, 1986.

b. **Suggested Searches:** Search for the following phrases in Google Images, Google Scholar, or an academic database to find images and additional resources: nursery in *Cherry Orchard*; Act 1 *Cherry Orchard*; dramatic action *Cherry Orchard*; indirect action *Cherry Orchard*.

7. **Self-dramatization among the characters simultaneously adds comic theatricality and pathos to the drama.** As a prime example, after announcing that he bought the cherry orchard at the end of Act 3, Lopákhin launches into a long speech in which he wishes that his father and grandfather, who beat him mercilessly as a child, could see him as a great success now. He, who had grown up poor and worked as a slave, had now bought "the most beautiful estate in the whole world" (1611). Lopákhin expresses rage and he puffs himself up as a gentleman landowner. Even as he vents such passion, however, he remains the lovesick boy whom Liubóv Andréyevna pitied and looked kindly upon many years

ago. The duality of Lopákhin's character is apparent immediately thereafter when he implores her with the words from the previously cited epigraph. Despite winning the bid for the cherry orchard, Lopákhin can never win Liubóv for himself. The perceived gap between who he is and who he pretends to be creates a comic response. What is true for Lopákhin is also true for the other characters. Their consistent inability to reconcile aspiration with reality is heartbreaking and hilarious at the same time.

  a. **Further Reading:** Beckerman, Bernard. "Dramatic Analysis and Literary Interpretation: *The Cherry Orchard* as Exemplum." *New Literary History* 2:3 (Spring 1971): 391–406.

  b. **Suggested Searches:** Search for the following phrases in Google Images, Google Scholar, or an academic database to find images and additional resources: pathos and comedy in *Cherry Orchard*; Zoë Wanamaker in *The Cherry Orchard*; self-dramatization in *The Cherry Orchard*; theatricality at the National Theatre.

In-Class Activities

1. Divide your students into small groups, and give the groups the creative task of determining what sort of situation Gurov and Anna are in ten years after the conclusion of *The Lady with the Dog*.

2. After handing out index cards to the class, ask half of the class to assume Anna's perspective and ask the other half of the class to assume the perspective of Gurov's wife. Then have each group write descriptions of Gurov from their assumed perspectives, and share some of these descriptions with the class. Discuss the different ways that Gurov might appear in positive or negative lights, and emphasize the importance of perspective.

3. Read aloud the scene near the end of Act 4 between Lopákhin and Várya. What supplies the tension in the dialogue? After all the talk about marriage, why doesn't Lopákhin actually propose to Várya?

4. The sound of the breaking string occurs twice in the play, and the characters give various explanations for its origin. If it is a symbol, what does it mean? If not, what else might the recurring sound signify?

5. Anton Chekhov called his play "almost a farce." How might that statement help stage Act 3? How should the action proceed?

Paper Topics/Suggestions for Writing

1. Write an essay in which you reflect on Gurov's initial attitude toward women in *The Lady with the Dog*, and the ways in which that attitude changes over the course of the story. Does Anna do anything in particular to make him change?

2. Write a paper in which you identify three significant similarities or shared themes between *The Lady with the Dog* and *The Cherry Orchard*.

3. *The Cherry Orchard* makes abundant references and allusions to time and time passing. What does the emphasis on time mean?

4. Acting is naturally associated with action, yet there is very little action of the traditional kind in this play. What challenges does paralysis of action pose for the actors? How can doing virtually nothing on stage interest an audience?

5. Arrivals to the rural Russian estate and departures from it structure the action. How are the "comings" and "goings" perfect organizing principles for a stage play but less effective for a film?

6. The playwright calls this play "almost a farce." Farce connotes both rapid pace and exaggerated expressions or behavior. Is it possible to defend Anton Chekhov's description of his play? Alternatively, is it possible to interpret the play as a tragedy?

7. Anton Chekhov is a master of irony. What is the principal irony of the drama, and what does it signify?

8. To what extent is it possible to believe Trofímov's vision of the glorious future? What complicates accepting his prophecies as truth?

9. Everyone assumes that Lopákhin will marry Várya. Act 4 builds up to a proposal, but Lopákhin does not ask her when he has the opportunity. Why not? What is particularly Chekhovian about the final exchange between Lopákhin and Várya?

Resources

Chekhov and the Moscow Art Theatre. Insight Media, 1982, VHS.
> This video features archival footage of the play as produced at the Moscow Art Theatre.

Chekhov: Comedy or Tragedy. Insight Media, 1968, VHS.
> In this video, Norris Houghton analyzes subtext in Chekhov.

Chekhov: Innovator of Modern Drama. Insight Media, 1968, VHS.
> This video features critic Norris Houghton explaining Chekhovian dramatic devices.

The Cherry Orchard. Dir. Michael Cacoyannis. Perf. Alan Bates, Charlotte Rampling. 1999. DVD. Kino Video, 2003.
> This is a film adaptation of the play, starring Charlotte Rampling as Liubóv Ranyéskaya and Alan Bates as Leoníd Gáyev.

The Cherry Orchard. Warner Home Video, 2007, DVD.
> This two-disc set features two separate productions, one with performances by Peggy Ashcroft and John Gielgud (1962) and the other with

Dorothy Tutin, Judi Dench, and Anna Massey (1981). Additional material includes a conversation between Dench and Sir Richard Eyre.

The Lady with the Dog. Dir. Iosif Kheifits. Lenfilm Studio, 1960.

This award-winning Soviet film is indicative of the ways in which Chekhov was appreciated in Russia even after the revolution in 1917.

Perspectives on European Empire

"I find no reason that I should obey you. I would
rather die."
—Machemba, "Letter to Major von
Wissmann"

Topics for Lecture or Discussion

1. **Several of the texts that advocate for European empires in this
   selection make use of thought drawn directly from Enlightenment
   thinkers and the philosophical attitudes which they spawned.** One
   example of this is Macaulay's progressive mentality in "Minute on
   Indian Education, February 2, 1835." He conceives of intellectual goods
   as best measured in terms of reason and scientific fact, with "reason"
   and "fact" understood in terms of a European, post-Enlightenment philosophical diction. Rational conclusions and the accumulation of facts
   are, for Macaulay, the measures of progress, and as such progress is
   assumed to be good; Europe is consequently regarded as better than the
   regions it is conquering. With such criteria for evaluating and rational-
   izing imperialism, Macaulay could not help but arrive at the conclusion
   that he does: "But when we pass from works of imagination to works in
   which facts are recorded, and general principles investigated, the superiority of the Europeans becomes absolutely immeasurable . . . In every
   branch of physical or moral philosophy, the relative position of the two
   nations is nearly the same" (1626–1627).
   a. **Further Reading:** Ghosh, P. R. "Macaulay and the Heritage of the
      Enlightenment." *The English Historical Review* 112:446 (1997):
      358–395.
   b. **Suggested Search:** At the Stanford Encyclopedia of Philosophy
      (http://plato.stanford.edu), a search for "Enlightenment" results in a
      helpful discussion of Enlightenment thought.

2. **In offering a critique of the warlike and wasteful ways of the progressive, colonialist leaders of his day, Garibaldi's "Memorandum"
   resorts to utopian visions of a united Europe.** Garibaldi criticizes
   the violence common in Europe at the end of the nineteenth century
   with simple but striking language: "Everyone speaks of civilization and
   progress . . . But to me it seems, excepting our elegance, that instead
   we do not differ much from primitive times, when men tore each other
   apart in order to possess themselves of another's prey" (1630). Garibaldi's
   suggestion requires the voluntary disarmament of the nations of
   Europe, and the voluntary submission of those nations to one overarching government, a view that many people would consider idealistic.

Garibaldi is aware that his vision might be dismissed as utopian (1632), and consciously or unconsciously he does echo some of the things that Raphael Hythloday describes in Thomas More's *Utopia*. These idealizations might be interpreted, however, as an exaggeration in order to convince Europe's countries to follow a more peaceful path.

a. **Further Reading:** More, Thomas. *Utopia*. Revised edition. Eds. George M. Logan and Robert M. Adams. Cambridge: Cambridge University Press, 2002.

b. **Suggested Search:** The Encyclopedia Britannica Academic Edition (http://www.britannica.com) has a helpful and brief biography of Garibaldi, including a picture.

3. **Despite the racial differences of the authors, Machemba's declaration of independence in the "Letter to Major von Wissmann" parallels Olive Schreiner's declaration about the Boers and residents of South Africa in several important ways.** The most obvious connection between the two works is that they are both letters, but this points toward the much more significant point that both Machemba and Schreiner are attempting to convey the thoughts and understanding of a different people to an expanding imperialist power. Machemba does not simply declare that he won't submit; he educates Wissman on the sorts of interactions that his people value: "I cannot recall that you ever gave me a paisa or a quarter paisa or a needle or a thread. I look for a reason why I should obey you, and I find not the slightest" (1634). Schreiner, too, attempts to convey the senses of despair, violation, and hopelessness of the South African populations: "The lands, the mineral wealth which should have been ours to build up the great Africa of the future, has gone into strange hands! And they use the gold they gain out of us to enslave us; they strike at our hearts with a sword gilded with South African gold" (1639–40).

a. **Further Reading:** Berkman, Joyce Avrech. *The Healing Imagination of Olive Schreiner: Beyond South African Colonialism*. Amherst, MA: University of Massachusetts Press, 1989.

b. **Suggested Search:** A Google search for "African Responses to Imperialism" results in many helpful links, including a page hosted by CUNY Brooklyn which compiles a variety of different Africans' quotes that are similar to Machemba's letter.

4. **The horrors that Mark Twain emphasizes in *King Leopold's Soliloquy* are some of the effects of imperialism that are conveniently ignored by those advocates of imperialistic expansion that we find in this selection.** Twain characterizes King Leopold as annoyed by the fact that certain details about the brutality of his administration are coming to the public's attention, but determined to ignore or contradict the reports. Yet in light of the slaughters and tortures that Twain

describes, claims like Kipling's sound not just hollow, but perverse: "Take up the White Man's burden— / Send forth the best ye breed— / Go bind your sons to exile / To serve your captives need; / To wait in heavy harness, / On fluttered folk and wild— / Your new-caught, sullen peoples, / Half-devil and half-child" (1640). Macaulay and Kipling are not Twain's Leopold, but their discussions of burdens and education while ignoring murder and slavery are a notable example of the tendency of human beings to ignore evils and see their own actions as good and helpful when in fact they are the opposite.

    a. **Further Reading:** Gilmour, David. *The Long Recessional: The Imperial Life of Rudyard Kipling.* New York: Farrar, Strauss, and Giroux, 2002.

    b. **Suggested Search:** A search at JSTOR for "Twain and Imperialism" results in several helpful articles.

In-Class Activities

1. Divide your students into six groups, and assign to each group a continent (excluding Antarctica). The groups must prepare a research presentation on the effects of imperialism on that continent, and deliver that presentation to the class.

2. Hold a debate in class about whether or not Olive Schreiner makes a persuasive argument. Be sure to address the fact that she ignores the indigenous black people entirely.

3. Hold a class discussion in which you weigh the claims that Macaulay makes about English literature and an education based upon the tradition in the west. Encourage your students to give a fair evaluation to his arguments, identifying aspects that are good and bad.

Paper Topics/Suggestion for Writing

1. Write a poetry analysis about Rudyard Kipling's "The White Man's Burden" in which you argue that he is, or is not, being serious.

2. Write an essay in which you reflect upon the idea of freedom in relation to the various texts included in this cluster.

3. What text most clearly identifies and condemns imperialism? What text most clearly identifies and defends imperialism? Which of the two is more persuasive, and why?

4. Write a biographical essay about Cecil Rhodes, in which you discuss his activities during his lifetime, the founding of the Rhodes scholarship, and the effects that Rhodes's wealth has had upon the world since his death.

5. Consider imperialism as a movement founded upon Enlightenment philosophy. To what degree is it racist? To what degree does it privilege Europeans? To what degree does it depend upon faulty philosophical assumptions, and to what degree does it reflect universal weaknesses in human nature?

Resources

Gregory, Brad. *The Unintended Reformation: How a Religious Revolution Secularized Society.* Cambridge, MA: Harvard University Press, 2012.
Gregory's work explains the context from which the Enlightenment emerged, and the impact that it has had upon the centuries that followed. It is tremendously helpful for understanding the confidence of imperialist thinkers and governments during the nineteenth and twentieth centuries.
Kipling, Rudyard. *The Jungle Book.* London: Macmillan & Co., 1946.
Readers wishing to understand Kipling's lasting popularity should turn to this volume, which presents some of the ideas debated in imperialist movements in a more interesting and colorful light.
Meredith, Martin. *Diamonds, Gold, and War: The British, the Boers, and the Making of South Africa.* New York: Public Affairs, 2007.
This history is both informative and accessible, and is recommended for both students and instructors.
Peterson, Derek R., ed. *Abolitionism and Imperialism in Britain, Africa, and the Atlantic.* Athens, OH: Ohio University Press, 2010.
This collection of essays provides a variety of views concerning the developments of imperialism and abolitionism at the turn of the century.

ORATURE

Topics for Lecture or Discussion

1. **The nineteenth-century European interest in folktales arose out of a recognition that a distinctly oral culture existed, a cultural truth that was first recognized by Enlightenment writers.** Medieval conceptions of spoken and written language often treated the two forms of communication as being essentially similar, obscuring any unique value to oral literature. As literacy grew in the seventeenth century, written communication became increasingly common, and new pressures, such as the growing need to standardize written language, pushed European writers to increasingly examine the differences between written and oral communication. Critic Nicholas Hudson writes, "With [the] separation of writing and speech in theories of language, European scholars . . . began to imagine oral and literate cultures as quite separate and dissimilar" (246). This shift toward understanding writing and speech as fundamentally dissimilar made possible a study of oral culture in the nineteenth century.

   a. **Further Reading:** Hudson, Nicholas. "Constructing Oral Tradition: The Origins of the Concept in Enlightenment Intellectual Culture." In *The Spoken Word: Oral Culture in Britain 1500–1850*, edited by Adam Fox and Daniel Woolf, 240–55. Manchester, UK: Manchester University Press, 2002.

   b. **Suggested Searches:** Samuel Johnson's *A Dictionary of the English Language* is a major document that came into existence due to the increased need to standardize written English. Images of Johnson's *Dictionary,* including introductory essays on grammar and the history of the English language, can be found in the University of Toronto's catalog at Internet Archive at http://archive.org/details /university_of_toronto. This can be found by clicking on the "Texts" tab on Internet Archive's home page, selecting "Canadian Libraries" on the search bar, and then searching for "Samuel Johnson" and "dictionary." Other copies of Johnson's *Dictionary* can be found on Internet Archive as well.

2. **"The Three Spinners" is one of several stories collected by the Brothers Grimm that concerns spinning. In their tales, spinning is shown to be common traditional work expected of women, making a story such as "The Three Spinners" one about society's expectations for a woman to be productive.** The story centers on the social expectation that the daughter spin flax. This social pressure clashes with the daughter's disinterest in spinning, and the story's conflict arises from the difference between the mother's claim that her daughter is a produc-

tive spinner and the daughter's actual disinterest in spinning. With this conflict between social expectations and private desires, a tale that valued productivity should punish the idle daughter, but "The Three Spinners" confounds these expectations and rewards the daughter.

   a. **Further Reading:** Bottigheimer, Ruth B. "Tale Spinners: Submerged Voices in Grimms' Fairy Tales." *New German Critique* 27 (August 1982): 141–50.

   b. **Suggested Searches:** Conduct a Google Images search for "Grimms' Fairy Tales" and "illustrations" to find images from the numerous versions of *Grimms' Fairy Tales*. Adding "Philipp Grot Johann" to the search will bring up some images from the first illustrator for the Grimm brothers' collection.

3. **In addition to collecting folklore, Joseph Jacobs argued for the context of the tales and a scholarly understanding of folklore. A number of his claims about folklore parallel the dominant beliefs of contemporary scholars, including an emphasis on the spread of folktales by diffusion.** Jacobs, who collected folktales such as "Tom Tit Tot" in our selection, also participated in scholarly debate regarding folktales. Many of Jacobs's views about folktales were broadly sociological, such as his belief that folktales were spread by diffusion. Diffusion offers an explanation as to why folktales in different regions appear to be similar, such as the resemblance of "Tom Tit Tot" to "Rumpelstiltskin." It argues that similarities between stories exist because folktales travel from region to region, being retold and slightly changed with each retelling. Diffusion should be contrasted with a belief that stories are uniquely invented in each region. While contemporary scholars may mix claims of invention and diffusion when comparing folktales, Jacobs's sociological argument of diffusion is a standard way to understand the spread of oral stories.

   a. **Further Reading:** Fine, Gary Alan. "Joseph Jacobs: A Sociological Folklorist." *Folklore* 98:2 (1987): 183–93.

   b. **Suggested Search:** "Tom Tit Tot" is retold in Book Two of *The Young and Field Literary Readers*, with beautiful illustrations by Maginel Wright Enright, the sister of famous architect Frank Lloyd Wright. The book can be found by searching for the title at Project Gutenberg (www.gutenberg.org). Book Two also contains illustrated stories of English, German, Hindu, French, Norse, Russian, and American Indian origin, as well as illustrated poems by Christina Rossetti, who is included in this volume in the section "Romantic Poets and Their Successors."

4. **Malagasy *hainteny* has primarily been recorded as literature and given no context for its performance, notes critic Lee Haring. Leaving out the context in which hainteny was used ignores its**

value to Merina communities, including its practical uses. One exception to this generalization is Jean Paulhan, who transcribed the haínteny that is translated for our selection. Paulhan also wrote about the situations in which he saw haínteny used, such as during disagreements in which the individuals disagreeing would duel or debate by speaking haínteny back and forth until a victor was determined. The rules of debating with haínteny were clear among members of the community, and even children could be seen using haínteny to resolve a disagreement.

  a. **Further Reading:** Haring, Lee. "Folklore and the History of Literature in Madagascar." *Research in African Literatures* 16:3 (Autumn 1985): 297–318.

  b. **Suggested Search:** The website Wild Madagascar (www.wildmada gascar.org) contains images and information about Madagascar, focusing on the island's wildlife. Clicking on the "Photos" link will lead to images focusing on the flora and fauna of Madagascar, as well as images of the people and villages of the island. Selecting the "People" link on the home page and then "History" will lead to a time line of major events in Madagascar.

5. **As a ceremony intended to heal an ill tribe member, "The Night Chant" demonstrates Navajo beliefs about the nature of health and the world. The ceremony demonstrates a Navajo belief in the interconnectedness of the entire universe.** "The Night Chant" is from a nine-day ceremony focused on healing a single member of the tribe, who is shown to be a part of the entire universe, and so the process of healing is a matter of bringing the individual into balance with the rest of the universe. "The Night Chant's" repetitions and lists show no creature to be solely an individual but to be an amalgam of qualities, often with landmarks locating the individual as one among others: "In the house made of the dawn, / In the house made of the evening twilight, / In the house made of the dark cloud, / . . . Oh, male divinity! / With your moccasins of dark clouds, come to us. / With your leggings of dark cloud, come to us. / With your shirt of dark cloud, come to us" (1676–77).

  a. **Further Reading:** Ramsey, Jarold. "The Poetry and Drama of Healing: The Iroquoian *Condolence Ritual* and the Navajo *Night Chant*." *Literature and Medicine* 8 (1989): 78–99.

  b. **Suggested Search:** Go to navajopeople.org for images and information about the Navajo. Images of the Navajo, Navajo land, and Navajo sand painting, and other related imagery, can easily be found through links on the left side of the home page.

6. **The trickster character of Anansi demonstrates how to fight against a stronger opponent through intelligence. The Anansi stories demonstrate practical tactics for slaves to use in resisting the dominat-**

ing power of slavery. In a society where physical abuse was legally sanctioned for slave owners and their employees, slaves had little hope of improving their daily condition through physical resistance. Among the Anansi tactics that critic Emily Zobel Marshall sees being used by slaves, according to historical documents, were those of lying to gain an advantage and acting unintelligent in order to be underestimated. In a society where it was impossible to win through direct force, the Anansi figure demonstrated how subtle manipulation could alter the behavior of a more powerful opponent.

    a. **Further Reading:** Marshall, Emily Zobel. "Anansi Tactics in Plantation Jamaica: Matthew Lewis's Record of Trickery." *Wadabagei: A Journal of the Carribbean and Its Diaspora* 12:3 (Fall 2009): 126–50.

    b. **Suggested Searches:** Anansi stories continue to be retold for children, and new versions of these stories can easily be found by searching for the character's name at youtube.com. A couple of retellings of Anansi stories can be found by searching for "Anansi" on the website Speakaboos at www.speakaboos.com.

In-Class Activities

1. "The Night Chant" is from a ceremony that lasts several days and includes extratextual elements such as sand paintings. How can we relate to translated text from this ceremony, taken out of its religious context? What does the poem tell you about a traditional Navajo worldview, and what remains obscure?

2. Contemporary versions of oral stories often present the stories as being primarily for children, but this is not historically or universally the originally intended audience. What aspects of the stories in the "Orature" section seem to be aimed at an adult rather than a child audience? How do you differentiate between an adult and a child audience for foreign cultures from different time periods?

3. "The Despotic Chiefs of Kau" focuses on the poor conduct of bad chiefs. What do we learn from these stories about how a chief is supposed to treat his people? What rights do common citizens hold?

Paper Topics/Suggestions for Writing

1. The Anansi stories continue to be retold to contemporary American children. Choose a nineteenth- or early twentieth-century telling of an Anansi story as well as a contemporary retelling of that story. Compare and contrast the two versions of the story, arguing for how each version relates to its particular audience.

2. An interpretation of folktales through the concept of archetypes was more common among scholarly work in the early to mid-twentieth

century with writers such as Carl Jung and Joseph Campbell than it is today. Review some writing on folktales from this scholarly point of view, and write on why this scholarly approach might have fallen out of favor. Consider both what might be unappealing and what might be valuable about a theory of archetypes.

3. The collecting of oral stories, such as the work done by Jacob and Wilhelm Grimm, is often done with the intent of preserving a traditional culture. This valuing of traditional culture has placed folktales in a relationship with nationalism in the nineteenth and twentieth centuries in places such as Ireland and Germany. Research the folklore of a country of your choosing, and write on the relationship between that nation's folklore and its recent political history.

4. A concern with social ills is shared by American slave spirituals and secular songs selected here and many of William Blake's *Songs of Innocence and of Experience* (in this volume). Compare one or more of the spirituals with one or more of Blake's poems.

5. Olaudah Equiano's *The Interesting Narrative* and Frederick Douglass's *Narrative* and "All God's Chillen Had Wings" (all in this volume) all depict the injustice of slavery. Examine "All God's Chillen Had Wings" alongside either Equiano's or Douglass's text. Argue for how each text might be valuable for its given audience.

6. As mentioned in the introduction to the Malagasy oral poetry, Jean Paulhan's translations of poems inspired French modernists such as Guillaume Apollinaire and Paul Éluard. Look at the selected Malagasy poems beside translations from Apollinaire's *Alcools* or Éluard's *Capital of Pain*. Argue for the aspects of the Malagasy poems that would be appealing to these French poets.

7. Consider gender in "The Three Spinners" or "Tom Tit Tot." Argue for whether these stories maintain or disrupt the norms of a patriarchal society, and examine the power given to and the limits placed on each story's heroine.

Resources

Calvino, Italo. *Italian Folktales*. Translated by George Martin. New York: Harcourt, 1980.
> This is a famous collection of Italian folktales by the major twentieth-century writer Italo Calvino.

Grimm, Jacob, and Wilhelm Grimm. *The Annotated Brothers Grimm*. Edited and translated by Maria Tatar. New York: W. W. Norton, 2004.
> This is a selection of tales collected by the Brothers Grimm, with annotated commentary on individual stories and classic illustrations.

Schmidt, Gary D., and Donald R. Hettinga, eds. *Sitting at the Feet of the Past: Retelling the North American Folktale for Children.* Westport, CT: Greenwood Press, 1992.

>This is a selection of essays on folktales told in America. While all the essays are scholarly in scope, several of them discuss contemporary issues regarding the retelling of folktales.

Tzara, Tristan. "Poèmes Nègres." In *4 X 1,* translated and edited by Pierre Joris, 15–72. Albany, NY: Inconundrum Press, 2002.

>This avant-garde French poet's collection of non-Western poetry (including a brief selection of hainteny) demonstrates the influence of African and oceanic literature on early twentieth-century French poetry.

IV. Modernity and Modernism, 1900–1945

JOSEPH CONRAD
Heart of Darkness

Topics for Lecture or Discussion

1. **Marlow's story is told as a frame narrative, a technique that challenges an objective understanding of reality and instead relies on individual perception.** The story of *Heart of Darkness* is presented through a complex narrative technique called a "frame narrative," or a story within a story. The tale of his own expedition is not told by Marlow firsthand, thus most of the text is in quotation marks. But the speaker is not omniscient and objective. He is an anonymous character in the story, one of the listening men on the *Nellie* who had heard and then reported to us Marlow's tale. Because this character repeats Marlow's narrative, which Marlow himself had to repeat after the events, the novel asks us to consider the flexibility of reality through perception. The readers are twice removed from the actual events and are forced to rely on the hearsay of characters, not God-like narrators. When Marlow derides women or looks indifferently at the suffering of the Africans, we must wonder about the reliability of this commentary as truth. Is it Marlow's or an embellishment by the narrator? Lies (like Marlow's to the Intended), disrupted narratives, twice-told stories, and failures of language (the "ciphers" in the Russian's book) are essential parts of communicating truth, a fact that Joseph Conrad celebrates and calls a "horror."
   a. **Further Reading:** Brooks, Peter. *Reading for the Plot: Design and Intervention in Narrative.* New York: Knopf, 1984.
   b. **Suggested Search:** Conduct a Google Images search for *"mise en abyme"* ("placing into infinity"). The results will show visual images of framing: art within art, mirror reflection within reflection, photograph within photograph. The most famous example is the painting *Las Meninas* by Velazquez.

2. **Though the Berlin Conference promised to abolish slavery and "civilize" the natives by the partitioning of Africa, the tyrant King Leopold II of Belgium brutally enslaved and killed millions of Africans in the Congo Free State, *Heart of Darkness*'s setting, to build his empire.** The partitioning of Africa, sometimes called the "Scramble for Africa," was a process of dividing African territory between European countries. In the 1870s, Europe controlled about 10 percent of Africa; by 1900, it controlled 90 percent. Though there were many origins for the scramble, like the pre–World War I nationalistic ideology surging through the continent, one of the largest influences was the amount of raw materials available in Africa, such as ivory, copper,

rubber, and tea. Europeans exploited territories for commercial gain, often enslaving the native residents. Ironically, the Berlin Conference of 1884–1885, which initiated the formal landgrab, listed abolishing slavery as one of its foremost goals, along with its "civilizing mission." The missionary David Livingstone, a possible prototype for Joseph Conrad's Kurtz, is the most famous example of an explorer who took on the "white man's burden." The phrase was popularly taken up after Rudyard Kipling's 1899 poem of the same name. In it he discusses the dangers of civilizing missions, but his irony was misunderstood as a justification for colonization. Under the pretense of ending slavery and civilizing the natives, King Leopold II's territory of the Congo Free State is infamous for its cruelty toward slaves that led to millions of deaths.

    a. **Further Reading:** Hochschild, Adam. *King Leopold's Ghost.* New York: Mariner, 1998.

    b. **Suggested Search:** Search for *"New World Encyclopedia* and Scramble." The first link will take you to a page that not only offers an extensive explanation of the partitioning but also political cartoons, photographs, and, most helpfully, a map like the one Joseph Conrad describes, showing the division of Africa between European states.

3. **The archetypal journey to the depths of Africa represents the process of discovering the corrupted European subconscious.** *Heart of Darkness* is often read in terms of mythological conceits. In this view, Marlow is the hero who journeys across a river to the guarded underworld to discover great truths from the damned. However, in this modernist work, the underworld can represent man's duplicitous consciousness. Through this psychoanalytic reading, Marlow is an Everyman, the average, universal figure to whom the audience relates. He makes the archetypal journey through his own interiority to discover his true subconscious, here the insane Kurtz. Kurtz is an amalgamation of the uncivilized European subconsciousness; as Marlow says, "All Europe contributed to the making of Kurtz" (1733). Images throughout the novel support this doubleness of identity. For example, Marlow imagines the Thames and now-civilized London as a "dark place" (1696); he calls Brussels a "whited sepulchre" (1700) that on the outside seems pure and clean but inside is a tomb, full of death and decay; and even the supposedly rational and socialized Europeans corrupt and destroy the Congo.

    a. **Further Reading:** Kartiganer, Donald M. "Freud's Reading Process: The Protagonist Narrative and the Case of the Wolf-Man." In *The Psychoanalytic Study of Literature,* edited by Joseph Reppen and Maurice Charney, 3–36. Hillsdale, NJ: The Analytic Press, 1985.

    b. **Suggested Search:** Search the web for *"Heart of Darkness* and webquest." This will guide students through the process of reading the novel. It can also be used to help guide instructors through certain types of interpretations, such as reader-response or psychoanalytical readings.

4. **Nigerian writer Chinua Achebe attacked both the novel *Heart of Darkness* and the prevailing literary interpretations of it for allowing Africans and Africa to function only as foils to whiteness and Europe.** In a 1975 lecture that was later published as "An Image of Africa," Achebe famously criticized metaphorical readings of Joseph Conrad's novel, especially psychoanalytical interpretations. To apply such a reading, he says, is to reduce an entire people to a literary device and to agree that Africa is the "antithesis to Europe and . . . civilization," a mere "metaphysical battleground" (4). As Achebe points out, Conrad denies Africans the power of language and facial expressions. Likewise, the African environment itself is "inscrutable" and "incomprehensible," words that imply that Africa is impossible to describe or understand. Achebe does not accept the argument that the characters, not Conrad, are racist. Instead, the frame narrative was Conrad's attempt to hide behind the moral views of his book. Marlow is not Conrad's ironic racist character; he is Conrad, another Enlightened European. Achebe's essay is one of the most influential criticisms on *Heart of Darkness* and still sparks much response. Theorist Edward Said, for example, replied to Achebe's claims in his book *Culture and Imperialism*, arguing that the book's position is anti-imperialistic; however, Conrad is a victim of his time and could not "grant the natives their freedom" (30).

   a. **Further Reading:** Achebe, Chinua. "An Image of Africa: Racism in Conrad's *Heart of Darkness*." In *Hopes and Impediments: Selected Essays*, 1–13. New York: Doubleday, 1989.

   b. **Suggested Search:** Go to the "Chinua Achebe: *Things Fall Apart* Study Guide" page at http://public.wsu.edu/~brians/anglophone /achebe.html, which gives an overview of Chinua Achebe's novel that many consider the nonracist version of Joseph Conrad's. It also offers the entirety of Yeats's poem "The Second Coming" and commentary on *Heart of Darkness*.

5. **The patriarchal ideology of the novel refuses complexity for the female characters.** A central focus of feminist and gender criticism is Marlow's lie to Kurtz's Intended. When she asks to hear Kurtz's last words, Marlow says "your name" and not "The horror! The horror!" Some critics read this moment through a Freudian lens, thus conflating her, European women, or women in general to "the horror." Other critics, such as Claire Kahane, have noted the similar pronunciations of "horror" and "whore," a similarity that denotes anger toward women or femininity. Whether the attitude toward them is hostile or not, the role of women in the novel is certainly not flattering. Joseph Conrad

includes only a handful of female characters, all of whom are nameless and some of whom are only identified by their relationship to men. The patriarchal atmosphere of the novel demotes women to their most basic functions. For example, Marlow's aunt, even though she helps Marlow obtain his position in the Company, represents foolish idealism and a "too beautiful . . . world of their own" (1702–03). And the characterless Intended and the Savage Mistress only represent opposite ends of the spectrum: frigidity and sexuality. In the same way that Africa is the foil to Europe, femininity foils masculinity.

 a. **Further Reading:** Mongia, Padmini. "Empire, Narrative, and the Feminine in *Lord Jim* and *Heart of Darkness*." In *Contexts for Conrad*, edited by Keith Carabine et al., 135–50. Boulder, CO: East European Monographs, 1993.

 b. **Suggested Searches:** Enter the phrase "Victorian women" in a Google Images search to find drawings and photographs of the typical nineteenth-century woman in England. Also search for "Women characters in heart of darkness slideshare." This slideshow discusses the role of women in the novel, moving through each character.

In-Class Activities

1. In the beginning of part 1, Marlow describes how London was once a "dark place" (1696) when the Romans conquered the Britons. He later likens the city of Brussels to a "whited sepulchre" (1700). Discuss both of these images and why Marlow would describe both of these major "civilized" cities in these two ways.

2. To introduce the frame narrative, ask students if they have encountered that narrative technique before. They might mention other works of literature, such as *The Thousand and One Nights*, parts of *The Odyssey*, *Canterbury Tales*, *Frankenstein*, *Wuthering Heights*, and *Turn of the Screw*. But you can also discuss films that use frame narratives, such as *Forrest Gump*, *Titanic*, and *Slumdog Millionaire*, or even the sitcom *How I Met Your Mother*. Discuss how the technique is used to different effects in those works and compared to *Heart of Darkness*. You can also show excerpts from film versions of the novel to emphasize the narrative effect.

3. Do any moments, images, or characters in the story seem mythological? You can discuss the women knitting outside of the office and the fates, the Congo as the River Styx, Marlow as the hero, and Kurtz as the anti-hero or Jungian "Shadow."

4. Explain the history of the colonization of Africa by European nations by beginning with Marlow's experience with the map as a child and then later when he is in the Company's offices. The website *New World Encyclopedia* includes an image of divided Africa in 1914 on the

"Scramble for Africa" page that could accompany the discussion (www .newworldencyclopedia.org/entry/Scramble_for_Africa).

5. Discuss the different ways to interpret Kurtz's famous last words, "The horror! The horror!" What was he referring to? How does the meaning change when Marlow tells Kurtz's Intended that his last words were her name?

Paper Topics/Suggestions for Writing

1. *Heart of Darkness* is presented as a frame narrative. In other words, an unknown narrator who knows Marlow tells the story of Marlow telling his own story. Explain how this frame narrative affects how the audience understands the events of the story. Why might Joseph Conrad want that effect?

2. T. S. Eliot, whose work is included in this volume, used the line "Mistah Kurtz—he dead" as the epigraph to his poem "The Hollow Men." The original epigraph to "The Waste Land," before poet Ezra Pound dissuaded Eliot, included the famous lines: "Did he live his life again in every detail of desire, temptation, and surrender during that supreme moment of complete knowledge? He cried in a whisper at some image, at some vision—he cried out twice, a cry that was no more than a breath—'The horror! the horror!'" (1748). Read one or both of these poems and discuss how *Heart of Darkness* relates to them.

3. Read Chinua Achebe's article "An Image of Africa." Explain his argument and then respond by agreeing or disagreeing. Support your response by referencing particular scenes from Joseph Conrad's novel.

4. In his book *King Leopold's Ghost*, Adam Hochschild argues that Joseph Conrad's story about a journey into the heart of darkness is not simply a literary metaphor for discovering the brutish consciousness of the individual. Instead, Hochschild says, it is a direct political commentary on imperialism based on Conrad's own experiences in the Congo. Do you believe that the novel functions better as a metaphor or as criticism? Does it function as both?

5. Compare the roles of the African female characters, such as the mistress and woman who launders the accountant's shirts, and the European female characters, such as the two knitters, Marlow's aunt, and Kurtz's Intended.

6. Kurtz writes a pamphlet that Marlow says "gave me the notion of an exotic Immensity ruled by an august benevolence." At the foot of the last page is scribbled, "Exterminate all the brutes!" (1733). Another marked book belongs to the Russian by the author "Towson or Towser."

Marlow discovers it and first believes that the notes are written in cipher or secret language. Explain how these two scenes with annotated written works contribute to the novel's concerns with truth, subjectivity, and perception.

Resources

Apocalypse Now. Dir. Francis Ford Coppola. Perf. Marlon Brando, Martin Sheen, and Robert Duvall. Paramount, 1979.

This acclaimed film is a modernized version of Joseph Conrad's novel, set in Vietnam during the war.

Hawkins, Hunt, and Brian Shaffer, eds. *Approaches to Teaching Conrad's "Heart of Darkness" and "The Secret Sharer."* New York: Modern Language Association, 2002.

This contemporary collection of essays offers twenty approaches to teaching Joseph Conrad.

Heart of Darkness. In Audio, 2004, CD.

This CD is an unabridged version of the novel, read by Ralph Cosham.

Joseph Conrad: Heart of Darkness. Films for the Humanities and Sciences, 1998.

Joseph Conrad scholars Bruce Harkness, Frederick Karl, Jerome Meckier, and Dwight Purdy discuss Conrad's life and times as an influence on *Heart of Darkness.*

The Joseph Conrad Society (UK). www.josephconradsociety.org.

The "Student Resources" section on this website is especially helpful. Look for overviews of criticism and suggestions for further reading, and see the links at the bottom of the page.

"Joseph Conrad's diary (hitherto unpublished) of his journey up the valley of the Congo in 1890." *Conrad First: The Joseph Conrad Periodical Archive.* Uppsala University, 2009. www.conradfirst.net/view/serialisation?id=164.

This site offers *The Blue Peter* 1925 publication of Joseph Conrad's diary entries when he traveled through the Congo. The content of the diaries will help draw autobiographical connections. The illustrations and the advertisements are also noteworthy.

Karl, Frederick. *Joseph Conrad: The Three Lives.* New York: Farrar, 1979.

This is one of the foremost critical biographies of Joseph Conrad.

King Leopold's Ghost. Dirs. Pippa Scott and Oreet Rees. 2006.

Based on Adam Hochschild's 1998 novel of the same name, this vivid and informative documentary describes King Leopold's Belgian Congo.

Orson Welles's The Mercury Theatre: Heart of Darkness. CBS, 1938, MP3.

Famous for its broadcast of *War of the Worlds*, Orson Welles's The Mercury Theater on the Air was a New York drama company that performed via radio broadcasts in the 1930s.

Said, Edward. *Culture and Imperialism.* New York: Vintage, 1993.

THOMAS MANN

Death in Venice

> It was a face reminiscent of Greek statues
> from the noblest period of antiquity; it com-
> bined perfection of form with a unique per-
> sonal charm that caused the onlooker to doubt
> ever having met with anything in nature or in
> art that could match its perfection.
> —Mann, *Death in Venice*

Topics for Lecture or Discussion

1. **Thomas Mann's psychological framework for his character Aschenbach is based on the Apollonian and Dionysian dichotomy.** In his
   1872 book *The Birth of Tragedy*, Friedrich Nietzsche introduces two
   types of artistic impulses: the Apollonian and the Dionysian. The Apollonian impulse is the desire to make order, while the Dionysian is the
   impulse to create and celebrate chaos. The former is defined by reason
   and boundaries, named after Apollo, the god of reason, while the latter
   is irrational, animalistic, and emotional, named after Dionysius, the
   god of wine and ecstasy. Nietzsche believes that ancient Greek tragedies perfectly combine these two impulses; this is what makes them the
   highest form of art. The music of the chorus, the Dionysian, and the
   dialogue, the Apollonian, balanced one another. Aschenbach's art and
   even Aschenbach himself never seem to achieve this perfect balance.
   When the novel begins, Aschenbach is a rigid, realistic, overly disci-
   plined man who is stricken with wanderlust. As Nietzsche would put it,
   he says "yes to life" (*Twilight of the Idols* [1889. Oxford University Press,
   1998], 80). The final scene shows Aschenbach passionately following a
   hallucination, which leads to his death. Because he can only live chasing one extreme or the other, Aschenbach is never the ideal artist.
   a. **Further Reading:** Picart, Caroline Joan. *Thomas Mann and Fried-
      rich Nietzsche: Eroticism, Death, Music, and Laughter.* Amsterdam:
      Rodopi, 1999.
   b. **Suggested Search:** Search Google for the site "Apollo vs. Dionysus:
      The Only Theme Your Students Will Ever Need in Writing about
      Literature" by Michael Thro. It includes a chart of Apollonian and
      Dionysian terms, as well as many applications of the scheme to
      literature.

2. **Although he felt "perturbed and diminished" by Sigmund Freud's
   ideas, Thomas Mann consciously used Freudian concepts such as**

the id and superego, or the "death drive." In 1925, Mann claimed that he wrote "under the direct influence of Freud" (Lewis A. Lawson, *A Gorgon's Mask: The Mother in Thomas Mann's Fiction*, 221). Aschenbach's psychology is a split between the Apollonian and Dionysian, but in Freudian terms, this is understood as the divide between the superego and the id. The superego is the part of the psyche that moralizes and restricts, while the id is guided by impulse. In the second chapter, when the narrator sketches Aschenbach as an artist and a person, he mentions the St. Sebastian-type hero Aschenbach prefers: "an intellectual and youthful manliness which grits its teeth in proud modesty and calmly endures the swords and spears as they pass through its body" (1763). His superego stresses hard work, discipline, and self-control, but this gives way to the id, beginning with his interaction with the red-haired stranger. Scholars have also applied Freud's theory of the death drive to Aschenbach's destructive behavior. According to scholar Jonathan Dollimore, the death drive operates both personally for Aschenbach and for civilization. His desublimation of desire leads to his own downfall and is also representative of the twentieth-century, World War I–era collapse of civilization.

  a. **Further Reading:** Dollimore, Jonathan. "Perversion, Degeneration, and the Death Drive." In *Sexualities in Victorian Britain*, edited by Andrew H. Miller and James Eli Adams. Bloomington, IN: Indiana University Press, 1996.

  b. **Suggested Search:** Conduct a Google search for "beyond the pleasure principle and modernism lab" to bring up the wiki for the Modernism Lab at Yale University, which provides a clear overview of Sigmund Freud's text that includes the death drive.

3. **Aschenbach's Venetian vacation and obsession with Tadzio were based on autobiographical elements, as well as on events from the works and life of Wolfgang von Goethe.** In *A Sketch of My Life*, Thomas Mann wrote, "Nothing in *Death in Venice* is invented: the traveller by the Northern Cemetery in Munich, the gloomy boat from Pola, the aged fop, the dubious gondolier, Tadzio and his family, . . . the cholera . . . everything was given, and really only needed to be fitted in" (*The Cambridge Companion to Thomas Mann*, ed. Ritchie Robertson [New York: Cambridge University Press, 2002], 101). In the spring of 1911, Mann traveled to Venice with his wife and brother. He, like Aschenbach, was fascinated by a young Polish boy and was inspired to write an essay on taste and culture, like his character's "page-and-a-half of choice prose" (1788). In this actual essay, Mann reconsiders his previous love of romanticism in Wagner and wishes for art that is "intellectually cooler, more refined and even healthier, something that does not seek greatness in Baroque grandeur nor beauty in intoxication—a new

classicism, I fancy, must come" (Robertson, 95). Mann uses Johann Wolfgang von Goethe as a model of order, balance, and harmony for his return to classicism. Goethe's own appreciation of Winckelmann and appreciation for "Greek love" inspired his comment that pederasty is at once rooted in nature and against nature. In Venice, Goethe found himself attracted to a boyish street performer. "Originally I had not planned anything less than telling the story of Goethe's last love, the love of the seventy-year-old for that little girl, whom he still absolutely wanted to marry" (*Letters of Thomas Mann*, 72).

a. **Further Reading:** Mann, Thomas. *Letters of Thomas Mann, 1889–1955.* Translated by Richard Winston and Clara Winston. Berkeley: University of California Press, 1990.

b. **Suggested Search:** Search on Google Books (books.google.com) for Doris Alexander's *Creating Literature Out of Life*. The first chapter is called "The Birth of Death in Venice" and begins with an explanation of the text's connection to Johann Wolfgang von Goethe.

4. **Much critical scholarship sees the novella as an embodiment of the pre-World War I European zeitgeist.** The very first sentence of *Death in Venice* prepares the reader for a political text: "On a spring afternoon in 19–, a year that for months glowered threateningly over our continent . . ." (1758). Although the novel is often read with aestheticism in mind, it is also a commentary on the degeneration of Europe. It was published just before the outbreak of World War I, and scholar Edward Timms says that it "fits the pattern of psychohistory. Germanic self-control succumbs to the lure of Slavonic sensuousness" (*Thomas Mann's Death in Venice*, 179). The Prussian ethos, he argues, suppresses emotional impulses, and this suppression is discernible in both Aschenbach and in his study of Frederick the Great. What Timms and other scholars are arguing is that Thomas Mann predicted the state of the West. In 1947, Wolfgang Grote wrote that *Death in Venice* "unexpectedly became a death in Europe, a thousandfold, divine-natural compensation for nationalistic drunkenness and unbrotherliness into which Herr von Achenbach's aesthetic kind was able to swell like the Flood!" (ibid., 49). One can see this "flood" in the cholera that infects Venice. It is first presented as a pestilence with "an increasing tendency to spread and roam," raging "persistently and with unusual ferocity throughout Hindustan; then it had spread eastwards to China and westwards to Afghanistan and Persia. . . . But while Europe was shaking in fear lest the specter should progress . . . it had emerged simultaneously in several Mediterranean port cites" (130, para. 3).

a. **Further Reading:** Shookman, Ellis. "Increasing Acceptance, 1915–55." In *Thomas Mann's Death in Venice: A Novella and Its Critics.* Rochester, NY: Camden House, 2003.

b. **Suggested Search:** Search for "Second Moroccan Crisis" on history .com. Described on this page are the events that led up to World War I, concurrent with Thomas Mann's writing of *Death in Venice*.

5. **Aschenbach tries to understand his attraction to Tadzio in terms of classical texts on art and beauty, such as Plato's *Phaedrus*. However, he manipulates the ideas to justify—or at to least address— his own sexual obsession.** The two most discussed thematic issues of *Death in Venice* are aesthetics and sexuality. Aschenbach seeks to understand his attraction to Tadzio in terms of Plato's dialogue and twice pretends to be Socrates lecturing to his young male pupil, Phaedrus. Only the first apostrophe accurately captures the arguments made in the original text. The second, just before his death, is simply an adoption of the framework, for it actually opposes Socrates's arguments to accommodate his impassioned desire for Tadzio. Aschenbach first says that beauty is the only aspect of the spiritual that we can sense physically; if we could sense other divinities—"reason and virtue and truth"—we would be "consumed by love" (1788). Beauty is the means for the sensitive man's, the artist's, transcendence to the spiritual. While this idea is taken directly from *Phaedrus*, the second passage manipulates Plato's dialogue to suit Aschenbach's moral degeneracy. Instead of beauty as a means to transcendence, beauty is all: "It [knowledge] has sympathy for the abyss; it is the abyss. Let us therefore resolutely reject it, and henceforth our efforts will be directed only toward beauty" (1806–07). He also says that beauty leads to "dissolution." By manipulating Plato's text, he justifies his sexual obsession that is now, by the end of the novella, free of artistic form.

a. **Further Reading:** Van Buren Kelley, Alice. "Von Aschenbach's Phaedrus: Platonic Allusion in Der Tod in Venedig." *Journal of English and Germanic Philology* 75:1/2 (1976): 228–40.

b. **Suggested Search:** Search for "CriticalLink Plato: Phaedrus." The resulting site (www.english.hawaii.edu/criticalink/plato/index.html) includes a general overview, an in-depth guide to each section, definitions for terms, Plato's biography, a timeline, and guiding questions on Phaedrus.

6. **As the novella progresses, the narrator's once-respectful but increasingly sarcastic tone toward Aschenbach indicates his moral deterioration.** One often overlooked "character" of the novella is the narrator because the mode of narration is so often free indirect discourse, "a technique whereby a narrative reports the speech or thoughts of a character, referring to that character in the third person but adopting the character's own idiom" (see "Free indirect discourse," *The Bloomsbury Dictionary of English Literature* [London: Bloomsbury Pub-

lishing Ltd., 1997]. Accessed on Credoreference.com, August 8, 2012).
For example, when Aschenbach goes to the English travel agency, the
narrator says, "The clerk was a wool-clad Briton, still young" (1800). It is
the image- and age-obsessed Aschenbach who would note that the clerk
is "still young." However, the narrator does seem to maintain his own
opinions of the main character, opinions that change throughout the
novella from respectful to ironic toward Aschenbach's immorality. In
the second chapter, when the narrator introduces us to Aschenbach, the
tone is especially reverent. He begins, "Gustav Aschenbach, the author
of the clear and vigorous prose epic on the life of Frederick the Great;
the patient artist who wove together with enduring diligence the novel-
istic tapestry *Maia* . . ." (1761). Compare this to the sarcasm of the passage on page 136 that precedes the death scene, beginning, "He sat
there, the master, the artist who had attained to dignity. . . ."

  a. **Further Reading:** Cohn, Dorrit. "The Second Author of Der Tod in
    Venedig." *Short Story Criticism* 80 (2005): 124–43.

  b. **Suggested Search:** The "Speech Presentation Checksheet" at
    www.lancs.ac.uk/fass/projects/stylistics/topic9/11checksheet.htm
    will help students identify types of narration, such as free indirect
    discourse.

In-Class Activities

1. Show to the class the 1971 film version of *Death in Venice*, directed by
   Luchino Visconti. Discuss the translation from page to screen. Does it
   capture the tone and themes of the novella?

2. Students might be uncomfortable with Aschenbach, an older man, lust-
   ing after a younger boy. Discuss the nature of his attraction to Tadzio. Is
   it only a sexual attraction? Is he jealous of youth? Aschenbach refers
   often to Greek mythology and art, so you might show some classical
   Greek images and sculptures to segue into a lecture on classical beauty.
   Include Spinario, the boy from the sculpture *Boy removing a thorn
   from his foot*.

3. The setting of Venice is important to the central themes of the novella.
   Show students a short documentary or photos of Venice to familiarize
   them with the city, and then discuss why Thomas Mann would set
   Aschenbach's decline into death there.

4. Benjamin Britten's last opera was based on and titled after Thomas
   Mann's *Death in Venice*. Students can find the entire opera, in English,
   as performed in Barcelona at the Gran Teatre del Liceu, on youtube
   .com. The video is broken into seventeen parts, with each part approximately 9 to 10 minutes long. Choose one or two scenes from the opera to

play in class, and then have students reflect on how Britten's music and this particular performance (the staging, lighting, costumes, and cast) capture the moods and themes of the novel. Is it an accurate translation of the novella?

5. Play the 1997 film *Love and Death on Long Island*, which is a contemporary retelling of Thomas Mann's novella, starring John Hurt as Giles De'ath, a well-known, older writer who is obsessed with a young actor played by Jason Priestley. Discuss how the movie maintained some of the essential features of Mann's story, such as the main relationship, the setting, or the tone.

Paper Topics/Suggestions for Writing

1. Consider the implications of the multiplicity of nationalities. Why did Thomas Mann set the story of Aschenbach's downfall in Venice? Why is Aschenbach German and Tadzio Polish?

2. Thomas Mann, like Charles Baudelaire, Stéphane Mallarmé, Paul Verlaine, Marcel Proust, and T. S. Eliot, was inspired by the composer Richard Wagner. How is this influence present in *Death in Venice*? Is it comparable to the influence on any of the aforementioned authors? You may want to read one of Wagner's essays, either "The Artwork of the Future" or "Opera and Drama."

3. Who is the stranger that Aschenbach sees in the first chapter? How does he create wanderlust in Aschenbach? Does he resemble other characters Aschenbach meets? What might he/these men represent?

4. Describe and contrast the two *Phaedrus* passages on pages 1848 and 1867. What does their opposition signify about Aschenbach's aesthetics? What is the aesthetic theory of the novella itself?

5. Explain the following quotation about Aschenbach through a Freudian lens: "A canny observer remarked about him to friends, 'You see, Aschenbach has always lived like this'—and the speaker closed the fingers of his left hand into a fist—'never like this'—and he let his open hand dangle comfortably from the arm of the chair" (1823, para. 3).

6. Who is the narrator? What is his or her opinion of Aschenbach? How would you describe the tone of the narrator? Does the narrator's opinion ever change? At what point do you see that change?

Resources

Berlin, Jeffrey B., ed. *Approaches to Teaching Mann's Death in Venice and Other Short Fiction*. New York: Modern Language Association, 1992.

This extremely helpful resource collects fifteen essays, including "Mann and the Modernist Tradition" and "Plato and Nietzsche in *Death in Venice*."

Death in Venice. Dir. Luchino Visconti. Alfa Cinematografica, 1971.

In Luchino Visconti's film version, which is much acclaimed for its visual and musical beauty, Aschenbach is not a writer but a composer.

Death in Venice. Opera by Benjamin Britten. 1973.

Benjamin Britten's last opera, based on Mann's novella, is available online, including on youtube.com.

Robertson, Ritchie. *The Cambridge Companion to Thomas Mann*. Cambridge: Cambridge University Press, 2002.

Ritchie Robertson's collection of essays on cultural, historical, and other thematic focuses also includes introductory notes on each major work, as well as diary entries.

Shookman, Ellis. *Thomas Mann's Death in Venice: A Reference Guide*. Westport, CT: Greenwood Press, 2004.

Ellis Shookman surveys *Death in Venice*'s reception from its publication in 1912.

MARCEL PROUST

Swann's Way

> And suddenly the memory appeared. That
> taste was the taste of the little piece of made-
> leine which on Sunday mornings at Combray
> (because that day I did not go out before it was
> time for Mass), when I went to say good morn-
> ing to her in her bedroom, my aunt Leonie
> would give me after dipping it in her infusion
> of tea or lime blossom.
>
> —Proust, "Overture" to *Swann's Way*

Topics for Lecture or Discussion

1. **In the "Overture" to *Swann's Way*, Marcel Proust depicts the synesthetic experience, or memory incited through the physical senses.**
"Overture," a musical term, describes an instrumental piece that introduces themes and motifs that will appear throughout the opera or sym-
phony. Proust's "Overture" both introduces and encapsulates the main
theme of *Remembrance of Things Past*, which is the harmony between
objects, senses, and experiences. This harmony is called "synesthesia"
and is defined as the simultaneous and involuntary stimulation of two
or more senses, such as taste and memory. Proust was influenced by
the poet Charles Baudelaire who used the term "correspondences" to
describe this process of sensory connections. In his 1857 poem titled
"Correspondences" (see Voume 2, p. 1043), Baudelaire writes, "Man wan-
ders among symbols in these glades / Where all things watch him with
familiar eyes" (lines 3–4). Marcel, similarly, says that "the past is hidden . . . in some material object . . . which we do not suspect" (1842).
Here the poet and the author state that synesthetic moments—when the
material, corporeal world awakens the ethereal, emotional world of
memory—are woven into life. Whether the stimulant is the physical
position of his limbs in bed or the taste of madeleine dipped in tea, Marcel is sensitive to associative thoughts, feelings, and memories.
   a. **Further Reading:** Weiner, Marc A. "Zwieback and Madeleine: Creative Recall in Wagner and Proust." *MLN* 95:3 (April 1980): 679–84.
   b. **Suggested Search:** Conduct a Google search for "Overture to Tristan
   and Isolde." The first result is an 11-minute video of the overture on
   youtube.com.

2. **Marcel Proust's concept of time is that it is fluid and moves between
past and present; it is not rigid or measurable.** Although he denied the

connection, many readers and scholars find helpful the comparisons between Henri Bergson and Marcel Proust. Bergson was a philosopher who authored, in 1889, the influential *Time and Free Will: An Essay on the Immediate Data of Consciousness*. In this essay, Bergson stresses the importance of *durée* ("duration"), or lived time, as the direct intuition of consciousness. Lived time, rather than sterile "clock time," which is mathematical and measurable, is what gives the overture such a fluid feel. He writes that "both the past and the present states form an organic whole, as happens when we recall the notes of a melody, melting, so to speak, into one another" (100). Marcel is able to "travel" to and from different points in his life because time "melts" and is not strict or linear. Many new readers struggle with the temporal setting of the "Overture" for this reason. One moment the adult narrator is discussing the role of memory in our daily lives and then transitions seamlessly into a childhood memory about "mother and grandmother" and his magic lantern.

a. **Further Reading:** Trigg, Dylan. "An Uncanny Memory." In *The Aesthetics of Decay: Nothingness, Nostalgia, and the Absence of Reason*. New York: Peter Lang Publishing, 2009.

b. **Suggested Search:** Search NPR.org for "time, memory, and Proust" to read and/or listen to an NPR program in which Linda Wertheimer interviews Alain de Botton, author of *How Proust Can Change Your Life*, about Proustian time.

3. **Marcel, Proust's narrator, shares his creator's name and childhood, but because Marcel Proust believed in the distinction between the private and social selves, he argued that the novel was not autobiographical.** Within the very first paragraph, Marcel mentions metempsychosis, the transmigration of the soul from one person to another, thus asking readers to question the existence of a single self. Proust believed that the aesthetic materials were readily available in the author's life or, rather, lives. In that case, the artist is a translator of life material into art material. This splintering of identities is a theme that runs throughout the novel, including the "Overture," beginning with the opening, when the narrator, Marcel, awakes and struggles to place or identify himself: "[T]hen it [my mind] would let go of the map of the place where I had fallen asleep and, when I awoke in the middle of the night, since I did not know where I was, I did not even understand in the first moment who I was" (1814–15). There is a division between the private self and the social self, and Proust uses the former as his narrating persona. Therefore, says Proust, biographical connections are a useless form of literary study, for we the readers cannot know the private self of the author.

a. **Further Reading:** Ellison, David R. "Who Is 'Marcel'?: Proust and the Question of Autobiographical Identity." *L'Esprit Createur* 20:3 (Fall 1980): 78–86.

b. **Suggested Search:** Conduct a Google search for "modernism lab and Proust." This will take you to Yale University's Modernism Lab wiki, where you will find an extensive biography, as well as articles on the entire novel.

4. **The "Overture" and subsequent novel are realistic sketches of the process of remembering.** New readers of Marcel Proust tend to feel frustration or at least initial confusion with the constant digressions and nesting of stories within stories. Individual sentences mimic this style so that one can lose track of the subject halfway through, sending the reader back and forth, stopping and starting. By writing in such a fluid, associative style, Proust encourages his readers to abide by his understanding of fluid, associative time. He admired this digressive manner in writer and aesthete John Ruskin, about whom he translated and wrote essays, which Walter Benjamin identified in Proust as "Penelope-work," continually weaving and unweaving the intellect and the memory. In the late nineteenth century, philosophers, critics, and writers were considering the nature of memory aesthetically, but scientists such as Hermann Ebbinghaus were also exploring the functions of memory. Ebbinghaus, in fact, discovered and studied what Proust would only later call "involuntary memory." Though it may seem paradoxical, the lack of "rational" design of Marcel's narration is one aspect of the novel's realism. It does not attempt an objective report of events, what Proust would call "data," but, rather, truthfully captures the sound of the thinking process.

a. **Further Reading:** Macksey, Richard. "Introduction." In *On Reading Ruskin* by Marcel Proust, edited and translated by Jean Autret, Phillip J. Wolfe, and William Burford, xii–liii. New Haven, CT: Yale University Press, 1989.

b. **Suggested Search:** Search for "The Adventures of Marcel Proust" on youtube.com.

5. **Marcel Proust distinguishes between voluntary and involuntary memory, the latter of which is essential to creating art, in the "Overture."** Voluntary memory is a forced remembrance and is often superficial and unreliable. Marcel says, "I could have answered anyone who asked me that Combray also included other things and existed at other times of day. But since what I recalled would have been supplied to me only by my voluntary memory, the memory of intelligence, and since the information it gives about the past preserves nothing of the past itself, I would never have had any desire to think about the rest of Combray" (1841). But involuntary memory happens naturally, without solicitation, spreading like the pieces of paper in the Japanese water game. The final image of the madeleine dipped into tea famously captures this involuntary process. Many scholars and readers compare this

process to a mystical or religious meditative state because it is a passive experience that transcends usual consciousness. However, the crucial difference is that involuntary memory can be grasped and re-created artistically. In this way, Proust's novel can be read either as his aesthetic theory—that memory is indispensable to the creation of art—or a kunstleroman, the story of the artist's development.

   a. **Further Reading:** Tukey, Ann. "Notes on Involuntary Memory in Proust." *French Review* 42:3 (1969): 395–402.

   b. **Suggested Search:** RadioProust (www.radioproust.org), through Bard College, offers a video about Molly Springfield's conceptual art piece, titled *Translation*, about the connection between physical objects and involuntary memory. To access this 21-minute video, which includes an introduction and discussion of the piece and of Proust by the artist and four Proust experts and art commentators, search for "Radio Proust a new translation."

In-Class Activities

1. The signature moment from the "Overture" is the taste of the madeleine and tea that triggers Marcel's involuntary memory. Ask students if they ever had a similar experience, typically called the "Proust effect." What sense inspired their involuntary memory? Was it a sound, like a song or someone's voice? A scent? A taste, like the narrator's? You could then ask students to capture that experience in writing.

2. To emphasize the plotlessness of the overture and novel, show the 1972 "All-England Summarize Proust Competition" from *Monty Python's Flying Circus*.

3. Play the overture to Richard Wagner's 1865 opera *Tristan und Isolde*. How is this piece similar to Marcel Proust's "Overture"? Why would he name what is usually in literature called a "Preface" or "Introduction" an "Overture"?

4. Marcel Proust filled out what is now known as the Proust Questionnaire twice in his life, at ages thirteen and twenty. Although he did not invent this questionnaire, it is appropriate in discussions of his literature, for the surveys encourage self-reflection and appreciation of the individual. You could distribute Proust's own surveys and discuss how his answers relate to the story of young Marcel (like his answer of "To be separated from Mama," in response to "What do you regard as the lowest depth of misery?"). You could also distribute blank questionnaires to your students and ask them to complete their own.

5. To explain the expanding and emerging memory, Marcel refers to "that game in which the Japanese amuse themselves by filling a porcelain

bowl with water and steeping in it little pieces of paper until then undifferentiated which, the moment they are immersed in it, stretch and bend, take color and distinctive form, turn into flowers" (1844). You can approximate this image by showing a video, available on you-tube.com, of blooming flower tea.

Paper Topics/Suggestions for Writing

1. Compare and contrast Marcel Proust's associative technique with stream of consciousness, a technique seen in William Faulkner's "Barn Burning" or Virginia Woolf's "A Room of One's Own," both of which are in this volume.

2. Read Charles Baudelaire's poem "Correspondences" (see Volume 2, p. 1043). How does the concept presented in the poem relate to "Overture"?

3. From what point of view is the story told? Is it young Marcel's point of view? Adult Marcel remembering his childhood? Both? Is the narrator Marcel Proust himself or an authorial persona? What is the difference? Why does Proust use this kind of narrative technique?

4. Choose one image or moment—such as Marcel waking, the magic lantern, or the dinner party—and explain the thoughts that precede and follow that moment or image. How does the narrator arrive at that image? Where does it lead? Use this exercise to comment on the chronological yet digressive narrative technique.

5. Who is M. Swann? How would you describe him? What is his effect on Marcel? How do others' opinions on Swann (like his aunt's) affect Marcel?

Resources

Bergson, Henri. *Time and Free Will: An Essay on the Immediate Data of Consciousness.* Trans. F. L. Pogson. New York: Macmillan, 1910.
This essay is available online at openlibrary.org.
Bloom, Harold, ed. *Marcel Proust.* Philadelphia: Chelsea House, 1987.
The 1987 edition includes critical essays by Samuel Beckett, Walter Benjamin, Rene Girard, and others, in addition to the introduction by Harold Bloom. The 2004 edition retains Bloom's introduction but updates the contents to include contemporary essays by Julia Kriteva, John Ruskin, and others.
Lehrer, Jonah. "Marcel Proust: The Method of Memory." In *Proust Was a Neuroscientist,* 75–95. New York: Houghton-Mifflin, 2007.
Jonah Lehrer's chapter on Marcel Proust discusses his prediction of twentieth-century neuroscience.

Painter, George. *Marcel Proust: A Biography*. New York: Random House, 1975.

    George Painter's work is a readable and anecdotal biography of Marcel Proust.

"The Proust Questionnaire Archive: A Tapestry of Memories and Thoughts and Emotions, Millions of Voices Murmuring." http://hoelderlin.org /Proust/fill_questionnaire.html.

    On this website, you can read Marcel Proust's responses to what is now known as the "Proust Questionnaire" as well as read other participants' answers and share your own answers.

Shapiro, Michael. "Contre Saint-Beuve." The Modernism Lab at Yale University. www.modernism.research.yale.edu.

    This wiki site, created by graduate students of literature at Yale University, gathers students' essays on certain works and artists of the modernist era. Michael Shapiro's essay "Contre Saint-Beuve" and Elyse Graham's "Marcel Proust" both offer extensive biographical information, as well as explanations of Marcel Proust's aesthetics.

Time Regained. Dir. Raoul Ruiz. Perf. Catherine Deneuve, John Malkovich. Gemini Films, 1999.

    Raoul Ruiz's film version of the last volume of *In Search of Lost Time* takes place in the mind of the dying author Marcel Proust.

James Joyce

The Dead

Topics for Lecture or Discussion

1. **James Joyce believed that Ireland, a longtime colony of England, lacked cultural identity and was paralyzed. "The Dead" is a microcosm of "the centre of paralysis," Dublin.** In a 1906 letter to his publisher, Joyce declared that his intention in the short story collection *Dubliners* "was to write a chapter of the moral history of my country and I chose Dublin for the scene because that city seemed to me the centre of paralysis" (*Letters of James Joyce*, ed. Richard Ellman, vol. 2 [New York: Viking Press, 1957], 134). By "paralysis," Joyce was referring to the modern condition of the culturally lacking Irish people who are oppressed by the Roman Catholic Church, poverty, and England's rule. As a product of British imperialism officially since 1800, Ireland, Joyce believed, lacked identity and suffered from cultural atrophy. The concluding story is aptly titled, for it reinforces the ineffectualness and impotence of Irishness, embodied especially in Gabriel Conroy, who must borrow quotations from other British writers, who wears galoshes like everyone on the continent, and who, compared to Michael Furey, is passionless. As a West Briton, an Irishman who considers Ireland a western province of Britain, Conroy's identity, like that of his snow-dampened nation, is unclear and, therefore, powerless.

   a. **Further Reading:** Kelleher, John V. "Irish History and Mythology in James Joyce's 'The Dead.'" *Review of Politics* 27:3 (1965): 414–33.

   b. **Suggested Searches:** Search the web for "Joyce's Dublin looking east or west." This will lead you to a podcast about Ireland's history and politics as an effect on "The Dead." The site, "Joyce's Dublin" (www.joycesdublin.ie), also features other podcasts and a slide show of James Joyce in Dublin.

2. **To fully understand James Joyce's "The Dead," one must appreciate the larger structure of *Dubliners*, the collection in which it appeared as the final story in the "public life" section. Joyce's interest in larger social networks composed of individuals exemplifies the story's use of disrupted contrasts.** Joyce carefully ordered the fifteen stories in *Dubliners*, positioning "The Dead" as the final story. He writes, "I have tried to present it [the center of paralysis, Dublin] to the indifferent public under four of its aspects: childhood, adolescence, maturity, and public life. The stories are arranged in this order" (*Letters of James Joyce*, 134). The setting of the story, a party, certainly aligns with this categorization, but by "public life," Joyce is referring to the community's

effect on the individual. For example, the snow falling "upon all the living and the dead" (1877) at once accentuates and diminishes Gabriel's own separateness, as it does for the living and the dead. Unified oppositions like this appear throughout the story: the long exchange of "good night" followed immediately by a description of morning, old Aunt Julia who sings "Arrayed for the Bridal" with a strong beautiful voice, or Gabriel who sexually longs for his death-preoccupied wife. By juxtaposing these oppositions, Joyce denies his readers and his characters the simplicity of opposition. A conversation between two individuals, like Gabriel and Ms. Ivors, then, is complicated by their social identities of unionist and nationalist, man and woman, friendly and bitter.

  a. **Further Reading:** Walzl, Florence L. "Pattern of Paralysis in Joyce's *Dubliners*: A Study of the Original Framework." *College English* 22: (1961): 221–28.

  b. **Suggested Search:** "Web resources for James Joyce's *Dubliners*" will yield a site (www.robotwisdom.com/jaj/dubliners) that contains e-text versions, summaries, and other media of all the stories in *Dubliners*.

3. **The technique for narrative resolution is an epiphany that concerns the private, public, and universal.** James Joyce adopts the religious term "epiphany," a term usually meaning the physical manifestation of Christ, to describe an event, or a non-event, that occurs in all fifteen of his *Dubliners* stories. To him, an epiphany is a sudden revelation of the spirit of a thing, including the self; it is when, as he writes in *Stephen Hero*, "the soul of the commonest object . . . seems to us radiant" (James Joyce, *Stephen Hero* [Norfolk, CT: New Directions, 1963], 213). Joyce's use of the epiphany falls in line with the modernist preference for interiority and eschewal of external action, plot, and conventional resolution. The ending here is not the classical active resolution but a realization had while staring out of a window. Gabriel's personal epiphany is that he does not know his wife and can never completely know her; this leads to a larger, more public epiphany when he recognizes "all the living and all the dead" (1877). Gabriel's leap from personal to universal is unanticipated and, therefore, unexplained, but one interpretation is that it represents his realization of the unknowability of everyone by everyone. Because this moment of awareness goes well beyond the individual (and even the public) and includes all people, alive or dead, it can be seen as the grand epiphany of the entire collection of individual epiphanies in *Dubliners*.

  a. **Further Reading:** Bowen, Zack. "Joyce and the Epiphany Concept." *Journal of Modern Literature* 9:1 (1981–1982): 103–14.

  b. **Suggested Search:** A search for "epiphany Victorian web" will take you to a brief overview of the literary epiphanic convention from the romantics to the Victorians to James Joyce on the website Victorian

Web (www.victorianweb.org). This page also includes suggestions for further reading.

4. **With free indirect discourse, the story emphasizes the internal lives of the characters. The climax, Gabriel's epiphany, is represented by a verbal shift in tone away from pettiness and toward a grand lyricism.** The story's main focus is the characters' interior lives, communicated through a narrative technique called "free indirect discourse." According to the *Bloomsbury Dictionary of English Literature* (available through Credo Reference [credoreference.com]), it is "a technique whereby a narrative reports the speech or thoughts of a character, referring to that character in the third person but adopting the character's own idiom." James Joyce employs this discourse from the first sentence, which claims that Lily was "literally run off her feet" (1848). The narrator uses the term "literally" to describe a figurative situation, a linguistic mistake that the caretaker's daughter, a member of an undereducated class, would make. Joyce's use of this modernist trend of painting the consciousness of individuals in their own voices stresses the moment of epiphany. Gabriel's language shifts from petty to lyrical, a verbal representation of his epiphanic moment. At the beginning of the story, he thinks—through the narrator—"He would fail with them just as he had failed with the girl in the pantry. He had taken up a wrong tone. His whole speech was a mistake" (1850). By the end, though, the voice is not at all weak or selfish; it is poetic and noble: "One by one they were all becoming shades. Better pass boldly into that other world, in the full glory of some passion, than fade and wither dismally with age" (1876).

   a. **Further Reading:** Murphy, Terence Patrick. "Monitored Speech: The 'Equivalence' Relation between Direct and Indirect Speech in Jane Austen and James Joyce." *Narrative* 15:1 (2007): 24–39.

   b. **Suggested Search:** The "Speech Presentation Checksheet" at www .lancs.ac.uk/fass/projects/stylistics/topic9/11checksheet.htm offers in-depth explanations and examples of speech and thought representations in literature.

5. **Irish identity exists in a language between Miss Ivors's propagandistic preference for Gaelic and Gabriel's dependence on English.** The Irish Revival, represented by Miss Ivors, was in full swing during the composition and publication of *Dubliners*. Celtic literary revivalists such as W. B. Yeats, Lady Gregory, and AE (George Russell) wrote idyllically about Ireland's peasantry and folklore, which James Joyce later claimed as an idealized vision of Ireland's past that could never be revived after years of colonization. Joyce briefly studied Gaelic and knew many nationalists, but he had no interest in their cause to create an Irish identity by preserving Gaelic as the official Irish language. Joyce wrote to his brother, "If the Irish programme did not insist on the Irish language I

suppose I could call myself a nationalist" (*Letters of James Joyce*, 187). In Gabriel Conroy, however, readers can see Joyce's hesitation in complete acceptance of the borrowed English language over Gaelic. For the lack of Ireland's own great writers, Conroy must borrow the words of England's Shakespeare or Browning and, post-epiphany, decides to "turn westward" toward the Irish-speaking Aran Islands. In later works, such as the semi-autobiographical *Portrait of the Artist as a Young Man*, Joyce would paint the artist as a "forger" of national identity; in "The Dead," Joyce gives the Irish people "one good look at themselves in my nicely polished looking glass" to inspire a need for that artist (*Letters of James Joyce*, ed. Richard Ellman, vol. 1 [New York: Viking Press, 1957], 63).

   a. **Further Reading:** Booker, M. Keith. "Shakespeare, Joyce's Contemporary: The Politics and Poetics of Literary Authority." In *Joyce, Bakhtin, and the Literary Tradition: Toward a Comparative Cultural Poetics*, 139–70. Ann Arbor, MI: University of Michigan Press, 1997.

   b. **Suggested Search:** Search for "Irish language and history" at irish-language.net. The page "History of the Irish Language" provides an overview of the Irish language movement popular while James Joyce was writing.

In-Class Activities

1. One major theme of the story is opposites and how they throw each other into relief. You can discuss these images (of life and death, youth and age, the individual and the community, present and past, the bourgeoisie and the impoverished) and then consider how the myriad oppositions support the theme.

2. Discuss Gabriel Conroy as a modernist anti-hero. How does he compare to T. S. Eliot's J. Alfred Prufrock or Thomas Mann's Gustav von Aschenbach?

3. Show all or parts of the film version of "The Dead," directed by John Huston, which is largely faithful to the original story. Discuss how the differences in media affect the meaning of the story, such as the loss of free indirect discourse or the ability to hear the music in the movie.

4. Discuss the metaphorical implications of the title for a story that is set at a party. How is this a social commentary on James Joyce's part?

Paper Topics/Suggestions for Writing

1. What is the role of music in the story? Look up the songs from the story ("Arrayed for the Bridal" and "The Lass of Aughrim"). Read the lyrics and/or listen to recordings. Discuss why James Joyce, a noted musician,

would choose those songs. Also consider why the fictional painting of Gretta that Gabriel imagines would be titled *Distant Music*.

2. Research James Joyce's biography. Discuss the similarities between Joyce and Gabriel and between Nora Barnacle and Gretta.

3. At the end of the story, after Gretta tells Gabriel about Michael Furey, the language seems to switch from free indirect discourse to the traditional authorial intrusion. Discuss whether this is, in fact, an authorial voice or if this is the voice of a "new" Gabriel, one who has had an epiphany. If so, what is the nature of that epiphany?

4. Explain the significance of Gabriel's comment to Molly Ivors, that "Irish is not my language" (1856). You may want to research "Irish Nationalism" or "Home Rule."

5. In a letter to his brother, James Joyce wrote, "Sometimes thinking of Ireland it seems to me that I have been unnecessarily harsh. I have reproduced (in *Dubliners* at least) none of the attraction of the city for I have never felt at my ease in any city since I left it except in Paris. I have not reproduced its ingenuous insularity and its hospitality." "The Dead" was composed after this letter. Discuss whether you believe that Joyce finally does express his attraction for Ireland in the story.

Resources

The Bloomsbury Dictionary of English Literature. Edited by Marion Wynne-Davies. London: Bloomsbury Publishing Ltd., 1997.
    This useful reference for literature terms and concepts is available online through http://corp.credoreference.com/component/book tracker/edition/362.html.
The Dead. Dir. John Huston. Vestron Video, 1988.
    John Huston's last film, his 1987 *The Dead*, starring Anjelica Huston as Gretta Conroy and Donal McCann as Gabriel Conroy, is a beautiful and faithful adaptation of James Joyce's story.
Ellmann, Richard. *James Joyce*. New York: Oxford University Press, 1983.
    Richard Ellmann's definitive biography of James Joyce offers a detailed, scholarly, and entertaining portrait of Joyce. This work also includes letters and photographs.
Fargnoli, A. Nicholas, and Michael Patrick Gillespie. *James Joyce A to Z: The Essential Reference to His Life and Work*. New York: Oxford University Press, 1995.
    This extensive encyclopedia offers concise and approachable entries on all aspects of James Joyce's works and life.
"James Joyce: The Brazen Head." The Modern Word. www.themodernword.com/joyce.

This comprehensive website includes links to criticism, reviews, biographies, images, links to audio recordings (including James Joyce reading his own work), and much more Joyce-related material.

"James Joyce: 1929 Reading of Anna Livia Plurabelle (Finnegans Wake)." youtube.com.

Here James Joyce reads a portion of his 1939 novel *Finnegans Wake*.

Joyce, James. *The Dead*. Edited by Daniel R. Schwarz. Boston: St. Martin's Press, 1994.

This work is an extremely helpful scholarly edition described as the "complete, authoritative text with biographical and historical contexts, critical history, and essays from five contemporary critical perspectives," which include psychoanalysis, reader response, new historicism, feminism, and deconstruction.

Joyce: The James Joyce Centre. www.jamesjoyce.ie.

This website for the Joyce Centre in Dublin provides information about Joycean events, lectures, and the annual Bloomsday celebration in honor of James Joyce's *Ulysses* character, Leopold Bloom, as well as important Joyce dates and a biography.

"Tony Awards—James Joyce's 'The Dead.'" youtube.com.

This 4-minute video clip is a performance from Richard Nelson's and Shaun Davey's 2000 musical *James Joyce's The Dead* at the Tony Awards.

FRANZ KAFKA
The Metamorphosis

Topics for Lecture or Discussion

1. **Though its symbols and events seem decipherable, "The Metamorphosis" resists any cohesive, singular interpretation.** The events in
Franz Kafka's story seem to easily lend themselves to metaphorical
equivalents. But the story itself is not metaphorical: Samsa *is* the bug.
With a journalistic and distant tone, the narrator reports the events but
never comments on or explains the biggest question: "Why?" The story
is unwilling either to provide a satisfactory answer or even to recognize that there is a question. For example, the narrator, almost immediately after beginning the tale, tries to shift our attention to a
picture of a woman hanging on Gregor's wall. The story seems oblivious to what actually interests us. Kafka forces the central absurd
event into normality and even dullness, almost claiming that it does
not deserve any conclusive interpretation. So, even though the story
is nightmare-like—frustrating, confusing, and grotesque—that interpretation is immediately rejected with the line "It was no dream"
(1880). Or, to the suggestion that the names "Samsa" and "Kafka" are
purposely similar, Kafka replied, "It is not a cryptogram. Samsa is not
merely Kafka, and nothing else" (Gustav Janouch, *Conversations with
Kafka* [New York: New Directions, 1971], 32). This statement can be
applied to the entire story: there is no one-to-one correspondence between
the events and the meaning. It is always already deconstructed for us.
   a. **Further Reading:** Ben-Ephraim, Gavriel. "Making and Breaking
      Meaning: Deconstruction, Four-Level Allegory and 'The Metamor-
      phosis.'" *Midwest Quarterly* 35:4 (1994): 450–68.
   b. **Suggested Search:** Search for "Franz Kafka" at The Modern Word
      (www.themodernword.com), which offers an extensive bibliography
      of (mutually exclusive) interpretations and criticisms, as well as pho-
      tographs and a biography.

2. **In his life and literature, Franz Kafka was especially concerned
   with the relationship between authority figures and those they subdue.** The term "Kafkaesque" has become a commonly used idiom to
   describe situations such as the nightmarish, oppressive, and frustrating
   ones found in Kafka's fiction. Though Gregor's transformation itself
   and the ensuing inability to communicate or eat are certainly vexing,
   Gregor's sharper and longer ingrained frustration is with his authority
   figures, a trait that harkens back to Kafka himself. In his forty-five-
   page *Letter to His Father* (Trans. Ernst Kaiser and Eithne Wilkins [New

York: Schocken Books, 1966]), Kafka explains his fear of the authoritative Hermann Kafka directly. He writes, "Even years afterward I suffered from the tormenting fancy that the huge man, my father, the ultimate authority, would come almost for no reason at all and take me out of bed in the night and carry me out onto the pavlatche [balcony], and that consequently I meant absolutely nothing as far as he was concerned" (17). Gregor's boss (and father), who undergoes his own transformation *to* power throughout the story, fills this role of senseless and heartless tormenter. Even Grete has recently been included in this topic of dominance, opening the story to feminist and gender studies.

    a. **Further Reading:** Straus, Nina Pelikan. "Transforming Franz Kafka's 'Metamorphosis.'" *Signs* 14:2 (1989): 651–67.

    b. **Suggested Search:** Search Google for "Franz Kafka letter to his father." The resulting page (www.kafka-franz.com/KAFKA-letter.htm) is the entirety of his letter. At the bottom of the page are links back to the home page, to photographs, and to articles on other subjects.

3. **The "very un-homelike" city of Prague both produced and trapped Franz Kafka, who explores the themes of alienation in his work.** Kafka's hometown, the melancholic Prague, perfectly suited the guilt-ridden and ineffective man. As a German-speaking Jew, Kafka never felt welcome in Prague, a predominately Catholic and anti-Semitic town in the Czech Republic. He wrote that Prague is "very un-homelike, a place of memories, of nostalgia, of pettiness, of shame, of seduction, of the misuse of power." Compared to the city, or the "little mother [that] has claws," Kafka proved weak (Mark Harman, "Missing Person: Two Little Riddles About Kafka and Berlin," *New England Review* 25:1/2 [2004]: 225). Though he succeeded as a law student, he never practiced. He worked as a civil servant for an insurance company, a stifling job that his father often mocked. He was engaged multiple times but never married. And, famously, Kafka asked his literary executor, Max Brod, to destroy his writings after his death. Because of his dejected temperament, scholars have often linked Kafka to the likewise impotent Gregor. Though Kafka argued that Samsa is not "merely" Kafka, readers can assume that Kafka translated his own feelings of suppression to his character, who is locked in his room, alienated from his Christian family.

    a. **Further Reading:** Bloom, Harold. "Introduction." In *Franz Kafka: Bloom's Modern Critical Views*, edited by Harold Bloom. New York: Chelsea House, 2010.

    b. **Suggested Search:** Search the Jewish Museum's website (www.thejewishmuseum.org) for "the City of K: Franz Kafka and Prague." This site includes videos, drawings, and photographs, and, through descriptions of the Jewish Museum's 2002–2003 exhibition on Franz Kafka, explains the role of Prague in Kafka's life.

4. **Franz Kafka's interest in the inner life of the mind and its physical manifestations is tied to the literary expressionism movement in form and content.** Like Kafka, German expressionists of the early twentieth century were interested in exploring authority and modernity. The paintings, films, and architecture of the movement distorted the physical world so that it better depicted the emotional state of that world. Though he cannot be unquestionably included as an expressionist, Kafka is clearly influencing and influenced by the movement. Visually, it is defined by sharp angles, awkward perspectives, warped forms, and two-dimensionality. The dysmorphia of the external communicates the underlying—yet superior—tonal or emotional reality. Kafka's story barely predates the apex of expressionism, and clearly so; one can see his own literary version that creates a haunting atmosphere through "physical" oddness. The one-dimensionality of the other characters, the detailed description of the apartment's architecture, and the straightforward language, for all their clarity, create an emotional undercurrent of disorientation and imprisonment. The bug itself, for example, is always described but never identified. Kafka uses vague terms to describe it— such as "bug" or "vermin"—and even disallowed his publisher from including an illustration of it on the cover. The emotional underpinning of grotesqueness, then, depends on the reader's own idea of grotesqueness, whether cockroach or beetle. In this way, he combines the impressionistic traits of modernism with his expressionism.

   a. **Further Reading:** "Expressionism." In *A Franz Kafka Encyclopedia*, edited by Richard T. Gray, et al., 86–88. Westport, CT: Greenwood Press, 2005.

   b. **Suggested Search:** Search Google Images for "Kafka Starke Verwandlung 1915." The top hit is an image of the first-edition book cover of "The Metamorphosis." Note the absence of the vermin, compared especially to most editions printed since then.

5. **The central oddness of "The Metamorphosis" is the lack of origin for the transformation. Scholars have combated the interpretation that Gregor's metamorphosis is un-self-motivated through literary schools such as psychoanalysis and existentialism.** One of Gregor's first thoughts upon waking is about his work. Using Freud's writing on accidents, scholars such as Walter H. Sokel argue that Gregor's transformation is an unaccidental accident. In other words, Gregor's extreme frustration with his job as a traveling salesman led to his transformation, an unconsciously made excuse to shirk his responsibilities. Franz Kafka was familiar with Freud's works and alluded to him in his diaries before writing "The Metamorphosis." Psychoanalytical readings of the story do carry weight but seem to do with finding an origin for the transformation. The preferred translation of the title to "The Metamorphosis" forces

readers to compare Gregor with the metamorphosed mortals in Ovid's *Metamorphoses*. This comparison with a collection of stories about capricious gods and their whimsical metamorphosing only highlights the lack of origin in Gregor's transformation. The lack of a "transformer" and psychoanalytical readings can overlap in existentialism. In the face of an absurd and a meaningless world of work, Gregor, a free agent, transforms himself into his authentic self. Gregor's doomed fate lay in his rejecting his decision that finally situated him in his rightful place.

    a. **Further Reading:** Sokel, Walter H. "Kafka's 'Metamorphosis': Rebellion and Punishment." *Monatshefte* 48:4 (1956): 203–14.

    b. **Suggested Search:** Search the Existential Primer (www.tameri.com /csw/exist/index.htm) for "Franz Kafka the absurdity of everything" to find a biography and essays on each of his works (including "The Metamorphosis") that concentrate on Franz Kafka's existentialism.

In-Class Activities

1. Begin the class by asking students to write a short in-class essay about what the story means. Ask them to share their responses, which typically conflict drastically. Use these dissimilarities to teach that no answer is satisfactory and that "the transformation is not a cryptogram."

2. The humor of the story is located in the matter-of-fact journalistic tone that reports the outrageous events. Because many students can become distracted by the events themselves, disregarding the disjunction between the action and the tone that creates the humor, you can alert them to the story's comical aspect. To illustrate this disjunction, introduce the police blotter or crime beat section of a local newspaper.

3. Show Steven Berkoff's television film *The Metamorphosis*. Discuss the similarities and differences, especially the choice to leave Gregor's character a man who acts like an insect.

4. Franz Kafka specifically refused an illustration of the vermin so that readers could imagine it for themselves. Supplement this information with the insect-less first-edition cover of the novella. Then ask students to draw Gregor as the insect. Compare their drawings to introduce the lecture on the theme of authority.

5. Play the satirical news report "Prague's Franz Kafka International Named World's Most Alienating Airport" from *The Onion* (www .theonion.com). Discuss how the news report parodies the "Kafkaesque." What Kafkaesque features are in "The Metamorphosis"?

Paper Topics/Suggestions for Writing

1. Explain the inverse ratio of Gregor's suffering and his family's happiness. How does this explain the ending?

2. Research German expressionism, such as the movie *The Cabinet of Dr. Caligari* or the paintings of Max Beckman and Franz Marc. Discuss the ways that Franz Kafka might have contributed to the movement.

3. Explore the scene in which Gregor reacts to his sister playing the violin. What does this scene imply for the story's position on beauty and art?

4. The word "metamorphosis" connotes a process or at least the moment of change, but Franz Kafka's story does not portray that moment. Gregor simply wakes up as the bug. How would the story change if Kafka had shown the audience the process of transformation? Why didn't he show the metamorphosis?

5. Research Franz Kafka's life in Prague, paying particular attention to the city's anti-Semitism and Kafka's relationship to his Judaism. How might this aspect of his biography have influenced "The Metamorphosis"?

Resources

Haugen, Hayley Mitchell Haugen, ed. *Readings on* The Metamorphosis. San Diego, CA: Greenhaven, 2002.
> This collection of fifteen critical essays offers various interpretations, from Freudian readings to gender studies.

Kuper, Peter. *The Metamorphosis*. New York: Three Rivers Press, 2003.
> Peter Kuper's illustrated adaptation of Franz Kafka's tale merges "American cartooning with German expressionism."

Metamorphosis. Films for the Humanities and Sciences, 2001, DVD/VHS.
> Jeff Goldblum narrates this educational video filmed in Franz Kafka's Prague. It combines reenactments of the story, critical commentary, and autobiographical information on Kafka.

"Metamorphosis," *a Study: Nabokov on Kafka*. Dir. Peter Medak. Library Video Company, 1989, DVD.
> This DVD, also available on youtube.com, stars Christopher Plummer as novelist Vladimir Nabokov, giving his famed lecture on "The Metamorphosis." It is both entertaining and insightful.

Preece, Julian, ed. *The Cambridge Companion to Kafka*. Cambridge: Cambridge University Press, 2002.
> This collection of fifteen essays contextualizes Franz Kafka and explores all of his works.

"Study Guide for 'The Metamorphosis.'" The Glencoe Literature Library. Available at www.glencoe.com/sec/literature/litlibrary/metamorphosis.html.
> This source, a pdf file approximately twenty pages long, is a teacher's guide with overviews and exercises to be used throughout the reading process.

LUIGI PIRANDELLO

Six Characters in Search of an Author

> Whatever is a reality today, whatever you
> touch and believe in and that seems real for
> you today, is going to be—like the reality of
> yesterday—an illusion tomorrow.
> —Luigi Pirandello, *Six Characters in Search
> of an Author*

Topics for Lecture or Discussion

1. **The conflict between the chaos of everyday life and the order of artistic representation underscores the Fascist political sympathies of the playwright.** As rightly pointed out in the headnote, the title is a bit of a misnomer due to the fact that an author has evidently created and written the characters. Instead of an author, the characters search for a theatrical form that will give their story shape and meaning. While life has no narrative shape (until its end, or death), an artistic representation of life has a defined beginning, middle, and end that can be reproduced each time that it is performed. The characters seek a strong director, or a benevolent dictator, who can tell them where to go and how to behave. The Producer in the play organizes the rehearsal time and space for the actors of the company, and the characters hope that he can fulfill the same function for them as he blends the literary with the performative. Just as the Producer holds sway over the various actors of his company, the Father functions as the *raisonneur*, or voice of reason, for the family of characters. The search for an Author, supplemented by the presence of both Producer and Father, expresses the desire for a powerful and patriarchal presence to regulate and shape the vagaries and vicissitudes of everyday living.

   a. **Further Reading:** Quinn, Michael L. "Relative Identity and Ideal Art: The Pirandello Conflict and Its Political Analogy." *Journal of Dramatic Theory and Criticism* 3:2 (Spring 1989): 73–106.

   b. **Suggested Searches:** Search for the following phrases in Google Images, Google Scholar, or an academic database to find images and additional resources: Pirandello and Mussolini; National Art Theatre of Rome.

2. **The modern metatheatrical structure belies the traditional melodramatic core of the play.** A play-within-the-play conceit frames the viewing of the entire play, since it takes place in a theater and there is no attempt to hide any theatrical devices. The lack of a stage curtain to

start the play and the stairs connecting the stage to the seats in the house, common conventions in today's theater, are two modern devices that visually set the world of the play in a theatrical environment. See the revised (2003) edition of Lionel Abel's *Tragedy and Metatheatre*, with an introduction by Martin Puchner, for a gloss on key concepts. The play's innovative form, however, contrasts with its rather prosaic and traditional content: a domestic family squabble rife with marital discord, sibling rivalry, hints of incest, and, ultimately, murder. The stylish form of the play diverts the reader or viewer from paying too much attention to the maudlin story.

   a. **Further Reading:** Cannon, Jo Ann. "The Question of the Frame in Pirandello's Metatheatrical Trilogy." *Modern Language Studies* 16:3 (Summer 1986): 44–56.

   b. **Suggested Searches:** Search for the following phrases in Google Images, Google Scholar, or an academic database to find images and additional resources: Rupert Goold production; Michael Billington on; at Gielgud Theatre in London 2008; Headlong Theatre production; Bristol Old Vic production.

3. **Characters and players struggle over the question of how best to bring a story to life on stage.** The characters narrate throughout the first part of the play to provide the players with the necessary exposition and explanation of past events. Beyond information, though, the often competing and conflicting accounts of what happened to them point out the complexity of human experience, urging the players to perform nothing but the truth, but the Producer explains that that is quite impossible to do on the stage: "Everything needs to be balanced and in harmony so that we can show what has to be shown! I know perfectly well that we've all got a life inside us and that we all want to parade it in front of other people. But that's the difficulty, how to present only the bits that are necessary in relation to the other characters: and in the small amount we show, to hint at all the rest of the inner life or the character!" (1945).

   The Producer argues that truth in art is not the same thing as truth in life. Art must sculpt life, chip some things away, and embellish other elements in order to make the representation clear and understandable to an audience. Constraints of time, space, and action, the three familiar Aristotelian unities, as well as restrictions of capital, force a creative team to create truth on stage that may well not correspond to the facts of observable reality.

   a. **Further Reading:** Lawrence, Kenneth. "Luigi Pirandello: Holding Nature Up to the Mirror." *Italica* 47:1 (Spring 1970): 61–77.

   b. **Suggested Searches:** Search for the following phrases in Google Images, Google Scholar, or an academic database to find images and

additional resources: Stacy Keach *Six Characters in Search of an Author* (video); Nobel Prize for Literature 1934; playwright of 1934 *Time* magazine.

4. **Notions of decorum and privacy resist displaying in public the spectacle of intimate, private family life.** The Son, alone among all the characters, refuses to participate in the dramatization of family secrets. To him it is unseemly to make entertainment out of personal sorrow and misfortune. While much of the play revolves around the question of how to represent a story on stage, a minor but an important point of view questions whether a private story should be represented in any fashion at all for others to see. To the Father's passion to present the truth as it really happened on stage, the Son says, "What's come over you? Why are you so frantic? Do you want to parade our disgrace in front of everybody? Well, I'm having nothing to do with it! Nothing! And I'm doing what our author wanted as well—he never wanted to put us on the stage" (1955). The author abandoned the characters, according to the Son, not because he could not put them on stage but because he ultimately did not want the story to be seen.

   a. **Further Reading:** Brustein, Robert. "Luigi Pirandello." In *The Theatre of Revolt*, 279–318. 1964. Chicago: Ivan R. Dee, 1991.

   b. **Suggested Searches:** Search for the following phrases in Google Images, Google Scholar, or an academic database to find images and additional resources: Robert Brustein adaptation of *Six Characters* at ART; National Theatre of Scotland production.

5. **The theatrical setting and context of the play ultimately make the opposition between fiction and reality irrelevant.** The characters and players debate the merits of truth versus illusion, life versus art, but the silent majority, the audience, mediates the division between the opposing sides by simply observing the spectacle and responding to what it sees. Near the end of the play, the Father defends the autonomy of the character by claiming, "he [the character] sometimes acquires a meaning that his author never dreamed of giving him" (1950). While much of the play concerns who controls and dictates the meanings of a theatrical representation, the Father implies here that an audience might interpret events counter to any stated intention by the author. The end of the play puts the question of interpretation squarely in the lap of the audience without dictating any particular meaning. The final image of the play casts the Producer alone on a dark stage, much like an audience member in a dark house, when suddenly the projected and very large images of the Characters appear behind a backdrop. Terrified by an illusion, the Director flees the theater. In the theater, where everything is false, human bodies construct images to make lasting impressions on the viewer's consciousness.

    a. **Further Reading:** Vargas, Margarita. "Staging Identity through Art." *CR: The New Centennial Review* 5:3 (Winter 2005): 65–82.

    b. **Suggested Searches:** Search for the following phrases in Google Images, Google Scholar, or an academic database to find images and additional resources: Aquila Theatre touring production 2011; Luigi Pirandello quotes; illusion and reality in Pirandello.

In-Class Activities

1. Divide small groups of eight into storytellers and performers. Instruct the performers to translate the story they hear into dramatic form. What does the initial story gain and lose when it changes from one form to another?

2. In many theatrical organizations, historically as well as currently, power is hierarchical and the actors submit to the authority of the playwright and the director. Who wields the ultimate power in the previous exercise? The "playwright"? The "director"? The "actors"?

3. Discuss how the various groups completed their tasks—through ensemble work or through the leadership of only one or two members of the group? Different organizational structures produce different methods and results. How might the working conditions and power structures vary in different settings such as the commercial, professional, community, or educational theater?

Paper Topics/Suggestions for Writing

1. Benito Mussolini and Fascism enthralled Luigi Pirandello. What relationship do you see between artistic form and political rule?

2. Male dominance in the family (the Father) and the theater (the Director) seem to align with Fascism in an attempt to establish and maintain order and control. What role might gender play in a critique of patriarchy and politics?

3. This play is justly famous and innovative for its play-within-a-play structure and the analogies it spawns between theater (form) and life (content). How does metatheatricality serve the themes of the drama?

4. Two of the play's concerns are the need for order and structure (on stage and in life). How might the idea of rehearsal and the dramatic performance of a fixed dramatic text resolve or disrupt the needs described previously?

5. All of the characters have a story to tell. What are the challenges and difficulties of transforming life into art?

Resources

Abel, Lionel. *Tragedy and Metatheatre: Essays on Dramatic Form*. New York: Holmes & Meier, 2003.

> This is the revised edition of Lionel Abel's *Metatheatre*—a classic work that coined the term "metatheatre"—with an introduction by Martin Puchner.

Italy: Origins of Theater to Pirandello. Insight Media, 1983, DVD.

> This video explores the theme of illusion and reality.

Six Characters in Search of an Author. Dir. Stacy Keach. Perf. John Houseman, Julie Adams, Andy Griffith. 1976. DVD. Broadway Theatre Archive, Kultur Video, 2002.

> This television adaptation stars John Houseman as the Director, Julie Adams as the Mother, and Andy Griffith as the Father.

Six Characters in Search of an Author. Insight Media, 1977, DVD.

> This BBC production includes the central section of the play and a condensed version of the opening.

Six Characters in Search of an Author. Perf. John Hurt. BBC, 1992, VHS.

> John Hurt stars as the Father in this BBC production.

VIRGINIA WOOLF
A Room of One's Own

Topics for Lecture or Discussion

1. **Virginia Woolf represents the concerns of both the "old feminists" and the "new feminists" of the 1920s, as well as her own ideas on female creativity throughout history.** In the 1920s, supporters of the women's movement were divided into two factions: "old" feminists, typically of the middle class, were still arguing for greater equality in education, while "new" feminists wanted to address more specific issues, such as contraception or aid for unmarried mothers. The former group feared that the latter was simply highlighting stereotypes of typical female roles, thus undermining its desire for equality; the "new" feminists, however, thought the "old" feminists were not addressing real problems and instead worried only about the ideological battle. Woolf, aware of this oft-reported debate, addresses both sides in her essay. Like the "old" feminists, she emphasizes education and independence; like the "new," she discusses the particulars of women's poverty, marriage, and motherhood. But Woolf also looks outside the temporal boundary of this two-sided argument with her exploration of female creativity and its long history of subjugation. She situates the problem of "Women and Fiction" within cultural and gender issues that are present not only within her own historical moment but also hundreds of years before and after. She added a complexity to the dichotomous presentation of contemporary women's issues.

   a. **Further Reading:** Briggs, Julia. "To the Women of the Future." In *Virginia Woolf: An Inner Life*, 216–37 . New York: Harcourt, 2005.

   b. **Suggested Search:** For a history of the feminism debates in 1920s England, search on Google for "Clio Talks Back: Should economic emancipation—the right to earn an independent living—be the most important priority for women today" on *Her Blue Print*, the official blog for the International Museum of Women (http://imowblog.blogspot.com/2010/11/clio-talks-back-should-economic.html).

2. **The experimental style and genre are essential features of Virginia Woolf's argument.** The first version of *A Room of One's Own* appeared as two lectures entitled "Women and Fiction," given by Woolf at Newnham College and then, six days later, at Girton College in 1928. When she later revises her talk into a draft of *A Room*, Woolf maintains the

lecturing voice through the narrator. This voice allows the text to work toward answering the question at hand while maintaining a stream-of-consciousness narrative full of interruptions, digressions, and the "twists and turns of [her] cogitations" (1968). Even the very first line is an interruption, as if the lecture or essay begins *in medias res*: "But, you may say . . . what has that got to do with a room of one's own?" (1960). By beginning with a contradiction and question, Woolf immediately represents her argument: women must interrupt, contradict, and think for themselves, questioning even the lecturer/writer. The opposition found in the first word establishes the theme of setting up strict binaries only to question and collapse them, including fact and fiction, like the narrator's story.

a. **Further Reading:** Seeley, Tracy. "Locating Woolf: Spatial Digression and Storytelling in *A Room of One's Own*." In *Locating Woolf: The Politics of Space and Place*, edited by Anna Snaith and Michael H. Whitworth, 31–45. New York: Palgrave, 2007.

b. **Suggested Search:** Search for "A Room of One's Own" on YouTube to find a clip (8:44) of Eileen Atkins as Woolf giving the lecture (www.youtube.com/watch?v=g5wJDLHgYeU). You can use this video to discuss with your class how the narrative style of the essay combines fact and fiction.

3. **The arguments can function metaphorically and literally, thus bringing practicality to aesthetics.** The text's images and ideas can be taken metaphorically as representations of female equality. For example, most students see that the "room" of the title could stand for the space a woman artist needs to create, and the 500 pounds might represent intellectual freedom. But the strength of Virginia Woolf's text is that these are not only imaginative devices but also function as literal suggestions, or even demands. In this way, Woolf's essay is one in a long line of suffrage pamphlets. During Woolf's life, she saw the passing of the Married Woman's Property Act in 1882 (the year of her birth), which allowed women to buy and sell their own property and keep the earnings; the Parliamentary Reform Act of 1918, which allowed women age thirty and older the vote; and the Sex Disqualification Removal Act, which opened more professions to women and allowed Parliament's first female member, Nancy Astor. But Woolf's discussion of aesthetics and literary history reminds her audience of the social, cultural, personal, and historical importance of the arts and that they too must be recognized as such. To request a room and 500 pounds—which, according to Hermione Lee's 1996 biography, was equivalent to 25,000 pounds—is a request to notice the essentialness of aesthetics in everyday life.

a. **Further Reading:** Zwerdling, Alex. *Virginia Woolf and the Real World*. Berkeley: University of California Press, 1986.

b. **Suggested Search:** Visit the site for A Room of Her Own: A Foundation For Women Writers and Artists, a non-profit organization inspired by Woolf that provides awards and programs for female artists (www.aroomofherownfoundation.org/home.php).

4. **Higher education represents intellectual exclusion for women and inculcation for men.** The fictional lecture of the essay takes place at Fernham, meant to represent the women's colleges of Cambridge, Girton, and Newnham. Unlike the long-founded men's colleges (Kings College, for instance, was founded in 1441), they were established in 1869 and 1871, respectively, a mere sixty years before Woolf's lectures. In addition, Cambridge did not confer degrees to women until 1948. Woolf herself was denied a formal education, unlike her brothers. In the essay, however, the narrator reflects not only on the effects of exclusion from higher education on women but also on the effects on men of inclusion into those same institutions, such as inculcation. The much-debated tail-less Manx cat from the Isle of Man that the narrator sees from the window of the men's college, which Woolf initially attributed to Sigmund Freud and her subconscious in the first draft, may in fact represent an invasion into a masculine space by one who is missing an essential part. To be shut in, in other words, leads to an inbred anger and a desire for superiority that drove World War I.

a. **Further Reading:** Hanley, Lynn T. "Virginia Woolf and the Romance of Oxbridge." *Massachusetts Review* 25:3 (1984): 421–36.

b. **Suggested Search:** Search on Google for a 2012 article from *Time* magazine entitled "Can Oxford and Cambridge Shed Their Elitist Images by Admitting More Poor Students?" (www.time.com/time/world/article/0,8599,2113589,00.html). This article is about a modern-day discrimination issue in the same universities that Woolf takes to task for gender discrimination, and it provides a solid understanding of the reputation of "Oxbridge."

5. **The text discusses and modifies patriarchal literary history.** When the narrator enters the British Museum Reading Room to research the role of women in history, she finds that only male academics have written on the topic (an idea meant to inspire the female members of her audience at the women's colleges). In addition to this clinical, academic cataloging of women, literary men have also discussed the role of women at great length. By alluding or directly referring to these actual male academics and authors throughout the text, Virginia Woolf inserts herself into literary history, which is predominantly male. One of the

most striking examples of this allusive insertion involves John Milton, with whom the narrator has especially taken issue for the self-deifying act of rewriting the story of Genesis. Woolf appropriates and alters a line from Thomas Gray's poem "Elegy Written in a Churchyard" to replace Milton with "some mute and inglorious Jane Austen" (1987). Woolf, too, speaks with the same reverence afforded Shakespeare (deferentially referred to as "Sh—p—re" in her novel of the same year, *Orlando*) toward *J____ H____*, or Jane Harrison, the classical scholar who first asserted that ancient Greece was matriarchal and Dionysian, who fought, unsuccessfully, for women to take degrees, and whose deathbed Woolf attended the same year.

a. **Further Reading:** Showalter, Elaine. *A Literature of Their Own.* Princeton, NJ: Princeton University Press, 1977. Also see: Gilbert, Sandra M., and Susan Gubar. "Milton's Bogey: Patriarchal Poetry and Women Readers." In *The Madwoman in the Attic*, 2nd edition, 187–212. New Haven, CT: Yale University Press, 2000; Peacock, Sandra J. *Jane Ellen Harrison: The Mask and the Self.* New Haven, CT: Yale University Press, 1988.

b. **Suggested Search:** Search for "Women in Literature—A Literary Overview" to find an essay by Elizabeth Lee on Elaine Showalter's argument that there are three stages of women's literature (www .victorianweb.org/gender/womlitov.html).

6. **Virginia Woolf carefully constructs a fictional, "legendary" narrator instead of narrating as herself.** Within the first paragraph, the narrator claims that she, like her story, is a fiction. By creating a fictional narrator, Woolf may have been rhetorically distancing herself from accusations of anger, like Professor von X's. In a letter to her friend Ethyl Smyth in 1933, she writes, "If I had said, Look here am I uneducated, because my brothers used all the family funds which is the fact—Well theyd have said; she has an axe to grind; and no one would have taken me seriously" (*The Letters of Virginia Woolf: Vol. 5*, eds. Nigel Nicholson and Joanne Trautmann [New York: Harcourt Brace, 1982], 195). She also reminds her audience of female students that they should decide for themselves the worth of her argument. With this repeated warning, Woolf forces attention onto the ideas and away from the authority figure, the speaker/writer, presenting the ideas. Finally, the nameless narrator may be an example of ironically embracing the "indifference of the world" (1989) that male writers fear and that female writers suffer.

a. **Further Reading:** Kamuf, Peggy. "Penelope at Work: Interruptions in *A Room of One's Own*." *Novel: A Forum on Fiction* 16:1 (1982): 5–18. Also see Fernald, Anne. "*A Room of One's Own*, Personal

Criticism, and the Essay." *Twentieth-Century Literature* 40:2 (1994): 165–90.

b. **Suggested Search:** On YouTube, search for "The Classical Feminist Tradition," a lecture by Yale professor Paul Fry (www.youtube.com /watch?v=wxZDA3M21OM). While the entire lecture is about Woolf's essay, "Chapter 3" of the video, which begins at 15:29, addresses the essay's structure and narrative style.

In-Class Activities

1. Show students the original book cover of the first edition, a woodcut by Virginia Woolf's sister, artist Vanessa Bell. Discuss the importance and possible origins in the text of the blue and pink coloring, the clock's hands at 10 and 2, the multileveled pedestal on which it sits, and the mirror (or window) in the background. Then ask students to design their own covers.

2. Play a recording or distribute a copy of the Scottish ballad "The Four Marys." After listening and/or reading, discuss how and why Virginia Woolf alludes to this ballad.

3. Debate about whether Virginia Woolf's main argument—that "a woman must have money and a room of her own if she is to write fiction"—is an ideal vision. Consider the motivating effects of censorship and hardship on Woolf and other artists as a source of creativity.

4. One of the best-known moments in *A Room of One's Own* is the story of Judith Shakespeare. The narrator says that she will imagine Judith's story "since facts are so hard to come by" (1986). What rhetorical purposes do this statement and the story serve?

5. In chapter 2, the narrator is attempting research on "Women and Poverty" in the British Museum, but she is quickly discouraged. Discuss this scene and what discourages the narrator. Consider Professor von X's book on women and the male student studying nearby. How does the narrator, at first, distinguish intellectual differences between men and women but later reconcile them?

Paper Topics/Suggestions for Writing

1. On the surface, Virginia Woolf's essay/speech seems to favor oppositions: fact and fiction, men and women, the material and spiritual. How does Woolf complicate these (and other) oppositions?

2. The phrase "of one's own" has been adopted frequently in popular culture. Search for books, movies, and even blogs and websites that allude to Virginia Woolf's title. Why have these other media appropriated the

phrase? Why does the title still resonate almost a century after publication?

3. Novelist Alice Walker (*The Color Purple*) responded to Virginia Woolf's argument in her 1974 article "In Search of Our Mothers' Gardens." Read Walker's article and discuss her opinion of Woolf's argument in relation to figures like Phillis Wheatley. How do race and racial subjugation fit into Woolf's ideas?

4. Of all possible writers, Virginia Woolf chose to fictionalize a sister for Shakespeare. Why is Shakespeare the most effective choice for Woolf's argument?

5. After the luncheon at the men's college, the narrator spots a tail-less Manx cat from the window; this leads her to think of "lack" and the war. Why does this scene take place at the men's college? How does the image connect to loss and World War I?

6. The narrator is constantly walking from location to location throughout the essay. What is the effect of this movement on the content of her thoughts? What might it have to do with the modernist narrative style of stream of consciousness?

Resources

"Blogging Woolf: Focusing on Virginia Woolf and Her Circle, Past and Present." The International Virginia Woolf Society. www.utoronto.ca/IVWS.
> The International Virginia Woolf Society, an allied organization of the Modern Language Association, provides an annually updated bibliography and lists of web links, news, and related societies on its website.

Briggs, Julia. "To the Women of the Future." In *Virginia Woolf: An Inner Life*, 216–37. New York: Harcourt, 2005.
> This biography revolves around Woolf's works. The chapter "To the Women of the Future" analyzes Woolf's thinking on the problems of the woman artist—and gender inequality more generally—in her novels *A Room of One's Own*, *To the Lighthouse,* and *Orlando*.

Gubar, Susan, ed. "Introduction." In *A Room of One's Own* by Virginia Woolf, Harcourt annotated edition, xxxv–lxi. New York: Harcourt, 2005.
> This introduction (and annotations) by Susan Gubar will help students decipher allusions in the text.

Lee, Hermione. *Virginia Woolf.* New York: Vintage, 1996.
> This is a thorough and evocative biography of Virginia Woolf's life.

A Room of One's Own (abridged). Read by Claire Bloom. CD.
> *A Room of One's Own* was born out of two papers Woolf read at the women's colleges Girton and Newnham. Play sections of the text to help students connect with the work.

A Room of One's Own. PBS Masterpiece Theatre. Perf. Eileen Atkins. 1991.
    This performance is based on Vanessa Bell's woodcut book cover of
    A Room of One's Own.
Rosenmann, Ellen Bayuk. *A Room of One's Own: Women Writers and the
    Politics of Creativity.* New York: Twayne, 1995.
    This book examines Virgina Woolf's feminism.
The Spoken Word. Read by Virginia Woolf. BBC, CD.
    This CD includes the sole surviving recording of Virgina Woolf. Listen
    to a 2-minute excerpt at http://news.bbc.co.uk/2/hi/7684201.stm.
Woolf, Virginia. *Women and Fiction.* Manuscript of *A Room of One's Own.*
    Transcribed and edited by S. P. Rosenbaum. Cambridge: Blackwell, 1992.
    This transcription of Woolf's manuscript retains passages that were
    not included in the published version.

WILLIAM FAULKNER

Barn Burning

Spotted Horses

> Then he was moving, running, outside the
> house, toward the stable: this the old habit,
> the old blood which he had not been permit-
> ted to choose for himself, which had been
> bequeathed him willy nilly and which had run
> for so long (and who knew where, battening
> on what of outrage and savagery and lust)
> before it came to him.
> —Faulkner, "Barn Burning"

1. **Flem Snopes—unknowable and incomprehensible to other characters, himself, and the readers—acts more as a symbol or mythological creature than a round, well-developed character.** "It wasn't
   ere a man knowed yet if Flem owned them things or not. They just
   knowed one thing: that they wasn't never going to know for sho if Flem
   did or not" (2010). This quotation captures Flem Snopes's unknowability; he is greeted always with a communal sense of his inscrutability
   and general suspicion. He seems to be less like a fully realized realistic
   character and more like a symbol or a mythological creature, as an
   objective correlative for an idea. But what idea or ideas does he represent? If readers see Snopes as a round character, then what are his
   flesh-and-blood motivations for his actions? Greed, of course, but the
   gargantuan extent of this greed seems cartoonish and demands an
   explanation. To say that Flem acts out of a sense of greed seems like
   saying Ahab acts out of a dearth of ambergris. What motivates Flem, if
   he has human motivations?
   a. **Further Reading:** Bassett, John E. "Yoknapatawpha Revised: Demys-
      tifying Snopes." *College Literature* 15:2 (Spring 1988): 136–52.
   b. **Suggested Search:** Search for "In Defense of Flat Characters" by
      George R. Clay through the International Fiction Review website
      (http://journals.hil.unb.ca/index.php/IFR/article/view/7655/8712).
      Clay does not address William Faulkner specifically, but he does dis-
      cuss "flatness" as meaning more than "undeveloped."

2. **Both "Barn Burning" and "Spotted Horses" complicate race and
   race relations, especially in the Snopes family, whose economic
   and social positions blur the conventional racial boundaries.** Issues
   of race interpenetrate the main concerns with class and economics in

these stories, since both blacks and the poor are outside of the social structure represented by the justice and the townspeople. How is race working in these two stories, "Barn Burning" in particular? Harris and the elder Snopes use the term "nigger" while the narrator uses the term "Negro," which suggests a disparity between their attitudes and therefore a quoted and an ironic interpretation on the part of the narrator, a distance between the perspective of Harris and the perspective of the narrator. De Spain is referred to as a "white man," whereas this description is never applied to the Snopes's father. Does the boy think this, with the narrator quoting his thoughts? If the boy does not think of his father as a white man, then what does he consider him? If these are the thoughts of the narrator, then the question still stands: What are the Snopes in opposition to "white men"?

a. **Further Reading:** Duvall, John Noel. "William Faulkner, Whiteface, and Black Identity." In *Race and White Identity in Southern Fiction: From Faulkner to Morrison*, 17–62. New York: Palgrave, 2008.

b. **Suggested Search:** Search on the *New York Times* website (www .nytimes.com) for the February 10, 2010, article "Faulkner Link to Plantation Diary Discovered" by Patricia Cohen.

3. **The narrative style of "Barn Burning" alternates between a first-person, stream-of-consciousness narration by Sarty Snopes and the voice of a third-person, omniscient narrator.** The narrator of "Barn Burning" often seems to be quoting the interior monologue of the Snopes boy, but just as frequently he will narrate the boy's thoughts or the thoughts of the judge, for instance, or narrate the events in general. He usually does so with a verbal dexterity alien to the illiterate boy. At one point, the narrator even refuses to relate an obscene word the narrator finds inappropriate for print; this suggests a particular point of view and a particular code of communal standards. The narrative voice seems to be using aspects of conventional third-person narration, aspects of stream of consciousness, some free indirect discourse, and some of the quirky verbal tics of a first-person narrator. Whose point of view does the narrative voice represent? Is it a limited third person? Is it a first-person plural, which William Faulkner has used in such stories as "A Rose for Emily"? Is it a communal voice reacting to the thoughts of the Snopes boy?

a. **Further Reading:** Ford, Marilyn Claire. "Narrative Legerdemain: Evoking Sarty's Future in 'Barn Burning." *Mississippi Quarterly* 51:3 (Summer 1998): 527–41.

b. **Suggested Search:** Search Google or www.openculture.com for "William Faulkner Reads from *As I Lay Dying*," which is considered a stream-of-consciousness novel. There are multiple audio files of William Faulkner's own narration.

4. **Although the setting is fastidiously detailed, William Faulkner places his stories and novels in the fictional Mississippi county of Yoknapatawpha, thus forcing it and the South in general into the mythic realm.** He provides the county with an elaborate history and mythology and fully peoples it with complex characters in complex socioeconomic structures. His complete geography—maps included—is imbued with all the psychology, history, myth, and socioeconomic and racial tensions operating by virtue of that soil. The mere placement of The Bear, for instance, near Sutpen's Hundred, holds for a reader steeped in Faulkner a redolence of Thomas Sutpen, his brutality and history, and his status as an objective correlative for a wide spectrum of political and historical issues: the moral underbelly of capitalist upward mobility and manifest destiny, miscegenation and slavery, and the loss of the feudal glory of the antebellum South. Why represent the South through this prism of invention rather than literally? What does Faulkner get out of this elaborate distancing? What is the difference between the poetry of mythology and the strict record of history?

   a. **Further Reading:** Doyle, Don H. *Faulkner's County: The Historical Roots of Yoknapatawpha.* Chapel Hill, NC: University of North Carolina Press, 2001.

   b. **Suggested Search:** Conduct a Google Images search for "Yoknapatawpha maps." Results will include many maps that William Faulkner himself drew of this fictional county.

5. **William Faulkner mourned the loss of Southern ideology that was replaced by the exploitative and morally weak "New South."** The Snopes in general and Flem in particular, a minor character in "Barn Burning" and a major one in "Spotted Horses," represent for Faulkner the financial rise of a lower class devoid of the chivalrous moral code that remained, vestigial and shrunken, in the ineffectual contemporary Southern aristocracy at whose expense they rose (the Compsons, for example). This new aristocracy itself is a travesty of the actual aristocracy of the feudal antebellum South (Colonel Sartoris, for example, the Snopes boy's namesake). The new justice renders judgment among cheeses, and Flem Snopes repeatedly outwits all of Jefferson, not just in "Spotted Horses" but also in the trilogy of novels *The Hamlet, The Town,* and *The Mansion.* What is Faulkner's attitude toward this New South and its avatars, the Snopes?

   a. **Further Reading:** Howe, Irving. "The Southern Myth and William Faulkner." *American Quarterly* 3:4 (Winter 1951): 357–62.

   b. **Suggested Search:** Search for "Property, Wealth, and the 'American Dream' in 'Barn Burning'" at the Center for Faulkner Studies through the Southeast Missouri State University website at www.semo.edu/cfs.

In-Class Activities

1. Find one of William Faulkner's several maps of Yoknapatawpha. Ask students to try to locate these stories specifically in Faulkner's geography and to figure out the historical, mythological, and socioeconomic indicators implied by the placement of various locales and events. Include in your discussion time line and genealogy schemas.

2. Ask students to draw Colonel Sartoris Snopes and Flem Snopes, looking carefully through the text for indicators of the purely visual appearance of the characters. Then try to read their appearances for larger historical and sociocultural cues.

3. Read an excerpt from *The Sound and the Fury*, and then have students watch part of the very different 1959 movie version starring Yul Brynner. By comparing the narrative methods of the movie (and movies in general, since students are often more familiar with classical Hollywood syntax than with any other narrative syntax) to the narrative methods of the text, begin to explain the virtues of the stream-of-consciousness style. Then try to apply this discussion to "Barn Burning."

4. Discuss the "American dream." What is that dream? In these stories, is William Faulkner critiquing the upward mobility on which America prides itself? If so, how?

5. Discuss with students other Southern literature they have read. Ask them how writers such as Mark Twain, Harper Lee, Eudora Welty, Flannery O'Connor, and Tennessee Williams are similar to William Faulkner. What makes them "Southern" writers? Is it just the setting and the characters' birthplace, or is there a quintessential Southernness to these authors' works?

Paper Topics/Suggestions for Writing

1. Is Flem Snopes a fully realized realistic character, or does he function more like a symbol or a mythological creature?

2. How is race working in these two stories, "Barn Burning" in particular? What is Sarty's view of race?

3. Whose point of view does the narrative voice of "Barn Burning" represent? Can this be considered a stream-of-consciousness narrative? Compare "Barn Burning" to other texts in this volume, such as James Joyce's "The Dead," Virginia Woolf's "A Room of One's Own," or Clarice Lispector's "The Daydreams of a Drunk Woman."

4. What does William Faulkner get out of the elaborate distancing of constructing a fictional county with its own fabricated history and mythol-

ogy? What is the difference between the poetry of mythology and the strict record of history?

5. Based on the evidence of these stories, what is William Faulkner's attitude toward this New South and its avatars, the Snopes?

6. Can "Barn Burning" be considered a coming-of-age story? At what point during the narrative does Sarty become a man? What is his rite of passage? Are there stylistic or textual cues that mark his transformation?

Resources

Barn Burning. Dir. Peter Warner. Perf. Tommy Lee Jones, Diane Kagan. The American Story Collection. 1980.

>Director Peter Warner's version of "Barn Burning" runs for 41 minutes and can be watched in under a single class period. Students can compare how the film handles certain aspects of the story, such as the narrative techniques.

Comprone, Joseph. "Literature and the Writing Process: A Pedagogical Reading of William Faulkner's 'Barn Burning.'" *College Literature* 9:1 (Winter 1982): 1–21.

>Joseph Comprone's article introduces a reading and writing process for students of literature and then uses "Barn Burning" to exemplify that process.

Greiner, Donald J. "Universal Snopeism: The Significance of 'Spotted Horses.'" *English Journal* 57:8 (November 1968): 1133–37.

>Donald Greiner's article offers a publication history of "Spotted Horses," as well as a clear, concise interpretation of the story as "universal."

Hahn, Stephen, and Robert W. Hamblin, eds. *Teaching Faulkner: Approaches and Methods.* Westport, CT: Greenwood Press, 2001.

>The nineteen essays collected in this volume approach William Faulkner and his works through multiple lenses, including historical, cultural, race, and gender.

Priddy, Anna, and Harold Bloom. *Bloom's How to Write about William Faulkner.* New York: Bloom's Literary Criticism, 2010.

>This book begins with a general description of how to write a good essay and then delves into many of William Faulkner's major works, including "Spotted Horses" and "Barn Burning." This would be a good resource for instructors and students alike.

The Good Woman of Setzuan

Dignity, dear colleagues, dignity! Never despair! As for this world, didn't we agree that we only have to find one human being who can stand the place?
—Bertolt Brecht, *The Good Woman of Setzuan*, interlude between scenes 9 and 10

Topics for Lecture or Discussion

1. **The gods desperately seek one good person in order to justify doing nothing to change the conditions of the world.** In a particularly Brechtian twist, the gods are lazy and descend to earth intent upon finding at least one good person, proof that goodness can exist. If they cannot find such a person, then they must agree that the material conditions are such that goodness cannot survive in the world as it is and that those same conditions must change in order for virtue to thrive. Their agenda is to find a person they can call good and thus relieve themselves of the responsibility and effort for changing the world. Ironically, the lowly and powerless prostitute Shen Te is the only one in the entire town who welcomes the gods and invites them to spend the night in her room. Quick to dodge the label of good that the gods pin on her, Shen Te claims that she cannot afford to be good and must sell herself to men in order to buy food and pay the rent. In a further irony, the gods hasten to give her money and depart, as if money were enough to maintain virtue. In fact, money, the capitalistic system, and the unequal and unfair distribution of wealth foster evil in the world.
   a. **Further Reading:** Barthes, Roland. "The Brechtian Revolution." 1955. In *Critical Essays*, translated by Richard Howard, 37–39. Evanston, IL: Northwestern University Press, 1972.
   b. **Suggested Searches:** Search for the following phrases in Google Images, Google Scholar, or an academic database to find images and additional resources: Brecht parable of morality and human society; Brecht's politics; Brecht and Communism; Brecht and social change.

2. **Shen Te invents her ruthless cousin, Shui Ta, to avoid complete exploitation.** Initially, Shen Te thinks that the large sum of money given to her by the gods solves all of her problems. Happily, she buys a tobacco shop and begins to set up a legitimate business. She learns quickly, however, that if having no money presents one set of problems, having some creates another set of difficulties. As soon as she had something to call

her own, people begged her favor. Unable to discern the truly needy from the merely opportunistic, she dons a male disguise and invents a male cousin in order to stave off financial ruin. The theatrical alternation of personas through change of costume, from the kind and gentle Shen Te to the ruthlessly savvy and efficient Shui Ta, manifests the critique of Western society: success in the business world, in a capitalistic system, demands aggressive, selfish behavior in which only the vicious shall survive.

   a. **Further Reading:** Rouse, John. "Brecht and the Contradictory Actor." *Theatre Journal* 36:1 (March 1984): 25–42.

   b. **Suggested Searches:** Search for the following phrases in Google Images, Google Scholar, or an academic database to find images and additional resources: performing Brecht; patriarchal dimensions of capitalism; Shen Te and Shui Ta.

3. **Bertolt Brecht's epic theater makes the dramatic event strange to provide aesthetic distance and spur the audience to form critical judgment.** Wang, the water-seller, functions as a narrator who develops a relationship with the theatrical audience as a storyteller. Rather than following traditional convention, which pretends the audience is not present, the narrator recognizes the audience and mediates the performance as if it were a demonstration of human phenomena in a scientific setting. In a dramatic, Aristotelian play, with its emphasis on plot, conflict, and the rising and falling action building to a final, often inevitable, conclusion, the audience gets lost in the fiction and, as in any good mystery, anticipates the end to find out what happened. In this play, however, Brecht presents a question regarding human behavior and moral virtue, and each scene offers evidence for the audience to reach a conclusion concerning the playwright's thesis. It is not so much *what* happens in the play that provokes interest but, rather, *how* it happens. Episodic scenes, recurring scenes with the gods, the exotic locale in China, the frequent songs, and the lack of any dramatic suspense are all techniques designed to provide the spectator with a perspective on the mechanics of human behavior. Above all else, the spectator must not view the dramatic outcome as inevitable in any way but as always the product of particular choices that could be changed to produce far different results.

   a. **Further Reading:** Brecht, Bertolt. "A Short Organum for the Theatre." In *Brecht on Theatre: The Development of an Aesthetic*, edited and translated by John Willett, 179–206. New York: Hill & Wang, 1964.

   b. **Suggested Searches:** Search for the following phrases in Google Images, Google Scholar, or an academic database to find images and additional resources: non-Aristotelian theater; epic theater.

4. **The trial scene at the end is a metatheatrical device that amplifies the playwright's dialectical methods.** A courtroom is inherently theatrical in that the staging is precise and proscribed, and each person plays a specific role: judge, defendant, plaintiff, prosecutor, defense attorney, member of the jury, and member of the audience of the court. The role each person plays is synonymous with the action that he or she performs. The courtroom setting functions metatheatrically, as a play-within-a-play. The juridical triad of prosecutor, defendant, and judge accords with Bertolt Brecht's dialectical critique in which the conflict of forces (A versus B) undergoes a final synthesis to reach a conclusion (C). In the drama, Shui Ta is accused of murdering Shen Te, an opposition that is solved with the revelation that Shen Te and Shui Ta are the same person and that the good persona had to disappear in order to survive. The gods originally asked for Shen Te to be good and to live. She discovers in the course of the action that it is impossible to do both. Unfortunately, the gods refuse to recognize the nuance of Shen Te's argument and flee the scene with blind conviction that their good person is alive and well.

   a. **Further Reading:** Jameson, Fredric. "Persistencies of the Dialectic: Three Sites." *Science & Society* 62:3 (Fall 1998): 358–72.

   b. **Suggested Searches:** Search for the following phrases in Google Images, Google Scholar, or an academic database to find images and additional resources: *Theater of War* John W. Walter (video); dialectical materialism and Brecht.

5. **The gods float away in a pink cloud, a comic send-up of the *deus ex machina* of Euripides as well as the staging devices of nineteenth-century melodramas, and leave humanity with the unresolved question of what to do now.** Typically the gods intervene at the end to save the day and make the world right or just again. Here, Bertolt Brecht's point is obvious: the supernatural cannot save humanity; only humanity can save itself. Rather than a theatrical ending that tidies up the action, Brecht writes an open ending and insists that the audience must decide how to write an ending that will be happy for all people. Once again, Brecht empowers the audience to consider what it has seen and to apply the lessons and insights to the problems of the real world that exist outside the theatrical space. Tellingly, it is asked in the epilogue whether change is possible and whether people can change. The preceding action suggests an affirmative answer, but each member of the audience must form an independent judgment and an individual commitment.

   a. **Further Reading:** Curran, Angela. "Brecht's Criticisms of Aristotle's Aesthetics of Tragedy." *Journal of Aesthetics and Art Criticism* 59:2 (Spring 2001): 167–84.

b. **Suggested Searches:** Search for the following phrases in Google Images, Google Scholar, or an academic database to find images and additional resources: *deus ex machina* in Brecht; Brechtian aesthetics; political theater; alienation effect in Brecht.

In-Class Activities

1. Collect masks (even Halloween masks are acceptable) and place them all together. Select one to wear and study it before putting it on. After putting it on, allow perception of the mask to suggest physical transformation and new movement and gesture patterns. Remove the mask and put it back on, continuing to allow perception of the mask to govern physical movement and gestures. Can you see how the mask could be the basis for characterization?

2. Look at Wang's speeches as the narrator of the play. How does he relate to the audience? What can the actor do physically to promote the relationship between the audience and him?

3. Discuss how this play is more like a scientific laboratory experiment than a traditional play in the theater. What is the hypothesis? How is the experiment conducted? What are your conclusions?

Paper Topics/Suggestions for Writing

1. Bertolt Brecht aspired to create a theater of pleasure in an age of science. He likened the theater to a sporting event such as a boxing match. From what aspects of this type of theater might an audience draw pleasure, and what might it learn in the process?

2. Actors, according to Bertolt Brecht, should objectively demonstrate the nature of human relationships rather than identify with their individual roles. What differences from standard theatrical practice do you detect in this approach, and what do you think such methods try to accomplish?

3. Shen Te is a nice person who discovers that she needs Shui Ta in order to survive. What does this dramatic doubling suggest about the fate of individual goodness in a corrupt world?

4. The gods are represented as lazy, petty, and quibbling. What does such a comic portrayal suggest about the modern world? If not from the gods, from where will salvation from human wrongs and problems come?

5. Business transactions and money exchanges dominate the action. What do these repeated gestures suggest to the audience about the performance?

6. Events in Bertolt Brecht's play are not fixed or inevitable in any way but are the outcome of particular choices and decisions. Political and social change is challenging, but possible and absolutely necessary. What changes are necessary in the world of this play in order to improve conditions for everyone?

Resources

Bertolt Brecht. Insight Media, 1996, VHS.
>This BBC video profiles the dramatist and discusses his development of a unique form of politically and socially minded drama.

Brecht on Stage. Insight Media, 1992, DVD.
>Hans Mayer discusses the staging of the original production of *Mother Courage* at the Berliner Ensemble.

JORGE LUIS BORGES
The Garden of Forking Paths

> The Pavilion of the Limpid Solitude stood in
> the center of a garden that was perhaps intri-
> cate; that circumstance could have suggested
> to the heirs a physical labyrinth. Ts'ui Pên
> died; no one in the vast territories that were
> his came upon the labyrinth; the confusion of
> the novel suggested to me that *it* was the maze.
> —Borges, "The Garden of Forking Paths"

Topics for Lecture and Discussion

1. **"The Garden of Forking Paths" is the first example of hypertextual literature.** It has all the trappings of detective fiction, including a secret agent on a mission, but it plays with the genre in the same way that Akutagawa Ryūnosuke does in "In a Bamboo Grove," which is included in this volume. Akutagawa had a strong influence on Jorge Luis Borges, and he alludes to both this story and to *Rashomon* throughout his own. For example, the protagonist says, "Thus I arrived before a tall, rusty gate. Between the iron bars I made out a popular grove and a pavilion" (2084). Both authors question objectivity and reality through the multiplicity of Truths. In Borges's studies, this effect is likened to hypertextuality, a term that is typically used to describe the "rhizomatic" structure of the World Wide Web, as well as a text arranged nonlinearly that "links" or branches to other nodes of information. In "The Garden of Forking Paths," Dr. Stephen Albert explains time hypertextually: "Each time a man is confronted with several alternatives, he chooses one and eliminates the others. . . . He creates, in this way, diverse futures, diverse times which themselves proliferate and fork . . . each [possible outcome] is the point of departure for other forkings" (2086).
   a. **Further Reading:** Sasson-Henry, Perla. "Jorge Luis Borges: A Fore-runner of the Technology of the New Millennium—Links and Fork-ing Paths." In *Borges 2.0: From Text to Virtual Worlds*, 23–37. New York: Peter Lang, 2007.
   b. **Suggested Search:** Search for "Choose your own adventure books and *Slate*." This Slate.com article by Grady Hendrix describes inter-active entertainment, starting with "The Garden of Forking Paths" and developing into children's interactive novels.

2. **Jorge Luis Borges's story collapses multiple possible narratives into one space, thus undermining the Fascism of the 1940s.** Although

he is considered an apolitical writer, some of his disdain for Fascism (especially his future hatred toward Argentinean president Juan Domingo Perón) may be discernible in "The Garden of Forking Paths." His general political stance was that any philosophical or political system proposes its own version of Truth. Fascism, however, forces its Truth. Like Pierre Menard of his "Pierre Menard, Author of Don Quixote," which was printed in 1941 with this short story, Borges believes that "historical truth . . . is not what took place; it is what we think took place" (Jorge Luis Borges, "Pierre Menard, Author of Don Quixote," *Ficciones* [New York: Grove Press, 1962], 53). By suggesting that time, and thus history, is fractured and many, Borges is undermining the totalitarian attempt to construct a single stable version of true history through propaganda and lies. This subversion is reinforced by the narration from Liddell Hart's *History of the First World War*, an actual historian's study, which begins Hsi P'êng's story. Despite his anti-Fascism, Borges remained supportive of Argentina, sharing Hsi P'êng's view as he walks to Albert's home: "I thought that a man can be an enemy of other men, of the moments of other men, but not of a country: not of fireflies, words, gardens, streams of water, sunsets" (2083–84).

a. **Further Reading:** González, José Eduardo. *Borges and the Politics of Form*. New York: Garland Publishing, 1998.

b. **Suggested Search:** The search term *"casa historia the perons"* will yield a page at www.casahistoria.net that collects many further sites, including audio and video, on Perón, the Fascist president of Argentina with whom Borges publicly and famously disagreed.

3. **Jorge Luis Borges was a cosmopolitan author, free from the restrictions of nation and race. "The Garden of Forking Paths" is the perfect text to guide a conversation on world literature in the modern world.** Borges says, "Gibbon observes that in the Arabian book par excellence, in the Koran, there are no camels. If there were any doubt as to the authenticity of the Koran, this absence of camels would be sufficient proof it is an Arabian work" (Borges, "The Argentine Writer and Tradition," 181). Instead of trying to capture and narrow what he calls the "flavor" of a certain place, which is Argentina for Borges, he accepts the cosmopolitanism of Buenos Aires, which has Western, European history, and cultural influences. Borges himself abandoned the nationalism of his early writing and wrote according to his cosmopolitan side that lived abroad, traveled extensively, and spoke many languages. This short story takes place in England, features Chinese characters, texts, and locations, and includes allusions to other national literatures, such as the German Johann Wolfgang von Goethe's and the Arabian *The Thousand and One Nights*. Borges does not insist upon his writing as Argentinean because it is nothing more than a simula-

crum of Argentina. Genuine Argentinean literature does not narrow itself internationally.

  a. **Further Reading:** Borges, Jorge Luis. "The Argentine Writer and Tradition." In *Labyrinths: Selected Stories and Other Writings*, edited by Donald A. Yates and James E. Irby, 177–85. New York: New Directions, 1964.

  b. **Suggested Search:** Search for *The Real Buenos Aires* at youtube .com. This two-part BBC documentary (about 20 min.) provides a nice overview of the city's cosmopolitanism.

4. **The labyrinth is the central image and structure of Hsi P'êng's fictional novel *The Garden of Forking Paths*, as well as Jorge Luis Borges's story "The Garden of Forking Paths."** A labyrinth is "a structure consisting of a number of intercommunicated passages arranged in bewildering complexity through which it is difficult or impossible to find one's way without guidance" (*Oxford English Dictionary*, 2nd ed.). The image and the idea of the labyrinth are essential to understanding the content and the form of the story. We realize, after Dr. Albert's explanation, that the tale we're reading is just one "fork" of time, chosen to be followed despite the other forks available to be followed. Within the first paragraph of Tsun's narrative, he lists the contents of his pockets: "The American watch, the nickel chain and the square coin, the key ring with the incriminating useless keys to Runeberg's apartment, the notebook, a letter which I resolved to destroy immediately (and which I did not destroy)" (2082). Each of those objects represents a branching off to another story. For example, why must the letter be destroyed but remains intact? People, too, represent these forkings. As Tsun walks through the coaches of the train, he says, "I remember a few farmers, a woman dressed in mourning, a young boy was reading with fervor the Annals of Tacitus, a wounded and happy soldier" (2082). Each of these characters' stories is explorable, yet unexplored by us. Why was the boy reading, so fervently, Tacitus? Why would a soldier be both wounded and happy?

  a. **Further Reading:** Zhang, Xuejun. "Borges and Contemporary Chinese Avant-Garde Writings." *Frontiers of Literary Study in China* 1:2 (2007): 272–86.

  b. **Suggested Search:** Search for "The Garden of Time" on youtube .com. Creators Caires and Cordoso explain their project as "an interactive video installation that pays an homage to . . . Borges."

5. **Jorge Luis Borges is considered one of the first writers of both magical realism and science fiction.** The term *magical realism* was coined in 1925 by German artist Franz Roh to describe postexpressionism. Latin American writers quickly adopted the term and re-created it as a literary genre. Massimo Bontempelli said that works in this genre must have "realist precision and magical atmosphere" (Luca Somigli,

"Italy," *The Cambridge Companion to European Modernism*, ed. Pericles Lewis [New York: Cambridge University Press, 2011], 88). Science fiction, like magical realism, is difficult to define, but it can be broadly understood as a text that posits the existence of alternate realities. In "The Garden of Forking Paths," the magical realism exists in the plurality of possible worlds. However, though Borges proposes alternative universes and stretches reality to its most magical point through plot verisimilitude, he followed only one central plotline in "The Garden of Forking Paths." In fact, as Harold Bloom notes, Borges was frustrated by his inability to create a simple, plot-based story.

a. **Further Reading:** Bowers, Maggie Ann. *Magic(al) Realism*. New York: Routledge, 2004.

b. **Suggested Search:** Search for "the guardian Borges's Google doodle." This will take you to the design on Google's home page that celebrated Jorge Luis Borges's 112th birthday on August 24, 2011. An article accompanies the design, as well as an animated YouTube video of the doodle.

In-Class Activities

1. "Remedial Chaos Theory" (episode 4, season 3) of NBC's sitcom *Community* features seven different possible time lines of the same evening. The 22-minute episode is a perfect example of parallel universes or alternative time lines represented in the Chinese book of *The Garden of Forking Paths*. Show the episode as an introduction to a lecture or a discussion on forking time.

2. Many critics argue that Jorge Luis Borges's fiction anticipates the hypertext of the Internet. Illustrate this theory in the classroom by projecting any Wikipedia entry and "Wikidrifting" by clicking on hyperlink after hyperlink. Ask students to share their own experiences of getting trapped in Internet surfing. How does that experience reflect "The Garden of Forking Paths"?

3. During an interview, Jorge Luis Borges said, "I remember having seen an engraving of the labyrinth in a French book—when I was a boy. It was a circular building without doors with many windows. I used to gaze at this engraving and think that if I brought a loupe close to it, it would reveal the minotaur" (Herbert A. Simon, *Models of My Life* [Cambridge, MA: MIT Press, 1996], 176). Borges is referring to the Cretan labyrinth of Greek mythology, the Palace of Knossos, which contained the minotaur. Familiarize your students with the myth of the minotaur, Ariadne, and Theseus, and show them images of labyrinths. Discuss how Borges's childhood fascination with the maze and myth may have affected the story. Is his fascination similar to Hsi P'êng?

4. Your students might be familiar with labyrinths from popular culture, such as the 1986 Jim Henson movie *The Labyrinth*, starring David Bowie, or the 2006 film *Pan's Labyrinth*. You can begin your lecture by referencing, or even showing clips from, either of these movies so that the central image has a familiar point of reference.

Paper Topics/Suggestions for Writing

1. Discuss the implications of Jorge Luis Borges's narrative technique. Who is the narrator? In what guise does he present himself? How does Borges blur the traditional distinctions between author, narrator, and character? Does this issue relate to Luigi Pirandello's play *Six Characters in Search of an Author*?

2. "The Garden of Forking Paths" and Naguib Mahfouz's "Zaabalawi" share elements, such as journeys through the city and gardens. Are there other imagistic similarities? What is the significance of those shared elements?

3. Jorge Luis Borges's work is often seen as the precursor to magical realism, a genre whose proponents include Gabriel Garcia Marquez, Julio Cortázar, and Isabel Allende. But Borges is also seen as a science fiction writer. Research the history and tenets of these genre modes. Does "The Garden of Forking Paths" fit into one, both, or neither of these genre conventions? Why?

4. "Labyrinth" can describe both the central image and narrative style of the story. How? What is a labyrinth? How is it different from a maze?

Resources

Bell-Villada, Gene H. *Borges and His Fiction: A Guide to His Mind and Art*. Austin: University of Texas Press, 1999.
> Gene Bell-Villada explains Jorge Luis Borges's writing through his biography.

Borges, Jorge Luis. *Selected Non-Fictions*. Edited by Eliot Weinberger. New York: Viking, 1999.
> This expansive collection of essays by Jorge Luis Borges spans topics from the act of reading, to James Joyce, to the idea of "reality."

Death and the Compass. Dir. Alex Cox. Perf. Peter Boyle. Estudios Churubusco Azteca S. A., 1992.
> This film is based on Jorge Luis Borges's short story "Death and the Compass," another pseudo-detective story.

Foster, David William. *Jorge Luis Borges: An Annotated Primary and Secondary Bibliography*. New York: Garland, 1984.
> This is an extensive collection of works by or about Jorge Luis Borges.

"The Garden of the Forking Paths." The Modern Word. www.themodernword .com/borges.

   This site offers a comprehensive collection of information, audio and video files, pictures, and essays on Jorge Luis Borges.

MODERNIST POETRY

These fragments I have shored against my
ruins.
—T. S. Eliot, "The Waste Land," line 431

Topics for Lecture or Discussion

1. **The twentieth century sees the shift from romantic poetry about the natural landscape to flaneurs writing about the "insidious streets" of the modern city.** At the turn of the century, the world was quickly modernizing. Modern cities became a literary focus. T. S. Eliot, in his "The Love Song of J. Alfred Prufrock," sets his narrator out through the "half-deserted streets," "Streets that follow like a tedious argument / Of insidious intent" into "sawdust restaurants with oyster shells" (2123, lines 4, 7, 9). And in Pablo Neruda's "Walking Around," the city is just as ominous for the walker: "And it shoves me along to certain corners, to certain deep houses / to hospitals where the bones come out of the windows, / to certain cobblers' shops smelling of vinegar, / to streets horrendous as crevices" (2169, lines 30–34). "I Speak of the City," by Octavio Paz, reads, "I speak of the buildings of stone and marble, of cement, glass and steel, of the people in the lobbies and doorways, of the elevators that rise and fall like the mercury in thermometers" (2184, lines 47–49). These scenes and landscapes are the interior psychic spaces of the speaker. They also fall into the long poetic tradition of talking about the experience of being on the street, surrounded by the profusion of the modern city as evidenced by the flaneur—a stroller, or a person who experiences life by walking the streets.
   a. **Further Reading:** Baudelaire, Charles. *The Painter of Modern Life.* London: Phaidon, 1964.
   b. **Suggested Search:** Conduct a Google search for "arcades project Baudelaire." One result will be the site "The Arcades Project: The Rhetoric of Hypertext." Go there for essays and images about the flaneur on a site template that encourages a cyber version of the act.

2. **Modernist poetry marked a break with traditional poetic forms and content.** Modernist poet Ezra Pound famously called on artists of his time to "make it new." Important to note about his suggestion is its origin: Pound took the phrase from Confucius, an act that fulfills the statement's very suggestion. Pound taught modernists that all ideas, images, and utterances originate elsewhere, so as artists they must make "it"—the old—new. The most illustrious example of this mantra is T. S. Eliot's "The Waste Land," which the poet dedicated to Pound with a quotation from Petronius's *Satyricon.* The quotation was originally spoken by Trimalchio, an ostentatious braggart, which is an ironic

allusion to make at the beginning of a poem that is a collection of allusions and quotations. By composing a poem of used lines, Eliot breaks down the traditional form of poetry. He continues this dismantling with discontinuity and disjunction, abutting lines and sections that have no clear narrative or logical connection. Much modernist poetry relied on images rather than on the discursiveness of the poetry of the recent past, the romantics and Victorians. Imagists like Eliot valued sparse wording and a directness in dealing with the object.

a. **Further Reading:** Perkins, David. *A History of Modern Poetry: From the 1890s to the High Modernist Mode.* Cambridge, MA: Belknap, 1976.

b. **Suggested Search:** Search for the article "Make It New: Originality and the Younger Poet" by Dana Levin on Poets.org.

3. **One way for readers to interrogate the literary classifications like "Modern Poetry" is to compare and contrast two authors and their approaches to the same topic, for instance, T. S. Eliot's and Federico García Lorca's disparate approaches to the role of emotion.** T. S. Eliot wrote that "[P]oetry is not a turning loose of emotion, but an escape from emotion." This comment can be attributed to the twentieth-century artist's suspicion and rejection of romantic emotionalism and Victorian sentimentality. Eliot argued that "[T]he only way of expressing emotion in the form of art is by finding an 'objective correlative'; in other words, a set of objects, a situation, a chain of events which shall be the formula of that particular emotion; such that when the external facts, which must terminate in sensory experience, are given, the emotion is immediately evoked" (T. S. Eliot, "Tradition and the Individual Talent," *Selected Prose of T. S. Eliot*, ed. Frank Kermode [New York: Harcourt, 1975], 43). Your students may find this idea—of applying a "formula" to evoke a particular emotion—too unsentimental. And perhaps they will find Eliot's confidence in his ability to produce the exact emotion he designs for in his readers off-putting or offensive. As an exercise, find passages in "The Waste Land" that are examples of the objective correlative, and then discuss Lorca's idea of *duende*, the state of heightened emotion that the artist experiences during the act of creation or performance. This conversation is a good introduction to questioning the classification of literature. Can both Eliot and Lorca, with such seemingly disparate opinions on the role of emotion in art, be considered "modernist"?

a. **Further Reading:** Lorca, Federico García. *In Search of Duende,* translated by Christopher Maurer and Norman Thomas di Giovanni. New York: New Directions, 1998.

b. **Suggested Search:** Conduct a Google search for T. S. Eliot's 1921 essay "Hamlet and His Problems." His definition and explanation of "objective correlative" begins in paragraph 7.

4. **Modernists such as Constantine Cavafy, William Butler Yeats, and Rainer Maria Rilke created or reinterpreted mythologies about aesthetics, history, and imagination.** A number of the modernist poets are interested in folklore, religion, and mythology, both their own and preexisting. Cavafy, for example, returns to Greek mythology in "Ithaka," but the return is imaginative. The excursion is only possible with the spiritual and intellectual internalization of Homer. And Yeats creates his own elaborate mythology about the progression of time that is not scientific or religious, in the sense that it accords to any preexisting religion. The gyres in "The Second Coming" interpenetrate, so that a new one begins only as its opposite concludes. Each gyre represents a cycle of history covering approximately two thousand years, but both gyres exist simultaneously, one always implying the other. The phrase "the second coming" will inspire students to discuss Christianity, but remind them that Yeats's interpretation of history is not a Christian one. Rather, discuss whether he has applied the Christian history to his model, or if he has appropriated the phrase. Rilke also creates a new mythology on top of an old one. In "Archaic Torso of Apollo," the god says, "You must change your life" (2117, line 14). Like Wallace Stevens in "Sunday Morning" (see www.poemhunter.com/poem/sunday-morning for the text of this poem), Rilke lays his own religion of aestheticism and imagination over the preexisting mythologies.
   a. **Further Reading:** Bell, Michael. *Literature, Modernism, and Myth: Belief and Responsibility in the Twentieth Century.* New York: Cambridge University Press, 1997.
   b. **Suggested Search:** Joseph S. Salemi's essay "Mythology and Modernism" is a personal narrative about discovering modernism's interest in the past, religions, and mythologies. A Google search for the title will yield the essay through *The Pennsylvania Review* (pennreview.com).

5. **Many modernist poets wrote about the politics that affected them personally and as artists.** Another way the modernist poets broke with the poetic tradition of their predecessors was the increased politicization of their poetry. Anna Akhmatova's "Requiem," for example, is about a Russian mother's pain during the Stalinist regime, writing in one of the poem's most striking sections, "But where the silent Mother stood, there / No one glanced and no one would have dared" (2155). The poem is begun under the pretense of a request: "Can you describe this?" asks a woman in the "Preface." Because of her question, the poem becomes a self-conscious literary response to the political situation. Pablo Neruda's poem "I'm Explaining a Few Things" is a result of his residence in Spain as the Chilean diplomatic consul during Franco's attack on the innocent people of Republican Spain. The arresting

opening lines dare the reader not to complain that the poem doesn't seem poetic: "You are going to ask: where are the lilacs? / and the poppy-petalled metaphysics?" (2169, lines 1–2). You can teach the poem alongside Pablo Picasso's painting *Guernica*, which is a depiction of the aerial bombing of the city of Guernica during the Spanish Civil War. Discuss the surrealistic quality of the painter's and poet's images. How do Neruda's tone, varying length of stanzas, and half lines parallel Picasso's painting?

   a. **Further Reading:** Ferrall, Charles. *Modernist Writing and Reactionary Politics*. New York: Cambridge University Press, 2001.

   b. **Suggested Search:** Conduct a Google search for "Guernica: Testimony of War." The resulting site at www.pbs.org/treasuresoftheworld /a_nav/guernica_nav/main_guerfrm.html includes an image of the painting as well as an explanation of why the usually nonpolitical Picasso turned to the bombing as subject matter.

In-Class Activities

1. According to Federico García Lorca, "The duende is a power and not a behavior, it is a struggle and not a concept. I have heard an old guitarist master say, 'The duende is not in the throat; the duende surges up from the soles of the feet.' It is not a matter of ability, but of real live form; of blood; of ancient culture; of creative action" (Lorca, *In Search of Duende*, 49). To introduce this elusive concept to students, show them one of the many videos of flamenco dancing on youtube.com. Discuss why flamenco dancing, like bullfighting, is associated with duende. You might also have students write about a time they felt the creative power of duende.

2. Choose a section of "The Waste Land." Have each student read a section. Discuss how reading the poem like this emphasizes T. S. Eliot's enjambment, alliteration, awkward rhymes, and lack of connections and transitions between images and scenes.

3. Poets such as Constantine Cavafy, William Butler Yeats, and Rainer Maria Rilke create their own imaginative mythologies built on top of or at least explained through preexisting mythologies. Yeats's gyres represent his cyclical model of the progression of history. Although it may seem complicated to students at first, show them the illustrations of the gyres to explain Yeats's view, and then ask them to reflect on their own theories of historical progression. Is it a Christian version? The "wave"? Evolutionary meliorism? The strictly linear teleology? Ask students to illustrate that model, like Yeats's.

Paper Topics/Suggestions for Writing

1. What is "modernist poetry"? Is there a way to classify poetry as modernist other than the period in which it was written?

2. In his 1919 essay "Hamlet and His Problems," T. S. Eliot says, "[T]he only way of expressing emotion in the form of art is by finding an 'objective correlative'; in other words, a set of objects, a situation, a chain of events which shall be the formula of that particular emotion; such that when the external facts, which must terminate in sensory experience, are given, the emotion is immediately evoked" (T. S. Eliot, "Hamlet," *Selected Prose of T. S. Eliot*, ed. Frank Kermode [New York: Harcourt, 1975], 48). What are the objects, situations, and events that evoke emotions in "The Love Song of J. Alfred Prufrock" and/or in "The Waste Land"? What are those emotions?

3. Research the political situations that inspired some of the poems in the selection. For example, you might look at William Butler Yeats's "Easter 1916," Anna Akhmatova's "Requiem," or Aimé Césaire's "Notebook of a Return to the Native Land," among others.

4. The most famous line of Rainer Maria Rilke's poem "Archaic Torso of Apollo" is the last line: "You must change your life" (line 14). Offer a reading of this poem, accounting for this striking last line.

5. Anna Akhmatova begins "Requiem" with a number of introductory sections, such as "Instead of a Preface." If this section is not a preface, then what is it? How does this section introduce the rest of the poem? What is "1935–1940," or "Dedication," or "Prologue"?

6. What view of the city emerges from Pablo Neruda's "Walking Around" and/or Octavio Paz's "I Speak of the City"? Compare the details that arouse the speakers' disgust with the details that J. Alfred Prufrock notices as he makes his way through the insidious streets.

7. Read Federico García Lorca's essay "The Duende: Theory and Divertissement" (Lorca, *In Search of Duende*; also available at http://literary movementsmanifesto.wordpress.com/text-2/garcia-lorcas-essay-the-duende-theory-and-divertissement). How does Lorca define *duende*? How would you define it in your own words? Does Lorca's "Lament for Ignacio Sánchez Mejías" have it?

Resources

"A Brief Guide to Modernism." Poets.org.
> This site offers a clear and succinct introduction to the modernist literary movement. The page also includes links to futurism, imagism, and other modernist authors.

Gay, Peter. *Modernism: The Lure of Heresy, from Baudelaire to Beckett and Beyond*. New York: Norton, 2008.

> This work is a cultural and artistic history that argues that modernist literature is based on a spirit of rebellion and subversion.

Whitworth, Michael H. *Reading Modernist Poetry*. Malden, MA: Wiley-Blackwell, 2010.

> This guide boasts about its ability to make modernist poetry less intimidating to new readers. It offers suggestions for considering literary techniques, information on modernism's predecessors, and clear explanations to lead readers through the poetry.

MANIFESTOS

Topics for Lecture or Discussion

1. **Filippo Tommaso Marinetti began the futurist movement to attack the old (i.e., the inherited and stored artifacts of previous generations' achievements) and to celebrate the new.** He uses a vocabulary of the geriatric and dilapidated to characterize traditional, established places and things and a festive and dynamic vocabulary to describe the modern: The tram is "ablaze with colored lights, as if villages in festive celebration," while the Canal is "ancient" and makes the sounds of "mumbled prayers" near palaces with their "creaking bones" (643). The modern world is beautiful and inspires Marinetti because of its filth and absurdity: his "face covered in repair-shop grime . . . with [his] arms all bruised and bandaged" (2201) inspires the dictation of 'The Foundation and Manifesto of Futurism." The tenets to be embraced include recklessness, rebellion, aggression and struggle, "speed" and transit, war as the "sole cleanser of the world" (2201), and the eradication of tradition and repositories of tradition. Marinetti, like Georges Sorel, was a supporter of anarchist and Fascist movements and codeveloped the Italian Fascist movement's first manifesto. People normally associate Fascism and anarchy as chaotic and negative movements. Do students perceive Marinetti's manifesto as provoking instability and evil?

   a. **Further Reading:** Rainey, Lawrence, Christine Poggi, and Laura Wittman, eds. *Futurism: An Anthology.* New Haven, CT: Yale University Press, 2009.

   b. **Suggested Search:** Search for "Manifestos" at the Italian futurism site, www.italianfuturism.org.

   c. **Suggested Search:** Search for "Filippo Tommaso Marinetti" at the Yale University Beinecke Library website, beinecke.library.yale.edu. The library houses 10,705 digitized slides taken from a microfilm of Martinetti's seven Libroni, or scrapbooks, compiled between 1905 and 1944, the year of his death. The Beinecke also houses a collection of his other papers, photographs, and postcards.

   d. **Suggested Search:** Search the Khan Academy database, at smarthistory.khanacademy.org, for "Italian Futurism." The website features various Futurist artworks and a video of the work 19th-century scientist and photographer Etienne-Jules Marey, whose innovative time-lapse photography is an example of this movement.

2. **Dadaism and surrealism were sibling movements that emphasized collaborative work and the avant-garde, anarchy, and antibourgeois**

sentiment and attacked the nihilistic and warmongering of the modern world. Dada was called an "anti-art," promulgated by Dadaists' inability to agree upon a shared ideology (or even a definition of the word "Dada"). Like fellow writers of manifestos, though, Tristan Tzara wrote about freedom and beauty in terms of the ugly and grotesque: "shrieking of contracted pains, intertwining of contraries, nonsequiturs: LIFE" (2204). André Breton as a surrealist was concerned with incongruity and fantasy as the basis of creativity; like other surrealists, he drew upon the Freudian theory of the unconscious and used psychological and parapsychological techniques such as "automatic writing" to achieve incongruous and fantastic compositions. In his manifesto, Breton commented on the impossibility of the term "real life," which exists only through the bourgeois lens of logic (2205). He argued that the Freudian focus on the dream state is as tenable as a focus on real experiences, because in his waking state "man is the plaything of his memory," whereas the resolution of reality and dreams forms "a kind of absolute reality, a surreality" (2207–08). Surrealism, finally, is defined as a belief in a superior reality that stems from the dream, or "psychic automatism in its pure state, by which one proposes to express . . . the actual functioning of thought" (2210). In what respects is surrealism an offshoot of Dadaism?

a. **Further Reading:** Hopkins, David. *Dada and Surrealism: A Very Short Introduction.* Oxford: Oxford University Press, 2004.

b. **Further Reading:** Gale, Matthew. Dada & Surrealism A & I (Arts and Ideas). London: Phaidon Press, 1997. This survey volume contains a full range of artistic production and ideas from Dadaism and Surrealism.

c. **Suggested Search:** Go to the International Dada Archive at www .lib.uiowa.edu/dada and search for Tristan Tzara's work in the "Digital Dada Library."

d. **Suggested Search:** Visit the Oxford Art Online archives at oxford-artonline.com to view artwork by different Dadaists and Surrealists. This database also contains essays and biographies of the major individuals involved in the two movements.

3. **"Creationism," a term coined by Vicente Huidobro in 1925, emphasizes the poet's expressive powers and view of the poem as a new and universally translatable work created for its own sake, not for any purposive or definitive meaning for the author or audience.** Defined as an aesthetic theory rather than a movement or a school, the creationists overlap with the Dadaists and their promotion of an "anti-art." Huidobro writes that the "first condition of the poet is to create, the second to create, and the third to create" (2213) and praises the mechanical ("in which each constituent part and everything together presents a

new fact") as a metaphor for poetry. Like the surrealists, Huidobro speaks of the poem as something real only "in the head of the poet," as something that "makes its own reality" and resembles nothing "in the external world" (2213). In order to achieve this method, a poet must humanize things, make the vague precise, make the abstract concrete and the concrete abstract, and create something "too poetic to be created" by changing its "customary meaning" (2215). How can something be "too poetic to be created," and how does following these four goals help the writer create poetry?

a. **Further Reading:** Huidobro, Vicente, and Jorge Garcia-Gomez. *The Poet Is a Little God: Creationist Verse.* Riverside, CA: Xenos Books, 1996.

b. **Suggested Search:** Go to the Getty Research Institute Library entry for "Vicente Huidobro papers, 1886–1968" at http://library.getty.edu /cgi-bin/Pwebrecon.cgi?BBID=361820. Professors should plan ahead and request materials several weeks in advance.

4. **The Black Panther Party approached protest in a more militant and dynamic manner than did Martin Luther King, who advocated nonviolent policies.** Founded in Oakland, California, in the 1960s by Huey Newton and Bobby Seale as a leftist organization that embraced Socialist and Communist doctrines, the party participated in the "black power" counterculture movement and created a Ten-Point Program to demand education and employment, to end crime, to end exploitation by the white man, to terminate conscription for black men, to receive fair housing, and to be given fair trial and treatment by the police (2220–21). The party created more than forty-five community "Survival Programs," including armed citizens' patrols and a free breakfast for children program to feed ten thousand inner-city youth before the school day. The party lost force after the 1970s, when details concerning some members' drug dealing and extortion methods were publicized. How does the Black Panther Party compare to other civil rights movements in terms of its demands and actions?

a. **Further Reading:** Ogbar, Jeffrey O. G. *Black Power: Radical Politics and African American Identity.* Baltimore, MD: Johns Hopkins University Press, 2004.

b. **Suggested Search:** Go to the official Black Panther Party website at www.blackpanther.org.

In-Class Activities

1. Designing a manifesto: Have students examine the style, structure, and content of the manifesto cluster, making note of the motivation to create and the expression of needs in these works. Students will then gather in groups (or individually) to declare a new movement,

culture, or ideology that they design and promote through a manifesto they design using the same elements as those found in the cluster readings.

2. Responding to a manifesto: Have students pretend they are journalists responding critically to one of these movements. Each student will write a news response to the declared movement, reacting to its declarations.

Paper Topics/Suggestions for Writing

1. Discuss the role of dream states and the unconscious in the formation of surrealist art.

2. Many of the writers included in the manifesto collection subscribed to Fascism, Socialism, or Communism. How do these political ideologies inform their aesthetic and artistic approaches?

3. Martin Luther King Jr. advocated nonviolent protest, which later disappointed Black Panther Party members. Discuss the Black Panther Party's response to other forms of civil rights protest, comparing its tenets to those expressed by other groups. Make sure to include a personal reaction expressing your support or disagreement with its strategies.

4. Discuss Filippo Tommaso Marinetti's obsession with "speed" in the context of both modern art and industrial culture.

5. What is "creationism" according to Vicente Huidobro, who wrote that one should "make a poem as nature makes a tree" (2216)?

Resources

Black Panther Party. www.blackpanther.org.
  This site contains background information on the Black Panther Party and its vision, the Ten-Point Program, FAQs, and images.
Dada and Surrealism: Masterworks of Western Art. Films for the Humanities, 1991, VHS.
  This is an overview of the movements, artists, and art works.
Getty Research Institute Library. Vicente Huidobro papers, 1886–1968.
  http://library.getty.edu/cgi-bin/Pwebrecon.cgi?BBID=361820.
  This site contains a collection of personal papers, correspondence with family, friends, and lovers, artwork, and manuscripts.
Italian Futurism. www.italianfuturism.org.
  This site contains manifestos, exhibitions, reviews, and interviews, as well as links to other futurism sites.

The University of Iowa Libraries. The International Dada Archive. http://
sdrc.lib.uiowa.edu/dada/digitaldadalib/index.html.

> This site contains an image library, biographies, links, a Dada/
> surrealism journal, and background information on both Dada
> and surrealism.

V. Postwar and Postcolonial
Literature, 1945–1968

LÉOPOLD SÉDAR SENGHOR

Topics for Lecture or Discussion

1. **Negritude ("blackness") developed to challenge colonial rule and to rehabilitate Africa and the black race.** Léopold Sédar Senghor believed (contrary to the French colonial education he received) that Africans "could teach each other and Europeans about their homeland rather than merely being beneficiaries of European civilization" (2232). In "Prayer to the Masks," Senghor introduces the mask as an ancestral protector and animal totem, both used to protect the people from the "wry, profane smiles" of the white colonists (line 6). The books, science, and humanity of the Western world during wartime in Paris become the police lines "at the borders of negritude" ("Letter to a Prisoner," lines 27–28) and evoke a period in which Senghor experienced racial discrimination during an "evening at the cinema" (lines 30–32). Ritual circumcision becomes proof of a man's civic and moral obligation in world cultures; Senghor's poem refers to the rite of passage from the African perspective, focusing on the dance, chant, and rhythm as part of the process to remove the excess foreskin, just as the colonists should be removed from Africa ("gets rid of its flesh, like trees in Europe under the winter sun . . . they obey only the measures of the ruler, the compass, the sextant," lines 31–33). What did the negritude movement offer black and African poets that would not have been accessible or permissible under Western or "white" poetic movements?
   a. **Further Reading:** Vaillant, Janet G. *Black, French and African: A Life of Leopold Sédar Senghor.* Cambridge, MA: Harvard University Press, 1990.
   b. **Suggested Search:** Go to the Leiden African Studies Center page for Léopold Sédar Senghor at www.ascleiden.nl/Library/Webdos siers/Senghor.aspx.

2. **Léopold Sédar Senghor's parents came from different ethnic backgrounds: his mother was a Peul, one of the pastoral and nomadic people from the northern savannah of western Africa, and his father was a Serer, the dominant ethnic group of his native region.** Though exposed to French Marxism, symbolism, and surrealism, Senghor's collaboration with Harlem Renaissance writers in the United States, including Aimé Césaire, led to the development of negritude. In "To New York" (written to be set to music as a type of spoken-word poem), Senghor describes his initial attraction to New York's "blue metallic eyes and icy smile" (line 3) and Harlem "teeming with sounds and ritual colors" (line 28); in the fashion of negritude, Senghor urges New York to allow black blood to "flow into" the city's veins in order to revive

it ("like an oil of life, let it give your bridges the curve of hips and supple vines," lines 54–55). "Songs for Signare" was written to be set to flute music to evoke the African pastoral tradition and though written based on the Western pastoral tradition, it evokes a Signare—a woman of mixed-race Portuguese and African descent. Does Senghor seem to applaud or disdain his mixed-ethnic background?

  a. **Further Reading:** Harney, Elizabeth. *In Senghor's Shadow: Art, Politics and the Avant-Garde in Senegal, 1960–1995.* Durham, NC: Duke University Press, 2004.

  b. **Suggested Search:** Search for the Lyon Academy site on Léopold Sédar Senghor at www.ascleiden.nl/Library/Webdossiers/Senghor .aspx#WEB LINKS.

3. **In Léopold Sédar Senghor's later poetry, readers will note his mastery of the interplay between the elegiac and lyrical that originated from his early works; Africa is poeticized, becoming an image of racial homeland and humanity's relationship to the universe.** Senghor's first volume of poetry, *Chants d'ombre* (*Shaded Songs*), forms a mental diary of his experience of cultural exile in Europe. Senghor uses long, loose verses that draw on biblical cadences and free verse with some use of rhyme. The wartime poems in *Hosties noires* (*Black Hosts*) carry religious overtones in the theme of nobility in suffering. Senghor's poetry post-1956 takes another turn, focusing on legendary African rule with no colonial references and comparing the African landscape to the artificial, concrete metropolises of the Western world. The poem "Night in Sine" makes reference to the Sine River along which Senghor's ethnic group settled: Africa's natural sounds, references to storytelling and African family life, the song element of nature, French African textiles ("milky pagne," line 14), and religious elders ("exiled like us, they do not want to die," line 20) create a sense of nostalgia for the poet, who wants to live through recollection of these cultural elements. "Letter to a Prisoner" opens with a direct address to the prisoner and wrestler named Ngom, a typical convention of oral poetry (line 1); though the poem is written to address the Africans who remained in the camps during wartime Paris, the references reflect African religion, culture, and poetic declamation practices ("lives off parchments," line 5; "whose voice is the color of flame," line 7). Wordplay and word creation appear in "Elegy of the Circumcised," in which the word *lamarque*, referring to civic and moral obligations, is formed from two foreign words that mean "landowner"— the Wolof word *lam* and the Greek word *archos* (line 46). How does the role of music work in these poems, and how does this relate to other poems of the period in which a musical setting is not utilized?

a. **Further Reading:** English, Parker. *What We Say, Who We Are: Leopold Senghor, Zora Neale Hurston and the Philosophy of Language.* Lanham, MD: Lexington Books, 2009.

b. **Suggested Search:** Go to the Senegal Guide entry on Léopold Sédar Senghor at http://isenegal.free.fr/senghor.htm.

In-Class Activities

1. Cultural awareness—Senegalese masks: In this activity, students will research the use of masks in the Senegalese culture, in which masks are used to represent the spirits of the ancestors. Students should examine the visual forms, gestures, colors, and materials used and compare them to Léopold Sédar Senghor's description of masks in "Prayer to the Masks" (2236). (Note: See the Senegal website link in the Resources section.)

2. Poetry in performance: Several of Léopold Sédar Senghor's poems in this collection are suggested parenthetically as being set to music (i.e., "To New York" [for jazz orchestra and trumpet solo] and "Songs for Signare" [for the flute]). In this activity, students will first discuss the musical elements of the poems and the ways in which music might be incorporated into the performance of the works. If the professor has access to jazz and African flute music, students might attempt improvised spoken-word performances of the works.

Paper Topics/Suggestions for Writing

1. Discuss the role of music in Léopold Sédar Senghor's poetry, including an examination of Western and African musical references and poem types (e.g., elegy, song, prayer).

2. Léopold Sédar Senghor writes at least two poems as letters ("Letter to a Prisoner" and "Letter to a Poet"). Explain his choice of titles, and discuss elements of letter or prose writing that might be present in these poems.

3. Define negritude and discuss its appearance in the poem cycle "To New York" and "Prayer to the Masks."

Resources

Académie de Lyon—Lettres. http://cddp49.crdp-nantes.fr/actions.asp?dep =ML&IDinfos=793.
  This site, maintained by Michel Balmont, contains links to Léopold Sédar Senghor, a bibliography of his works, bibliographies of works about him (books, articles, theses), and a list of books and articles on negritude and African literature and on Senegal.

Leiden African Studies Center. www.ascleiden.nl/Library/Webdossiers /Senghor.aspx#WEB LINKS.

> This archive site contains a biography, a bibliography, and links to websites on Léopold Sédar Senghor, as well as a list of abstracts on the writer.

Senegal Guide. http://isenegal.free.fr/senghor.htm.

> This site offers a presentation, biography, bibliography, and information on negritude and francophone studies related to Léopold Sédar Senghor, as well as information on Senegal culture, politics, and history, with images and links. The site is in French but is easy to navigate for non-French speakers.

JULIO CORTÁZAR
House Taken Over

"I had to shut the door to the passage. They've taken over the back part." "In that case," she said, picking up her needles again, "we'll have to live on this side."
—Cortázar, "House Taken Over"

Topics for Lecture or Discussion

1. **"House Taken Over" is an unironic allegory of the invasion of the working class into Buenos Aires under Juan Perón's Populism that pushed out the bourgeois class.** In a 1979 speech, Julio Cortázar spoke on purely aesthetic literature that avoids politics: "When a reader reads my fantastic stories, he knows that I am not trying to tear him away from history and anaesthetize him with a literature of evasion and of renunciation; if he follows me along my most unreal and most experimental paths, it is because he knows that I have never tried to deceive him, to distance him from his own historical responsibility" (John H. Turner, "Sexual Violence in Two Stories of Julio Cortázar: Reading as Psychotheraphy?," *Latin American Literary Review* 15.30 [1987]: 43–56). In "House Taken Over," Cortázar is asking his readers to pay attention to the political climate, in Perónism. Under Perón's Populist rule, the bourgeois has no societal value. The siblings—unmarried, childless, with no servants, and no jobs—are an allegorization of the bourgeoisie. The house, representative of Argentina, no longer requires stamp-collecting, book-reading intellectuals whose only industry is to clean and obsess over their own inheritance. Cortázar sympathized with the intellectuals, once saying of the working class that migrated to Buenos Aires, "I was exasperated by this type of invasion of the lower classes of the population of the capital and of what I call the monsters who were called at that time the 'little black heads'" (Jean Franco, "Comic Stripping: Cortázar in the Age of Mechanical Reproduction," *Julio Cortázar: New Readings*, ed. Carlos J. Alonso [New York: Cambridge University Press, 1998], 36–75). The year that the story was published was the year of Perón's election as president and Cortázar's emigration from Argentina.

   a. **Further Reading:** Levinson, Brett. "Populism, Aesthetics, and Politics for Cortázar and for Us: Houses Taken Over." *Latin American Literary Review* 32:64 (2004): 99–112.

   b. **Suggested Search:** Conduct a Google search for "Vimeo video" and "Argentina: The Rise and Fall of Perónism" to find a lecture by

Stephen Volk that explains the ideology of Perónism that Julio Cortázar initially rejected (http://vimeo.com/10670748).

2. **From his first publication, Julio Cortázar was considered a writer of magical realism.** "House Taken Over," or "Casa Tomada," was his first published story. Jorge Luis Borges published it in his magazine *Los Anales de Buenos Aires* in 1946. Before that, Cortázar had published poetry, mostly sonnets, and a couple of short stories under the pseudonym Julio Denis. In an interview, Cortázar said, "One of my first and most popular stories, 'House Taken Over,' is a nightmare I had. I got up immediately and wrote it. But in general, what comes out of the dreams are fragments of references. That is, my subconscious is in the process of working through a story—when I am dreaming, it's being written inside there" ("Julio Cortázar, The Art of Fiction No. 83," *The Paris Review*). It is the dreamlike beginning and nature of the text that gave him entry to the group of Latin American writers who began or predicted the genre of magical realism. Artist Massimo Bontempelli said that works in this genre must have "realist precision and magical atmosphere" (Luca Somigli, "Italy," *The Cambridge Companion to European Modernism*, ed. Pericles Lewis [New York: Cambridge University Press, 2011], 90). Later in his career, he was a part of the Latin American Boom, which was a literary movement of the 1960s and 1970s in which Latin American writers became extremely popular internationally. Along with Cortázar, the boom included other writers in this volume, such as Carlos Fuentes and Gabriel García Márquez.

   a. **Further Reading:** Cortázar, Julio. "The Present State of Fiction in Latin America." *Books Abroad* 50:3 (1976): 522–32.

   b. **Suggested Search:** Conduct a Google Images search for the terms "Norah Borges" and "Casa Tomada." The first result is the illustration by Jorge Luis Borges's sister that accompanied the first publication of "Casa Tomada" in Borges's journal.

3. **The siblings' passive reaction to the invasion of their house is a metaphor for passive reading.** In his study *Understanding Julio Cortázar*, Peter Standish addresses the author's idea of how we understand reality: "According to Cortázar, a gentleman's agreement has come into operation between man and reality: a man is left in the comfort of his routines and in exchange agrees not to keep prodding and questioning" (Peter Standish, "Break: Cortázar on Literature," *Understanding Julio Cortázar*, 83). This explanation suits perfectly "House Taken Over" and its befuddling Kafkaesque predicament. The oddness is not simply in that the house is invaded by unidentified forces; rather, it is the lack of resistance from Irene and the narrator that seems fantastic. Despite being denied the comfort of their routines, the siblings still refrain from questioning the nature of reality. One could read their apathy as an

extreme case of a willing suspension of disbelief. Readers are frustrated by their indifferent acceptance because they do not, like us, recognize the fantastic. The story, then, might be a metatextual meditation on the act of reading fantastic fiction. Julio Cortázar wrote other fiction and nonfiction essays about passive readers, or as he has deemed them, "female readers." By leaving blank spaces in his story, Cortázar is encouraging his reader to participate in the fantastic, not intellectually or critically but creatively.

   a. **Further Reading:** Standish, Peter. *Understanding Julio Cortázar.* Columbia, SC: University of South Carolina Press, 2001.

   b. **Suggested Search:** A Google search for "Julio Cortázar and the Twilight Zone" will take you to a page (http://cocopreme.hubpages .com/hub/Cortazar-and-The-Twilight-Zone) that includes an essay and video clips that compare Julio Cortázar's fiction with the 1950s television show.

4. **The potentially incestuous relationship between Irene and the narrator opens up "House Taken Over" to psychoanalytical study.** When the narrator says that cleaning the house made him and his sister think "at times, that that was what had kept us from marrying," he implies that they, the brother and sister, were kept from marrying one another. This ambiguous phrasing reinforces the odd, nearly incestuous relationship between Irene and the narrator. Lanin A. Gyurko reads "House Taken Over," or "Casa Tomada," psychoanalytically. The noises that the siblings hear are not real people but psychological manifestations of their own incest or, at least, incestuous thoughts. The house is a metaphor for their own minds. But they can no longer repress those thoughts, and, like Adam and Eve banished from the Garden of Eden, Irene and the narrator banish themselves from their own home, guilty of their desires. Some feminist critics take the idea further and see Irene as a replacement mother figure with whom the narrator can complete his oedipal desires now that he has been rejected by the house, the womb of his mother. In its original Spanish, "house," a feminine noun, is often referred to as "she" rather than "it," as in "It was she that kept us from marrying."

   a. **Further Reading:** Gyurko, Lanin A. "Destructive and Ironically Redemptive Fantasy in Cortázar." *Hispania* 56:4 (December 1973): 988–99.

   b. **Suggested Search:** Search for "Freud Oedipus" on youtube.com, which will provide a 2-minute overview of Freud's Oedipus complex (www.youtube.com/watch?v=X0mNd5U8QiY).

5. **Julio Cortázar's Western influences, including Edgar Allan Poe and John Keats, reveal the themes of frozen time and physical confinement in "House Taken Over."** Because Cortázar and his homeland are both recognized for their cosmopolitanism, it is no surprise that the author lists Western authors among his influences. Poe

and Keats seem particularly instrumental in Cortázar's development as a writer. In her study of their influence, Ana Castillo explains Cortázar's stories' connections to these Western writers' texts, including "House Taken Over." Poe's 1839 story "The Fall of the House of Usher" features Usher and his sister, a couple whose home confines them: "He [Usher] was enchained by certain superstitious impressions in regard to the dwelling which he tenanted, and whence, for many years, he had never ventured forth . . . an influence which some peculiarities in the mere form and substance of his family mansion, had, by dint of long sufferance, he said, obtained over his spirit" (Castillo, "Woman as Death," *Keats, Poe, and the Shaping of Cortázar's Mythopoesis*, 51). The siblings go mad from this confinement, and, like it is one of them, the house sinks in the waters that surround it. This same theme of confinement might be discernible in Cortázar's interest in Keats, especially in Keats's poem "Ode on a Grecian Urn." Cortázar's now-forgotten essay "On a Grecian Urn" argues that the poem describes an urn that depicts the scene of a woman's sacrifice. The woman, in a sense, is trapped within the urn and in time, forever in the process of being sacrificed.

a. **Further Reading:** Castillo, Ana. *Keats, Poe, and the Shaping of Cortázar's Mythopoesis*. Amsterdam, The Netherlands: John Benjamins BV Publishing Company, 1981.

b. **Suggested Search:** Search for "The Fall of the House of Usher Part 1" on youtube.com to find the 1979 made-for-TV version of the Edgar Allan Poe story, featuring Martin Landau. You will also find many videos of Keats's "Ode on a Grecian Urn."

In-Class Activities

1. Your students might feel confused or frustrated by the events of the story. Begin the discussion by asking some provoking questions, such as "Who invaded the house?" or "Why didn't Irene and the narrator confront the invaders?"

2. To introduce your lecture on Julio Cortázar's anti-Populism, ask your students to discuss the symbolic importance of the siblings' daily activities. What do cleaning, knitting, stamp collecting, and reading old tomes symbolize individually and together? How can you classify the brother and sister socially based on these activities?

3. Have the students draw the layout of the house, which the narrator describes on page 2245. Discuss the two phases of the takeover and which parts of the house were affected.

4. Play a recording of John Keats's "Ode on a Grecian Urn." Discuss the themes of frozen time and metatextuality in both the poem and in Julio Cortázar's story.

Paper Topics/Suggestions for Writing

1. Jorge Luis Borges was a mentor to and influence on Julio Cortázar. Read Borges's "The Garden of Forking Paths," included in this volume. What are the thematic and textual connections between Borges's story and "House Taken Over"?

2. Irene and the narrator quickly adapt and change their lifestyle to suit those taking over. Why didn't they resist the invasion?

3. Who was in the house? Is there a chance that their house was not being invaded?

4. Julio Cortázar argued that he does not want to distance his reader from "his own historical responsibility." What sorts of contexts are available to his readers in this story?

5. Explain Irene's obsessive knitting habit. Why is Irene always knitting but unwilling to sell or even use what she makes? And when they are escaping from the house, what is the symbolic significance of dropping the thread when she realizes the ball of yarn is still inside the house? How do both of their habits and pastimes classify them socially and culturally?

6. Tanizaki Jun'ichirō and Julio Cortázar both read and translated the works of Edgar Allan Poe, who was an influence on the Japanese and Argentinean writers. Explain the nature of this influence. Are the writers influenced by the same elements?

Resources

Bloom, Harold, ed. *Julio Cortázar.* Philadelphia: Chelsea House Publishers, 2005.
> This collection includes an introduction by Harold Bloom, eleven critical essays, and Julio Cortázar's bibliography and chronology.

Julio Cortázar: Argentina's Iconoclast. Films Media Group, 1999.
> This 1999 documentary explores Julio Cortázar's experimental literature through historical context, archival material, and interviews.

Standish, Peter. *Understanding Julio Cortázar.* Columbia: University of South Carolina Press, 2001.
> Peter Standish's eight-chapter study discusses Julio Cortázar's work, from his earliest life and works to his posthumous publications. This is an extremely readable and helpful study by a knowledgeable scholar.

Stavans, Ilan. *Julio Cortázar: A Study of the Short Fiction.* New York: Twayne Publishers, 1996.
> In this study, Ilan Stavans analyzes the short stories through Julio Cortázar's recurrent themes and symbols. It also includes three of Cortázar's nonfiction essays.

Tadeusz Borowski

This Way for the Gas, Ladies and Gentlemen

Topics for Lecture or Discussion

1. **The publication of this story was, at the time, itself a politically charged act.** By the time "This Way for the Gas, Ladies and Gentlemen," was published, the concentration camps were public knowledge and still fresh and shocking; at the same time, the Cold War was in full swing, and publishing anything in Soviet-controlled Poland was a politically charged act. The most disturbing aspect of this story was its depiction of prisoners' inhumanity to their fellow prisoners—rather than suffering saints, the victims of the Nazis became themselves part of the machinery of death. In Soviet Poland, the Communist Party wanted publications with clear moral messages; this story provided the opposite. Tadeusz Borowski was immediately invited to join and take advantage of the Communist Party and its opportunities. He did so and produced propagandistic journalism in favor of Communism, the Soviet state against the West, in the hope that a new Communist regime would help stand against the possibilities of further atrocities such as Auschwitz. But as time went on, he began to see his activist writing as compromising his own literary gifts; stories such as this one, in which all parties seem guilty, refuse to agitate for any particular political action or social order.

   a. **Further Reading:** Kott, Jan. "Introduction." In Tadeusz Borowski's *This Way for the Gas, Ladies and Gentlemen*. New York: Penguin, 1976.

   b. **Suggested Search:** Search the JSTOR database at jstor.org for an article version of Jan Kott's introduction, "Afterword," in *The American Poetry Review*.

2. **Tadeusz Borowski's life and experience span many of the political crises and humanitarian disasters of the early twentieth century.** Although his life, in part due to the subject matter of his most famous work, is generally known through the lens of the Holocaust, he also was caught up in both the Soviet Gulag as well as in Cold War politics. Born into a Polish community in the Ukraine, war shaped his life long before World War II—both his parents were sent to Soviet labor camps. This was a period of collectivization and famine. Eventually Borowski and his parents were able to resettle in Poland. In the aftermath of the war, he participated not just in Communist journalism but in espionage on behalf of the party; he also saw the utopian dream begin to turn sour, as the purges of suspected dissidents began to take down his

friends. He killed himself in 1951 at age twenty-eight. This story was initially published with works by other fellow camp survivors under the title *We Were in Auschwitz*—this is an idea of literature as witness to a specific historical moment, as part of a collective, broad story.

    a. **Further Reading:** Drewnowski, Tadeusz, ed. *Postal Indiscretions: The Correspondence of Tadeusz Borowski*. Translated by Alicia Nitecki. Evanston, IL: Northwestern University Press, 2007.

    b. **Suggested Search:** Search Google for Ian Baruma's *New York Review of Books* article, "The Hell of Victory," a review-essay that uses Tadeusz Borowski's life and writing to address the history of displaced persons following World War II.

3. **The story is not just testimony to atrocity; it is also confessional.** Tadeusz Borowski was perpetually on the periphery of historical atrocity: his parents were transported while he lived with an aunt; in the camps, as this story relates, because he was not Jewish he was able to gain some measure of privilege over those destined for death; and in Soviet Poland, he gained safety from prosecution by furthering the aims of the government. His work, including this story, does not merely reflect a parade of atrocity but shows the difficulty of avoiding complicity with it. As the critic Christopher Bigsby puts it, "His survival depended on the deaths of others" (*Remembering and Imagining the Holocaust*, 347). It is very difficult to separate Borowski the author from Borowski the narrator of the story: To what degree does this story ask us to pass judgment on its narrator and characters? Or, does it suggest that judgment becomes impossible in such circumstances? The Nuremberg Trials were taking place when this story first appeared: the story suggests that where complicity is everywhere, it is almost impossible to find standards with which to judge.

    a. **Further Reading:** Bigsby, C. W. E. *Remembering and Imagining the Holocaust: The Chain of Memory*. Cambridge: Cambridge University Press, 2006.

    b. **Suggested Search:** Search jstor.org for Theodore Ziolkowski's 1977 *Sewanee Review* article "The Literature of Atrocity," which reviews Tadeusz Borowski's work in the context of the developing field of Holocaust literature studies.

4. **The story's different styles of narration alternate between stressing the immediacy of events and striving for critical distance from them.** In the middle of the story, the narrator focuses on the SS officer, who is keeping track of the trucks in his notebook. "The transports swell into months, years. When the war is over, they will count up the marks in their notebooks—all four and a half million of them" (701). Suddenly the speaker seems to speak with knowledge of the future. For the most part, however, the story is in an intense present tense: when the transport doors open, the narrator perceives "People . . . inhumanly

crammed, buried under incredible heaps of luggage" (2255). That ellipsis is the author's, suggesting that the story is tracking the moment-by-moment process of the narrator's perceptions. The sense of constant shifting between the immediate moment and the historical distance highlights the difficulties of coming to terms with these events: the details of individual victims and their lives are contrasted with the scale of death. The story can only switch between these perspectives; it asks us to struggle over the impossibility of reconciling them.

a. **Further Reading:** Hatley, James. *Suffering Witness: The Quandary of Responsibility after the Irreparable.* Albany, NY: State University of New York Press, 2000.

b. **Suggested Search:** Search Google for Ernst van Alphen's article "Caught by images: on the role of visual imprints in Holocaust testimonies" in the *Journal of Visual Culture.*

5. **Tadeusz Borowski's work is about the effect of atrocity on the mind; it addresses the difficulty of representing events of overpowering horror.** Does this story suggest any particular way of viewing the world? It has been called absurdist, cynical, and despairing, a production of "almost impersonal horror" (Ascherson, "Graves Everywhere"). It also has seemed like merely the raw stuff of experience: "this 'story' seems hardly to have had time to be processed through the memory" (Bigsby, 346). Does the story seem like a coherent artistic expression of a perspective, or is it an untransmuted fact? Theodor Adorno famously declared, "Writing poetry after Auschwitz is barbaric." Adorno later retracted the quote, but the idea that the Holocaust was an event that somehow defies artistic representation has remained powerful (even as artistic representations of the Holocaust continue to proliferate). When Borowski's narrator describes men carrying a corpse, "kick[ing] out of their way some stray children who have been running all over the ramp, howling like dogs" (2260), the baldly physical language on one level seems inadequate to represent the suffering implied behind this scene; on another, it represents precisely the effect this world has had on the narrator's thinking, where corpses and howling children become merely physical inconveniences rather than individuals with lives of their own. How does Borowski's story foreground the difficulties of representing atrocity, as well as the power of such representations?

a. **Further Reading:** Adorno, Theodor W. *Prisms.* Cambridge, MA: MIT Press, 1983. (The opening essay contains the statement about Auschwitz.)

b. **Suggested Search:** Search Google for the *New York Review of Books* review of the 1976 re-publication of Tadeusz Borowski's work, an article entitled "Graves Everywhere" by Neal Ascherson.

In-Class Activities

1. Have students collectively make a list of all the people from the transports who are described. Discuss the role played by each. How does Tadeusz Borowski use these capsule portraits to create the arc of the story?

2. Photocopy the October 6, 1945, letter from *Postal Indiscretions*. Ask students to compare the tone of the letter to the story and discuss the differences between a personal and public audience.

3. Have students read the section of *Night* where Elie Wiesel describes his family's arrival at Auschwitz-Birkenau. Compare and contrast Tadeusz Borowski's portrayal of the same scene.

Paper Topics/Suggestions for Writing

1. Analyze the girl who "appears" in the story "above the teeming crown" (704). What makes her seem different from the other prisoners? Why does Tadeusz Borowski include her as a figure of dignity alongside his portraits of ugliness and degradation?

2. Analyze the use of different languages in this piece. The story was written in Polish; fragments of German and French appear as well. How does the author, as well as the character, use foreign language fragments?

3. "[T]he gallows humor of Borowski's grim tales represents a reaction to atrocity, both existential and literary, that is unique" (Ziolkowski, 140). Discuss Tadeusz Borowski's use of humor.

4. "Sir, what's going to happen to us?" (2255). Discuss the use of the future tense in the story.

5. "Below us, naked, sweat-drenched men crowd the narrow barracks aisles" (2251). Discuss the imagery of physical bodies in this story.

Resources

Borowski, Tadeusz. *This Way for the Gas, Ladies and Gentlemen*. Trans. Barbara Vedder. New York: Viking Penguin, 1967.
    This collection of Borowski's stories has been published and reprinted by Viking/Penguin over the years.
Miloscz, Czeslaw. *Captive Mind*. Trans. Jane Zielonko. New York: Knopf, 1953.
    This work includes the chapter "Beta the Disappointed Lover," which is a thinly disguised depiction of Tadeusz Borowski.

Siedlecki, Janisz Nel, Krystyn Olszewski, and Tadeusz Borowski. *We Were in Auschwitz*. Trans. Alicia Nitecki. New York: Welcome Rain Publishers, 2000.

> Written in 1945, this is a first-hand account of life for the inmates of a Nazi concentration camp by Tadeusz Borowski and two other survivors.

The United States Holocaust Memorial Museum. ushmm.org.

> This site includes a "Holocaust Encyclopedia," which has an entry for Auschwitz that includes photographs and videos.

ALAIN ROBBE-GRILLET

The Secret Room

Topics for Lecture or Discussion

1. **By dedicating *The Secret Room* to the painter Gustave Moreau, Alain Robbe-Grillet reinforces the pictorial qualities of his fiction.** Robbe-Grillet's *The Secret Room* proceeds by describing scenes from particular angles, as if the reader is actually viewing a painting or film. The opening sentence seizes control of the reader's vision by beginning "The first thing to be seen . . ." (2264), and as the particular scene shifts to different moments of time, it also shifts to different angles. These scenes are described in a way that one might describe a painting, as the narrator talks about the foreground and background, lighting, things that are obstructed from a particular point of view, etc. Similarly, the narrator's diction repeatedly identifies things by their shape and color, rather than by their proper name; hence the woman's breasts are described as hemispheres and globes, and the pooling blood is "a red stain" (2264). Robbe-Grillet may also have dedicated *The Secret Room* to Gustave Moreau because the latter's paintings, with their often unusual scenes that are not entirely clear, may have been an inspiration for the author.

    a. **Further Reading:** Hellerstein, Marjorie H. *The Art of Alain Robbe-Grillet*. Cranbury, NJ: Associated University Presses, 1998.

    b. **Suggested Search:** At http://www.musee-moreau.fr, you can find a variety of pictures of Moreau's paintings and sketches, as well as pictures of his home.

2. **In conjunction with the pictorial elements of Alain Robbe-Grillet's *The Secret Room*, the story for the most part moves backwards through time.** It begins with the man on the stairs leaving, then it describes him looking back at the woman's body as he approaches the stairs to leave, and then it describes him leaning over the woman as he stabs her with a knife. This regression through time corresponds conversely with the reader's dawning comprehension regarding aspects of the scene being described (although, importantly, the reader never fully learns the context or details of the killing). The final scene that the narrator describes is the last one chronologically, however, as the body is alone and has stiffened in death. In presenting the reader with only a limited amount of information that is given in a scrambled manner, Robbe-Grillet sought to present in prose the different ways that humans come to understand their experiences, including misconceptions, limited perceptions, and only partially grasped details.

a. **Further Reading:** Robbe-Grillet, Alain. "Time and Description in Fiction Today." In *For A New Novel*, 143–156. Evanston, IL: Northwestern University Press, 1989.

b. **Suggested Search:** Search for "Robbe-Grillet" at the Paris Review (http://www.theparisreview.org) for the transcript of an interesting interview with the author.

3. **Robbe-Grillet consciously sought to combine erotic and horrific or violent elements in his fiction, and this is an important factor in the unsettling nature of his work.** Robbe-Grillet spends a considerable amount of time in *The Secret Room* describing the woman's body, repeatedly emphasizing her nudity with several references to her genitals and detailed descriptions of her breasts. Yet these descriptions are always joined to violent action or the evidence of violence. For example, describing several streams of blood on the woman's body, Robbe-Grillet writes, "Three or four tiny veins have reached the hollow between the legs, meeting in a sinuous line, touching the point of the V formed by the outspread legs, and disappearing into the black tuft" (2267). Presenting the woman's body as a site of violence, the descriptions of the nude body become associated with violation and suffering rather than the erotic or the sensual.

a. **Further Reading:** Fragola, Anthony N., and Roch C. Smith. *The Erotic Dream Machine: Interviews with Alain Robbe-Grillet On His Films*. Carbondale, IL: Southern Illinois University Press, 1995.

b. **Suggested Search:** A YouTube search for "Robbe-Grillet" will result in several clips taken from his movies that demonstrate his unsettling approach to sexual things and violence (students may find these clips disturbing, and there is nudity and violence in several of them, so be advised).

4. **As a writer who espoused the ideas of the *nouveau roman* (or "new novel") movement, an important part of Robbe-Grillet's craft was his attention to detail, and particularly the way his narrative focuses upon objects rather than thoughts or feelings.** The tableau that is described in *The Secret Room* is striking both because it is mysterious—why is the woman being killed? Does she know her killer? Where are they?—but also because readers are given substantial details about particular objects that are part of this mysterious scene. For instance, we learn that there are oriental rugs with thick, dark-colored cushions (2265), and while we don't know why the woman is chained, we are given particular details about how she is chained (2266). The paucity of information regarding the thoughts or emotions of the people in *The Secret Room* stands in sharp contrast to the plenitude of information about the objects that fill the scene. This exemplifies the shift of focus from the subjects that are traditionally described in literature, and is a hallmark approach of the new novel movement.

a. **Further Reading:** Babcock, Arthur E. *The New Novel in France: Theory and Practice of the Nouveau Roman.* New York: Twayne Publishers, 1997.

b. **Suggested Search:** At the New York Times website (http://www .nytimes.com) a search for "He Was Nouveau When It Was New" results in an article about Robbe-Grillet's life and work (the article was occasioned by the author's death in 2008).

5. **Even the title of the story, *The Secret Room*, provides information that must then be questioned and reconsidered in light of the rest of the details that the reader is given.** As the room is gradually described and more things are revealed to the reader, it becomes apparent that this woman's body is not necessarily in a room at all. The narrator tells us that the stairway coming down into the room is very large, that the dimensions of the room itself are unclear because the distances fade in the dark, and that "considerable space must in reality extend all around, right and left, as it does toward the faraway browns and blues among the columns standing in line, in every direction, perhaps toward other sofas, thick carpets, piles of cushions and fabrics, other tortured bodies, other incense burners" (2265). Rather than a room, this could be a dungeon, a catacomb, a crypt, or any number of other expansive, dark places with colonnades. Similarly, readers might question what "secret" in the title indicates. From whom is this location secret? Why is it secret? Or is this a place that keeps secrets?

a. **Further Reading:** Robbe-Grillet, Alain. "New Novel, New Man." In *For A New Novel*, 133–142. Evanston, IL: Northwestern University Press, 1989.

b. **Suggested Search:** A YouTube search for "Alain Robbe-Grillet's lecture" results in an interesting lecture that he delivered in 1989 at San Francisco University.

In-Class Activities

1. As a creative exercise, ask each of your students to draw a map of the room, as it might be viewed from above. Compare the different maps to discuss where things are situated, and how big each student conceives the room to be.

2. Ask each of your students to find another of Robbe-Grillet's stories (either online or in the library), and to compare its narrative style with that of *The Secret Room.*

3. In class, watch one of Robbe-Grillet's movies (warning: they are often unsettling and may contain nudity or violence). Discuss the ways his film does or does not correspond with his fiction.

Paper Topics/Suggestions for Writing

1. Write a creative addition to *The Secret Room* in which you explain the context of the killing that takes place.

2. How should the narrator's description of the woman as a "young sacrificial victim" (2263) be interpreted? Is this a religious ceremony? Is she actually sacrificial? Find evidence in the text that does or does not support the idea that this was a religious killing.

3. Consider the different changes of angle and time in *The Secret Room*. Which is more important for conveying information to the reader? Is time treated differently than space in this story?

4. Write a journal entry in which you discuss when and why you realized that there was a dead body in the room. What are the clues in the early part of the text?

5. What is the relationship between the erotic and the violent in *The Secret Room*? Is Robbe-Grillet's story sensual? Or is it violent? How are nudity and vulnerability related to violence and domination? Is *The Secret Room* a critique of violence or eroticism?

Resources

Robbe-Grillet, Alain. "New Novel, New Man." In *For A New Novel*, 133–142. Evanston, IL: Northwestern University Press, 1989.
> This volume is a collection of Robbe-Grillet's essays that discuss his ideas about fiction. It is extremely helpful for understanding his unusual approach to literature.

Smith, Roch C. *Understanding Alain Robbe-Grillet*. Columbia, SC: University of South Carolina Press, 2000.
> Smith considers Robbe-Grillet's theoretical and creative work in this book, and while it may be difficult for most students, it is a good volume for instructors who are unfamiliar with these works.

Stoltzfus, Ben. *Alain Robbe-Grillet: The Body of the Text*. Cranbury, NJ: Fairleigh Dickinson University Press, 1985.
> Stoltzfus collects several of his essays in this volume, and he discusses both Robbe-Grillet's fiction and films.

Oppenheim, Lois, ed. *Three Decades of the French New Novel*. Chicago: University of Illinois Press, 1986.
> This collection of papers is the result of a colloquium that was held at New York University, and Robbe-Grillet was in attendance. Certain essays will be difficult for a typical undergraduate student.

ITALO CALVINO
From *Invisible Cities*

Topics for Lecture or Discussion

1. **While our selection from *Invisible Cities* does not make the interlocking numerical structure of the work apparent, it does show that there is a frame narrative—the interactions between Marco Polo and Kublai Khan that are in italics—and that because of its philosophical overtones, it invites comparison with other philosophical dialogues.** Students are often initially baffled by *Invisible Cities*, and it can be helpful to draw a comparison between it and other philosophical dialogues (for example, you might mention Plato's *Symposium* or Thomas More's *Utopia* in Volume 1 of this anthology), and to draw attention to the formal structure of the work. Marco Polo and Kublai Khan's conversation is about cities and empire, and Kublai Khan "*thought he was on the verge of discovering a coherent, harmonious system underlying the infinite deformities and discords*" (2270). This might be compared to Plato's philosophic dialogues, with their conception of ideal forms, and the frame narrative can be fruitfully contrasted with *The Thousand and One Nights* or Boccaccio's *Decameron*.
   a. **Further Reading:** Brera, Matteo. "At the Court of Kublai Kan: Storytelling as Semiotic Art in *Le citta invisibili* by Italo Calvino." *Symposium* 65:4 (2011): 271–289.
   b. **Suggested Search:** At www.ferigo.it/maze/ITALO-CALVINO.pdf, there is a helpful outline/discussion of *Invisible Cities*.

2. **Marco Polo's descriptions of the cities are essentially prose poems; that is, they are written as prose but they read, and should be read, as poetry.** For example, in the "Cities & Names" section, Marco Polo concludes with language that is highly metaphorical: "For those who pass it without entering, the city is one thing; it is another for those who are trapped by it and never leave. There is the city where you arrive for the first time; and there is another city which you leave never to return. Each deserves a different name; perhaps I have already spoken of Irene under other names; perhaps I have spoken only of Irene" (2271). This passage is not as rich in meaning or implication if it is only interpreted literally, or as a simple prose narrative. Instead, Calvino presents a poetic paradox to the reader: Polo states that the same city deserves different names depending upon a person's relationship with it (just arriving, forever leaving, etc.), but on the other hand, perhaps all cities are the same and perhaps Polo has only been describing Irene.

a. **Further Reading:** Bloom, Harold, ed. *Italo Calvino: Comprehensive Research and Study Guide.* Broomall, PA: Chelsea House Publishers, 2002.

b. **Suggested Search:** At www.prose-poems.com you can find a variety of prose poems that might be a good contrast to Calvino's description of the cities.

3. **In the "Continuous Cities" section, Calvino records a bleak, perhaps despairing, response to modernity's urban sprawl and the drab uniformity of a global economy dominated by huge businesses.** Calvino writes, "The suburbs they drove me through were no different from the others, with the same little greenish and yellowish houses. Following the same signs we swung around the same flower beds in the same squares. The downtown streets displayed goods, packages, signs that had not changed at all. This was the first time I had come to Trude, but I already knew the hotel where I happened to be lodged" (2272). Students should be encouraged to consider whether the tone of this passage is better interpreted as vehement condemnation or quiet discouragement. As a continuous city, Trude raises further questions: Why should Marco Polo continue to travel given the uniformity of everything from airport to stores to hotels?

a. **Further Reading:** Hume, Kathryn. *Calvino's Fictions: Cogito and Cosmos.* Oxford: Clarendon, 1992.

b. **Suggested Search:** A Google Images search for Italo Calvino results in several different pictures of the author.

4. ***Invisible Cities* investigates many of the different ways in which humans communicate with one another.** In our selection, after the description of the cities Marco Polo surprises Kublai Khan by speaking, and the narrator tells us, "*Until then the Great Khan had not realized that the foreigner knew how to express himself fluently in his language, but it was not this fluency that amazed him*" (2273). Khan is amazed by what Polo has communicated, not how he has communicated; also important is the fact that so much information has been exchanged between Polo and Khan without the use of language until this point. Instead of language, the chess game is a model for, and mirror of, reality that is also the medium of communication: "*Knowledge of the empire was hidden in the pattern drawn by the angular shifts of the knight, by the diagonal passages opened by the bishop's incursions, by the lumbering, cautious tread of the king and the humble pawn, by the inexorable ups and downs of every game*" (2270).

a. **Further Reading:** Francese, Joseph. *Narrating Postmodern Time and Space.* Albany, NY: State University of New York Press, 1997.

b. **Suggested Search:** At the Paris Review (http://www.theparisreview
.org) a search for Italo Calvino results in the transcription of an
interesting interview with the author.

In-Class Activities

1. Dividing the class into five groups, assign one city to each, and ask them to
create a poster that might function as an advertisement for the city, drawing upon the details in the text as the guide for how the city should look.

2. As a class, catalogue the words that are indicators of emotion and discuss whether these are particularly associated with a certain city or
character.

3. Ask the students to identify real cities that they think at least partially
match the descriptions that Calvino writes. Discuss the ways in which
Calvino has identified common truths about modern cities.

4. To impress the nature of the prose poems on the class, arrange to have
the section "Cities & the Sky 3" read aloud to the class prior to a discussion of Calvino's literary style. This exercise is most helpful if it is
read either by you or one of your students who reads texts aloud with
ease; if the passage is stumbled over while read, it can make the work
even more difficult to understand.

Paper Topics/Suggestions for Writing

1. Imitate the style of Calvino's prose poems and write descriptions of two
more fictional cities.

2. What is the relationship between chess and language in the story?
Between chess and empire? Between chess and the imagination?

3. Write an essay in which you consider the relationship between Marco
Polo and Kublai Khan. What are the most important features of their
relationship? What sorts of things do they exchange?

4. What is the relationship between the narrative parts (that are in italics), and the descriptions of the cities? How does the variation between
these shape or change the narrative and tone of *Invisible Cities*?

5. Write an analysis of the prose poems included in this selection from
Invisible Cities. Is there a primary metaphor or image that Calvino makes
use of? What do these poems show us about Marco Polo?

Resources

Bloom, Harold, ed. *Italo Calvino: Comprehensive Research and Study Guide*.
Broomall, PA: Chelsea House Publishers, 2002.

While less comprehensive than its title would make one hope, this is a helpful introductory volume for studying Calvino's works, and is recommended for students and instructors.

Calvino, Italo. *Italian Folktales*. Trans. George Martin. New York: Harcourt, 1980.

This is an excellent volume for demonstrating Calvino's considerable range and the reasons for his lasting popularity. Students are often quickly captivated by these folktales, and they will see both similarities and substantial differences with Calvino's narrative style in *Invisible Cities*.

Calvino, Italo. *Hermit in Paris: Autobiographical Writings*. Trans. Jonathan Cape. New York: Random House, 2003.

While this volume does not offer a comprehensive biographical account of Calvino, it is entertaining and provides readers with valuable information with respect to his imagination and works.

Hume, Kathryn. *Calvino's Fictions: Cogito and Cosmos*. Oxford: Clarendon, 1992.

Instructors who seek a more thorough understanding of Calvino's philosophical approach to literature should turn to this volume. It is too advanced for most undergraduate students.

PAUL CELAN

Topics for Lecture or Discussion

1. **The theme of suffering and loss in Paul Celan's poems relates to his experiences as a survivor of the Holocaust.** Raised in a Zionist, traditional Jewish household with his mother's love of German litera-ture, Celan was a polyglot who lost both of his parents during World War II to Soviet labor camps and spent part of his life in a labor camp in German-allied Romania. He worked earnestly as a translator into German of Kafka, Shakespeare, and other important writers, and he later moved to Paris, where he taught German literature. Celan's life was rife with self-loathing as a result of the irony in which he wrote poetry, taught and translated into the German language, which represented the language of his oppressors and the murderers of his people. The poem "Aspen Tree" suggests a resentment for and commemoration of his mother's untimely death in a Ukrainian camp, where she died young ("her hair never turned white," line 2), was never seen by her son again (she "did not come home," line 4), and where she was shot by a guard for her inability to work (her "heart was hurt by lead," line 8). The poem "Shibboleth" incorporates Spanish words and references into the Span-ish Civil War (1936–1939) to make universal (or perhaps represent) his own wartime suffering through a foreign lens. Are elements of Judaism or Jewish identity present in these poems, or does Celan seem preoc-cupied with something other than his heritage?

   a. **Further Reading:** Felstiner, John. *Paul Celan: Poet, Survivor, Jew.* New Haven, CT: Yale University Press, 2001.

   b. **Suggested Search:** A recording of Paul Celan reading "Todesfuge" and other select poems is available at www.yes2art.com/DACH/todes _dead.html.

2. **Paul Celan's poetry often incorporated religious and political allu-sions and early on reflected a Germanic lyricism; his late poetry was monosyllabic and disjointed and incorporated more German neologisms in an attempt to "reinvent" German, perhaps as a cop-ing mechanism for writing in the language of his oppressors.** In "Aspen Tree," students will notice the couplet singsongy nature of the poem and the poet's use of a first-line natural reference ("tree," "dande-lion," "rain cloud," "star," "oaken door") to parallel (or contrast) his mother's character and her life (family pillar, young and innocent, weeping, burned out, violently destroyed). Lyricism and elements of German romanticism are present in "Corona," in which the relationship between lovers is compared to flora and fauna ("like poppy and memory, we slumber like wine in seashells," lines 9–10). The poem title "Tenebrae"

refers to Jesus's Crucifixion; the repetition of the end word "Lord" in most of the lines recalls not only Jewish prayer (many, especially confessional and in supplication, that take a call-and-response form) but also the African American slave chants performed during heavy labor. The poem "Psalm" is not only a reference to the biblical Psalms ("songs") written in praise of or as pleas to God but also suggests a poem to be set to music. Celan's "Psalm" makes use of wordplay—sight/spite, God as "No One" and man as "No One's Rose"—and of botanical references not to a rose but, rather, to the buckthorn and rush from which Jesus's crown of thorns was fashioned; Celan refers to anatomical parts of the plants—the pistil, stamen, and corona (lines 14–20)—perhaps to reflect the impotence of emotion and man's attempt to find meaning in the face of events such as the Holocaust. In "World to be stuttered after," which is not a title but, rather, the first line of an unnamed poem, contrary motion is presented in the poet-as-guest whose name is "sweated down" a wall on which a "wound licks up high" (lines 4–5); though the poem is allusive, students might propose different interpretations of it, which include the wall as a sheet of paper on which the writer's identity is traced through poetry that (because it relives his Holocaust experiences) opens and expands the painful wound of memory. Is Celan a universal poet who attempted to find parallels of suffering in other cultures, or are his experiences as a Holocaust survivor untranslatable?

a. **Further Reading:** Derrida, Jacques. *Sovereignties in Question: The Poetics of Paul Celan.* 3d ed. New York: Fordham University Press, 2005.

b. **Suggested Search:** Go to the Barbez website at www.barbez.com /celan.html and listen to an excerpt of their *Force of Light* album, based on Paul Celan.

3. **"Deathfugue" is Paul Celan's first published and most famous poem, referring to the dance music that an SS commander forced prisoners to play during marches and executions at the Janowska camp in L'vov, Ukraine.** The elements of a fugue include the development of a theme that is repeated in different pitches throughout the composition; fugues usually include three sections—exposition, development, and recapitulation—and usually are applied to imitative works. The theme "death" is echoed as a motif throughout the three sections of the poem: in the exposition (lines 1–15), the redundancy of drinking "black milk" and the commander's demand for the Jews to "shovel a grave" as they "play up a dance" are introduced, and counterpoint is added in the comparison of the German woman Margareta to the Jewish woman Shulamith (lines 12–15). The development (lines 16–24) includes an

episode (repeated material) reiterating "black milk of daybreak" and the voices of Margareta and Shulamith (lines 18–23); during the development, the commander "shouts" several commands to dig the earth, sing and play, stick spades, play death more sweetly, and scrape the instrument strings darker. The recapitulation, or coda (closing section), represents a cadence: the language of the first two parts is intermixed and varied, and the final two lines are simply the women's golden and ashen hair (lines 34–35). How does the camp commander's mandate that Jews perform dance tunes while digging graves compare to the content and impetus to create African American hymns and tunes that were sung by slaves during their labor?

   a. **Further Reading:** Daive, Jean. *Under the Dome: Walks with Paul Celan.* Providence, RI: Burning Deck, 2009.

   b. **Suggested Search:** See the Holocaust Research Project entry on Janowska, particularly the image of the orchestra, at www.holocaust researchproject.net/othercamps/janowska.html.

In-Class Activities

1. Poetry performance: Have different students enact Paul Celan's "Deathfugue" by reading it aloud, perhaps assigning the roles of an SS commander and a Jewish orchestra member. How do the intonation, use of pauses, and style of performance affect the students' understanding and appreciation of the poem?

2. Interview the poet: Each student should generate a question that she or he would like to ask Paul Celan if he were still alive and had arranged to visit the class to present his work. Share the questions anonymously as a class and discuss not only how Celan would likely have responded but also what the questions say about modern reader responses.

Paper Topics/Suggestions for Writing

1. Offer an original interpretation of the untitled poem that begins "World to be stuttered after" (2276).

2. Paul Celan committed suicide by drowning after years of struggling with post-Holocaust paranoia. Interpret the theme of death and martyrdom in at least two poems from this collection.

3. Read the poem "Zurich, at the Stork," which Paul Celan wrote for Nelly Sachs, a German Jewish playwright with whom he was friends and held a theological conversation at the Stork Hotel. Knowing that both writers were Jewish, what do you believe was the theological debate between the two? Use evidence from the poems to support your argument.

Resources

Force of Light. Produced and performed by Barbez. Available at www.barbez
.com/things.html.

 The website provides information about the project's relationship to
Paul Celan and his work.

Holocaust Research Project. www.holocaustresearchproject.net/other
camps/janowska.html.

 Entries on this site include photographs, background, readings, information and hyperlinks on all things related to the Holocaust and
concentration camps.

Paul Celan's "Todesfuge." www.yes2art.com/DACH/todes_dead.html.

 This site features Paul Celan's reading of "Todesfuge" and other
selected poems.

DORIS LESSING

The Old Chief Mshlanga

> That was his name for our district: "The Old
> Chief's Country"; he did not use our name for
> it—a new phrase which held no implication of
> usurped ownership.
> —Lessing, "The Old Chief Mshlanga"

Topics for Lecture or Discussion

1. **The political background of the story—the colonization of Rhodesia and the exploitation of the natives—is explained through the European perspective of a young girl who is only just realizing that "her" country, England, is an unjust one.** There is a harsh economic history behind the social relationships and final conflict in the story. Until 1923, Southern Rhodesia was administered by a British Chartered Company that divided all land into "alienated" property—owned and occupied by white settlers or by Africans who paid a tax to both the settler and the company—and "unalienated" African property, which could be appropriated by whites with permission of the company. If natives resided on "reserves" on unalienated land, they also paid taxes. After the company yielded control to the British government's Land Apportionment Act of 1930, Africans were pushed off more and more newly appointed "European" land. In 1956, Doris Lessing wrote that only 46 percent of the land was still owned by Africans. In the story, the young girl reads about this process: "As I read more books about the time when this part of Africa was opened up, not much more than fifty years before, I found Old Chief Mshlanga had been a famous man" (2287). But by the end of the story, the chief and his people moved from one small tract of land to a reserve two hundred miles away.
   a. **Further Reading:** Raftopoulos, Brian, and Alois Mlambo, eds. *Becoming Zimbabwe: A History from the Pre-Colonial Period to 2008.* Johannesburg: Jacana Media, 2009.
   b. **Suggested Search:** Search Google for "Zimbabwe's struggle for liberation" to find a page by the Emory University English department at www.english.emory.edu/Bahri/Zimb.html that contains background on the colonization and insurrection in former Rhodesia.

2. **Doris Lessing portrays the culturally ingrained and necessary racism of colonizers.** The Jordan family's unquiet racism and disrespect toward the African people may make some students uncomfortable or even angry. The mother mocks the chief's son, who works in her

kitchen, and disrespects his family line. The final scene between the father and Chief Mshlanga shows Mr. Jordan's heartlessness. Though the young girl also exhibits racist behavior, her feelings are much more complex than her family's: "It was this instilled consciousness of danger, of something unpleasant, that made it so easy to laugh out loud, crudely, if a servant made a mistake in his English, or if he failed to understand an order—there is a certain kind of laughter that is fear, afraid of itself" (2285). And unlike her mother, who scoffs at the boy's lineage, the girl researches Chief Mshlanga and teaches herself about his and his people's past. She even wants to visit and speak to him again. Though readers never see the girl as a perfect model of social justice, she does progress away from hostile racism to the opposite extreme, naively assuming that all race issues can be easily solved. The final image of a new white settler arriving on the old chief's land shows the girl thinking about the complicated race relations and history in a more sophisticated way.

   a. **Further Reading:** Louw, Patricia. "The Vexed 'Colour Problem': Doris Lessing and the 'African Renaissance.'" *Inkanyiso: Journal of Humanities and Social Sciences* 1:1 (2009): 18–21.
   b. **Suggested Search:** Search on youtube.com for the 8:46 video "How the British Stole Zimbabwe," about Cecil Rhodes, after whom Rhodesia was named.

3. **Nkosikaas's maturation is marked by a shift from third-person to first-person narration.** A bildungsroman is a novel that follows the moral, spiritual, or psychological education or development of its main character, typically from youth to adulthood. Though "The Old Chief Mshlanga" is not a novel, it does track the development of its sometime narrator, whom we know only by Nkosikaas, or "Chieftainness." It might be considered a snapshot of the moment of her crucial education, like the moment James Baldwin explores in "Notes of a Native Son." The pivotal moment of growth is couched in a gradual process. When readers first meet Nkosikaas, she is totally removed from the African landscape and its people; she lives in a fairy-tale world of medieval castles, oak trees, snow, and Northern witches. The African landscape is unreal, and its people are an amorphous, faceless mass, "as remote as the trees and rocks" (2285). During this part of her story, when she walks through the countryside with the protection of two dogs and a gun, the girl is referred to as "a small girl," "a white child," and "she." The beginning of her shift into maturity is marked by a switch from third-person to first-person narration. The latter half, narrated by "I," the girl, shows her reaching out personally, even visiting Chief Mshlanga. By the end of the story, she completes her education, realizing that she is one of the destroyers of the African land.

a. **Further Reading:** Hotchkiss, Jane. "Coming of Age in Zambesia." In *Borders, Exiles, Diasporas*, edited by Elazar Barkan and Marie-Denise Shelton, 81–91. Stanford, CA: Stanford University Press, 1998.

b. **Suggested Search:** Search Google for "Bildungsroman Novels for Young Adults" to find a page on the Louisiana State University website (www.lsu.edu/faculty/jpullia/3223bildungsroman.htm) that contains a list of contemporary books and their plot summaries with which students may already be familiar.

4. **Doris Lessing gives her main character her own childhood naiveté about race relations.** Much of Lessing's fiction is autobiographical, including "The Old Chief Mshlanga." Like her main character, Lessing grew up in Rhodesia, the daughter of white settlers from England. She says of her childhood, "I was brought up on the farm in the bush, which was the best thing that happened; it was just a wonderful childhood. One of my most formative experiences was listening to my mother playing Beethoven and Chopin on the piano and listening to the drums playing in the compound: two kinds of music playing together. And as a child, I didn't see any reason why they shouldn't be played together; you had to be much older to understand that African drums and Chopin weren't really a part of the same phenomenon" (BBC World Serve site on Women Writers: Doris Lessing, www.bbc.co.uk/worldservice/arts /features/womenwriters/lessing_life.shtml). She gives her main character this same youthful misunderstanding: "But I thought: this is my heritage, too; I was bred here; it is my country as well as the black man's country; and there is plenty of room for all of us, without elbowing each other off the pavements and roads" (2287). When she finds that her visit does not please the chief, the landscape becomes menacing. It tells her, "You walk here as a destroyer" (2291). This is when the girl realizes that she cannot "dismiss the past with a smile in an easy gush of feeling" (2291).

a. **Further Reading:** Lessing, Doris. *Under My Skin: Volume One of My Autobiography.* New York: HarperCollins, 1994.

b. **Suggested Search:** Conduct a Google search for "Virginia Woolf and Doris Lessing" to find Lynda Scott's essay on how both writers approach autobiography (available on the University of Otago website at www.otago.ac.nz/DeepSouth/vol3no2/scott.html).

5. **A significant effect of the girl's evolution and maturation is her ability to recognize and appreciate the African landscape instead of escaping into English poetry and novels for Western nature scenes.** The main character slowly opens herself up to the people of Rhodesia, but Doris Lessing seems to give equal weight to her gradual appreciation of the landscape as well. The opening image is clearly the African landscape, but the voice we hear is that of a young girl singing

from "The Lady of Shalott," a poem by Alfred Lord Tennyson, England's poet laureate, and based on an Arthurian legend. She replaces the "green aisles of the mealie stalks" with "Northern forests" and the "msasa tree" for "the leaves of an ash or an oak" (2284). Only after meeting Chief Mshlanga does the young girl put down European books and start reading about her own country. After this point, she slowly begins to see and feel the African landscape for itself. She says, walking toward the chief's *kraall*, meaning village or homestead, "I had read of this feeling, how the bigness and silence of Africa, under the ancient sun, grows dense and takes shape in the mind, till even the birds seem to call menacingly, and a deadly spirit comes out of the trees and rocks" (2289). She has lost her envy of Europe for the sublimity of this overwhelming landscape. The story's ending opposes its beginning: the narrator recognizes the lushness and beauty of the "warm valley" (2292).

  a. **Further Reading:** Louw, Pat. "Landscape and the Anti-pastoral Critique in Doris Lessing's African Stories." *English Academy Review: South African Journal of English* 27:1 (2010): 36–44.

  b. **Suggested Search:** Conduct a Google Images search for "Zimbabwe landscape." You will find a great number of photographs that illustrate the setting of the story.

In-Class Activities

  1. List and describe the different landscapes. How and why do they differ? What do they each symbolize? What are the political implications of these symbols?

  2. As a creative writing project, ask students to write their own personal narrative about a time when their childhood concepts of other people changed. Encourage students to mimic Doris Lessing's style and techniques, including the setting descriptions and the change in narration from third person to first person. When did they decide to make the switch? What does the setting have to do with their story?

  3. Watch Caroline Link's 2001 film *Nowhere in Africa*, which is based on Doris Lessing's 1950 novel *The Grass Is Singing*. Like "The Old Chief Mshlanga," the film and the novel take place in Rhodesia and describe the relationship between African natives and European farmers. Discuss how situations and images from the movie parallel the story.

Paper Topics/Suggestions for Writing

  1. When the story begins, third-person narration is used but then it switches to first-person narration. When does this switch happen? Why? Does it ever switch back?

2. Describe the main character's relationship with the natives. Do these relationships change after she meets the chief?

3. What signs of colonial government are included in the story? Why are they not given more prominence?

4. Doris Lessing's "The Old Chief Mshlanga," Albert Camus's "The Guest," and Tadeusz Borowski's "This Way for the Gas, Ladies and Gentlemen" are about the genocidal assaults on cultural communities. Compare and contrast in these texts the view of the oppressor and the oppressed. How do the oppressors gain and maintain power? How are the victims also collaborators?

5. Discuss the significance of the final image of the "unsuspected vein of richness" (2292). How does this description oppose the opening image? What does this contrast represent about the girl's growth?

6. Why does the chief seem displeased about the girl's visit to his village? Why does she think he is displeased? At what point is she in her evolution when she visits?

7. What does the loss of the goats mean to Chief Mshlanga? What does it mean to Mr. Jordan? What is implied when Mr. Jordan says, "Go to the police, then" (2291)? Why is there no further discussion?

Resources

Hanford, Jan. *Doris Lessing: A Retrospective.* www.dorislessing.org.
> This website collects information about Doris Lessing and is divided into the categories "Her Books," "Her Life & Biography," "Periodicals, Essays, Articles, Collections," "Video," and "Interviews and Articles."

Lessing, Doris. "Nobel Lecture: On Not Winning the Nobel Prize." The Official Web Site of the Nobel Prize, 2007. www.nobelprize.org/nobel_prizes /literature/laureates/2007/lessing-lecture_en.html.
> Doris Lessing gave her Nobel acceptance speech of this same title to draw attention to its messages about the importance of literature, the need for reading material in developing countries such as Zimbabwe, and to condemn President Robert Mugabe's "reign of terror" on literature and education.

Lessing, Doris, and Thomas Frick. "Doris Lessing, The Art of Fiction No. 102." *Paris Review* 106 (Spring 1988).
> This article is a lengthy, engaging interview with Doris Lessing about her childhood, her politics, and her many writing projects.

World of Ideas: Doris Lessing. Films for the Humanities & Sciences, 2005.
> This documentary film about Doris Lessing includes segments such as "Life in Rhodesia," "Fiction versus Autobiography," and "Lessing's Ideas and Themes."

James Baldwin

Notes of a Native Son

> I saw nothing very clearly but I did see this:
> that my life, my real life, was in danger, and
> not from anything other people might do but
> from the hatred I carried in my own heart.
> —Baldwin, "Notes of a Native Son"

Topics for Lecture or Discussion

1. **James Baldwin's narrative technique of flashbacks, associations, and Proustian memories imitates the disorder of his own life.** In this autobiographical essay, the organization of events is only roughly chronological. Its order might be best described as Proustian: a series of flashbacks and associations. In addition to the ordering of the events, Baldwin's essay resembles Marcel Proust's *In Search of Lost Time* because it features a Proustian, or an involuntary, memory. Like Marcel's bite into the madeleine that sparked the memory of his childhood, Baldwin hears a song and is sent back to his own youth: "Then someone began singing one of my father's favorite songs and, abruptly, I was with him, sitting on his knee, in the hot, enormous crowded church. . . . With this image, a host of others came" (2305). Among the din in his mind—"Snatches of popular songs, indecent jokes, bits of books I had read, movie sequences"—and the noise of a rioting city—"muggings, stabbings, shootings, assaults, gang wars, and accusations of police brutality"—Baldwin is able to find a significant stimulus (2305, 2301, respectively). In light of these narrative techniques the "Notes" part of the title becomes ironic. Though it implies that the essay will be a distant record of an anonymous person, Baldwin's story is a highly personal account of his experience as a black man.
   a. **Further Reading:** Porter, Horace. "The Significance of 'Notes of a Native Son.'" *James Baldwin*, edited by Harold Bloom, 69–80. New York: Chelsea House, 2007.
   b. **Suggested Search:** Search youtube.com for the video "James Baldwin: The Price of the Ticket," which intersperses video recordings of Harlem with photographs of James Baldwin's life and interviews with him.

2. **James Baldwin's father represents a cultural predecessor as an African American, not an African heritage.** When Baldwin writes of "inheritance" and "birth right," he is not interested in his African heritage. He is not a "native son" of Africa; he is, instead, a native African

American, or "Negro." In "Stranger in the Village," Baldwin writes, "The time has come to realize that the interracial drama acted out on the American continent has not only created a new black man, it has created a new white man, too" (Baldwin, "Stranger in the Village," *Notes of a Native Son*, 175). His later distrust of negritude writers, such as Léopold Sédar Senghor or Aimé Césaire, is also traceable in "Notes of a Native Son." Of his father, Baldwin writes, "But he looked to me, as I grew older, like pictures I had seen of African tribal chieftains: he really should have been naked, with war-paint on and barbaric mementos, standing among spears" (2295). By this Baldwin does not mean that he is the progeny of a native African but the progeny of someone who is as distant and foreign to him as an African. What he does inherit, though, is his father's bitterness and anger, and what every American inherits: "the conundrum of color" (Baldwin, "Preface to the 1984 Edition," *Notes of a Native Son*, xxi).

a. **Further Reading:** Baldwin, James. "Introduction: The Price of the Ticket." In *The Price of a Ticket: Collected Nonfiction, 1948–1985*, ix–xx. New York: St. Martin's Press, 1985.

b. **Suggested Search:** Search for the MSNBC article by Jesse Washington titled "Some blacks insist: 'I'm not African-American' " (www.msnbc.msn.com/id/46264191).

3. **James Baldwin believed that his writing was both artistic and honest about race, unlike other African American "protest novels" in which the authors are complicit in creating and maintaining racist attitudes.** Although the title of his essay echoes Richard Wright's 1940 novel *Native Son*, "Notes of a Native Son" is not an homage to Wright's novel. Rather, it could be considered a revision. In "Everybody's Protest Novel," another essay in the collection *Notes of a Native Son*, Baldwin says that Wright's novel and Harriet Beecher Stowe's *Uncle Tom's Cabin* are "both badly written and wildly improbable" (13) and do not challenge racism because they sentimentalize and dehumanize African-Americans. In fact, they comfort their readers: "The protest novel, so far from being disturbing, is an accepted and comforting aspect of the American scene, ramifying that framework we believe to be so necessary" (19). Baldwin's essay, though, reconciles artistic and social responsibility by depicting an actual black experience during the riots of 1943. The riots began, as Baldwin recounts, with the shooting of an African American soldier by a white policeman. By couching the Harlem riots within the main story of his father's death, and by doing so without sentimentality or rage, Baldwin gives complexity to his character and weaves his particular experience into social history.

a. **Further Reading:** Baldwin, James. "Everybody's Protest Novel." In *Notes of a Native Son*. Boston: Beacon Press, 1984.

b. **Suggested Search:** Conduct a Google search for the video "Remembering James Baldwin" (www.thomhartmann.com/users/shallhenry/blog/2010/09/remembering-james-baldwin-rare-video).

4. **Though his story mostly takes place in all-black Harlem, James Baldwin's essay discusses the role of blacks throughout America.** The larger frame of Baldwin's story is personal, but nested within the story of a father and son is a portrait of black society in America, not only Harlem, in the 1940s. He mentions the "Negro boys in uniform" and their families, who "felt, mainly, a peculiar kind of relief when they knew that their boys were being shipped out of the south, to do battle overseas" (2302). It wasn't until 1941 that Franklin D. Roosevelt issued Executive Order 8802, which allowed full participation in the defense of the United States without racial discrimination. However, this mandate was controversial and, according to *The Oxford Companion to World War II*, some units did not integrate "on the grounds that it would undermine the morale of white soldiers" ("African Americans at war," *Oxford Companion to World War II*, eds. I. C. B. Dear and M. R. D. Foot [New York: Oxford University Press, 2001], 4). At training camps in the South, where segregation was legally enforced (unlike Northern de facto segregation) through the Jim Crow laws, the soldiers were treated with harsh injustices and violence by the armed forces and civilians. Baldwin recounts his own experience with segregation in a New Jersey restaurant when he is told, "We don't serve Negroes here" (741).

a. **Further Reading:** de Jongh, James. *Vicious Modernism: Black Harlem and the Literary Imagination.* Cambridge: Cambridge University Press, 2009.

b. **Suggested Search:** Conduct a Google search for the pdf document "Letters from African-American Soldiers during World War II."

5. **James Baldwin's essay may be highly personal and about a very specific time and place, but one of its themes—the search for identity as one approaches adulthood—is ubiquitous.** One major concern of the essay is the individual's quest for identity in the transitional period between childhood and adulthood. Symbolically important to this point is the temporal setting of the story: the intersection of a birth and a death concurrent with Baldwin's own birthday. For Baldwin, part of that odyssey toward identity had to do with his relationship with religion. He did not openly consider himself a religious writer, but scholars have noted that "much of the symbolism, language, archetypal rhythm, and thematic call for justice in his essays are . . . steeped in Christian ethics" (Sondra A. O'Neale, "Fathers, Gods, and Religion," *Critical Essays on James Baldwin*, 127). On the surface, he is indisputably hostile toward Christianity: "Perhaps many of those legends, including

Christianity, to which the world clings, began their conquest of the world with just some such concerted surrender to distortion" (2307). In the essay, though, Baldwin the character is in the middle state: he has violently broken with the religion that he accepted and even preached as a child, yet he has not discovered how that Christianity will affect him as a writer and a thinker. At age nineteen, Baldwin the writer has not yet emerged. For this, Horace Porter has compared Baldwin's process to the prodigal son of Jesus's parable (Porter, *Stealing the Fire: The Art and Protest of James Baldwin* [Middleton, CT: Wesleyan University Press, 1989], 23–24).

   a. **Further Reading:** O'Neale, Sondra A. "Fathers, Gods, and Religion: Perceptions of Christianity and Ethnic Faith in James Baldwin." In *Critical Essays on James Baldwin*, edited by Fred L. Standley and Nancy V. Burt. Boston: G. K. Hall, 1988.
   b. **Suggested Search:** Conduct a Google search for James Tackach's "The Biblical Foundation of James Baldwin's 'Sonny's Blues.'"

In-Class Activities

1. Have students work together to create an outline of the story and then share the order of events that James Baldwin creates. Discuss why Baldwin's life events are reported outside of typical chronology.

2. James Baldwin concludes his essay by arguing that to overcome prejudice, "one would have to hold in the mind forever two ideas which seemed to be in opposition" (2308). What are those two opposed ideas? Ask students to discuss Baldwin's suggestion. What does it look like in practice?

3. James Baldwin's "Notes of a Native Son" is an insightful political essay about racial discrimination, but it is effective because it is told as a son's highly personal meditation on his relationship with his father. Have your students imitate Baldwin's approach of uniting the personal and the political through sketching their own essays that tackle a larger issue, such as racism or sexism, through a personal framework.

4. James Baldwin was a wonderful orator and interviewee. Numerous recordings and videos are available online, particularly on youtube.com. Play one of these videos or recordings and then ask students to discuss how Baldwin, as an orator and a writer, marries social activism and art.

Paper Topics/Suggestions for Writing

1. Scholar Horace Potter likens James Baldwin's character of his younger self to Marcel Proust's Marcel. Read Proust's "Overture" to *Swann's Way*, included in this volume. Do you believe that the characters are

similar authorial personas? Are there other similarities between the texts, such as theme or narrative technique?

2. Research the race riots of 1943 in Detroit and New York. How does this contextualization affect your reading of James Baldwin's story?

3. In his essay "Everybody's Protest Novel," James Baldwin takes to task authors Harriet Beecher Stowe and Richard Wright for their artistically and politically nonengaging novels. Read this essay and then revisit "Notes of a Native Son" through its opinions. Do you think that this essay is artistic and political? Does it meet Baldwin's own requirements?

4. What role does the teacher play in James Baldwin's life? What role does she play in the story of his life?

5. Explain the role of illness, both physical and mental, in the essay. How does James Baldwin use gangrene and amputation to explain anger? What is the "chronic disease" that Baldwin contracts on page 2299? Is it a literal disease, or is he speaking metaphorically? Are the implications of that disease physical only?

6. When James Baldwin tells the story of the black soldier being shot by a white policeman, he says that people preferred an untruthful version of the story: "They preferred the invention because this invention expressed and corroborated their hates and fears so perfectly. It is just as well to remember that people are always doing this" (2307). Is Baldwin casting doubt on his own story in this anecdote and commentary, or is he mentioning it so that we trust that he is not guilty of invention?

7. Why is James Baldwin's essay titled "Notes of a Native Son"? What does the word "Notes" imply? What does it mean that Baldwin is a "native son"? "Native" to whom or where?

Resources

Baldwin's Nigger. Dir. Horace Ové. Infilms, 1969.
> Horace Ové, in his first documentary, simply films a conversation between James Baldwin and Dick Gregory in London on the black experience in America in the 1960s, as well as how it might relate to the black Caribbean experience in Britain.

Balfour, Katherine Lawrence. *The Evidence of Things Not Said: James Baldwin and the Promise of American Democracy.* Ithaca, NY: Cornell University Press, 2001.
> In this study, Katherine Balfour recasts James Baldwin's creative works, including *Notes of a Native Son*, as political theory.

Dimitriadis, Greg, and Cameron McCarthy. "A Talk to Teachers: James Baldwin as Postcolonial Artist and Public Intellectual." In *Promises to Keep:*

Cultural Studies, Democratic Education, and Public Life, edited by Greg Dimitriadis and Dennis Carlson, 115–24. New York: RoutledgeFalmer, 2003.

This pedagogical chapter discusses James Baldwin as an essential postcolonial figure who is not restricted by categorization in life or in writing. The authors argue that Baldwin "serves as a shining light in an educative field that typically stresses genre confinement in writing, elides personal narrative, addresses narrowly defined circumscribed audiences, and atomizes the role of an intellectual" (116).

Go Tell It on the Mountain. Dir. Stan Lathan. ABC, 1985.

The American Playhouse television series created a made-for-television movie version of James Baldwin's *Go Tell It on the Mountain*, a semi-autobiographical novel about growing up in Harlem.

ALBERT CAMUS

The Guest

> This is the way it was: bare rock covered three quarters of the region. Towns sprang up, flourished, then disappeared; men came by, loved one another or fought bitterly, then died. No one in this desert, neither he nor his guest, mattered. And yet, outside this desert neither of them, Daru knew, could have really lived.
>
> —Camus, "The Guest"

Topics for Lecture or Discussion

1. **In "The Guest," Albert Camus both presents his absurdist philosophy and rejects the existentialist view.** Absurdism is the philosophical belief that life has no inherent meaning and, therefore, social rules or moral codes that purport to abide by that meaning are moot. And even if there were an inherent meaning in life, it is not humanly possible to discover that meaning. All efforts to reconcile the two will inevitably fail. Camus, a self-proclaimed absurdist, did not believe in existential thought, which proposes that there is absolutely no inherent meaning, but that one must build meaning through actions and decisions. For Camus and for Daru, there are no good or bad decisions. But the world will not accommodate inaction or the decision not to decide which stand to take. This is Camus's philosophical rebuttal to existentialism's premise of making meaning through action. From the moment of his assignment, Daru is apathetic and unwilling to participate. When it seems he must, he engages in the most noncommittal way possible by providing the prisoner with a means of escape, like the door that remained unlocked overnight. Despite Daru's uninvolved involvement, the "brothers" read Daru's nonactions as decisive actions and, therefore, threaten him for them. This ending proves the impossibility of inaction in a world that demands meaning.
   a. **Further Reading:** Sefler, George F. "The Existential vs. the Absurd: The Aesthetics of Nietzsche and Camus." *Journal of Aesthetics and Art Criticism* 32:3 (1974): 415–21.
   b. **Suggested Search:** Search for "Albert Camus" in the *Stanford Encyclopedia of Philosophy* (http://plato.stanford.edu). One of the many helpful sections on the "Albert Camus" page includes "Criticism on Existentialists."

2. **Like Daru, Albert Camus preferred to remain neutral on the Algerian question.** "The Guest" is set on the eve of a violent rebellion by Algerians, headed by the Front de Liberation (FLN), against their French colonizers. The Algerian Revolution began in 1954 after over 120 years of French rule. Camus died in 1960, two years before Algeria achieved independence, but, like Daru, Camus did not take a side during the revolution. He was born to European parents in Algeria and lived and worked there exclusively until he was twenty-seven. Though he was interested in and concerned about the Algerian question, he refused to support either a violent revolution or the restriction of individual freedom. During the conflict, he concentrated only on sparing innocent civilians. In a 1956 lecture capped "Appeal for a Civilian Truce in Algeria," Camus argued, "What do we want? Simply to get the Arab movement and the French authorities, without having to make contact or to commit themselves to anything else, to declare simultaneously that for the duration of the fighting the civilian population will on every occasion be respected and protected" (Camus, "Appeal for a Civilian Truce in Algeria," *Resistance, Rebellion, and Death*, trans. Justin O'Brien [New York: Modern Library, 1964], 100). Because he was the most well-known Algerian in both France and Algeria, both sides depended heavily on his support. "The Guest" might be considered his attempt to express the personal difficulties he felt in judging the Algerian situation.

   a. **Further Reading:** Carroll, David. *Albert Camus the Algerian: Colonialism, Terrorism, Justice.* New York: Columbia University Press, 2008.

   b. **Suggested Search:** Search youtube.com for the video "Camus, The Nobel Prize & Algerian War."

3. **As a teacher for the French government in Algeria, some critics believe that Daru is the "Ideological State Apparatus" that leads the prisoner to turn himself in.** One of the first pieces of information we are given about Daru is that he is a schoolmaster. Shortly after, readers are given a description of his classroom: "On the blackboard the four rivers of France, drawn with four different colored chalks, had been flowing toward their estuaries for the past three days" (2312). The narrator reminds us again at the end of the story that it is "among the winding French rivers" that the brothers have written "the clumsily chalked-up words" (2320). We are being asked to notice that Daru teaches lessons in French geography (and probably history, literature, etc.), not Algerian. In his study of Daru as a teacher, Daniel K. Muhlestein calls Daru an "Ideological State Apparatus" or "ISA," a term borrowed from theorist (and fellow Algerian) Louis Althusser that describes the consciousness of individuals as products of society's own ideologies. In other words, a society creates its own subjects through an ISA

such as family, church, or school. The prisoner turns himself in, then, because Daru, an ISA of France and a professional teacher, helps create a subject who acts according to the state's desires. Muhlestein says that "Daru's tragedy, then, is that while he is a good man, he is an even better teacher" (232).

   a. **Further Reading:** Muhlestein, Daniel K. "A Teacher and His Student: Subversion and Containment in Camus's 'The Guest.'" *Studies in Short Fiction* 99:36 (Summer 1999): 223–35.

   b. **Suggested Search:** Search youtube.com for Ron Strickland's lecture "Cultural Theory: Althusser's Concept of Ideology."

4. **Both the prisoner and Daru are each judged according to cultural standards to which they do not adhere.** Most critics tend to classify the prisoner as primitive, passive, and even "a little stupid" (Griem, "Albert Camus's 'The Guest'," *Studies in Short Fiction*, 95). He doesn't even know why he killed, argues Diana Festa-McCormick. But Eberhard Griem's article "Albert Camus's 'The Guest': A New Look at the Prisoner" asks readers to reconsider the prisoner as a man who acted intentionally and honorably according to Islamic law. When Daru asks if he is sorry for murdering his cousin, the prisoner "stared at him openmouthed. Obviously he did not understand" (2317). He did not understand because, according to his culture, he responded in accordance to custom: should a man run away instead of taking responsibility, it is another man's responsibility to kill the man who brought shame to the family by stealing. The prisoner's decision to take the path to his trial, then, means that he, like the threatened Daru, is being charged for a crime he feels he did not commit.

   a. **Further Reading:** Griem, Eberhard. "Albert Camus's 'The Guest': A New Look at the Prisoner." *Studies in Short Fiction* 30 (1993): 95–98.

   b. **Suggested Search:** Search your library's academic database for Peter Roberts's "Teaching, Learning and Ethical Dilemmas: Lessons from Albert Camus" for an article that relates Daru's predicament to the dilemmas that teachers face.

In-Class Activities

1. Ask students to apply archetypal roles to the characters of the story. Who is the villain? The hero? Why did they apply those particular roles to the characters of their choice? Does it have to do with the characters' sense of morality or with the students' ideas of morality?

2. As an introduction to the characters, especially Daru's apathetic and unwilling nature, begin class with a performance or dramatic reading of the dialogue between Daru and Balducci on pages 2314–2316. How did the actors capture the characters? Ask students to explain how they

decided to portray their characters. What are the differences between Daru and Balducci?

3. Have students write a personal reflection on the "moral" of the story. Is there a moral? If there is, what is it? If there does not seem to be one, then what is Camus's message? What is he trying to tell readers through Daru's experience?

4. Students may be new to philosophical schools. To introduce and familiarize students with absurdism and existentialism, show a film that embodies the philosophies, such as 2009's *A Serious Man* or 1993's *Groundhog Day.*

5. Play the music video for the song "Killing an Arab" by the Cure, which is based on Albert Camus's novel *The Stranger.* Discuss the philosophies that the images support.

Paper Topics/Suggestions for Writing

1. Why does Albert Camus set the story on a remote outpost in Algeria, just after a freak snowstorm has isolated it even more profoundly than usual? How does he use descriptions of the landscape to reinforce Daru's isolation? Do the descriptions of the landscape suggest its beauty? Why or why not?

2. Why does Daru give the Arab the opportunity to escape? Why does he choose not to escape? Why does he choose not to take the road to the Arab lands at the end of the story?

3. Why is this piece called "The Guest"? In what ways is the Arab treated as a guest by Daru? In what ways is Daru a guest in Algeria? Note that in French the title "L'Hôte" means both "the guest" and "the host." How would you translate the title? Why?

4. From this story, can you discern Albert Camus's personal position on the Algerian question?

5. Relate "The Guest" to Doris Lessing's short story "The Old Chief Mshlanga," also included in this volume. Pay attention to themes and motifs about the injustice of colonialism. How does the physical setting of each story embody those themes?

6. Read Albert Camus's 1942 essay "The Myth of Sisyphus," in which he defines and explains the "absurd hero." What is an absurd hero? Why is Sisyphus his prime example? Is Daru an absurd hero? Why or why not?

7. Essayist Gaëtan Picon wrote that the short story collection *Exile and the Kingdom* "is not based upon a contradiction, and herein lies its

success. The exile and the kingdom are not two continents separated by an ocean: they are two aspects of the same breath and heartbeat. The kingdom is in the exile, the exile is a path toward the kingdom—in fact, exile could actually be the kingdom" (Gaëtan, "Exile and the Kingdom," *Camus: A Collection of Critical Essays*, ed. Germaine Brée [Englewood Cliffs, NJ: Prentice-Hall, 1962], 155). Respond to this statement. How do you understand "exile" and "kingdom" in "The Guest"?

Resources

Hughes, Edward Joseph. *The Cambridge Companion to Camus*. New York: Cambridge University Press, 2007.

This collection of fourteen essays explores Albert Camus's works in three sections: "Biography and Influences," "Themes, Preoccupations, and Genres," and "Texts and Contexts."

Kamber, Richard. *On Camus*. Belmont, CA: Wadsworth/Thomson, 2001.

Richard Kamber's study for students, part of the Wadsworth Notes Series, clearly and succinctly explains Albert Camus's philosophy and works.

Perrine, Laurence. "Camus' 'The Guest': A Subtle and Difficult Story." *Studies in Short Fiction* 1:1 (Fall 1963): 52.

Laurence Perrine writes from the perspective of a teacher whose students struggled with "The Guest." He offers a helpful summary of the story and then addresses the main mistakes or oversimplifications that students tend to make when they discuss the story.

Stacy, Gerald. "Teaching Camus's 'The Guest.'" *Eureka Studies in Teaching Short Fiction* 3:2 (Spring 2003): 87–91.

This short, helpful article leads students through a close reading with guiding questions about Albert Camus's intended response from his audience: commiseration with Daru.

SAMUEL BECKETT

Endgame

Topics for Lecture or Discussion

1. **Theater of the absurd arose in Europe during the 1960s as an existentialist response to the meaninglessness and purposelessness of human existence** (students should not confuse this form with Existentialism, though there is an overlap). The "absurd" stems from Albert Camus's "The Myth of Sisyphus," in which Camus presents the absurd as man's reaction to the world. Features of absurdist plays include grotesque devices, vaudeville, repetitive and meaningless gestures, and nonsensical language and parody. Important playwrights of the genre include Samuel Beckett, Eugene Ionesco, Jean Genet, Tom Stoppard, and Edward Albee. Absurdist characters abandon reason and often act as automatons in response to the crisis and chaos of the world; therefore, "imprisonment" is often a common element in these works ("It's the same time as always," 2326), and Hamm's parents are imprisoned in ash bins. Language in Beckett's work is playfully twisted to highlight misunderstandings and dark humor ("It's time for your painkiller. . . . There's no more painkiller. You'll never get any more pain killer," 2349), or clichés are employed to complement the monotony of characters' daily lives; plot, too, is monotonous and deemphasized, as there is no purpose or lesson to be derived ("When I fall I'll weep for happiness," 2352). Wordplay presents in the characters' names: Nagg (nagging, nail), Hamm (Hamlet, hammer), and Clov (nail, clown). Which events make the twentieth century a prime breeding ground for absurdist writing?
    a. **Further Reading:** Ackerley, C. J., and S. E. Gontarski, eds. *The Grove Companion to Samuel Beckett.* New York: Grove Press, 2004.
    b. **Suggested Search:** Watch *Breath*, Samuel Beckett's 25–45-second play, at www.youtube.com/watch?v=Y1ZON66BbB0&feature=results _main&playnext=1&list=PLA29AD9E1B25B508D.

2. **Samuel Beckett's later work explores "nothingness," a concept that was equally important to the French poet Stéphane Mallarmé.** Mallarmé, in the poem's opening line "The virginal, vibrant, and beautiful dawn" (Volume 2 in this anthology, 1089), uses the swan's struggle ("struggling to resist / For never having sung of a land in which to exist," lines 6–7) to symbolize the poet's futile quest for the absolute Sign ("its quivering neck will shake free of the agonies / inflicted on the bird by the space it denies," lines 9–10). Though the poem is a formally structured sonnet, the futility and barrenness of life are apparent ("hopelessly," "never having sung of a land in which to exist," "sterile winter," and "space it denies"

are among the terms that suggest a void). The obsession with nothing-ness is reflected in Beckett's increasing preference to write in the French language, of which he said "in French it is easier to write without style" (2322) to reflect the bare bones of language without embellishment. Absence and emptiness present as themes in absurdist theater: in Beck-ett's *Waiting for Godot*, for example, Godot never appears, and the sec-ond act is virtually identical to the first. The title "Endgame" already suggests that the play is entering the final phase, by which time the end is already predictable, yet the actions must still be completed to resolve the game. Finality ("The end is terrific!," 2341), nihilism ("no more"), and the lack of newness in spite of the passage of time (which is always bleak) ("All life long, the same inanities," 2340) signify nothingness in this play. How does the concept of nothingness and voidness evolve from late nineteenth-century and early modern works into Beckett's work?

a. **Further Reading:** Fletcher, John. *About Beckett*. London: Faber and Faber, 2006.

b. **Suggested Search:** See the Beckett exhibition at www.hrc.utexas .edu/exhibitions/web/beckett.

3. **Samuel Beckett's poem "Whoroscope" established his lifelong con-cern with the dualism between mind and body, which again fea-tures in *Endgame*.** Hamm is crippled yet orders around Clov. Since he represents the king piece (which is moved only a single space at a time, and is moved very little during a chess match, similarly how Hamm is moved around by Clov in short distances), Hamm is forever compelled to sit, yet he is the only character aware of his life as a performance ("I'll soon have finished with this story. Unless I bring in other charac-ters," 2343). This is another characteristic of absurdist theater; again, as in chess, preserving the king's life is the endgame and resolution. Clov is forever compelled to stand and perpetuate the master–slave dialectic with Hamm ("This is what we call making an exit," 2352). Beckett measured his own worth as a writer in comparison to James Joyce, whom he considered the greatest writer of the modern era; though he admired Joyce's work, Beckett later commented that Joyce preferred to add to his work, while he (Beckett) preferred to eliminate from his work. What appears to be eliminated from *Endgame* that stu-dents might like to see added or extended?

a. **Further Reading:** Murray, Christopher, ed. *Samuel Beckett: Play-wright & Poet*. New York: Pegasus Books, 2009.

b. **Suggested Search:** Read about Beckett as the recipient of the Nobel Prize (1969) at www.nobelprize.org/nobel_prizes/literature/laure ates/1969/press.html#.

4. **In spite of his concern with meaninglessness and nothingness, Samuel Beckett paradoxically required that his stage directions for**

Endgame **be impeccably maintained.** In 1984, JoAnne Akalaitis directed *Endgame* for the American Repertory Theater in Cambridge, Massachusetts; her production featured Phillip Glass's music and was set in a subway tunnel. Beckett sued over and settled out of court to add an insert into the production's program, in which he wrote, "The American Repertory Theater production, which dismisses my directions, is a complete parody of the play as conceived by me. Anybody who cares for the work couldn't fail to be disgusted by this" (McCarthy 2009, 102). How do students respond to Beckett's uncompromising demands and control over his works? Is he justified or hypocritical in forbidding directors from altering the stage setting of his works?

   a. **Further Reading:** McCarthy, Sean. "Giving Sam a Second Life: Beckett's Plays in the Age of Convergent Media." *Texas Studies in Literature and Language* 51:1 (2009): 102–17.

   b. **Suggested Search:** Watch the roundtable participants discuss Samuel Beckett at www.youtube.com/watch?v=u5UF2-2kqaw&feature=related.

In-Class Activities

1. Performance appreciation: Before watching performances, ask students to share some ideas about how they envision the presentation of the works based on Samuel Beckett's use of stage directions and the play's content and characters. Students will then watch one or more performances of Beckett's works (see the Resources section). Are the performances as students imagined?

2. Comparative drama: In this activity, students will compare the style, form, and performance of Bertolt Brecht's *The Good Woman of Setzuan* (this volume, 2025–78) to Samuel Beckett's play. How is Brecht's idea of breaking the fourth wall iterated in Beckett's play?

3. Field trip: Students will visit the Samuel Beckett online exhibition (see the Resources section) and write a reflective response after the trip is completed. What have students learned through the visual presentation of Beckett and his work?

Paper Topics/Suggestions for Writing

1. Define three characteristics of the theater of the absurd, and discuss their relevance in Samuel Beckett's play.

2. What does "nothingness" represent for Samuel Beckett? Use evidence from the play to support your argument.

3. Compare Samuel Beckett's use of language and gesture in *Endgame* to Bertolt Brecht's in *The Good Woman of Setzuan*.

4. Explain the duality of mind and body in Samuel Beckett's work, and use examples to support your arguments.

Resources

Beckett on Film. Directed by Aton Egoyan, Walter Asmus, et al. Ambrose Video, 2003, DVD (4 disks).

This DVD set comprises nineteen stage works written by Samuel Beckett, presented by nineteen directors and showcasing famous actors. Included are interviews with playwrights, actors, and directors and a stills gallery.

"Fathoms from Anywhere." A Beckett Centenary Exhibition. Harry Ransom Center, the University of Texas–Austin. www.hrc.utexas.edu/exhibitions/web/beckett.

This online exhibition features an introduction to Samuel Beckett and includes images, a time line, and suggested reading.

"I'll Go On: An Afternoon of Samuel Beckett." November 22, 2008. www.youtube.com/watch?v=u5UF2-2kqaw&feature=related.

This roundtable discussion about Samuel Beckett features Edward Albee, Tom Bishop, Alvin Epstein, Lois Oppenheim, and John Turturro.

National Portrait Gallery. London. www.npg.org.uk/collections/search/person.php?LinkID=mp00332.

Found on this site are thirty-seven portraits of Samuel Beckett by various artists.

Nobel Prize official website. www.nobelprize.org/nobel_prizes/literature/laureates/1969/press.html#.

Featured on this site is Samuel Beckett's 1969 receipt of the Nobel Prize, with a biography, an introductory speech, and background information on his life and suggested influences.

VLADIMIR NABOKOV

The Vane Sisters

> Sybil's personality, she said, had a rainbow
> edge as if a little out of focus. She said that
> had I known Sybil better I would have at once
> understood how Sybil-like was the aura of
> minor events which, in spells, had suffused
> her, Cynthia's, existence after Sybil's suicide.
> —Nabokov, "The Vane Sisters"

Topics for Lecture or Discussion

1. **The narrator's unreliability is relieved only when the Vane sisters'
   spirits cause his lyrical reflection.** When readers first meet the narrator, his reflections are lyrical and perceptive. Consider the beauty of his
   icicle journey: "This twinned twinkle was delightful but not completely
   satisfying; or rather it only sharpened my appetite for other tidbits of
   light and shade, and I walked on in a state of raw awareness that seemed
   to transform the whole of my being into one big eyeball rolling in the
   world's socket" (2356). This lyricism gives way to his true character: a
   pedantic and misogynistic instructor who takes pleasure in judging
   others. When she receives his letter that "poke[s] a little Latin fun at
   some of her guests," Cynthia says "that I was a prig and a snob, that I
   only saw the gestures and disguises of people" (2363). After seeing his
   true colors immediately after the end of part 2, when he refers to the
   students' exams as "that stuff" and coldly relates Sybil's and D.'s relationship, readers recognize that he is not a trustworthy or reliable narrator. Cynthia's estimation of his inability to see people, when it finally
   arrives at the end of part 5, is exactly right. As we learn by the end,
   though, he need not be reliable, for the Vane sisters have possessed his
   experiences and explanations of them—they were the ones who caused
   his lyricism.
   a. **Further Reading:** Eggenschwiler, David. "Nabokov's 'The Vane Sis-
      ters': Exuberant Pedantry and a Biter Bit." *Studies in Short Fiction*
      18:1 (1981): 33–39.
   b. **Suggested Search:** Conduct a Google search for the article
      "Hitchcock/Nabokov," which is about the similarities in using dop-
      pelgängers and unreliable narrators.

2. **Although the story is told in the first person, the acrostic in the last
   paragraph alerts the reader to the possession of the narrator by
   the Vane sisters.** The narrator, disbelieving of Cynthia's faith in the

supernatural, says, "I wish I could recollect that novel or short story (by some contemporary writer, I believe) in which, unknown to its author, the first letters of the words in its last paragraphs formed, as deciphered by Cynthia, a message from his dead mother" (2361). The perceptive reader will remember this moment when they reach the last paragraph of Vladimir Nabokov's story, which, as he says in a letter to *The New Yorker*, abruptly changes style to further warn us of the acrostic, which says "Icicles by Cynthia. Meter from me Sybil" (807). Nabokov had a lifelong love of games, riddles, and puzzles; that love found its way into his writing through concealed meanings and codes. Of "The Vane Sisters," Nabokov said that he used a system of composition "wherein a second (main) story is woven into, or placed behind, the superficial, semitransparent one" (Brian Boyd, *Vladimir Nabokov: The American Years* [Princeton, NJ: Princeton University Press, 1993], 195). In this case, the "superficial" story is the narrator's; the real story is the Vane sisters haunting the narrator. "My difficulty," said Nabokov, "was to smuggle in the acrostic without the narrator's being aware that it was there, inspired to him by the phantoms" (Wayne C. Booth, "The Uses of Authorial Silence," *The Rhetoric of Fiction* [Chicago: Chicago University Press, 1983], 301).

a. **Further Reading:** Quinn, Brian. "The Elusiveness of Superficial Reality in Nabokov's 'The Vane Sisters.'" *Studies in Languages and Cultures* 20 (2005): 83–91. https://qir.kyushu-u.ac.jp/dspace/bit stream/2324/5611/1/slc020p083.pdf.

b. **Suggested Search:** Search *Wired* magazine's website (wired.com) for the article "Nabokov's Final Riddle."

3. **The literary allusions (made either by the sisters, the narrator, the sisters controlling the narrator, or Vladimir Nabokov) create a rich metafictional story about the relationship between life and art.** This story, like all of Nabokov's fiction, is peppered with literary allusions. When the narrator likens himself to "one big eyeball rolling in the world's socket" (2356), he is alluding to Ralph Waldo Emerson's idea of the "transparent eyeball." From then on, we hear of the person from Porlock, who interrupted Samuel Taylor Coleridge's "Kubla Khan," William Shakespeare's sonnets, and even Leo Tolstoy's and Oscar Wilde's presences at the séance. Another allusion to Oscar Wilde's *The Picture of Dorian Gray* is through the name Sybil, or, in Wilde's case, Sibyl Vane. Dorian becomes engaged to the Shakespearean actress Sibyl Vane, but when he breaks the engagement because of her unconvincing portrayal of Juliet, she kills herself. Lord Henry comforts Dorian, saying, "The girl never really lived, and so she has never really died. To you at least she was always a dream, a phantom that flitted through Shakespeare's plays and left them

lovelier for its presence. . . . Mourn for Ophelia if you like. . . . But don't waste your tears over Sibyl Vane. She was less real than they are" (*The Complete Works of Oscar Wilde: Volume 3* [New York: Oxford University Press, 2005], 80). This particular allusion among so many others calls the reader's attention to the relationship between life and art. The narrator, unlike Dorian Gray, refuses to see the beauty and mystery of life and is therefore constantly guided to the aesthetic by the ghost of Sybil Vane, the "plagiarized" version of Sibyl Vane, through allusions.

   a. **Further Reading:** Murray, Isobel. "'Plagiatisme,' Nabokov's 'The Vane Sisters,' and *The Picture of Dorian Gray.*" *Durham University Journal* 70 (December 1977): 69–72.

   b. **Suggested Search:** Conduct a Google search for "The Figure in the Crypt," an essay about annotating and interpreting Vladimir Nabokov's allusions.

4. **Vladimir Nabokov gives metaphysical weight to everyday objects, thus uniting the supernatural and the superficial.** In a letter he explains what he calls his best story: "My French professor, a somewhat obtuse scholar and a rather callous observer of superficial planes of life, unwittingly passes (in the first pages) through the enchanting and touching 'aura' of dead Cynthia" (*Vladimir Nabokov: Selected Letters, 1940–1977*, ed. Dmitri Nabokov and Matthew Joseph Bruccoli [New York: Harcourt Brace Jovanovich, 1989], 115). Because the narrator is so unsympathetic, readers tend to discredit his views, like his sarcastic report of the séance and his disbelief of auras. Instead of the superficial, then, readers accept the supernatural. For Nabokov, the supernatural is the metaphysical: ghosts penetrate the superficial plane to make physical surroundings supernatural. The most obvious physical metaphysical objects are the icicles and the parking meter. But, upon rereading, others, such as Sybil's exam book, stand out as spiritually imbued objects: "And then, holding that limp notebook as if it were a kind of passport to a casual Elysium (where pencil points do not snap and a dreamy young beauty with an impeccable complexion winds a lock of her hair on a dreamy forefinger, as she meditates over some celestial test), Cynthia led me upstairs" (2358).

   a. **Further Reading:** Rutledge, David. S. *Nabokov's Permanent Mystery: The Expression of Metaphysics in His Work.* Jefferson, NC: McFarland & Co., 2010.

   b. **Suggested Search:** Search for the article "Nabokov's Letters: 'Let Me Explain a Few Things'" at nytimes.com.

5. **Although "The Vane Sisters" was initially overlooked and deemed unsophisticated for the acrostic, Vladimir Nabokov uses playfulness as an integral aspect of his aesthetic.** After Nabokov received a

rejection letter from *The New Yorker* saying that it would not publish "The Vane Sisters," he wrote back to Katharine White to explain its meaning and the acrostics. She haughtily replied, "We did not work out your acrostic, to be sure, that being rather out of the *New Yorker's* line" (*Vladimir Nabokov: Selected Letters, 1940–1977*, 118). Some readers do represent the presence of puzzles as silly, precious, or unsophisticated for their "serious" literature. But this sense of playfulness is essential to Nabokov's aesthetic theory, not simply his penchant for games shining through. In a 1964 speech, Nabokov listed "freedom of art," "freedom of speech," and "freedom of thought" as the three permanent elements in his political creed. Playfulness allows his art to be free. He said, "And when we actually play—whether we throw peas at a tin battalion or approach the net barrier in tennis—what we feel in our muscles is the essence of that play which possesses the marvelous juggler who tosses from hand to hand in an unbroken sparkling parabola—the plants of the universe" (Thomas Karshan, "December 1925: Nabokov Between Work and Play," *Nabokov Studies* 10.1 (2006): 1–25).

   a. **Further Reading:** Karshan, Thomas. "Nabokov and Play." D.Phil. thesis, Oxford University, 2006. http://eastanglia.academia.edu /ThomasKarshan/Papers/615498/Nabokov_and_Play.

   b. **Suggested Search**: Search for "Playful, Subversive Covers Give Nabokov's Books New Life" at theatlantic.com.

In-Class Activities

1. Vladimir Nabokov believed that play is an essential aspect of art and life, and so he would include puzzles in his work like the acrostic at the end of this story. You can begin class with a competitive game, such as Hangman or even just tossing wads of paper in the trash bin for points. Then ask students to reflect on the experience of play, especially in a serious space like a classroom or in a work of literature. How does playfulness affect a room or a work of art? How can puzzles and games be such an essential part of Nabokov's aesthetics?

2. The narrator is unaware of the story behind the story, which is that he is being guided by the Vane sisters. Your students might be incredulous about this point. Ask your students to complete the following writing exercise before starting your lecture on the message in the acrostic: "Are there moments in the narrator's story that seemed poetic? Find lines or paragraphs that are especially lyrical and elegant for a prudish French professor with a usually straightforward and clinical writing style. Consider his descriptions of the icicle, the painting of a windshield, or the final three paragraphs. Why would Nabokov have his narrator fluctuate between two different styles?"

3. Divide the class into four groups. Give each group the text (or a relevant excerpt) to which Vladimir Nabokov alludes in "The Vane Sisters": Oscar Wilde's *The Picture of Dorian Gray*, William Shakespeare's LXX, CXX, LXXXVIII, and CXXXI sonnets, Ralph Waldo Emerson's "Nature," and Samuel Taylor Coleridge's "Kubla Khan." Ask each group to read the selection and then work together to explain how the allusion affects the meaning of the story. Does each group provide a different meaning? Why else might Nabokov use so many obvious literary allusions?

Paper Topics/Suggestions for Writing

1. Some critics have called "The Vane Sisters" a type of detective story. Compare it to other works in this volume that play with the genre of mystery fiction, such as Jorge Luis Borges's "The Garden of Forking Paths."

2. How would you describe the narrator's personality? How is he different from the Vane sisters? Is it important to Sybil that he is a professor of French literature? Why does he give such a lengthy, unflattering description of Cynthia? As a reader, with whom do you sympathize?

3. What role does "D." play? Was it a coincidence that the narrator, thinking of him during his icicle walk, runs into D. shortly afterward?

4. What is the significance of the narrator's favorite painting by Cynthia: "*Seen Through a Windshield*—a windshield partly covered with rime, with a brilliant trickle (from an imaginary car roof) across its transparent part and, through it all, the sapphire flame of the sky and a green-and-white fir tree" (2359)? Consider the point of view in works of art, especially in this story itself.

5. Some readers and critics have found the secret acrostic too precious. Do you agree with this opinion? Why or why not?

6. Compare and contrast Cynthia Vane's understanding of auras with those presented in Carlos Fuentes's *Aura*, included in this volume.

Resources

Kellman, Steven G., and Irving Malin, eds. *Torpid Smoke: The Stories of Vladimir Nabokov*. Atlanta, GA: Rodopi, 2000.
    This collection of essays ranges in topics from memories and dreams to supernaturalism. It also includes an interesting and engaging essay by Linda Wagner-Martin called "'The Vane Sisters' and Nabokov's 'Subtle and Loving' Readers."
Vladimir Nabokov. BBC Worldwide, 2010.
    This brief but informative documentary film discusses Vladimir Nabokov's biography and the central themes in his most famous works, such as *Lolita* and *Pale Fire*.

Wood, Michael. *The Magician's Doubts: Nabokov and the Risks of Fiction.* Princeton, NJ: Princeton University Press, 1997.

Michael Wood's book approaches Vladimir Nabokov's works with both their playfulness and seriousness in mind. The chapter "The Cruelty of Chance: Bend Sinister, 'Signs and Symbols,' 'The Vane Sisters,'" will be especially helpful.

CLARICE LISPECTOR
The Daydreams of a Drunk Woman

Topics for Lecture or Discussion

1. **Clarice Lispector was a Brazilian modernist writer who focused on the difference between perceived sensory reality that we attach to a thing (i.e., its color, its flavor) and the internal "thingness" of an object that is unknowable.** Throughout the story, readers are both entrenched in the narrator's physical life as a promiscuous alcoholic and in her interior as a woman who has married to escape physical poverty but now suffers from an emotional and a moral impoverishment. In a relevant description, the narrator has become drunk after eating a Sunday lunch, and "all things which by their true nature are separate from each other—the smell of oil on the one hand, of a male on the other . . . became strangely linked by their true nature" (2369). Does Lispector seem to express disgust or approval of the interior and exterior worlds?

   a. **Further Reading:** Moser, Benjamin. *Why This World: A Biography of Clarice Lispector.* New York: Oxford University Press, 2009.

   b. **Suggested Search:** Go to the Clarice Lispector official website at www.claricelispector.com.br.

2. **Clarice Lispector uses interior monologue to evoke the immediacy of subjective consciousness in her characters.** Her style is intense and tightly structured, with an emphasis on sensuous perception to attain intuitive knowledge; it has been called "feminine writing" because of its exploration of immediate bodily experience in relation to language. Lispector's characters experience bodily sensations and experiences in reality, but they live in a world separate from the objective and observed shared world in which all people participate. She is both angry, haughty, and offended that her home is absent and silent during the day; "still in bed, peaceful and casual," she uses that physical abandonment and silence as a time to daydream about the man "whom she would love one day" (2368). She plays out different potential conversations with and responses to a businessman who invites her to dinner (2370) and then makes reference to her obesity—or being "full" of emotion—using pregnancy-related terms ("she was plump and heavy and generous to the full") in comparison to the thin, "barren" people in the restaurant (2370) and closing with the lines in which her "husband's friend saw her so pretty and plump" in comparison to the nauseating image she had of herself just prior (2372). How does interior monologue as a narrative form enhance the reader's appreciation of this work's theme?

    a. **Further Reading:** Tompkins, Cynthia, and David Foster, eds. *Notable Twentieth-Century Latin American Women*. Westport, CT: Greenwood, 2001, 165–69.

    b. **Suggested Search:** Search for the film *The Hour of the Star* (see the Resources section).

3. **Clarice Lispector was the child of Russian Jews who had been victims of the pogroms and migrated to Brazil; though her Jewish heritage does not present in "The Daydreams of a Drunk Woman," students may note the woman's identity crisis as she abandons her original heritage (as a poor *rapariga*) and struggles with her newfound identity.** Lispector's parents changed her name from the Hebrew "Chaya" to the Christian name "Clarice." She entered law school, became the first female reporter at a major newspaper, and won her first literary prize at age twenty-three. She married a diplomat but separated from him, writing "The Daydreams of a Drunk Woman" as part of the short story collection *Family Ties* (1960). The narrator of the short story may present as passive-aggressive and appears to indulge in sadomasochistic experiences; at one point, she attacks her husband for fawning over her ("Don't paw me!") and is "vaguely flattered" when he replies that she is "ill" (2368). Suggestions that she is mentally ill feature in the closing physical description, in which her hearing is both magnified and distorted ("life suddenly becoming loud and magnified in its smallest movements" (2372), and she dissociates from reality to the extent that she compares formerly sensuous and positive attention from her husband to noisy and nauseating experiences of the present. Is there a moral to this story or a lesson to be learned from it (an ontological purpose), or does the story relate the crisis of modernism—that life is chaotic and meaningless?

    a. **Further Reading:** Fitz, Earl. *Sexuality and Being in the Poststructuralist Universe of Clarice Lispector*. Austin: University of Texas Press, 2001.

    b. **Suggested Search:** Go to www.youtube.com/watch?v=9ad7b6kqyok for a three-part video interview with Clarice Lispector.

In-Class Activities

1. Interview the author: Each student develops a question that she or he would like to ask Clarice Lispector in a "meet the author" visit to the classroom. Questions are read aloud and the class discusses how the author would likely have responded and what these questions tell us about modern reader responses to the work.

2. Role-play: In this collaborative activity, students are paired off (or put into groups of three); one student plays the role of the therapist and the

partner(s) plays the role of the narrator (and her husband, in a group of three). Students role-play a therapy session and afterward share their experience—was the narrator (and her husband) able to resolve some of the issues presented? What changes will she or he make to achieve fulfillment?

Paper Topics/Suggestions for Writing

1. Discuss the metaphor of pregnancy alluded to throughout the story. How does the narrator's use of pregnancy-related terms typify the work as "feminine writing"?

2. Discuss the role of interior monologue in the story.

3. Is the narrator mentally ill, or is her response to her predicament rational? Use evidence from the story to support your argument.

4. How are interior and observable identity contrasted in this story? Use evidence from the story to support your argument.

5. Critics have pointed to "ontological questioning" as an important element of Clarice Lispector's work, in which a question about the meaning of existence is answered with another question. What types of ontological questions do you believe are tried and answered throughout "The Daydreams of a Drunk Woman"? Provide both hypothetical questions and proof of the answers as given in the text.

Resources

Clarice Lispector official website. www.claricelispector.com.br.
   This site, in Portuguese, is maintained by Rocco Publishers and includes a biography, chronology, and list of works, as well as audio recordings and images.
Clarice Lispector video interview. Panorama, 1977. www.youtube.com/watch?v=9ad7b6kqyok.
   This video is a three-part interview, in Portuguese, with Clarice Lispector by journalist Junio Lerner.
The Hour of the Star (Hora da Estrela). Dir. Suzana Amaral. Kino International, 1987.
   This film is an adaptation of Clarice Lispector's novella of the same title.

CHINUA ACHEBE

Chike's School Days

> It did not matter to their dancing that in the
> twentieth century Caesar was no longer ruler
> of the whole world.
> —Achebe, "Chike's School Days"

Topics for Lecture or Discussion

1. **Chinua Achebe believes that Africans with a colonial education, like Chike, are in need of fiction for cultural reeducation.** He often wrote about education in both his fiction and nonfiction. So what is the nature of Chike's education? The narrator says, "He developed a strong hatred for arithmetic. But he loved stories and songs. And he liked particularly the sound of English words, even when they conveyed no meaning at all" (2378). Can obsessing about words such as "periwinkle" and "constellation" be considered education? His teacher also shares this obsession: "Chike's teacher was fond of long words. . . . His favourite pastime was copying out jaw-breaking words from his Chambers' Etymological Dictionary" (2378). Is this actually education or infatuation, which inspires Chike only to babble meaninglessly? Contrasted with the diviner's wisdom, the teacher's lessons seem shallow: "Those who gather ant-infested faggots must be prepared for the visit of lizards" (2376), the diviner tells Chike's grandmother. As a novelist, Achebe saw himself foremost as an educator to the African colonized. In his 1965 essay "The Novelist as Teacher," Achebe concludes, "I would be quite satisfied if my novels . . . did no more than teach readers that the past—with all its imperfections—was not one long night of savagery from which the first Europeans acting on God's behalf delivered them" (45).
   a. **Further Reading:** Achebe, Chinua. "The Novelist as Teacher." In *Hopes and Impediments*, 40–46. New York: Anchor Books, 1990.
   b. **Suggested Search:** Search for the article "Western Education in Africa: The Igbo Experience, 1900–1960" by C. N. Ubah at JSTOR (jstor.org).

2. **Mr. Brown, the English missionary, inhabits a complicated role: he initiates the chain of events that leads to Chike's colonial, non-Igbo education, but he also disregards the oppressive Osu caste system that Chinua Achebe derided, and this is still in effect today.** Mr. Brown, the missionary in "Chike's School Days," is also the missionary in Achebe's famous novel *Things Fall Apart*. Here Mr. Brown may seem like a prototype of his later, fuller manifestation in the novel

to students who have read *Things Fall Apart*. But despite his smaller role in the story, he is still a significant presence for Chike, his family, and his culture. He represents the British who had been colonizing Nigeria since the 1870s. With this colonization came an overwhelming number of Igbo conversions to Christianity. Though students may first read Mr. Brown as a detriment to Igbo culture, they should be encouraged to consider him in a positive light as well. The narrator says, "The only person who supported Amos in his mad marriage venture was Mr. Brown, the white missionary" (2376). Chike's mother is an Osu, a member of the untouchable class, said to be slaves to the deities. Achebe has written about this caste system in his fiction and nonfiction. In *No Longer at Ease*, he writes, "Our fathers in their darkness and ignorance called an innocent man Osu, a thing given to the idols, and thereafter he became an outcast, and his children, and his children's children forever" (Achebe, *No Longer at Ease* [New York: Anchor Books, 1994], 151).

   a. **Further Reading:** Oko, Ebele O. "Chinua Achebe and Colonial Christianity: A Case of Subtle Ambiguity." In *Emerging Perspectives on Chinua Achebe: Isinka, The Artistic Purpose: Chinua Achebe and the Theory of African Literature*, edited by Ernest Emenyonu and Iniobong I. Uko, 209–24. Trenton, NJ: Africa World Press, 2004.

   b. **Suggested Search:** Conduct a Google search for "The Imperial Archive Nigeria." The resulting site through Queen's University Belfast (www.qub.ac.uk/imperial/nigeria/nigeria.htm) explains and collects links about "The Colonial and Postcolonial History and Literature of Nigeria."

3. **Chinua Achebe suggests the careful use of the English language to express the experiences of a colonized African person through Chike's careless—and humorous—obsession with English.** Like Chike, Achebe has a keen interest in language. Only one sentence after the narrator says that he and the other students were impressed with and never forgot the phrase "explosive mechanism," he says, "Chike was naturally impressed by [the] teacher's explosive vocabulary" (2378). The integration of the word "explosive" in this case seems to imply that Chike, or a fellow Igbo, Chike-like character like Achebe himself, is the narrator. He represents the African who is interested in language. Though he loves the English language, it is the same language that spoke of Africans as barbarians, the type of comments that inspired Achebe to write an African novel against Joseph Conrad's *Heart of Darkness* and Joyce Cary's *Mister Johnson*. In "The African Writer and the English Language," Achebe says, "I feel that the English language will be able to carry the weight of my African experience. But it will have to be a new English, still in full communion with its ancestral home but altered to suit its new African surroundings" (*African Intellectual*

Heritage, eds. Molefi Kete Asante and Abu S. Abarry [Philadelphia: Temple University Press, 1996], 384). Achebe's fiction is an example of English, resuited to accommodate a bicultural space. Instead of using words ostentatiously and without thought, Achebe—the grown Chike—learns to control them for his own purpose.

a. **Further Reading:** Gikandi, Simon. *Reading Chinua Achebe: Language & Ideology in Fiction*. Portsmouth, NH: Heinemann, 1991.

b. **Suggested Search:** Conduct a Google search for "The African Writer and the English Language" to find the full text of Chinua Achebe's 1964 essay.

4. **The narrator's seeming digressions from the main story force the audience to see how larger social, cultural, and ancestral issues affect individual lives.** Most of the story "Chike's School Days" is not, in fact, about Chike's school days. The story is initially a succession of digressions about Chike's family and tribe, digressions that at first seem only tangentially related to the subject matter of the title. The narrator himself often acknowledges these asides, saying, for example, "We have wandered from our main story" (2377). One effect of the digressive nature of the text is the echoing of the oral storytelling tradition, important to the Igbo culture. Some readers may initially feel like the real subject is suspended while they read through the family history, but it is worth pausing to consider how the background stories—dramatic stories about religious conversion, colonialism, social status, cultural integration, and family—actually are about the less dramatic, more quotidian schooling of a young boy. Were the story only about Chike as a student of English, readers would understand less the major political and cultural changes that caused his family's change and his own infatuation with the West.

a. **Further Reading:** Ogede, Ode. "Oral Tradition and Modern Storytelling: Revisiting Chinua Achebe's Short Stories." *The International Fiction Review* 28:1 (2001): 67–77. http://journals.hil.unb.ca/index.php/IFR/article/view/7692/8749.

b. **Suggested Search:** Search http://news.bbc.co.uk for the BBC News article "Achebe: Oral Tradition Not Needed."

5. **Chinua Achebe began writing children's fiction to pay honor to the child, as well as to achieve his goal of reeducation in Nigeria.** Achebe would return to his character Chike six years after completing this story. He is probably best known as the main character in "Chike and the River," Achebe's first of many children's stories, published in 1966. He turned to this genre because the Nigerian children, who play an important—almost sacred—role in Igbo culture, were still reading foreign, and sometimes derogatory, fiction. In an interview, Achebe explained that "if there is a constant coming and going between us and

the world of ancestors, which is what my people believe, then it's in fact the child who can tell you about that world since it's coming from there—it's not the old man who's going there but the child who's coming from there" (Achebe, "Chinua Achebe: At the Crossroads," by Jonathan Cott, *Conversations with Chinua Achebe* [Jackson, MS: University Press of Mississippi, 1997], 87). The name "Chike" may hold extra importance because it includes the word "chi," which in Igbo means one's "individual spirit," or one's "separate identity," that lives in the spirit world. "Chike" is short for "Chinweike," which means "She has the strength." Though he did not realize the dire need for children's literature to instruct the youth of Nigeria morally and intellectually until years after this story's publication, Achebe's esteem for the child is evident.

a. **Further Reading:** Emenyonu, Ernest N. "Nurturing the Cradle: Chinua Achebe's Fiction for Children." In *Goatskin Bags and Wisdom: New Critical Perspectives on African Literature*, edited by Ernest N. Emenyonu, 239–54. Trenton, NJ: Africa World Press, 2000.

b. **Suggested Search:** Search for the entry "Chinua Achebe: Chike and the River" on the blog *We Too Were Children* (http://wetoowere children.blogspot.com) for a summary and an explanation of the plot of the story, as well as the original illustrations.

In-Class Activities

1. Show the 61-minute film *Chinua Achebe: Africa's Voice*. Discuss how Chike's life and experiences reflect Chinua Achebe's.

2. Outline the order of events in the story. Discuss why Chinua Achebe digresses and moves back and forth in time in a story that is ostensibly about "Chike's school days."

3. As an introduction to the digressive nature of the story, begin with a writing exercise based on the following prompt: "Chike probably does not realize the major social, political, cultural, and religious changes that affected his family and consequently led to his English education. Now consider your own childhood. Can you relate to Chike's situation? Think of the larger social issues that may have affected your family and their decision to send you to a certain school, play a certain sport, join a certain club, and so on."

4. The 2005 BBC News article "Achebe: Oral Tradition Not Needed" reports that Chinua Achebe believes "if it's [oral storytelling] not going to work any more in the future, then rather than sit and weep and mourn, why don't we find out what has come to replace it?" Divide the class in half to debate this point. If orality is historically and culturally important to Igbo people, should it not be preserved? Why would Achebe, whose work often mimics oral storytelling, be willing to lose it?

5. To introduce Chinua Achebe's concepts of language, read the passages from *Heart of Darkness* by Joseph Conrad or *Mister Johnson* by Joyce Cary (which *Time* magazine called "the best novel ever written about Africa" [October 20, 1952]) that Achebe excerpts in his essay "My Home under Imperial Fire." For example, you might read this passage from *Mister Johnson*: "Its people would not know the change if time jumped back fifty thousand years. They live like mice or rats in a palace floor; all the magnificence and variety of the arts, the ideas, the learning and the battles of civilization go on over their heads and they do not even imagine them" (Joyce Cary, *Mister Johnson* [Alexandria, VA: Time Reading Program, 1981], 121). Discuss how an African writer might write in a language that also captured that idea.

Paper Topics/Suggestions for Writing

1. Chinua Achebe's greatest-known work is the 1958 novel *Things Fall Apart*, in which he "rewrites" Joseph Conrad's 1899 novel *Heart of Darkness*, included in this volume. Achebe explains the need to rewrite the novel in his essay "An Image of Africa." Read this essay and then explain Achebe's depictions of Africans in this story compared to Conrad's in *Heart of Darkness*.

2. What is this story about? Is it only about Chike and his school days? Why does the speaker include the stories of Chike's grandmother, father, and his mother, who refuses to let him eat "heathen food" (2376)? Are these digressions from the main story about Chike, or are they somehow integral to the story?

3. What is the role of language in the story? Explain Chike's obsession with English words and songs. For Chinua Achebe's ideas, refer to his 1964 essay "The African Writer and the English Language." Note that he concludes this essay with a quotation from James Baldwin, the author of "Notes of a Native Son." Are Baldwin's and Achebe's stories comparable on the issue of language?

4. Research Chinua Achebe's childhood. What connections can you draw between Chike and Achebe as a child? What are the implications if "Chike's School Days" is autobiographical?

5. Examine "Chike's School Days" as a comment on children who grow up in a bicultural land. Compare Chinua Achebe's story to others in this volume with a similar concern for culture and childhood, such as Doris Lessing's "The Old Chief Mshlanga," Salman Rushdie's "The Perforated Sheet," Jamaica Kincaid's "Girl," or Junot Díaz's "Drown."

6. Research the Osu caste system. What is the history of the Osu people? Is this caste system still in effect today? Is Chinua Achebe commenting

on the Igbo culture's treatment of the "untouchables," as Premchand comments on the Indian caste system in "The Road to Salvation," by discussing Dalits, or, as Kawabata Yasunari comments on Japan's rigid social system in "The Izu Dancer," by discussing the Hinin class? If yes, what is Achebe saying? If not, what role does the caste system play in the story?

7. Who is the narrator? What can you glean about the person telling the story by the tone, type of information shared, and so on?

Resources

Achebe, Chinua. "Chike's School Days." *The Rotarian* (April 1960).
    "Chike's School Days" was first published in the magazine *The Rotarian* in 1960. You can access the original story, with illustrations, through Google Books (books.google.com) by searching for "Chike's school days Rotarian."

Achebe, Chinua, and Bernth Lindfors. *Conversations with Chinua Achebe.* Jackson: University Press of Mississippi, 1997.
    This collection of over twenty interviews with Chinua Achebe addresses both his life and work.

Onwuejeogwu, M. A. *An Igbo Civilisation: Nri Kingdom and Hegemony.* London: Ethnographica, 1981.
    This anthropological study describes in detail the Igbo politics, religion, and social system. It includes drawings, photographs, and maps.

CARLOS FUENTES

Aura

> Now you know why Aura is living in this
> house: to perpetuate the illusion of youth and
> beauty in that poor, crazed old lady. Aura, kept
> here like a mirror, like one more icon on that
> votive wall with its clustered offerings, pre-
> served hearts, imagined saints and demons.
> —Fuentes, *Aura*

Topics for Lecture or Discussion

1. **The second-person voice and present tense push *Aura* into the realm of postmodernity for the story's metafictional awareness of its own readers.** This story is unusual beginning with its first sentence: "You're reading the advertisement" (2380). *Aura* is one of the very few works of literature that is written in the second person, as if the narrator is guiding or directing you as Felipe Montero. Furthermore, the story that "you" are told is in the present tense; the action happens as you read it. The result of these two textual elements together is hypnotic, as if Carlos Fuentes were putting us into a trance. Because Fuentes requires the reader's participation, *Aura* is often read as a postmodern work, which is often metafictional and draws attention to itself as a work of art. Just as Montero recognizes himself in the photographs, we discover ourselves in the text: "Aura doesn't look as young as she did in the other picture, but it's she, it's he, it's . . . you. [. . .] You cover General Llorente's bear with your finger, and imagine him with black hair, and you discover only yourself: blurred, lost, forgotten, but you, you, you" (2399).
   a. **Further Reading:** Williams, Raymond L. "Fuentes the Modern; Fuentes the Postmodern." *Hispania* 85:2 (May 2002): 209–18.
   b. **Suggested Search:** Search the *Writer's Digest* website (writersdi gest.com) for the article "The POV Commitment" (March 11, 2008).

2. **The supernatural elements—such as Consuelo's and Llorente's reincarnations in Aura and Felipe Montero—are connected to feminine power.** The epigraph to Aura is taken from Jules Michelet's 1862 book *La Sorcière*, or *Satanism and Witchcraft*. In this book, Michelet describes the evolution of medieval sorceresses and their spells, which would help people revisit dead loved ones. Janice Titiev argues that the narrator is the spellbinder and the novel itself is the spell that reincarnates Llorente in Felipe, or at least makes him realize he has always been the

reincarnation of Consuelo's husband. This, she says, "explains the very concentrated action and the choppy quality of much of the prose. Verbs predominate, often appearing in [a] series of short phrases with only the essential modifiers, and frequently beginning the sentence or phrase" (400). The connection to Michelet's book also explains the constant references to the color green; it is "Satan's color, and an important step in the medieval woman's evolution to sorceress is the acquisition of a green dress" (401). The reference to a text in which only women hold supernatural powers invites discussion not only on Carlos Fuentes's interest in the magical but also in the power dichotomy between man and woman. Though he dreams of himself as a hero who will save Aura, the young, robust man is subject to the desires of the elderly and sickly woman.

   a. **Further Reading:** Titiev, Janice Geasler. "Witchcraft in Carlos Fuentes' *Aura*." *Revista de Estudios Hispanicos* 15:3 (October 1981): 395–405.

   b. **Suggested Search:** Search for "La Sorciere" on archive.org to access the full text version of Jules Michelet's book in English.

3. **Carlos Fuentes challenges the typical view of history. Instead of a linear progression of grand events, *Aura* privileges personal history, presented in a timescape that collapses present, past, and future.** When the story begins, one of the first pieces of information we have about "you," Felipe Montero, is that he is a historian. Readers later find out the nature of his interest: he wants to write a "great, inclusive work on the Spanish discoveries and conquests in the New World. A work that sums up all the scattered chronicles, makes them intelligible, and discovers resemblances among all the undertakings and adventures of Spain's Golden Age, and all the human prototypes and major accomplishments of the Renaissance" (2389). In the face of this grand idea of history, the General's life seems "tedious" to Montero. This tedious, small, personal history, though, is his own. The novella also challenges how time moves, making "history" a slippery term. The house, and therefore the story itself, is in a loop of time, wherein the General can allude to the future through his letters, Consuelo can return to the past through Aura, and Montero can maintain a feeling of "memory and premonition" at once (2396). The present contains past, present, and future, which challenges Montero's and our traditional view of history and the ability to write a linear, intelligible, and Casaubon-esque *The Key to All Mythologies.*

   a. **Further Reading:** Frenk, Susan F. "Rewriting History: Carlos Fuentes' *Aura*." *Modern Language Studies* 30:3 (1994): 256–76.

   b. **Suggested Search:** Search Google Books (books.google.com) for chapter 1 of Chalene Helmuth's *The Postmodern Fuentes*, "Approaching Postmodernism," to find a discussion of time and history in *Aura*.

4. **As an urban writer interested in the life of the city, Carlos Fuentes creates the house in Aura to represent the collective unconscious of Mexico City.** In an interview for the *Paris Review*, Fuentes said, "I am a city writer and I cannot understand literature outside the city. For me it is Mexico City and its masks and mirrors, the twitchy little images I see when I look at the base of this totem-city, in the mud of the city" ("Carlos Fuentes, The Art of Fiction No. 68," *Paris Review* 82 [Winter 1981]). Although Aura may seem divorced from the "real" world, it is important to remember that the story begins in a coffee shop in Mexico City, a modern city that Felipe Montero must navigate by bus before reaching the house in the center of the city, where "the juke-boxes don't disturb them. The mercury streetlights don't shine in" (2381). The old house, untouched by the passing of time, is the center or base of the city. Scholars such as Gloria B. Duran and Richard J. Callan have applied Carl Jung's idea of archetypes to *Aura* so that Montero is the hero figure, Consuelo the Great Mother, and Aura the anima (the feminine aspect of a man's personality). The house, the heart of Mexico City, contains these archetypes. Given Fuentes's interest in the "totem-city," which means that Mexico City is the inhabitants' supernatural ancestor or original progenitor that embodies their spirit, maybe the house in Aura is the object that contains Mexico City's collective unconscious.
   a. **Further Reading:** Duran, Gloria B. "Aura and Its Precedents in Fuentes's Earlier Works." In *The Archetypes of Carlos Fuentes: From Witch to Androgyne*, 43–63. North Haven, CT: Archon Books, 1980.
   b. **Suggested Search:** Search the *New World Encyclopedia* (www.newworldencyclopedia.org), for "totemism."

5. **Carlos Fuentes's own particular version of the broad label "magical realism" concentrates on the more realistic "second reality" that is hidden behind our everyday experiences.** As a leading figure of the Latin American Boom of the 1960s, Fuentes was considered part of the magical realism genre. Latin American fiction was politically subversive and dealt with what he called a "second reality": "I have always attempted to perceive behind the spectral appearance of things a more tangible, more solid reality than the obvious everyday reality" (Wendy B. Faris, "Short Fiction and Theater: Magical Realism, Symbolic Action," *Carlos Fuentes* [New York: Frederick Ungar Publishing, 1983], 69). According to the arguments of Jaime Alazraki, this world is "an authentic and unexplored dimension that hides behind our everyday lives and that only can be briefly glimpsed through epiphanic moments" (Santiago Juan-Navarro, *Archival Reflections: Postmodern Fiction of the Americas [Self-Reflexivity, Historical Revisionism, Utopia]* [Cranbury, NJ: Associated University Press, 2000], 196). In Aura, Felipe Montero briefly glimpses

the second reality when he witnesses Consuelo miming Aura's slaughter of a goat or when he recognizes himself in the old photographs. Fuentes recognized that the fictionalization of the second reality placed him in the magical realism camp, but later he came to resent the term. He said, "so-called 'magical realism,' which, invented by Alejo Carpentier, had been applied indiscriminately as a label to too many Hispanic American novelists, although truly it became the personal stamp of only one: Gabriel Garcia Marquez."

    a. **Further Reading:** Zlotchew, Clark. *Varieties of Magic Realism.* Eatontown, NJ: Academic Press ENE, 2007.

    b. **Suggested Search:** Search janushead.org for Wendy B. Faris's "The Question of the Other: Cultural Critiques of Magical Realism."

In-Class Activities

1. As an introductory exercise, ask your students to explain the plot. They may need time to figure out exactly what happens in the fantastic *Aura*.

2. Show students an episode of the BBC sitcom *Peep Show*. This show takes place in the "second person," as if the viewer were the main character. Ask students how this element affected their viewing experience. How does it relate to the narrative style of *Aura*?

3. Carlos Fuentes, in his essay about composing *Aura*, "How I Wrote One of My Books," compares his characters to Miss Havisham from Charles Dickens's novel *Great Expectations*. Show students a clip of Miss Havisham from a movie version. Portions of the BBC version with Gillian Anderson as Miss Havisham are available on youtube.com. What sorts of archetypes are Miss Havisham and Consuelo?

4. "How I Wrote One of My Books" also mentions the 1953 Japanese film *Ugetsu Monogatari*, directed by Kenji Mizoguchi, as an influence; Carlos Fuentes says that he shows "the emotion that lies within all that is ghostly" (Fuentes, *This I Believe: An A to Z of a Life*, 49). Show students the film and discuss the connections between the film and the novella. What do you think Fuentes means by "ghostly"?

Paper Topics/Suggestions for Writing

1. How does the epigraph from Jules Michelet's *La Sorcèrie*, known as *Satanism and Witchcraft*, affect your understanding of *Aura*? Read and/or research Michelet's text. Why does Carlos Fuentes take his epigraph from this history book? Does it change the meaning of the story for you?

2. Why is the story narrated in the second-person voice, and why does the narrator only report events in the present tense? What effect did this have on you as you read the story? Who is the narrator?

3. Carlos Fuentes sees himself as the rescuer of Aura. How is this ironic?

4. What is the role of Consuelo's pet rabbit, which she calls, like she calls Aura, her "companion"? What about the cats and rats?

5. Like Gabriel García Márquez, Julio Cortázar, and Jorge Luis Borges, Carlos Fuentes is a magical realist whose fiction blends the lines between reality and fantasy. Compare and contrast Fuentes's version of magical realism with one of these other writers.

Resources

Carlos Fuentes. Films for the Humanities and Sciences, 2007.
> This is an interview with Carlos Fuentes about writing as a Mexican author during the Latin American Boom.

Carlos Fuentes: At Home in the Americas. Films for the Humanities and Sciences, 1999.
> This film offers a broad survey of Carlos Fuentes's interests and biography, from "Fuentes' Childhood in Mexico" to "In Adoration of Women and Films."

Fuentes, Carlos. "On Reading and Writing Myself: How I Wrote *Aura*." *World Literature Today* 57:4 (1983): 531–39.
> This essay is extremely helpful in locating the artistic and biographical influences that echo throughout the novella.

Van Delden, Maarten. *Carlos Fuentes, Mexico, and Modernity*. Nashville, TN: Vanderbilt University Press, 1998.
> Maarten van Delden uses Carlos Fuentes's fiction and nonfiction writing to explore his relationship with modernity, which he sees as a tension between cosmopolitanism and nationalism.

Williams, Raymond L. *The Writings of Carlos Fuentes*. Austin: University of Texas Press, 1996.
> Raymond Williams "traces the themes of history, culture, and identity in Fuentes' work" (publisher's description). He also considers Carlos Fuentes's political involvement and interest in Latin American identity.

ALEXANDER SOLZHENITSYN
Matryona's Home

> We had all lived side by side with her and had
> never understood that she was the righteous
> one without whom, as the proverb says, no vil-
> lage can stand. Nor any city. Nor our whole
> land.
> —Solzhenitsyn, "Matryona's Home"

Topics for Lecture or Discussion

1. **Because of its open attack on Soviet bureaucracy and the coopera-
   tive farm system, "Matryona's Home" was the first work of the Village Prose movement of the 1960s and 1970s, a literary movement
   in which writers questioned collective societies and looked with
   nostalgia back to traditional Russian villages.** Matryona and the other
   villagers in Torfoprodukt work on a *kolkhoz*, or a collective farm. Joseph
   Stalin began enforcing collectivization in 1927 as part of his plan to
   completely socialize Soviet Russia. Although a collective was supposedly
   voluntary, many peasants were forced through bureaucratic red tape to
   participate at the risk of losing their land. Alexander Solzhenitsyn
   attacked the collective farm system as inefficient and callous. The lack
   of peat, which Matryona must have for fuel during the insufferably
   cold Russian winter, is particularly suggestive because it forces the old
   women of the village to gather their courage and steal it from the
   bogs—where it is being kept for more privileged members of the Soviet
   "classless" society. Matryona's vain and exhausting attempts to get her
   pension ("They shove me around, Ignatich" [2410]) reemphasize the
   point, as does her experience trying to get train tickets.
   a. **Further Reading:** Parthe, Kathleen. *Russian Village Prose: The Radi-
      ant Past.* Princeton, NJ: Princeton University Press, 1992.
   b. **Suggested Search:** Search Google for "The Peasant on the Farm" to
      find a 1931 article by Gareth Jones, a reporter who stayed on a Rus-
      sian collective (www.garethjones.org/soviet_articles/peasant_on_the
      _farm.htm).

2. **To Alexander Solzhenitsyn, technological advancements—especially
   the railroad—are "an extremely intricate trial of our free will."** Solzhenitsyn's disgust with the machine age is clear. The narrator says,
   "When they announced on the radio that some new machine had been
   invented, I heard Matryona grumbling out in the kitchen, 'New ones all

the time, nothing but new ones. People don't want to work with the old ones any more, where are we going to store them all?'" (2415). The narrator's camera seems to transform Matryona, a symbol of goodwill, into a cold person: "More important to me was the smile on her roundish face, which I tried in vain to catch when at last I had earned enough to buy a camera. As soon as she saw the cold eye of the lens upon her, Matryona assumed a strained or else an exaggeratedly severe expression" (2409). The most effective and suggestive symbol of the callousness and greed of the machine age, though, is the train. Matryona tells of a time she had to beg for tickets from the ticketmaster, only to ride the train with "its big eyes popping out and the rails humming away" (2413). Because of her distrust and avoidance of technology, Matryona's death is ironic. She, like her house, is destroyed by technology and greed.

  a. **Further Reading:** Ericson, Edward E. *Solzhenitsyn and the Modern World*. Washington, DC: Regnery Gateway, 1993.

  b. **Suggested Search:** Conduct a Google search for "Solzhenitsyn Harvard Address" to find his speech "A World Split Apart."

3. **Matryona is an embodiment of pre-Soviet Russia.** According to scholar Sheryl Spitz, "Matrenin Dvor" is often translated as either "Matryona's Home" or "Matryona's House." However, "dvor" can be more accurately translated as "homestead," a word that connotes what Americans might understand as a term of the Western frontier. Spitz argues that "Matryona's Home" embodies "Russian-ness," like the tales of the American West that are "the locus of the American myth" (167). When the narrator begins his narrative, he says he wants to find Russia, "to lose myself in deepest Russia . . . if it was still anywhere to be found" (2404). What he finds is Matryona, which is the colloquial spelling of the name "Matrona," meaning "Mother"; she is the avatar or embodiment of Mother Russia. In his essay "Matryona's Home: The Making of a Russian Icon," Robert Louis Jackson says the Matryona is pre-revolutionary Russian icon that has somehow survived into the Soviet period. She is extremely superstitious about thunder and trains, and even snowstorms signal a suicide; her folktale-like beliefs define her as a pre-Soviet Russian woman. Not only does Matryona embody this folksiness, but the story itself is colloquial and full of Russian idioms.

  a. **Further Reading:** Spitz, Sheryl A. "The Impact of Structure in Solzhenitsyn's 'Matryona's Home.'" *Russian Review* 36:2 (April 1977): 167–83.

  b. **Suggested Searches:** First conduct a Google Images search for "Mother Russia." Then search for "Mother Motherland." Use these two different images to explore the different personifications of Russia both pre-revolution and post-revolution.

4. **"Matryona's Home" is semi-autobiographical, based on Alexander Solzhenitsyn's return from the Gulag.** Through the brief, intriguing introductory section, readers learn that the first-person narrator is telling his story of Matryona six months after it ends. The prologue immediately pulls us into the mystery of why the trains slow down and the significance of that spot, like a detective story might. We share in the bewilderment of the passengers who ask, "Was the line under repair, or what?" and "Would the train be late?" (2404). The most glaring question, though, is who is the "I" telling the story? In fact, the narrator shares a lot in common with Solzhenitsyn, who spent eight years in a Soviet prison camp called the "Gulag." He was exiled there in 1945 for creating anti-Soviet propaganda and agitation, after a letter in which he criticized Joseph Stalin was intercepted by a government censor. After he was released, he took a job as a schoolteacher in rural Ryazan, near Moscow. During his tenure there, he apparently became friendly with a person who was the basis for Matryona. The train accident that appears in "Matryona's Home" is said to be based on what happened to that friend.

   a. **Further Reading:** Pearce, Joseph. *Solzhenitsyn: A Soul in Exile.* Grand Rapids, MI: Baker Books, 2001.

   b. **Suggested Search:** Search on Google or nobelprize.org for "Solzhenitsyn autobiography" which will lead you to the author's self-authored life story for the Nobel Prize site.

5. **The story's Christian, moral didacticism inspired many Russians to convert to Christianity, but the story was critically condemned for its anti-Communist message.** Grigory Pomerants, a samizdat historian, claimed that "for a million people[,] Christianity began with reading 'Matryona's House'" (Peter Duncan, *Russian Messianism: Third Rome, Holy Revolution, Communism, and After* [New York: Routledge, 2000], 63). The anti-materialistic and selfless Matryona became a symbol of Christian saintliness, emulated as "the righteous one without whom, as the proverb says, no village can stand" (2429). "Matryona's Home" has even been called hagiography—the story of the life of a saint. Others, however, condemned the story for "failing to educate youth by positive examples" that would lead the youth "to communism" (Pearce, *Solzhenitsyn*, 171). Clearly, some Russians found his message was, as Aleksandr Tvardovsky, writer and editor of *Novy Mir* literary magazine, put it, "a bit too Christian" (ibid., 162). In his essay "Post-Stalin Trends in Russian Literature," scholar Victor Erlich explains, "Solzhenitsyn's positive message—his emphasis on personal 'righteousness,' on unaggressive goodness, so clearly at odds with the 'struggle'-oriented and stridently public Soviet ethos—[was] objectionable" (Erlich, "Post-Stalin Trends in Russian Literature," *Slavic Review* 23.3 [1964]:

411). The story was attacked because it supposedly offered a distorted version of Soviet village life. The claim was that Alexander Solzhenitsyn insisted that capitalistic competitiveness was still present in the countryside.

   a. **Further Reading:** Dunlop, John B., Richard Haugh, and Alexis Kilmoff, eds. *Aleksandr Solzhenitsyn: Critical Essays and Documentary Materials*. New York: Collier, 1975.

   b. **Suggested Search:** Search images.spectator.co.uk for "Russia's Ignorant Still Hate Solzhenitsyn," an article by Owen Matthews in the *Spectator*.

In-Class Activities

1. With the class, create a character list. Then, one by one, ask students to describe each character's history, behaviors, and personality, referencing particular passages in the novella. How does the main character, Matryona, seem to differ from her family and the other townspeople?

2. Begin class with the following writing exercise prompt: "What is your concept of utopia? In other words, what is the most ideal way that society could possibly function? What does Alexander Solzhenitsyn's utopia look like, according to this story? How do you know? Refer to specific passages in the novella."

3. As an introduction to your lecture or discussion on *kolkhoz* and Soviet Russia, show an image of Vera Mukhina's stainless steel sculpture *Worker and Kolkhoz Woman*, created for the 1937 Paris World's Fair. From this image, ask students to determine Russian ideology.

Paper Topics/Suggestions for Writing

1. In the beginning of his narrative, the speaker says, "I wanted to efface myself, to lose myself in deepest Russia . . . if it was still anywhere to be found" (2404). Why does he want to do this? Does he ever find Russia? If so, in what ways?

2. How is narrative understatement used in the story? Is it effective? What would be the effect of writing about such a saintly woman in inflated language?

3. How does Matryona die? Considering her beliefs and personality, did you find the cause and nature of her death ironic? Why or why not?

4. According to scholar Sheryl Spitz, "Matrenin Dvor" is most accurately translated as "Matryona's Homestead." How does this translation of the title affect your understanding of the novella? Would you translate the

title with the word "home"? "House"? "Homestead"? Or, would you choose another translation? Explain.

5. Analyze the symbolic significance of the tearing apart of Matryona's home. For what original purpose had the top room been built? Compare the use of architecture in other texts in this volume, such as Borges's "The Garden of Forking Paths," Lessing's "The Old Chief Mshlanga," or Cortázar's "House Taken Over."

6. How does the narrator's hobby of photography work as a metaphor for his relationship with Matryona and his epiphany about her at the end of his tale?

7. Research Russian politics during the time of this story. How does the political context affect your understanding of the story? You can also research Alexander Solzhenitsyn's political activity prior to writing "Matryona's Home." How did his interactions with the government result in this story? Compare this narrator's experience with Anna Akhmatova's "Requiem" (in this volume), which was also published in 1963.

Resources

Aleksandr Solzhenitsyn: In Love with Mother Russia. Films Media Group. (49 min.), 2006.

> This biographical and critical documentary features interviews by Andrei Vassilievsky, Nikita Struve, and Alexander Solzhenitsyn.

Curtis, James M. *Solzhenitsyn's Traditional Imagination.* Athens: University of Georgia Press, 1984.

> Discussed in this work are the literary traditions and writers, both Russian and non-Russian, influencing Alexander Solzhenitsyn's work.

Ericson, Edward E. "The Enduring Achievement of Aleksandr Solzhenitsyn." *The Constitutionality of Faith-Based Prison Units: Law and Culture* 6:2 (Spring 2008): 513–26.

> Edward Ericson's article addresses Alexander Solzhenitsyn's "influence on history, the power of his thought in general, and his contribution as a mission-driven literary artist."

Jackson, Robert Louis. "'Matryona's Home': The Making of a Russian Icon." In *Solzhenitsyn: A Collection of Critical Essays*, edited by Kathryn Feuer, 60–70. Englewood Cliffs, NJ: Prentice Hall, 1976.

> This essay discusses Matryona as a symbolic figure. The collection also includes essays exploring other aspects of Solzhenitsyn's work.

Secret History: The Gulag Archipelago. Dir. Jean Crepu and Nicolas Miletitch. 2009. Available at factualtv.com.

> This documentary film tells the story of the publication history of Alexander Solzhenitsyn's novel *The Gulag Archipelago*.

ALICE MUNRO

Walker Brothers Cowboy

> The 1930s. How much this kind of farmhouse,
> this kind of afternoon seem to me to belong to
> that one decade in time, just as my father's hat
> does, his bright flared tie, our car with its run-
> ning board (an Essex, long past its prime).
> —Munro, "Walker Brothers Cowboy"

Topics for Lecture or Discussion

1. **The adult narrator tells the story of her childhood in the voice of her younger self and in the present tense. This conflation reinforces the theme of complicated and multiple histories.** "Walker Brothers Cowboy" begins by eschewing the formalities of narrative introduction and at once plunges the reader into a familiar relationship with the narrator. She uses the present tense, as she does throughout the story, except for a couple of significant lapses, to quote her father's cryptic question: "Want to go down and see if the Lake's still there?" (2432). Though we recognize that the narrator is young and the father's question is quirky and fun, it still strikes readers as ominous, as if this family's world is so vulnerable and defenseless that even the lake might disappear. The introductory section, even before it transitions into the story, establishes the theme of susceptibility of the world to change. The narrator speaks childishly and in the present tense, but she seems at times to be looking back as an adult on this childhood memory. She says, "The 1930s. How much this kind of farmhouse, this kind of afternoon seem to me to belong to that one decade in time" (2436). This reflection from the future suggests that the narrator is now an adult who is telling us about the day that she realized the lasting effects of the past on people's lives.
   a. **Further Reading:** Rasporich, Beverly Jean. *Dance of the Sexes: Art and Gender in the Fiction of Alice Munro.* Edmonton, Canada: University of Alberta Press, 1990.
   b. **Suggested Search:** Search Google Books (books.google.com) for Brad Hooper's *The Fiction of Alice Munro: An Appreciation.* In the chapter "She Begins Her Career," Hooper includes a discussion of Alice Munro's narrators, including the girl from "Walker Brothers Cowboy."

2. **The girl's three excursions—to the lake, shopping with her mother, and to Nora—introduce her to various types of histories, from the universal to the personal.** One of the most striking passages from the

story is the girl's reflection on time as she stares at the lake with her father. He simultaneously teaches her how past events imprint themselves upon us (the Great Lakes come from the mark left by the ice on a flat plain) and how faint the signs of the influence are (mimicking the ice's encroachment on the plain, the father's fingers make hardly any impression at all, prefiguring the faint, unreadable mark that Nora will make on the dusty car fender). When they travel to Nora's house and she sees him as a person with his own complicated history, she must reconsider her initial response to the bigness of history. She initially said, "Even my father, who sometimes seems to me to have been at home in the world as long as it has lasted, has really lived on this earth only a little longer than I have, in terms of all the time there has been to live in" (2433). The father's initial lake speech, and her imaginative response to it, and the subsequent trip to Nora's house initiate the girl into the complicatedness of history; she is now one who must recognize the existence of the past.

    a. **Further Reading:** Martin, Walter Rintoul. *Alice Munro: Paradox and Parallel*. Edmonton, Canada: University of Alberta Press, 1987.

    b. **Suggested Search:** Search Google for "Dragged into the Past: A Major Motif in Walker Brothers Cowboy." This article, by Hal Blythe and Charlie Sweet, succinctly explains the role of history in the story.

3. **Though Nora seems a better romantic partner for Ben than his wife, they did not marry because of religious differences.** Because the story is narrated from a child's point of view, readers are never explicitly told the nature of Nora and Ben's relationship. However, we can infer that they have a romantic history: Nora seems flustered at his arrival and changes from her cleaning clothes into a dress that "is flowered more lavishly than anything my mother owns" (2438). Alice Munro carefully distinguishes between Nora and Ben's wife. Nora laughs at his jokes and songs and shares a drink with him, and they talk with ease. This is in stark contrast to his wife, who "would laugh finally, unwillingly" and doesn't know he drinks (2436). It is not until the narrator notices the picture hanging on Nora's wall that we begin to understand why Ben did not marry her. The picture is "of Mary, Jesus' mother—I know that much—in shades of bright blue and pink with a spiked band of light around her head. I know that such pictures are only found in the homes of Roman Catholics and so Nora must be one" (2439–40). When Irish settlers moved to Ontario, they brought their religious prejudices with them, so that Protestants and Catholics, who "dig with the wrong foot," cannot marry (2440). The narrator unknowingly discovers that her father's history is a personal tragedy caused by those social prejudices.

    a. **Further Reading:** Redekop, Magdalene. *Mothers and Other Clowns: The Stories of Alice Munro.* New York: Routledge, 1992.

    b. **Suggested Search:** Conduct a Google search for "Why are Catholics sometimes called left-footers" for a Guardian article about the origin of the phrase "dig with the wrong foot" (www.guardian.co.uk /notesandqueries/query/0,5753,-1121,00.html).

4. **Because of Alice Munro's interest in how imagination alters everyday objects and landscapes, her stories often border on magical realism.** The story takes place in rural Canada near Lake Huron during the 1930s. At this point, the economy was still suffering from the Depression. The father failed at the fox fur business and had to take a much less glamorous job selling salves and ointments from door to door. For most of the story, Ben does not seem downtrodden, but the mother suffers with embarrassment at the state of their clothes. This desolation is captured in the landscape: "We have to roll up the windows because of dust. The land is flat, scorched, empty. Bush lots at the back of the farms hold shade, black pine-shade like pools nobody can ever get to" (2435). Her descriptions of the landscape always border on magical realism. She says, for example, "The street is shaded, in some places, by maple trees whose roots have cracked and heaved the sidewalk and spread out like crocodiles into the bare yards" (2431). Her stories, in fact, have been compared to paintings by the Canadian artist Alex Colville, who also emphasizes the magic of the ordinary. The girl's final epiphany is when she looks over the landscape and considers what it might look like "when your back is turned" (2441).

    a. **Further Reading:** Stubbs, Andrew. "Fictional Landscape: Mythology and Dialectic in the Fiction of Alice Munro." *World Literature Written in English* 23:1 (1984): 53–62.

    b. **Suggested Search:** Conduct a Google Images search for the artist "Alex Colville" to compare his depiction of magical ordinariness with Alice Munro's.

5. **The narrator is telling the story of becoming an artist.** The only female character with a name is Nora, which is a significant name in literature. She shares the name with Henrik Ibsen's main character in *A Doll's House*, Nora Helmer, who represents the self-emancipated woman. Though Alice Munro's Nora does not exit with a "door slam heard 'round the world," like Ibsen's Nora, she does leave her impression, "making an unintelligible mark in the dust there" on the fender (2440). She disregards Ben's directions to his house in favor of making this inscrutable, barely noticeable yet unarguably made mark. Scholars Hal Blythe and Charlie Sweet make another argument about Nora's name, this one about her last name, Cronin, which they liken to "crone." They say Nora as a crone represents a mythological figure who controls

men's—in this case, Ben's—fate. Overall, critics tend to read Nora as an important female figure in the story. She has clearly made an impression on Ben's life, symbolized by her mark on the car or even her name, but the young narrator seems to recognize that, however slight, Nora has changed history. She may have even inspired the young artist—who grew up to write this story—to try and make her own mark on history.

a. **Further Reading:** Rasporich, Beverly Jean. *Dance of the Sexes: Art and Gender in the Fiction of Alice Munro*. Edmonton, Canada: University of Alberta Press, 1990.

b. **Suggested Search:** Search youtube.com for the video "Alice Munro in Conversation with Diana Athill" to find an interview about the author wanting to read and write as a child.

In-Class Activities

1. As a creative writing exercise, assign to students the following prompt: "Do you have a childhood memory in which you saw or did something that you didn't understand until you were older? First, write about that memory from your current perspective as an adult. Then, rewrite that memory from your perspective as a child." You can share some of their stories and then discuss how Alice Munro uses both perspectives.

2. By giving Nora a blind, oblivious mother, Alice Munro suggests the possibility of metaphorical blindness in other characters. With the class, create a list of characters that might be considered "blind." Select passages or moments from the text that support your choices.

3. Go to youtube.com for a 5-minute video called "Alice Munro in Conversation with Diana Athill." Alice Munro discusses in this video reading and writing as a very young child. Show this video to students to begin a discussion about the artist as a young child or the process of becoming or realizing artistry as a child.

Paper Topics/Suggestions for Writing

1. Compare and contrast the following observation by Stephen Albert at the end of Jorge Luis Borges's "The Garden of Forking Paths" (in this volume) with Alice Munro's treatment of time and space as exemplified by the father's description of time: "In contrast to Newton and Schopenhauer, your ancestor did not believe in a uniform, absolute time. He believed in an infinite series of times, in a growing, dizzying net of divergent, convergent, parallel times" (2087).

2. William Faulkner's "Barn Burning" and Doris Lessing's "The Old Chief Mshlanga" (both in this volume) are also about the transition from

adolescence to adulthood. Compare and contrast one or both of these stories with "Walker Brothers Cowboy."

3. How old is the narrator? Explain how this confusion reinforces the story's interest in time.

4. Who is Nora? How does the narrator's father know her? How would you describe their relationship? How would you compare it to her father and mother's relationship? Why does the narrator say that Nora "digs with the wrong foot" (2439)?

5. Why does the father name himself the "Walker Brothers Cowboy"? What are some connotations of the word "cowboy"? Do those connotations suit his behavior in any parts of the story?

6. Describe the father's attitude and behavior. How do they change throughout the story? Why do they change?

7. Alice Munro's fiction has been compared to Zhang Ailing's (also known as Eileen Chang), the author of "Sealed Off" (in this volume). Explain how both writers use magic in their stories.

Resources

Bloom, Harold, ed. *Alice Munro*. New York: Chelsea House, 2009.
　　This collection includes an introduction by Harold Bloom and ten scholarly essays on topics such as "Wilderness and Social Code" and "Memory, Identity, and the Aesthetics of Connection."
Carscallen, James. *The Other Country: Patterns in the Writing of Alice Munro*. Toronto, Canada: ECW Press, 1993.
　　James Carscallen tracks Alice Munro's works through a single interpretive model, arguing that Munro is concerned with "great human myths, but as half-concealed . . . behind a surface of ordinariness."
Mazur, Carol, and Cathy Moulder. *Alice Munro: An Annotated Bibliography of Works and Criticism*. Lanham, MD: Scarecrow Press, 2007.
　　This is a great resource that catalogs Alice Munro's fiction, through 2005, interviews, nonfiction, and critical and academic publications on Munro.
Thacker, Robert. *Alice Munro: Writing Her Lives: A Biography*. Toronto, Canada: McClelland & Stewart, 2005.
　　This work concentrates on how Alice Munro's life and stories intertwine.

VI. Global and Local in Contemporary World Literature

DEREK WALCOTT

Topics for Lecture or Discussion

1. **In his essay "Meanings" (1970), Derek Walcott wrote of a dualism in his work: as a "split writer" he is divided between the narrative and gestural, on the one hand, and the literary and classical, on the other.** Walcott's work reflects a struggle to discover historical heroes for his nation who could compete with traditional European monuments. Walcott was trained initially as a painter, and readers will note a disparity between the oral-performative and visual-calligraphic in Walcott's work. In an interview, Walcott commented that "metaphor is almost calligraphic: when it is pronounced, you can almost see it," explaining that his entire childhood was based on a race "renaming something that had been named by someone else and giving that object its own metaphoric power" (287). In "Crusoe's Journal," Walcott uses a painterly language to describe his people's gestural and performative acts to adopt Western rituals and myths: they recite the New Testament and receive the Eucharist ("parroting our master's style and voice . . . we learn to eat the flesh of Christ," lines 20–26); they embrace and recant the colonial works by Henty, Marryat, and R. L. S. (lines 36–42); and they fashion a new culture out of the debris washed ashore (lines 50–56). How does Walcott's painterly writing compare to the practice of ekphrasis, in which objects are described through rich poetic description (e.g., the Shield of Achilles, "Ode on a Grecian Urn")? What benefit does painterly writing serve for the reader?
    a. **Further Reading:** Baugh, Edward. "Of Men and Heroes: Walcott and the Haitian Revolution." *Callaloo* 28:1 (2005): 45–54.
    b. **Suggested Search:** Go to www.nobelprize.org/nobel_prizes/litera ture/laureates/1992/walcott-lecture.html to listen to Derek Walcott's Nobel lecture.

2. **Derek Walcott's style reflects not only a mastery of and passion for standard English but also a "creolization" of language.** The Caribbean represents a multicultural region inhabited (largely due to slavery and colonization) by Africans, Asians, and Europeans. England and France shared possession of Saint Lucia at least a dozen times, which affected language use and language evolution. In interviews, Walcott often speaks of the fragmentation of the Caribbean to the extent that nationalist literature arises on islands rather than as a West Indian entirety. He often employs "punning syntax," for example, by giving adjectives a verbal status, or by altering the traditional English phrasal structure, as in "The Sea Is History" ("Sir, it is locked in them sea sands," line 34), and in the play on French and English *singe* (monkey)/

singe (to burn) in "North and South" (line 128). Metaphors take on new meaning as a result of language disparity, he states in his essay "Meanings," using the example "ciseau la mer" ("scissor of the sea") instead of "tern" because "it is much more startling, much more exciting" (287). There is a parallelism between Europe and the Caribbean; in "As John to Patmos," the Evangelist's divine experience of Patmos's landscape is compared to Walcott's own experience on Saint Lucia, where he too is inspired to "praise lovely, the living and the brown dead" (line 16). In "The Almond Trees," the sea almond plants become a metaphor first for the beautiful brown girls whose "forked limbs" are toasted by the sun, and then for the black people as having survived enslavement and colonial oppression to become sturdy and tempered ("they're cured, they endured their furnace," lines 19–32). The Caribbean becomes a "hammock swung between Americas" in "Elegy" (line 1), through which not only is Robert Kennedy elegized, but the poet also laments America's romanticized revisions of historical tragedies (American violence and poverty, line 509; displacement of the Native Americans, lines 25–28); in this poem, Walcott condemns the white man as a wolf in sheep's clothing ("like Calvin's saints . . . gripping the devil's pitchfork," lines 29–32). "Omeros" makes reference to the histories of Africa, Ireland, and Saint Lucia, transposing world myths and heroic deeds from the Caribbean perspective. Achilles becomes a humble Saint Lucian fisherman who navigates West Indian consciousness; like his Greek counterpart, he and another local fisherman, Hector, dispute over Helen. Achilles's descent into the underworld (Chapter VIII) becomes a metaphor for the descent into the tumultuous, dark history of the Caribbean. Which characters and values from Western mythology appeal most to Walcott?

    a. **Further Reading:** King, Bruce. *Derek Walcott: A Caribbean Life.* Oxford: Oxford University Press, 2000.

    b. **Suggested Search:** Read Derek Walcott's interview with Edward Hirsch at www.theparisreview.org/interviews/2719/the-art-of-poetry -no-37-derek-walcott.

3. **Affliction is an important theme in Derek Walcott's work.** In "Ruins of a Great House," Walcott revisits the decaying architecture of a former slave plantation as a place where the Bible and sword, where imperial explorers such as Raleigh and Drake, are rotten like the limes "whose stench became the charnel galleon's text" (line 36). In "North and South," New York City becomes the epitome of Western oppression and colonization (lines 11–20) from ancient through modern times ("even when spring comes with its rain of nails . . . the world will be one season older but no wiser," lines 30–32); New York is like Conrad's "heart of darkness," a foreign land where the poet longs for home—the "cacophonous seaports" built, ironically, around a British

colonial monument (lines 50–54). As the poet shifts southward into Virginia, additional references are made to the Holocaust and Nazi regime: the bread truck breaks like a broken swastika (line 93), the KKK is compared to the Gestapo (line 98), and racial tension is apparent in the cashier's reaction as she places change in his hands (lines 125–28). Do students agree with Walcott that affliction is a universal theme, and is it appropriate to compare a situation like the Holocaust to colonial oppression? Do students enjoy or dislike Walcott's recycling of Western myths and history into a new Caribbean work?

    a. **Further Reading:** Breslin, Paul. *Nobody's Nation: Reading Derek Walcott.* Chicago: University of Chicago Press, 2001.

    b. **Suggested Search:** See the British Council entry on Derek Walcott at http://literature.britishcouncil.org/derek-walcott.

4. **Scholars have noted that Methodism and spirituality are important facets of Derek Walcott's work.** Nathaniel Gilbert III brought Methodism to the Caribbean in 1760, when he returned to his sugar plantation in Antigua. Walcott's mother was the head teacher at a Methodist school, though the Catholic majority population on the island undermined the Methodist community. In an interview with Edward Hirsch (see the Resources section), he speaks of a poet's ecstasy as (quoting Yeats) "a benediction, a transference, it's gratitude . . . the more of that a poet keeps, the more genuine his nature." Of Crusoe (see "Crusoe's Journal," 2457), Walcott explains that poets and writers are all Crusoes in the sense that they survey and possess islands and experience the despair of solitude ("time, that makes us objects, multiplies our natural loneliness," line 40, and "God's loneliness moves His smallest creatures," line 70). In "The Almond Trees," the poet appears as a castaway, unappreciated and unheeded by his larger community. Walcott denounced fellow black Caribbean writers, such as Brathwaite, for their self-pity and focus on healing from colonial oppression but, like them, rewrites some Western characters for Caribbean culture (Walcott's Philoctetes comes from the Greek figure, Brathwaite rewrites Uncle Tom, and Aime Cesaire refashions Caliban from Shakespeare's *The Tempest*). How is "Omeros" a work of benediction and transference?

    a. **Further Reading:** Thieme, John. *Derek Walcott.* New York: Manchester University Press, 1999.

    b. **Suggested Search:** Go to the Harvard course Wiki on Derek Walcott at https://coursewikis.fas.harvard.edu/aiu18/Derek_Walcott.

In-Class Activities

1. Understanding myth: Students will compare the Achilles of Homer's *The Iliad* to Derek Walcott's Achilles. Greek heroes displayed courage,

valor, and honor in battle and loyalty to their nation and their fellow warriors, and they sought glory. In Greek myth, Achilles (whose name means "grief of the people") was born of a nymph and Myrmidon; he was physically immortal except for a weakness in his heel, which was the only body part his mother Thetis had not dipped into the River Styx. Homer depicts Achilles as the greatest but also the most wrathful warrior, and he possessed superior armor fashioned by the god Hephaestus (described in *The Iliad*, Book 19, 478–608).

2. Responding to a literary lecture: Listen to and read about Derek Walcott's attack on V. S. Naipaul's writing at www.radioopensource.org/calabash-08-first-the-fireworks. What bone does Walcott pick with Naipaul's writing? If students were to interview Walcott on his criticisms, what questions would they ask?

3. Comparing literature: Daniel Defoe wrote *Robinson Crusoe* in 1719, a story in which a castaway initially on a slave expedition to Africa is shipwrecked on an island near Trinidad; recalled in the narrative are his experiences with the natives and with British mutineers who return him to Europe. In this activity, students will compare Derek Walcott's poem "Crusoe's Journal" (2457) to the Defoe original. (Note: If an original copy of *Crusoe* is not available, students might use the excerpt that prefaces Walcott's poem.)

Paper Topics/Suggestions for Writing

1. Discuss Derek Walcott's references to one of the following in the anthology poems: the Holocaust; Greek mythology; American history and politics.

2. Discuss the themes "forgetfulness" and "affliction" in Derek Walcott's poems.

3. Derek Walcott criticized his peers for wallowing too much in the sadness and self-pity they experienced as a result of colonial oppression and its aftereffects. Where in Walcott's poetry do you see evidence of a refusal to focus on this victimization? How did Walcott depict the colonial and postcolonial events that shaped his nation?

4. How is landscape used as a symbol in Derek Walcott's poetry? Provide at least four examples to support your argument.

5. Léopold Sédar Senghor and Derek Walcott both visited New York City and wrote of their experiences there. Discuss the poet's response to the metropolis in Senghor's "To New York" (2238) and Walcott's "North and South" (2464). How does each poet use style, content, and topography to describe his experiences?

Resources

"Derek Walcott." British Council on Literature. http://literature.britishcoun
cil.org/derek-walcott.
    This page offers a biography, bibliography, and criticism of Derek
    Walcott.
Hirsch, Edward. "Derek Walcott, The Art of Poetry No. 37." *Paris Review* 101
    (Winter 1986). www.theparisreview.org/interviews/2719/the-art-of-poetry
    -no-37-derek-walcott.
    Edward Hirsch interviews Derek Walcott on Saint Lucia in June 1985
    about Walcott's work habits, inspiration, and family background.
"The Nobel Prize in Literature 1992: Derek Walcott." The Official Web
    Site of the Nobel Prize. www.nobelprize.org/nobel_prizes/literature/lau
    reates/1992/walcott-bio.html#.
    This page features Derek Walcott's biography and lecture, as well as
    links to other Nobel Prize recipients.

Seamus Heaney

Topics for Lecture or Discussion

1. **Seamus Heaney created his mature work during the "Troubles" events that took place in Northern Ireland and affected England and parts of mainland Europe.** From the 1960s until 1998 (when the Belfast "Good Friday" Agreement was made), Protestant unionists and Catholic nationalists in Ireland arose as a result of the Protestant majority discriminating against the Catholic minority and the desire for independence from British rule in Northern Ireland with a reunited Irish Republic. In 1972, Heaney moved to Dublin, which at the time was perceived as sympathizing with the nationalist cause to create a unified Irish Republic. Like the Israeli poet Yehuda Amichai, Heaney sometimes uses myth and folklore from his region not for sacred purposes but, rather, to indicate a parallel with modern, mundane culture (e.g., "Punishment" compares Iron Age society to violence during the Troubles). Heaney combines ancient folklore and modern events in "The Strand at Lough Beg," written in memory of Heaney's cousin, Colum McCartney, who was killed in sectarian violence: like the pagan Irish king Sweeney, who killed a Christian monk and fled before the bloodied heads, Heaney imagines McCartney "leaving the white glow of filling stations" and fleeing for the same hills (lines 1–6). A personal mythology—of the family as agricultural laborers and shepherds—appears in the second stanza, in which it is suggested that McCartney, coming from a family where guns were used by hunting duck shooters (lines 17–19), and where the family "fought shy" and "could not crack the whip or seize the day" (lines 23–25), was a pacifist. In folk tradition, and to indicate a resurrection or commemoration, Heaney cleans his dead cousin's body, adorning it with scapulars that he fashions from the fresh rushes sprouting around the corpse (lines 43–44). Heaney has been criticized for a perceived neutrality to political instability in his country. Do you agree with this criticism based on the content in his poetry, and do you believe that a poet is obligated to take a political stance in his or her artwork?
   a. **Further Reading:** O'Driscoll, Dennis. *Stepping Stones: Interviews with Seamus Heaney.* New York: Farrar, Straus and Giroux, 2010.
   b. **Suggested Search:** Listen to Heaney's Nobel Prize acceptance speech at www.nobelprize.org/nobel_prizes/literature/laureates/1995/heaney -lecture.html.

2. **The Northern Irish landscape of Seamus Heaney's youth plays a central role in his poetry. Heaney's use of sound appears in the pronunciation of place-names and in the use of alliteration and assonance.** Alliteration creates movement and sensory evocation in

"Digging," in which the poet writes "spade sinks," "gravelly ground," "curt cuts" (lines 4, 26); the family tradition of agricultural labor, recalling his "roots," is continued ("living roots awaken in my head," line 27) through the writing of poetry and the digging of pen upon paper (lines 29–30). "Anahorish" represents not only a landscape description but also a kind of linguistic analysis of the place-name as a "soft gradient of consonant, vowel-meadow" (lines 7–8); in "Broagh," the place-name represents not only a riverbank but also the musicality produced by this word, making a "low tattoo" (drumbeat, line 10) and ending with the letters "gh," which "the strangers found difficult to manage" (lines 16–17). The poem "The Haw Lantern" is an unrhymed sonnet in free verse and represents a period of abstract symbolist writing: the "small people" refer not only to the Northern Irish but also to the poet as an individual who must speak out for justice ("wanting no more from them but that they keep the wick of self-respect from dying out," lines 3–4). "The Tollund Man" and "Punishment" recall oral folk and ballad forms, and words from the Anglo-Saxon (which Heaney studied in college and translated into modern English, including *Beowulf*). How does the theme "history and homeland" play a role in Heaney's modern poetry?

a. **Further Reading:** O'Donoghue, Bernard, ed. *The Cambridge Companion to Seamus Heaney*. Cambridge: Cambridge University Press, 2009.

b. **Suggested Search:** Watch Paul Muldoon's interview with Seamus Heaney at www.newyorker.com/online/blogs/festival/2008/10/history-and-hom.html.

3. **For Seamus Heaney, the Bog People and their resting places symbolize the untimely death and struggle associated with political turmoil and death in modern Northern Ireland.** Bog People, known also as Bog bodies, are corpses that have been naturally preserved by the environmental conditions in which they are buried (the acidic water preserves and darkens their skin and dissolves their bones). More than eighteen hundred Bog bodies have been discovered in Northern Europe, are usually dated to the Iron Age, and generally show signs of ritual sacrifice or execution. The Tollund Man was discovered in 1950 in what was ancient Scandinavia (fourth century B.C.E.); a noose around the body's neck and special vegetable-seed soup discovered in his bowels indicated that the man was killed as part of a ritual sacrifice, punishment, or some other special purpose. Heaney had seen photographs of the Tollund Man, and in his poem "The Tollund Man" he accurately describes the corpse and its intestinal contents (lines 7–8) and suggests that he has been ritually sacrificed ("Bridegroom to the goddess," line 12). He associates the Tollund Man's martyrdom for the turf-cutters with the execution of "four young brothers" (lines 5–12) who represent

Irish nationalist brothers killed in the 1920s. Why does the speaker feel "lost, unhappy and at home" (line 24), and how do readers make sense of these contradictory words ("lost"/"at home")?

  a. **Further Reading:** Coles, Byrony. *People of the Wetlands: Bogs, Bodies and Lake-Dwellers.* London: Thames and Hudson, 1989.

  b. **Suggested Search:** See images and background on the Tollund Man at www.pbs.org/wgbh/nova/ancient/tolland-man.html.

4. **Seamus Heaney's preoccupation with the Bog People, particularly with the sexualized female corpse in "Punishment," bears resemblance to Edgar Allan Poe's necrophilia writings but offers a compellingly different view of death than in Charles Baudelaire's "A Carcass."** In "A Carcass" (Volume 2, 1045), Baudelaire describes a morning walk with his beloved, during which they discover a putrid carcass that is sexually reclined "like a lecherous whore" (line 5) being penetrated and revived by flies and maggots, and ravaged by a dog (lines 17–20, 32–35). In grotesque manner, Baudelaire uses the decaying body to introduce the inevitability of his beloved's death, whose memory he will valorize and immortalize in poetry. Heaney paints the drowned adulteress's body in all its ugliness ("frail rigging of her ribs," "shaved head like a stubble of black corn," lines 7, 17–18) but does not desubjectivize the female body as Baudelaire does in his poem; instead, the body is honored, and its noose becomes the wedding ring that stores "the memories of love" (lines 21–22; she has been drowned because of her adultery). Heaney revives the corpse through a description of her beauty prior to death ("you were flaxen-haired, undernourished," lines 25–26); rather than use the dead body to sublimate a real, living woman, he uses it as a means to judge himself (I "would have cast, I know, the stones of silence" and "would understand the exact and tribal, intimate event," lines 29–30, 40–42). Ask students to read Baudelaire's "A Carcass" and Robert Browning's "Porphyria's Lover" (Volume 2). How are death, female sexuality, and male desire treated in these two works and in Heaney's work? What does this tell us about changes in aesthetics and perception from the late romantic period (Baudelaire) to the Victorian period (Browning) to the modern (Heaney) period?

  a. **Further Reading:** Haffenden, John. "Seamus Heaney and the Feminine Sensibility." *Yearbook of English Studies* 17 (1987): 89–116.

  b. **Suggested Search:** See the Robert Browning "gender matters" entry on the Victorian Web at www.victorianweb.org/authors/rb/index.html.

In-Class Activities

1. Interviewing an author: Students will first watch Paul Muldoon's interview with Seamus Heaney (see the Resources section). In groups, students will choose themes for an interview they might hold with

Heaney and then create a set of questions that might be asked during that interview. The purpose of this activity is to get students thinking about how to conduct successful interviews and to draw out information on particular themes, structures, and styles from an artist's work.

2. Irish mythology and folklore lesson: Students will be placed in groups to research the landscape, myth, and traditions of Northern Ireland (including place-names, burial rites, and early agricultural life). Each group will present its findings to expand its appreciation of Seamus Heaney's cultural background.

Paper Topics/Suggestions for Writing

1. What is the poet's reaction to the woman stoned for adultery in "Punishment," and how does he use language and structure to express his response?

2. Discuss the elements of local landscape and folklore as parallels to modern warfare and the Troubles in "The Strand at Lough Beg."

3. Interpret the metaphor of the fish in "The Guttural Muse," using examples from the poem to support your analysis.

4. "The Haw Lantern" is not a traditional sonnet in content or form. Analyze the sonnet, making sure to include a discussion about how this poem differs from traditional sonnets in content and form.

Resources

"History and Homeland." Interview with Seamus Heaney. New Yorker Festival, October 15, 2008. www.newyorker.com/online/blogs/festival/2008/10/history-and-hom.html.
>   Paul Muldoon interviews Seamus Heaney on the theme of "history and homeland" during the New Yorker Festival.

National Portrait Gallery of London. www.npg.org.uk/collections/search/person/mp05395/seamus-justin-heaney.
>   This page includes twenty-two portraits of Seamus Heaney by various artists.

"The Nobel Prize in Literature 1995: Seamus Heaney." The Official Web Site of the Nobel Prize. www.nobelprize.org/nobel_prizes/literature/laureates/1995/heaney-lecture.html.
>   This page features an audio recording of Seamus Heaney's Nobel lecture.

Seamus Heaney: Collected Poems. RTÉ and Lannan Foundation, 2009, CD.
>   This boxed set comprises fifteen CDs of Seamus Heaney reading his collected works, with 556 tracks and a fifty-eight-page essay about Heaney by Peter Sirr.

INGEBORG BACHMANN

The Barking

Topics for Lecture or Discussion

1. **Ingeborg Bachmann conceived of a literary cycle called *Ways of Death* that would present a world in which characters reappeared and moved between different novels and stories.** This sort of approach to writing fiction was most famously attempted by Honoré de Balzac, though it is also evident in the works of writers like Anthony Trollope and William Faulkner. For *The Barking*, knowledge of other stories and the world surrounding Frau Jordan and Franziska can be helpful, but is not necessary for understanding the story. For example, by the end of *The Barking*, the reader is told that both Franziska and Frau Jordan have died, though the story does not say how they died. In fact, the ways that they die are not important, for the story emphasizes simply that death is the bleak result of the corrupt and tyrannical behavior of Dr. Jordan. Yet we do learn elsewhere in *The Franza Case* that Franziska died due to her emotional collapse after separating from Dr. Jordan and then being raped by a group of strangers in Egypt.
   a. **Further Reading:** Achberger, Karen. "Three Paths to the Lake." In *Understanding Ingeborg Bachmann*, 143–172. Columbia, SC: University of South Carolina Press, 1995.
   b. **Suggested Search:** A YouTube search for "Interview with Elfriede Jelinek (on Ingeborg Bachmann)" results in an interesting interview about Bachmann's work.

2. **The Barking is, in part, a story of discovery and growth in self-knowledge.** Both Frau Jordan and Franziska make gradual discoveries about themselves and each other as they have their conversations. Franziska also has important realizations about Leo Jordan; in fact, it is important that as Franziska comes to understand more about her relationship with Leo, she also grows in self-knowledge. Frau Jordan, on the other hand, refuses to truly consider or reflect upon the truths that the women approach in their conversations, and she consequently does not make the same deep discoveries about herself that Franziska does. Precisely because she is his mother, the barking that Frau Jordan imagines might be understood as a defensive mechanism that distracts her from facing the reality that her son is a brute.
   a. **Further Reading:** McMurtry, Aine. *Crisis and Form in the Later Writing of Ingeborg Bachmann.* London: Modern Humanities Research Association, 2012.

b. **Suggested Search:** A Google search for the "Ingeborg Bachmann Center" results in the webpage for the Center at the University of London. The page includes a variety of links and podcasts that examine Austrian literature, including Ingeborg Bachmann's works.

3. **While the primary characters in *The Barking* are Frau Jordan and Franziska, the looming figure of Leo Jordan in all of their conversations reflects the degree to which their lives are dominated by this man.** When Franziska first starts visiting Frau Jordan, the two women talk exhaustively of the famous doctor: "The old woman and Franziska talked almost exclusively about Leo, because he was the only productive topic the two of them had" (2499). Though Leo exists only in the background at this point, he still dominates the conversation of the women, and when the reader is told that "after a while the topic 'the good son' had been exhausted and Franziska repeatedly steered the conversation to the old woman herself" (2500), nevertheless, the topics eventually reverted to, or touched upon, Leo.

   a. **Further Reading:** Boa, Elizabeth. "Reading Ingeborg Bachmann." *Postwar Women's Writing in German*, edited by Chris Weedon, 269–289. Providence, RI: Berghahn Books, 1997.

   b. **Suggested Search:** A search on JSTOR (www.jstor.org) for "Ingeborg Bachmann" results in several helpful articles.

4. **In *The Barking*, Bachmann utilizes indirect discourse and a partial stream of consciousness narrative style to offer a more psychological account that also obscures certain details.** The conversations that take place between Frau Jordan and Franziska are almost entirely recounted as indirect discourse (that is, we are not told exactly what is said with quotation marks separating the statements, but instead we are told about what is said). Similarly, some of Franziska's thought is presented in a partial stream of consciousness: for example, "On the way home she made one detour after the other, in a state of inner turmoil, this poor woman shouldn't sell her brooch while she and Leo spent money freely, went on trips, entertained. She kept debating what she should say to Leo, but a first, faint alarm sounded inside her, because even though the old woman had her quirks and exaggerated things, she must be right about something, and so in the end she didn't say a word about it at home and only reported cheerfully that his mother was doing very well" (2503). Both of these aspects of Bachmann's narrative style contribute to a sense of the narrator's emotional distance from the events, and while it gives readers important clues for understanding Franziska's relationship with her husband, it does not offer a direct characterization of any person in the story.

   a. **Further Reading:** Mahrdt, Helgard, and Jeanette Clausen. "'Society Is the Biggest Murder Scene of All': On the Private and Public

Spheres in Ingeborg Bachmann's Prose." *Women in German Year-book* 12 (1996): 167–187.

b. **Suggested Search:** A Google Images search for "Ingeborg Bach-mann" results in several pictures of the author, including one of her with Paul Celan.

In-Class Activities

1. Hold a class discussion in which you analyze the different moments when Frau Jordan begins to hear barking. What is the barking associ-ated with?

2. Ask your students to find and bring to class a poem by Bachmann that can be fruitfully compared with *The Barking*.

3. Ask each student to write a journal entry in which they consider Bach-mann's claims about fascism and relationships between men and women.

Paper Topics/Suggestions for Writing

1. What is the significance of the title of *The Barking*? Is there particular symbolism associated with barking, dogs, and animals?

2. Write an essay in which you explain the gradual revelations or realiza-tions that Franziska has over the course of the story. What is the earli-est point at which her attitude toward Leo changes?

3. Write a character analysis of Leo Jordan. What details about his char-acter are revealed to the reader? Why is he intimidating to his mother?

4. How does the narrative style contribute to the tone and moral attitude of *The Barking*? How does it affect the reader's response to the charac-ters and their situations?

5. Write an essay in which you compare *The Barking* to Leslie Marmon Silko's *Yellow Woman*. Be sure to address the relationships between men and women in both stories.

Resources

Achberger, Karen. *Understanding Ingeborg Bachmann*. Columbia, SC: Uni-versity of South Carolina Press, 1995.

This volume is an excellent introduction to Bachmann's work, and it includes analysis of her poetry, prose, and a helpful annotated bibliography.

Bachmann, Ingeborg. *The Book of Franza & Requiem for Fanny Goldmann*. Trans. Peter Filkins. Chicago: Northwestern University Press, 1999.

Students and instructors who wish to read more of the work from which *The Barking* is taken can turn to this volume.

Bachmann, Ingeborg. *Darkness Spoken: Collected Poems of Ingeborg Bachmann.* Trans. Peter Filkins. Brookline, MA: Zephyr Press, 2005.

Well-known for her poetry as well as prose, this volume is recommended, and has facing pages of the original German and the English translation.

Lennox, Sarah. *Cemetery of the Murdered Daughters: Feminism, History, and Ingeborg Bachmann.* Boston: University of Massachusetts Press, 2006.

This volume analyzes Bachmann's writing from a feminist perspective, and argues that Bachmann did not just see women as victims.

GABRIEL GARCÍA MÁRQUEZ
Death Constant Beyond Love

Topics for Lecture or Discussion

1. **Magical realism as a genre blends fantasy, myth, and the paranormal with reality and actuality.** Laws of physics, the facts associated with historical events, and our understanding of the observable universe are challenged in this genre, which twists or invades the real world to create an extraordinary yet plausible situation. The term "magical realism" was used in its current sense in 1955 as a form of "uncanny realism" and originated in Latin America. Characteristics of the genre include plentitude (embellishment or use of the fanciful), hybridity (blending time periods or constellatory realities), metafiction (the reader and text directly enter each other's worlds), and unreliable narrator (the narrator withholds or does not justify events or characters' viewpoints). In Gabriel García Márquez's story, word substitutes mark plentitude: "sweat" is called "soup," the only real rose present in the city is named "Rosal del Virrey" (Rosebush of the Viceroy), brought in and worn by Senator Sanchez, and the "fixed term" refers to death rather than to a senatorial term (2511). Students will note the implausibility of the scene in which Senator Sanchez fashions a paper butterfly that flies out of the room, unfolds, and becomes permanently plastered to the wall (2514).

   a. **Further Reading:** Schroeder, Shannin. *Rediscovering Magical Realism in the Americas.* New York: Praeger, 2004.

   b. **Suggested Search:** *Lo Magia de lo Real* (see the Resources section).

2. **Gabriel García Márquez initially worked as a journalist, largely influenced by his grandfather's political views.** His grandfather had protested the banana massacres that took place in 1927 (the United Fruit Company demanded better working conditions, and the Columbian army opened fire on the strikers and their families just after Sunday mass, its leader arguing that it had attacked to prevent the foreign United States from invading to protect its own interests) and had been a liberal veteran of the Thousand Days' War (based not only on falling coffee prices but also on liberals' contention that conservatives, then in rule, were using fraudulent methods to win elections; the United States also threatened involvement in this war due to its interests in the Panama Canal). Márquez later commented in interviews that his grandfather's tales of the civil war and its horrors shaped his storytelling process as a socialist and anti-imperialist. Márquez also became a member of the Barranquilla Group, a collective of writers and philoso-

phers in Colombia fictionalized as the "four friends" in Márquez's *One Hundred Years of Solitude*. In "Death Constant Beyond Love," Márquez treats political corruption (going through the motions and illusions necessary to achieve reelection) and a character's denial of his impending death by engaging in love affairs and going through the motions of reelection in order to avoid the preparation and acceptance of dying. This is a recurrent theme in other works, including *Love in the Time of Cholera*.

  a. **Further Reading:** Gerald, Martin. *Gabriel Garcia Márquez: A Life*. London: Bloomsbury, 2008.

  b. **Suggested Search:** Go to the Nobel Prize website and read Gabriel García Márquez's Nobel lecture, "The Solitude of Latin America," at www.nobelprize.org/nobel_prizes/literature/laureates/1982 /Márquez-lecture.html.

3. **In an interview with Raymond Leslie Williams, Gabriel García Márquez states that, in his writing, he needs "everything idealized" (131).** Like Faulkner, Márquez is interested in representing subjective experience and using stream-of-consciousness techniques that reveal interior thoughts and feelings. Nelson Farina is an unreliable narrator, and readers will find this in his observation of the speech from his hammock— through his lens, Farina's background as a murderer and his view of the speech from the "back side of the farce" blend two time periods and two simultaneous perspectives of the senator's speech. The senator also creates an illusory farce with promises of rainmaking machines and other devices that will improve the agriculture and industry of the small town ("When he saw that his fictional world was all set up, he pointed to it. . . . An ocean liner made of painted paper," 2512). What does the paper ocean liner, which is superimposed on a decaying cardboard "artificial city," represent in the context of a politician making empty promises in a dusty town? What is being idealized in this story—death, the characters, love, a sense of hope, or something else? Students should make note of the senator's statement that there will be nothing for politicians to do in the dusty town once real improvements are made (2514).

  a. **Further Reading:** Williams, Raymond Leslie. "The Visual Arts, the Poetization of Space and Writing: An Interview with Gabriel García Márquez." *PMLA* 104:2 (1989): 131–40.

  b. **Suggested Search:** Read Peter H. Stone's interview with Márquez at www.theparisreview.org/interviews/3196/the-art-of-fiction-no-69 -gabriel-garcia-marquez.

In-Class Activities

1. Understanding magical realism: In this activity, students will first identify the elements of magical realism. Next they will be divided into

small groups, and each group will brainstorm (or compose) a short story in this genre, based on the historical events, culture, and myth of its locality.

2. Understanding metafiction: In this activity, readers will now become writers who interrupt and contribute to Gabriel García Márquez's narrative by developing a metafiction in which they expand Nelson Farina's and Laura Farina's stories or add a section in which the senator's wife appears and confronts his love affair.

Paper Topics/Suggestions for Writing

1. Define plentitude and hybridity, and discuss their role in Gabriel García Márquez's story.

2. Discuss the theme of solitude in the story, paying particular attention to the senator and Nelson Farina.

3. Analyze the important dichotomy between nature and artifice in the story, including a discussion of unreliable narrator.

Resources

Lo Magia de lo Real. Films for the Humanities. Prod. Harold Mantell. Applause Video, 1982. In Spanish and English.
   This film includes conversations recorded with Gabriel García Márquez that examine his life, influences on his narrative style, and inspirations for his plots and characters.
Márquez: Tales beyond Solitude. Prod. Holly Aylett. Homevision, 2000, VHS.
   In this documentary, Gabriel García Márquez speaks about his role in Latin American cinema and his storytelling talents.
"The Nobel Prize in Literature 1982: Gabriel García Márquez." The Official Web Site of the Nobel Prize. www.nobelprize.org/nobel_prizes/literature/laureates/1982.
   This page contains Gabriel García Márquez's biography and speech, a bibliography, a photo gallery, and resources, as well as links to other Nobel Prize winners.
Stone, Peter H. "Gabriel Garcia Marquez, The Art of Fiction No. 69." *Paris Review* 82 (Winter 1981). www.theparisreview.org/interviews/3196/the-art-of-fiction-no-69-gabriel-garcia-marquez.
   This interview covers Marquez's writing style, literary influences, and experiences lecturing abroad.

V. S. Naipaul

One Out of Many

Topics for Lecture or Discussion

1. **V. S. Naipaul has been criticized for his controversial views on postcolonial countries and their governments and cultures, often by displaying a nostalgia for colonial times.** Born in Trinidad and Tobago to Indian parents and a family of writers, Naipaul's controversial life and apolitical views (in his Nobel lecture, he says that "to have a political view is to be prejudiced") have inspired critics, including Salman Rushdie, a fellow Nobel laureate, to denounce Naipaul as a Fascist and misogynist (he has commented that women's writing is inferior and banal). Naipaul developed a love-hate relationship with his family—his father was a struggling and depressed journalist, and his mother and grandmother were domineering and distanced themselves from his father. Nostalgia presents in the opening scene of the story, where the protagonist laments that his employer has been promoted, which may lead to Santosh being fired and sent back to his wife and children in the village and end his ideal life as a man who "lives in the street," sleeps on the pavement, and shares the clay pipe with homeless friends (2518–19). After living in America, Santosh becomes nostalgic for Bombay and the "happy times," however, he does not want to return (2530). Through Priya, readers sense an urgency to retain one's heritage; the two characters reenact their home cultures by together moving into Priya's cubby and working in an Indian restaurant where non-Indians are dressed in Indian garb (2531–33). As Santosh becomes more Indian again, he loses his looks and health ("My face had become pudgy and sallow," 2534) and reverts to calling his equal friend "sahib" ("owner," "proprietor"). Is Santosh able to escape his native identity and redefine his life, or does he simply reinvent his original life in American terms?
   a. **Further Reading:** French, Patrick. *The World Is What It Is: The Authorized Biography of V. S. Naipaul.* New York: Random House, 2008.
   b. **Suggested Search:** Listen to V. S. Naipaul's Nobel lecture at www .nobelprize.org/nobel_prizes/literature/laureates/2001/naipaul-lec ture.html.

2. **V. S. Naipaul's work is compared to Joseph Conrad's writing because of the political and psychological reactions to exile, colonization, and violence that permeate his work.** As a travel writer, Naipaul used observations from his travels as the basis for his fiction. "One Out of Many" is atypical for Naipaul, who sets the story in the

United States. The first-person narrative is an immigration story that deals with racial tensions and discrimination associated with cultural assimilation as Santosh, the protagonist, meets *hubshi*, a pejorative Hindi term for an African American. Psychologically, Santosh cannot cope with the adjustment to Western living—he refers to the airplane bathroom as the "hissing room at the back" (2520), does not understand the rules of purchasing alcohol on a plane ("That took me by surprise. I had no money, only a few rupees," 2520), and collects condiments as if they are religious artifacts ("I had been collecting them throughout the journey," 2521). He is willing to sleep in a cubby, viewing it as an upgrade from his living accommodations in Bombay rather than as an insult by the government (2523). His perception of the *hubshi* woman is both as Kali, the Indian goddess of death and destruction, and as a grossly obese, lower-class black woman (2537). Naipaul's character responds to life in America as both an "imprisonment" and a "freedom." Which of these two qualities seems to better define his perception of his new life by the story's end?

a. **Further Reading:** Hayward, Helen. *The Enigma of V. S. Naipaul: Sources and Contexts*. New York: Macmillan, 2002.

b. **Suggested Search:** Go to the Emory Postcolonial Studies Project entry on V. S. Naipaul at www.english.emory.edu/Bahri/Naipaul .html.

3. **The Indian social caste practice affects Santosh's perception of social hierarchy in the United States, even among the assimilated Indians.** The narrator notes a "disturbing thought" as he observes the "half-caste appearance of the dancers," based on either their poor pronunciation of Sanskrit or their dialect; he imagines that they have forgotten their roots due to being enslaved like the blacks or becoming nomadic like the gypsies (2524). Santosh is mortified to discover that his status has been diminished further as a result of traveling to the land of dreams—he is now an indentured servant who is working off the cost of his airline ticket, a "prisoner" who has spent half of his advance on morning breakfast and a movie (2525). The *hubshis* are described as a militant people who work as guardsmen, represent the blue-collar workers carrying parcels and groceries for others, and are unwelcoming of others in their community. Santosh's impressions of social hierarchy are further formed by the commercials he watches on television than by the observable world ("If by some chance I saw an American on the street I tried to fit him or her into the commercials . . . as people not quite real," 2526). His first exposure to English language is through an African American cashier and, later, a black maid, both of whom like his scent and teach him to distrust law enforcement. He is slowly drawn into the American obsession with appearance and com-

modities—he becomes desirable to the *hubshi* women, with whom it is "indecent and wrong for a man of our blood to embrace," solely because he has marijuana to sell them (2526–27, 2529). What do the *hubshis* represent for Santosh by the story's end—imprisonment and degradation, or freedom and enlightenment?

    a. **Further Reading:** Said, Edward. *Intellectuals in the Post-Colonial World*. New York: Salmagundi, 1986.

    b. **Suggested Search:** Watch V. S. Naipaul read from his novel *Half a Life* at www.c-spanvideo.org/program/Half.

In-Class Activities

1. Critical response: In this activity, each student will write a letter from the perspective of Santosh's wife and children, who still live in India and have been made aware that Santosh has married a *hubshi* woman to acquire U.S. citizenship. The letters are shared anonymously so that students will appreciate the complex views developed in relation to identity, assimilation, and immigration.

2. Revising an ending: In this activity, students will pretend that Santosh is deported to Bombay. How does he react when reintroduced to his native culture? Students will share their alternate endings and determine how the story's theme and reader appreciation change according to these modified versions.

3. Critical response: Critics, including other postcolonial writers, have accused V. S. Naipaul of having controversial responses to postcolonial culture. In this activity, students will first discuss Naipaul's approach to postcolonial issues as represented in "One Out of Many." Next, each student will compose a letter of response to a critic who has evaluated Naipaul's works as being contradictory, inconsistent, or misogynistic; the letter can be one of consensus or disagreement.

Paper Topics/Suggestions for Writing

1. Explain the original meaning of "One Out of Many" (*E pluribus unum*, a phrase on the official seal of the United States) and its significance as a title and theme in V. S. Naipaul's short story.

2. Discuss the role of urban life in V. S. Naipaul's short story.

3. Compare Santosh's transformation to that experienced by Gregor Samsa in Kafka's *Metamorphosis*. How do work ethic and loyalty to one's family (or owner) contribute to the characters' identity and deformity?

4. Compare Santosh's statement that "far from gaining my freedom, I had begun to accept death not as the end but as the goal" (2536) to the

senator's radical acceptance of his impending death in Gabriel García Márquez's "Death Constant Beyond Love" (2509).

5. Santosh might be compared to Siddhartha, who became a great Buddha by renouncing life—he became enlightened (freed) by eliminating expectations (translated often as "desire"), which led to suffering. Do you believe that by the story's end Santosh is enlightened? Has he truly renounced life and eliminated all desires, or does he maintain his identity under the guise of a married American citizen? Use evidence from the story to support your argument.

6. Does the story have a happy ending? Use examples to support your argument.

Resources

Emory University English Department. Post Colonial Studies Project. www .english.emory.edu/Bahri/Naipaul.html.

> This entry on V. S. Naipaul includes a biography, a bibliography, and related themes and links.

Half a Life. October 29, 2001. C-Span Video Library. www.c-spanvideo.org /program/Half.

> In this video, V. S. Naipaul reads from his book *Half a Life*.

The Mystic Masseur. Dir. Ismail Merchant. Merchant Ivory Productions, 2001.

> This film, based on V. S. Naipaul's work by the same title, is a comedy set in Trinidad about a masseur who cures illness and later becomes a colonial politician.

"The Nobel Prize in Literature 2001: V. S. Naipaul." The Official Web Site of the Nobel Prize. www.nobelprize.org/nobel_prizes/literature/laure ates/2001/naipaul-lecture.html.

> Sir V. S. Naipaul delivers this lecture at the Swedish Academy in 2001.

LESLIE MARMON SILKO

Yellow Woman

Topics for Lecture or Discussion

1. **The short story emphasizes female sexual desire as a topic of fiction.** From the opening line—"My thigh clung to his with dampness" (2542)—Leslie Marmon Silko focuses graphically on the unnamed protagonist's blend of physical desire and uncertainty about Silva. The protagonist both mysteriously desires Silva and wants to leave and return home. Where in some of the original versions of the story, Yellow Woman is unambiguously abducted and/or raped by a spirit attacker, Silko makes it quite clear that to the extent Silva has power over her, it is more through his influence on her mind rather than his physical threat. At the same time, in the story it is ambiguous whether this influence is the familiar material of human love and lust, or something more mysterious emanating from the power of the myth she seems to find herself enacting. As the story progresses, the sexual encounters become more forcible and frightening. Silko's story suggests that myth has its roots in the most intimate of human realities; it also asks us to see our reality as always potentially mythic. Silko has argued against seeing her story as being about a woman striking out for freedom from social norms; instead, she says, the story is about "this attraction, this passion, this connection between the human world and the animal and spirit worlds" (*Conversations with Leslie Marmon Silko*, 77).

   a. **Further Reading:** Arnold, Ellen L., ed. *Conversations with Leslie Marmon Silko.* Jackson: University Press of Mississippi, 2000.

   b. **Suggested Search:** Search for Leslie Marmon Silko's essay "Yellow Woman and A Beauty of the Spirit," initially published in the *Los Angeles Times*.

2. **The short story is an adaptation of traditional Laguna Pueblo stories and mythology.** "Yellow Woman" is a recurring figure in Laguna oral tradition; oral versions of Yellow Woman abduction stories were recorded in the 1920s by the anthropologists Franz Boas and Ruth Benedict. The stories vary greatly in their details. The Yellow Woman of myth and religion "represents all women," according to Leslie Marmon Silko, and in many versions of abduction stories she returns home pregnant with a child from her captor. Silko mentions Yellow Woman stories in this short story both as abductions and seductions; at times the protagonist thinks of her grandfather's stories as being about Yellow Woman, "[s]tolen by a ka'tsina" away from her home (2546); at another point she recalls a favorite story in which the male figures (Badger and Coyote) are

away from home and find a woman in a mysterious house (2543). Yellow Woman is both victim and seductress, mysterious being away from normal life and the representative of normal life snatched away into a different realm. Silko's story deliberately incorporates visions of the myth that it does not represent in its main plot. How does this foregrounding of alternatives change our interpretation of Silko's version of the story?

   a. **Further Reading:** Allen, Paula Gunn, ed. *Spider Woman's Granddaughters: Traditional Tales and Contemporary Writing by Native American Women.* Boston, MA: Beacon Press, 1989.

   b. **Suggested Search:** Search the JSTOR database at jstor.org for "Silko's Originality in *Yellow Woman*" by Peter G. Beidler, which contains the results of a class exercise requiring students to compare the story to one of the old myths.

3. **Leslie Marmon Silko emphasizes the incongruity of the world of highways and nature coexisting.** After the protagonist follows Silva, she thinks of Yellow Woman: "she is from out of time past and I live now and I've been to school and there are highways and pickup trucks that Yellow Woman never saw" (2544). Yet it is not just the physical signs of human presence that the protagonist envisions as inimical to the myth; it is the people themselves: "I will see someone, and then I will be certain that he is only a man" (2544). The natural world into which she and Silva venture is opposed not just to trucks and modernity but is estranged from human existence more broadly, and the vitality of the myth is dependent on the isolation of their encounter—on the protagonist not thinking about her husband and family. Yet the roles of Yellow Woman and the ka'tsina spirit are deeply ingrained in Laguna Pueblo society, and, as Silko herself says, Yellow Woman crosses the boundaries to the spirit world "in order to save the Pueblo" ("Yellow Woman and A Beauty of the Spirit"). Does this story allow any room for the mythological dimensions of its action to impact on or connect with the reality to which the narrator returns at the conclusion?

   a. **Further Reading:** Sando, Joe S. *Pueblo Nations: Eight Centuries of Pueblo Indian History.* Santa Fe, NM: Clear Light, 1992.

   b. **Suggested Search:** Conduct a Google Images search for "Lee Marmon," a photographer and the father of Leslie Marmon Silko, who has created many famous images of Laguna Pueblo and its inhabitants.

4. **The outside world has a political dimension in this story.** Silva declares explicitly that he steals from the Texan and Mexican cattle ranchers near the reservations, which the protagonist sees as part of the human rather than the supernatural world: "I didn't believe that there were highways or railroads or cattle to steal" (2546), she thinks,

after waking up in the isolated house. But Leslie Marmon Silko's work more broadly suggests connections between ancient myths and the modern crises of the Native American political situation. Her epic second novel, *Almanac of the Dead* (1991), centers around a vision of Tucson, Arizona, as a decadent, corrupt metropolis; full of violence and sexual cruelty, the novel portrays Euro-American society heading toward apocalyptic self-destruction and revolution, prophesied in the novel by various native mythologies. When the protagonist in the story leaves Silva during his confrontation with the rancher, she sees "something ancient and dark" in his eyes. It remains an open question whether the confrontation between white and native people, with all the strife and historical context it implies, is in this story part of the ordinary human world or worked into a new myth of Yellow Woman.

   a. **Further Reading:** Silko, Leslie Marmon. *Almanac of the Dead*. New York: Simon & Schuster, 1991.

   b. **Suggested Search:** Search the JSTOR database at jstor.org for Adam Sol's article "The Story as It's Told: Prodigious Revisions in Leslie Marmon Silko's *Almanac of the Dead*."

5. **The history of interpretation of stories like this one is in part a history of feminist literary criticism.** Paula Gunn Allen's 1986 book *The Sacred Hoop* made the provocative claim that "gynocracy"—society organized by the authority of women—was the major form of tribal social organization throughout North America before encounters with Europeans. This claim has since been vigorously disputed, and certainly does not apply to all the societies to which Allen attempted to attribute it, but initially it was tremendously influential; critics and students and Native American literature and culture found allies in feminism, and texts like Leslie Marmon Silko's became important feminist objects of analysis. It also had a particular relevance and strength in those tribes that did follow matrilineal or matrifocal social organizations. The Laguna Pueblo people, to which both Silko and Allen belong, are matrilineal. Yet although this short story represents its female protagonist striking out away from her home and family, it does not focus on *her* power, and the gender differences between Silva and her are strongly marked. Does this story offer a vision that frustrates or reinforces the gender roles of modern America—or of Laguna Pueblo?

   a. **Further Reading:** Allen, Paula Gunn. *The Sacred Hoop: Recovering the Feminine in American Indian Traditions*. Boston, MA: Beacon Press, 1986.

   b. **Suggested Search:** Search the JSTOR database at jstor.org for the article "Yellow Women and Leslie Marmon Silko's Feminism" by Louise Barnett.

In-Class Activities

1. Have students read Leslie Marmon Silko's essay "Yellow Woman and a Beauty of the Spirit." Ask them to compare and contrast the versions of Yellow Woman in the story and in the essay.

2. Ask students to underline all the noun phrases in the story used to refer to Silva and the narrator (e.g., "he," "I," "Yellow Woman," "ka'tsina," "Silva"). Discuss when and how the different words and phrases appear.

3. Have students read one of the other versions of the story in *Spider Woman's Granddaughters*. Ask them to compare and contrast the old myths with Leslie Marmon Silko's version.

Paper Topics/Suggestions for Writing

1. "I never heard anyone talk about 'women's work' until after I left Laguna for college" ("Yellow Woman and A Beauty of the Spirit"). How does the presentation of gender in the story compare to Leslie Marmon Silko's assertion that gender distinctions are relatively unmarked in Laguna Pueblo culture?

2. "It's stories that make this a community" (*Conversations with Leslie Marmon Silko*, 12). How does the short story seem to reflect—or to reject—the process of community building?

3. "Native Americans acknowledge no borders; they seek nothing less than the return of all tribal lands" (Silko, *Almanac of the Dead*, 15). Discuss the relationship between myth and history in this story.

4. "Someday they will talk about us, and they will say, 'Those two lived long ago when things like that happened'" (2545). Discuss the relationship between the past, present, and future in the story.

5. "Many Yellow Woman tales highlight her alienation from the people" (Allen, *The Sacred Hoop*, 227). How does the possibility of alienation appear in this story?

Resources

Barnett, Louise K., and James L. Thorson, eds. *Leslie Marmon Silko: A Collection of Critical Essays*. Albuquerque: University of New Mexico Press, 1999.

> This essay collection surveys and introduces Leslie Marmon Silko's major works.

Porter, Joy, and Kenneth M. Roemer, eds. *Cambridge Companion to Native American Literature*. Cambridge: Cambridge University Press, 2005.

This book provides a good general background on Native American literary studies and includes a chapter surveying Leslie Marmon Silko.

Silko, Leslie Marmon. *Ceremony*. New York: Viking Penguin, 1977.

Leslie Marmon Silko's first novel is still her most famous, juxtaposing Native American culture and mythology with the situation of a returning Vietnam War veteran.

NGUGI WA THIONG'O
Wedding at the Cross

Topics for Lecture or Discussion

1. **"Wedding at the Cross" is one of the final works Ngugi wa Thiong'o wrote in English before turning entirely to writing in Gikuyu, arguing that in order to "decolonize the mind" African writers had to write in indigenous African languages.** "Wedding at the Cross" was written shortly before an important moment of literary revolution in Ngugi's career. In the late 1970s, Ngugi turned away from English as a writing language, arguing in *Decolonising the Mind* that African writers should write in African languages. (The Gikuyu audience he sought to affect with his writing could speak, but not read, English.) The short story itself is an anatomy of the ways in which the "colonization of the mind" works—Wariuki's humiliating experience with Douglas Jones leads him not to rebel against the values of the British but to attempt to succeed according to their terms: to succeed by fighting for the British, by cooperating with them, by adopting their religion, and, most prominently, by taking their language for his own name, becoming Dodge W. Livingstone. Ngugi suggests in this story that the mental impact of colonization leads to a fundamental change in the self—when the protagonist becomes Livingstone, he "cast[s] away Wariuki" (2556). At the climax, Miriamu pronounces that Wariuki "is dead" (2560). Ngugi's own life reverses the name change at the center of the story: his initial works were published under the Anglicized name "James Ngugi"; only in the late 1970s did he insist on being published and known as "Ngugi wa Thiong'o."

   a. **Further Reading:** Ngugi wa Thiong'o. *Decolonising the Mind: The Politics of Language in African Literature*. London: James Currey, 1986.

   b. **Suggested Search:** Search for Ngugi wa Thiong'o's article "The Language of African Literature" in the *New Left Review*, 1985 (an early version of one chapter of *Decolonising the Mind* that focuses on the historical background of the suppression of native languages).

2. **"Wedding at the Cross" is part historical fiction, telling a story that begins decades before the moment of its writing and publication.** The short story begins in the period before World War II and covers the years through the war, the Mau Mau Uprising, uhuru (independence, in 1963), and beyond. In part, the story of the marriage of Miriamu and Wariuki is also the story of Kenyan history in the mid-twentieth cen-

tury. The mental effects of colonialism are not just a singular fact but also a historical process: Wariuki's mind is slowly shaped by the different experiences he has in different periods of time. Though the story constantly returns to his driving motive—the memory of his interview with Douglas Jones—the elements of his character change come from specific historical moments: World War II allows him to feel like an ally of the British; Mau Mau becomes a reason to resent the struggles of his fellow impoverished Kenyans; and Christianity steps in at a moment when he is grateful not to be accused of being a collaborator. The two novels Ngugi wa Thiong'o wrote around this period cover much of the same material: *Grain of Wheat* (1967) describes the ethical dilemmas and compromises of Mau Mau and independence, and *Petals of Blood* (1977) focuses on the post-uhuru reality of those Africans who had collaborated the most with the British, profited from their departure by stepping into their roles of economic power, and left those who had fought for independence struggling to survive.

    a. **Further Reading:** Ngugi wa Thiong'o. *Grain of Wheat.* London: Heinemann, 1967; *Petals of Blood.* London: Heinemann, 1977.

    b. **Suggested Searches:** Search for the *London Review of Books* article "How Did They Get Away with It?" by Bernard Porter, as well as for the many letters in response that indicate the still-incendiary nature of a historical discussion of Mau Mau.

3. **Although the Christian wedding becomes a figure for the English colonization of Wariuki's mind, the story also suggests that Christianity might be associated with the downtrodden and oppressed African working class.** Christianity in this story is closely associated with two contrasting economic perspectives—at the end of the story, Wariuki sees Christianity as a sign of his newly found prosperity and new English customs and names, while Miriamu sees it as the "Religion of Sorrows," emphasizing care for the poor and oppressed of the earth: "They seemed united in a common labour and faith" (2557). Ngugi wa Thiong'o has held many different ideological positions over his career; two of the most important changes are his abandonment of Christianity and his adoption of Marxism. The Religion of Sorrows, which opposes a quasi-Marxist Christianity with a colonial Christianity of capitalism, complicates these divisions. In 1967, while a student at Leeds University, Ngugi had read Frantz Fanon's *The Wretched of the Earth*, which outlined the possibility of postcolonial nationalist movements becoming repressive neocolonial states. Ngugi's Marxism provided a lens through which he began to understand the strife of Kenyan history—not through the lens of colonizer and colonized but as a more general problem of privilege and oppression. The dual role of Christianity in the story suggests these tensions.

    a. **Further Reading:** Gikandi, Simon. *Ngugi wa Thiong'o*. Cambridge: Cambridge University Press, 2000.

    b. **Suggested Search:** Search for the *Internet Encyclopedia of Philosophy*'s article on Frantz Fanon, which provides an overview of his ideas and includes a brief discussion of their influence on Ngugi wa Thiong'o.

4. **The story shifts constantly in its point of view, forcing the reader to see events through many perspectives.** It begins with a collective, external viewpoint on the protagonists Wariuki and Miriamu: "Everyone said of them: . . ." Much of the climactic scene is told through Miriamu's internal monologue: "A spasm of guilt. But only for a time. It did not matter. Not now" (2560). These techniques are often associated with Ngugi wa Thiong'o's attempt to balance a colonizing European literary heritage with a native African one; Byron Caminero-Santangelo has suggested that in the novel *Grain of Wheat* the replacement of an individualized perspective with the collective narrative *we* reflects the rejection of the European realist novel in favor of the values of Gikuyu collectivity. (The motto of Kenya is *Harambee*, Swahili for "all pull together.") Yet in this story the collective viewpoint is the subject of heavy irony: by the end of the story we will see the limitations of what "everyone said." Yet the stream-of-consciousness point of view is equally problematic: it is not only the source of Miriamu's climactic moment of clarity but is also the way Ngugi depicts the catastrophic interview that haunts (and destroys) Wariuki: "A buzz in his head, a blurring vision, and he heard the still gracious voice" (2552). Ngugi's narrative variants, rather than representing literary traditions, are tools for manipulating the reader's sense of irony and sympathy.

    a. **Further Reading:** Caminero-Santangelo, Byron. *African Fiction and Joseph Conrad: Reading Postcolonial Intertextuality*. Albany, NY: State University of New York Press, 2005.

    b. **Suggested Search:** Search the JSTOR database at jstor.org for the article "The Use of Popular Forms and Characterisation in Ngugi's Postcolonial Narrative" by James Ogude.

5. **Ngugi wa Thiong'o is an advocate for the study of African literature as opposed to European literature.** In 1968 the so-called Nairobi Revolution resulted in the abolishment of the English department of the University of Nairobi in favor of a literature department that heavily emphasized African literature. Ngugi was one of three lecturers whose memo demanding a curriculum that did not force students of literature to focus on English literature set in motion the change. European authors were still taught afterward, but not privileged. Ngugi was nevertheless a wide and thorough reader of classic European works; Joseph Conrad was one of his favorite novelists and an acknowledged

influence on many of his works. Throughout the 1970s, Ngugi was intensely involved in debates on the nature and content of African education, specifically in literature: Was the task of literature to further African nationalism, or was it to allow young Africans access to global (Eurocentric) discourse? What other options were available? This short story, written in English, was originally published in *Ghala* (a regular literary edition of *East Africa Journal*), aimed at an audience of Africans in several countries who knew English. How does the story, which valorizes the Gikuyu laborers who could not read it and uses many literary styles drawn from the colonial powers whose culture it in part condemns, fit into these debates?

  a. **Further Reading:** Amoko, Apollo Obonyo. *Postcolonialism in the Wake of the Nairobi Revolution.* New York: Palgrave Macmillan, 2010.

  b. **Suggested Search:** Search for "Literature and Society: The Politics of Canon" by Ngugi wa Thiong'o, posted online at several sources and also available in his book *Writers in Politics.*

In-Class Activities

  1. List the broader historical events mentioned in the story (e.g., Mau Mau, independence). Divide students into groups to research the contrast between the portrayal of an event in the story with a widely available historical understanding or common knowledge. Have each group present its findings to the class.

  2. Discuss the parable of the wise and foolish virgins that Miriamu thinks about (2559) in the climactic scene. Ask the class why her rejection of the "wedding at the cross" should be accompanied by a biblical parable, and use this discussion to open up the complexities of "decolonizing" the mind.

  3. Ask students how they would divide the story into three sections if they had to. Collect all of their answers and display them to the class. This should produce different ways of interpreting the story (e.g., some will divide according to key historical events, while others will pick divisions at the moments of psychological tension or crucial plot choices). Use this exercise to prompt students to consider the different kinds of interpretation available to them, and the different kinds of stories that Ngugi wa Thiong'o builds upon.

Paper Topics/Suggestions for Writing

  1. "Ngugi is unique among African writers of his generation in his refusal to invoke a precolonial world as the site of a stable culture and identity" (Simon Gikandi, 14). How does Ngugi wa Thiong'o invoke Gikuyu

culture—or what is the importance of Gikuyu cultural features in his work—if not through imagining a precolonial past?

2. How does Ngugi wa Thiong'o use free indirect discourse to further his aims in this story?

3. "Perhaps the crucial question is not that of the racial, national, and class origins of the novel, but that of its development and the uses to which it is continually being put" (Ngugi, *Decolonising the Mind*, 65). How does Ngugi wa Thiong'o treat European cultural products in this story? Does he view them in light of their origins, their uses, or both?

4. Why does Miriamu, raised in a life of Westernized privilege, seem to suffer no ill effects in giving that life up, while Wariuki, who has never known such a life, longs for it? Compare and contrast the different effects colonial life has on the minds of these two characters.

5. "Ahh, well, well—no man was born with wealth—wealth was in the limbs you know and you, you are so young" (Douglas Jones to Wariuki, 2552). Discuss the difference in this story between speech or external appearance and inner self or real intention.

Resources

Ngugi wa Thiong'o official website. www.ngugiwathiongo.com.
   This site contains a complete bibliography and capsule biography of Ngugi wa Thiong'o.
Sander, Reinhard, and Bernth Lindfors, eds. *Ngugi wa Thiong'o Speaks*. London: James Currey, 2006.
   This is a wide-ranging collection of interviews with Ngugi wa Thiong'o.
Sicherman, Carol, ed. *Ngugi wa Thiong'o: The Making of a Rebel—A Source Book in Kenyan Literature and Resistance*. London: Hans Zell, 1990.
   This is a useful set of primary sources relating to Kenyan history, with a focus on Ngugi wa Thiong'o.
Williams, Patrick. *Ngugi wa Thiong'o*. Manchester, UK: Manchester University Press, 1999.
   Like Simon Gikandi's more recent work (referenced in topic 1 in this module), this survey does not treat "Wedding at the Cross" in any detail, but its concluding chapter in Ngugi wa Thiong'o's novel *Petals of Blood* provides an overview of issues relevant to the story.

WOLE SOYINKA

Death and the King's Horseman

> Life has an end. A life that will outlive
> Fame and friendship begs another name.
> What elder takes his tongue to his plate,
> Licks it clean of every crumb? He will
>   encounter
> Silence when he calls on children to fulfill
> The smallest errand! Life is honour.
> It ends when honour ends.
> —Wole Soyinka, *Death and the King's Horseman*

Topics for Lecture or Discussion

1. **Elesin's joy in living prevents him from the timely fulfillment of his duty.** The king died thirty days earlier and awaits final burial, but, according to Yoruban custom, the king's chief horseman, Elesin, must commit suicide in order to accompany the king to heaven. The action of the play begins with Elesin's pursuit of sensual pleasures before he must depart from among the living. A smiling, laughing, and charismatic figure, Elesin walks through the market, a metaphor for the world, wrapped in colorful tribal clothes, enjoying the attention given him by throngs of women. As one of his last requests, Elesin solicits a new bride, a young woman already betrothed to the son of Iyaloja, leader of the market women. She grants his desire, despite her obvious conflict of interest, with a final declaration designed to hasten the ritual to an obligatory end: "Now we must go prepare your bridal chamber. Then these same hands will lay your shrouds" (2574). Iyaloja proposes an abrupt and dramatic transition between life and death. It is unclear in the dramatic text at what point the British rulers intervene and prevent Elesin from completing his ritualistic obligation, but Elesin's lust for life and his impromptu "marriage" offer enough delay for Pilkings to stop the anticipated suicide. Elesin progresses as far as a self-induced trance in a transitional state from life to death, but bad timing results in failure and a calamity for the Yoruban people.

   a. **Further Reading:** Booth, James. "Self-Sacrifice and Human Sacrifice in Soyinka's *Death and the King's Horseman*." *Research in African Literatures* 19:4 (Winter 1988): 529–50.

   b. **Suggested Searches:** Search for the following phrases in Google Images, Google Scholar, or an academic database to find images and

additional resources: National Theatre production (London) 2009; Soyinka passage from life to death; Yoruba ritual suicide.

2. **The initial scenes contrast native Yoruban and British colonialist rituals.** The opening scene with Elesin and the market women stretches a Western audience's capacity to understand and comprehend what is happening. The ritual is foreign, the metaphors are obscure, and the references to Yoruban myth, language, and culture are dauntingly numerous and frequent. Only at the end does it seem clear that Elesin must turn quickly from a marriage bed to a deathbed. Act 2, set in the District Officer's bungalow, makes the prior scene clear in retrospect. Not only does a native officer explain to Pilkings and his wife about the nature of the Yoruban ritual, but the British couple themselves are preparing to attend a ritual of their own, an elaborate costume ball to be staged as a relief from the war (World War II) effort. Indeed, Pilkings and his wife, Jane, appear dancing the tango in fancy dress that seems to mock the native inhabitants of the colony. As this first scene might have initially confused the theatrical audience, the second scene confounds the native sergeant who enters with a message and witnesses the event. Significantly, the Yoruban ritual is latent with meaning that becomes abundantly clear in the course of the action; the English ball, patterned after a Jonsonian masque, but lacking the political importance of those sixteenth-century events, is a ritual too, but it is one that is merely a silly diversion for the ruling class to pass the time.

   a. **Further Reading:** Olakunle, George. "Cultural Criticism in Wole Soyinka's *Death and the King's Horseman.*" *Representations* 67 (Summer 1999): 67–91.

   b. **Suggested Searches:** Search for the following phrases in Google Images, Google Scholar, or an academic database to find images and additional resources: British and Nigerian culture clash in Soyinka; Soyinka Nobel Prize literature 1986; Yoruba ritual video; Washington Shakespeare Company production 2006; British colonialism in Africa.

3. **Setting the drama during World War II highlights a conflict between the one and the many.** While the actual source story of the play dates from 1946, the playwright moved his play back for strategic reasons. The dialogue between Olunde, Elesin's son, and Jane Pilkings illustrates the inability and perhaps the unwillingness of the colonizers to recognize the autonomy, culture, and values of the colonized. The English prevent a single man, Elesin, from killing himself in a ritual sacrifice because, as Jane says, "Life should never be thrown deliberately away" (2594). She and, by extension, her husband and all the British, fail to see the nobility of self-sacrifice, even when Olunde cites a recent example of a captain's willingness to blow himself up so that

innocent people in the surrounding harbor would remain safe. Elesin's death is part of a ceremony meant to preserve the future health of an entire society. The death of one preserves the health and prosperity of many. Jane cannot understand the practice of ritual suicide, but alluding to the wartime strategy of generals sending young soldiers to slaughter, Olunde pointedly asks: "Is that worse than mass suicide?" (2595). In this context, the Yoruban ritual that sacrifices only one man seems civilized, and the Western nations seem barbaric.

a. **Further Reading:** Ojalde, Tanure. "Teaching Wole Soyinka's *Death and the King's Horseman* to American College Students." *College Literature* 19/20: 3/1 (October 1992–February 1993): 210–14.

b. **Suggested Searches:** Search for the following phrases in Google Images, Google Scholar, or an academic database to find images and additional resources: Soyinka and identity; Soyinka and non-Western drama; British colonialism in Nigeria; Frank Rich on Lincoln Center production 1987.

4. **The tragic death of Olunde is inevitable and ironic.** The young, sap-filled shoot of the plantain that replaces the withering leaves of the parent stalk is a dominant metaphor for the proper rotation of the human life cycle in the play. Early in the drama, Elesin speaks in verse: "Women, let my going be likened to / The twilight hour of the plantain" (2573). Accusing Pilkings of blame at the end, Iyaloja declares: "The gods demanded only the old expired plantain but you cut down the sap-laden shoot to feed your pride" (2610). Colonial interference and intervention of the Yoruban ritual keep Elesin from performing his duty, but they allow Olunde, his son, to take his place. Stepping in for the father reverses the natural order of things. It is a horrible revelation for Elesin to witness the presentation of his son's body, and this leads directly to his own suicide as well. The crime against nature and the natural order is further ironic because Olunde left his country, at the behest of the Pilkings and against his father's will, as a young man to train as a doctor in the West. The prodigal son returns home to take his father's place in death. Olunde's tragic death, however, is not the product of bad timing. He decided to come home to bury his father in the wake of the king's death. Certain that his father also is now dead, Olunde registers shock to discover him still alive. "I have no father, eater of left-overs," is all he can muster in response and these are his last lines of the drama (2600). All that is left to uphold family honor and fill the societal breach created by Elesin is for Olunde himself to commit suicide and fulfill his father's function.

a. **Further Reading:** Jain, Jasbir. "The Unfolding of a Text: Soyinka's *Death and the King's Horseman." Research in African Literatures* 17:2 (Summer 1986): 252–60.

b. **Suggested Searches:** Search for the following phrases in Google Images, Google Scholar, or an academic database to find images and additional resources: Soyinka and Greek tragedy; Oregon Shakespeare Festival production 2009.

5. **The final lines of the play advise the Bride to focus on the future.** The ritual of suicide by the king's horseman is geared toward the preservation of the Yoruban people, culture, and society. For an extended account of the power of ritual, see Andrew Apter's *Black Critics and Kings: The Hermeneutics of Power in Yoruba Society* (1992). Iyaloja acknowledges that damage has been done and that outside interference has perhaps altered the future. She blames the foreigners, British colonialists such as Pilkings, who "believe that the stain of death will not cling to you" (2610), yet the closing lines offer hope for a return and restoration of order. "Now forget the dead, forget even the living. Turn your mind only to the unborn," advises Iyaloja (2610). This coda to the action comes immediately following her screams addressed to Pilkings and functions as a transition for the audience from the world of the theater to the mundane world outside.

a. **Further Reading:** McLuckle, Craig. "The Structural Coherence of Wole Soyinka's *Death and the King's Horseman.*" *College Literature* 31:2 (Spring 2004): 143–63.

b. **Suggested Searches:** Search for the following phrases in Google Images, Google Scholar, or an academic database to find images and additional resources: Yoruba marriage ritual; folk ritual and Soyinka; history of British colonization and decolonization of Nigeria.

In-Class Activities

1. The plantain is one of the recurring images in the play. Trace its use from beginning to end in order to see what it means. Identify and trace the use of other recurring images as well.

2. Why is the play particularly difficult to understand and follow in the opening scenes, and why might this be by design? Locate some representative passages of difficulty as evidence and try to explicate them. If the process of interpretation becomes easier over time, what does that indicate?

3. Why does the role of Elesin require a very charismatic performer? At the same time, his son, Olunde, lacks this same quality. Examine the text to see why this is so and what bearing it has on the meanings of the drama.

Paper Topics/Suggestions for Writing

1. Life and death are often considered extreme opposites, and for obvious reasons. This play celebrates the subtle transition between life and

death. How do the elements of fate, obligation, duty, hesitation, and bad timing mark that transition and carve a thematic path for the drama?

2. The English clearly consider the Africans primitive and culturally inferior people. Can you detect any irony in the depiction of the English masquerade party?

3. None of the colonists suspect that Olunde will sacrifice his life to fulfill his father's obligation. Instead, they assume that he will behave just like them since he was educated in the West. How do Olunde's actions fulfill or complicate the conflict between nature and culture?

4. Elesin's desire for earthly pleasures and his last requests disgust Iyaloja. How do male and female perspectives differ regarding the death ritual?

5. Amid the mass destruction and genocide of World War II, in which the civilized Western powers wage war against each other, Pilkings tries to save one man from committing a ritualistic suicide as part of his cultural obligation. What does this gesture, which ensures the tragic end of the play, suggest about the arrogance of Western imperialism?

Resources

Apter, Andrew Herman. *Black Critics and Kings: The Hermeneutics of Power in Yoruba Society*. Chicago: University of Chicago Press, 1992.
> This book is an extended examination of the power of ritual in Yoruba society.

Oba Koso: Nigerian Drama. Insight Media, 1975, VHS.
> This video includes excerpts from the National Theater of Nigeria's production of folkloric Yoruba drama/musical/dance about a wicked man who tries to overthrow a king.

BESSIE HEAD

The Deep River

Topics for Lecture or Discussion

1. **Women's rights (or lack thereof) and the theme of otherness are primary issues in Bessie Head's work.** Head had moved as a refugee to Serowe, Botswana, in 1964. Serowe was the country's largest village and capital of the Bamangwato people, who represent one of eight principal tribes; Head may at times have been ostracized as an "outsider," and at one point she was committed to a mental hospital for denouncing the first president of Botswana, Seretse Khama, as an assassin. Sebembele's declaration of love for Rankwana is ridiculed (he "made the second blunder. In a world where women were of no account . . . a man who is influenced by a woman is no ruler," 2613–14). The story's plot is built around the tribe members' demand that Sebembele renounce his child (2615), and it climaxes with his exile and refuge in Bamangwato. Though established as the Botalaote, the tribe's men still hold a grudge over their displacement from the Monemapee kingdom and loss of birthright "over a woman" (2616). In the footnote, Head states that the story is a "romanticized and fictionalized version" of Botalaote tribal history. Should this story be read as historical fiction or entertainment, or for a didactic purpose?
   a. **Further Reading:** Eilersen, Gillian Stead. *Bessie Head: Thunder Behind Her Ears—Her Life and Writings.* London: Heinemann, 1996.
   b. **Suggested Search:** Visit Bessie Head's official website at www.bessiehead.org/index.html.

2. **Apartheid shaped Bessie Head's early life.** Head's mother gave birth to her in a mental asylum, having been committed for engaging in sexual relations with a black man. By state law, only black or mixed-race parents could raise a mixed-race child, and Head was raised unaware of her biological parents until her teen years. Historically, apartheid was enforced racial segregation by the National Party of South Africa from 1948 to 1994, though segregation itself began during the Dutch and British colonial rule during the nineteenth century. Under apartheid, black people were deprived of citizenship and political representation, public services were segregated and inferior service was offered to blacks, people were forced to live in separate townships, marriage was prohibited and sexual relations with a person of a different race (African, Indian, or mixed race) were deemed a criminal offense, and education for blacks was limited to preparation for blue-collar labor. Black women under apartheid were severely oppressed—they had no legal

rights, they could not own property, and they were denied education and fair wages relative to their male counterparts. Issues of illegitimacy and immorality are present in the opening section of "The Deep River": Sebembele is installed as chief of the tribe but wrongfully claims his father's youngest wife for himself, and her son as conceived by him. This leads not only to questions of the chief's death but also to concerns about seniority and claims to the throne (2613). Which elements of modern apartheid are transposed in this narrative's conflict and resolution?

    a. **Further Reading:** Louw, Eric. *The Rise, Fall and Legacy of Apartheid.* New York: Praeger, 2004.

    b. **Suggested Search:** Visit the Johannesburg Apartheid Museum at www.apartheidmuseum.org.

3. **The Pan-African Association, of which Bessie Head was a member, called for the unity of all African peoples against slavery, colonialism, and discrimination.** Henry Sylvester-Williams organized the association in 1887 to refer not only to the unity of the continent but also to dispersed Africans. Literary members often call for a return to traditional values and practices, as well as a new understanding of African history based on an African rather than a colonial perspective. Important members have included W. E. B. DuBois, Marcus Garvey, Bob Marley, Colonel Gaddafi, and Malcolm X. Pan-Africanism is represented in the opening lines of "The Deep River," which relate the history of the universal Monemapee people to which the Talaote and other tribes belonged prior to "a conflict ruffl[ing] their deep river" (2612) and, at the story's end, when resentment brews over the loss of one's heritage ("And the name Talaote was all they were to retain of their identity as the people of the kingdom of Monemapee," 2616). In what ways are history, unity, and tradition emphasized in this story?

    a. **Further Reading:** Walters, Ronald. *Pan-Africanism in the African Diaspora: An Analysis of Modern Afrocentric Political Movements.* Detroit, MI: Wayne State University Press, 1997.

    b. **Suggested Search:** Read about the agenda and vision of the All-African People's Revolutionary Party at www.aaprp-intl.org.

In-Class Activities

1. Understanding apartheid: Students will take a virtual field trip to the Apartheid Museum (see the Resources section) to examine the images and primary documents collected. Each student will then write a short reflection piece that discusses the experience and responds to the materials accessed. How did the visit enrich students' understanding of Bessie Head's writing?

2. Music appreciation: Though they lived worlds apart, both Bessie Head and Bob Marley were proponents of Pan-Africanism. In this activity, students will listen to Bob Marley's "Africa Unite" and discuss the lyrics in the context of the Pan-African movement. How does Marley's vision relate to Head's discussion of "unity and conflict" in her short story?

3. Reenacting tribal practice: The tribal males in this story both create and resolve conflict that they blame on one man's love for a woman. In this activity, students will role-play: Assign a head chief, three males in line to rule, and a new mother claimed as wife by the new head chief. The characters have to interact with each other to present their arguments, make claims, and resolve differences (they do not need to behave according to Talaote tribal values). Each group will share its outcomes. Are the renunciation of the child or of one's throne and exile the only possible solutions? What concerns arose as each character presented his or her demands and concerns? What does this tell us about human values and interpersonal relationships when issues of identity and sovereignty arise?

Paper Topics/Suggestions for Writing

1. Should Bessie Head's story be categorized as historical fiction or pure entertainment, or does it serve a didactic or moral purpose? Use evidence from the story to support your argument.

2. How are the history of apartheid and the ideologies of the Pan-African movement embedded in Bessie Head's story? Use evidence from the story to support your argument.

3. Discuss the relationship between identity and otherness as a theme in Bessie Head's story.

4. Why is exile viewed as a loss of one's identity? Is selfhood defined in tangible terms of place and time, or can culture be carried elsewhere? Use evidence from the story, as well as your personal experiences, to support your argument.

Resources

All-African People's Revolutionary Party. www.aaprp-intl.org.
    This site includes background information, press releases, resources, and a video gallery related to the party, which calls for the "total liberation and unification of Africa."

Apartheid Museum. www.apartheidmuseum.org.
    This site contains some collections, background information, and resources and helpful YouTube video interviews on South Africans' responses to their history.

Bessie Amelia Head website. www.bessiehead.org/index.html.
  This site features a biography, photos, excerpts, papers, and related
  services through the Bessie Head Heritage Trust.
Botswana official website. www.gov.bw.
  This site has information on citizens, business, travel, government,
  and useful links.

Salman Rushdie
The Perforated Sheet

Topics for Lecture or Discussion

1. **Salman Rushdie has lived in exile and in diasporas, which have defined the migrant, culturally homogeneous, and hybrid nature of his writing; his writing often traverses time periods and perceptions of history.** Rushdie has lived abroad due to a religious decree ordered by the Ayatollah Khomeini in 1989, obligating Muslims to murder Rushdie for blasphemy. Rushdie was born into a wealthy Muslim family at the end of British colonial rule but received his undergraduate and graduate degrees in Islamic studies at the University of Cambridge. Corresponding to the story, Rushdie, like Aziz, receives a Western European education (Aziz earns a medical degree from Heidelberg University, Germany, 2627). Readers of the novel *Midnight's Children*, which includes "The Perforated Sheet," find that World War I ends the same day that Aziz and Naseem first gaze upon each other (he "saw a soft face that was not at all ugly," 2631). Saleem will narrate the remainder of the story in an urgent stream-of-consciousness state ("I must work fast, faster than Scheherazade, if I am to end up meaning—yes, meaning—something," 2619–20). Do students perceive Rushdie's story as politically motivated, or do they categorize it as entertainment, educational, speculative, or something else?
   a. **Further Reading:** Kane, Jean M., and Salman Rushdie. "The Migrant Intellectual and the Body of History: Salman Rushdie's *Midnight's Children*." *Contemporary Literature* 37:1 (1996): 94–118.
   b. **Suggested Search:** Visit Salman Rushdie's official website at www.salman-rushdie.com.

2. **Magical realism as a genre blends fantasy, myth, and the paranormal with reality and actuality.** Laws of physics, the facts associated with historical events, and our understanding of the observable universe are challenged in this genre, which twists or invades the real world to create an extraordinary, yet a plausible, situation. The term "magical realism" was used in its current sense in 1955 as a form of "uncanny realism" and originated in Latin America. Characteristics of the genre include plentitude (embellishment or use of the fanciful), hybridity (blending time periods or constellatory realities), metafiction (the reader and text directly enter each other's worlds), and unreliable narrator (the narrator withholds or does not justify events or characters' viewpoints). Gabriel García Márquez (this volume, 2511) wrote "Death Constant Beyond Love," which treats political corruption (going through the

motions and illusions necessary to achieve reelection) and a character's denial of impending death, by having his characters engage in love affairs and go through the motions of reelection in order to avoid the preparation and acceptance of dying. Salman Rushdie's "The Perforated Sheet" unfolds the story of Saleem's life as a precise parallel to the collective history of India: his birth coincides with the birth of the independent Indian nation, with the birth of his nemesis Shiva (corresponding to India's neighboring Pakistan), and the conflict arising between the Hindu–Muslim identities in those countries ("I had been mysteriously handcuffed to history, my destinies indissolubly chained to those of my country," 2619). In *Midnight's Children*, readers discover that the Heidelberg bag represents not only the foreign part of Aziz's background as a medical student in Germany but will later represent his loss of faith and create a physical stigma by bruising him during the Amritsar massacre. Do Rushdie and Márquez use the same form and elements of magical realism?

    a. **Further Reading:** Sharma, Shailja. "Salman Rushdie: The Ambivalence of Migrancy." *Twentieth Century Literature* 47:4 (2001): 596–618.

    b. **Suggested Search:** Watch part of an in-depth interview with Salman Rushdie at www.c-spanvideo.org/program/Salman.

3. **Salman Rushdie's characters are often allegorical.** Saleem Sinai embodies India: his nose is shaped like the country's peninsula, and his body threatens to break into 580 million pieces, representing India's population at the time Rushdie composed the story. Sinai, in a biblical sense, is also the Mount on which Moses (considered one of the four great prophets in Islam) received the Ten Commandments from God; Saleem, too, is born (like the thousand other midnight children) with magical powers and the ability to communicate with others telepathically (divinely). Aadam Aziz represents the progenitor of Saleem's universe, and the hole (representing emptiness, "a vacancy in a vital inner chamber," 2620) is initially formed by the penetration of Aziz's nose into the icy earth while praying (described as "the place where the outside world meets the world inside you," 2626; compare the magical properties of Aziz's nose, mucus, and spittle to the Greek myth of the birth of Venus through Uranus's castration and drops of blood to form Venus and sea foam, as here they form rubies and diamonds). The hole symbolizes doubt (2622) and nostrils (2623), and it forms the scope through which Aziz will imagine and desire the universe of his patient's body, which he has seen only in fragmented form. Rushdie also hints that the hole has been used not only to modestly reveal the daughter's body but perhaps also to mirror the Old Testament myth of Eve being formed from Adam's rib (thereby creating a hole in his torso) and the

monotheistic practice in some cultures of using a perforated sheet to cover all but the genitalia of a woman's body during sexual intercourse. Tai has been said to represent "timelessness" in the work—his role as a ferryman (2624) parallels Greek and European folklore and myth about the ferryman who eternally travels the river that flows between the land of the living and the land of the dead. Why are universal myths integrated into the story when its characters dismiss and/or create a farce of religion and belief?

  a. **Further Reading:** Dayal, Samir. "Talking Dirty: Salman Rushdie's *Midnight's Children*." *College English* 54:4 (1992): 431–45.

  b. **Suggested Search:** Go to the entry on fragmentation and Salman Rushdie at www.postcolonialweb.org/pakistan/literature/rushdie/hol lett.html.

In-Class Activities

1. Perception: Students are placed into pairs and then make a small hole in a sheet of paper. They hold the perforated sheet between them, examining and revealing fragments of their faces to each other. How does this activity affect their understanding of being both voyeur and exhibitionist? What feelings and thoughts arise during this process, and how do they relate to the feelings and perceptions that Aziz and Naseem experience in the story?

2. Imagining the remainder of the story: "The Perforated Sheet" is only a fragment of Salman Rushdie's first successful novel, *Midnight's Children*. Based on the content excerpted in this anthology, what do students believe will happen next? How do they anticipate the novel unfolding and resolving (if at all)? Readers have been assured that Saleem is going to meet his death soon. Do they believe that he will die at the novel's end? Would that make the work tragic? Ask students to write a short paragraph describing their vision (based on the small perforation they have created in the novel by reading the short story) and have them share the results as a class.

3. Film/Literary comparison: Students will watch the film rendition of *Midnight's Children* (see the Resources section) and afterward will discuss how magical realism is transposed in the visual form and what works effectively or poorly compared to the original written text.

Paper Topics/Suggestions for Writing

1. Both Salman Rushdie and Gabriel García Márquez are writers belonging to the magical realism genre. Discuss the theme of "personal destiny and the unfolding of a nation's political history" in both "Death Constant Beyond Love" and "The Perforated Sheet."

2. Which elements of Salman Rushdie's biography are integrated into the story, and why are they relevant to our understanding of the story's theme and characters' desires?

3. Saleem states that "above all things, I fear absurdity" (2620). How does this statement reflect and/or contradict the plot, character, and narration in Salman Rushdie's story?

4. What does the "perforated sheet" symbolize? Use evidence from the story to support your argument.

5. Discuss at least two elements of magical realism as they are used in the story, citing examples to support your contentions.

6. Salman Rushdie once stated that writing is a sacrament that "fills the hole left by the departure of God." What does the "hole" symbolize both for the author and for various characters in the story?

Resources

"In Depth with Salman Rushdie." December 5, 2010. C-Span Video Library. www.c-spanvideo.org/program/Salman.
> The three-hour interview on this site features a discussion about Salman Rushdie's career, life, and work.

Midnight's Children. Dir. Deepa Mehta. David Hamilton Productions, 2012.
> This film, released in October 2012, is loosely based on Salman Rushdie's novel of the same title.

"Salman Rushdie." Postcolonial Web. www.postcolonialweb.org/pakistan /literature/rushdie/rushdieov.html.
> This entry on Salman Rushdie offers a biography, history, visual arts, works, related Web resources, and links to other writers.

Salman Rushdie official website. www.salman-rushdie.com.
> This site features books, news, and media as well as background and contact information.

JAMAICA KINCAID

Girl

> . . . don't squat down to play marbles—you are
> not a boy, you know.
> —Kincaid, "Girl"

Topics for Lecture or Discussion

1. **The body of advice narrated in "Girl" indicates some of the forms in which traditional cultural knowledge is frequently transmitted.** This advice comes in the form of explicitly stated directions (e.g., "Don't walk barehead in the hot sun," 2633), example (e.g., "This is how you set a table for dinner with an important dinner guest," 2633), and parental guidance through knowledge of the particular child (e.g., "Is it true that you sing benna in Sunday school?" 2633 [benna is a form of Antiguan folk music that often has sexual and political themes, thus presumably is inappropriate for Sunday school]). In combining into one brief narrative these various forms of cultural transmission and education, Jamaica Kincaid indicates the vitality and strength of the Antiguan culture even if, at the same time, she indicates certain contradictions (topic 2 here elaborates on the contradictions). As is evident in the many proscriptions in "Girl" that relate to public behavior, the Antiguan culture had a great influence on the social interactions between its members, but it similarly guided the private lives of Antiguans in comfort and hygiene. Part of the artistry of this story, then, is that in such a brief work Kincaid deftly illustrates both the vigor of the culture of Antigua and its various modes of preservation and transmission.

   a. **Further Reading**: Ferguson, Moira. "A Lot of Memory: An Interview with Jamaica Kincaid." *Kenyon Review* 16:1 (1994): 163–88.

   b. **Suggested Searches:** Perform a Google Maps (maps.google.com) search for "Antigua" for satellite images of the island, and use this tool to illustrate both the small size of the island and its geographical location. Also, the Antigua and Barbuda government website (http://ab.gov.ag/index.php) contains further information about the government, as well as festivals and photos emphasizing the tourism industry.

2. **The speaker of "Girl" offers advice that is sometimes given in a contradictory spirit, and these moments of apparent opposition not only invite the reader to question the authority of the speaker but also illustrate the shifting nature of advice that is given over an extended period of time.** The most apparent example is in relation to

the sexual advice given by the speaker. The speaker refers three different times to "the slut you are so bent on becoming" (2633): she cautions the listener about a certain care and modesty in relation to how she walks, how to hem her dress (2633), and how to behave around men who do not know her well (2634). In contrast to this cautious social attitude, the speaker teaches the private techniques of abortifacient concoctions (e.g., "This is how to make a good medicine to throw away a child even before it becomes a child," 2634), and sexual knowledge is implied in her statement, "This is how to love a man" (2634). The contradictions that are implied between the private and the public behavior of the listener who is being advised should prompt the reader to question the authority and wisdom of the speaker.

   a. **Further Reading:** Booth, Wayne. *The Rhetoric of Fiction*. Chicago: University of Chicago Press, 1961.

   b. **Suggested Search:** A search at Literature Online (lion.chadwyck.com) for "unreliable narrator" results in several helpful articles and reference entries.

3. **"Girl" is a work that is not easily categorized within any particular genre.** It might justly be called a short story insofar as it does develop a context in which two characters and the surrounding culture are apparent. The reader can infer a considerable amount of detail about the characters, particularly the speaker, through the advice that is given; for example, the speaker might be characterized as confident, bossy, self-content, and desirous to be helpful, among other things. But "Girl" does not develop a plot in any regular sense; rather, it is told in one long sentence and has a striking linguistic rhythm, repeating certain phrases with only minor variation, for example: "This is how you smile to someone you don't like too much; this is how you smile to someone you don't like at all; this is how you smile to someone you like completely" (2633). All of these unusual features indicate that "Girl" might be better understood as a prose poem, a hybrid genre that is written in prose form that extends to the right margin of the page (rather than the typical line breaks of poetry) but that makes use of metaphorical or rhythmically structured prose and does not follow typical grammatical rules.

   a. **Further Reading:** Simmons, Diane. "The Rhythm of Reality in the Works of Jamaica Kincaid." *World Literature Today* 68:3 (Summer 1994): 466–72.

   b. **Suggested Search:** A Google search for "Mutable Boundaries: On Prose Poetry" results in a helpful article by Karen Volkman at poets.org that discusses the genre and history of prose poems.

4. **The primary speaker of "Girl" is briefly interrupted twice by the listener, and both of these interruptions are essential to understanding the deeper tensions in the story.** In the first interruption,

the listener interjects "*but I don't sing benna on Sundays at all and never in Sunday school*" (emphasis in original, 2633), responding to the apparently false suggestion by the primary speaker. The second interruption is unlike the first, as the listener does not attempt to correct the speaker but seeks clarification about the advice given, asking, "*But what if the baker won't let me feel the bread?*" (emphasis in original, 2634). The primary speaker's response to this question is to rebuke the girl for being too timid, an interesting contrast to the suggestion that she is too bold in singing benna at Sunday school. Both of these interruptions also imply that the speaker does not know the listener as well as she thinks, for while she is quite loquacious, she does not actually have knowledge of the worries, temperament, and character of the one she is advising.

a. **Further Reading**: Caton, Louis F. "Romantic Struggles: The *Bildungsroman* and Mother-Daughter Bonding in Jamaica Kincaid's *Annie John*." *MELUS* 21:3 (Autumn 1996): 125–42.

b. **Suggested Search**: A search for "Jamaica Kincaid" at www.charlierose.com results in two different video interviews that Charlie Rose held with her. The 1996 interview discusses Kincaid's *The Autobiography of My Mother* (28 min.) and the 1997 interview discusses her work *My Brother* (16 min.).

5. **While "Girl" does not explicitly identify the location at which it takes place, several details indicate that it is Jamaica Kincaid's native Antigua, and in this respect Kincaid's story is part of the larger canon of literature from or about the Caribbean islands.** In "Girl," details such as the cooking advice (2633), the mention of benna (2633), and the identification of the "okra tree" (2633) indicate the tropical, and likely Antiguan, location of the story. Such local detail and color are important in the story, as they provide an identifiable sense of place in Kincaid's writing (and this same sense also can be consistently found in her other works). A similar sense of the importance of place is often found in world literature from various regions, and Kincaid's use of place might be fruitfully compared to Derek Walcott's (Walcott is a fellow Caribbean writer) (see *Omeros*, 2469–2487), or the American regionalism so apparent in William Faulkner's writing (see "Spotted Horses," 2009–2020). Important points of emphasis for all of these writers are the ways in which the history and physical geography of a place shape human culture and life.

a. **Further Reading**: Kincaid, Jamaica. *My Garden*. Illustrated by Jill Fox. New York: Farrar, Straus, and Giroux, 1999.

b. **Suggested Search**: At the website vimeo.com, a search for "Jamaica Kincaid" results in several videos, including "A Reading by Jamaica Kincaid" at Columbia University, with insightful introductory comments given by Dr. Saidiya Hartman. (Note that part of the selection

Kincaid reads includes profanity.) A question and answer session of considerable interest is included in this video.

In-Class Activities

1. Begin class with the following writing exercise prompt: "If your mother, father, guardian, or other mentor were to give you advice to initiate you into your culture's idea of adulthood—like the girl's mother does in 'Girl'—what would he or she say? Write an impression of 'Girl,' replacing the advice meant for the girl with advice meant for you." After students complete the exercise, ask them to reflect on the type of advice given: Was it supportive, moral, inspiring, practical, or chastising? Did the student allow her or his voice to come through in the story? If one were to read the student's imitation, how would one describe the student's life? Is it one of oppression, like the girl's?

2. Play Jamaica Kincaid's reading of "Girl," available online at virtuaLit Fiction Audio Player (http://bcs.bedfordstmartins.com/virtualit). Discuss Kincaid's rendition. Is this how the students imagined the mother's voice? If they were to give a dramatic reading, how would they perform the mother's voice?

3. Ask the students to separate into small reading groups, and ask each group to choose another short work of fiction from this volume. Each group should prepare and deliver a brief presentation on the differences of genre and style that it finds between Jamaica Kincaid and its chosen author.

Paper Topics/Suggestions for Writing

1. Write a reader response essay in which you react to the narrative style of "Girl." How did the mother's direct address to you, as if you were her daughter, affect your understanding of the story? Did it reinforce any of the major themes of the story?

2. How would you classify the mother's advice? Is it nurturing and supportive? Is it condemning and admonishing? Is it both? What does the nature of the mother's advice tell you about growing up as a woman in Antigua?

3. Analyze this quotation by Jamaica Kincaid, using research on the history of colonization in Antigua: "I've come to see that I've worked through the relationship of the mother and the girl to a relationship between Europe and the place that I'm from, which is to say, a relationship between the powerful and the powerless. The girl is powerless and the mother is powerful. The mother shows her how to be in the world, but at the back of her mind she thinks she never will get it. She's deeply

skeptical that this child could ever grow up to be a self-possessed woman and in the end she reveals her skepticism; yet even within the skepticism is, of course, dismissal and scorn. So it's not unlike the relationship between the conquered and the conqueror" (Vorda, 12).

4. Although the mother repeats instructions for how to avoid being "the slut I know you are so bent on becoming," she also instructs her daughter about "how to love a man" and "how to throw away a child before it even becomes a child" (2634). Is the mother unknowingly contradicting herself, or does she consciously doubt that her daughter will follow her repeated advice not to be a slut? How do the issues of being a slut and aborting a child relate to the other advice given? Is there a particular moral code implied in this story?

5. Discuss the fluid form of the story. What is a prose poem? Why is the sentence-long story punctuated with semicolons? Why does "Girl" rely on rhythm sporadically?

6. What is the setting of the story? Is the mother addressing the daughter at the present time, giving her this advice as a rite of passage into adulthood? Or could the daughter be reminiscing about her mother's guidance, collapsing the advice into one memory or one speech?

Resources

Bloom, Harold, ed. *Jamaica Kincaid*. New York: Infobase Publishing, 2008.
This volume is a collection of critical essays about Jamaica Kincaid and her works, edited by Harold Bloom. As Bloom observes in his "Editor's Note," "all the contributors to this volume . . . value her primarily upon an ideological basis" (vii). In this context, Bloom's brief introduction, which praises her style and imagination, is refreshing and recommended.

Bouson, J. Brooks. *Jamaica Kincaid: Writing Memory, Writing Back to the Mother*. Albany: State University of New York Press, 2006.
This book mentions "Girl," but it does not offer an extended reading of the story. However, many of Jamaica Kincaid's other works, like "Girl," are about the relationship between mothers and daughters. The readings of those texts here offer a nice thematic cohesion to her oeuvre.

Kincaid, Jamaica. *Annie John*. New York: Farrar, Straus, and Giroux, 1985.
This coming-of-age novel shares many important themes with Jamaica Kincaid's "Girl," including the mother-daughter relationship that echoes the relationship between the colonizer and the colonized.

Kincaid, Jamaica. *A Small Place*. New York: Farrar, Straus, and Giroux, 1988.

Jamaica Kincaid's *A Small Place* is part memoir and part essay about Antigua's history as a colony of England and how the history still affects the nation through tourism and a corrupt government. Like Kincaid's "Girl," it addresses the lingering effects of colonialism.

Vorda, Allan. "An Interview with Jamaica Kincaid." *Mississippi Review* 20:1–2 (1991): 7–26.

This interview can be used as a source for Paper Topic 3.

Toni Morrison

Recitatif

> And it shames me even now to think there was
> somebody in there after all who heard us call
> her those names and couldn't tell on us.
> —Morrison, "Recitatif"

Topics for Lecture or Discussion

1. **By titling this story "Recitatif," Toni Morrison reinforces the theme of the integration of disparate parts.** A "recitatif" (French), or the more common "recitative" (English), is a term for a form of music that balances the spoken and the sung. A recitative is commonly found in opera as a type of dialogue or narration; it is sung, but the words follow speech patterns and rhythms rather than the more typical structural inversions that occur in songs. This balance of distinct parts that a recitative accomplishes is usually essential for the development and progression of the plot. In referring to this musical term, Morrison indicates the necessary balance and integration between different races. Furthermore, the structure of the story constitutes five distinct parts that narrate five different moments when Twyla and Roberta meet, and one might infer that the friendship and antagonism narrated in these moments must be similarly balanced in the manner of a recitative.

   a. **Further Reading:** Obadike, Mendi Lewis. "Music." In *The Toni Morrison Encyclopedia*, edited by Elizabeth Ann Beaulieu, 225–30. Westport, CT: Greenwood Press, 2003.

   b. **Suggested Searches:** Go to youtube.com and search for the video "What Is a recitative?" (4:40). A further search for "Recitative and Aria" results in many examples from various operas and oratorios.

2. **The themes of motherhood and the relationship between parent and child are central elements in "Recitatif."** The opening sentence of the story establishes this theme, as both of the main characters are identified through the descriptions of their mothers: "My mother danced all night and Roberta's was sick" (2636). Because both Roberta's and Twyla's mothers are still alive, the girls are regarded as distinct from the other children at the orphanage, and when the mothers visit them, the girls' friendship contrasts with the immediate hostility between their mothers (and this is itself a forecast of the antagonism between Twyla and Roberta). As adults, Twyla and Roberta find themselves on opposing sides of the school desegregation issue, both because of race and

because of their disagreements about what is good for their children. Roberta says, "It's not about us, Twyla. Me and you. It's about our kids" (2646), but in fact this central theme of motherhood involves both Roberta and Twyla, their mothers, and their children. Other points that are pertinent to a discussion of motherhood in the story are that Roberta is a stepmother, whereas Twyla is a biological mother, and that as a child Twyla called her mother by her first name, Mary.

   a. **Further Reading:** Androne, Helane Adams. "Revised Memories and Colliding Identities: Absence and Presence in Morrison's 'Recitatif' and Viramontes's 'Tears on My Pillow.'" *MELUS* 32:2 (Summer 2007): 133–50.

   b. **Suggested Search:** Go to the National Public Radio website at www .npr.org and search for "Toni Morrison: A Mother, A Stranger, 'A Mercy'" for a four-part recording of Toni Morrison reading and discussing one of her recent novels, *A Mercy*, which shares with "Recitatif" the central theme of motherhood.

3. **By informing the reader that Twyla and Roberta are black and white, but never stating which character is which race, Toni Morrison invites reflection about the role that race plays in understanding characters and interpreting their actions.** The childhood friendship between the girls takes place despite the suggested racism of their mothers, as the narrator admits that her mother will not be pleased that she was roommates with a member of a different race (2637). Similar racial elements persist throughout the story, though they rarely take center stage; even when Twyla and Roberta are on opposing sides of the picket line protesting elements of school desegregation, Morrison paints their disagreement in terms of their rights as mothers and their children's wishes: "They want to take my kids and send them out of the neighborhood. They don't want to go" (2646). By obscuring the specific races of the characters in the story—including Maggie's (even Twyla and Roberta find Maggie's race confusing)—Morrison challenges the reader to contemplate the role that race plays in one's identity and also emphasizes a common humanity among Twyla, Roberta, and Maggie.

   a. **Further Reading:** Bennett, Juda. "Toni Morrison and the Burden of the Passing Narrative." *African American Review* 35:2 (Summer 2001): 211–17.

   b. **Suggested Search:** Go to charlierose.com and search for "A Conversation with author Toni Morrison" for a 2008 interview with Charlie Rose (31 min.).

4. **Roberta's exclamation at the end of the story, "What the hell happened to Maggie?" (2649), illustrates the different perceptions and memories that people can have concerning the same event.** When,

as adults, Roberta tells Twyla that Maggie's fall was not accidental, but that the older girls had pushed her down, Twyla becomes confused and thinks to herself, "Roberta had messed up my past somehow with that business about Maggie. I wouldn't forget a thing like that. Would I?" (2645). Then when Roberta later claims, "You kicked her. We both did. You kicked a black lady who couldn't even scream" (2647), both Roberta and Twyla become confused about Maggie's race and what exactly happened when Maggie fell. At the conclusion of the story, Roberta admits that they did not kick Maggie (2649), though her account that the older girls did push and kick her still conflicts with Twyla's original account (2637), and neither woman can properly remember Maggie's race. All of these elements demonstrate both the difficulty of properly remembering and understanding past events, especially when events are influenced by great emotion, and the challenge to readers to question the accuracy and reliability of the narrator.

a. **Further Reading:** Sklar, Howard. "'What the Hell Happened to Maggie?': Stereotype, Sympathy, and Disability in Toni Morrison's 'Recitatif.'" *Journal of Literary and Cultural Disability Studies* 5:2 (2011): 137–54.

b. **Suggested Search:** A search at Literature Online (lion.chadwyck .com) for "unreliable narrator" results in several helpful reference entries and articles.

5. **There was great civil and political strife over the racial desegregation of schools during the 1970s and 1980s; "Recitatif" illustrates that these tensions, on a very personal level, destroyed friendships and made evident the growth of racial prejudice.** As children, Roberta and Twyla recognized their racial differences but did not view them as a barrier to their friendship. When, later, Roberta acts rudely to Twyla at Howard Johnson's, her behavior is not overtly racist but merely ill will. So, too, when they meet at the food emporium, they are once again friendly and there is no sense of racial tension. Yet when the school desegregation occurs, the women end up on different sides, and though they couch their arguments in terms of their children, they also become racially antagonistic toward each other, with both of them asking, "I wonder what made me think you were different?" (2646). Tragically, Twyla and Roberta adopt racial prejudices that fill the political environment around them rather than behave in the more rational and humane manner to which they had been accustomed.

a. **Further Reading:** Morrison, Toni. *Remember: The Journey to School Integration.* New York: Houghton Mifflin, 2004.

b. **Suggested Search:** Go to c-span.org and search for "Toni Morrison," which results in a video of a talk that Toni Morrison delivered regarding the desegregation of schools and *Brown v. Board of Education.*

6. **The treatment of Maggie at the hands of Roberta and Twyla illustrates the human tendency to despise those less fortunate than oneself, and this parallels the racial themes throughout the story.** As Twyla narrates her childhood, she describes her attitude by recalling, "Maggie fell down there once. . . . We should have helped her up, I know, but we were scared of those girls with lipstick and eyebrow pencil" (2637). Yet Roberta and Twyla also call Maggie names, and Twyla states, "I think she could hear and didn't let on. And it shames me even now to think there was somebody in there after all who heard us call her those names" (2638). Recognizing their cruelty as children is only part of the realization that Twyla and Roberta share at the conclusion of the story, for they both also come to the realization that they projected hateful aspects of their lives onto Maggie: "I didn't kick her; I didn't join in with the gar girls and kick that lady, but I sure did want to. We watched and never tried to help her and never called for help. Maggie was my dancing mother. Deaf, I thought, and dumb. . . . Nobody who would hear you if you cried in the night" (2648). Seeing part of themselves in Maggie did not provoke pity in them when they were young, and only as adults did they realize with horror their attitude toward the disabled and unfortunate.

   a. **Further Reading:** Stanley, Sandra Kumamoto. "Maggie in Toni Morrison's 'Recitatif': The Africanist Presence and Disability Studies." *MELUS* 36:2 (Summer 2011): 71–88.

   b. **Suggested Search:** Go to youtube.com and search for "Toni Morrison Talks about Her Motivation for Writing," which results in several interesting interviews in which Toni Morrison discusses her craft.

In-Class Activities

1. Students should work independently to complete the following exercise: First, ask students to choose one scene from the story that features both Roberta and Twyla. Instruct them to draw or illustrate that scene. Then, ask students to respond to the following writing exercise prompt: "In your illustration, is Roberta white or black? How did you know? Is Twyla white or black? How did you know?" One of Toni Morrison's goals with this, her only short story, was to reveal any latent prejudicial thinking her readers may still maintain. Use this exercise—and subsequent discussion, if students are comfortable—to reveal any persistent stereotypes.

2. Have students work in groups to track any shifts in narrative style from the beginning to the end of the story. Does Twyla's voice or tone change as she and Roberta age, or is her narrative style consistent? Students should excerpt specific passages from each segment to support their argument.

3. Play the video "Toni Morrison: Challenges as a Female Writer" (2:57). In this excerpt of an interview, Toni Morrison discusses why she insists on being a black female writer. After showing this interview, discuss how this point coincides with "Recitatif." How does Morrison's aesthetic and professional role in the literary canon resemble the central concerns of the short story?

Paper Topics/Suggestions for Writing

1. Why is the story titled "Recitatif"? In what way does this story combine speech and song?

2. Did you notice that Toni Morrison does not assign a race to Twyla and Roberta, other than to say that one is black and one is white? If so, did you try to figure out or at least assume the race of the characters? How did you do so? Did this reveal any racial biases you unknowingly maintain? After considering the lack of knowledge with which you as a reader had to contend, explain why Morrison would leave out this information.

3. Analyze the role of motherhood in the story. Consider Twyla's and Roberta's mothers, but also consider Twyla and Roberta as mothers. Why are Twyla's signs (especially those that read "HOW WOULD YOU KNOW?" and "IS YOUR MOTHER WELL?") so disturbing to Roberta? Is the struggle with mothers and/or motherhood a racial issue for Toni Morrison like fatherhood is for James Baldwin in "Notes of a Native Son"?

4. Is Twyla a reliable narrator? Why are readers given her version of the story when both she and Roberta are the main characters? How do you think the story would have been told differently if Roberta were the narrator?

5. Who is Maggie? What details does the story provide about her? Why is she so important to Twyla and Roberta's relationship from childhood to adulthood? How do they empathize with her?

6. "Part 1. Combray" of Marcel Proust's *Swann's Way* is often referred to as the "Overture" to the work. Toni Morrison's "Recitatif" is also named after a musical piece. What themes do these works share? Consider childhood perspectives of the adult world, mother and child relationships, and memory. Why do musical terms help capture those themes?

Resources

Li, Stephanie. *Toni Morrison: A Biography*. Santa Barbara, CA: Greenwood Press, 2010.

This brief biography of Toni Morrison is accessible and concise enough to be of substantial assistance to students wanting to learn more or trying to further contextualize Morrison's work.

Nicol, Kathryn. "Visible Differences: Viewing Racial Identity in Toni Morrison's Paradise and 'Recitatif.'" In *Literature and Racial Ambiguity*, edited by Teresa Hubel and Neil Edward Brooks, 209–32. New York: Rodopi, 2002.

> Kathryn Nicol's essay offers readers a theoretical approach to the possibility of racial ambiguity in Toni Morrison's work and contains several illuminating quotes from her other works that will help students understand "Recitatif."

Patterson, Robert J. "Disrupting Racial Discourse: Teaching 'Recitatif.'" In *The Fiction of Toni Morrison: Reading and Writing on Race, Culture, and Identity*, edited by Jami L. Carlacio, 97–107. Urbana, IL: National Council of Teachers of English, 2007.

> Robert Patterson's work should prove helpful in presenting the story to students who may be coming face-to-face with lingering beliefs about racial stereotypes. The other essays in this volume also are helpful for instructors teaching Toni Morrison's works.

Talley, Justine, ed. *The Cambridge Companion to Toni Morrison*. New York: Cambridge University Press, 2007.

> The selection of essays in this volume orients and contextualizes Toni Morrison's work; this volume is recommended for students and instructors alike. Abena P. A. Busia's essay "The Artistic Impulse of Toni Morrison's Shorter Works" (101–14) is recommended for classes reading "Recitatif."

Taylor-Guthrie, Danille, ed. *Conversations with Toni Morrison*. Jackson: University Press of Mississippi, 1994.

> Danille Taylor-Guthrie presents in this volume a collection of twenty-four interviews and conversations with Toni Morrison that paint a complete picture of the author's aesthetic theories, politics, and biography.

ISABEL ALLENDE

And of Clay Are We Created

> I recognized the precise moment at which Rolf gave up the fight and surrendered to the torture of watching the girl die. I was with them, three days and two nights, spying on them from the other side of life.
>
> —Isabel Allende, "And of Clay Are We Created"

Topics for Lecture or Discussion

1. **Isabel Allende's "And of Clay Are We Created" is a powerful story in part because it deftly intertwines three characters' distinct struggles and suffering in one brief narrative.** An important question for readers is to ask whether there is a main character in the story. The narrator is the woman, Eva Luna, but her experience of the tragedy is partially mediated through the television and her distance from the event. In contrast, the trapped girl, Azucena, is certainly at the center of the action in the story, but she is relatively unknown to the narrator and not given the psychological complexity that Rolf Carle is given. In fact, Allende has described her various drafts of the story, in which her understanding of her story evolved from being about Azucena, to being about Rolf, to being about Eva Luna and the changes that she undergoes while watching the tragedy on television (see the Further Reading selection for Allende's interview).

   a. **Further Reading:** Iftekharuddin, Farhat. "An Interview with Isabel Allende." In *Speaking of the Short Story: Interviews with Contemporary Writers*, edited by Farhat Iftekharuddin, Maurice Lee, and Mary Rohrberger, 314. Jackson, MS: University Press of Mississippi, 1997.

   b. **Suggested Search:** Go to youtube.com and search for "Isabel Allende Interview (Artist Toolbox)" for an interview (12 min.) in which Allende speaks about art and her approach to writing.

2. **Isabel Allende's story examines the media in two distinct respects: the role of the media at the scene of a tragedy, and the role of the media in conveying a tragedy to individuals far from the actual place where it occurred.** Rolf Carle is important for both portrayals of the media, for while all of the other cameras simply follow the story and attempt to interview Azucena, he is moved to action and attempts to save her in whichever way he can. The media are more generally interested in the news story rather than in the reality of human suffering,

but this is not wholly reprehensible because the attention that the media bring to the tragedy is itself the source of aid from other countries (2656–57). In this respect, the media also bridge the gap of space and emotional distance that would otherwise exist between Eva Luna (the narrator) and Rolf, as she is able to follow his actions and suffering with close attention: "National Television began receiving sharper pictures and clearer sound; the distance seemed suddenly compressed, and I had the horrible sensation that Azucena and Rolf were by my side, separated from me by impenetrable glass" (2655).

a. **Further Reading:** Gough, Elizabeth. "Vision and Division: Voyeurism in the Works of Isabel Allende." *Journal of Modern Literature* 27:4 (Summer 2004): 93–120.

b. **Suggested Search:** Go to youtube.com and search for "Isabel Allende discusses the writing process" for an interview in which she discusses her particular process of research, writing, and inspiration.

3. **Rolf Carle's emotional suffering as he watches Azucena slowly die is not only indicative of his compassionate nature but, as Eva Luna realizes, it prompts him to face his own difficult memories.** Rolf's memories about his tragic childhood in Eastern Europe under the Nazis and Communists had been buried, and Azucena's situation reawakens what not even he could consciously call to mind. Azucena overcomes "the obstacles that had blocked his consciousness for so long" (2656), and Eva Luna realizes that "the girl had touched a part of him that he himself had no access to, a part he had never shared with me" (2657). Rolf deeply struggles with himself and his memories, and Eva Luna realizes this and gives him time to recover in the following months. However, when she addresses him in her comments at the conclusion of the story, the reader must wonder if she really understands: "Beside you, I wait for you to complete the voyage into yourself, for the old wounds to heal. I know that when you return from your nightmares, we shall again walk hand in hand, as before" (2658). Do all old wounds heal? Perhaps the narrator is overly hopeful.

a. **Further Reading:** Maier, Linda S. "Mourning Becomes *Paula*: The Writing Process as Therapy for Isabel Allende." *Hispania* 86:2 (May 2003): 237–43.

b. **Suggested Search:** A search for "Isabel Allende" at www.metroactive.com results in an article discussing Allende's work *Paula*, in which she struggles with her own memories and the death of her daughter.

4. **"And of Clay Are We Created" is based on true events. In 1985, the volcano Nevado del Ruiz erupted, and the ensuing landslides and mudslides buried the surrounding towns, most notably Armero, killing more than twenty thousand people.** Commonly called the "Armero

Tragedy," this event was the basis of Isabel Allende's story in several ways, including the fact that seismologists had warned that the volcano was becoming particularly active. As Allende writes, "Geologists had set up their seismographs weeks before and knew that the mountain had awakened again. For some time they had predicted that the head of the eruption could detach the eternal ice from the slopes" (2652). Similarly, a thirteen-year-old girl named Omayra Sanchez was caught in the mud. Three days later, she was photographed by journalist Frank Fournier and became a symbolic face for the tragedy and the general difficulties and governmental incompetence in dealing with the situation. Allende was deeply moved by the event, and since the publication of her story, she has said that she was haunted by Omayra's eyes as she was stuck in the mud.

    a. **Further Reading:** "Picture Power: Tragedy of Omayra Sanchez." BBC News. September 30, 2005. http://news.bbc.co.uk/2/hi/4231020 .stm.

    b. **Suggested Search:** A search for "Armero Tragedy" at youtube.com results in many videos and news stories about the tragic situation.

5. **"And of Clay Are We Created" is told in the form of a first-person narrative, but several passages in the story describe what could not possibly be known by the narrator.** As the narrator, Eva Luna, describes Rolf Carle's first efforts at freeing Azucena, she indicates that her knowledge is from watching Rolf in the television broadcast: "Despite the quality of the transmission, I could hear his voice break, and I loved him more than ever" (2653). Yet in the following passages, the narrator transitions to present her knowledge as omniscient, recounting Rolf's thoughts at the time: "He thought, she's already too old for dolls, and I don't know what would please her; maybe a dress. I don't know much about women, he concluded, amused, reflecting that although he had known many women in his lifetime, none had taught him these details" (2654). Eva Luna's narration of Rolf's thoughts, feelings, and memories—things that she admits "he had never shared with me" (2657)—should encourage the reader to question the accuracy of her narration and whether she is imposing her own interpretation of things upon Rolf.

    a. **Further Reading:** Gregory, Stephen. "Scheherazade and Eva Luna: Problems in Isabel Allende's Storytelling." *Bulletin of Spanish Studies: Hispanic Studies and Researches on Spain, Portugal and Latin America* 80:1 (2003): 81–101.

    b. **Suggested Search:** A search for "Isabel Allende Interview" at bigth ink.com results in a helpful interview in which Allende discusses nationality, her letter writing, and its influence on her fiction.

In-Class Activities

1. By doing a simple Google Images search for "Armero Tragedy," you can show your students that many results are of photographs of Omayra Sanchez, who has become a media icon of that disaster. Discuss other tragedies and the famous images that the media made iconic. Students might mention Kim Phuc burned by napalm, Thich Quang Duc's self-immolation, the destruction of the Twin Towers on 9/11, the man standing up to the tanks in Tiananmen Square, the mother of the Great Depression (Florence Owens Thompson), or "The Last Jew of Vinnitsa" photo. Discuss how these images come to represent those events. Have they become less impactful because of their widespread presence?

2. Begin class with the following writing exercise prompt: "Describe a major event that you only experienced through the media. Then describe an event for which you were actually present. Was there a difference for you between those two experiences? In the age of such advanced technology, does 'being there' really matter? Explain how the speaker of the short story might describe the differences."

3. Show Isabel Allende speaking at TED.com. The 18-minute video is titled "Isabel Allende Tells Tales of Passion." In it she discusses passion's role in life and art. After playing the video, discuss her aesthetic theory and how it relates to "And of Clay Are We Created."

Paper Topics/Suggestions for Writing

1. The narrator describes events at which she was not physically present. Analyze this narrative in terms of technology's and the media's effects on genuine experience.

2. The narrator of this story is Eva Luna, the main character of Isabel Allende's earlier novel, *Eva Luna*. In that novel, Eva Luna is a great storyteller, compared by many critics to Scheherazade from *The Thousand and One Nights*. Connect this story's theme of media sensationalism and audience-tailored stories to Allende's allusion to *The Thousand and One Nights*. The narrator says, "I was able to follow events hour by hour; I knew everything my love did to wrest the girl from her prison and help her endure her suffering; I overheard fragments of what they said to one another and could guess the rest; I was present when she taught Rolf to pray, and when he distracted her with the stories I had told him in a thousand and one nights beneath the white mosquito netting of our bed" (2655).

3. What role does the president of the Republic play in the events of the story? What does he symbolize for the story itself? Is he comparable to

the senator from Gabriel García Márquez's "Death Constant Beyond Love"?

4. Why didn't the townspeople evacuate when the geologists learned from their seismographs that the volcano would soon erupt? What does it mean that their warnings "sounded like the tales of frightened old women" (2652)?

5. Analyze Rolf Carle's response to Azucena's situation. How does his perspective change throughout the story? Why do his own memories suddenly wash over him? How does his response differ from his partner's, who narrates the story?

6. The title of the story alludes to both Eastern and Western religious myths about the creation of humankind. Discuss why Isabel Allende would title this story based on the belief that humans are made of earth and will one day return to earth. Why does the title begin with the word "And"?

7. In an interview, when asked if her works include elements of magical realism, Isabel Allende said, "In world literature, including modern U.S. fiction, written, for example, by women of ethnic minorities, African-American women, Chinese-American women, there are elements of the imagination as extraordinary as the ones employed by those [writers] of Latin America's 'Boom.' These occur in Scandinavian sagas, in German Gothic literature, in all parts of the world. By incorporating these elements of the imagination, literature, precisely, enriches reality" (Zapata-Whelan). Analyze this statement. Do you agree that literary works from other parts of the world—especially those written by "women of ethnic minorities"—are as magical as Allende's story, as well as Latin American literature in general? In your answer, refer to other works that you have read this semester.

Resources

Bloom, Harold, ed. *Isabel Allende*. Philadelphia: Chelsea House Publishers, 2003.
> This collection of fourteen critical essays also includes a short biography, a chronology of Isabel Allende's life and publications, and an introduction by Harold Bloom. Edna Aguirre Rehbein's essay "Isabel Allende's Eva Luna and the Act/Art of Narrating" is particularly recommended, as certain elements are equally applicable to "And of Clay Are We Created."

Correas de Zapata, Celia. *Isabel Allende: Life and Spirits*. Trans. Margaret Sayers Peden. Houston, TX: Arte Publico Press, 2002.

Though slightly dated now, this volume is an informative biography interspersed with interviews and is recommended for both students and instructors seeking a larger context for understanding Isabel Allende's work.

Cox, Karen Castellucci. *Isabel Allende: A Critical Companion*. Westport, CT: Greenwood Press, 2003.

This volume is a helpful collection of chapters on each of Isabel Allende's major works. Offered are summaries and interpretations that are straightforward thematic discussions. The first chapter is a brief (twelve-page) biography that is recommended for those unfamiliar with Allende's life.

Zapata-Whelan, Carol. "The Difference between Fantasy and Imagination: A Conversation with Isabel Allende." *Margin: Exploring Modern Magical Realism*. www.angelfire.com/wa2/margin/nonficCZWEnglish.html.

This interview can be used as a source for Paper Topic 7.

JUNOT DÍAZ

Drown

> One teacher, whose family had two grammar
> schools named after it, compared us to the
> shuttles. A few of you are going to make it.
> Those are the orbiters. But the majority of you
> are just going to burn out. Going nowhere. He
> dropped his hand onto his desk. I could already
> see myself losing altitude, fading, the earth
> spread out beneath me, hard and bright.
> —Junot Díaz, "Drown"

Topics for Lecture or Discussion

1. **A central theme of Junot Díaz's "Drown" is the difficulty of changing one's place in life, despite the recognition that there are preferable alternatives that might be achieved with hard work.** The story begins, "My mother tells me Beto's home, waits for me to say something, but I keep watching TV" (2659), and in a symbolic manner the narrator's persistence in simply watching TV reflects what is later revealed, as the narrator had skipped school and spent much of his time watching television (2664). Despite the fact that the narrator admits "I want to be away from here" (2664), he does not take any particular course of action in changing his position, including avoiding the military recruiter who offers a viable and honorable alternative to life as a drug dealer. In many respects, he himself is the primary obstacle for bettering his situation. When Beto goes to college, the narrator remembers, "You can't be anywhere forever, was what Beto used to say, what he said to me the day I went to see him off" (2667), yet when Beto gives him a book, he simply throws it away. The story concludes without any significant change in, or even an attempt to change, his situation.

    a. **Further Reading:** Frydman, Jason. "Violence, Masculinity, and Upward Mobility in the Dominican Diaspora: Junot Díaz, the Media, and Drown." *Columbia Journal of American Studies* 8 (Spring 2007): 99–118.

    b. **Suggested Search:** Go to youtube.com and search for "Junot Díaz 2009 National Book Festival," which results in a video of Díaz answering questions and discussing his craft.

2. **Junot Díaz's use of English, Spanish, and "Spanglish" emphasizes the cultural interactions that take place in the story.** These interactions reflect a variety of elements, including economic, sexual, and

racial differences. When the narrator describes Beto by saying, "He's a pato now but two years ago we were friends and he would walk into the apartment without knocking" (2659), the use of Spanish slang to describe Beto as a homosexual emphasizes both the sexual differences between the boys and the cultural elements of the narrator's immigrant family. Similarly, the narrator recalls the sign by the edge of the pool: "*No Horseplay, No Running, No Defecating, No Urinating, No Expectorating*. At the bottom someone has scrawled in *No Whites, No Fat Chiks*" (2661, emphases and misspelling in original). Elements of antagonism between races parallel the tensions between different sexual orientations, as well as the dramatic differences between those able to go to college and those who work part time and use drugs.

a. **Further Reading:** Torres, Lourdes. "In the Contact Zone: Code-Switching Strategies by Latino/a Writers." *MELUS* 32.1 (Spring 2007): 75–96.

b. **Suggested Search:** A search for "Junot Díaz on becoming an American" at www.npr.org results in an interview with Díaz (audio and text available) in which he speaks of his experience as an immigrant.

3. **As noted in the introduction to Junot Díaz in our anthology (2658), certain aspects of the relationship between the narrator and his parents are reminiscent of Telemachus's situation in Homer's *The Odyssey*.** Odysseus's long absence from Ithaca leaves his son Telemachus in the unenviable position of defending his mother, Penelope, and their family possessions from many aggressive and disrespectful suitors. The narrator of "Drown," like Telemachus, cares for his mother, giving her money, paying some of her bills, escorting her on trips to the mall, and constantly checking to make sure the windows are securely shut: "She drags us through the apartment to make sure the windows are locked. She can't reach the latches so she has me test them . . . putting my hand on the latch is not enough—she want[s] to hear it rattle. This place just isn't safe, she tells me" (2662). In addition to the fulfillment of these filial duties, the narrator guides his mother in her relationship with his father and remembers his father's tough but correct lessons: "He was a charmer, my pop, a real asshole, but he was right" (2663). Apart from the more apparent similarities between the families in "Drown" and *The Odyssey*, however, it is also important to consider the implications of Díaz's story in its use of epic references. Is this story part of an epic about immigration, or about the struggles of youth in New Jersey?

a. **Further Reading:** Homer. *The Odyssey*. In *The Norton Anthology of World Literature*, 3rd ed., Volume A, edited by Martin Puchner et al., 332–85. New York: W. W. Norton & Company, 2012.

b. **Suggested Search:** At the Poets and Writers website (www.pw.org), a search for "Chasing the Whale: A Profile of Junot Díaz" results in an interesting article about Díaz and his writing process for *Drown* (the volume of short stories from which our story "Drown" is taken) and his Pulitzer Prize–winning novel *The Brief Wondrous Life of Oscar Wao.*

4. **Throughout the story, a sharp dichotomy between the narrator and Beto is emphasized, but the vibrancy of their friendship is in counterpoint to these many differences.** Beto is presented as studious and serious about school, whereas the narrator attempts to avoid his studies since he is not good at them. When, for example, they wait for the bus in the morning, the narrator recalls, "He [Beto] was already standing on line. I just stood back and grinned, my hands in my pockets" (2664). Despite playing hooky, however, the boys remain friends, and the narrator looks forward to seeing Beto when he returns from school. Indeed, their differences allow each to contribute something distinctive to their friendship, as Beto is particularly adept at shoplifting and confidently talking to adults, and the narrator is clever enough to investigate those things that do interest him: "He hated when I knew something he didn't . . . he thought I didn't read, not even dictionaries" (2661). Despite the striking differences between the boys, then, their friendship flourishes.
   a. **Further Reading:** Moreno, Marisel. "'The Important Things Hide in Plain Sight': A Conversation with Junot Díaz." *Latino Studies* 8:4 (2010): 532–42.
   b. **Suggested Search:** Go to youtube.com and search for "Colgate Living Writers: Junot Díaz," which results in a video of Díaz reading some of his work and answering questions (Díaz begins speaking shortly after the nine-minute mark).

5. **The title of this story, "Drown," is somewhat enigmatic—it encourages the reader to consider its potential metaphorical meanings.** An obvious referent for "drown" is the community pool where the neighborhood children swim at night, and at an important moment the narrator does come close to drowning. When he tells Beto that "expectorating" means spitting, he recalls, "He hated when I knew something he didn't. He put his hands on my shoulders and pushed me under. . . . He was stronger than me and held me down until water flooded my nose and throat" (2661). Though this is merely horseplay, common for boys in swimming pools, its relevance to the title of the story helps emphasize that the fundamental differences between the boys—Beto's desire to know things and the narrator's unambitious nonchalance—would later become a fundamental division between the friends. The title "Drown" can also be metaphorically understood as referring to the immigrants' new culture, the narrator's inability to escape from his situation, and the loss of the boys' friendship due to the cultural and intellectual distances between them.

a. **Further Reading:** Cespedes, Diogenes, and Silvio Torres-Saillant. "Fiction Is the Poor Man's Cinema: An Interview with Junot Díaz." *Callaloo* 23:3 (Summer 2000): 892–907.

b. **Suggested Search:** Go to youtube.com and search for "Junot Díaz Interview with Rafael Pi Roman," which results in a two-part video interview with Díaz.

In-Class Activities

1. Instruct students to work independently to track images of stagnation, confinement, and failure. Discuss these many images—the locked windows, the space shuttle, the swimming pool and its crowdedness—and their significance.

2. Begin class with the following writing exercise prompt: "Have you ever felt trapped, like Yunior? What circumstances kept you from leaving that situation? Compare your situation with Yunior's. Why couldn't—or didn't—he leave?"

3. Divide the students into research groups and then have each group prepare a brief presentation of points of similarity and dissimilarity between "Drown" and other works read in class, for example, Homer's *The Odyssey*, Virginia Woolf's *A Room of One's Own*, Samuel Beckett's *Endgame*, and William Faulkner's "Barn Burning."

Paper Topics/Suggestions for Writing

1. Analyze the following excerpt to determine Yunior's relationship with Beto and with his own Latino identity: "I sit near the sign that runs the pool during the day: *No Horseplay, No Running, No Defecating, No Urinating, No Expectorating*. . . . Beto hadn't known what expectorating meant though he was the one leaving for college. . . . Even then I didn't tell him; he thought I didn't read, not even dictionaries" (2661, emphasis in original). Is he ashamed of his ability to read?

2. Why is the story told in a combination of Spanish and English? Consider the epigraph to *Drown*, the short story collection in which "Drown" appeared, by Cuban writer Gustavo Perez-Firmat: "The fact that I / am writing to you / in English / already falsifies what I / wanted to tell you" (see Resources).

3. "Drown" closes with two parallel scenes: the narrator and Beto watch a pornographic movie together, and then the narrator and his mother watch a classic movie dubbed in Spanish. Analyze the significance of these parallel moments. How are they similar? How are they different?

4. Could this be classified as a coming-of-age story, though Yunior does not seem to actually "come of age"? Compare "Drown" with other similarly

themed texts about growing up, such as William Faulkner's "Barn Burning," James Baldwin's "Notes of a Native Son," or Alice Munro's "Walker Brothers Cowboy."

5. Why is the story entitled "Drown"? Did you expect a character to drown at the public pool? What sorts of metaphorical drowning are present in the story?

Resources

Díaz, Junot. *Drown*. New York: Riverhead Books, 2006.

This volume is a collection of ten of Junot Díaz's short stories, including "Drown," from which the collection takes its name. Many of the themes and ideas present in "Drown" resonate in the larger collection of stories. This work is recommended reading for both students and instructors and can be used as a source for Paper Topic 2.

Paravisini-Gebert, Lizabeth. "Junot Díaz's *Drown*: Revisiting 'Those Mean Streets.'" In *U.S. Latino Literature: A Critical Guide for Students and Teachers*, edited by Harold Augenbraum and Margarite Fernandez Olmos, 163–74. Westport, CT: Greenwood Press, 2000.

Though this essay is dated, insofar as it was written before the publication of Junot Díaz's Pulitzer Prize–winning novel, *The Brief Wondrous Life of Oscar Wao*, it is very helpful in that it addresses the issues in the collection of stories *Drown*. Other essays within this volume might also be of assistance in contextualizing Díaz and his work.

Saez, Elena Machado, and Raphael Dalleo. "Movin' On Up and Out: Lowercase Latino/a Realism in the Work of Junot Díaz and Angie Cruz." In *The Latino/a Canon and the Emergence of Post-Sixties Literature*, 73–106. New York: Palgrave Macmillan, 2007.

This chapter contains an analysis of Junot Díaz's distinctive use of a language and realism as a means of progressive thought and assumes a political approach to literature. This book is more appropriate for the instructor or the advanced student.

Roberto Bolaño

Sensini

> In one of his letters Sensini said he was worried that he might have run his race. I misunderstood; I thought he meant he was running out of competitions to enter.
> —Roberto Bolaño, "Sensini"

Topics for Lecture or Discussion

1. **In "Sensini," both the narrator and Sensini face the difficult issue of using literature or, more broadly, art as a commodity through which the artist makes money.** When the narrator first decides to enter a writing competition, he does so because he needs money, but he attempts to retain a part of his respect for the art of literature, as he states, "First I thought about trying for the poetry prize, but I felt it would be demeaning to send what I did best into the arena with the lions" (2669). His idea that it is demeaning to compete with one's finest work reserves some element of literature as art for its own sake. Sensini also struggles between the purely utilitarian approach to literature and a sense of higher accomplishment, as he is readily willing to be called a professional prize hunter, but he retains a sense of better and worse art, and he wrote to the narrator that "the little world of letters is terrible as well as ridiculous" (2672). This statement implies his own understanding of the demeaning aspect of using one's art for financial competition. On the other hand, he was living in poverty and deeply felt the pressing need of money for food and rent.
   a. **Further Reading:** Villoro, Juan. "Roberto Bolaño: The Future Battle." *Literature and Arts of the Americas* 43:1 (2010): 9–18.
   b. **Suggested Search:** A search for "Roberto Bolaño Advice on the Art of Writing Short Stories" at www.molossus.co results in the short, semicomical essay by Bolaño about his craft.

2. **The litany of authors to which the narrator refers when discussing both his and Sensini's artistic taste and talent is important because it indicates an understanding of literature as a partial reflection of other writers that an author has read.** Most undergraduates will be unfamiliar with such references as "I had read Abelardo Castillo's plays and the stories of Daniel Moyano and Rodolfo Walsh (who was killed under the dictatorship, like Conti) . . . they didn't have the stature of Borges or Cortázar, and were soon overtaken by Manuel Puig and Osvaldo Soriano" (2670). Yet the association between authors—and the

fact that they are understood as part of a tradition and as representatives of literary or historical movements—is important, and the narrator himself clearly expresses this sentiment when stating his honor at having placed in a competition with Sensini: "My favorite was Sensini, and having been his fellow runner-up in a provincial literary competition—an association I found at once flattering and profoundly depressing—encouraged me to make contact with him" (2670). Even if they never meet, as is the case with the narrator and Sensini, the web of influences between various authors is stressed and understood as a formative part of one's own art.

a. **Further Reading:** Villalobos-Ruminott, Sergio. "A Kind of Hell: Roberto Bolaño and the Return of World Literature." *Journal of Latin American Cultural Studies* 18:2–3 (2009): 193–205.

b. **Suggested Search:** A Google search for "Roberto Bolaño Infrarealist Manifesto" results in several links to English translations of the difficult, quixotic declaration about art and poetry.

3. **Like William Shakespeare's use of the name in his play *The Tempest*, Roberto Bolaño names Sensini's daughter "Miranda" as a reference to the long tradition associated with the word "wonder."** Etymologically, this name has Latin roots (*admirare, mirari*), meaning "to behold" or "to wonder," and a long tradition in Western literature understands wonder as a passion that is the result of recognizing one's ignorance (it is more simply stated as a sudden, powerful fear of ignorance). The person who wonders is led, consequently, to seek knowledge, and such knowledge can be gained through either the philosophical or the poetic act. Notably, just as Shakespeare's Miranda inspires wonder in others and is herself repeatedly filled with wonder, so too Sensini's daughter Miranda fills the narrator of the story with wonder. Miranda is described as "insatiably curious" (2673), and the narrator finds the picture of her "both moving and disturbing" (2674). The narrator states, "The photo and the photocopy lived on my desk for a long time. I would sit there staring at them or take them to the bedroom and look at them until I fell asleep" (2674). Similarly, while the narrator gazes with wonder at the picture, he is moved to the poetic act, writing, "a very long, very bad poem, full of voices and faces that seemed different at first, but all belonging to Miranda" (2674).

a. **Further Reading:** Quinn, Dennis. *Iris Exiled: A Synoptic History of Wonder.* Lanham, MD: University Press of America, 2002.

b. **Suggested Search:** The full text of William Shakespeare's *The Tempest* can be accessed at http://shakespeare.mit.edu. In Act 1, Scene II, one can see that Miranda is repeatedly filled with wonder over her father's stories.

4. **Roberto Bolaño's "Sensini" combines elements of epistolary narrative and the more direct realist narrative of a character recalling what has transpired.** Both narrative techniques are important elements of the story because they emphasize certain central themes. For example, epistolary narrative—narrative that is told through the form of letters between characters—is a literary form that is associated with the early stages of the genre of the novel, as Samuel Richardson's epistolary novel *Pamela* was extraordinarily popular in eighteenth-century England. "Sensini" includes certain elements of this epistolary form, including building suspense between the reception of various letters and limiting the reader's knowledge to that written by the correspondents in their letters. The reader is constrained to the narrator's knowledge of Sensini, and, like the narrator, the reader never comes to know Sensini directly. The direct, first-person narrative that is combined with these epistolary elements is presented in realist terms, as the narrator, like any person, does not perfectly remember details and only gives the reader a general sense of the information in the letters: "I remember thinking, what a strange letter. I remember reading a few chapters of *Ugarte*" (2671). These limitations of memory are important for the narrative, as they parallel the sorrowful memories that Sensini has of his lost son.
   a. **Further Reading:** Fludernik, Monika. "Letters as Narrative." In *Routledge Encyclopedia of Narrative Theory*, edited by David Herman, Manfred Jahn, and Marie-Laure Ryan, 227. London: Routledge, 2010.
   b. **Suggested Search:** A search for "The Face in the Mirror Roberto Bolaño" at the website for the *San Francisco Bay Guardian* (www .sfbg.com) results in a helpful article by Marcelo Ballvé that discusses certain elements of Bolaño's narrative technique.

5. **Roberto Bolaño's political views and activism inform elements of "Sensini," as the horrors that occurred in Argentina during the Dirty War under Jorge Rafael Videla are the cause of the disappearance of Sensini's son, Gregorio.** Bolaño's treatment of Videla's reign is not overtly political in this story, but through allusions to the disappearance of activists and intellectuals, and through the eventual discovery of the probable remains of Gregorio in a mass grave, Bolaño presents the reader with hints of the atrocities that occurred in Argentina. Similarly, the narrator remembers his final letter from Sensini: "He had written to say good-bye. He was going back to Argentina; with the return of democracy he would be safe now, so there was no point staying away any longer. And it was the only way he would be able to find out for sure what had happened to Gregorio" (2675). The fall of Videla's dictatorship in 1983 allowed the reformation of a democratic government, and this allowed the return of many who had fled the terrorizing

regime. Yet part of the power of Bolaño's fiction is that rather than dwelling upon the larger political picture, he portrays the situation through the particular human tragedy of Sensini and his son.

   a. **Further Reading**: Lewis, Paul H. *Guerrillas and Generals: The "Dirty War" in Argentina*. Westport, CT: Praeger, 2002.

   b. **Suggested Searches**: A Google Videos search (www.google.com/videohp) for "Argentina's Dirty War" results in a variety of videos and documentaries describing the various horrors of the war. A search at www.npr.org for "Argentina's Dirty War Still Haunts Youngest Victims" results in a recent story (audio and text, 2010) about how the ramifications of the Dirty War are still being felt.

In-Class Activities

1. Sensini—like his creator, Roberto Bolaño—is cynical toward the literary marketplace. Debate the following question: Is art really art if it is produced solely for economic means, for fame, or for some other ulterior motive? What do Bolaño's characters believe? What does Bolaño seem to believe?

2. Although he was hostile toward magical realism, Roberto Bolaño praised Jorge Luis Borges and Julio Cortázar, claiming that they had a great influence on his work. Have students work in pairs to compare and contrast "Sensini" with either Borges's "The Garden of Forking Paths" or Cortázar's "House Taken Over."

3. Distribute to the class the manifesto that Roberto Bolaño wrote for infrarealism, available online. Students should read it individually, working on a definition of the word "infrarealism." After they are finished reading the manifesto, discuss its genre and form. How do those two elements reinforce Bolaño's messages? Then discuss with students infrarealism. How did students define it? What passages particularly elucidate the movement? Finally, pose the following question: Can "Sensini" be considered a work of infrarealism? Why or why not?

Paper Topics/Suggestions for Writing

1. From this story, what can you glean from Roberto Bolaño's opinion of the literary world? Consider his criticisms of other writers, including Pablo Neruda, Gabriel García Márquez, and Isabel Allende.

2. What does it mean for Sensini to be dismissed as "Kafka in the colonies" by Spanish critics (2670)? Why would Roberto Bolaño allude so directly to Franz Kafka's "The Metamorphosis"? And why would Sensini give his son the namesake Gregor Samsa? How are the two stories—and the two characters—similar?

3. Analyze the speaker's obsession with Sensini and his later interest in Sensini's daughter, Miranda.

4. Research the Argentine Dirty War and the junta. Explain their effects on the characters in "Sensini."

5. What is the narrator's relationship to writing and the writing career? What is Sensini's relationship? Compare and contrast their ideas about the art with Elizabeth Costello's in J. M. Coetzee's "The Novel in Africa" or the narrator's in Chu T'ien-hsin's "Man of La Mancha."

Resources

Bolaño, Roberto. *Last Evenings on Earth*. Translated by Chris Andrews. New York: New Directions Books, 2007.

This volume is a collection of fourteen of Roberto Bolaño's short stories, selected from 1997's *Llamadas Telefonicas* and 2001's *Putas Asesinas*; they are highly recommended for those who wish to read additional works by Bolaño.

Corral, Will H. "Roberto Bolaño: Portrait of the Writer as Noble Savage." *World Literature Today* 80:6 (2006): 47–50.

This brief but helpful article discusses Roberto Bolaño as "savage," or his reputation as a difficult and provocative writer and personality.

Echevarria, Roberto Gonzalez. *Modern Latin American Literature: A Very Short Introduction*. Oxford: Oxford University Press, 2012.

While this work only briefly discusses Roberto Bolaño, it should be an excellent aid for instructors or students who wish to understand the larger context of the Latin American literature of which Bolaño was a part.

Pollack, Sarah. "Latin America Translated (Again): Roberto Bolano's *The Savage Detectives in the United States*." *Comparative Literature* 61:3 (2009): 346–65.

This essay is about Latin American writers and how their works are chosen for translation and publication in the United States.

Stavans, Ilan. "Roberto Bolaño's Ascent." *Chronicle of Higher Education* 55:17 (December 19, 2008): B20–B21.

Ilan Stavans's article discusses Roberto Bolaño's overnight rise to great popularity in academia and could be useful for prompting students to discuss the manner in which works are chosen for anthologies and how they enter into or fall out of the canon of what is typically read.

J. M. Coetzee
Elizabeth Costello

> The African novel is thus, I would claim, in its
> very being, and before the first word is writ-
> ten, a critique of the Western novel.
> —J. M. Coetzee, "The Novel in Africa"

Topics for Lecture or Discussion

1. **A central aspect of Elizabeth Costello's critique of Emmanuel Egudu is that he insincerely emphasizes his "exotic" nature as an African novelist for the success of his career, all the while blaming Western cultures and readers for forcing exoticism upon him and other African novelists.** As Costello thinks, "All of Emmanuel's talk of an oral novel . . . is just another way of propping up the mystique of the African as the last repository of primal human energies. Emmanuel blames his Western publishers and his Western readers for driving him to exoticize Africa; but Emmanuel has a stake in exoticizing himself" (2690). Egudu is able to follow a luxurious career without serious intellectual labor because he is treated as an exotic African, and he purposefully emphasizes this in lieu of actually grappling with the more difficult questions concerning the nature of the novel and its relation to different cultures. During his lecture, Costello thinks, "*Negritude*: she had thought Emmanuel would grow out of that pseudo-philosophy. Evidently he has not. Evidently he has decided to keep it as part of his professional pitch" (2686, emphasis in original).

   a. **Further Reading:** Bell, Michael. "What Is It Like to Be a Nonracist? Costello and Coetzee on the Lives of Animals and Men." In *J. M. Coetzee and the Idea of the Public Intellectual*, edited by Jane Poyner, 172–92. Athens, OH: Ohio University Press, 2006.

   b. **Suggested Search:** A search for "J. M. Coetzee, The Historical, and The Literary" at youtube.com results in a lecture about Coetzee given by Dominick LaCapra at Cornell University.

2. **While the title of J. M. Coetzee's story, "The Novel in Africa," is the title of Emmanuel Egudu's talk, the title of Elizabeth Costello's talk, "The Future of the Novel," is also important, and taken together the titles indicate the important point of contention throughout the story: What is a novel? How does one define a novel?** Several different definitions of the genre of the novel are given, as Elizabeth states, "The novel, the traditional novel . . . is an attempt to understand human fate one case at a time, to understand how it comes about that some

fellow being, having started at point A and having undergone experiences B and C and D, ends up at point Z" (2682). In contrast, Emmanuel states, "The African novel, the true African novel, is an oral novel" (2685), and he contrasts it to the "form of writing" (2685) that is the European novel. Elizabeth challenges this loose definition, seeking to distinguish between forms of live performance and the written medium of the novel (2688). A final, distinct understanding of the novel is also alluded to by Steve, the Englishman at their table, when he states, "You treat writing as a business. You identify a market and then set about supplying it. I was expecting something different" (2689). "The Novel in Africa" is, in these respects, a short story about the definition of a novel.

   a. **Further Reading:** McKeon, Michael, ed. *Theory of the Novel: A Historical Approach.* Baltimore, MD: Johns Hopkins University Press, 2000.

   b. **Suggested Search:** A search for "African novel" at Literature Online (lion.chadwyck.com) brings up many helpful results, especially reference entries from the *Encyclopedia of the Novel.*

3. **"The Novel in Africa" was first delivered by J. M. Coetzee as an Una's Lecture at the University of California at Berkeley, and the ability of the work to function as a lecture within a story, or conversely as a story within a lecture, is an important element of its structure.** Many readers will be struck by the fact that most of the story is simply a summary or transcription of the talks that Elizabeth Costello and Emmanuel Egudu deliver, and that much of the friction in the story is developed through the narration of Elizabeth's silent, intellectual disagreements with Emmanuel's points. In many ways, consequently, the work can easily function as a lecture delivered by Coetzee. Yet it also incorporates elements usually foreign to lectures, such as the development of debate within the work itself, and the important revelation at the end of the story of the past relationship between the story's characters. If "The Novel in Africa" addresses the important question of the definition of a novel (see topic 2), it also challenges a typical understanding of the genres of the short story and lecture.

   a. **Further Reading:** Clarkson, Carrol. *J. M. Coetzee: Countervoices.* New York: Palgrave Macmillan, 2009.

   b. **Suggested Search:** A search for "The Novel in Africa J. M. Coetzee" at http://townsendcenter.berkeley.edu results in a page describing his lecture, as well as a link to a pdf of "The Novel in Africa," with a helpful, brief introduction by Randolph Starn.

4. **Elizabeth Costello's talk about the future of the novel juxtaposes conceptions of the past and future that are important in understanding her character.** She states, "What is miraculous about the past is that we have succeeded . . . in making thousands and millions of

individual fictions, fictions created by individual human beings, lock well enough into one another to give us what looks like a common past, a shared story" (2682). She emphasizes the past, then, as a particularly meaningful conception of human life and action, but she disparages the idea of the future, for "we do not possess a shared story of the future. . . . Compared with our fiction of the past, our fiction of the future is a sketchy, bloodless affair" (2682). While these distinctions are important for several reasons—including the understanding of meaning as something created and dependent upon collective agreement—they are also important because as a philosophy, she finds them intellectually enervating: "She is not sure, as she listens to her own voice, whether she believes any longer in what she is saying" (2682). In contrast to this element of intellectual ambivalence that borders on despair, when she stumbles on an albatross on Macquarie Island, she thinks (with a possible reference to the albatross in Samuel Taylor Coleridge's "The Rime of the Ancient Mariner"), "Before the fall . . . this is how it must have been before the fall. I could miss the boat, stay here. Ask God to take care of me" (2691).

 a. **Further Reading:** Lenta, Margaret. "Coetzee and Costello: Two Artists Abroad." *English in Africa* 31:1 (May 2004): 105–19.

 b. **Suggested Searches:** A Google search for "The Rime of the Ancient Mariner" results in several links to the text of the poem. A Google Images search for "Gustave Dore The Rime of the Ancient Mariner" results in many of Dore's illustrations for the poem, including depictions of the albatross.

5. **The revelation at the conclusion of the story that Elizabeth Costello had slept with Emmanuel Egudu when they were younger complicates the friction between the characters throughout the story.** Elizabeth's anger toward Emmanuel and her doubt concerning the degree of his artifice ("Egudu smiles his big smile. . . . But she cannot believe it is a true smile, cannot believe it comes from the heart" (2687) are both presented in the story as an indignant but a rational disagreement with Emmanuel's thoughts and behavior. As she recalls her history with him at the beginning of the story, Elizabeth thinks, "Their acquaintance goes back more years than she cares to remember, to a PEN conference in Kuala Lumpur. Egudu had been loud and fiery then, political; her first impression was that he was a poseur. Reading him later on, she had not changed her mind" (2681). Without any hint toward their intimacy at the Kuala Lumpur conference, the reader is forced to reconsider Elizabeth's irritation with Emmanuel throughout the story when it is revealed that she had slept with him. Do they disagree with each other because of rational positions, or are Elizabeth and Emmanuel antagonistic toward one another because of their intimate and possibly emotional past?

a. **Further Reading:** Moses, Michael Valdez. "'King of the Amphibi-ans': Elizabeth Costello and Coetzee's Metamorphoric Fictions." *Journal of Literary Studies* 25:4 (2009): 25–38.

b. **Suggested Search:** A search for "J. M. Coetzee lecture" at www .utexas.edu results in an interesting talk he delivered at the Univer-sity of Texas (his alma mater).

In-Class Activities

1. If this text has been read at a late point in the semester, your students most likely have read some other African writers, such as Chinua Achebe, Ngugi wa Thiong'o, Bessie Head, and Niyi Osundare. Divide the class into two sides and have each side join the debate between J. M. Coetzee's characters, making reference to any other pertinent texts they have studied. Allow students time to discuss their assigned posi-tions. Ask these questions: What does Egudu believe about the African novel? And Elizabeth? With whom does Coetzee seem to agree?

2. Present students with the following writing exercise prompt: "Elizabeth claims that Egudu and all African novelists 'perform your Africanness at the same time as you write.'" Explain what Elizabeth means here. How can one "perform" an aspect of one's identity, such as nationality, race, or gender? Do you "perform," or have you ever "performed," an aspect of your identity? How? Why?

3. After lecturing or discussing J. M. Coetzee's interest in dismantling genre conventions, ask each student to analyze and explain "The Novel in Africa" as one of eight "lessons" included in *Elizabeth Costello*. Does "The Novel in Africa" teach Elizabeth a lesson? Is it a lesson she teaches us? Is it a lesson Coetzee has learned or is learning, or is it an arbitrary designation, meant to challenge our understanding of genre divisions?

Paper Topics/Suggestions for Writing

1. What is your impression of Elizabeth as a writer and teacher? Would you want to take a literature class with her? Why or why not? What is your impression of Emmanuel? Would you take a literature class from him?

2. Why is the setting of this story important? Why would J. M. Coetzee set these events on a cruise ship and, briefly, on Macquarie Island?

3. The final section of the story seems to imply that Elizabeth and Emmanuel's contentious professional relationship is a pretense of their personal relationship. Do you agree with this reading? Does this inter-pretation completely invalidate their literary arguments?

698 | *Global and Local in Contemporary World Literature*

4. Although Elizabeth is Australian, her novel, titled *The House on Eccles Street*, is, only presumably in this story, about the Irish author James Joyce and his novel *Ulysses* (elsewhere in the collection of stories *Elizabeth Costello*, readers learn that it is a retelling of *Ulysses* from the perspective of Leopold Bloom's wife, Molly Bloom). Note that Elizabeth also refers to England as "the mother country" (2680). Discuss her relationship to her own nationality, especially compared to Emmanuel's. What role does race play in this issue? What is the difference between race and nationality?

5. Is this story a critique of the commodification of postcolonial literature, world literature, or literature in general? Discuss your experience in this class: Have the works you have read thus far struck you as commodities that exploit postcoloniality or nationality?

6. What is this text's genre? Explain why J. M. Coetzee might nest lectures inside of fiction. Does this aspect support or undermine Elizabeth's opinion that "a novel about people who live in an oral culture . . . is not an oral novel. Just as a novel about women isn't a women's novel" (2690)?

7. Discuss the role of "audience" in the story. Consider both the readership about which Elizabeth and Emmanuel debate over dinner and the audience's reactions to both writers' lectures. You might also consider the extratextual readership, J. M. Coetzee's audience.

Resources

Boehmer, Elleke, Robert Eaglestone, and Katy Iddiols, eds. *J. M. Coetzee in Context and Theory*. New York: Continuum International Publishing Group, 2009.

    This volume is a collection of fourteen essays divided between issues of "Context" and "Theory" in J. M. Coetzee's oeuvre to date. Essays of particular interest might include "Elizabeth Costello as a Post-Apartheid Text" (pp. 20–35) and "Authenticity: Diaries, Chronicles, Records as Index-Simulations" (pp. 173–84).

Coetzee, J. M. *Doubling the Point: Essays and Interviews*. Edited by David Attwell. Cambridge, MA: Harvard University Press, 1992.

    J. M. Coetzee's essays and interviews are pieced together here to create a literary biography on a full range of topics. Though some may seem unrelated to Coetzee's literary development or persona, for example, "Triangular Structures of Desire in Advertising 1980," they work together to form a story of Coetzee's aesthetic theories and interests.

Coetzee, J. M. *Elizabeth Costello*. New York: Viking, 2003.

This volume is the full collection of the eight "lessons" featuring Elizabeth Costello. "The Novel in Africa" is the second story of the collection, and this is recommended for those seeking a deeper understanding of Costello's character.

Head, Dominic. *The Cambridge Introduction to J. M. Coetzee*. Cambridge: Cambridge University Press, 2009.

This work is a helpful introduction that includes chapters of J. M. Coetzee's life, the context in which he wrote, and chapters on his works. A helpful bibliography also is included.

Index

Achebe, Chinua, 475, 477, 600–605, 697

Aeneid (Virgil), 10, 26, 89–93, 96, 124, 146, 156, 166, 287, 338

Aeschylus, 39–44, 50, 65, 76, 77

Aesop, 29–32, 99, 143

Agamemnon (Aeschylus), 39–44, 64, 65, 280, 611

Airs, Waters, Places, 75–76, 77

[*A journey across many seas and through many nations*] (Catullus), 86

Akhmatova, Anna, 533, 535, 615

Alfonso X, 163

All alone am I, and alone I wish to stay (Christine de Pizan), 161, 164

Allende, Isabel, 529, 678–682, 692

All God's Chillen Had Wings, 469

Almond Trees, The (Walcott), 624, 625

Al-Zahra (Ibn Zaydun), 162

Anahorish (Heaney), 629

Anaxagoras, 5, 7

And of Clay Are We Created (Allende), 678–682

Antigone (Sophocles), 43, 48, 52–57, 82

Apuleius, 109–112

Archaic Torso of Apollo (Rilke), 533, 535

Archipoeta, 163

Ariosto, Ludovico, 228–231, 287

Aristophanes, 61, 64–67, 73, 79, 82

Arnaut Daniel, 163

Art of Love, The (Arnaut Daniel), 163

[*As I composed this little book*] (de Castro), 408–409

As John to Patmos (Walcott), 624

Aspen Tree (Celan), 567

Augustine, 113–116, 188, 361

Aura (Fuentes), 595, 606–610

"Authun and the Bear," 155–159

Bachmann, Ingeborg, 632–634

Baldwin, James, 572, 576–580, 676, 688

Barbauld, Anna Laetitia, 409, 410

Barking, The (Bachmann), 632–634

Barn Burning (Faulkner), 490, 515–519, 619–620, 687, 688

Bartleby, the Scrivener: A Story of Wall-Street (Melville), 398–401, 434

Battles of the Pen and the Scissors, The (Shem Tov Ardutiel), 163

Baudelaire, Charles, 112, 403, 404, 405, 409, 484, 486, 490, 630

Beatrice of Dia, 161, 164

Beattie, James, 297

Beckett, Samuel, 587–590, 687

Behn, Aphra, 321–324, 346

Bello, Andrés, 409

Beowulf, 123–127, 130, 131, 145, 156, 192, 290

Bernart de Ventadorn, 161

Bertran de Born, 139

Bible, Christian, 103–108, 142

Bible, Hebrew, 4, 14–20, 86–87, 103, 105, 118, 119, 121, 131, 139

Blake, William, 370, 405, 408, 409, 469

Boccaccio, Giovanni, 97, 109, 140, 147, 149, 166, 177–180, 182, 183, 184, 185, 201, 203, 243, 246, 563

Boethius, Ancius Manlius Severinus, 123, 161–162

Bolaño, Roberto, 689–693

Bolívar, Simón, 355, 358–359

Book of the City of Ladies, The (Christine de Pizan), 136, 139, 200–204

Book of the Courtier, The (Castiglione), 238–242

Borges, Jorge Luis, 525–529, 553, 595, 610, 615, 619, 692
Borowski, Tadeusz, 554–557, 575
Brecht, Bertolt, 520–524, 589
Breton, André, 538
Broagh (Heaney), 629
Browning, Elizabeth Barrett, 403–404, 408
Browning, Robert, 408, 410, 630
Bunina, Anna, 409
Burke, Edmund, 355, 358, 359

Calvino, Italo, 563–565
Camus, Albert, 400, 575, 582–586, 587
Candide, or Optimism (Voltaire), 221, 251, 343–347, 348–349, 351, 380, 418
Canterbury Tales, The (Chaucer), 97, 113, 169, 178, 182–189, 243, 476
Carcass, A (Baudelaire), 630
Castiglione, Baldassare, 238–242
Catullus, 72, 84–87, 164
Cavafy, Constantine, 533, 534
Celan, Paul, 567–569
Cervantes, Miguel de, 229, 248, 258–262, 426
Charles d'Orleans, 163
Chaucer, Geoffrey, 97, 113–114, 140, 145, 146, 149, 166, 177, 178, 182–189, 192, 243, 246, 315–316
Chekhov, Anton, 454–459
Cherry Orchard, The (Chekhov), 454–459
Chike's School Days (Achebe), 600–605
Chimney Sweeper, The (Blake), 405, 408, 409
Chrétien de Troyes, 146, 150–154, 425, 426
Christian Bible, The, 103–108, 142
Christine de Pizan, 136, 139, 161, 164, 200–204
Coetzee, J. M., 693, 694–698
Coleridge, Samuel Taylor, 361, 362, 406, 409, 410, 592, 595, 696
[*Come, you hendecasyllables, in force now,*] (Catullus), 86
Commedia (Dante Alighieri), 166

Confessions (Augustine), 113–116, 177, 361
Confessions (Rousseau), 355, 361–365, 390, 394, 401, 420, 423
Conrad, Joseph, 473–478, 601, 604, 639, 650–651
Consolation of Philosophy, The (Boethus), 123, 161–162
Conversation Between Me and the Women (Bunina), 409
Corona (Celan), 567
Correspondences (Baudelaire), 486, 490
Cortázar, Julio, 529, 549–553, 610, 615, 692
Crusoe's Journal (Walcott), 623, 625, 626
Cry of the Children, The (Browning), 408
Cult of Love, The (Hadewijch of Brabant), 161

D'Alembert, Jean le Rond, 296, 299, 329
Dancing Girl (Walther von der Vogelweide), 162
Dante Alighieri, 113–114, 124, 146, 166–171, 183, 184, 185, 188, 191, 192, 285
Darío, Rubén, 404, 409
Daydreams of a Drunk Woman, The (Lispector), 518, 597–599
Dead, The (Joyce), 492–496, 518
Death and the King's Horseman (Soyinka), 653–657
Death Constant Beyond Love (Márquez), 636–638, 642, 662–663, 682
Deathfugue (Celan), 568–569
[*Deathless Aphrodite of the spangled mind*] (Sappho), 35
Death of Ivan Ilyich, The (Tolstoy), 377, 423, 431–434, 447, 453
Decameron (Boccaccio), 97, 109, 147, 177–180, 182, 201, 243, 563
de Castro, Rosalía, 408–409
Declaration of Independence, 356, 358, 359, 365
Declaration of Sentiments (Stanton), 355–356, 358, 393, 409

Declaration of the Rights of Man and of the Citizen, 358, 359, 365
Deep River, The: A Story of Ancient Tribal Migration (Head), 658–660
Defense of Poetry (Shelley), 410
de La Fayette, Marie de la Vergne, 307–310
Descartes, René, 296, 299
Dessalines, Jean-Jacques, 359
Díaz, Junot, 604, 684–688
Dickinson, Emily, 407–408, 409
Dictionary of the English Language, A (Johnson), 465
Diderot, Denis, 296, 299, 329
Digging (Heaney), 629
Divine Comedy, The (Dante Alighieri), 113, 124, 166–171, 188
Donne, John, 284, 285, 338
Don Quixote (Cervantes), 109, 111, 229, 230, 248, 258–262, 426
Dostoyevsky, Fyodor, 377, 420–423, 434
Douglass, Frederick, 111, 356, 357–358, 359, 364–365, 366, 369, 392–396, 452, 453, 469
Drown (Díaz), 604, 684–688
Du Bellay, Joachim, 208, 209, 210

Easter 1916 (Yeats), 535
Eighteen Hundred and Eleven, a Poem (Barbauld), 409
Elegy (Walcott), 624
Elegy of the Circumcised (Senghor), 546
Eliot, T. S., 477, 484, 495, 531–532, 534, 535
Elizabeth Costello: Eight Lessons (Coetzee), 693, 694–698
Empedocles, 5, 7
Empty Garlic, An (Rumi), 164
Encyclopédie, The (Diderot and D'Alembert), 296, 299
Endgame (Beckett), 198, 587–590, 687
England in 1819 (Shelley), 409
Enuma Elish, 3, 5, 7
Epic of Gilgamesh, The, 8–13, 18, 24, 26, 73, 108, 126, 146, 158, 344
Epistle 47 (Seneca), 74, 76, 77

Equiano, Olaudah, 111, 359, 366–370, 390, 452, 453, 469
Erasmus, Desiderius, 218–221
Essay on Man, An (Pope), 339, 340–341, 342
Essays (Montaigne), 253–257
Euripides, 30, 43, 50, 58–62, 522
Everyman, 195–198
Exodus, 103, 121

Fables (Aesop), 29–32, 99, 143
Facundo (Sarmiento), 359, 370, 385–391
Fanon, Frantz, 649
Faulkner, William, 490, 515–519, 619–620, 632, 637, 668, 687, 688
Faust (Goethe), 372–375
Ferdowsi, Abolqasem, 108, 129–132
First New Chronicle and Good Government, The (Poma), 265
Flaubert, Gustave, 380, 385, 418, 423, 425–430, 446
Florentine Codex, The, 265, 267
Flowers of Evil, The (Baudelaire), 405
Franco, Veronica, 214
Franklin, Benjamin, 298, 300
Freedom (Verga), 441–444
Frost at Midnight (Coleridge), 361, 362, 406
Fuenteovejuna (Lope de Vega), 269–274
Fuentes, Carlos, 550, 595, 606–610

Garcilaso de la Vega, 214
Garden of Forking Paths, The (Borges), 525–529, 553, 595, 615, 619, 692
Gargantua and Pantagruel (Rabelais), 210
Garibaldi, Giuseppe, 461–462
Genesis, 4, 6, 14–15, 18, 73, 98, 121, 263, 267, 511
Gentle Now, Doves (Ibn 'Arabi), 162
Girl (Kincaid), 604, 666–670
Goblin Market (Rossetti), 409
Goethe, Johann Wolfgang von, 248, 372–375, 481, 526
Gogol, Nikolai, 380, 382–385
Golden Ass, The (Apuleius), 109–112

Good Woman of Setzuan, The (Brecht), 520–524, 589

Great Hymn to the Aten, The, 3, 4, 5, 6, 7

Guest, The (Camus), 575, 582–586

Guido Cavalcanti, 163, 167

Guido Guinizzelli, 163

Gulliver's Travels (Swift), 331–333, 335, 336, 339, 342, 344, 346, 347

Guttural Muse, The (Heaney), 631

Hadewijch of Brabant, 161

Hafez, 164

HaLevi, Yehuda, 162

Half of Life, The (Hölderlin), 407

Hamlet, Prince of Denmark (Shakespeare), 43, 58, 198, 275–280, 313

Hautot and His Son (Maupassant), 445–448

Haw Lantern, The (Heaney), 629, 631

Head, Bessie, 658–660, 697

Heaney, Seamus, 125, 628–631

Heart, in his beauty's garden (Jahan Khatun), 163

Heart of Darkness (Conrad), 473–478, 601, 604

Hebrew Bible, The, 4, 14–20, 86–87, 103, 105, 108, 118, 121, 131, 139

Hedda Gabler (Ibsen), 436–440

Heine, Heinrich, 420

Heinrich von Morungen, 161

Heptameron (Marguerite de Navarre), 243–246, 250

Heraclitus, 5, 7

Her Hair (Baudelaire), 112

Herodotus, 75–76, 77, 78

[He seems to me equal to gods that man] (Sappho), 34, 36

Hesiod, 3, 4, 5, 6, 7, 24, 73, 95, 98, 183, 184

Hildegard of Bingen, 162

His Confession (Archipoeta), 163

Histories (Herodotus), 75–76, 78

History of a Voyage to the Land of Brazil (Léry), 265, 267

History of Rasselas, Prince of Abissinia, The (Johnson), 348–351

Hölderlin, Friedrich, 407

Homer, 10, 21–27, 30, 37, 90, 92, 93, 166, 167, 183, 184, 229, 263, 287, 312, 338, 625–626, 685, 687

Horace, 77, 339

House Taken Over (Cortázar), 549–553, 615, 692

Hugo, Victor, 415–418, 426, 429

Huidobro, Vicente, 538–539, 540

Hume, David, 297

Hymn to Holy Women, A (Notker), 162–163

Ibn 'Arabi, 162

Ibn Zaydun, 162

Ibsen, Henrik, 436–440, 618

[If anything ever came through for one who so longingly] (Catullus), 85

If you wish to sell your kisses (Charles d'Orleans), 163

Iliad (Homer), 21–22, 23, 24, 25, 26, 27, 62, 91, 92, 126, 166, 287, 338, 625–626

I'm Explaining a Few Things (Neruda), 533–534

In Praise of War (Bertran de Born), 136, 139

Interesting Narrative of the Life of Olaudah Equiano, Or Gustavus Vassa, the African, Told by Himself (Equiano), 359, 366–370, 452, 469

[I simply want to be dead] (Sappho), 34

I Speak of the City (Paz), 531, 535

Ithaka (Cavafy), 533

Jahan Khatun, 163, 164

Job, 4, 15–16, 18

John, 103, 104, 106

Johnson, Samuel, 348–351, 465

Joyce, James, 25, 492–496, 518, 588, 698

Kafka, Franz, 498–502, 567, 641, 692

Kant, Immanuel, 295, 299

Keats, John, 405, 409, 551, 552

Kincaid, Jamaica, 604, 666–670

King Leopold's Soliloquy (Twain), 462–463

Kipling, Rudyard, 463, 474
Kubla Khan (Coleridge), 592, 595

Labé, Louise, 214
La Belle Dame sans Merci (Keats), 409
lady asks me, A (Guido Cavalcanti), 163
Lady of Shalott, The (Tennyson), 574
Lady with the Dog, The (Chekhov),
454–459
La Fontaine, Jean De, 317–319
Lais (Marie de France), 145–149, 202
Lament for Ignacio Sánchez Mejías
(Lorca), 535
Lazarillo de Tormes, 109, 111, 230, 245,
248–251, 258
Leaves of Grass (Whitman), 404
Leopardi, Giacomo, 409
Léry, Jean de, 265, 266, 267
Les Misérables (Hugo), 415–418,
426, 429
Lessing, Doris, 571–575, 585, 604,
615, 619–620
Letter to a Poet (Senghor), 547
Letter to a Prisoner (Senghor), 545,
546, 547
Letter to Francesco Vettori (Machia-
velli), 209
Letter to Major von Wissmann
(Machemba), 462
Liberty or Death (Dessalines), 359
Life of Lazarillo de Tormes and of His
Fortunes and Adversities, The,
248–251
*Lines Composed a Few Miles above Tin-
tern Abbey* (Wordsworth), 362,
405, 406
Lispector, Clarice, 518, 597–599
Little Black Boy, The (Blake), 370
Lope de Vega, 269–274
Lorca, Federico García, 532,
534, 535
Love always repairs to the noble heart
(Guido Guinizzelli), 163
Lover's Prize, A (Beatrice of Dia), 161
Love Song of J. Alfred Prufrock, The
(Eliot), 531, 535
Lucretius, 3, 4, 5, 6–7, 99
Luke, 103, 104–105, 106, 107

Luther, Martin, 282, 285
Lysistrata (Aristophanes), 61, 64–67,
79, 82

Macaulay, Thomas Babington, 461,
463
Machado de Assis, Joaquim Maria,
449–453
Machemba, 462
Machiavelli, Niccolò, 207, 209,
223–226, 233, 237, 239, 242
Madame Bovary (Flaubert), 380, 385,
418, 425–430, 446
Mallarmé, Stéphane, 403, 404, 406,
484, 587–588
Mann, Thomas, 479–484, 495
Marguerite de Navarre, 140,
243–246, 250
Marie de France, 145–149, 179, 202
Marinetti, F. T., 537, 540
Mark, 103, 104, 107
Márquez, Gabriel García, 550, 609,
610, 636–638, 642, 662–663, 664,
682, 692
Marquis de Sade, 298, 299
Martí, José, 404
Matryona's Home (Solzhenitsyn),
611–615
Matthew, 103–104, 105, 106–107
Maupassant, Guy de, 445–448
Medea (Euripides), 30, 43, 50, 58–62
Melville, Herman, 398–401, 434
Memorandum (Garibaldi), 461–462
Metamorphoses (Ovid), 95–99, 143, 287
Metamorphosis, The (Kafka), 498–502,
641, 692
Milton, John, 124, 287–291, 313, 511
Minute on Indian Education, February
2, 1835 (Macaulay), 461
Modest Proposal, A (Swift), 331, 333–
334, 335, 336
Molière (Jean-Baptiste Poquelin),
301–306, 380
Montaigne, Michel Eyquem de,
253–257
More, Thomas, 208, 221, 233–237,
238, 332, 344, 462, 563
Morrison, Toni, 672–676

[*Mourn, Cupids all, every Venus, and whatever*] (Catullus), 85
Munro, Alice, 616–620, 688
My Last Duchess (Browning), 408

Nabokov, Vladimir, 591–595
Naipaul, V. S., 626, 639–642
Narrative of the Life of Frederick Douglass, An American Slave (Douglass), 356, 359, 364–365, 369, 392–396, 452, 469
Neruda, Pablo, 404, 531, 533–534, 535, 692
New Sappho, The (Sappho), 37
New Testament, 113, 118, 119, 143
New Testament Gospels, The, 103–108, 142
Ngugi wa Thiong'o, 648–652, 697
Night Chant, The, 467, 468
Night in Sine (Senghor), 546
North and South (Walcott), 624–625, 626
Notes from Underground (Dostoyevsky), 377, 401, 420–423, 434
Notes of a Native Son (Baldwin), 572, 576–580, 676, 688
Notker Balbulus, 162–163

Ode on a Grecian Urn (Keats), 552, 623
Ode on Intimations of Immortality (Wordsworth), 361
Ode to a Nightingale (Keats), 405
Odyssey (Homer), 10, 21–22, 23–25, 26, 27, 30, 32, 92, 131, 138, 156, 158, 166, 167, 263, 287, 312, 313, 338, 344, 476, 685, 687
Oedipus the King (Sophocles), 43, 46–51, 52, 59, 61, 72, 198, 280, 312
Old Chief Mshlanga, The (Lessing), 571–575, 585, 604, 615, 619–620
Olympe de Gouges (Marie Gouzes), 355, 356, 358, 409
Omeros (Walcott), 624, 668
[*Once on a time pine trees from Pelion's summit*] (Catullus), 84–85, 87
One Out of Many (Naipaul), 639–642
On the Nature of Things (Lucretius), 3, 4, 6–7, 99

Orlando Furioso (Ariosto), 228–231, 287
Oroonoko; or, The Royal Slave (Behn), 321–324, 346
Out of the Cradle Endlessly Rocking (Whitman), 400
Overcoat, The (Gogol), 380, 382–385
Ovid, 86–87, 95–99, 141, 143, 145, 160, 162, 183, 184, 287

Paradise Lost (Milton), 124, 287–291, 313
Paz, Octavio, 531, 535
Perceval (Chrétien de Troyes), 150–154
Perforated Sheet, The (Rushdie), 604, 662–665
Persians (Aeschylus), 76, 77
Petrarch, Francis, 167, 183, 207, 212–216, 328, 329
Petrus Alfonsi, 108, 121, 140–143, 164
Phèdre (Racine), 312–316, 406
Philosophical Satire (Sor Juana Inés de la Cruz), 328
Philosophy in the Bedroom (Marquis de Sade), 298
Pirandello, Luigi, 503–506, 529
Plato, 29, 69–73, 76, 92, 126, 202, 220, 233, 238, 313, 482, 563
Plautus, 79–82
Poet's Answer to the Most Illustrious Sor Filotea de la Cruz, The (Sor Juana Inés de la Cruz), 326–327
Poma de Ayala, Guaman, 265
Pope, Alexander, 112, 331, 338–342
Popol Vuh (Quiché Maya), 263, 267
Porphyria's Lover (Browning), 408, 630
Praise of Folly, The (Erasmus), 218–221
Prayer to the Masks (Senghor), 545, 547
Prelude, The (Wordsworth), 359
Prince, The (Machiavelli), 223–226, 233, 237, 239, 242
Princess of Clèves, The (de La Fayette), 307–310
Proust, Marcel, 406, 484, 486–490, 487, 576, 579–580, 676
Psalm (Celan), 568
Psalms, 16–17, 18, 86–87
Pseudolus (Plautus), 79–82

Punishment (Heaney), 629, 630, 631
Pushkin, Alexander Sergeyevich,
     377–380

Queen of Spades, The (Pushkin),
     377–380
Question, The (Rumi), 164
Qur'an, The, 117–121, 138, 174,
     175, 526

Rabelais, François, 207, 208, 210
Racine, Jean, 312–316, 406
Rape of the Lock, The (Pope), 112, 331,
     336, 338–339, 341
Recitatif (Morrison), 672–676
Reflections on the Revolution in France
     (Burke), 358, 359
Reply of a South American to a Gentle-
     man of This Island (Bolívar), 358–359
Requiem (Akhmatova), 533, 535, 615
Responsory for the Virgin (Hildegard of
     Bingen), 162
Rhodes, Cecil, 463
Rights of Woman, The (Olympe de
     Gouges), 355, 356, 358, 365, 409
Rilke, Rainer Maria, 533, 534, 535
Rimbaud, Arthur, 409
Rime of the Ancient Mariner, The
     (Coleridge), 409, 696
Robbe-Grillet, Alain, 559–562
Rod of Justice, The (Machado),
     449–453
Room of One's Own, A (Woolf), 490,
     508–513, 518, 687
Rossetti, Christina, 409
Rousseau, Jean-Jacques, 248, 355,
     361–365, 390, 394, 401, 420, 423
Ruin, The, 163
Ruins of a Great House (Walcott), 624
Rumi, Jalâloddin, 129, 164
Rushdie, Salman, 604, 639, 662–665

San Juan de la Cruz, 283–284
Sappho, 30, 34–37, 72, 86–87
Sarmiento, Domingo Faustino, 359,
     370, 385–391, 409
Scholar's Guide (Petrus Alfonsi), 108,
     121, 140–143, 164

Schreiner, Olive, 462, 463
Scorpions, The (Alfonso X), 163
Sea Is History, The (Walcott), 623–624
Second Coming, The (Yeats), 533
Secret Room, The (Robbe-Grillet),
     559–562
Seneca, 74, 76, 77
Senghor, Léopold Sédar, 545–547,
     577, 626
Sensini (Bolaño), 689–693
Shahnameh (Ferdowsi), 107, 129–132
Shakespeare, William, 43, 58, 98,
     179, 183, 212, 213, 215, 275–280,
     315, 316, 322, 338, 393, 396, 406,
     511, 513, 567, 592, 595, 690
Shelley, Percy Bysshe, 403, 409, 410
Shem Tov Ardutiel, 163
Shibboleth (Celan), 567
Silko, Leslie Marmon, 634, 643–646
Sir Gawain and the Green Knight, 126,
     185, 190–194, 202
Six Characters in Search of an Author
     (Pirandello), 503–506, 529
Solzhenitsyn, Alexander, 611–615
[*Some men say an army of horse and*
     some men say an army on foot] (Sap-
     pho), 35
Song of Roland, 134–139, 202, 230
Songs for Signare (Senghor), 546, 547
Songs of Experience (Blake), 469
Songs of Innocence (Blake), 469
Sophocles, 43, 46–51, 52–57, 61, 82
Sor Juana Inés de la Cruz, 326–330
Soyinka, Wole, 653–657
[*Sparrow, precious darling of my sweet-*
     heart,] (Catullus), 85
Spotted Horses (Faulkner), 515–519,
     668
Story of the Grail, The, 425, 426
Strand at Lough Beg, The (Heaney),
     628, 631
Swann's Way (Proust), 486–490,
     579–580, 676
Swift, Jonathan, 331–336, 344, 346
Symposium (Plato), 69–73, 563

Tale of the Shipwrecked Sailor, 74, 77
Tartuffe (Molière), 301–306, 380

Tenebrae (Celan), 567–568
Tennyson, Alfred, Lord, 25, 408, 574
Teresa of Ávila, 282–283, 285
Thales, 5, 7
Theogony (Hesiod), 3, 5, 95
"Thidrandi Whom the Goddesses Slew," 155–159
This Way for the Gas, Ladies and Gentlemen (Borowski), 554–557, 575
Thousand and One Nights, The, 97, 109, 140, 143, 146, 147, 169, 172–176, 177, 178, 179, 182, 476, 526, 563, 681
Three Spinners, The, 465–466, 469
Throw of the Dice Will Never Abolish Chance, A (Mallarmé), 403
To Ibn al-Mu'allim (HaLevi), 162
Tollund Man, The (Heaney), 629–630
Tolstoy, Leo, 377, 423, 431–434, 446–447, 453, 592
Tom Tit Tot, 466, 469
To New York (Senghor), 545–546, 547, 626
To Roosevelt (Darío), 409
To Toussaint L'Ouverture (Wordsworth), 359
Twain, Mark, 462–463, 518
Tzara, Tristan, 538

Ulysses (Tennyson), 25, 408
[Up yours both, and sucks to the pair of you] (Catullus), 86
Utopia (More), 221, 233–237, 238, 332, 344, 462, 563

Vane Sisters, The (Nabokov), 591–595
Verga, Giovanni, 441–444
Verlaine, Paul, 404, 484
Vindication of the Rights of Woman, A (Wollstonecraft), 327

Virgil, 10, 26, 89–93, 96, 113, 115, 166, 167, 183, 184, 229, 287, 338
Voltaire, 251, 343–347, 348–349, 351, 380, 418

Walcott, Derek, 623–626, 668
Walker Brothers Cowboy (Munro), 616–620, 688
Walking Around (Neruda), 531, 535
Walther von der Vogelweide, 162
Waste Land, The (Eliot), 477, 531, 534, 535
We Are Seven (Wordsworth), 385
Wedding at the Cross (Ngugi), 648–652
What Is Enlightenment? (Kant), 295
When I see the lark stretch out (Bernart de Ventadorn), 161
White Man's Burden, The (Kipling), 463, 474
Whitman, Walt, 399, 400, 404, 407–408
[Who's the dedicatee of my new witty] (Catullus), 84, 85
Wollstonecraft, Mary, 297, 299, 327, 330
Woolf, Virginia, 490, 508–513, 518, 687
Wordsworth, William, 359, 361, 362, 385, 405, 406, 410
Works and Days (Hesiod), 3, 4, 6
[World to be stuttered after] (Celan), 568, 569
Wound of Love, The (Heinrich von Morungen), 161
Wretched of the Earth, The (Fanon), 649

Yeats, William Butler, 494, 533, 534, 535
Yellow Woman (Silko), 634, 643–646

Zurich, at the Stork (Celan), 569